The Big Book of Coding Interviews

Interviews

in C & C++

Interview Druid Publishing

Third Edition: 2018

The Big Book of Coding Interviews in C & C++

If you spot any mistakes in the book, please e-mail them to interviewdruid@gmail.com

Contents

List of Coding Problems

1.1 Linked Lists

1.2 Stacks and Queues

1.3 Trees

1.6 Bitwise operations

1.7 Application of Data Structures

2.1 Searching

2.2 Sorting

List of Puzzles

Preface

Dear reader,

This book is a collection of interesting programming interview questions. All aspects and elements of programming interviews including data structures, searching and sorting, algorithms, math, object design, programming language concepts, computer science concepts, puzzles and personality have been exhaustively covered.

Frankly, there is no limit to the number of questions that an interviewer can choose from in an interview. However, some questions are asked more frequently than others. So questions in this book have been carefully chosen after analyzing several interviews so that they represent the frequently asked interview questions.

To make this book a delectable treat to read, I have added plenty of examples, diagrams and tables to help you figure out the solutions.

There are bound to be areas for improvement. Please send me your invaluable feedback to interviewdruid@gmail.com. I will try my best to incorporate your feedback into the subsequent revisions of the book. **If you liked reading the book, I beg you to PLEASE, PLEASE, PLEASE give your review comments on Amazon.**

The link to the github project is

https://github.com/parineeth/tbboci-3rd-edition-c-and-cpp

The complete source code for the coding problems is available at the following URLs

https://goo.gl/EiUQr3

https://goo.gl/d45yXc

http://www.interviewdruid.com/3rd-edition-c-and-cpp.zip

https://www.dropbox.com/s/6s21rm9vgt7b7b8/3rd-edition-c-and-cpp.zip

I hope you enjoy reading this book and successfully crack the coding interviews ahead of you!

Preliminaries

1. The link to the github project is

https://github.com/parineeth/tbboci-3rd-edition-c-and-cpp

The complete source code for the coding problems is available at the following URLs

https://goo.gl/EiUQr3

https://goo.gl/d45yXc

http://www.interviewdruid.com/3rd-edition-c-and-cpp.zip

https://www.dropbox.com/s/6s21rm9vgt7b7b8/3rd-edition-c-and-cpp.zip

2. In the code when we refer to the sort function, we make generally use of quicksort as shown below

```
/*Function for comparing two elements. This function used while sorting*/
int cmp_function(const void *p1, const void *p2)
{
    int *x = (int *)p1;
    int *y = (int *)p2;

    if (*x < *y)
        return -1;
    else if (*x == *y)
        return 0;
    else
        return 1;
}


void sort(int a[], int length)
{
    qsort(a, length, sizeof(int), cmp_function);
}
```

3. Non-decreasing order indicates that the elements will be arranged from smallest to biggest and there can be repetition of elements in the input. For instance {1, 2, 2, 3, 5} is in non-decreasing order.

Non-increasing order indicates that the elements will be arranged from biggest to smallest and there can be repetition of elements in the input. For instance {5, 5, 4, 2, 1} is in non-increasing order.

1. Data Structures

A linked list is a sequence of nodes, where each node is linked to its neighboring node.

In a singly linked list, a node is linked to only one of its neighbors. The nodes can be traversed in one direction only. In a circular linked list, the last node in the linked list is linked with the first node in the linked list. By making the linked list circular, it is possible to reach any node in the linked list from any starting node. The circular linked list is still traversed in one direction only. In a doubly linked list, each node is linked to its previous neighbor and its next neighbor. The nodes in the doubly linked list can be traversed in both directions.

The advantage of linked lists over arrays is that insertion and deletion operations on linked lists are inexpensive. Insertion and deletion operations using arrays on the other hand require moving the array elements and are significantly more expensive. If the number of elements is not known before hand in an array, when the array becomes full the entire array will have to be resized which is a costly operation.

The main drawback of linked lists is that they don't provide random access to elements whereas arrays provide random access. Also additional memory is consumed by linked lists compared to arrays since each node in the linked list will have to maintain the pointer to the neighbor.

A linked list can have different types of nodes in it. Also the same node can be a part of many linked lists.

Stack is a data structure with the Last In First Out (LIFO) semantics. The stack can be implemented as an array or a linked list. The main operations on a stack are push, pop and peek. All operations on a stack happen at only one end of the stack – at the top of the stack. The code for a stack that is implemented using a linked list is shown below

```
int push(stack  *s, node *new_element) {
    new_element->next = s->top;
    s->top = new_element;
    return 0; /*Return success*/
}

node* pop(stack *s) {
    node *popped_element = s->top;
    if (s->top) {
        s->top = s->top->next;
        }
        return popped_element;
```

```
}
```

Queue is a data structure with the First In First Out (FIFO) semantics. Queue can also be implemented as an array or a linked list. When using arrays, queues are implemented using circular arrays. Elements are inserted at the rear end of the queue (enqueue) and removed from the front end of the queue (dequeue). The code for a queue implemented using a linked list is shown below

```
int enqueue(struct queue *q, struct node *new_element) {
    new_element->next = NULL;
    if (!q->head) {
        q->head = new_element;
        q->tail = new_element;
        return 0; /*Return the result code indicating success*/
    }
    q->tail->next = new_element;
    q->tail = new_element;
    return 0; /*Return the result code indicating success*/
}

struct node *dequeue(struct queue* q) {
    struct node *removed_element = q->head;
    if (q->head) {
        q->head = q->head->next;
        if (!q->head)
            q->tail = NULL;
    }
    return removed_element;
}
```

Tree is a connected acyclic graph. The two most commonly used techniques to traverse a tree are depth first search and breadth first search. Depth First Search can be implemented by placing the nodes of the tree in a stack. Breadth First Search can be implemented by placing the nodes of the tree in a queue.

A binary tree is a tree where each node has at most two child nodes. A balanced binary tree is a binary tree where for each node, the depth of its left sub-tree and the depth of right sub-tree differ by at most 1 node. By maintaining a balanced binary tree, the depth of the tree is minimized. Two of the most popular data structures for maintaining balanced binary trees are Red Black trees and AVL trees

A binary search tree is a binary tree where for each node X in the tree, the nodes in the left sub-tree of X store elements less than the element stored in X and the nodes in the right sub-tree of X store elements greater than the element stored in X.

A binary tree can be traversed using pre-order, in-order or post-order traversal techniques. In pre-order traversal, the root is first processed, followed by the left sub-tree and then the right sub-tree. In in-order traversal, the left sub-tree is first processed, followed by the root and then the right sub-tree. In post-order traversal, the left sub-tree is first processed, followed by the right sub-tree and then the root. It is important to note that in-order traversal can be ambiguous. For instance, although the two trees below are different, they have the same in-order result BAC.

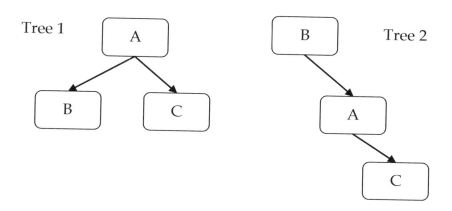

An array is a collection of similar objects which are stored in a set of contiguous memory locations. An element of the array is accessed using the element's index in the array. Both sequential and random access of elements is possible using an array. Arrays may be one-dimensional (if they use a single index) or multi-dimensional (if they use more than one index).

Arrays have two main drawbacks

1. Only a fixed number of elements can fit into an array. When the array is completely full and we still need to store more elements in it, the entire array has to be copied to a new bigger space in memory. Copying the entire array can be a costly operation if the size of the array is large.

2. When an element is deleted in an array it results in a vacant slot in the array. Over several delete operations, the vacant slots can be strewn all over the array. Additional data structures will be needed to efficiently handle the holes in the array.

Strings are a collection of characters. Searching for a sub-string (pattern) in a long string (text) is commonly encountered in strings. This is also referred to as searching for a needle in a haystack. A brute force approach has a time complexity of $O(nm)$ where n is the length of pattern and m is the length of the text. To speed up string searching, algorithms try to skip characters in the text. The main approaches for solving the exact string match problem are Knuth Morris Pratt algorithm and the Boyer Moore Algorithm.

In the Knuth Morris Pratt algorithm, the pattern is compared with the text from left to right. A lookup table is pre-computed on the pattern which indicates by how many characters the pattern can be advanced if there is a mismatch. The worst case time complexity is $O(n+m)$

In the Boyer Moore algorithm, the pattern is compared with the text from right to left. This helps speed up the algorithm since many more characters in the text can be skipped when a mismatch occurs. The algorithm uses two rules: the bad character rule and the good suffix rule, to advance the search. The worst case time complexity is $O(nm)$. However in most practical cases Boyer Moore runs faster than Knuth Morris Pratt algorithm. So Boyer Moore algorithm is preferred to the Knuth Morris Pratt algorithm. If the pattern is very long, Boyer Moyer algorithm is most likely to be the most efficient exact string match algorithm

A hash table maps a key to a value using a hash function as shown.

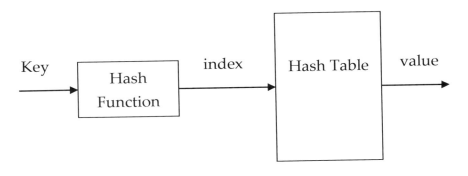

Different kinds of hash functions can be used to generate the index from the key. For instance, a commonly used hash function divides the numeric key value with a prime number and the resulting remainder forms the index (index = key mod prime number). The prime number should preferably not be close to a power of 2. Cyclic Redundancy Check (CRC) functions are also good hash functions

An ideal hash function should map each key to a unique index. In practice, ideal hash functions are rare. An overflow can occur if two keys are mapped to the same index. One of the techniques used to handle overflows is to maintain a linked list for all the keys that are mapped to the same index.

For an ideal hash table, the time complexity is listed below

Insert time complexity: O(1)

Delete time complexity: O(1)

Search time complexity: O(1)

The problem with hash tables is that information about the order of elements can't be preserved in the hash table. So we can't store sequences using hash tables.

Heap is a complete binary tree (every node other than the leaves have 2 children). There are two types of heaps: a max-heap and a min-heap. In a max heap, each parent node is >= any of its children. In a min-heap, each parent node is <= any of its children. A max-heap is shown below

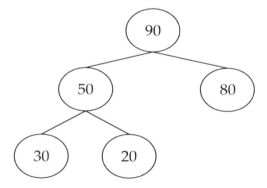

Heaps are generally represented using simple arrays. If the parent node is stored at index i, then the left child is stored at index 2*i and the right child is stored at index (2*i)+1.

Using a heap the maximum or minimum element can be easily identified since it will be at the root of the heap. A heap does not maintain all the elements in the sorted order.

The time complexity of different operations on a heap is given below

Insert operation - O(log n)

Delete min/max - O(log n)

Find minimum or maximum - O(1)

1.1 Linked Lists

1. Reverse a linked list

A linked list can be reversed without using recursion by maintaining 3 nodes: prev_node, cur_node and next_node. As we traverse the linked list, we update the 3 nodes and the links in the linked list are reversed. The time complexity is O(n).

```
/*Reverses the linked list without using recursion
head: first node in the original linked list
Return value: the first node of the reversed linked list
*/
struct node* reverse_linked_list(struct node *head) {
    struct node *cur_node, *prev_node, *next_node;

    cur_node = head;
    prev_node = NULL;

    while (cur_node) {
        /*Store the next node in a temporary variable*/
        next_node = cur_node->next;

        /*Reverse the link so that current node points to the previous node*/
        cur_node->next = prev_node;

        /*Update the previous node to the current node */
        prev_node = cur_node;

        /*Proceed to the next node in the original linked list*/
        cur_node = next_node;
    }

    /*
    Once the linked list has been reversed, prev_node will be
    pointing to the new head. So return it
    */
    return prev_node;
}
```

The linked list can also be reversed using recursion. However this approach takes up additional memory that is proportional to the size of the linked list and so is not preferred. Sometimes interviewers explicitly ask for a recursive solution to reverse a linked list. So we are discussing the recursive solution also. Given the head node in a linked list consisting of n nodes, to reverse it using recursion, we first reverse the remaining n-1 nodes in the list recursively and then connect up the head node to the end of the reversed list. The steps are shown in the diagrams below:

1. Initially cur_node points to the head of the list

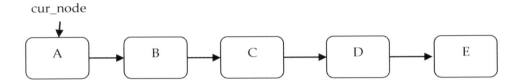

2. Recursively reverse the remaining list (BCDE becomes EDCB)

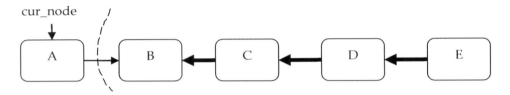

3. Set cur_node->next->next = cur_node. Here cur_node = A.
So A->next->next = A. But A->next is B. So B->next = A. So B now points to A.
Then set cur_node->next = NULL. So A->next = NULL

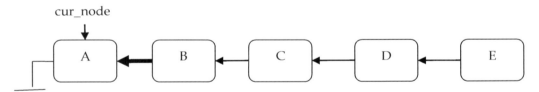

```
/*cur_node: current node of the linked list being processed
Return value: new head to the reversed linked list*/
struct node* reverse_linked_list_r(struct node *cur_node) {
    struct node *new_head;
    if (!cur_node || !cur_node->next)
        return cur_node;/*return last node in original linked list as new head*/

    /*Recursively reverse the remaining nodes in the linked list*/
    new_head = reverse_linked_list(cur_node->next);

    /*Connect up the current node to the reversed linked list*/
    cur_node->next->next = cur_node;
    cur_node->next = NULL;
    return new_head;
}
```

2.   Reverse every k nodes in a linked list. So if the input is A->B->C->D->E->F->G->H and k is 3, then the output should be C->B->A->F->E->D->H->G

Both recursive and non-recursive solutions exist to reverse every k nodes with O(n) time complexity. Although the recursive solution takes more space, we will use it here since it is simpler. If there are n nodes in the linked list, we reverse the first k nodes and then recursively process the remaining n - k nodes. Let the linked list be A->B->C->D->E->F->G->H and k = 3. The diagram below illustrates the technique.

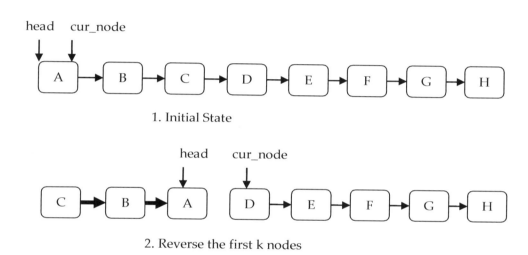

1. Initial State

2. Reverse the first k nodes

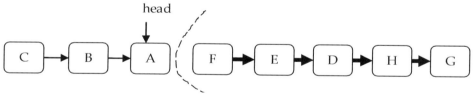

3. Recursively reverse the remaining nodes

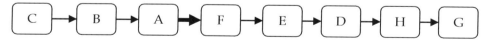

4. Connect the two linked lists

9

```
/*
head: the first node of the linked list
k: how many nodes should be reversed
Return value: first node of the new linked list after reversing every k nodes
*/
struct node * k_reverse_list(struct node *head, int k)
{
    struct node *cur_node,  *prev_node, *temp_node;
    int i = 0;

    if (!head || k == 0)
        return head;

    cur_node = head;
    prev_node = NULL;

    while (cur_node && i < k) {
        /*Store the next node in a temporary variable*/
        temp_node = cur_node->next;

        /*Reverse the link */
        cur_node->next = prev_node;

        /*Update the previous node to the current node */
        prev_node = cur_node;

        /*Proceed to the next node in the original linked list*/
        cur_node = temp_node;

        ++i;
    }

    /*
    We have reversed k nodes. cur_node points to the (k+1)th node
    and head points to the kth node.
    Now recursively process the remaining nodes from cur_node onwards
    and assign the result to head->next.
    */
    if (cur_node)
        head->next = k_reverse_list(cur_node, k);

    /*prev_node will point to first node in linked list after reversal*/
    return prev_node;
}
```

3. Find the kth node from the end of a linked list

We can treat the last node in the linked list as either the 0th node from the end or we can treat the last node as the 1st node from the end. So k can begin from 0 or 1. In the function below, we are treating the last node as the 1st node from the end. To find the kth node from the end, we first find the length of the linked list. Then we again traverse through the linked list to find the (length – k +1)th node from the beginning which corresponds to the kth node from the end. If the length of the linked list is n, then in the worst case we will access 2n nodes. The time complexity is O(n)

```
/*
head: first node of the linked list
k: node position from the end. k starts from 1 onwards
Return value: kth node from end if it exists, NULL otherwise
*/
struct node* find_kth_node_from_end(struct node *head, int k)
{
    struct node *n1;
    int i, length;

    length = 0;
    n1 = head;
    while (n1 != NULL) {
        length++;
        n1 = n1->next;
    }

    n1 = head;
    for (i = 1; i <= length; ++i) {
        if (i == length - k + 1) {
                return n1;      /*n1 is the kth node from end. So return it*/
        }
        n1 = n1->next;
    }

    /*k value passed doesn't match with the linked list. So return NULL */
    return NULL;
}
```

4.
Swap the kth node from the end with the kth node from the beginning of a linked list

If the length of the linked list is n, then k can take values from 1 to n. We can solve the problem in O(n) using the following steps:

1. Find the kth node from the start of the linked list (k1) and its previous node (prev1).

2. Find the kth node from the end of the linked list (k2) and its previous node (prev2).

3. Swap k1 and k2. While swapping we have to handle three possible cases:

- k1 and k2 are identical. In this case we don't have to swap
- k1 and k2 are neighbors (either k1->next = k2 or k2->next = k1)
- k1 and k2 are not neighbors

Note that if k is 1, then we have to swap the head of the linked list with the tail of the linked list. In this case, the head of the linked list will change. Also note that the node k1 may lie before or after k2. For instance, if linked list length is 10 and k = 3, then k1 is before k2. But if linked list length is 10 and k = 9, then k1 is after k2.

```
/*Helper function which swaps two neighbors n1 and n2
head: first node in the linked list
prev: node previous to n1
n1: first node to be swapped
n2: second node to be swapped. n2 occurs immediately after n1
Return value: head of the result linked list after swapping neighbors
*/
struct node* swap_neighbors(struct node *head, struct node *prev,
              struct node *n1, struct node *n2)
{
    /*Swap n1 and n2*/
    n1->next = n2->next;
    n2->next = n1;

    if (prev) {
        prev->next = n2;
    } else {
        head = n2; /*If prev doesn't exist, update head to n2*/
    }
    return head;
}
```

```
/*Main function for swapping the kth node from beginning and end
head: first node in the linked list
k: which node in the linked list should be swapped
length: number of nodes in the linked list
Return value: head of the result linked list on success, NULL on error
*/
struct node* swap_kth_node(struct node *head, int k, int length)  {
    struct node  *temp;
    struct node *k1, *k2, *prev1, *prev2;

    if (!head || k < 1 || k > length)
        return NULL;

    prev1 = prev2 = NULL;

    /*k1 is the kth node from begining and prev1 is previous to k1*/
    k1 = find_kth_node_from_begin(head, k, &prev1);

    /*k2 is the kth node from end and prev2 is previous to k2*/
    k2 = find_kth_node_from_end(head, k, length, &prev2);

    if (k1 == NULL || k2 == NULL)
        return NULL; /*the k value is incorrect*/

    if (k1 == k2)
        return head; /*both nodes are the same. So no need to swap*/

    /*Handle the case where k1 and k2 are neighbors and return*/
    if (k1->next == k2)
        return swap_neighbors(head, prev1, k1, k2);

    if (k2->next == k1)
        return swap_neighbors(head, prev2, k2, k1);

    /*k1 and k2 are not neighbors. So swap k1.next with k2.next*/
    temp = k1->next;
    k1->next = k2->next;
    k2->next = temp;

    if (prev1) {
        prev1->next = k2;
    } else  {
        head = k2; /* After swap, k2 becomes new head*/
    }

    if (prev2) {
        prev2->next = k1;
    } else  {
        head = k1; /* After swap, k1 becomes new head */
    }

    return head;
}
```

5. Delete a node in a linked list given only a pointer to that node

Let us say that we are given only a pointer n1 to the node that needs to be deleted. We don't know the node previous to n1. If we delete the node that n1 points to, then we can't update the next pointer of the node preceding n1. So we can't directly delete n1, but we have to employ a trick to do the job.

To solve the problem, let n2 be the pointer to the node next to n1. We copy n2->data into n1->data. We also copy n2->next into n1->next. Now n1 points to a node that is exactly identical to the node pointed by n2. Now instead of deleting n1, we delete n2. This achieves the required result.

This solution will not work if the node being deleted is the last node in the linked list and the last node points to NULL. One possible approach to make this solution work for all nodes in the linked list is to use a circular linked list.

```
/*
n1: pointer to the node to be deleted
Return value: 0 on success, -1 on failure
*/
int delete_node(struct node *n1)
{
    struct node *n2;

    if (n1->next) {
        /*Get the pointer to the next node*/
        n2 = n1->next;

        /*Copy the contents of the next node into the current node*/
        n1->data = n2->data;
        n1->next = n2->next;

        /*Free the next node*/
        free(n2);

        /*Return indicating the operation is successful*/
        return 0;
    }

    /*return indicating the operation failed*/
    return -1;
}
```

6. Remove duplicates from a linked list

For removing duplicates, we can try two approaches

1. Use brute force. Pick each node (let's call it current node) in the linked list, then check the nodes that occur after the current node and remove those nodes that are identical to the current node. The time complexity is O(n²). We don't need additional memory.

2. Use a hash table. As we traverse the linked list, we store the data of the nodes in the hash table. If the data of a node has already been stored in the hash table, then it is a duplicate and we delete the node from the linked list. The time complexity is O(n) but we will use additional memory because of the hash table.

The code for the brute force approach is given below

```
/*
head: first node in the linked list
*/
void remove_duplicates(struct node *head)
{
    struct node *cur_node, *iter_node, *prev_node;

    /*If there are 0 or 1 nodes in linked list, then simply return*/
    if (head == NULL || head->next == NULL)
        return;

    cur_node = head;
    while (cur_node) {
        /*Iterate from node after cur_node to the end of the linked list*/
        iter_node = cur_node->next;
        prev_node = cur_node;

        while (iter_node) {
            if (cur_node->data == iter_node->data) {
                /*iter_node is a duplicate of cur_node. So remove it*/
                prev_node->next = iter_node->next;
                free(iter_node);
                iter_node = prev_node->next;
            } else {
                prev_node = iter_node;
                iter_node = iter_node->next;
            }
        }

        cur_node = cur_node->next;
    }
}
```

15

7. Rotate a linked list by k positions

Consider the linked list A->B->C->D->E. If we rotate the linked list by k = 2 positions, then the linked list will become D->E->A->B->C. To perform the rotation we do the following:

1. Locate the kth node from the end (let's call this node the pivot). If k = 2, we have to locate the second last node which in this case is D.

2. Make the node previous to the pivot point to NULL. So in this case C will point to NULL.

3. Traverse until the end of the linked list and make the last node point to the head of the linked list. So the last node E will point to the head A.

4. Make the pivot the head of the new linked list. So D will now become the new head.

Note that if k = length of linked list, then after rotation we end up with the original linked list. So we apply the formula, k = k % length to figure out the actual rotation required.

```
/*
head: first node of the linked list
k: by how many positions the linked list should be rotated
length: number of nodes in the linked list
Return value: first node of the rotated linked list
*/
struct node* rotate_list(struct node *head, int k, int length)
{
    struct node *pivot, *prev, *last;

    /*If there are 0 or 1 nodes in the linked list, then simply return*/
    if (length < 2)
        return head;

    /*If we shift by k times, then we get back the same linked list. So we
    just have to shift k % length times*/
    k = k % length;

    /*If k is 0, then no need to shift*/
    if (k == 0)
        return head;

    /*Find the kth node from the end. If k = 1, then pivot will have
    the last node and prev will be the node previous to last node*/
    prev = NULL;
```

```
pivot = find_kth_node_from_end(head, k, length, &prev);

/*Find the last node in the linked list*/
last = pivot;
while (last->next)
    last = last->next;

/*Make the last node point to head and the node previous to pivot
point to NULL*/
last->next = head;
prev->next = NULL;

/*pivot will be the new head*/
return pivot;
}
```

rotate 2

```
        2.     1.
1 → 2 → ③ → ④ → 5
 4.      5.        3.
  4   5 →1    2    3 → X
```

0. k = k % length   return now if 0
1. find K from end (4) and its pNode (3)
3. pNode → next = NULL
4. k from end becomes new head
5. old tail points at old head

17

8. Two linked lists merge at a common node. Given the heads of the two linked lists, find the node where the linked lists merge. In the diagram below, the two linked lists ABCXYZ and PQXYZ merge at node X.

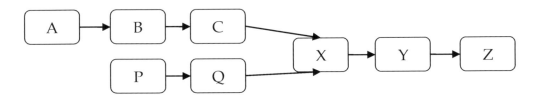

Using a brute force approach, we can pick each node in the first linked list and compare it with every node in the second linked list in sequential order. If we get a match, then we have found the first common node between the two linked lists. If one linked list has m nodes and the other has n nodes, this takes O(mn) time.

However there are better techniques to solve the problem. Two approaches which can perform better than the brute force approach are described below

Approach 1: Marking the nodes

An extra field is maintained in each node to indicate if the node has been visited or not. Initially the nodes in both linked lists have the field set to 0 indicating that they have not yet been visited. The nodes of the first linked list are then traversed and the visited field in the first linked list nodes is set to 1 indicating that they have been visited. Then the nodes of the second linked list are traversed in sequential order. As soon as we encounter a node in the second linked list with the visited field set to 1, we have found the first node that is common to both the linked lists. The time taken by this approach is O(m+n) and it requires additional space in each node to store the visited field

Approach 2: Counting

The lengths of the two linked lists are first computed. Let m be the number of nodes in the longer linked list and n be the number of nodes in the shorter linked list. n1 is made to point to the head of the longer linked list and n2 is made to point to the head of the shorter linked list. The absolute difference in the lengths of the two linked lists m-n is then computed. n1 is advanced in the longer linked list by m-n nodes. Now the number of remaining nodes starting from n1 in the longer linked list is equal to the number of nodes in the shorter linked list. If n1 and n2 point to the same node, we have found the

18

first common node. If not, we advance n1 and n2 by one node in their respective linked lists and compare them. This process is repeated until we get a match or we reach the end of the linked lists. The time taken by this approach is also O(m+n) and requires no additional space. So this approach is the preferred solution and is given below.

```
/*
head1: first node of linked list1
head2: first node of linked list2
Return value: first common node between the two linked lists
*/
struct node * find_intersection_node(struct node * head1, struct node *head2)
{
    struct node *n1, *n2;
    int length1, length2, diff;

    /*Find the length of the two linked lists*/
    length1 = find_length(head1);
    length2 = find_length(head2);

    /*store head of the longer linked list in n1 and head of shorter
    linked list in n2*/
    if (length1 >= length2) {
        n1 = head1;
        n2 = head2;
    } else {
        n1 = head2;
        n2 = head1;
    }

    /*Find the difference in length of the two linked lists. Then advance
    n1 by the difference*/
    diff = abs(length1 - length2);
    while (diff > 0) {
        n1 = n1->next;
        --diff;
    }

    /*Go on comparing the nodes in linked list1 starting from n1 and
    linked list2 starting from n2 until n1 and n2 match*/
    while (n1 && n2 && n1 != n2) {
        n1 = n1->next;
        n2 = n2->next;
    }

    /*n1 will have the common node if it exists, otherwise n1 will be NULL*/
    return n1;
}
```

9. Find out if there is a cycle in a linked list. Also find the node where the cycle begins

We can maintain the is_visited field in each node. Initially the is_visited field in all the nodes is set to 0. When a node is traversed in the linked list, the is_visited field is changed from 0 to 1. While traversing the linked list, the moment we encounter a node whose is_visited field is already 1, we know that there is a cycle in the linked list and the cycle begins at this node. The drawback of this approach is that it uses additional memory.

To solve the problem without using additional memory, we use the following idea. Suppose two runners take part in a race, one of them being faster than the other, the faster runner will overtake the slower runner as soon as the race starts. If the race track is a loop, then later in the race, the faster runner will again meet the slower runner and overtake him. Similarly, we can traverse the linked list using a fast pointer and a slow pointer. At each step, the fast pointer is moved ahead by 2 nodes, whereas the slow pointer is moved ahead by 1 node. If there is a loop in the linked list, the two pointers will meet at a common node.

To find where the loop starts, we need to do the following: Let n1 be the fast pointer and n2 be the slow pointer. When n1 and n2 meet, initialize a third pointer n3 to point to the beginning of the linked list. So n1 is ahead of n3 in the linked list. Now ignore n2 and advance n1 and n3 one node at a time. The node where n1 and n3 meet is where the loop starts. The proof for this is given below

Proof:

Finding the node where the loop starts requires some mathematical jugglery. You can skip this portion if you want to. Let n1 be the faster pointer and n2 be the slower pointer. Initially both pointers point to the beginning of the linked list. n1 is two times faster than n2. So in each step, n1 advances by 2 nodes and n2 advances by 1 node. Let the number of nodes from the beginning of the linked list (node A) to the node where the loop starts (node B) be K. Let the length of the loop (BCDB) be L.

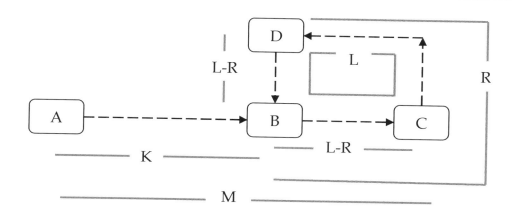

When n2 reaches the start of the loop (node B), n2 has traversed K nodes. Since n1 is twice as fast as n2, n1 has traversed 2K nodes and reached node D. The first K nodes that n1 has traversed are the nodes before the loop whereas the next K nodes that n1 has traversed are nodes inside the loop. The K nodes that n1 has traversed inside the loop can be written as K = nL + R where n indicates the number of times n1 has completed the loop and R indicates by how many nodes n1 is ahead of n2 inside the loop.

So inside the loop, n1 is R nodes ahead of n2. Since we are dealing with a loop, we can instead view the same information as n1 is behind n2 by L-R nodes inside the loop. If n1 is behind n2 by X nodes, then by the time n2 advances by X nodes, n1 will advance by 2X nodes, make up for the lost ground and meet exactly with n2. Now since n1 is behind n2 by L-R nodes, by the time n2 advances by L-R nodes and reaches node C, n1 will advance 2(L-R) nodes and both will meet exactly at node C. Let the number of nodes from the beginning of the loop (node A) to the node where the two pointers meet (node C) be M.

M = K + (L-R)

But we already have K = nL + R. Substituting for K, we have

M = n*L + R + L- R

M = (n+1)L

So M is a multiple of the length of the loop.

So to find the node where the loop starts, when n2 and n1 meet at node C, initialize a third pointer n3 to point to the beginning of the linked list. n1 is M nodes ahead of n3. Now ignore n2 and advance n1 and n3 one node at a time. By the time n3 traverses K nodes and reaches node B at the beginning of the loop, n1 also traverses K nodes and n1 is still M nodes ahead of n3. But M is a multiple of the loop length. So if n3 is at node B, M nodes ahead of B corresponds to node B itself. So n1 is also at B. So n1 and n3 meet at node B exactly where the loop starts.

```
/*head: first node of the linked list
Return value: first node in loop if loop exists, NULL otherwise
*/
struct node* find_loop( struct node *head)
{
    struct node *n1 = head, *n2 = head, *n3;
    int found_loop = 0;

    /*n1 is the fast pointer. So advance it by two steps
    n2 is slow pointer. So advance it by one step
    */
    while (n1 != NULL) {
        n1 = n1->next;
        if (n1) {
                n1 = n1->next;
                n2 = n2->next;
        }

        /*If n1 and n2 meet then there is a loop in the linked list*/
        if (n1 == n2) {
                found_loop = 1;
                break;
        }
    }

    if (!found_loop)
        return NULL;

    /*Find the beginning of the loop*/
    n3 = head;
    while (n1 != n3) {
        n1 = n1->next;
        n3 = n3->next;
    }

    return n1;
}
```

10. Interleave two linked lists

Let's consider two linked lists, L1 having the members A->B->C->D and L2 having the members X->Y->Z. Interleaving the two linked lists will result in the single linked list A->X->B->Y->C->Z->D, wherein the first node of L2 is placed next to the first node of L1, second node of L2 is placed next to second node of L1 and so on. If the sizes of the two linked lists are m and n, then interleaving can be done in O(m+n)

```
/*
n1: head of the first linked list
n2: head of the second linked list
Return value: head of the result interleaved linked list
*/
struct node* interleave_lists( struct node *n1, struct node *n2)
{
    struct node *result,  *temp1, *temp2;

    if (!n1) {
        return n2; /*If linked list1 is empty, return n2 */
    }

    if (!n2) {
        return n1; /*If linked list2 is empty, return n1*/
    }

    /*Process the two linked lists*/
    result = n1;
    while (n1 != NULL && n2 != NULL) {
        temp1 = n1->next;
        temp2 = n2->next;

        /*Place node of second linked list next to the node
        of the first linked list*/
        if (n1->next)
                n2->next = n1->next;
        n1->next = n2;

        n1 = temp1;
        n2 = temp2;
    }
    return result;
}
```

11. Merge two sorted linked lists into a single sorted linked list

Let the nodes of the two linked lists be sorted in non-decreasing order. We can merge the linked lists in a single pass. We go on traversing the two linked lists and keep adding the smaller node in the two linked lists to the result. When we run out of nodes in one of the linked lists, we append the remaining portion of the other linked list to the result. If linked list1 has m nodes and linked list2 has n nodes, then the time complexity is O(m+n)

```
/*
n1: head of the first linked list
n2: head of the second linked list
Return value: head of the merged linked list
*/
struct node* merge_lists( struct node *n1, struct node *n2)
{
    struct node *prev_merge_node, *result;

    if (!n1)
        return n2; /*If linked list1 is empty, return n2 */

    if (!n2)
        return n1; /*If linked list2 is empty, return n1*/

    /*Make the result point to the node with the smaller value */
    if (n1->data <= n2->data) {
        result = n1;
        prev_merge_node = n1;
        n1 = n1->next;
    } else {
        result = n2;
        prev_merge_node = n2;
        n2 = n2->next;
    }

    /*Process the two linked lists*/
    while (n1 != NULL && n2 != NULL) {
        if (n1->data <= n2->data) {
                prev_merge_node->next = n1;
                n1 = n1->next;
                prev_merge_node = prev_merge_node->next;
        } else {
                prev_merge_node->next = n2;
                n2 = n2->next;
                prev_merge_node = prev_merge_node->next;
        }
    }
```

```
    /*
    If there are still nodes present in linked list1 or linked list2, then
    append them to the result list
    */
    if (n1)
        prev_merge_node->next = n1;
    else
        prev_merge_node->next = n2;

    return result;
}
```

12. Each node in a linked list has two pointers. One of the pointers points to the next element in the linked list, while the other pointer points to a random element in the linked list. Create another copy of this linked list in O(n) time using constant extra space

Let the next pointers in the linked list be connected as: A->B->C (indicated by solid lines in diagram below). Let the random pointers be connected as: A->C, C->B and B->A (indicated by the dashed lines in diagram below). Let the newly created nodes of the cloned linked list be represented as A', B' and C'

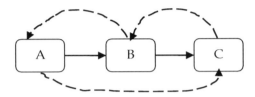

Solution 1: to solve the problem we can make use of a hash table.

1. First create the new linked list from the original linked list and fill in the correct next pointers in the new linked list nodes.

2. As we traverse the original linked list, store the address of the original node (say A) as the key and the address of the corresponding new node (A') as the value in a hash table.

3. Next traverse the original linked list and new linked list simultaneously using the next pointers in the respective linked lists. For each node in the original linked list (A), pick up its random pointer (C) and lookup the random pointer in the hash table. This will give us the address of random node (C') in the new linked list. Fill up this address as the random pointer for the current node (A') in the new linked list.

The time complexity is O(n). The problem with this solution is that it uses additional space that is proportional to the size of the linked list.

Solution 2: to solve the problem in O(n) using constant extra space, we do the following:

1. For each node in the original linked list, make a copy of the node and store it next to the original node. So the linked list A->B->C, now becomes A->A'->B->B'->C->C'

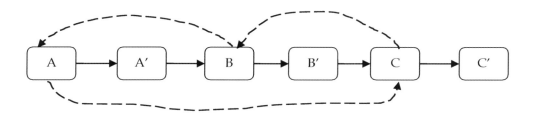

2. Next traverse the linked list again and for each of the <u>original</u> nodes do the following: ptr->next->random = ptr->random->next.

For instance, if ptr=A, then A->next->random = A->random->next
So A'->random = C->next [since A->next is A' and A->random = C]
So A'->random = C' [since C->next is C']

So we end up connecting the correct random pointer for the new nodes

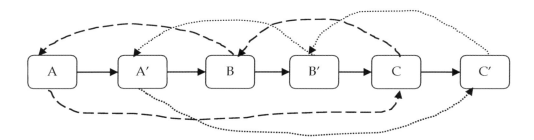

3. Remove the new nodes A' B' and C' from the original linked list and form a new linked list with them. We end up with two identical linked lists.

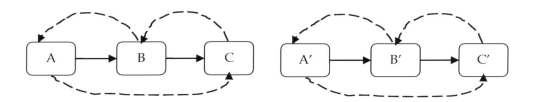

The code for the second solution is given below

```
/*
original_head: head of the original linked list
Return value: head of the newly created linked list
*/
struct node* clone_list(struct node *original_head)
{
    struct node *n1, *n2, *new_head = NULL, *next_node;
    /*
    For each node in original linked list, create a new node. The new node
    initially will be placed next to the original node
    */
    n1 = original_head;
    while (n1) {
        next_node = n1->next;

        n2 = (struct node*) malloc(sizeof(struct node*));
        if (!n2) {
                return NULL;
        }
        n2->data = n1->data;

        if (!new_head)
                new_head = n2;
        n1->next = n2;
        n2->next = next_node;
        n1 = next_node;
    }

    /*Set the random pointer correctly for the new nodes*/
    n1 = original_head;
    while (n1) {
        n1->next->random = n1->random->next;
        n1 = n1->next->next;
    }

    /*Disconnect new nodes from original linked list and form
    a new linked list for them*/
    n1 = original_head;
    while (n1) {
        n2 = n1->next;
        n1->next = n1->next->next;
        if (n2->next)
                n2->next = n2->next->next;

        n1 = n1->next;
    }
    return new_head;
}
```

13. Check if a linked list is a palindrome in O(n) time

To check if a linked list is a palindrome in O(n), we use the following approach

1. Find the length of the linked list and the middle node of the linked list.

2. Reverse the second half of the linked list. Then compare the first half of the linked list with the reversed second half. If the linked list is a palindrome then the nodes in the first half and the reversed second half should have the same data

3. Reverse the second half of linked list again so that we get back the original linked list

```
/*
head: first node of linked list.
Returns: 1 if linked list is a palindrome, 0 otherwise
*/
int is_list_palindrome(struct node *head)
{
    struct node *p, *q, *r, *temp;
    int i, length, is_palindrome;

    if (!head)
        return 0;

    /*Advance p by two nodes and q by one node in each loop.
    So when p reaches the end of linked list, q will point to middle of
    the linked list*/
    p = q = head;
    length = 0;
    while (p != NULL) {
        ++length;
        p = p->next;
        if (p) {
            ++length;
            p = p->next;
        }

        if (p) {
            q = q->next;
        }
    }

    /*Reverse the second half of the linked list*/
    temp = r = reverse_linked_list(q->next);
    p = head;

    /*Compare first half with reverse of second half*/
    is_palindrome = 1;
```

29

```
    for (i = 0; i < length / 2; ++i) {
        if (p->data != r->data) {
                is_palindrome = 0;
                break;
        }
        p = p->next;
        r = r->next;
    }

    /*Reverse the second half of linked list to get back the original
    linked list*/
    reverse_linked_list(temp);

    return is_palindrome;
}
```

14. Each node of a linked list stores one digit of a number. The head of the linked list has the most significant digit. Find the sum of two such linked lists (result is also a linked list)

The head of the input linked list stores the most significant (MS) digit. However, we perform addition from the least significant (LS) digit to the most significant digit. So we have to reverse the input linked lists to perform an efficient addition in O(m+n) where m and n are the sizes of the two input linked lists. The procedure is:

1. Reverse the two input linked lists

2. Add the digits of the two input linked lists. A new node is created to store the result of the addition of two nodes and the new node is appended to the result linked list. The carry obtained by adding two nodes is carried forward to the next nodes.

3. Once the addition is done, we may have still have a non-zero carry. In this case, create a new node to store the carry and append it to the result linked list

4. Reverse the two input linked lists to get back the original input linked lists

Note that we are constructing the result linked list with pointers pointing from most significant to least significant direction. So there is no need to reverse the result linked list. The diagram below illustrates the addition of 23 with 89

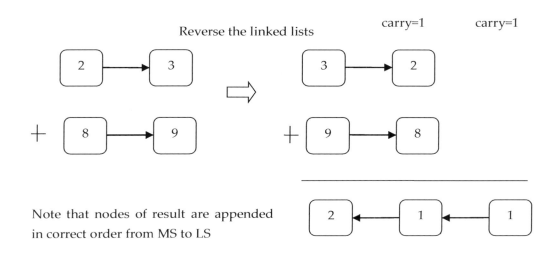

Note that nodes of result are appended in correct order from MS to LS

```
/*
n1: head of the first linked list
n2: head of the second linked list
Return value: head of new linked list having the result of addition of
    the two linked lists
*/
struct node* add_lists(struct node *n1, struct node *n2)
{
    struct node *p1, *p2, *h1, *h2;
    struct node *new_node, *result_node;
    int sum, carry;

    /*Reverse the two input linked lists*/
    h1 = p1 = reverse_linked_list(n1);
    h2 = p2 = reverse_linked_list(n2);

    /*Add the nodes of the two linked lists*/
    sum = 0;
    carry = 0;
    result_node = NULL;
    while (p1 != NULL && p2 != NULL) {
        new_node = (struct node*) calloc(1, sizeof(struct node));
        new_node->next = result_node;
        result_node = new_node;

        sum = p1->data + p2->data + carry;
        new_node->data = sum % 10;
        carry = sum / 10;

        p1 = p1->next;
        p2 = p2->next;
    }

    /*If one of the two input linked lists still has nodes to be processed
    then make p1 point to the leftover input linked list*/
    if (p2 != NULL)
        p1 = p2;

    /*Process the remaining input linked list*/
    while (p1) {
        new_node = (struct node*) calloc(1, sizeof(struct node));
        new_node->next = result_node;
        result_node = new_node;

        sum = p1->data + carry;
        new_node->data = sum % 10;
        carry = sum / 10;
        p1 = p1->next;
    }
```

```
    /*If carry is non-zero, then store the carry in the result linked list*/
    if (carry) {
        new_node = (struct node*) calloc(1, sizeof(struct node));
        new_node->next = result_node;
        result_node = new_node;
        new_node->data = carry;
    }

    /*Reverse back the two input linked lists*/
    reverse_linked_list(h1);
    reverse_linked_list(h2);

    /*The result  node already points to MS node.
    So no need to reverse result linked list*/
    return result_node;
}
```

15.

Each node of a linked list stores one digit of a number. The head of the linked list has the most significant digit. Find the product of two such linked lists (result is also a linked list)

The head of the input linked list stores the most significant digit. However, we perform multiplication from the least significant digit to the most significant digit. So we have to reverse the input linked lists to perform an efficient multiplication. The time complexity is O(mn) where m and n are the sizes of the two input linked lists. The procedure is

1. To simplify processing, we first pre-create nodes of the result linked list and zero fill them. If sizes of input linked lists are m and n, then result linked list will have m+n nodes.

2. Reverse the two input linked lists

3. Consider the diagram below. Take the digit in second linked list (node 9) and multiply it with the first linked list (3->2). Add the result to the nodes in the result linked list (from node a onwards). Then move to the next node in the second linked list (node 8) and the next node in result (node b). Repeat this step for all the nodes in the second linked list.

4. Reverse the two input lists and the result list.

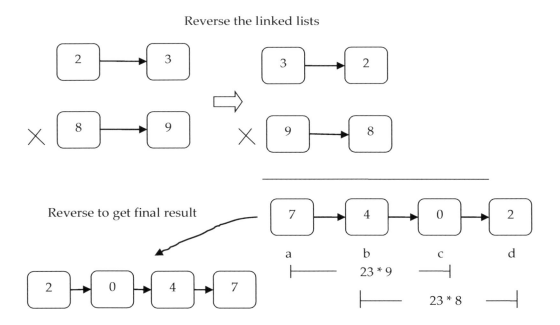

```
/*n1, n2: head of the first and second linked list
count1, count2: num elements in first and second linked list
Return value: head of new linked list having the result of multiplication*/
struct node* multiply_lists(struct node *n1, struct node *n2, int count1,
                int count2)
{
    struct node *p1, *p2, *h1, *h2;
    struct node *cur_res_node, *result_head, *result_start_node;
    int i, product, sum, carry;

    /*Reverse the two input linked lists*/
    h1 = reverse_linked_list(n1);
    h2 = reverse_linked_list(n2);

    /*Pre-create the result linked list*/
    i = 0;
    result_head = NULL;
    while (i < count1 + count2 ) {
        cur_res_node = (struct node*) calloc(1, sizeof (struct node*));
        cur_res_node->next = result_head;
        result_head = cur_res_node;
        ++i;
    }

    /*Perform the multiplication*/
    result_start_node = result_head;
    p1 = h1;
    while (p1 != NULL) {
        cur_res_node = result_start_node;
        p2 = h2;
        carry = 0;
        while (p2 != NULL) {

                product = p1->data * p2->data;
                sum = product + cur_res_node->data + carry;
                cur_res_node->data = sum % 10;
                carry = sum / 10;

                p2 = p2->next;
                cur_res_node = cur_res_node->next;
        }

        cur_res_node->data = carry;

        p1 = p1->next;
        result_start_node = result_start_node->next;
    }
    /*Reverse back the two input linked lists*/
    reverse_linked_list(h1);
    reverse_linked_list(h2);

    /*Reverse the result linked list*/
    result_head = reverse_linked_list(result_head);
    return result_head;
}
```

16.

Construct a doubly linked list with just a single pointer in each node for traversing it

The nodes in a doubly linked list use two pointers: a pointer to the previous node and a pointer to the next node. However it is possible to traverse the doubly linked list in both directions with just a single pointer in each node. The idea is to use the XOR operation which has the following properties: 1.) A XOR A = 0, 2.) A XOR 0 = A.

Each node maintains a single field called neighbor whose value is given by the formula
neighbor field value = address of previous node XOR address of next node

So in the example below, node A stores 0 XOR address of node B in the neighbor field. 0 is used since A has no previous node. Node B stores address of A XOR address of C.

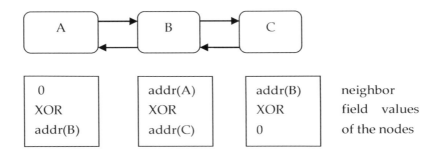

0 XOR addr(B)	addr(A) XOR addr(C)	addr(B) XOR 0	neighbor field values of the nodes

While traversing the list we apply the following formula to get the address of next node:
next node address = neighbor field value of current node XOR previous node address

Let us say that we are traversing the list starting from node A. Then next node address =
= (neighbor field of A) XOR (0) = 0 XOR addr(B) XOR 0

= addr(B) [Reason: 0 XOR 0 = 0, addr(B) XOR 0 = addr(B)]

We have obtained address of node B. To move to the node next to B, we do the same:
next node address = neighbor field of B XOR addr(A) = addr(A) XOR addr(C) XOR addr(A)

= addr(C) [Reason: addr(A) XOR addr(A) = 0, addr(C) XOR 0 = addr(C)]

Similarly traversal in the reverse direction is also possible

1.2 Stacks and Queues

1. Implement a queue using stacks

To implement a queue using stacks, we have to perform the enqueue and dequeue operations of the queue using the push and pop operations supported by the stacks.

Let us say that we internally use stack S1 to implement a queue. When elements are added to the queue, they are pushed onto the internal stack S1. However when we have to remove an element from the queue, if we pop the element from S1, we will be returning the most recently added element instead of the element first added to the queue. We solve this problem by using an additional internal stack S2 that stores the elements to be removed from the queue in correct order. So S2 should store the elements in reverse order of S1. By popping each element from S1 and immediately pushing it into S2, S2 will store the elements in reverse order of S1. To remove an element from the queue, we will have to just pop the element from S2.

For instance, let us say that elements A, B and C are added to the queue. Then S1 will contain A, B and C while S2 will be empty as shown in the diagram below.

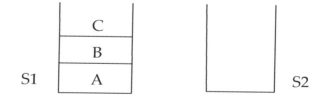

Now if an element has to be removed from the queue, since S2 is empty, each element of S1 is popped and immediately pushed into S2 as shown in the diagram below.

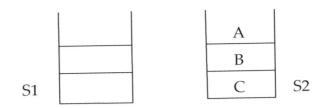

The top of stack S2 (which is element A) is then popped to remove the element from the queue.

It is important to note that, elements should be popped from S1 and pushed into S2 only when S2 is completely empty. For instance, after A is removed, let the element D be added to the queue. D is first added to S1. Suppose D is popped from S1 and pushed to S2 even before S2 is empty, then the state of the stacks is shown below

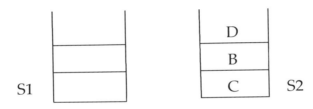

Clearly this results in an incorrect behavior since the next element that will be removed from the queue is D as D is at the top of S2 whereas the correct element to be removed from the queue is the element B. The code for a queue class using stacks is given below:

```
template <class T> class QueueUsingStacks
{
    private:
    stack<T> s1;
    stack<T> s2;

    public:
    QueueUsingStacks() {

    }

    void add(T new_element) {
        /*Add elements only to stack s1*/
        s1.push(new_element);
    }

    T remove() {
        T e;
        if(s2.empty()) {
                /*We remove elements only from stack s2. So
```

```
                if s2 is empty, then pop all the elements from s1 and
                push them into s2.*/
                while(!s1.empty()) {
                        e = s1.top();
                        s1.pop();
                        s2.push(e);
                }
        }

        if (s2.empty())
                throw exception();

        /*If s2 is not empty, then remove the element from top of s2.
        This element corresponds to the head of the queue*/
        e = s2.top();
        s2.pop();
        return e;
    }

    bool empty() {
        /*Queue is empty only if both stacks are empty*/
        if (s1.empty() && s2.empty())
                return true;
        return false;
    }

};
```

Note that each element that is added to the queue and removed from the queue later, will be first pushed into S1, then popped from S1, then pushed to S2 and finally popped from S2 thereby undergoing a total of 2 push and 2 pop operations.

2. Implement a stack using queues.

To implement a stack using queues, we have to perform the push and pop operations of the stack using the enqueue and dequeue operations supported by the queues.

A stack can be implemented using two internal queues Q1 and Q2. There are two ways to achieve this: one where the push operation is more efficient than the pop operation and the other where the pop operation is more efficient than the push operation.

Case 1: Push is more efficient than pop

When an element is pushed to the stack, the element is enqueued in Q1

When an element is popped from the stack, dequeue the first N-1 elements from Q1 (N is the number of elements currently present in Q1) and enqueue them in Q2, one element at a time. Dequeue the last element from Q1 and return it as the element popped from the stack. Now rename Q1 as Q2 and Q2 as Q1.

For instance, let us say that the elements A, B and C are added to the stack. Then A, B, C will be enqueued into Q1 as shown in the diagram below

Now if an element must be popped from the stack, dequeue A and B from Q1, then enqueue A and B in Q2. Finally dequeue the last element in Q1 which is C and return it as the popped element. Once this is done, the state of Q1 and Q2 are shown below

In the last step of the pop operation, Q1 is renamed as Q2 and Q2 is renamed as Q1 as shown below

Q1

| A | B | |

front

Q2

| | | |

front

The code for implementing a stack class using queues where push is efficient is given below.

```
template <class T> class StackUsingQueues
{
    private:
    queue<T> *q1;
    queue<T> *q2;

    public:
    StackUsingQueues() {
        q1 = new queue<T>();
        q2 = new queue<T>();
    }

    ~StackUsingQueues() {
        delete q1;
        delete q2;
    }


    bool empty() {
        /*Stack is empty only if both queues are empty*/
        if (q1->empty() && q2->empty())
                return true;

        return false;
    }


    void push(T new_element) {
        /*Add element to the end of queue q1*/
        q1->push(new_element);
    }
```

41

```
T pop() {
    /*If stack is empty, then throw an exception*/
    if (empty())
            throw exception();

    T e;
    /*Remove all elements from q1 and add it to q2 except the last item*/
    while (q1->size() > 1) {
            e = q1->front();
            q1->pop();
            q2->push(e);
    }

    /*Remove the last element in q1. It will contain the top of stack*/
    e = q1->front();
    q1->pop();

    /*Swap the queues q1 and q2*/
    queue<T> *temp = q1;
    q1 = q2;
    q2 = temp;

    return e; /*Return the top of the stack*/
}

};
```

Case 2: Pop is more efficient than push

When an element is pushed to the stack, the element is enqueued in Q1. All the elements of Q2 are dequeued and enqueued in Q1. Rename Q1 as Q2 and Q2 as Q1. So Q2 will always contain elements in the reverse order of insertion.

When an element is popped from the stack, a dequeue operation is performed on Q2 to obtain the element at the top of the stack.

3. Implement N stacks in an array

If there are just two stacks, the bottoms of the stacks can be at the opposite ends of the array and the stacks will grow in opposite direction towards the middle of the array. This way, the free space of the array is common to both the stacks and any stack can make use of the free space in between. So there will be no wastage of space.

bottom	top	top	bottom
S1	Free Space		S2

If 3 or more stacks should be stored in an array, the possible size that each stack can grow to can be initially guessed. Based on the initial guess, the bottom of each stack is decided in the array. To fully utilize the free space in the array, the bottom of one or more stacks and their elements can be shifted at run time.

For instance, let us say that we have to implement 3 stacks in an array. The guess estimate for the sizes of stack S1 is 2, S2 is 3, and S3 is 4. Then the diagram below shows the initial layout of the array.

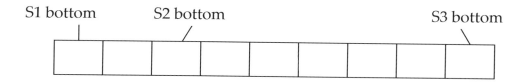

At run time let us say that the state of the stacks is as shown and we want to add C to S1

Stack S1 is full. However there is still space available between S2 and S3. Stack S1 can make use of this space for storing C, if the bottom of stack S2 and elements in S2 are shifted as shown below.

S1 bottom		S1 top	S2 bottom	S2 top			S3 top	S3 bottom
A	B	C	X	Y	Z		Q	P

4. Implement a circular queue using arrays. Take care of resize of the queue in-case the queue becomes full

In a circular queue implemented using arrays, we keep track of the head (index of first element) and tail (index of last element) of the queue. The time complexity of enqueue and dequeue operations is O(1). When we resize the array of size N, we can't directly copy the first N locations of the old array into the first N locations in the new array. Instead we have to copy the elements from head to tail in the old array into the locations 0 to N-1 in the new array. The implementation for a circular queue using arrays is given below:

```
template <class T> class queue
{
    private:
    int head; /*index of the first element in queue. -1 if queue is empty*/
    int tail; /*index of last element in queue. -1 if queue is empty*/
    int count; /*Number of elements currently present in the queue*/
    int max_size; /*Maximum number of elements that can be stored in the queue*/
    T *buffer; /*buffer for storing elements */

    public:

    queue():head(-1), tail(-1), count(0), max_size(1) {
        buffer = new T[max_size];
    }

    ~queue() {
        delete [] buffer;
    }

    int add(int new_element) {
        if (count == max_size) {
                /*If the queue is full, then resize the queue*/
                T *new_buffer = new T[max_size * 2];
                int old_pos = head;
                int new_pos = 0;

                /*Copy from the old queue buffer to the new buffer*/
                while (new_pos < count) {
                        new_buffer[new_pos] = buffer[old_pos];
                        ++new_pos;
                        old_pos = (old_pos + 1) % max_size;
                }

                delete [] buffer;

                buffer = new_buffer;
                head = 0;
```

```
                tail = count - 1;
                max_size = max_size * 2;
        }

        /*Advance the tail and insert the element at the tail of the queue*/
        tail = (tail + 1) % max_size;
        buffer[tail] = new_element;

        if (count == 0)
                head = tail;

        count++;

        /*Return the result code indicating success*/
        return 0;
    }

    T remove() {
        T removed_element;

        /*Can't remove an item from an empty queue*/
        if (count <= 0)
                throw exception();

        removed_element = buffer[head];

        if (head == tail) {
                /*There was only 1 item in the queue and that item has
                been removed. So reinitialize head and tail to -1*/
                head = -1;
                tail = -1;
        } else {
                /*Advance the head to the next location*/
                head = (head + 1) % max_size;
        }

        count--;

        return removed_element;
    }

};
```

5. Implement get minimum functionality in a stack which returns the smallest value stored in the stack in constant time.

We can find the smallest value stored in a stack in constant time by maintaining an additional stack called the min_stack. The top of the min_stack always has the smallest value stored so far in the main_stack.

When a push operation is performed on the main_stack, the item is first added to the main_stack. Then if the min_stack is empty or if the item being added is smaller than or equal to the item at the top of the min_stack, then the item is also pushed on to the min_stack.

When a pop operation is done on the main_stack, the top element is first removed from the main_stack and the value of this element is compared with the value of the top element of the min_stack. If both values match, then topmost element of min_stack is also popped.

To get the minimum value in the main_stack at any point of time, we just have to peek at the top of the min_stack.

```
/*
main_stack: the main stack
min_stack: the additional stack for getting the minimum element
data_to_add: data to be added to the stack
*/
void add_element(stack<int>& main_stack, stack<int>& min_stack, int data_to_add)
{
    /*Push the node being inserted onto the main stack*/
    main_stack.push(data_to_add);

    /*
    If the min_stack is empty or the data being inserted is <=
    to the top of the min_stack, then add the data to the min_stack
    */
    if (min_stack.empty() || data_to_add <= min_stack.top()) {
        min_stack.push(data_to_add);
    }
}
```

```
/*
main_stack: the main stack
min_stack: the additional stack for getting the minimum element
Return value: data at the top of the main stack, -1 if the main stack is empty
*/
int remove_element(stack<int>& main_stack, stack<int>& min_stack)
{
    int popped_element, min_val;

    /*If main stack is empty we can't remove element*/
    if (main_stack.empty())
        throw exception();

    /*Remove the topmost element from the main stack*/
    popped_element = main_stack.top();
    main_stack.pop();

    /*Peek at the minimum value, which is stored at the top of the min_stack*/
    min_val = min_stack.top();

    /*
    If value popped from the main stack matches the value at the top
    of min_stack, then remove the topmost element from the min_stack
    */
    if (popped_element == min_val)
        min_stack.pop();

    return popped_element;
}
```

6. Sort the elements in a stack using the push, pop, peek and is_empty operations

Let the original stack be S1. We will use an additional stack S2 for sorting the elements of S1. The final sorted result will be stored in S2. Let the elements 3, 1, 2 be stored in S1.

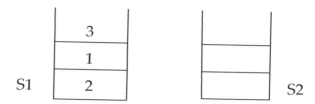

Initially S2 is empty. So 3 is popped from S1 and pushed into S2. Then 1 is popped from S1 and compared with the top element of S2 which is 3. Since 1 is <= 3, by pushing 1 on to S2, we can continue to maintain the sorted order of elements in S2. So 1 is also pushed into S2. Next 2 is popped from S1 as shown below.

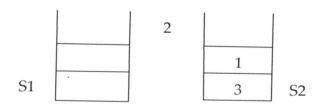

Then 2 is compared with the top element of S2 which is 1. Since 2 > 1, if we push 2 onto the stack, we can't maintain sorted order. So we pop elements from S2 and push them into S1 until we find an element >= 2 in S2 or until S2 becomes completely empty. So 1 is popped from S2 and pushed into S1. Next since 2 < 3, we have found the position where 2 can be inserted into S2 and we push 2 into S2 as shown below

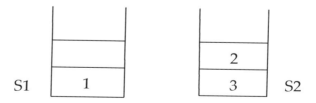

Then 1 is popped from S1 and compared with top of S2. Since 1 < 2, 1 is pushed into S2

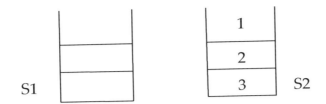

Now S2 contains the sorted elements. The code is given below

```
/*
Input elements are stored in original_stack. At the end of the operation,
original_stack will be empty and sorted stack will have elements in sorted order
*/
void stack_sort(stack<int>& original_stack, stack<int>& sorted_stack) {
    int e1, e2;

    while (!original_stack.empty()) {
        e1 = original_stack.top();
        original_stack.pop();

        /*If sorted stack is empty OR e1 <= top element of
        sorted stack, then push e1 onto the sorted stack */
        if (sorted_stack.empty()) {
            sorted_stack.push(e1);
            continue;
        }

        e2 = sorted_stack.top();
        if (e1 <= e2) {
            sorted_stack.push(e1);
            continue;
        }

        /*While e1 > top element of sorted stack, remove the top
        element of sorted stack and push it onto the original stack.
        */
        while (!sorted_stack.empty()) {
            e2 = sorted_stack.top();
            if (e1 > e2) {
                sorted_stack.pop();
                original_stack.push(e2);
            }
            else {
                break;
            }
        }
        sorted_stack.push(e1); /*Push e1 onto the sorted stack */
    }
}
```

7. Given a string consisting of opening and closing braces '{', '}', opening and closing brackets '[', ']' and opening and closing parenthesis '(' and ')', check if the opening and closing characters are properly nested

To check if the opening and closing characters are properly nested we make use of a stack. Traverse the characters in the string and do the following

1. If we get an opening character in the string, then push it on to the stack

2. If we get a closing character in the string, then the corresponding opening character must be present on top of the stack. So if we get ')' in the string, '(' should be present on top of the stack. Otherwise, the nesting is not proper. After checking the top of stack, pop the stack.

After processing all characters in the string, the stack should be empty. If the stack still has elements in it, then the nesting is not proper

```
/*
Verify if the braces, brackets and parenthesis are properly nested
str1: input string containing braces, brackets and parenthesis
Return value: 1 if the nesting is proper, 0 otherwise
*/
int validate_nesting(const char *str1) {
    stack<char> s;
    int i = 0;

    while (str1[i]) {
        char c, top_char;

        c = str1[i];
        if (c == '{' || c == '[' || c == '(') {
            /*If we get an opening brace, bracket or parenthesis
            in string, then push it on to the stack*/
            s.push(c);
        } else if (c == '}' || c == ']' || c == ')') {
            /*If we get a closing brace, bracket or parenthesis
            in string, then the character on top of stack should be
            the corresponding opening character*/
            if (s.empty())
                    return 0;

            top_char = s.top();
            if (c == '}' && top_char != '{')
                    return 0;
            else if (c == ']' && top_char != '[')
                    return 0;
            else if (c == ')' && top_char != '(')
                    return 0;
```

51

```
            /*Since we have matched the opening and closing character,
            remove the opening character from the stack*/
            s.pop();
    } else {
            /*We found a character other than a brace, bracket
            or parenthesis*/
            return 0;
    }
    ++i;
}

/*At the end of processing, the stack should be empty*/
if (!s.empty())
    return 0;

return 1;
}
```

1.3 Trees

1. Convert a binary tree into its mirror image

An example of a binary tree and its mirror image is shown below.

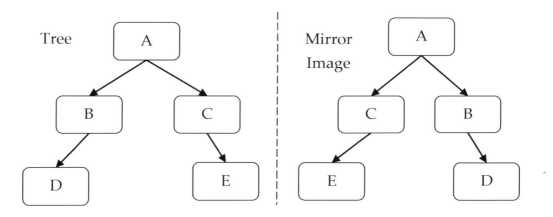

So to convert the binary tree to its mirror image, the left child and the right child of each node in the tree should be swapped.

```
/*
cur_node: current node of the tree whose mirror image should be computed
*/
void compute_mirror_image(struct node *cur_node) {
    struct node *temp_node;

    if (cur_node) {
        /*Swap the left child and right child of the current node*/
        temp_node = cur_node->left;
        cur_node->left = cur_node->right;
        cur_node->right = temp_node;

        /*Recursively compute the mirror image */
        compute_mirror_image(cur_node->left);
        compute_mirror_image(cur_node->right);
    }
}
```

2. Find if a binary tree is symmetric

A binary tree is symmetric, if the left sub-tree of each node is a mirror image of the right sub-tree. An example of a symmetric binary tree is given below

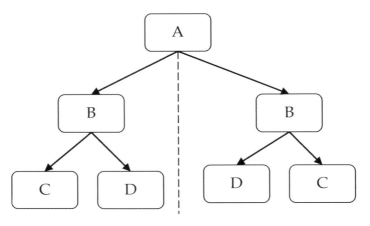

```
int compare_nodes ( struct node *n1, struct node *n2) {
    if (!n1 && !n2)   /*If both the nodes are NULL */
        return 1;   /* return symmetric*/

    if ( (n1 && !n2) || (!n1 && n2)) /*If one node is NULL and other is not*/
        return 0; /*return not symmetric*/

    if (n1->data != n2->data) /*If data of two nodes don't match */
        return 0; /* return not symmetric */

    if (!compare_nodes (n1->left, n2->right))
        return 0;

    if (!compare_nodes (n1->right, n2->left))
        return 0;

    return 1; /*Return symmetric*/
}

/*Returns 1 if the tree is symmetric, 0 otherwise*/
int is_symmetric(struct node * root) {
    if (!root)
        return 1;

    return compare_nodes(root->left, root->right);
}
```

3. Find if a binary tree is balanced

A binary tree is balanced if at every node in the tree, the absolute difference between the height of the left-subtree and the height of the right sub-tree doesn't exceed 1. To solve the problem we recursively traverse the tree and calculate the height of the nodes in a bottom up manner. If at any node, the difference between the height of the left and right sub-trees exceeds 1, we report that the tree is unbalanced.

```
/*cur_node: node of the binary tree being checked
height: height of the current node is returned here
Return value: 1 if the tree is balanced, 0 otherwise
*/
int is_balanced(struct node *cur_node, int *height)
{
    int is_left_balanced, is_right_balanced;
    int left_height, right_height;

    if (!cur_node) {
        *height = 0;
        return 1;
    }

    is_left_balanced = is_balanced(cur_node->left, &left_height);
    is_right_balanced = is_balanced(cur_node->right, &right_height);

    if (!is_left_balanced || !is_right_balanced)
        return 0;

    /*If the difference between height of left subtree and height of
    right subtree is more than 1, then the tree is unbalanced*/
    if (abs(left_height - right_height) > 1)
        return 0;

    /*To get the height of the current node, we find the maximum of the
    left subtree height and the right subtree height and add 1 to it*/
    *height = max(left_height, right_height) + 1;

    return 1;
}
```

4. Find if a binary tree is a binary search tree

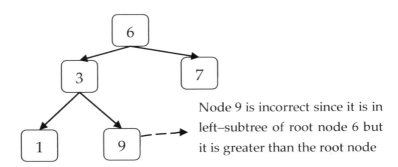

Node 9 is incorrect since it is in left–subtree of root node 6 but it is greater than the root node

The initial approach that comes to mind is to check if the left child node is smaller than the parent node and the right child node is greater than the parent node for all the nodes in the tree. However this solution will not work as shown in the binary tree above. Every node satisfies the condition that the left child is smaller than the parent and the right child is greater than the parent. But the tree is still not a binary search tree since node 9 is incorrect. To correctly find out if a tree is a binary search tree, we should traverse the tree in-order and check if the nodes are present in ascending order.

```
/*cur_node: current node whose left and right sub-trees need to be checked
prev_node_pp: the in-order predecessor of cur_node
Return value: 1 if the tree is a binary search tree, 0 otherwise
*/
int is_bst(struct node *cur_node, struct node ** prev_node_pp)
{
    if (!cur_node)
        return 1;

    /*Check if the left sub-tree is a BST*/
    if (!is_bst(cur_node->left, prev_node_pp))
        return 0;

    /*If data in cur_node is <= to previous node then it is not a BST*/
    if (*prev_node_pp && cur_node->data <= (*prev_node_pp)->data)
        return 0;

    /*Update previous node to current node*/
    *prev_node_pp = cur_node;

    /*Check if the right sub-tree is a BST*/
    return is_bst(cur_node->right, prev_node_pp);
}
```

5. Print the nodes of a binary tree in level order

To print the nodes of the binary tree in level order, we start with the root node and then print the child nodes in each level from left to right. Consider the binary tree below

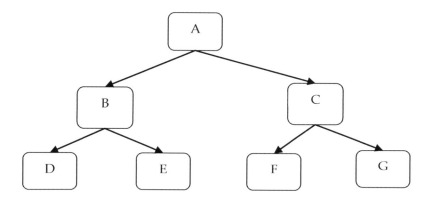

The level order printing will result in the following output: ABCDEFG. To achieve this we make use of a queue and use the following strategy:

1. Add the root node to the queue
2. Remove the head element of the queue and print it. Then add the children of the removed element back to the queue. Repeat step-2 until the queue becomes empty.

1. Add root of tree to queue

2. Remove A, print it and add its children B and C to the queue

3. Remove B, print it and add its children D and E to the queue

4. Remove C, print it and add its children F and G to the queue

```
/*
root: root node of the tree
q: queue that helps in printing in level order
*/
void print_level_order(struct node *root, queue<struct node*>& q)
{
    struct node *n;
    int num_nodes_in_cur_level, num_nodes_in_next_level;

    if (!root)
        return;

    /*Add the root node to the empty queue*/
    q.push(root);
    num_nodes_in_cur_level = 1;
    num_nodes_in_next_level = 0;

    /*Process the nodes in the queue in Breadth First manner*/
    while (!q.empty()) {

        /*Remove the node at the head of the queue*/
        n = q.front();
        q.pop();

        print_data(n->data); /*print the data in the node*/

        /*Add the left child to the end of the queue*/
        if (n->left) {
                q.push(n->left);
                num_nodes_in_next_level++;
        }

        /*Add the right child to the end of the queue*/
        if (n->right) {
                q.push(n->right);
                num_nodes_in_next_level++;
        }

        num_nodes_in_cur_level--;

        /*go to next line, if all nodes in current level are processed*/
        if (num_nodes_in_cur_level == 0) {
                cout << endl;
                num_nodes_in_cur_level = num_nodes_in_next_level;
                num_nodes_in_next_level = 0;
        }
    }
}
```

6. Print the nodes of a binary tree in spiral (zigzag) order

Consider the following binary tree

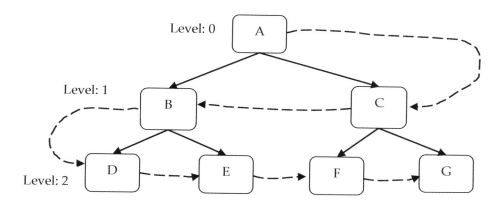

To print in spiral (zigzag) order, we have to print the nodes from right to left in one level and left to right in the next level. So the output for this tree is ACBDEFG. To achieve this, we make use of two stacks Stack-0 and Stack-1. Stack-0 is used when printing nodes at an even level and Stack-1 is used when printing nodes at an odd level. The algorithm that we use to print spirally is as follows:

1. Initially push the root into Stack-0 and start processing Stack-0

2. For an even level, pop an element from Stack-0 and print it. Then add its left child followed by its right child into Stack-1. Repeat step-2 until Stack-0 becomes empty

3. For an odd level, pop an element from Stack-1 and print it. Then add its right child followed by its left child into Stack-0. Repeat step-3 until Stack-1 becomes empty

The algorithm comes to a halt when both stacks become completely empty

The steps of the algorithm are shown below. First push root node into Stack-0.

Then pop A from Stack-0 and print it. Push its left child (B) followed by its right child (C) onto Stack-1.

Since Stack-0 has become empty, we start processing Stack-1. Pop C from Stack-1 and print it. Then push its right child (G) followed by its left child (F) onto Stack-0

Pop B from Stack-1 and print it. Then push its right child (E) followed by its left child (D) onto Stack-0

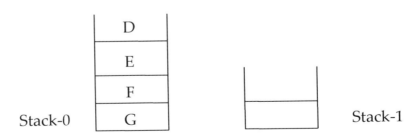

Since Stack-1 is empty, start processing Stack-0. Since the nodes in Stack-0 have no children, we end up popping and printing them and finally both stacks become empty.

```
/*Helper function for printing in zig zag order
print_stack: stack used for printing the nodes
store_stack: stack that stores the children of nodes in print_stack
left_to_right: if set to 1, left child is stored first followed by right child
*/
void process_stacks(stack<struct node*>& print_stack,
        stack<struct node*>& store_stack, int left_to_right)
{
    struct node * cur_node;

    while (!print_stack.empty()) {

        cur_node = print_stack.top();
        print_stack.pop();
        print_data( cur_node->data);

        if (left_to_right) {
                if (cur_node->left)
                        store_stack.push(cur_node->left);
                if (cur_node->right)
                        store_stack.push(cur_node->right);
        } else {
                if (cur_node->right)
                        store_stack.push(cur_node->right);
                if (cur_node->left)
                        store_stack.push(cur_node->left);
        }
    }
}

/*root: root of the binary tree to be printed spirally
s0, s1: stacks used for storing nodes of the binary tree
*/
void print_zig_zag(struct node *root, stack<struct node*>& s0,
        stack<struct node*>& s1)
{
    if (!root)
        return;

    /*Push root into stack s0 and start processing*/
    s0.push(root);

    while (!s0.empty()) {
        /*s0 is used for printing. The children of nodes in s0 are
        stored in s1 in left to right direction*/
        process_stacks(s0, s1, 1);
        cout << endl;

        /*s1 is used for printing. The children of nodes in s1 are
        stored in s0 in right to left direction*/
        process_stacks(s1, s0, 0);
        cout << endl;
    }
}
```

7. Find the least common ancestor for two nodes in a tree given only parent pointers

Each node in the tree has a parent pointer. To find the least common ancestor of two nodes N1 and N2 in the tree we use the following procedure:

1. Find the depths of the two nodes N1 and N2 by traversing up the tree using the parent pointers until we reach the root node

2. Let us say that N1 is deeper than N2. Pick the deeper node N1 and traverse up the parent pointers until we reach a node whose depth is equal to the depth of the shallower node N2.

3. If the nodes in the two paths are the same then the common node is the least common ancestor. Otherwise go up the tree by one level on both paths and repeat this step until we reach a common node

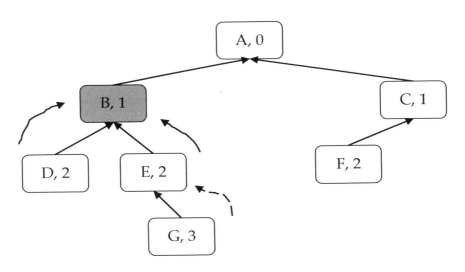

Consider the following tree, where the depth of the nodes are indicated for each node. Node A has depth of 0, node B and C have a depth of 1 and so on. Suppose we have to find the least common ancestor of node D and node G. D has a depth of 2 while G has a depth of 3. Since G is the deeper node, we find the ancestor of G which is at the same depth as the shallower node D. In this case E has the same depth as D. Then we advance from D and E by one node up along both paths until we reach a common node. So we reach node B along both paths. So B is the least common ancestor of nodes D and G.

```
/*n: node in the binary tree
Return value: depth of the node
*/
int find_depth(struct node *n)
{
    int depth = 0;

    while (n->parent) {
        n = n->parent;
        ++depth;
    }
    return depth;
}

/*Find the Least Common Ancestor of a BINARY TREE
n1 and n2 are two nodes in the tree
Return value: least common ancestor node of n1 and n2
*/
struct node *lca(struct node *n1, struct node *n2)
{
    int depth1, depth2;

    depth1 = find_depth(n1);
    depth2 = find_depth(n2);

    /* If n1 is deeper than n2, then move n1 up the tree
    until the depth of n1 and n2 match
    */
    while (depth1 > depth2) {
        n1 = n1->parent;
        depth1--;
    }

    /* If n2 is deeper than n1, then move n2 up the tree
    until the depth of n1 and n2 match
    */
    while (depth2 > depth1) {
        n2 = n2->parent;
        depth2--;
    }

    /*Move n1 and n2 up the tree until a common node is found*/
    while (n1 != n2 ) {
        n1 = n1->parent;
        n2 = n2->parent;
    }

    return n1;
}
```

8. Convert a sorted array into a binary search tree with least depth.

Let the elements of the input array {1, 2, 3, 4, 5} be sorted in ascending order. If we store the first element of the array in the root of the binary search tree, then place the next element to the right of the root and so on, we will end up with the tree shown below.

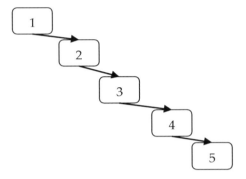

Although this is still a valid binary search tree, the tree is too deep. The tree is now more like a linked list and we can't get the speed up while searching it. So to build a binary search tree with the least depth, we use the following approach

1. Place the middle item in the array into the root of the tree

2. Recursively construct the left sub-tree using elements between (start, middle – 1) and the right sub-tree using the elements between (middle + 1, end)

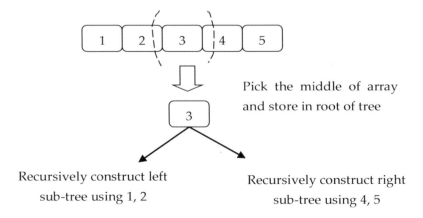

Pick the middle of array and store in root of tree

Recursively construct left sub-tree using 1, 2

Recursively construct right sub-tree using 4, 5

```c
/*
parent: parent of the BST node currently being constructed
values: sorted array to be converted into BST
low, high: lower and upper index of the array region being operated upon
Return value: BST node created that corresponds to values[(low+high)/2]
*/
struct node* construct_bst(struct node *parent, int values[], int low, int high)
{
    struct node *new_node;
    int middle = (low + high) / 2;

    if (low > high)
        return NULL;

    new_node = (struct node*) calloc(1, sizeof(struct node));
    if (!new_node)
        return NULL;

    /*Construct the new node using the middle value*/
    new_node->data = values[middle];
    new_node->parent = parent;

    /*Construct the left sub-tree using values[low] to values[middle-1]*/
    new_node->left = construct_bst(new_node, values, low, middle - 1);

    /*Construct the right sub-tree using values[middle+1] to values[high]*/
    new_node->right = construct_bst(new_node, values, middle + 1, high);

    return new_node;
}
```

9. Convert a sorted doubly linked list in place into a binary search tree with least depth

Each node has 2 members: left and right. In the doubly linked list, left stores the previous node and right stores the next node. In the BST, left stores the left child and right stores the right child. We reuse the doubly linked list nodes to create the BST. The procedure is:

- Find the middle node in the doubly linked list
- Recursively construct left sub-tree using the nodes that are before the middle node and connect the left sub-tree to the middle node
- Recursively construct right sub-tree using the nodes that are after the middle node and connect the right sub-tree to the middle node

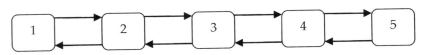

1. Given doubly linked list to be converted to BST

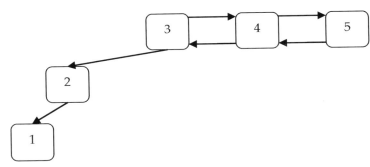

2. Recursively compute left sub-tree and connect to middle node

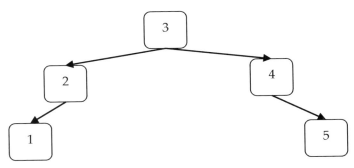

3. Recursively compute right sub-tree and connect to middle node

The code to convert a doubly linked list to a binary search tree is given below.

```
/*
list_node_pp: node for traversing the doubly linked list
start: index of node in linked list at the beginning of region being operated on
end: index of node in linked list at the end of region being operated on
Returns: root of the binary search tree
*/
struct node * list_to_bst (struct node **list_node_pp, int start, int end)
{
    int middle;

    struct node *middle_node, *left_child;

    if (start > end)
        return NULL;

    middle = (start + end) / 2;

    /*Recursively construct the left subtree using the nodes before the
    middle node and get the root of the left sub-tree*/
    left_child = list_to_bst(list_node_pp, start, middle - 1);

    /*list_node_pp will now be pointing to the middle node*/
    middle_node = *list_node_pp;

    /*Connect the left sub-tree to the middle node*/
    middle_node->left = left_child;

    /*Advance to the next node after the middle node*/
    *list_node_pp = (*list_node_pp)->right;

    /*Recursively construct the right subtree using the nodes after the
    middle node and connect the root of right subtree to middle node*/
    middle_node->right = list_to_bst(list_node_pp, middle + 1, end);

    return middle_node;
}
```

10. Convert a binary search tree in place into a sorted doubly linked list

Each node has 2 members: left and right. In the doubly linked list, left stores the previous node and right stores the next node. In the BST, left stores the left child and right stores the right child. We reuse the BST nodes to create the doubly linked list. The procedure is:

1. Recursively convert left sub-tree into a doubly linked list and connect it to the root

2. Recursively convert right sub-tree into a doubly linked list and connect it to the root

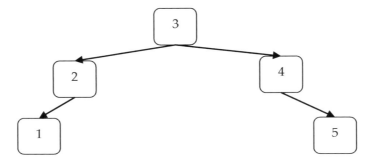

1. Given BST to be converted to doubly linked list

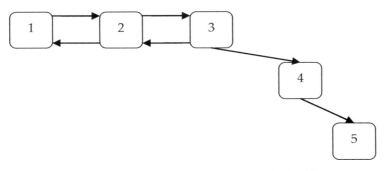

2. Recursively convert left sub-tree to doubly linked list

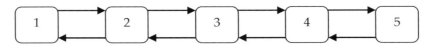

3. Recursively convert right sub-tree to doubly linked list

The code to convert a binary search tree to a doubly linked list is given below.

```c
/*
cur_node: the current BST node being processed
prev_node_pp: node that is previous to the current node in linked list
list_head_pp: head of the result linked list
Returns: 0 on success
*/
int bst_to_list(struct node *cur_node, struct node **prev_node_pp,
        struct node **list_head_pp)
{
    if (!cur_node)
        return 0;

    /*In-Order Traversal of the BST*/

    /*Convert the left sub-tree of node to linked list*/
    bst_to_list(cur_node->left, prev_node_pp, list_head_pp);

    /*Link the previous node and the current node*/
    cur_node->left = *prev_node_pp;

    if (*prev_node_pp) {
        (*prev_node_pp)->right = cur_node;
    } else {
        /*Since previous node is NULL, this is the first node of the list
        So make head point to it */
        *list_head_pp = cur_node;
    }

    /*Make the current node the previous node*/
    *prev_node_pp = cur_node;

    /*Convert the right sub-tree of node to linked list*/
    bst_to_list(cur_node->right, prev_node_pp, list_head_pp);

    return 0; /*return success*/
}
```

11. Given a node in a binary search tree, find its previous and next nodes

We can traverse to the previous and next node of a given node in a binary search tree provided that the nodes maintain the parent pointers.

To find the previous element in a binary search tree, we will encounter two cases.

Case-1: the current node has a left child. Suppose we have to find the node previous to node 5 in the diagram below. Node 5 has a valid left child. In this case, the previous node is the rightmost node in the left sub-tree of the current node. So to find the element previous to 5, we find the rightmost element in the left sub-tree of 5 which in this case is 4.

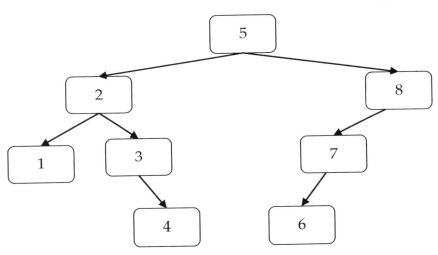

Case 2: the current node doesn't have a left child. For instance, in the diagram above, node 6 has no left child. In this case, we have to keep on traversing up the tree until we find the ancestor node whose right sub-tree has the current node. The ancestor node whose right sub-tree has the current node is the previous element of the current node. So to find the element previous to 6, we traverse up the tree since 6 has no left child. 6 is in the left sub-tree of 7. So we continue up to reach node 8. Again 6 is in the left sub-tree of 8. We continue up again to reach node 5. 6 is in the right sub-tree of 5. So the element previous to 6 is 5.

```
/*
x: node in the binary search tree
Return value: the node previous to node x
*/
struct node* get_previous(struct node *x)
{
    struct node *y;

    /*Handle Case-1, left child exists*/
    if (x->left) {
        y = x->left;
        while (y->right) {
                y = y->right;
        }
        return y;
    }

    /*Handle Case-2, left child doesn't exist*/
    y = x->parent;
    while (y && y->left == x) {
        x = y;
        y = y->parent;
    }

    return y;
}
```

To find the next element in a binary search tree, we will again encounter two cases.

Case-1: the current node has a valid right child. Suppose we have to find the node next to node 5. Node 5 has a valid right child. In this case, the next node is the left most node in the right sub-tree of the current node. So to find the element next to 5, we find the leftmost element in the right sub-tree of 5 which in this case is 6.

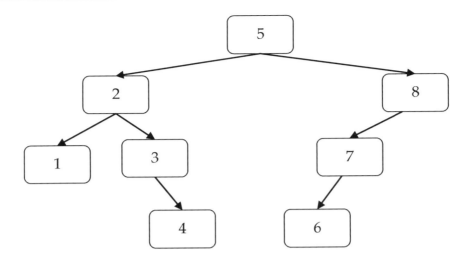

Case-2: the current node doesn't have a right child. For instance, in the diagram above, node 4 has no right child. In this case, we have to keep on traversing up the tree until we find the ancestor node whose left sub-tree has the current node. The ancestor node whose left sub-tree has the current node is the next element of the current node. So to find the element next to 4, we traverse up the tree since 4 has no right child. 4 is in the right sub-tree of 3. So we continue up to reach node 2. Again 4 is in the right sub-tree of 2. We continue up again to reach node 5. 4 is in left sub-tree of 5. So the element next to 4 is 5.

```
/*x: node in the binary search tree
Return value: the node after node x
*/
struct node* get_next(struct node *x)
{
    struct node *y;

    /*Handle Case-1: right child exists*/
    if (x->right) {
        y = x->right;
        while (y->left) {
                y = y->left;
        }
        return y;
    }

    /*Handle Case-2: right child doesn't exist*/
    y = x->parent;
    while (y && y->right == x) {
        x = y;
        y = y->parent;
    }

    return y;
}
```

12. Find the kth largest element in a binary search tree

The largest element in a binary search tree is the rightmost element in the tree. To find the kth largest element, we first find the largest element and then traverse the k-1 elements previous to the largest element. For instance, to find the 3rd largest element, we find the largest element and then traverse 2 nodes before the largest element. We make use of the get_previous function described in page 71

```
/*
root: the root node of the binary search tree
k: indicates the kth largest value. k >= 1
Return value: kth largest node in the binary search tree
*/
struct node* find_kth_largest(struct node *root, int k)
{
    struct node *n;
    int i;

    if (!root || k < 1)
        return NULL;

    /*Find the node with the maximum value*/
    n = root;
    while (n->right)
        n = n->right;

    /*Find the k-1 previous nodes */
    for (i = 1; i < k; ++i) {
        n = get_previous(n);
        if (!n) {
            return NULL;
        }
    }

    return n;
}
```

13. Find if the sum of any two nodes in a binary search tree equals K

Suppose instead of a binary search tree, we were given a sorted array A = {0, 1, 3, 4, 6, 7, 8, 9} and asked to find if any two numbers sum up to 11. Then we can do the following.

- Initialize left = 0 and right = number of elements in A - 1
- Compute sum = A[left] + A[right]. If the sum is equal to 11 then we have found the pair
- If the sum is less than 11, then we have to increase the sum. So left = left + 1
- If the sum is greater than 11, then we should decrease the sum. So right = right - 1

This process is repeated until we find the pair whose sum is k or left becomes >= right. The running time of this algorithm is O(n).

The same algorithm can be extended to binary search trees since a binary search tree is also a data structure meant for representing sorted data. We make use of the get_previous function and get_next functions described on pages 71 and 72.

```
/*
root: the root of the binary search tree
k: sum of two nodes should equal k
result1: first result node that sums to k is returned
result2: second result node that sums to k is returned
*/
void find_pair_sum_to_k(struct node *root, int k, struct node **result1,
                struct node **result2)
{
    struct node *n1, *n2;

    *result1 = NULL;
    *result2 = NULL;

    if (!root)
        return;

    /*Store the leftmost node in n1*/
    n1 = root;
    while (n1->left)
        n1 = n1->left;

    /*Store the right most node in n2*/
    n2 = root;
    while (n2->right)
        n2 = n2->right;
```

```
    /*Process the tree by picking one node from left and one node from right*/
    while (n1 != n2) {
        int sum = n1->data + n2->data;

        /*check if the left node and right node sum to k*/
        if (sum == k) {
                *result1 = n1;
                *result2 = n2;
                break;
        }

        if (sum < k) {
                /*Pick the next higher value node from the left*/
                n1 = get_next(n1);
        } else {
                /*Pick the next smaller value from the right*/
                n2 = get_previous(n2);
        }
    }
}
```

14. In each node of a binary search tree, store the sum of all nodes that are greater than it

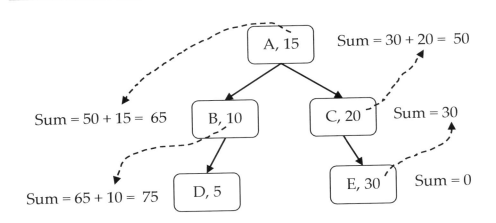

In the above diagram, the values of the nodes in a binary search tree are shown. Node E is the rightmost node and there are no nodes greater than it. So the sum for node E is 0. Node E is greater than node C. So the sum stored in C is 30. Nodes C and E are greater than A. So the sum stored in A = 20 + 30 = 50.

To compute the sum of all the nodes greater than a node, we initialize sum to zero, traverse the tree in post-order and use the following approach at each node starting with the root

wrong. post-order is left right visit

1. First process the right sub-tree of the current node and add the values of the nodes in the right subtree

2. In the current node, store the sum of the values in the right sub-tree

3. Add the value of the current node to the sum

4. Pass the sum to the left subtree of the current node and recursively process the left subtree.

```
/*
cur_node: current node of the binary search tree
sum_p: sum of nodes greater than current node is returned here
*/
void compute_sum_of_greater_nodes(struct node *cur_node, int *sum_p)
{
    if (!cur_node)
        return;

    /*Since greater elements are in the right sub-tree, first process the
    right sub-tree*/
    compute_sum_of_greater_nodes(cur_node->right, sum_p);

    /*Assign the sum of the greater nodes*/
    cur_node->sum = *sum_p;

    /*Add the current nodes data to the sum*/
    *sum_p += cur_node->data;

    /*Process the left sub-tree*/
    compute_sum_of_greater_nodes(cur_node->left, sum_p);
}
```

15. Compute the vertical sum of a binary tree

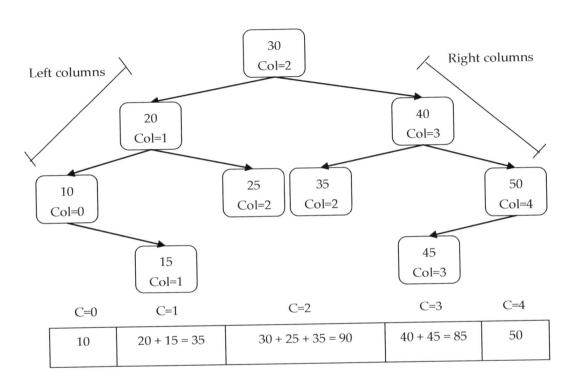

C=0	C=1	C=2	C=3	C=4
10	20 + 15 = 35	30 + 25 + 35 = 90	40 + 45 = 85	50

The number of left columns in the tree can be found by repeatedly traversing left in the left sub-tree of the root. In this example, the number of left columns = 2 (corresponding to nodes 20 and 10). Similarly the number of right columns can be found by repeatedly traversing right in the right sub-tree of the root. In this example, the number of right columns = 2 (corresponding to the nodes 40 and 50). The total columns of the tree including root = 1 + left columns + right columns = 1+ 2+ 2 = 5

Each node in the tree above is also assigned a column number as follows:

- the Col. number of the root is initialized to the number of left columns = 2
- if node is left child of its parent, its Col. number = Col. number of parent − 1
- if node is right child of its parent, its Col. number = Col. number of parent + 1

The procedure to find the vertical sum is:

1. Create the sum array whose size is equal to the total number of columns in the tree. Initialize the sum array to 0 for all columns.

2. Assign the column numbers for each node in the tree as we traverse the tree. Use the column number assigned to a node as the index into the sum array and add the value of the node to the sum array. After traversing all nodes in the tree, the sum array will have the vertical sum for each column.

```
/* Helper function to find the vertical sum
cur_node: current node being processed in the binary tree
col: column of the current node
sum_array: array containing the sum of nodes in each column
*/
void process_sum(struct node *cur_node, int col, int *sum_array)
{
    if (!cur_node)
        return;

    sum_array[col] += cur_node->data;

    /*column number of left child is col - 1*/
    process_sum(cur_node->left, col - 1, sum_array);

    /*column number of right child is col+1*/
    process_sum(cur_node->right, col +  1, sum_array);
}

/* Main function to find the vertical sum
root: root of the binary tree
sum_array_pp: array which contains the vertical sum will be returned here
Return value: number of columns in the binary tree
*/
int compute_vertical_sum(struct node *root, int ** sum_array_pp)
{
    struct node *cur_node;
    int num_left_cols= 0, num_right_cols = 0, root_col, total_num_cols;

    *sum_array_pp = NULL;
    if (!root)
        return 0;


    /*Compute the number of left columns*/
    cur_node = root->left;
    while (cur_node) {
        ++num_left_cols;
        cur_node = cur_node->left;
    }
```

```
    /*Compute the number of right columns*/
    cur_node = root->right;
    while (cur_node) {
        ++num_right_cols;
        cur_node = cur_node->right;
    }

    total_num_cols = num_left_cols+ num_right_cols + 1;

    /*Dynamically create the array for storing the column sum*/
    *sum_array_pp = (int*) calloc(total_num_cols, sizeof(int));

    root_col = num_left_cols;

    /*Compute the vertical sum starting with the root*/
    process_sum(root, root_col, *sum_array_pp);

    return total_num_cols;
}
```

16. Remove all nodes in a binary tree that don't lie in a K-heavy path

K-heavy path is a path in which the sum of the values of the nodes in the path is at least K. Suppose K = 10, then in the binary tree below, the path ABDH has a net value of 3+ 2+ 2+ 1 = 8 and so is not a K-heavy path. On the other hand, path ACG has a net value of 3+ 2+ 7 = 12 and is a K-heavy path.

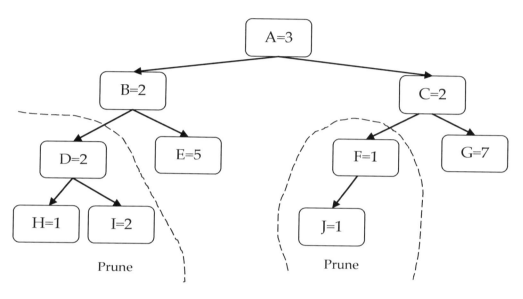

In this problem, we have to prune out the nodes that don't lie in any K-heavy path.

Consider node D. The paths running through D from the root are ABDH with a net value of 8 and ABDI with a net value of 9. Since none of the paths through D are at least 10, the node D should be completely pruned.

Consider node B. The path ABE through the node B has a net value of 10. Since there is at least one path through node B with net value >= K, node B should not be pruned.

To remove nodes that are not in a K-heavy path, traverse the tree and perform the following at each node

- Compute the value (X) of the path from the root to the current node
- Compute the longest path from the current node to any of its leaf nodes in its left and right sub-trees (Y)
- If X+Y < K, then prune the node

Consider node D. Then value of path from root to D = 3 + 2 + 2 = 7. The longest path from D to leaf = 2. So X+Y = 7 + 2 which is less than 10. So D should be pruned.

```
/*
cur_node: current node of the binary tree
above_sum: sum of the nodes from root to the parent of current node
k: the threshold path value for retaining the nodes
Return value: length of the longest path from root to leaf in which current
        node is present
*/
int k_heavy_path(struct node *cur_node, int above_sum, int k)
{
    int max_left_path, max_right_path, longest_path;

    if (!cur_node)
        return above_sum;

    above_sum += cur_node->data;

    /*Find the longest path in left sub-tree that contains the current node*/
    max_left_path = k_heavy_path(cur_node->left, above_sum, k);

    /*If longest left sub-tree path is below threshold, prune left sub-tree*/
    if (max_left_path < k)
        cur_node->left = NULL;

    /*Find longest path in right sub-tree that contains current node*/
    max_right_path = k_heavy_path(cur_node->right, above_sum, k);

    /*If longest right sub-tree path is below threshold, prune right sub-tree*/
    if (max_right_path < k)
        cur_node->right = NULL;

    longest_path = max(max_left_path, max_right_path);

    /*If all paths through node are below k, then free the node*/
    if (longest_path < k)
        free(cur_node);

    return longest_path;
}
```

17. Find the diameter of a binary tree

The diameter of a binary tree is the number of nodes in the longest path between any two leaves in the tree. It is not necessary that the diameter of the binary tree should pass through the root of the tree. For instance, the diameter in the binary tree below is IGDBEHJ and it doesn't pass through the root node A

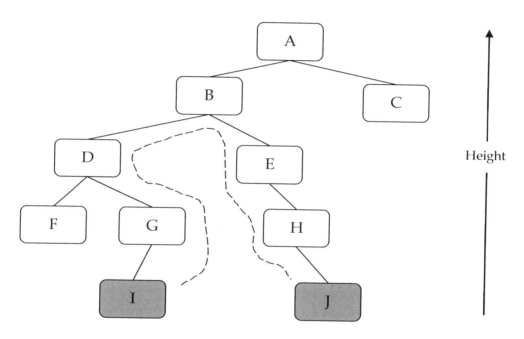

To calculate the diameter we need to know the left and right height of a node. The left height of a node is the maximum number of nodes in a path from the node to any leaf in left sub-tree of the node. So the left height of D is 1 (path F)

Similarly the right height of a node is the maximum number of nodes in a path from the node to any leaf in right sub-tree of the node. So right height of D is 2 (path GI)

Height of a node is 1 + max(left height, right height). So the height of D is 1 + max (1, 2) = 1 + 2 = 3.

We can compute the left and right height of the nodes in the tree in a bottom up manner. So if we know the heights of the children, we can calculate the height of the parent.

Once we know the left height and the right height of a node X, we can find the longest path between any two leaves passing through this node X using the formula longest path through node = 1 + left height + right height.

So longest path through D = (1 + left height of D + right height of D) = 1+ 1+ 2 = 4. The longest path through B = (1 + left height of B + right height of B) = 1+ 3+ 3 = 7.

The diameter of the tree is the maximum longest path among all nodes in the tree.

```
/*
cur_node: current node of the binary tree
height: height of current node is returned here. Leaf node has a height of 1
diameter: the diameter of the tree is returned here
*/
void find_diameter(struct node *cur_node, int *height, int *diameter)
{
    int left_height, right_height;
    int longest_path;

    if (!cur_node) {
        *height = 0;
        return;
    }

    /*Find the height of the left sub-tree*/
    find_diameter(cur_node->left, &left_height, diameter);

    /*Find the height of the right sub-tree*/
    find_diameter(cur_node->right, &right_height, diameter);

    /*Calculate height of cur_node*/
    *height = 1 + max(left_height, right_height);

    /*Calculate longest path between any two leafs passing through cur_node*/
    longest_path = left_height + right_height + 1;

    /*If the length of longest path through cur_node is greater than
    the current diameter, then assign it to the diameter*/
    if (longest_path > *diameter)
        *diameter = longest_path;
}
```

18. Form a binary tree given its in-order and pre-order traversals

We can reconstruct a binary tree in the following cases

- in-order and pre-order traversals are known
- in-order and post-order traversals are known
- in-order and level-order traversals are known

Note that if in-order traversal is not known, then even if we have pre-order, post-order and level-order traversal, we still can't reconstruct the tree. In the current problem, we know the in-order and pre-order traversals. So we can reconstruct the binary tree. Let the in-order traversal = {B,D,A,E,C,F} and pre-order traversal = {A,B,D,C,E,F}. The traversals are stored in arrays. The procedure to reconstruct the binary tree is as follows:

1. Choose the first element (A) in the pre-order array as the pivot. Since the root of the binary tree is stored as the first element of the pre-order array, pivot A is the root of the tree. So we create the root node with data equal to A

2. Next find the location of the pivot A in the in-order array.

3. The elements {B, D} that are to the left of A in the in-order array will be in the left sub-tree. Advance to the next element in the pre-order array (B) and form the left sub-tree recursively on the left in-order sub-array {B, D}. When the left subtree processing is complete, we would have advanced to element C in pre-order array

4. The elements {E, C, F} that are to the right of A in the in-order array will be in the right sub-tree. Advance to the next element in the pre-order array (E) and form the right sub-tree recursively on the right in-order sub-array {E, C, F }.

Pre-order = **A**, B, D, C, E, F

In-order = B, D, **A**, E, C, F

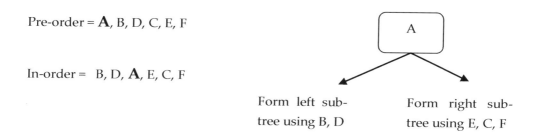

Form left sub-tree using B, D

Form right sub-tree using E, C, F

85

```c
/*
pre_order: array containing the data of nodes of the binary tree in pre-order
in_order: array containing the data of nodes of the binary tree in in-order
in_start: starting index of current region in the in_order array
in_end: ending index of current region in the in_order array
pre_pos: index in the pre-order array
Return value: newly created binary tree node
*/
struct node* construct_tree(int * pre_order, int * in_order, int in_start,
                int in_end, int *pre_pos)
{
    struct node *new_node;
    int in_location;
    int pivot;

    /*Termination condition for recursion*/
    if (in_start > in_end)
        return NULL;

    /* Assign the pivot from pre-order array*/
    pivot = pre_order[*pre_pos];

    /*Find pivot in in-order array*/
    for (in_location = in_start; in_location <= in_end; ++in_location) {
        if (in_order[in_location] == pivot) {
                break;
        }
    }

    /*Create the new node and assign the pivot data*/
    new_node = (struct node*) calloc(1, sizeof(struct node));
    new_node->data = pivot;

    /*Advance to the next member in the pre-order array*/
    (*pre_pos)++;

    /*First recursively construct the left sub-tree */
    new_node->left = construct_tree(pre_order, in_order, in_start,
                                    in_location - 1, pre_pos);

    /*Recursively construct the right sub-tree*/
    new_node->right = construct_tree(pre_order, in_order, in_location + 1,
                                    in_end, pre_pos);

    return new_node;
}
```

19. Serialize and Deserialize a binary tree

Serialization converts a data structure into a format that can be stored in persistent memory (such as a file) or that can be sent across a network. The process of reconstructing the format back to get the original data structure is called deserialization.

In our case, we will convert the binary tree into a format so that it can be stored in a file. As we traverse the nodes of the binary tree, the data in each node is written to a file. If a node has no child, then a special value (say #) is written to the file in place of the child.

Since in-order traversals are ambiguous, pre-order tree traversal is used.

Consider the tree below

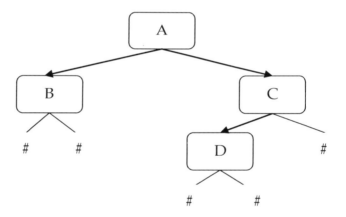

The output written to the file using pre-order traversal and the special value # for empty nodes is A B # # C D # # #.

To deserialize the tree, the file is read and the tree is constructed in pre-order.

```
/*cur_node: current node of the binary tree
fp: file where the binary tree should be stored
Return value: 0 on sucess
*/
int serialize_tree(struct node *cur_node, FILE *fp) {
    /*If cur_node is NULL, then store the special character and return*/
    if (!cur_node) {
        fprintf(fp, "%d\n", SPECIAL_CHARACTER);
        return 0;
    }

    /*Traverse the nodes in pre-order*/
    /*First print the data of the node into the file*/
    fprintf(fp, "%d\n", cur_node->data);

    /*Traverse the left subtree*/
    serialize_tree(cur_node->left, fp);

    /*Traverse the right subtree*/
    serialize_tree(cur_node->right, fp);

    return 0;
}

/* fp: file where the data about binary tree was stored
Return value: the reconstructed node of the binary tree
*/
struct node *deserialize_tree(FILE *fp) {
    struct node *new_node;
    int value;

    fscanf(fp, "%d", &value);

    /*If the special character is read, then return NULL */
    if (value == SPECIAL_CHARACTER)
        return NULL;

    /*Traverse in pre-order*/
    /*Store the value read from the file in the new_node*/
    new_node = (struct node*) calloc(1, sizeof(struct node));
    new_node->data = value;

    new_node->left = deserialize_tree(fp); /*Construct the left subtree*/

    new_node->right = deserialize_tree(fp); /*Construct the right sub-tree*/

    return new_node;
}
```

20. Print the border nodes of a binary tree

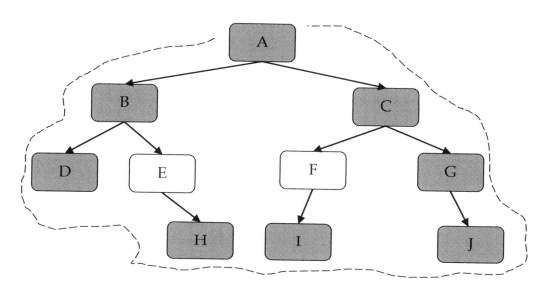

The border nodes in a binary tree consist of

- the left border nodes: the root node and all nodes that we can reach by starting from the root and repeatedly traversing left constitute the left border nodes. In the diagram above, A, B and D are left border nodes
- the right border nodes: the root node and all nodes that we can reach by starting from the root and repeatedly traversing right constitute the right border nodes. In the diagram above, A, C, G and J are right border nodes.
- the leaf nodes: in the diagram above, D, H, I and J are leaf nodes

Note that node D is a left border node and also a leaf node. Similarly node J is a right border node and also a leaf node. These nodes should be printed only once. So the convention we follow is that when printing left/right border nodes, we don't print the leaf nodes to avoid printing the same node twice. To print the border nodes to form a continuous boundary, we print in the following order

- the non-leaf left border nodes starting from the top of the tree (A, B)
- the leaf nodes (D, H, I, J)
- the non-leaf right border nodes in bottom up manner (G, C, A)

```c
/*Print the left border nodes of the tree*/
void print_left_border(struct node *cur_node)
{
    /*Keep traversing left and print the non-leaf nodes*/
    while (cur_node) {
        /*If node has a left or right child, then it is a non-leaf node*/
        if (cur_node->left || cur_node->right)
                print_data( cur_node->data);

        cur_node = cur_node->left;
    }
}

/*Print the leaf nodes of the tree*/
void print_leaf_nodes(struct node *cur_node)
{
    if (!cur_node)
        return;

    if (!cur_node->left && !cur_node->right)
        print_data(cur_node->data);

    print_leaf_nodes(cur_node->left);
    print_leaf_nodes(cur_node->right);
}

/* Print the right border nodes of the tree*/
void print_right_border(struct node *cur_node)
{
    if (!cur_node)
        return;

    /*First reach the deepest right node and then start printing bottom-up*/
    print_right_border(cur_node->right);

    /*If the node has a left or right child, then it is a non-leaf node.
    So print it*/
    if (cur_node->left || cur_node->right)
        print_data(cur_node->data);

}


/*Main function that prints the border nodes of a binary tree*/
void print_border_nodes(struct node *root)
{
    if (!root)
        return;

    print_left_border(root);
    print_leaf_nodes(root);
    print_right_border(root);
}
```

21. Print the right view of a binary tree

The right view of a binary tree consists of the last nodes at each level of the tree. For instance, for the tree below, the right view is ACF.

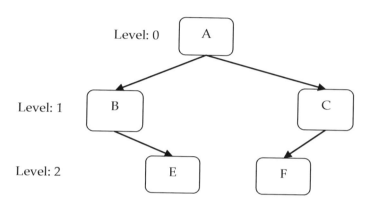

To print the right view, we will first traverse the right child of a node and then the left child of the node. By doing this we will now have to print the first node that we encounter in each level as we traverse the tree instead of printing the last node in each level. We will also keep a track of the level of the current node and the maximum level reached in the tree. If the level of the current node exceeds the max level reached in the tree so far, then we have reached a new level and we will print the current node.

```
/*cur_node: current node in the tree being processed
cur_level: the depth of the current node. Root node of tree has a level of 0
max_level: Maximum level seen in the tree so far. We pass -1 for the root node
*/
void print_right_view(struct node *cur_node, int cur_level, int *max_level) {
    if (!cur_node)
        return;

    /*If the current node is the first node we have observed in current level,
    then print it*/
    if (*max_level < cur_level) {
        print_data(cur_node->data);
        *max_level = cur_level;
    }

    /*First expand the right child and then the left child*/
    print_right_view(cur_node->right, cur_level + 1, max_level);
    print_right_view(cur_node->left, cur_level + 1, max_level);
}
```

22. Given two binary trees t1 and t2, find out if t2 is the sub-tree of t1

To check if tree t2 is a sub-tree of t1, we pick each node (let's call it the chosen node) from t1 and check if all nodes of t2 are present under the chosen node in the same manner. To achieve this we make use of two recursive functions. The first recursive function (is_sub_tree) first traverses the tree t1 to pick the chosen node of t1 from where to start the comparison and then invokes the second recursive function (compare_nodes) which compares the sub-tree under the chosen node of t1 with the nodes of t2.

There is one boundary condition we need to take care of. If t2 is empty, then we treat t2 as a sub-tree of t1.

If t1 has m nodes and t2 has n nodes, then the worst case time complexity is $O(m*n)$. However if the root of t2 occurs only k times in t1, then the time complexity reduces to $O(m + (n*k))$.

```
/*Helper function that compares the nodes
n1: node belonging to the main tree
n2: node belonging to sub-tree being searched
Return value: 1 if sub-tree of n1 matches sub-tree of n2. 0 otherwise
*/
int compare_nodes(struct node *n1, struct node *n2)
{
    if (n1 == NULL && n2 == NULL)
        return 1;

    if (!n1 || !n2)
        return 0;

    if (n1->data != n2->data)
        return 0;

    return (compare_nodes(n1->left, n2->left)
        && compare_nodes(n1->right, n2->right));
}
```

```
/*Main function that checks if tree under root2 is a subtree of tree under root1
root1: main tree node
root2: root of the sub-tree being searched
Return value: 1 if tree under root2 is present in tree under root1, 0 otherwise
*/
int is_sub_tree(struct node *root1, struct node *root2)
{
    /*empty tree is treated as a sub-tree of the main tree*/
    if(root2 == NULL)
        return 1;

    if (!root1)
        return 0;

    if (compare_nodes(root1, root2))
        return 1;

    /*Check if sub-tree being searched is present in left sub-tree of root1
    or in right sub-tree of root1*/
    return (is_sub_tree(root1->left, root2)
        || is_sub_tree(root1->right, root2));
}
```

23.

Two nodes of a binary search tree have been accidentally swapped. How will you correct the tree?

Let us not worry about the binary search tree and just consider the sorted data (10, 20, 30, 40, 50). Suppose two members in this data get accidentally swapped. Then there are two possibilities

1. Non-adjacent members are swapped. 20 and 40 are not adjacent to each other. If they get swapped, then we get (10, 40, 30, 20, 50). In this case, when we traverse the data and compare the previous element with the current element, we will get two inconsistencies. The first inconsistency is when we compare current element 30 with previous element 40. The second inconsistency is when we compare current element 20 with previous element 30. To get back the original sorted data, we have to swap the previous element of the first inconsistency (40) with the current element of the second inconsistency (20).

2. Adjacent members are swapped. 20 and 30 are adjacent to each other. If they get swapped, then we get (10, 30, 20, 40, 50). In this case, when we traverse the data and compare the previous element with the current element, we will get only one inconsistency. The inconsistency happens when we compare the current element 20 with the previous element 30. To get back the original sorted data, we have to swap the previous element (30) and current element (20).

If we are given a binary search tree, then we have to traverse the tree in-order and keep comparing the previous node with the current node to find the inconsistencies. When we find the first inconsistency, we will store the previous node as error node 1 and current node as error node 2. When the second inconsistency happens, we will store the current node of the second inconsistency as error node 2. Finally we swap the data of error node 1 and error node 2 to correct the binary search tree.

```
/*Helper function for finding the error nodes in a Binary Search Tree
cur_node: current tree node
prev_node_pp: node that is the in-order predecessor of cur_node
error1_pp, error2_pp: the two error nodes are returned here
*/
void find_error_nodes(struct node *cur_node, struct node ** prev_node_pp,
              struct node **error1_pp, struct node **error2_pp)
{
    if (!cur_node)
       return;

    /*Check for error node in the left sub-tree*/
    find_error_nodes(cur_node->left, prev_node_pp, error1_pp, error2_pp);

    /*cur_node should be greater than previous node. So if data in cur_node
      is less than or equal to previous node then we have found an error */
    if (*prev_node_pp && cur_node->data <= (*prev_node_pp)->data) {
        if (*error1_pp == NULL) {
                *error1_pp = *prev_node_pp;
                *error2_pp = cur_node;
        } else {
                *error2_pp = cur_node;
                return;
        }
    }

    /*Update previous node to current node*/
    *prev_node_pp = cur_node;

    /*Check for error node in the right sub-tree*/
    find_error_nodes(cur_node->right, prev_node_pp, error1_pp, error2_pp);
}


/*Main function for correcting the Binary Search Tree
root: root node of the Binary Search Tree in which two nodes have been swapped
*/
void correct_bst(struct node *root)
{
    struct node *error1, *error2, *prev_node;
    int temp_data;

    error1 = error2 = prev_node = NULL;

    /*Find the two error nodes*/
    find_error_nodes(root, &prev_node, &error1, &error2);

    /*If we found two error nodes, then swap their data*/
    if (error1 != NULL && error2 != NULL) {
        temp_data = error1->data;
        error1->data = error2->data;
        error2->data = temp_data;
    }
}
```

24. Traverse a binary tree in-order without using recursion

For traversing the tree without recursion, we make use of a stack. We start with the current node initialized to the root node and push it on to the stack. Then we push on to the stack all the nodes that we encounter by repeatedly traversing left from the current node. Once we can no longer travel left, we pop the node from the top of the stack, make it the current node, process it and then traverse to the right of the current node.

```
/*
root: root node of the binary tree
s: stack for storing the nodes for in-order traversal
*/
void non_recursive_in_order(struct node *root, stack<struct node*>& s)
{
    struct node *cur_node;

    cur_node = root;
    while (cur_node || !s.empty()) {

        if (cur_node) {
                /*push the current node onto stack*/
                s.push(cur_node);

                /*Traverse to the left sub-tree*/
                cur_node = cur_node->left;

        } else {
                /*remove the node from top of stack and process it*/
                cur_node = s.top();
                s.pop();

                /*process or print the node in-order*/
                process(cur_node);

                /*Traverse to the right sub-tree*/
                cur_node = cur_node->right;
        }
    }
}
```

25. Traverse a binary tree in-order without using recursion and without using a stack

To traverse a binary tree without using recursion and without using a stack, we make use of threaded binary trees. In threaded binary trees, if a node does not have a right child, then instead of storing a NULL pointer for the right child, a link (also referred to as a thread) is stored pointing to the in-order successor of the node. For instance, consider the binary tree below.

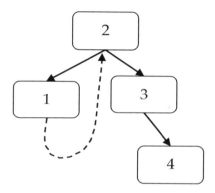

There is a thread shown as a dotted line from node 1 to node 2 (node 2 is the in-order successor of node 1). The main idea is that when we hit a dead end while traversing the tree, the threads help us figure out the next node. So for instance, we reach the node 1 from the root node 2. Without using a stack and without recursion, we reach a dead end at node 1. However if we maintain a thread from node 1 to node 2, we can continue the traversal. So to avoid using stacks and recursion, we construct the threads as we traverse the tree and once we no longer need the threads, we remove the threads during the tree traversal itself. This method of tree traversal is called Morris traversal. In Morris traversal, we start from the root node and perform the following:

1. If the current node has no left child, then process this node and go to the right child of the current node

2. If the current node has a left child, then find the predecessor of the current node in its left sub-tree and do the following

- If the predecessor has no right child, then we have not yet traversed this portion of the tree. Construct a thread linking the right child of predecessor and the current node so that when we reach the predecessor, we can then follow the thread to reach back the current node. Then proceed to the left child of current node

- If the predecessor has a right child, then it is a thread that we had actually formed earlier to help us traverse the tree. Now that we have finished traversing this portion of the tree, we can remove the thread. So make the right child of the predecessor NULL. Process the current node. Then proceed to the right child of the current node.

Let us take an example and work out the details.

1. We start with the root (Node-2) as the current node. Node-2 has a left child. So we find the predecessor of Node-2 in its left sub-tree. The left predecessor of Node-2 is Node-1. Node-1 has no right child. So we construct a thread from Node-1 to the current node (Node 2). The left child of Node-2 which is Node-1, then becomes the current node

2. The current node (Node-1) has no left child. So we immediately process it. The right child of Node-1 which in this case is Node-2 (because of the thread we constructed) then becomes the current node.

3. The current node (Node-2) has a left child. So we again find the predecessor of Node-2 in its left sub-tree. The left predecessor of Node-2 is Node-1. But now, Node-1 has a right child. So make the right child of Node-1 equal to NULL. Process the current node (Node-2) and then move to its right child (Node-3).

4. The current node (Node-3) has no left child. So immediately process it and move to its right child (Node-4)

5. The current node (Node-4) has no left child. So immediately process it and move to its right child (NULL)

6. Since current node is NULL, we have finished the processing.

```
/*
root: root node of the binary tree
*/
void morris_traversal(struct node *root)
{
    struct node *cur_node, *left_pre;

    cur_node = root;
    while (cur_node) {
        /*If cur_node has no left sub_tree, then print/process the cur_node
        then move over to cur_node->right and continue*/
        if (!cur_node->left) {
                print_morris(cur_node);
                cur_node = cur_node->right;
                continue;
        }

        /*cur_node has a left sub-tree. First store the left predecessor
        of cur_node in left_pre. Left predecessor can be found by
        traversing to the left of current node and then repeatedly going
        to the right until we hit a leaf node
        */
        left_pre = cur_node->left;
        while (left_pre->right != NULL && left_pre->right != cur_node)
                left_pre = left_pre->right;

        if (left_pre->right == NULL) {
                /*If left predecessor points to NULL, it means we have not
                yet traversed the left sub-tree of current node. So create
                a thread from left_pre->right to current node to remember
                that on reaching left_pre the next in-order node is current
                node. Then proceed to cur_node->left
                */
                left_pre->right = cur_node;
                cur_node = cur_node->left;
        } else {
                /*If left predecessor does not point to NULL, then it means
                that we have finished traversing the left sub-tree of
                cur_node. So remove the thread from left_pre->right to
                cur_node. The current node is the in-order node to be
                processed. So process it and then move to right sub-tree
                of cur_node
                */
                left_pre->right = NULL;
                print_morris(cur_node);
                cur_node = cur_node->right;
        }
    }
}
```

99

26. Merge two binary search trees

To merge two binary search trees, we do the following

1. Convert each binary search tree into a doubly linked list (binary search tree to doubly linked list conversion has already been solved on page 69).

2. The two doubly linked lists will be sorted. Now merge the two sorted linked lists into one result doubly linked list (merging two sorted linked lists has already been solved on page 24).

3. Convert the result doubly linked list back into a binary search tree (doubly linked list to binary search tree conversion has already been solved on page 67).

1.4 Arrays

1. Replace each element in an array with the next greatest

Consider the array A = {0, 2, 8, 1, 3, 5, 4}.

The greatest number after 0 in A is maximum of {2, 8, 1, 3, 5, 4} = 8. So 0 is replaced by 8.

The greatest number after 8 in A is maximum of {1, 3, 5, 4} = 5. So 8 is replaced with 5.

4 is the last number in A. There are no more elements to its right. So 4 is replaced by an invalid number or the smallest possible number.

So the resulting array is = {8, 8, 5, 5, 5, 4, INVALID_NUMBER}.

The brute force approach will try to compute the next greatest of an element by scanning all the elements to its right. This will have a time complexity of $O(n^2)$.

However we can achieve the same in $O(n)$ by traversing from the end of the array to the beginning and maintaining the maximum element seen so far. The code is given below

```
/*
a: array in which each element should be replaced with next greatest
n: number of elements in the array. n >= 1
*/
void replace_with_next_greatest(int a[], int n) {
    int i, next_greatest, temp;

    next_greatest = a[n-1];
    a[n-1] = INVALID_NUMBER;

    /*Process the array from backwards*/
    for (i = n-2; i >= 0; --i) {
        temp = a[i];

        a[i] = next_greatest;

        if (temp > next_greatest)
                next_greatest = temp;
    }
}
```

2. Given an array, remove all occurrences of an element from the array

Suppose the given array is A = {1, 4, 2, 1, 5, 2} and we have to remove all occurences of 1 from it, then the result array is {4, 2, 5, 2}. The element to be removed from the array can be present in multiple locations. We can efficiently remove all occurrences of the element in O(1) space and O(n) time in a single pass through the array by doing the following:

1. Maintain a variable called fill_pos to keep track of where we should store the next element of the array that should not be deleted. Initialize fill_pos to 0.

2. Traverse through the array. If the current element in the array should be deleted then skip it. If current element in the array should not be deleted, then store the current element at fill_pos in the array and increment fill_pos.

```
/*
a: input array from which all occurences of an element should be removed
length: number of elements in array a
x: element to be removed
Return value: number of elements in a after removing x
*/
int remove_element(int a[], int length, int x)
{
    int i, fill_pos;

    fill_pos = 0;
    for (i = 0; i < length; ++i) {
       if (a[i] != x) {
               a[fill_pos] = a[i];
               fill_pos++;
       }
    }

    return fill_pos;
}
```

3. Given an array, remove all the duplicates from the array.

Suppose the given array is A = {1, 4, 2, 1, 5, 2} and we have to remove all duplicates from it, then the result array is {1, 4, 2, 5}. All duplicates in an array A can be removed using the following approaches

1. Brute force approach. Pick every element in A and remove all the duplicates of that element. Removing all duplicates of one element can be done in O(n). Since we have to do this for n elements, the time complexity will be O(n²) and no extra space is needed

2. Hash table approach. Traverse the elements in A and add the elements to a hash table. If we encounter an element which is already in the hash table, then we exclude it from the result. The time complexity is O(n) but we will need extra space for the hash table.

3. Sorting. Sort the array A. After sorting, the duplicates will be arranged next to each other. Then iterate through the sorted array and retain an element in A only if it is different from the previous element. We will be using this approach in the code below. The time complexity is O(nlog(n)) and we don't need additional space.

```
/*
a: non-empty array from which duplicates should be removed.
    this array will be modified in-place
length: number of elements in array a
Returns: number of elements in array a after removing duplicates
*/
int remove_duplicates(int a[], int length)
{
    int i, fill_pos;                     if (! length)
                                           return 0;
    /*Sort the array*/
    sort(a, length);

    fill_pos = 1;
    for (i = 1; i < length; ++i) {
        if (a[i] != a[i - 1]) {
                a[fill_pos] = a[i];
                fill_pos++;
        }
    }

    return fill_pos;
}
```

103

4. Move all the zeroes in an array to the right end of the array

We can move all the zeroes to one end of the array (in this case, the right end) in O(n) using the following technique:

1. Scan for the first zero from the left side of the array.

2. Scan for the first non-zero from the right side of the array.

3. Swap the zero and non-zero provided that the zero appears to the left of the non-zero.

```
/*
a: input array in which the zeroes should be moved to one end
length: number of elements in array a
*/
void move_zeroes(int a[], int length)
{
    int left, right;

    left = 0;
    right = length - 1;

    while (left < right) {
        /*Locate the first zero from the left*/
        while (left < length && a[left] != 0)
            left++;

        /*Locate first non-zero from the right*/
        while (right >= 0 && a[right] == 0)
            right--;

        if (left < right) {
            /*Swap a[left] and a[right]*/
            int temp = a[left];
            a[left] = a[right];
            a[right] = temp;
        }
    }
}
```

$k = 3$

☆ trick

1,2,3,4,5   3,4,5,1,2

5,4,3,2,1

3,4,5,1,2

5. Rotate an array by k times

Consider the array {10, 20, 30, 40, 50}. Suppose we rotate the array once, we have to move the elements 10, 20, 30, 40 right by 1 position and move the last element 50 to the beginning to get {50, 10, 20, 30, 40}. So if we have an array of size n, then for 1 rotate operation we will need n moves. If we rotate the array k times then there will be k*n moves. There is a faster method for rotating an array. Let the array be A = {10, 20, 30, 40, 50} and the number of rotations k = 2. The procedure is:

1. Reverse the entire array. So we get {50, 40, 30, 20, 10}

2. Reverse the array in the region 0 to k -1. If k = 2, we reverse the region A[0] to A[1]. So we get the array {40, 50, 30, 20, 10}

3. Finally reverse the array in the region k to n-1 where n is the length of the array. If k=2, we reverse the region A[2] to A[4]. So we get the required result {40, 50, 10, 20, 30}.

With this technique, we always need 2*n moves irrespective of the value of k.

```
/*Main function to rotate a 1 dimensional array
a: array which should be rotated.
length: number of elements in the array. Should be > 0
num_rotations: how many times to rotate the array. Should be >= 0
*/
void rotate_array(int a[], int length, int num_rotations)
{
    /*Suppose an array has a length of 5, every time we rotate by 5
    locations, we end up with the same array. So obtain num_rotations
    value from 0 to length - 1*/
    num_rotations = num_rotations % length;

    if (num_rotations == 0)
        return;

    reverse_array(a, 0, length - 1);

    reverse_array(a, 0, num_rotations - 1);

    reverse_array(a, num_rotations, length - 1);
}
```

10, 20, 30, 40, 50

1
2 40, 50, 10, 20, 30
3 30, 40, 50, 10, 20
4
5 50, 40, 30, 20, 10

$k = 3$:   30, 40, 50, 10, 20

1. reverse array
   50, 40, 30, 20, 10
2. reverse 1st k
   30, 40, 50, 20, 10
3. reverse last k
   30, 40, 50, 10, 20 ✓

105

```
/*Helper function which reverses an array in region (low, high)
a: array which needs to be reversed
low: lower index of region to be reversed
high: higher index of region to be reversed
*/
void reverse_array(int a[], int low, int high)
{
    int temp;

    while (low < high) {
        temp = a[low];
        a[low] = a[high];
        a[high] = temp;
        low++;
        high--;
    }
}
```

Can't subtract small-large e.g. 599 −521 doesn't work!!

6. An array is used to store the values of the digits of a large number. So if the number is 789, then a[0] = 7, a[1] = 8, a[2] = 9. Perform subtraction of two such arrays and store the result in an array

We do the following

1. Find the larger of the two numbers. The array which has more elements will have the larger number. If both arrays have the same number of elements, then compare the digits from the most significant digit to the least significant digit to find the larger number.

2. Subtract the smaller number from the larger number. Initialize borrow to 0 and start finding the difference of the digits of the two numbers from least significant digit to most significant digit. The difference between the digits of the two numbers at a particular position = digit of larger number − digit of smaller number − borrow. If the difference is negative, then add 10 to the difference and set borrow to 1.

3. If the user has requested (smaller number − larger number), then the result will be negative.

```
/*
num1 and num2: arrays which store the digits of the two numbers.
    The two arrays store numeric value of the digits and not ascii values
length1 and length2: number of digits in arrays num1 and num2
result: result array which contains num1 - num2
is_negative: indicates if the result is negative or not
*/
int large_subtract(char num1[], int length1, char num2[], int length2,
            char result[], char *is_negative)
{
    int i, difference, borrow, temp_length;
    int pos1, pos2;
    char *temp_ptr;

    *is_negative = 0;

    /*Store larger number in num1
    So if num1 is smaller than num2, then swap num1 and num2*/
    if (is_smaller(num1, length1, num2, length2) ) {
        /*Swap num1 and num2*/
        temp_ptr = num1; num1 = num2; num2 = temp_ptr;

        /*Swap length1 and length2*/
        temp_length = length1; length1 = length2; length2 = temp_length;

        /*If num1 was smaller than num2, then result will be negative*/
        *is_negative = 1;
    }
```

```
    for (i = 0; i < length1; ++i)
        result[i] = 0;

    /*Perform the subtraction for all the digits in num2*/
    pos1 = length1 - 1;
    pos2 = length2 - 1;
    borrow = 0;
    while (pos2 >= 0) {
        difference = num1[pos1] - num2[pos2] - borrow;
        if (difference < 0) {
                difference += 10;
                borrow = 1;
        } else {
                borrow = 0;
        }
        result[pos1] = difference;
        pos1--;
        pos2--;
    }

    /*Process any digits leftover in num1*/
    while (pos1 >= 0) {
        difference = num1[pos1] - borrow;
        if (difference < 0) {
                difference += 10;
                borrow = 1;
        } else {
                borrow = 0;
        }
        result[pos1] = difference;
        pos1--;
    }

    return length1;
}
```

☆ Cool trick

7. Given an array, find the power set of the elements in the array

The power set will contain all subsets of the array including the empty set. Consider the array = {A, B, C}. The power set consists of {}, {A}, {B}, {C}, {A,B}, {A,C}, {B,C}, {A, B, C}.

We can generate the power set either non-recursively or recursively. The non-recursive method is as follows: Initialize an integer to 0. Then go on incrementing the integer until we reach $2^n - 1$, where n is the number of elements in the array. Each integer generated represents one subset. If the ith bit in the integer is set to 1, then the ith element in the array is included in the subset, otherwise the ith element is excluded from the subset. So when the integer is 0, it represents the empty subset. The code for the non-recursive method is given below

```
/*Helper function for printing a subset
input: array containing the input elements
selection: if bit i is 1 in selection, then element i is present in subset
length: number of elements in the array
*/
void print_subset(int input[], int selection, int length) {
    int i;
    printf("{");

    for (i = 0; i < length; ++i) {
        if (selection & (1u << i))
            printf("%d ", input[i]);
    }

    printf("}\n");
}


/*Main function for generating the subsets
input: array containing the input elements
length: number of elements in the array
*/
void generate_subsets(int input[], int length)
{
    int i = 0;
    int num_subsets = 1u << length;

    while (i < num_subsets) {
        print_subset(input, i, length);
        ++i;
    }
}
```

8. Given an array of N elements, produce all the subsets of size R that can be formed from the elements.

To find the subset of size R, we will use recursion. Cycle through all elements in the array recursively. First exclude the current item from the subset and recursively fill the remaining items into the subset until the subset contains R items. Then include the current item in the subset and recursively fill the remaining items into the subset until the subset contains R items.

```
/*
input: input array containing the elements
is_selected: if is_selected[i] = 1, then the ith element of
    the input array is present in the current subset
pos: current position in the input
length: total number of elements present in input
subset_size: total number elements that should be present in the final subset
cur_num_selections: currently how many elements have been selected
*/
void generate_combinations(int input[], char is_selected[], int pos, int length,
            int subset_size, int cur_num_selections)
{
    if (cur_num_selections == subset_size) {
        print_combination(input, is_selected, length, subset_size);
        return; /*Terminate the recursion*/
    }

    if (pos >= length) {
        return; /*Terminate the recursion*/
    }

    /*Exclude the item from the subset*/
    is_selected[pos] = 0;

    generate_combinations(input, is_selected, pos+1, length, subset_size,
                cur_num_selections);

    /*Include the item in the subset*/
    is_selected[pos] = 1;

    generate_combinations(input, is_selected, pos+1, length, subset_size,
                cur_num_selections + 1);
}
```

9. Find the intersection and union of two arrays

We can find the intersection of two arrays, A (size = m) and B (size = n) using the following techniques

1. Brute force approach: For every element in A, check if the element is present in B and if yes add it to the result. The time complexity will be O(mn) and no extra space is needed.

2. Hash table approach: Add elements of A to a hash table. Then search the elements of B in the hash table. If the element of B is found in the hash table, then add it to the result. The time complexity is O(m+n) but we will need extra space.

3. Sorting: Sort the arrays A and B. This can be done in O(mlogm) and O(nlogn). Then iterate through the sorted arrays and pick the elements that are common to both arrays. This can be done in O(m+n). We don't need additional space. We will be using this approach in the code below.

To find the union of two arrays we can again apply the same 3 techniques

1. Brute force approach: Pick each element of A and if it is not already present in the result then add it to the result. Then pick each element of B and if it is not already in the result, then add it to the result. The time complexity is O(mn) and we don't need additional space.

2. Hash table: Add the elements of A and B to a hash table. Then iterate through all the elements of the hash table and add them to the result. The time complexity is O(m+n) but we need extra space.

3. Sorting: Sort the two arrays and then pick up the unique elements from the two arrays and add them to the result. Sorting can be done in O(mlogm) and O(nlogn). Adding the unique elements to the result can be done in O(m+n). We will be using this approach in the code below. Note that we don't need additional space but since we sort the input arrays, they will get modified. Suppose we don't want the input arrays to get modified, then we can do the following: Add all the elements of A and B into the result array. Then sort the result array. This can be done in O((m+n)log(m+n)). Then remove the duplicates from the result. If there are any duplicates in the result, they will be next to each other. So removal of the duplicates can be done in O(m+n).

111

In the code below, we use the sorting approach to find the intersection of arrays

```
/*
a, b: two input arrays whose intersection has to be found
length1, length2: number of elements in array a and b
result: array containing the result of intersection of a and b
Returns: number of elements in the result array
*/
int find_intersection(int a[], int length1, int b[], int length2, int result[])
{
    int i, j, result_pos;

    /*Sort the two arrays in non-decreasing order*/
    sort(a, length1);
    sort(b, length2);

    i = j = result_pos = 0;
    while (i < length1 && j < length2) {
        /*Check if the elements in a and b match*/
        if (a[i] == b[j]) {
            /*Add only unique elements to the result*/
            if (i == 0 || a[i] != a[i - 1]) {
                result[result_pos] = a[i];
                ++result_pos;
            }
            ++i;
            ++j;

        } else if (a[i] < b[j]) {
            ++i;
        } else {
            ++j;
        }
    }
    return result_pos;
}
```

In the code below, we use the sorting approach to find the union of two arrays

```
/*
a, b: two input arrays whose union has to be found
length1, length2: number of elements in array a and b
result: array containing the result of union of a and b
Returns: number of elements in the result array
*/
int find_union(int a[], int length1, int b[], int length2, int result[])
{
    int i, j, pos;

    if (length1 + length2 <= 0)
        return 0;

    /*Sort the two input arrays in non-decreasing order*/
    sort(a, length1);
    sort(b, length2);

    /*Process as long as there are elements in both a and b.
    Pick the smaller element among a[i] and b[j] and if it
    doesn't match with previous element in result, then add it to result*/
    i = j = pos = 0;
    while (i < length1 && j < length2) {
        if (a[i] <= b[j]) {
            if (pos == 0 || a[i] != result[pos - 1])
                    result[pos++] = a[i];

            if (a[i] == b[j])
                    ++j; /*advance b*/
            ++i;
        } else {
            if (pos == 0 || b[j] != result[pos - 1])
                    result[pos++] = b[j];
            ++j;
        }
    }

    /*Process the remainder elements in a*/
    while (i < length1) {
        if (pos == 0 || a[i] != result[pos - 1])
            result[pos++] = a[i];
        ++i;
    }

    /*Process the remainder elements in b*/
    while (j < length2) {
        if (pos == 0 || b[j] != result[pos - 1])
            result[pos++] = b[j];
        ++j;
    }

    return pos;
}
```

10. An unsorted array of size N, contains elements whose values are between 0 to K − 1 where K <= N. Find the most frequently occurring element in O(n) time and O(1) space. For instance if N = 5 and K = 4, given the array {1, 3, 0, 2, 0}, then 0 is the most frequently occurring element

The main idea is to use the element value in the array as an index into the array. It is safe to do so since the value of an element in the array is less than the size of the array (K <= N). To solve the problem, we iterate through the elements in the array a and do the following

1. Compute index = a[i] % K

2. Add K to a[index].

Once we have processed all the elements in the array, we find the maximum element in the array. The index of the maximum element will give the most repeated element.

Note that to calculate the index in step 1 above, we perform a[i] % K. This is because by the time we come to location i, we might have already added K to the value at this location one or more times. So we take a[i] % K to get the original value at location i.

Also note that the elements in the array have been modified. To get back the original elements, we simply perform a[i] = a[i] % K for each element in the array

Let a = {1, 3, 0, 2, 0}. N = 5 and K = 4. The table below illustrates how we calculate the most repeated element

i	a[i]	index = a[i] % K	Add K to a[index]
0	1	1 % 4 = 1	a = {1, **3+4**, 0, 2, 0}, So a = {1, **7**, 0, 2, 0}
1	7	7 % 4 = 3	a = {1, 7, 0, **2+4**, 0}, So a = {1, 7, 0, **6**, 0}
2	0	0 % 4 = 0	a = {**1+4**, 7, 0, 6, 0}, So a = {**5**, 7, 0, 6, 0}
3	6	6 % 4 = 2	a = {5, 7, **0+4**, 6, 0}, So a = {5, 7, **4**, 6, 0}
4	0	0 % 4 = 0	a = {**5+4**, 7, 2, 6, 0}, So a = {**9**, 7, 2, 6, 0}

So the maximum value in array a is 9 which is present at index 0. So 0 is the most repeated element in the array.

```
/*
```

```
a: array consisting of numbers. A number can have a value between 0 to k-1
n: number of elements in the array
k: k should be <= num elements in array
*/
int find_most_repeated(int a[], int n, int k)
{
    int i, index, most_repeated, max_value;

    /*For each number found in the array, go to the index corresponding
    to the number and add k to the value at the index. */
    for (i = 0; i < n; ++i) {
        /*By the time we come to location i, we might have already added
        k to the value at this location one or more times. So take
        a[i] % k to get the original value
        */
        index = a[i] % k;
        a[index] += k;
    }

    most_repeated = -1;
    max_value = MIN_INT;

    for (i = 0; i < n; ++i) {

        if (a[i] > max_value) {
                /*Note that index i will give the most repeated number*/
                most_repeated = i;
                max_value = a[i];
        }

        /*Get back the original value in the array*/
        a[i] = a[i] % k;
    }

    return most_repeated;
}
```

11. Find the lowest absolute difference between any two elements in an array

Using the brute force approach, we can compute the absolute difference between every pair of elements in the array and find the lowest absolute difference in $O(n^2)$. However there is a faster technique as described below

1. Sort the array in non-decreasing order. This can be done in $O(nlogn)$

2. Find the difference between adjacent pairs of elements, i.e. $(a[1] - a[0])$, $(a[2] - a[1])$, etc. This can be done in $O(n)$.

The lowest difference between the adjacent pairs of elements gives the lowest absolute difference between any two elements in the array. The overall time complexity is $O(nlogn)$.

```
/*
a:input array
length: number of elements in array a
Returns: the least absolute difference between any two elements in the array
*/
int find_least_difference(int a[], int length)
{
    int i;
    int least_difference;

    assert (length > 1);

    /*Sort the array in non-decreasing order*/
    sort(a, length);

    least_difference = a[1] - a[0];
    for (i = 1; i < length - 1; ++i) {
        if (a[i+1] - a[i] < least_difference)
            least_difference = a[i+1] - a[i];
    }

    return least_difference;
}
```

12. Given an array of integers, find a 3-element subset that sums to S

A minor variation of this problem is to find if any 3 elements in an array sum up to zero.

Using a brute force approach, it is possible to solve the problem with a time complexity of $O(n^3)$ by generating all the 3-element subsets. There is a more efficient solution that uses sorting as described below:

1. Sort the input array A in non-decreasing order. This can be done in $O(n\log n)$.

2. Pick each element x in the array A. Let the index of the element x in array A be i. Let the total number of elements in the array be n. Then start picking one element A[low] from i+1 in the forward direction, where low >= i + 1 and another element A[high] from n-1 in the backward direction, where high <= n - 1. Let total = x + A[low] + A[high]. If total is equal to S, then we have found the sum. If total is less than S, then we increment low. If total is greater than S, then we decrement high. For one element this can be done in $O(n)$. For n elements this can be done in $O(n^2)$

The total time complexity is $O(n^2)$ and we don't need additional space. We will however end up sorting the input array.

```
/*
a: input array
length: number of elements in the array
S: the addition of any 3 elements in array should be equal to S
Return value: Number of 3 elements subsets where sum of 3 elements is equal to S
*/
int find_3_element_sum(int a[], int length, int S)
{
    int i, low, high, count;

    /*Sort the array in non-decreasing order*/
    sort(a, length);

    count = 0;
    for (i = 0; i < length - 2; ++i) {
        /*Choose a[i]. Start picking the other two elements from
        opposite ends. So start choosing from i+1 on one side and
        length - 1 on the other side
        */
        low = i + 1;
        high = length - 1;

        while (low < high) {
```

```
            int total = a[i] + a[low] + a[high];
            if (total == S) {
                    count++;
                    /*print result indicating that a[i], a[low] and
                    a[high] will sum to S*/
                    print_result(a[i], a[low], a[high], S);
                    ++low;
                    --high;
            } else if (total > S) {
                    --high; /*We need to pick a smaller element*/
            } else {
                    ++low; /*We need to pick a larger element*/
            }
        }
    }

    return count;
}
```

13. Find the maximum product of any 3 numbers in an array

We can find the highest 3 numbers in the array and multiply them to get the maximum product of 3 numbers in the array. However if the array contains negative numbers, then we may not get the correct result. For instance, consider the array {-10, -9, 1, 2, 3}. The product of the highest 3 numbers is 1 * 2 * 3 = 6. But the maximum product that we can get is -10 * -9 * 3 = 270. So the maximum product of 3 numbers in an array is either the product of the 3 highest numbers OR the product of the 2 lowest numbers and the highest number.

So we need to find the 2 lowest numbers and the 3 highest numbers in the array. We can do this in a single scan of the array. We will maintain the array called max_values for storing the 3 highest numbers. max_values[0] will store the highest value, max_values[1] will store the second highest number and max_values[2] will store the third highest number. Similarly, we will maintain the array called min_values for storing the 2 lowest numbers. min_values[0] will store the lowest value and min_values[1] will store the second lowest value. The code is given below

```
/*
a:input array
length: number of elements in array a
Returns: the maximum product of 3 elements in the array
*/
int find_max_product(int a[], int length)
{
    int i;
    int max_value[3];
    int min_value[2];

    assert (length >= 3);

    max_value[0] = max_value[1] = max_value[2] = MIN_INT;
    min_value[0] = min_value[1] = MAX_INT;

    for (i = 0; i < length; ++i) {
        /*Check if a[i] is among the 3 largest values*/
        if (a[i] > max_value[0]) {
            max_value[2] = max_value[1];
            max_value[1] = max_value[0];
            max_value[0] = a[i];
        } else if (a[i] > max_value[1]) {
            max_value[2] = max_value[1];
            max_value[1] = a[i];
```

119

```
        } else if (a[i] > max_value[2]) {
                max_value[2] = a[i];
        }

        /*Check if a[i] is among the 2 smallest values*/
        if (a[i] < min_value[0]) {
                min_value[1] = min_value[0];
                min_value[0] = a[i];
        } else if (a[i] < min_value[1]) {
                min_value[1] = a[i];
        }
    }

    return max(max_value[0] * max_value[1] * max_value[2],
            min_value[0] * min_value[1] * max_value[0]);
}
```

14. For every element in an array, efficiently find the product of all other elements except that element. Division is not allowed. For instance, given A = {2, 6, 4, 5}, the product of all elements except 2 is 6*4*5 = 120. So if we do this for every element, we get {120, 40, 60, 48}

For one element, we can find the product of all elements except itself in O(n). If we do this for all elements, we can find the result in $O(n^2)$. However there is an efficient solution that can do the job in O(n). The idea is as follows:

1. In the first pass through the array A, we process it from left to right and keep multiplying the adjacent elements from the left. In result[i], we store the product of elements from A[0] to A[i-1]   *get product of all elements to the right of the A[i] element*

2. In the second pass through the array A, we process it from right to left and go on accumulating the product of adjacent elements from the right. So at location i, we will have the product of elements from A[n-1] to A[i+1]. We multiply this product with result[i] which already has A[0] *...*A[i-1]. So result[i] will now have A[0] * ... A[i-1] * A[i+1] * .... * A[n-1]   *get " " left*

and add to the step 1 result

```
/*a: input array
length: number of elements in the array
result: result[i] will contain product of all elements of array a except a[i]
*/
void compute_product(int a[], int length, int result[])
{
    int i, product;

    /*Compute the product of elements of array a in forward direction.
    Store product of a[0] to a[i-1] in result[i]*/
    product = 1;
    for (i = 0; i < length; ++i) {
        result[i] = product;
        product = a[i] * product;
    }

    /*Next compute the product of elements of array a in reverse direction
    So we now compute product of a[n-1] to a[i+1] and multiply it with
    value in result[i]. In this way result[i] will contain product of
    a[0]...a[i-1]*a[i+1]....a[n-1]*/
    product = 1;
    for (i = length - 1; i >= 0; --i) {
        result[i] = result[i] * product;
        product = a[i] * product;
    }
}
```

15. Efficiently find the equilibrium point in an array. The equilibrium point is the location where the sum of elements to the left of the location equals the sum of the elements to the right of the location. For instance, given A = {-50, 100, 80, 30, -60, 10, 70}, the equilibrium point is 2, since sum of elements to left of index 2 = -50 + 100 = 50 and sum of elements to the right of index 2 = 30 – 60 + 10 + 70 = 50

excluding equilibrium value

We can apply the brute force approach and check if each point is an equilibrium point. We can find if one point is an equilibrium point in O(n) and since we have to do this for n points, the complexity of brute force approach is O(n²). There is a more efficient way that gives the equilibrium point in O(n) that is described below:

1. First compute the sum of all elements in the array A. This value will be stored in right_sum. Next initialize left_sum to 0.

2. Process the elements of the array from left to right. When we pick A[i], we subtract A[i] from right_sum so that right_sum has sum of all elements to the right of index i. Then we compare left sum and right sum. If they match, we have found the equilibrium point. If not, we increment left_sum with A[i] and go to the next element.

```
/*a: input array whose equilibrium point has to be found.
n: number of elements in array a
Return value: index of the equilibrium point if it exists, -1 otherwise*/
int find_equilibrium_point(int a[], int n) {
    int left_sum, right_sum, i;

    /*Compute the sum of all elements and store in right_sum*/
    right_sum = 0;
    for (i = 0; i < n; ++i) {
        right_sum += a[i];
    }

    /*Go on computing sum of all elements from the left to right
    and compare with right sum */
    left_sum = 0;
    for (i = 0; i < n; ++i) {
        /*Subtract a[i] from right_sum to find out sum of the
        elements to the right of i*/
        right_sum -= a[i];

        if (left_sum == right_sum) {
                return i; /*We have found the equilibrium point*/
        }
        left_sum += a[i];
    }
    return -1;
}
```

16. In an array consisting of 0's and 1's, find the longest sub-array which has equal number of 0's and 1's

Consider the array {1, 1, 0, 1, 0, 1, 1, 1, 1, 0}. The longest sub-array with equal 0's and 1's is {1, 0, 1, 0} from index 1 to index 4.

To find the longest sub-array, we first compute the running sum of 0's and 1's. The running sum is initialized to 0 and every time we get a 1, we increment the running sum by 1 and if we get a 0, we decrement the running sum by 1. So if there are N elements in the array and all of them are 0's we get a running sum of –N. If all the N elements are 1's, then we get a running sum of N. So the running sum for an array can vary from –N to N. We normalize the running sum from the range (–N, N) to the range (0, 2*N) by adding N to the running sum.

We maintain the first_ix_for_sum array that gives the first index in the array at which we observed a particular normalized sum. Initially first_ix_for_sum array is initialized with MIN_INT.

first_ix_for_sum[N] corresponds to normalized running sum of N. Normalized running sum of N corresponds to running sum of 0. We can consider that we have already observed a running sum of 0 at index of -1 ie, before starting to process the array. So first_ix_for_sum[N] is initialized to -1.

The array {1, 1, 0, 1, 0, 1, 1, 1, 1, 0} has N = 10 elements in it. Consider the first 5 elements of the array.

Index	Element	Running Sum	Normalized Sum = Running sum + N	Is first occurrence of normalized sum	Action
0	1	1	11	Yes	first_ix_for_sum[11] = 0
1	1	2	12	Yes	first_ix_for_sum[12] = 1
2	0	1	11	No	
3	1	2	12	No	
4	0	1	11	No	

Each time that we obtain a normalized running sum that we have already observed, it means that we have traversed an equal number of 0's and 1's between the index corresponding to the first occurrence of the normalized running sum and the current index. For instance, we observe the normalized running sum of 11 for the first time at index 0 . Subsequently we observed normalized running sum of 11 again at index 2. So there are equal number of 0's and 1's in between index 1 to index 2. We again observe normalized running sum of 11 at index 4. So again there are equal number of 0's and 1's from index 1 to index 4.

So every time we hit a normalized sum that we have already encountered before, the difference between the current index and the index when we first observed the normalized sum will give us the length of the region with equal 0's and 1's. The longest such region will give us the result.

```
/*
a:input array
num_elements: number of elements in array a
start_index: start index of longest subarray of equal 0's and 1's is returned
end_index: end index of longest subarray of equal 0's and 1's is returned
Returns: the length of the longest subarray with equal 0's and 1's
*/
int find_sub_array(int a[], int num_elements, int *start_index, int *end_index)
{
    int i, running_sum, max_length;
    int *first_ix_for_sum = (int*) malloc((2*num_elements + 1) * sizeof (int) );
    int normalized_sum;

    /*first_ix_for_sum will store the first seen index for a particular
    normalized running sum. Initialize the sum table. MIN_INT should be < -1
    normalized running sum = num_elements + running_sum*/
    for (i = 0; i < (2 * num_elements + 1); ++i)
        first_ix_for_sum[i] = MIN_INT;

    /*Before we start processing, we say that at index -1, running sum is 0
    The normalized running sum =  num_elements + running_sum = num_elements
    + 0 = num_elements. So first_ix_for_sum[num_elements] is set to -1*/
    first_ix_for_sum[num_elements] = -1;
    max_length = running_sum = 0;
    *start_index = *end_index = -1;
    for (i = 0; i < num_elements; ++i) {
        /*If we get a 1, increment the running sum. If we get a 0
        then decrement the running sum*/
        if (a[i])
                running_sum++;
        else
                running_sum--;

        /*If there are 10 elements, then running sum can vary from -10
        to +10. Normalize the running sum into an index from 0 to 20*/
```

```
        normalized_sum = num_elements + running_sum;
        if (first_ix_for_sum[normalized_sum] == MIN_INT) {
                /*We are observing the normalized running sum
                for the first time. Store the index in first_ix_for_sum*/
                first_ix_for_sum[normalized_sum] = i;
        } else {
                /*We have already observed the normalized running sum
                before. Suppose we have a normalized running sum of 3
                at index 10 and we again observe normalized running sum
                of 3 at index 18, then there are equal 0's and 1's
                from index 11 to index 18*/
                int first_index = first_ix_for_sum[normalized_sum];
                if (i - first_index > max_length) {
                        max_length = i - first_index;
                        *start_index = first_index + 1;
                        *end_index = i;
                }
        }
    }

    free(first_ix_for_sum);
    return max_length;
}
```

17. Rotate a two dimensional square matrix by 90 degrees

To rotate a square matrix in the clockwise direction by 90° we have to take the first row in the original matrix and make it the last column in the rotated matrix. The second row becomes the second last column and so on. This can be done easily by using an additional matrix. But we want to rotate the matrix in-place without using up a lot of additional memory.

To solve this problem, we do the following

- choose one quadrant of the square matrix
- take each element in the chosen quadrant and circularly rotate the corresponding elements in all the quadrants

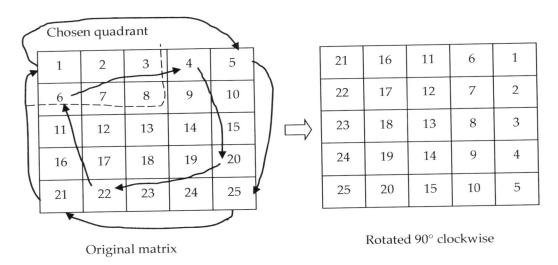

Original matrix

Rotated 90° clockwise

So in the diagram above, 1, 5, 25, 21 are circularly swapped (1 moves to 5, 5 moves to 25, 25 moves to 21 and 21 moves to 1). The other circular movements are

- 6->4->20->22
- 2->10->24->16
- 7->9->19->17
- 3->15->23->11
- 8->14->18->12

The code for rotating 90° clockwise is given below

```
/*
m: 2d matrix to be rotated by 90 degrees in clockwise direction
n: number of rows or cols in the matrix. n is equal to MAX_NUM_COLS
*/
void rotate_square_matrix_90(int m[][MAX_NUM_COLS], int n)
{
    int i, j, temp;
    int max_i, max_j ;

    /*max_i and max_j have the boundaries of the first quadrant*/
    max_i = (n/2) - 1;
    max_j = ((n+1)/2) - 1;

    for (i = 0; i <= max_i; ++i) {
        for (j = 0; j <= max_j; ++j) {

                /*Perform  a four way swap*/
                temp = m[i][j];

                m[i][j] = m[n - j - 1][i];

                m[n - j - 1][i] = m[n - i - 1][n - j - 1];

                m[n - i - 1][n - j - 1] = m[j][n - i - 1];

                m[j][n - i - 1] = temp;
        }
    }
}
```

There is another technique that uses matrix transpose for rotating a matrix in-place. The transpose of a matrix interchanges the rows and columns (so first row becomes first column, second row becomes second column and so on).

To rotate a matrix by 90° clockwise using matrix transpose, do the following:

- take the transpose of the matrix
- then interchange the columns: interchange first column and last column, interchange the second column and second last column and so on

To rotate a matrix by 90° anti-clockwise using matrix transpose, do the following:

- take the transpose of the matrix
- then interchange the rows: interchange first row and last row, then interchange the second row and second last row and so on

To rotate a matrix by 180°, do the following

- interchange the rows: interchange first row and last row, then interchange the second row and second last row and so on
- interchange the columns: interchange first column and last column, interchange the second column and second last column and so on

Note that for 180°, the direction of rotation does not matter (we will get the same result if we rotate a matrix by 180° clockwise or 180° anti-clockwise). So to get a matrix rotated by 180° we can also first interchange all the columns and then interchange all the rows.

18. Print the elements of a two dimensional matrix in spiral order

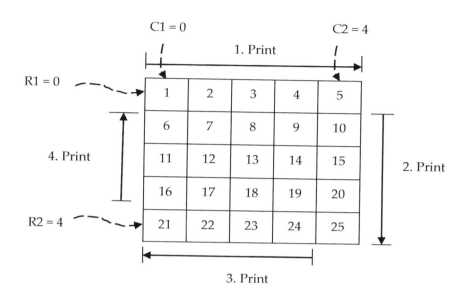

Consider the matrix above. To print in spiral order we have to print 1, 2, 3, 4, 5, 10, 15, 20, 25, 24, 23, 22, 21, 16, 11, 6, 7, 8, 9, 14, 19, 18, 17, 12 and 13.

The start row R1 is initialized to 0, end row R2 is initialized to number of rows − 1 = 5 - 1 = 4, start column C1 is initialized to 0 and end column C2 is initialized to number of columns − 1 = 5 − 1 = 4. The algorithm to print the matrix spirally is:

- print the cells in R1 (0) from columns C1 (0) to C2 (4). So we print 1, 2, 3, 4, 5.
- increment R1 (R1 becomes 1).
- print the cells in C2 (4) from rows R1 (1) to R2 (4). So we print 10, 15, 20, 25
- decrement C2 (C2 becomes 3)
- print the cells in R2 (4) from columns C2 (3) to C1 (0). So we print 24, 23, 22, 21.
- decrement R2 (R2 becomes 3)
- print the cells in C1 (0) from rows R2 (3) to R1 (1). So we print 16, 11, 6
- increment C1 (C1 becomes 2)

The above steps are repeated as long as R1 <= R2 and C1 <= C2.

```
/*
m: 2d matrix that should be printed spirally
num_rows: number of rows in the matrix
num_cols: number of columns in the matrix (num_cols is equal to MAX_NUM_COLS)
*/
void print_spiral(int m[][MAX_NUM_COLS], int num_rows, int num_cols)
{
    int r1 = 0, r2 = num_rows - 1;
    int c1 = 0, c2 = num_cols - 1;
    int cur_row, cur_col;

    while (r1 <= r2 && c1 <= c2) {
        /*Print row r1*/
        cur_row = r1;
        for (cur_col = c1; cur_col <= c2; ++cur_col) {
                printf("%d ", m[cur_row][cur_col]);
        }
        ++r1; /*Advance r1 to next row*/

        /*Print column c2*/
        cur_col = c2;
        for (cur_row = r1; cur_row <= r2; ++cur_row) {
                printf("%d ", m[cur_row][cur_col]);
        }
        --c2; /*Advance c2 to previous column*/

        if (r1 != r2) {
                /*Print row r2*/
                cur_row = r2;
                for (cur_col = c2; cur_col >= c1; --cur_col) {
                        printf("%d ", m[cur_row][cur_col]);
                }
                --r2;   /*Advance r2 to previous row*/
        }

        if (c1 != c2) {
                /*Print column c1*/
                cur_col = c1;
                for (cur_row = r2; cur_row >= r1; --cur_row) {
                        printf("%d ", m[cur_row][cur_col]);
                }
                ++c1; /*Advance c1 to next column*/
        }
    }
}
```

19. A two dimensional matrix M consists of 0's and 1's. If M[i][j] is 1, then make all the elements in row i and all elements in column j equal to 1 using minimal additional space.

We can solve this problem by having two additional arrays: row_array and colum_array. The row_array[i] will be set to 1 if there is at least one cell in row i of matrix M that is set to 1. The column_array[j] will be set to 1 if there is at least one cell in column j of matrix M set to 1. Once the arrays are computed, we go ahead and modify the matrix as follows:

- If row_array[i] = 1, then make all the cells in row i of matrix M to 1
- If column_array[j] = 1, then make all cells in column j of matrix M to 1

There is a better solution that requires just two variables instead of two arrays. By having these two variables, it is possible to use the first row of the matrix M to serve as row_array and first column of matrix M to serve as column_array. The steps of this solution are:

1.) Maintain the variables is_1_in_first_row (which is set to 1 if there is at least one cell in the first row set to 1) and is_1_in_first_col (which is set to 1 if there is at least one cell in the first column set to 1). In the input matrix below, is_1_in_first_col is set to 1 since there is a 1 in first column and is_1_in_first_row is set to 0 since all the cells are 0 in the first row.

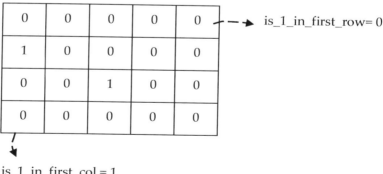

is_1_in_first_col = 1

2.) Now scan the region M[1][1] to M[num_rows-1][num_cols-1] and check the cells. If M[i][j] is set to 1, then make M[i][0] = 1 and M[0][j] = 1

0	0	0	0	0
1	0	0	0	0
0	0	1	0	0
0	0	0	0	0

0	0	1	0	0
1	0	0	0	0
1	0	1	0	0
0	0	0	0	0

Scan this region for 1's

If M[i][j] = 1, make M[i][0] and M[0][j] = 1

3. Go through the first column of M and if M[i][0] is 1, then set all cells in row i to 1. Also go through the first row of M and if M[0][j] is 1, then set all cells in column j to 1.

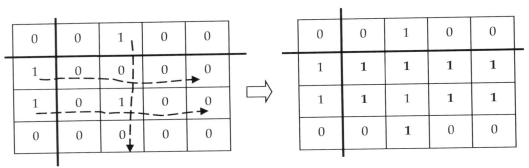

Set the cells to 1 based on first row and first column of M

4. If is_1_in_first_col is 1, then set all cells in first column to 1. If is_1_in_first_row is 1, then set all cells in the first row to 1.

0	0	1	0	0
1	1	1	1	1
1	1	1	1	1
0	0	1	0	0

1	0	1	0	0
1	1	1	1	1
1	1	1	1	1
1	0	1	0	0

is_1_in_first_col = 1

```c
/*m: 2d matrix to be processed
num_rows: number of rows in the matrix
num_cols: number of columns in the matrix (equal to MAX_NUM_COLS)
*/
void process_matrix(int m[][MAX_NUM_COLS], int num_rows, int num_cols)
{
    int i, j, is_1_in_first_row = 0, is_1_in_first_col = 0;

    /*Check if any cell in the first row is set to 1*/
    for (i = 0; i < num_rows; ++i)
        if (m[i][0]) {
                is_1_in_first_row = 1;
                break;
        }

    /*Check if any cell in first column is set to 1*/
    for (j = 0; j < num_cols; ++j)
        if (m[0][j]) {
                is_1_in_first_col = 1;
                break;
        }

    /*Scan the matrix. If m[i][0] is equal to 1 then, set m[i][0] to 1
    and set m[0][j] to 1*/
    for (i = 1; i < num_rows; ++i)
        for (j = 1; j < num_cols; ++j)
                if (m[i][j]) {
                        m[i][0] = 1;
                        m[0][j] = 1;
                }

    /*Mark the cells as 1 as indicated by m[i][0] and m[0][j]*/
    for (i = 1; i < num_rows; ++i)
        for (j = 1; j < num_cols; ++j)
                if (m[i][0] || m[0][j])
                        m[i][j] = 1;

    /*If there was a 1 initially in first column, set 1 in all the cells
    of first column*/
    if (is_1_in_first_col)
        for (i = 0; i < num_rows; ++i)
                m[i][0] = 1;

    /*If there was a 1 initially in first row, set 1 in all the cells
    of the first row*/
    if (is_1_in_first_row)
        for (j = 0; j < num_cols; ++j)
                m[0][j] = 1;
}
```

20. A two dimensional matrix M represents a maze. If M[i][j] is -1, then the cell is blocked. Find how many paths are present between M[0][0] and M[num_rows - 1] [num_cols-1]

Consider the grid in the diagram below. We are treating M[num_rows-1][num_cols-1] as the source and M[0][0] as the destination. We have three possible movements from a cell:

- we can move above to the previous row
- we can move to the left to the previous column.
- we can move diagonally to the cell in the previous row and previous column

destination

(0, 0)

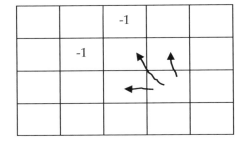

source

(num_rows -1, num_cols-1)

We can solve this problem using recursion. At each cell, we apply the following steps

- if we reach a cell that is marked with -1, then we stop traversing on that path and backtrack to the previous cell we had traversed
- if we reach a normal cell, then we explore all possible paths through the cell. So we first jump to the cell above and try to recursively traverse further to reach the destination. We then jump to the cell to the left and try to recursively traverse further to reach the destination. We then jump to the diagonally above cell and recursively try to reach the destination.

```
/*
m: matrix that has to be navigated
cur_row: row of the current cell
cur_col: column of the current cell
num_paths: the total number of paths possible is returned here
*/
void navigate_maze(int m[][MAX_NUM_COLS], int cur_row, int cur_col,
                    int *num_paths)
{
    if (cur_row < 0 || cur_col < 0)
        return;

    if (m[cur_row][cur_col] == -1)
        return; /*We can't traverse this cell, so simply return*/

    if (cur_row == 0 && cur_col == 0) {
        /*We have reached the destination*/
        (*num_paths)++;
        return;
    }

    /*Try continuing the path by going to the cell in previous row*/
    navigate_maze(m, cur_row - 1, cur_col, num_paths);

    /*Try continuing the path by going to the cell in previous col*/
    navigate_maze(m, cur_row, cur_col - 1, num_paths);

    /*Try continuing the path by going to the diagonally above cell*/
    navigate_maze(m, cur_row - 1, cur_col - 1, num_paths);
}
```

1.5 Strings

1. Find if two string words are anagrams of each other

Two strings are anagrams of each other if re-arrangement of characters in one string results in the other string. This implies that two string words are anagrams if for each character, the number of times the character occurs in the first string is equal to the number of times it occurs in the second string. The code for finding if two words are anagrams is given below

```
/*str1, str2: the two non-NULL strings which we want to compare
Return value: 1 if the two strings are anagrams, 0 otherwise
*/
int are_strings_anagrams( char *str1, char *str2)
{
    int count1[NUM_CHARACTERS], count2[NUM_CHARACTERS];
    int is_anagram, i;

    /*Initialize the counts to zero */
    memset(count1, 0, sizeof(int) * NUM_CHARACTERS);
    memset(count2, 0, sizeof(int) * NUM_CHARACTERS);

    /*Compute the character counts for str1 and str2*/
    while (*str1) {
        count1[(int)*str1]++;
        str1++;
    }

    while (*str2) {
        count2[(int)*str2]++;
        str2++;
    }

    /*Compare the counts*/
    is_anagram = 1;
    for (i = 0; i < NUM_CHARACTERS; ++i) {
        if (count1[i] != count2[i]) {
                is_anagram = 0;
                break;
        }
    }
    return is_anagram;
}
```

2. Count the number of words in a string

We will define a word as a collection of one or more characters from a-z and A-Z. The words in a string can be separated by multiple spaces, tabs, punctuation marks etc. To count the number of words, as we traverse the string, we will keep track of the previous character and the current character. If the previous character is not an alphabet from a-z and A-Z and the current character is an alphabet from a-z and A-Z, then we have encountered a new word and we increase the word count by 1.

```
/*
str1: string in which the number of words have to be counted
Return value: number of words in the string
*/
int count_words(char *str1)
{
    int num_words, pos;
    char cur_char, is_prev_char_alphabet;

    if (!str1)
        return 0;

    num_words = 0;
    pos = 0;
    cur_char = str1[pos];
    is_prev_char_alphabet = 0;
    while (cur_char != '\0') {
        int is_cur_char_alphabet = is_alphabet(cur_char);

        /*If previous character is not an alphabet and current character
        is an alphabet then we have found a new word*/
        if (!is_prev_char_alphabet && is_cur_char_alphabet) {
            ++num_words;
        }

        is_prev_char_alphabet = is_cur_char_alphabet;

        pos++;
        cur_char = str1[pos];
    }

    return num_words;
}
```

```
/*Helper function which checks if a character is an alphabet(a-zA-Z)*/
int is_alphabet(char c)
{
    if (c >= 'A' && c <= 'Z')
        return 1;

    if (c >= 'a' && c <= 'z')
        return 1;

    return 0;
}
```

3. Convert a string to an integer without using built-in functions.

The function for converting a string to an integer is given below:

```c
/*
str: string to be converted to an integer
Result: integer value of the string
*/
int function_atoi(const char * str)
{
    int i, length;
    int val = 0;
    int is_negative = 0;

    if (!str)
        return 0;

    length = strlen(str);
    i = 0;
    if (str[0] == '-') {
        is_negative = 1;
        ++i;
    }

    while (i < length ) {
        if (str[i] >= '0' && str[i] <= '9') {
                val = (val * 10) + (str[i] - '0');
        }
        else {
                break;
        }
        ++i;
    }

    if (is_negative)
        val = -1 * val;

    return val;
}
```

139

4. Given a number from 0 to 999,999,999, print the number in words. So 200,145,700 should be printed as two hundred million one hundred forty five thousand seven hundred

---

We will break the input number into millions, thousands and the remaining 3 least significant digits. So in this case 200,145,700 gets broken down to 200, 145 and 700. Then we make use of a helper function that prints 3 consecutive digits.

```
/*
Helper function to print number from 1 to 999
number: number from 1 to 999
*/
void print_3_digits(int number)
{
    int hundreds_digit, tens_digit, unit_digit, remainder;

    /*basic_lookup[0] is empty. We want basic_lookup[1] to map to "One"
    and so on. */
    char *basic_lookup[] = {"", "One", "Two", "Three", "Four", "Five", "Six",
            "Seven", "Eight", "Nine", "Ten", "Eleven", "Twelve",
            "Thirteen", "Fourteen", "Fifteen", "Sixteen", "Seventeen",
            "Eighteen", "Nineteen"};

    /*tens_lookup[0] and tens_lookup[1] are empty.
    We want tens_lookup[2] to map to "Twenty" and so on. */
    char *tens_lookup[] = {"", "","Twenty", "Thirty", "Fourty", "Fifty",
            "Sixty", "Seventy", "Eighty", "Ninety"};

    /*Suppose number is 987, then hundreds_digit is 9*/
    hundreds_digit = number / 100;
    if (hundreds_digit > 0) {
        printf("%s Hundred ", basic_lookup[hundreds_digit]);
    }

    /*Suppose number is 987, then remainder will be 87*/
    remainder = number % 100;
    if (remainder > 0) {
        if (remainder <= 19) {
            printf("%s ", basic_lookup[remainder]);
        } else {
            tens_digit = remainder / 10;
            unit_digit = remainder % 10;
            printf("%s ", tens_lookup[tens_digit]);
            printf("%s ", basic_lookup[unit_digit]);
        }
    }
}
```

```
/*
Main function to print the number in words
number: any number from 0 to 999999999
*/
void print_num_in_words(int number)
{
    int millions, thousands, remainder;

    /*If number is 0, handle it here and return*/
    if (number == 0) {
        printf("Zero \n");
        return;
    }

    /*Suppose number is 123456789, then millions = 123, remainder = 456789*/
    millions = number / 1000000;
    remainder = number - (millions * 1000000);

    /*Suppose remainder = 456789, then thousands = 456, remainder = 789*/
    thousands = remainder / 1000;
    remainder = remainder - (thousands * 1000);

    if (millions > 0) {
        print_3_digits(millions);
        printf("Million ");
    }

    if (thousands > 0) {
        print_3_digits(thousands);
        printf("Thousand ");
    }

    if (remainder > 0) {
        print_3_digits(remainder);
    }

    printf("\n");
}
```

5. Convert a string having Roman numerals into an integer.

The integer equivalent for the Roman numerals is given below

Roman numeral	Integer value
I	1
V	5
X	10
L	50
C	100
D	500
M	1000

To find the integer equivalent of a string containing Roman numerals, we process the string from the rear. This simplifies the computation. If the current Roman numeral is greater than the next numeral, we add the current numeral to the result. For instance consider XI. When processing X, since X is greater than I, we add 10 to the result. If the current Roman numeral is less than the next numeral, then we subtract the current numeral from the result. For instance consider IX. When processing I, since I is less than X, we subtract 1 from the result.

```
/*Helper function that returns the numeric value of a Roman alphabet*/
int get_numeric_value(char c)
{
    int result;

    switch(c) {
        case 'I': result = 1; break;
        case 'V': result = 5; break;
        case 'X': result = 10; break;
        case 'L': result = 50; break;
        case 'C': result = 100; break;
        case 'D': result = 500; break;
        case 'M': result = 1000; break;
        default: result = 0; break;
    }
    return result;
}
```

```
/*
Main function that converts a Roman string into an integer
str1: valid input string with Roman alphabets
Return value: integer equivalent of the Roman string
*/
int roman_to_int(char *str1)
{
    int i, result;

    /*Process the string from the rear*/
    i = strlen(str1) - 1;
    if (i < 0)
        return 0;

    result = get_numeric_value(str1[i]);
    --i;
    while (i >= 0) {
        int cur_value = get_numeric_value(str1[i]);
        int next_value = get_numeric_value(str1[i+1]);

        if (cur_value < next_value)
                result -= cur_value;
        else
                result += cur_value;

        --i;
    }

    return result;
}
```

6. Compress a string using run length encoding. So the string "aaabcccbbbb" becomes "a3b1c3b4"

We start at the beginning of the input string and traverse it. Each time we encounter a character, we parse out all identical characters that are adjacent to it and find out the count of identical characters. The character and the count are then written out to the result.

```
/*Performs run length encoding on a string
str1: input string (example: "aaabb")
str2: output string (example: "a3b2")
*/
void run_length_encode(char *str1, char *str2)
{
    char c;
    int pos1, pos2, count;

    if (str1 == NULL || str2 == NULL)
        return;

    pos1 = pos2 = 0;
    while (1) {
        c = str1[pos1];
        if (c == '\0') /*If we have reached end of string, then break*/
            break;

        /*Count the number of consecutive occurences of character c*/
        count = 0;
        while (c == str1[pos1]) {
            count++;
            pos1++;
        }

        /*Store character c in the output string*/
        str2[pos2] = c;
        pos2++;

        /*Store the count in the output string. sprintf returns the
        number of characters appended to str2. So add it to pos2 */
        pos2 += sprintf(&str2[pos2], "%d", count);
    }
    str2[pos2] = '\0';
}
```

A variation of this question is, given the run length encoded string "a3b2" decode it back to the original string "aaabb"

7. Remove all duplicate characters in a string

If we are given the string "hehllho", after removing the duplicate characters we get "helo". We can remove all the duplicate characters in a string s1 in O(n) as indicated below:

1. Maintain an array called was_char_observed which indicates if a character has been observed in s1 until now. Initialize fill_position to 1.

2. Traverse s1 starting with s1[1], and if the was_char_observed array indicates that the current character has not been observed so far, then move the current character into the fill_position and advance fill_position to the next location.

```c
/*str1: string from which duplicate characters should be removed*/
void remove_duplicates(char *str1) {
    int i, length, fill_pos;
    char c, was_char_observed[MAX_NUM_CHARACTERS];

    if (!str1)
        return;

    length = strlen(str1);
    if (length < 2)
        return;

    memset(was_char_observed, 0, MAX_NUM_CHARACTERS * sizeof(char));

    c = str1[0];
    was_char_observed[(int)c] = 1;
    fill_pos = 1;
    for (i = 1; i < length; ++i) {
        c = str1[i];

        /*Only if current character was not observed so far, add the
        current character to fill position and advance fill position*/
        if (!was_char_observed[(int)c]) {
                str1[fill_pos] = c;
                fill_pos++;
        }
        was_char_observed[(int)c] = 1;
    }
    /*Insert the termination \0 at the end of str1*/
    str1[fill_pos] = 0;
}
```

A variation of this question is to remove all the characters of string s2 from string s1. In this case we fill was_char_observed using the characters in s2 and use above approach.

8. Replace all spaces in a string with "%20"

When a URL is sent to a web server, the space characters (' ') in it are first converted to "%20" and then sent. Each space occupies 1 character whereas "%20" occupies 3 characters. So the result will be longer than the original string. To solve the problem with least number of moves, we process the string from the rear as described below:

1. Count the number of spaces in the original string.

2. Initialize fill_position to original string length + (2 * number of spaces) - 1

3. Go on copying the characters from the rear of the original string to the fill_position and keep decrementing the fill_position. If we encounter a space in the original string, then we insert the characters "%20" at the fill_position.

```
/*str1: string in which space characters (' ') should be replaced with %20.
    There is sufficient free space at the end of the string to
    accomodate the extra characters needed
*/
void replace_space(char *str1)
{
    int i, num_spaces, length, fill_pos;

    /*Count the number of spaces*/
    i = num_spaces = 0;
    while (str1[i]) {
        if (str1[i] == ' ')
                num_spaces++;
        ++i;
    }
    length = i;

    fill_pos = length + (2 * num_spaces);
    str1[fill_pos] = 0; /*Insert the string termination character*/
    fill_pos--; /*fill_pos is now at original length + (2*num_spaces) - 1*/

    /*Keep copying characters from rear of original string to fill position*/
    i = length - 1;
    while ( i >= 0) {
        if (str1[i] == ' ') {
                /*If we get a space, then place "%20" at fill position*/
                str1[fill_pos] = '0';
                str1[fill_pos - 1] = '2';
                str1[fill_pos - 2] = '%';
                fill_pos = fill_pos - 3;
        } else {
                /*Copy the character to fill position*/
```

```
                str1[fill_pos] = str1[i];
                fill_pos--;
            }
        --i;
        }
    }
}
```

9. Given two strings, find if one string can be formed by rotating the characters in the other

*trick - can do same without O(N) space by doing modulo read with loop bound of slen*2

Let the strings be str1 and str2. We need to check if str2 can be formed by rotating str1. If the two strings are not of the same length, then we can immediately conclude that str2 is not a rotation of str1. If the two strings are of equal length, then we can generate every rotation of str1 and compare with str2. If the size of str1 is n, then there are n possible rotations and each comparison takes O(n). So the total time complexity is O(n²).

We can find out if str2 is a rotation of str1 in O(n), if we are allowed to use additional space. The algorithm is as follows:

1. If the two strings have different lengths then return indicating str2 is not a rotation of str1.

2. Form a new string str3 and copy str1 into str3. Then again concatenate str1 into str3.

3. Search for str2 in str3. If str2 is found in str3, then str2 is a rotation of str1.

For instance, let str1="PQR" and str2 = "QRP". Then str3 will be str1 repeated twice which in this case is "PQRPQR". The rotations of str1 are "PQR", "RPQ" and "QRP". str3 will have all the rotations of str1 in it as shown below.

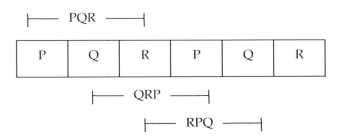

So all the rotations of str1 are present in str3. So when we check if str2 is present in str3, we will find it if str2 is a rotation of str1.

```
/*
str1 and str2 are the two strings which need to be checked
Return value: 1 if the two strings are rotations of each other, 0 otherwise
*/
int is_string_rotation(char *str1, char *str2)
{
    char *str3;
    int is_rotation;
    int length1, length2;

    if (!str1 || !str2)
        return 0;

    length1 = strlen(str1);
    length2 = strlen(str2);

    /*If lengths of two strings are not equal, then they can't be rotations*/
    if (length1 != length2)
        return 0;

    str3 = (char*) malloc(2*length1 + 1);

    strcpy(str3, str1);
    strcat(str3, str1);

    is_rotation = 0;

    /*
    strstr(str3, str2) returns the pointer to first occurence of str2 in str3.
    So if strstr returns a non-null pointer, then str2 is a substring of str3
    */
    if (strstr(str3, str2))
        is_rotation = 1;

    free(str3);

    return is_rotation;
}
```

10.

Reverse the words in a string in-place. So the string "Hello how are you" should become "you are how Hello"

We can reverse the words in a string in O(n) without using additional space, by doing the following:

1. Reverse the entire string. So if the input string is "Hello how are you", after reversal it becomes "uoy era woh olleH".

2. Then reverse all the words in the string. So "uoy era woh olleH" now becomes "you are how Hello"

```
/*Helper function which reverses a string between indexes low and high
str1: string which needs to be reversed
low: lower index of region to be reversed
high: higher index of region to be reversed
*/
void reverse_string(char str1[], int low, int high)
{
    char temp;

    while (low < high) {
        temp = str1[low];
        str1[low] = str1[high];
        str1[high] = temp;
        low++;
        high--;
    }
}

/*Helper function which checks if a character is an alphabet(a-zA-Z)*/
int is_alphabet(char c)
{
    if (c >= 'A' && c <= 'Z')
        return 1;

    if (c >= 'a' && c <= 'z')
        return 1;

    return 0;
}
```

```
/*Main function to reverse the words in a string
str1: the string in which the words have to be reversed
*/
void reverse_words(char str1[])
{
    int length, low, high, pos;

    length = strlen(str1);
    if (length < 2)
        return;

    /*Reverse the entire string*/
    reverse_string(str1, 0, length - 1);

    /*Reverse the individual words in the string*/
    pos = 0;
    while (pos < length) {
        if (is_alphabet(str1[pos])) {
                low = pos;
                while (pos < length && is_alphabet(str1[pos])) {
                        pos++;
                }
                high = pos - 1;
                reverse_string(str1, low, high);
        } else {
                pos++;
        }
    }
}
```

11. Find the first non-repeating character in a string. For instance, in string "ABBCAEEF", the first non-repeating character is C.

To find the first non-repeating character in the string, we use the following approach which has a time complexity of O(n):

1. First scan the string and count the number of occurrences for each character

2. Next scan the string again from left to right and the first character that we encounter with a count of 1 is the first non-repeating character.

```c
/*
str1: non-NULL character array to be searched
Return value: first unique character if it exists, '\0' otherwise
*/
char find_first_unique_char(char *str1)
{
    int i, count[MAX_NUM_CHARS];
    int length = strlen(str1);
    char cur_char, first_unique_char;

    for (i = 0; i < MAX_NUM_CHARS; ++i)
        count[i] = 0;

    /*count the number of occurences of each character*/
    for (i = 0; i < length; ++i) {
        cur_char = str1[i];
        count[(int)cur_char]++;
    }

    /*traverse str1 and find first character which occurs only once*/
    first_unique_char = 0;
    for (i = 0; i < length; ++i) {
        cur_char = str1[i];
        if (count[(int)cur_char] == 1) {
                first_unique_char = cur_char;
                break;
        }
    }

    return first_unique_char;
}
```

12. Find the first non-repeating character in a stream of characters

When we are given a stream of characters, we can inspect only one character at a time. To find the first non-repeating character in a stream, we need to maintain information about the characters that we have observed previously in the stream. For each character, we maintain:

- the first position of the character observed in the stream. If we have not yet observed the character in the stream, we store -1 as the first position
- whether the character has been repeated in the stream, i.e. the character has already appeared two or more times in the stream

We also maintain the current first unique (non-repeating) character in the stream. If there are no unique characters in the stream, we store a special character, say '#', as the first unique. When we process the current character in the stream, we do the following

1. If the first position of the current character is -1, then we update the first position of the character to the current position. If the first unique doesn't exist, then the current character becomes the first unique.

2. If the first position of the current character is not -1, then we have already observed the character. So we mark the character as a repeated character. If the current character is the first unique, then we need to find the new first unique. Scan the first positions and character repeated information of all characters to find the new first unique. If there are m characters in the alphabet, then each scan can be done in $O(m)$ and we will have to do at most m such scans. So the complexity of scanning is $O(m^2)$

If the length of the stream is n, then the total complexity of the algorithm is $O(n + m^2)$. If n is very large compared to m^2 then the complexity reduces to $O(n)$.

```
struct stream_param {
    /*If we have seen the character 2 or more times in the stream,
    then is_repeated[character] = 1*/
    char is_repeated[MAX_NUM_CHARS];

    /*For every character, we maintain the position of its first
    occurence. If the character has not yet occured in stream, we store -1 */
    int first_pos[MAX_NUM_CHARS];
    char first_unique; /*the first unique character in the stream*/
    int cur_pos;      /*the current position in the stream*/
};
```

```
/*
stream_param: contains the parameters for processing the stream
cur_char: indicates the current character in the stream
Returns: first unique character in the stream if it exists, # otherwise
*/
char first_unique_in_stream(struct stream_param *p, char cur_char)
{
    if (p->first_pos[(int)cur_char] == -1) {
        /*We are seeing the character for the first time in the stream. So
        update its first position*/
        p->first_pos[(int)cur_char] = p->cur_pos;

        /*If there are no unique characters in the stream, then make this
        the first unique character*/
        if (p->first_unique == '#') {
                p->first_unique = cur_char;
        }

        p->cur_pos = p->cur_pos + 1;
        return p->first_unique;
    }

    /*We have already seen this character before*/
    p->is_repeated[(int)cur_char] = 1;

    /*If the current character is the first unique character in the stream,
    then we need to replace it with next unique character*/
    if (p->first_unique == cur_char) {
        int i, smallest_pos;

        /*Find the first character that occurs only once in stream*/
        smallest_pos = MAX_POS;
        p->first_unique = '#';
        for (i = 0; i < MAX_NUM_CHARS; ++i) {
                if (p->is_repeated[i] == 0 && p->first_pos[i] != -1
                    && p->first_pos[i] < smallest_pos) {
                        smallest_pos = p->first_pos[i];
                        p->first_unique = i;
                }
        }
    }

    p->cur_pos = p->cur_pos + 1;
    return p->first_unique;
}
```

13. Find the length of the longest palindrome in a string

To find the length of the longest palindrome we use the following procedure:

1. Pick each character in the string and treat it as the middle of a possible palindrome.

2. Then keep extending the substring, one character at a time, in the left and right directions from the chosen character until there is a mismatch in the characters on the left end and right end of the substring. This is the longest possible palindrome with the chosen character at the center.

3. The longest amongst all palindromes generated is the longest palindrome in the string

It is important to note that when we pick a character as the middle of a possible palindrome, the chosen character may be the middle of an odd length palindrome or an even length palindrome. For example, in the string ABCBACDEED, C is the middle of the odd length palindrome ABCBA and E is the middle of the even length palindrome DEED. We have to check for both possibilities at each character. So we do the following:

- to find the longest odd length palindrome with location p as center, simply extend in the left direction (from p-1 onwards) and the right direction (from p+1 onwards) by one character at a time until the left most and right most characters mismatch

- to find the longest even length palindrome with location p as center, first choose the next character p+1 as well. If the characters at p and p+1 match, then extend in the left direction (from p-1 onwards) and the right direction (from p+2 onwards) by one character at a time until the left most and right most characters mismatch

The time complexity of this approach is $O(n^2)$

```
/*str1: non-NULL input character string
Return value: length of longest palindrome
*/
int find_longest_palindrome(char *str1)  {
    int n, left, pos, right, max_pal_len, cur_pal_len;

    n = strlen(str1);
    max_pal_len = 0;
    for (pos = 0; pos < n; ++pos)  {
        /*Check for odd length palindromes by comparing the characters
        to the left of pos with the characters to the right of pos
        */
        left = pos - 1;
        right = pos + 1;
        cur_pal_len = 1;
        while (left >= 0 && right <= n - 1)  {
                if (str1[left] != str1[right])
                        break;
                cur_pal_len += 2;
                --left;
                ++right;
        }

        if (cur_pal_len > max_pal_len)
                max_pal_len = cur_pal_len;

        /*Check for even length palindromes. If str1[pos], matches
        with str1[pos+1], then compare the characters to the left of
        pos with the characters to the right of pos+1
        */
        if (str1[pos] == str1[pos + 1])  {
                left = pos - 1;
                right = pos + 2;
                cur_pal_len = 2;
                while (left >= 0 && right <= n - 1)  {
                        if (str1[left] != str1[right])
                                break;
                        cur_pal_len += 2;
                        --left;
                        ++right;
                }

                if (cur_pal_len > max_pal_len)
                        max_pal_len = cur_pal_len;
        }
    }
    return max_pal_len;
}
```

14. Find if any permutation of a string is a palindrome. For instance, the string "EVELL" has a permutation "LEVEL" which is a palindrome

The permutations of a string are all the possible rearrangements of the characters in the string. We can check if any permutation of a string is a palindrome in O(n) as follows:

1. For each character in the string, count the number of times it occurs in the string

2. If the number of characters that appear odd number of times is less than 2, then at least one permutation of the string will form a palindrome.

For instance in "EVELL", E occurs 2 times, L occurs 2 times and V occurs once. So the number of characters that occurs odd number of times is 1 (which is less than 2). So at least one permutation of "EVELL" will form a palindrome

```
/*Returns 1 if there is at least one permutation of string str1 which is a
    palindrome, 0 otherwise*/
int is_permutation_palindrome(char str1[])
{
    int i = 0, num_odd_char;
    int count[NUM_CHARACTERS];

    for (i = 0; i < NUM_CHARACTERS; ++i)
        count[i] = 0;

    /*Find out how many times a character appears in the string*/
    i = 0;
    while(str1[i]) {
        count[(int)str1[i]]++;
        i++;
    }

    num_odd_char = 0;
    for (i = 0; i < NUM_CHARACTERS; ++i) {
        if (count[i] % 2 == 1)
                num_odd_char++;

        /*If there are 2 or more characters that appear odd number of
        times then we can't form a palindrome with any permutation of
        the string*/
        if (num_odd_char >= 2)
                return 0;
    }

    return 1;
}
```

review

15. Print all the substrings in a string

Let S be the input string of length n and let S(x, y) denote the substring of S starting at position x and ending at position y. We first generate the substrings S(0,0), S(0, 1), S(0, 2), ... S(0, n-1). We then generate the substrings S(1,1), S(1,2), ... S(1, n-1) and so on.

```c
/*
str1: string whose substrings should be printed
*/
void print_all_sub_strings(char *str1)
{
    int  i, j, pos, n;

    n = strlen(str1);

    /*Generate all pairs (i,j) where i <= j*/
    for (i = 0; i < n; ++i) {
        for (j = i; j < n; ++j) {

            /*print the substring string[i] to string[j]*/
            for (pos = i; pos <= j; ++pos)  {
                printf("%c", str1[pos]);
            }
            printf("\n");

        }
    }
}
```

Suppose we are asked to generate all the repeating substrings (also referred to as repeating sequences) in a string, we can maintain a hash table. Every time a substring is generated, the count for the substring in the hash table is incremented. At the end, all substrings in the hash table whose count is 2 or more are the repeated substrings.

printf ("%.*s", sublength, &s[i])

16. Generate all permutations of the characters in a string

The permutations of a string are all the possible rearrangements of the characters in the string. The permutations will have the same length as the original string. There are n! permutations for a string with length n. Consider the string ABC. The permutations are ABC, ACB, BCA, BAC, CAB, and CBA

To generate all the permutations of a string, we make use of recursion. Each call to the recursive function at level i will cycle through all the possible characters at position i. To prevent the same character from being added more than once to the permutation, we maintain a visited array where visited[i] = 1 if i^{th} character in the input string has already been added to the current permutation.

```
/*
str1: valid input string whose permutations have to be formed
buf: array for storing the current permutation
pos: current position in the buf array
visited: indicates if character in input string has already been visited
length: length of the input string
*/
void generate_permutations(char *str1, char *buf, unsigned int pos,
                int *visited, unsigned int length)
{
    unsigned int i;

    /*Recursion termination condition*/
    if (pos == length) {
        buf[pos] = 0;
        printf("%s\n", buf);
        return ;
    }

    for (i = 0; i < length; ++i) {
        if (visited[i] == 0) {
            buf[pos] = str1[i];
            visited[i] = 1;
            generate_permutations(str1, buf, pos+1, visited, length);
            visited[i] = 0;
        }
    }
}
```

17.

You are playing the scrabble game. Given a bunch of characters, generate all possible strings that you can form using the characters.

If we are given the characters A, B, C, then we will have to generate A, B, C, AB, BA, AC, CA, BC, CB, ABC, ACB, BAC, BCA, CAB, and CBA. To achieve this we make use of recursion. Each call to the recursive function at level i will cycle through all the possible characters at position i. To prevent the same character being added more than once to the permutation, we maintain a visited array where visited[i] = 1 if i^{th} character in the input has already been added to the current permutation. The solution to this problem is similar to the previous problem where we generated all the permutations of a string. The only difference is that, if there are n characters in the input, then we don't need to wait until all n characters have been generated in the output. During recursion, all strings that we construct having 1 to n characters are treated as output strings.

```
/*
str: valid input string from which words have to be generated
buf: array for storing the current word that has been generated
pos: current position in the buf array
visited: indicates if character in input string has already been visited
length: length of the input string
*/
void generate_words(char *str, char *buf, unsigned int pos,
                int *visited, unsigned int length)
{
    unsigned int i;

    /*Output all strings that we generate*/
    buf[pos] = 0;
    printf("%s\n", buf);

    /*Recursion termination condition*/
    if (pos >= length) {
        return;
    }

    for (i = 0; i < length; ++i) {
        if (visited[i] == 0) {
            buf[pos] = str[i];
            visited[i] = 1;
            generate_words(str, buf, pos+1, visited, length);
            visited[i] = 0;
        }
    }
}
```

18.

Print all possible interleavings of two strings. For instance if str1 = "abc" and str2 = "123", then "abc123", "a1b2c3", "ab123c", "12a3bc", etc. are all valid interleavings.

When we interleave two strings str1 and str2, the order of characters in each string should be preserved. For instance, if character 'a' appears before character 'b' in str1, then the same should hold good in the interleaved string. To generate all possible interleavings of str1 and str2, we make use of recursion. At each position of the interleaved string, we can choose between the current character in str1 and str2. So first choose the current character from str1 at the position and recursively process the next positions. Then choose the current character from str2 at the position and recursively process the next positions.

```c
/*
str1, str2: two non-NULL input strings that have to be interleaved
buffer: string that contain the result of interleaving
pos: current position in the buffer
*/
void string_interleave(char *str1, char *str2, char *buffer, int pos)
{
    /*If we have finished processing both strings, print the buffer and
    terminate the recursion*/
    if (!str1[0] && !str2[0]) {
        buffer[pos] = '\0';
        printf("%s\n", buffer);
        return;
    }

    /*If we have finished processing str2, concatenate str1 to the buffer,
    print the buffer and terminate the recursion*/
    if (!str2[0]) {
        buffer[pos] = '\0';
        strcat(&buffer[pos], str1);
        printf("%s\n", buffer);
        return;
    }

    /*If we have finished processing str1, concatenate str2 to the buffer,
    print the buffer and terminate the recursion*/
    if (!str1[0]) {
        buffer[pos] = '\0';
        strcat(&buffer[pos], str2);
        printf("%s\n", buffer);
        return;
    }

    /*Include the next character of str1 into the buffer*/
```

```
    buffer[pos] = *str1;
    string_interleave(str1+1, str2, buffer, pos + 1);

    /*Include the next character of str2 into the buffer*/
    buffer[pos] = *str2;
    string_interleave(str1, str2+1, buffer, pos + 1);
}
```

19. On the telephone keypad, digit 2 represents characters "ABC", digit 3 represents the characters "DEF" and so on. Given a telephone number, find all the strings that can be generated from it. For instance, if the telephone number is 23, we can form the strings "AD", "AE", "AF", "BD", "BE", "BF", "CD", "CE" and "CF".

The digits 0 and 1 don't have any alphabetical character associated with them. So we assume digit 0 represents "0" and digit 1 represents "1". To generate all possible strings, we make use of recursion and for each digit in the telephone number, we cycle through all possible characters that we can assign to the digit.

```
/*Helper function for printing the words corresponding to the telephone number
digits: array of digits from 0-9
num_digits: number of digits in the array
key_pad: contains the characters corresponding to each digit
buf: contains the word formed corresponding to the telephone digits
pos: current position in buf and digits
*/
void keypad_string_gen(int digits[], int num_digits, char *keypad[],
                char buf[], int pos)
{
    int cur_digit, i;
    char *key_string;

    if (pos == num_digits) {
        /*We have processed all the digits. So print the
        word and terminate the recursion*/
        buf[pos] = 0;
        printf("%s\n", buf);
        return;
    }

    cur_digit = digits[pos];
    key_string = keypad[cur_digit];

    /*key_string is the string corresponding to the current digit
    So if current digit is 2, key_string will be "ABC".
    Cycle through all the characters in the key_string.*/
    i = 0;
    while (key_string[i]) {
        buf[pos] = key_string[i];
        keypad_string_gen(digits, num_digits, keypad, buf, pos+1);
        i++;
    }
}
```

```
/*Main function for printing the words corresponding to the telephone number
digits: array of digits from 0-9 in the telephone number
num_digits: number of digits in the array
*/
void telephone_digits_to_string(int digits[], int num_digits)
{
    /*Create a temporary buffer for storing the words corresponding
    to the digits*/
    char *buf = (char*) calloc(1, num_digits+1);

    /*digit 2 corresponds to ABC, 3 corresponds to DEF and so on*/
    char *keypad[] = {"0", "1", "ABC", "DEF", "GHI", "JKL", "MNO", "PQRS",
                "TUV", "WXYZ"};

    keypad_string_gen(digits, num_digits, keypad, buf, 0);

    free(buf);
}
```

20.

Generate all valid permutations of N opening braces '{', brackets '[', parenthesis '(' and N closing braces '}', brackets ']' and parenthesis ')'

To generate all valid permutations of braces, brackets and parenthesis we use recursion. At the current position in the output string, we can either pick an opening character or a closing character using the conditions given below:

1. If the number of the opening characters in the output string is less than N, then we are free to choose any of the opening characters in the current position

2. While picking the closing character, we have to ensure that the opening and closing characters are properly nested. So we first check the most recent unmatched opening character and place the equivalent closing character at the current position. For instance, if we have generated the string "{[()". Then the most recent unmatched opening character is '['. So we can place ']' at the current position

```
/*Helper function for finding the nearest unmatched opening character
str1: input string containing braces, brackets and parenthesis
pos: we will search for unmatched opening character from pos - 1 to 0
Return value: index of the first unmatched character when traversing from
    pos - 1 to 0  if it exists, -1 otherwise*/
int find_unmatched(char str1[], int pos)
{
    int back_pos = pos - 1;
    int n_braces = 0, n_brackets = 0, n_parenthesis = 0;

    /*When we get a closing character, decrement the count by 1,
    when we get an opening character, increment the count by 1*/
    while (back_pos >= 0) {
        if (str1[back_pos] == '{')
                n_braces++;
        else if (str1[back_pos] == '[')
                n_brackets++;
        else if (str1[back_pos] == '(')
                n_parenthesis++;
        else if (str1[back_pos] == '}')
                n_braces--;
        else if (str1[back_pos] == ']')
                n_brackets--;
        else if (str1[back_pos] == ')')
                n_parenthesis--;

    /*If we encounter more opening characters than closing
    characters as we traverse backwards, then we have found
    the location of the mismatch*/
    if (n_braces > 0 || n_brackets > 0 || n_parenthesis > 0)
            return back_pos;
```

use a stack instead

if (open < n) '('
buf[w] =
push (')')
recursion()
pop ()
if open-closed is empty (stack)
pop()
buf[w] = popped val
recursion popped val
push

165

```
            back_pos--;
    }
    return -1;
}

/*Main function for printing the braces, brackets and parenthesis
str1: string used to store braces, brackets and parenthesis
pos: next free position in the string str1
n_max: maximum number of opening characters (equal to max closing characters)
n_open: number of opening characters currently in str1
n_close: number of closing characters currently in str1
*/
void print_nesting(char *str1, int pos, int n_max, int n_open, int n_close) {
    /*Condition for terminating the recursion*/
    if (n_close == n_max) {
        str1[pos] = 0;
        process_string(str1);
        return;
    }

    if (n_open < n_max) {
        /*Add an opening brace and call print_nesting recursively*/
        str1[pos] = '{';
        print_nesting(str1, pos+1, n_max, n_open + 1, n_close);

        /*Add an opening bracket and call print_nesting recursively*/
        str1[pos] = '[';
        print_nesting(str1, pos+1, n_max, n_open + 1, n_close);

        /*Add an opening parenthesis and call print_nesting recursively*/
        str1[pos] = '(';
        print_nesting(str1, pos+1, n_max, n_open + 1, n_close);
    }

    int unmatched_pos = find_unmatched(str1, pos);
    if (n_open > n_close && unmatched_pos >= 0) {
        /*to balance the characters, add the closing character corresponding
        to nearest unmatched character and call print_nesting recursively*/
        char unmatched_char = str1[unmatched_pos];

        if (unmatched_char == '{') {
            str1[pos] = '}';
            print_nesting(str1, pos+1, n_max, n_open, n_close + 1);
        } else if (unmatched_char == '[') {
            str1[pos] = ']';
            print_nesting(str1, pos+1, n_max, n_open, n_close + 1);
        } else if (unmatched_char == '(') {
            str1[pos] = ')';
            print_nesting(str1, pos+1, n_max, n_open, n_close + 1);
        }
    }
}
```

1.6 Bitmaps

1. Given an unsigned integer, a.) set a particular bit position to 1, b.) reset a particular bit position to 0 and c.) toggle a particular bit position

---

Let n be the unsigned integer and pos be the position of the bit

To set a bit to 1: n = n | (1u << pos)

To reset a bit to 0: n = n & ~(1u << pos)

To toggle a bit: n = n ^ (1u << pos)

2. Efficiently count the number of bits set in an integer   ☆ *memorize this*

One way to find the number of bits set in an integer is to check each bit. However there is a faster method to count the number of bits set using the function below

```
unsigned int count_num_bits_set(unsigned int n)
{
    unsigned int count = 0;

    while (n) {
        n &= n - 1;
        count++;
    }

    return count;
}
```

The following code works because each time we perform the operation n &= n - 1, the first bit that has a value of 1 from the right (from the least significant bit) is reset to 0.

For instance if n = 1100, then

n	= 1 1 0 0
n – 1	= 1 0 1 1
n & (n-1) =	1 0 0 0

So 1100 is converted to 1000 wherein, the first bit that has a value of 1 from the right in 1100 is now reset to 0.

3. Find if an integer is a power of 2 using bit wise operators

The condition (x & (x-1) == 0) checks if an integer is a power of 2 or not. From the previous question, we know that x & (x-1) will reset the first bit that has a value of 1 from the right to 0. If x is a power of 2, then only one of the bits will be set to 1 and all the remaining bits will be set to 0 (for instance, 8 is a power of 2 and 8 in binary is 1000). So x & (x-1) will reset the only bit that has a value of 1 resulting in 0.

x & (x-1) == 0 however incorrectly indicates that 0 is also a power of 2, since (0 & (0 − 1)) = (0 & 0xffffffff) = 0. Since 0 is not a power of 2, we modify the condition as shown below

```
(x != 0) && (x & (x-1) == 0)
```
Memorize
this

4. Reverse the bits in an integer

We can reverse the bits in an integer one bit at a time. However there is a faster technique. To reverse the bits in an integer efficiently, a lookup table is pre-computed to give the reverse values for every byte. This lookup table is then referred to for performing the reversal of the integer. The code for this is given below

```
/*
input_value: the integer that has to be reversed
reverse_table: lookup table that has the reversed values for every byte.
     Example - reverse_table[0x1] = 0x80, since reverse of 00000001 is 1000000
Return value: integer that is the reverse of the input integer
*/
unsigned int reverse_integer(unsigned int input_value,
                        unsigned char reverse_table[])
{
    unsigned int result = 0;
    int i = 0;
    int num_bytes = sizeof(int);

    for (i = 0; i < num_bytes; ++i) {
        /*Get the least significant byte from the input*/
        int cur_byte_value = input_value & 0xFF;

        /*Left shift the result by 8 and append the reverse of the
        least  significant byte of input*/
        result = (result << 8) | reverse_table[cur_byte_value];

        /*Right shift out the least significant byte from the input*/
        input_value = input_value >> 8;
    }
    return result;
}
```

5. Given two integers, find the number of bits that are different between the two integers

Consider the integers 2 (0010 in binary) and 9 (1001 in binary). Three bits are different and one bit is identical. To efficiently find the number of bits that are different, we do the following

1. XOR the two integers.

2. In the result of the XOR, if the bit is 1, then the two integers are different at this bit position. So the number of 1's present in the result gives the number of different bits between the two integers. For counting the number of 1's in the result, we make use of the technique we described in page 167

```
/*
a, b: the two input integers
Return value: Number of bits that have different values in a and b
*/
unsigned int count_different_bits(unsigned int a, unsigned int b)
{
    unsigned int c = a ^ b;
    unsigned int count = 0;

    /*Since c = a xor b, the positions where a and b are different will
    be set to 1 in c. So by counting the number of 1's in c, we will get the
    number of bits that are different between a and b*/
    while (c != 0) {
        count++;
        c = c & (c - 1);
    }

    return count;
}
```

6. Given an integer, swap the bit at position 1 with the bit at position 2

We first extract the bits at position 1 and position 2. We then have to swap the two bits only if the two bits are different. The code for swapping the bits is given below

```
/*
x: integer in which the bits should be swapped
pos1: position of first bit to be swapped
pos2: position of the second bit to be swapped
*/
unsigned int swap_bits(unsigned int x, int pos1, int pos2)
{
    /*get the bits at position pos1 and pos2*/
    int bit1 = (x >> pos1) & 1;
    int bit2 = (x >> pos2) & 1;

    /*swap the bits if the bits are different*/
    if (bit1 != bit2) {
        x = write_bit(x, bit1, pos2);
        x = write_bit(x, bit2, pos1);
    }

    return x;
}
```

```
/*writes the bit_value (0/1) into position pos in x and returns the result*/
unsigned int write_bit(unsigned int x, int bit_value, int pos)
{
    unsigned int mask = 1 << pos;
    if (bit_value)
        x = x | mask;
    else
        x = x & ~mask;

    return x;
}
```

7. Given an integer, compute the parity bit for the integer

There are two types of parity bit schemes

1. Even parity: if the total number of 1's is odd, then the parity bit will be 1 to make the total number of 1's (including the parity bit) even

2. Odd parity: if the total number of 1's is even, then the parity bit will be 1 to make the total number of 1's (including the parity bit) odd.

We will implement an even parity scheme here. We count the number of 1's in the integer using the scheme described in page 167.

```
/*
x: input integer
Return value: parity bit, 1 if there are odd number of 1's, 0 otherwise
*/
unsigned int compute_parity(unsigned int x)
{
    /*for each bit set to 1 in x, toggle the parity bit*/
    unsigned int parity = 0;
    while (x != 0) {
        parity = parity ^ 1;
        x = x & (x - 1);
    }

    return parity;
}
```

8.

Copy the bits between the specified start bit and end bit positions of one integer into another integer. For instance if source integer is 0xBBB and destination integer is 0xAEC and we copy the bits from 4 to 7 from source to destination, the result is 0xABC

Let the source integer be 0xBBB, destination integer be 0xAEC and we have to copy bits from position 4 to 7. The strategy we use is as follows:

1. Construct a mask (let's call it ones mask) in which all the bits are initially set to 1. If we need to copy n bits and the total number of bits in the integer is m, then right shift the ones mask by (m-n). So if we need to copy 4 bits between bit 4 and bit 7, and total number of bits in integer is 32, we perform ones_mask >> (32 – 4). So ones_mask will have a value 0xF.

2. Left shift the ones mask to the starting position from where we have to copy the bits. The ones mask will now have 1's from the start bit position to the end bit position. In this example, starting bit position is 4, so we perform (ones_mask << 4) = (0xF << 4) = 0xF0.

3. Construct a zeroes mask which is the complement of the ones mask. The zeroes mask will have 0's from the start bit to the end bit. So if ones mask is 0xF0, then zeroes mask will be 0xFFFFFF0F.

4. AND the destination integer with the zeroes mask to clear out the bits in the destination from start bit to end bit. So if destination is 0xAEC, then 0xAEC & 0xFFFFFF0F will give 0xA0C

5. AND the source integer with the ones mask so that only the bits from start and end bit positions remain and the rest of the bits are cleared. If the source integer is 0xBBB, then 0xBBB & 0xF0 will give 0xB0

6. OR the source and destination. So 0xA0C | 0xB0 will give 0xABC

```
/*
dest: destination integer into which the bits have to be copied
src: source integer from which the bits have to be copied
end_pos: Most Significant bit position upto where the bits should be copied
start_pos: Least Significant bit position from where the bits should be copied
    end_pos should be >= start_pos
Return value: result integer after copying bits from source to destination
*/
unsigned int copy_bits(unsigned int dest, unsigned int src,
               unsigned int end_pos, unsigned int start_pos)
{
    unsigned int num_bits_to_copy = end_pos - start_pos + 1;
    unsigned int num_bits_in_int = sizeof(unsigned int) * 8;
    unsigned int zeroes_mask;
    unsigned int ones_mask = ~((unsigned int) 0); /*all ones*/

    /*Use the bit-wise right shift operator to remove the excess 1's
    in the mask*/
    ones_mask = ones_mask >> (num_bits_in_int - num_bits_to_copy);

    /*Left shift the 1's to the starting position. ones_mask will contain 1's
    from start_pos to end_pos*/
    ones_mask = ones_mask << start_pos;

    /*zeroes_mask will contain 0's from start_pos to end_pos*/
    zeroes_mask = ~ones_mask;

    /*clear the bits in destination from start_pos to end_pos*/
    dest = dest & zeroes_mask;

    /*retain the bits in source from start_pos to end_pos and clear the
    remaining bits*/
    src = src & ones_mask;

    /*copy the source bits into the destination*/
    dest = dest | src;

    return dest;
}
```

article

9. Implement circular shift left and circular shift right on an unsigned integer

Let n be the number of bits to shift. Let m be the total number of bits present in the integer. If we circular shift an integer m times, then we get back the original integer. So the actual number of shifts we need to perform is n % m.

The functions for circular shift left (also called left shift rotate) and circular shift right (right shift rotate) are given below

```
/*
input: input value which has to be circularly shifted left
n: number of positions to shift
Return value: result after circularly left shifting input
*/
unsigned int circular_left_shift(unsigned int input, int n)
{
    unsigned int size = sizeof(unsigned int) * 8;
    unsigned int result;

    n = n % size;
    result = input << n | input >> (size - n);
    return result;
}
```

$X = 0110, \quad n = 2$

$y = X << n \quad 1000$

$y |= X >> (4-n) \quad 100)$

```
/*
input: input value which has to be circularly shifted right
n: number of positions to shift
Return value: result after circularly right shifting input
*/
unsigned int circular_right_shift(unsigned int input, int n)
{
    unsigned int size = sizeof(int) * 8;
    unsigned int result;

    n = n % size;
    result = input >> n | input << (size - n);
    return result;
}
```

10.

Find the maximum of 2 integers without using if-else or any other comparison operator

We can find the maximum of 2 integers without making use of if else or any comparison operator using the function below

```
/*Returns the maximum of x and y without using if-else and comparison*/
int find_max(int x, int y) {
    int difference = x - y;
    int sign_bit =    (difference >> 31) & 0x1;
    /*
    Sign bit can be 0 or 1
    If sign bit is 0, max = x - (0 * difference) = x
    If sign bit is 1, max = x - (1 * (x-y)) = x - x + y = y
    */
    int max = x   - (sign_bit * difference);
    return max;
}
```

First we compute the difference between x and y. Next we find the sign bit of the difference. In the 2's complement notation, the most significant bit indicates the sign of the number. If the sign bit is 0, then the number is positive and if the bit is 1, then the number is negative.

If $x >= y$, then the difference $x - y$ is positive and so the sign bit of the difference is 0. If $x <$ y, then the difference $x - y$ is negative and sign bit of the difference is 1.

Then we compute max = x - (sign_bit * difference).
If $x >= y$, then sign_bit = 0 and max = x - (0 * difference) = x. So we return x as the maximum value
If $x < y$, then sign_bit = 1 and max = x - (1 * difference) = x - difference = x - (x - y) = y. So we return y as the maximum value

11. Implement addition without using the addition (+) operator

When we add two bits X and Y, the result consists of the sum bit and the carry bit as shown in the table below

X	Y	Sum	Carry
0	0	0	0
0	1	1	0
1	0	1	0
1	1	0	1

So we find that Sum = X XOR Y, Carry = X AND Y. When adding two integers, we go on computing the Sum and Carry for all bits in the integers until the Carry becomes 0 as shown in the code below

```
/*
x, y: two integers, can be negative. x may be bigger, equal or smaller than y
Return value: x + y
*/
int add(int x, int y)
{
    int carry;

    while (y != 0) {
        /*compute the carry bits for all the bits in x and y*/
        carry = x & y;

        /*compute the sum bits for all the bits in x and y*/
        x = x ^ y;

        /*If a carry is present at current bit position, we would have
        marked a 1 in current bit position. But the carry needs to be
        added from the next bit position. So left shift the carry bits
        by 1 and then add the carry in the next iteration
        */
        y = carry << 1;
    }
    return x;
}
```

12. Implement subtraction without using the subtraction (-) operator

When we subtract two bits X and Y, the result consists of the difference bit and the borrow bit as shown in the table below

X	Y	Difference	Borrow
0	0	0	0
0	1	1	1
1	0	1	0
1	1	0	0

So we find that Difference = X XOR Y, Borrow = (~X) AND Y. When subtracting two integers, we go on computing the Difference and Borrow for all bits in the integers until the Borrow becomes 0 as shown in the code below

```
/*
x, y: two integers, can be negative. x may be bigger, equal or smaller than y
Return value: x - y
*/
int subtract(int x, int y)
{
    int borrow;

    while (y != 0) {
        /*compute the borrow bits for all the bits in x and y*/
        borrow = (~x) & y;

        /*compute the difference bits for all the bits in x and y*/
        x = x ^ y;

        /*If a borrow is needed at current bit position, we would have
        marked a 1 in current bit position. But the borrow needs to be
        subtracted from the next bit position. So left shift the borrow
        bits by 1 and then subtract the borrow in the next iteration
        */
        y = borrow << 1;
    }
    return x;
}
```

13. Implement multiplication without using the multiplication operator (*)

Let us say that we have to evaluate X * Y. We do the following

1. Initialize the result to 0.

2. Examine the least significant bit of Y. If the least significant bit is 1, then add X to the result

3. Shift out the least significant bit of Y and double the value of X.

4. Repeat steps 2 and 3 until Y becomes 0.

```
/*x, y: two integers >= 0
Return value: x multiplied with y */
int multiply(int x, int y) {
    int result;

    result = 0;
    while (y) {
        /*if the least significant bit of y is 1, then add x to result*/
        if ((y & 1) == 1) {
            result += x;
        }
        y = y >> 1;/*shift out the least significant bit of y*/
        x = x << 1; /*Double the value of x*/
    }
    return result;
}
```

14.

Implement division without using the division (/) or mod (%) operators. The answer should return the quotient and remainder

The code to evaluate a / b without using division or mod operators is given below

```
/*
a, b: a is an integer >= 0. b is an integer > 0
quotient_p: quotient of a / b will be returned here
remainder_p: remainder of a / b will be returned here
Return value: 0 on success, non-zero value on error (such as division by zero)
*/
int integer_division(int a, int b, int *quotient_p, int *remainder_p) {
    int quotient, remainder;
    char next_bit;
    int i, max_bit_pos = (sizeof(int) * 8) - 1;

    if (b == 0)
        return DIVISION_BY_ZERO_ERROR; /*we can also throw an exception*/

    quotient = remainder = 0;
    for (i = max_bit_pos; i >= 0; --i) {
        remainder = remainder << 1;   /*double the remainder*/

        /*Find the value of the next bit in the dividend a.
        In first iteration, we find value of the Most Significant Bit*/
        next_bit = 0;
        if (a & (1u << i)) {
                next_bit = 1;
        }

        /*Copy the value of the next bit into the least significant
        bit of remainder*/
        if (next_bit)
                remainder = remainder | 1;

        /* If the remainder is now greater than the divisor b,
        then subtract the divisor b from the remainder and
        set the appropriate quotient bit*/
        if (remainder >= b) {
                remainder = remainder - b;
                quotient = quotient | (1u << i);
        }
    }
    *quotient_p = quotient;
    *remainder_p = remainder;
    return 0;
}
```

15.

In a set of integers, all integers are repeated even number of times except one integer which is repeated odd number of times. Find the integer that occurs odd number of times in O(n) time and O(1) space. For instance in the array {1, 4, 8, 4, 6, 8, 1}, 6 occurs once (odd number of times) while the remaining integers occur even number of times

For this problem we make use of the XOR operator. For any integer A, the XOR operator has the following properties

A XOR A = 0

A XOR 0 = A

To find the integer that occurs odd number of times, we XOR all the integers in the set. By doing this, all the integers that are repeated even number of times will cancel each other out (since A XOR A = 0). So the result of XORing all the integers in the set will give us the integer that occurs odd number of times.

```
/*
a: array consisting of numbers, where one element occurs odd number of times
      while remaining elements occur even number of times
n: number of elements in the array
Return value: element that occurs odd number of times
*/
int find_odd_occurence(int a[], int n)
{
    int i, result;

    /*XOR all the elements*/
    result = 0;
    for (i = 0; i < n; ++i) {
        result = result ^ a[i];
    }

    return result;
}
```

16.

In a set of integers, all integers are repeated even number of times except **two** integers which are repeated odd number of times. Find the two integers that occur odd number of times in O(n) time and O(1) space. For instance in the array {1, 4, 3, 8, 4, 7, 8, 1}, 3 and 7 occur once (odd number of times) while the remaining integers occur even number of times

To solve the problem we do the following

1. XOR all the integers in the set. The integers that occur even number of times will cancel each other out since A XOR A = 0. So the result of the XOR is actually the XOR of the two integers that occur odd number of times

2. Choose any bit position in the result of the XOR whose bit value is 1. This represents the bit where the two integers that occur odd number of times differ. For instance in the example array {1, 4, 3, 8, 4, 7, 8, 1}, the result of the XOR of all elements is 4 (100 in binary). This implies that the two odd occurring integers differ at bit position 2 (the least significant bit is treated as bit 0). We can verify this. 3 and 7 occur odd number of times. 3 (011 in binary) and 7 (111 in binary) indeed differ at bit position 2.

3. We initialize result0 and result1 to 0. Then we iterate through all the elements in the array. If the element has 0 at the chosen bit position, then we XOR it with result0, otherwise we XOR it with result1. In this way we are partitioning the elements into two sets. Note that a repeated element will always go into the same set and if it occurs even number of times then it cancels out due to the XOR operation. So at the end, result0 will contain one integer that occurs odd number of times and result1 will contain the other integer that occurs odd number of times.

```
/*
a: input array where 2 elements occur odd number of times and the remaining
   occur even number of times
n: number of elements in a
result: the two numbers that occur odd number of times will be returned here
*/
void find_odd_occurences(unsigned int a[], int n, unsigned int result[])
{
    unsigned int all_xor, mask;
    int i;

    all_xor = 0;
    for (i = 0; i < n; ++i) {
        all_xor = all_xor ^ a[i];
    }
```

```
/*Find the first bit in the XOR result that is set to 1. The two odd
occuring numbers will differ at this bit position. So if difference
is at bit position 3, then mask will be ...00001000
*/
mask = all_xor & ~(all_xor - 1);

/*Separate out values in list a such that, values that have a 1 at the
different bit will be XORed with result[0] and values that have a 0
at the different bit will be XORed with result[1]
*/
result[0] = result[1] = 0;
for (i = 0; i < n; ++i) {
    if (a[i] & mask)
            result[0] = result[0] ^ a[i];
    else
            result[1] = result[1] ^ a[i];
}

/*result[0] and result[1] will now contain the two numbers that
occur odd number of times*/
}
```

1.7 Application of Data Structures

1. What data structure would you choose for implementing priority queues?

In a priority queue, the node with the highest priority is processed first. If two nodes have the same priority then, they are processed in the order in which they are stored in the queue. A priority queue should support the following operations

1. Insert an element with a given priority into the priority queue
2. Process/Remove the element with the highest priority in the priority queue

A heap is the ideal data structure for representing a priority queue. If higher numeric value indicates higher priority, then a max-heap should be used to represent the priority queue. If lower numeric value indicates higher priority, then a min-heap should be used to represent the priority queue.

2. What data structure would you choose for implementing an English dictionary?

An English dictionary can be represented using a hash table or a trie or a binary search tree. Each data structure has its own pros and cons.

If we use a hash table, the access time to find the meaning of a word is O(1). However the drawback is that the hash table doesn't store the information about the neighboring words. So if we want to display a word and its adjacent neighbors, we can't achieve it by using a hash table alone. One alternative is to have an additional linked list that stores the words in dictionary sequence order. This increases the memory usage.

We can use a trie, where each node has 26 children corresponding to the 26 characters in the English alphabet. The access time depends on the number of characters in the word. We can display the neighboring words using the trie. However the memory consumed by the trie would be quite huge since each node has to maintain 26 pointers.

We can use a binary search tree to store the words in the English dictionary. The access time would be O(logn) where n is the number of words. So if we are storing 100,000 words then we will need about 17 accesses on an average to find a particular word. So the access time is more than the hash table and the trie. However the memory requirements of a binary search tree are much smaller than a trie and it is also possible to find the adjacent neighbors of a word by traversing the binary search tree.

3. Design a data structure which can perform each of the following operations in O(1): insert, delete, fetch and get_random

---

The insert, delete and fetch operations can be performed in O(1) using a hash table.

To perform the get_random operation in O(1) we use an extra doubly linked list along with the hash table. The hash table will store the pointer to the node and the nodes will be connected to each other in the doubly linked list. The operations are described below:

- Insert: the pointer to the node is added to the hash table. The node is then randomly connected either to the head of the doubly linked list or to the tail of the doubly linked list. This can be done in O(1). This way we can randomize the order of nodes in the doubly linked list

- Delete: the pointer to the node is removed from the hash table. Using the pointer to the node, the node is deleted from the doubly linked list. This can be done in O(1).

- Fetch: the fetch operation is performed on the hash table and the pointer to the node is returned

- Get_Random: A separate iterator pointer is maintained for traversing the linked list. It is initialized to the head of the doubly linked list. When get_random() is invoked, the iterator pointer is returned and the iterator is advanced to the next member in the doubly linked list. This can be done in O(1). Since the order of nodes in the linked list is random, we will be returning random nodes.

4. Design a data structure for an LRU cache?

A Least Recently Used cache has a fixed number of slots in it. Once all the slots in the LRU cache are used up and we need to store a new node in the LRU cache, then the least recently used node is removed and the new node is added to the LRU cache.

An LRU cache can be implemented using two data structures: a hash table (given the key for the node, the hash table returns the address of the node) and a doubly linked list (the most recently used node is maintained at the head and the least recently used node is maintained at the tail of the doubly linked list)

The operations that the LRU cache will support are

lru_add – adds a node to the cache. If the LRU cache is already full, then the least recently used node which is present at the tail of the doubly linked list is removed from the doubly linked list and the node pointer is also removed from the hash table. The new node is then added to the head of the doubly linked list and the pointer to the new node is added to the hash table

lru_get – returns the node given the key. The key is used to access the hash table and obtain the address of the node. Using the address of the node, the node is then removed from the doubly linked list and added to the front of the doubly linked list since it is now the most recently accessed node.

The structure of the LRU cache and the implementation of lru_add and lru_get are given below

```
struct lru_cache
{
    int max_size; /*Maximum number of nodes that the cache can hold*/
    int count; /*current number of nodes in the cache*/
    struct node *head; /*Head of the doubly linked list*/
    struct node *tail; /*Tail of the doubly linked list*/
    unordered_map<int, struct node*> *ht; /*hash table*/
};
```

```
/*
cache - the LRU cache
new_item - new node to be added to the LRU cache
Return value: 0 on success
*/
int lru_add(struct lru_cache *cache, struct node *new_item)
{
    if (cache->count == cache->max_size) {
        /*The cache is full. So remove the last node from the linked list */
        struct node *temp = cache->tail;

        cache->tail = cache->tail->prev;

        if (cache->tail == NULL)
                cache->head = NULL;
        else
                cache->tail->next = NULL;

        cache->count--;

        /*Remove the last node from the hash table*/
        cache->ht->erase(temp->key);

        delete temp; /*Free the last node*/
    }

    /*Add the new node to the front of the linked list*/
    new_item->prev = NULL;
    new_item->next = cache->head;

    if (cache->head)
        cache->head->prev = new_item;

    cache->head = new_item;

    if (!cache->tail)
        cache->tail = new_item;

    cache->count++;

    /*Add the new node to the hash table*/
    cache->ht->emplace(new_item->key, new_item);

    return 0;
}
```

```
/*
cache - LRU cache
key - key for the node that should be fetched from the cache
Return value: node corresponding to the key
*/
struct node* lru_get(struct lru_cache *cache, int key)
{
    struct node *cur_node;

    /*Get the node pointer from the key using the hash table
    "auto" is used to automatically find the type of the variable "it"
    based on the return value of the stl hash table find function */
    auto it = cache->ht->find(key);

    /*it is an iterator. If it == cache->ht->end(), then it is invalid
    and it means that the key was not found in the hash table */
    if (it == cache->ht->end())
        return NULL;

    /*it->first gives the key and it->second gives the data which in
    this case is the node corresponding to the key*/
    cur_node = it->second;

    /*If the node being fetched is at the head of the linked list, then
    simply return*/
    if (cache->head == cur_node)
        return cur_node;

    /*
    The node being fetched is not at the front. So detach it from the linked
    list and add it to the beginning. If the node was removed from the tail,
    then update the tail
    */
    if (cache->tail == cur_node)
        cache->tail = cur_node->prev;

    cur_node->prev->next = cur_node->next;
    if (cur_node->next)
        cur_node->next->prev = cur_node->prev;

    cur_node->prev = NULL;
    cur_node->next = cache->head;
    cache->head->prev = cur_node;
    cache->head = cur_node;

    return cur_node;
}
```

5. What data structure will you use for finding out if a person is connected to another person on LinkedIn/Facebook?

A graph data structure can be used to find out if a person is connected to another person. The graph can be represented using any of the following:

- Incidence matrix: the rows of the matrix represent persons and the columns of the matrix represent edges. If the edge k connects person i with person j, then matrix[i][k] = 1 and matrix[j][k] = 1
- Adjacency matrix: the rows and columns represent persons. If person i is connected to person j, then matrix[i][j] and matrix[j][i] will be set to 1.
- Adjacency list: for each person, a list of his/her friends is maintained.

The problem with incidence matrix and adjacency matrix is that they are sparse and this leads to a lot of wasted memory. So the preferred data structure is the adjacency list. We can perform depth first search or breadth first search on the adjacency list to find if two persons are connected.

2. Sorting and Searching

The summary of different sorting techniques is given below. A **stable** sorting algorithm will preserve the relative order between two equal elements even after sorting.

	Average case	Best case	Worst Case	Stability
Bubble sort	$O(n^2)$	$O(n)$	$O(n^2)$	Stable
Insertion sort	$O(n^2)$	$O(n)$	$O(n^2)$	Stable
Heap sort	$O(n\log n)$	$O(n\log n)$	$O(n\log n)$	Not stable
Merge sort	$O(n\log n)$	$O(n\log n)$	$O(n\log n)$	Stable
Quick sort	$O(n\log n)$	$O(n\log n)$	$O(n^2)$	Stable

Counting sort is an integer sorting algorithm that can be applied only if the range of integers present is small. The time complexity is $O(n)$.

Radix sort is also an integer sorting algorithm where the individual digits of the integers are sorted either from most significant to least significant digit or vice versa. The time complexity is O(kn), where k is the number of digits in the integer. Although radix sort has a better time complexity compared to quicksort, quicksort is preferred since radix sort requires additional memory.

If all the elements to be sorted can't fit into the main memory at once, then external storage devices must be used for sorting. Sorting done using external storage is referred to as external sorting.

2.1 Searching

1. Find the smallest and second smallest numbers in an array

We can find the smallest and second smallest numbers in a single scan of the array. We will maintain another array called min_values for storing the 2 smallest numbers. min_values[0] will store the smallest value and min_values[1] will store the second smallest value. min_values[0] and min_values[1] are initialized to MAX_INT. As we traverse the main array, we do the following

- If the current element is smaller than min_values[0], then we move min_values[0] to min_values[1] and store the current element in min_values[0]
- If the current element is larger than min_values[0] but smaller than min_values[1], then we store the current element in min_values[1]

The code is given below:

```
/*
a:input array
length: number of elements in array a
min_value: the two smallest values will be returned here
*/
void find_two_smallest(int a[], int length, int min_value[])
{
    int i;

    min_value[0] = min_value[1] = MAX_INT;

    for (i = 0; i < length; ++i) {
        if (a[i] < min_value[0]) {
                min_value[1] = min_value[0];
                min_value[0] = a[i];
        } else if (a[i] < min_value[1]) {
                min_value[1] = a[i];
        }
    }
}
```

2.

Find the maximum and minimum elements in an array using the least number of comparisons

In the simple approach, we will compare each element of the array with the maximum value and minimum value obtained so far. So for every element, we need 2 comparisons.

In the efficient approach, we pick all pairs of consecutive numbers in the array and first compare the numbers within each pair. Then we compare the highest in the pair with the maximum value and the lowest in the pair with the minimum value. So we need 3 comparisons for 2 elements instead of 4 comparisons needed by the simple approach.

Since we will be picking pairs of consecutive numbers, if we have odd number of elements in the array, the last element will be left unpaired. To avoid this problem, if we have odd elements, we will initialize the max value and the min value to the first element in the array and then go on picking pairs of numbers from the second element onwards.

```
/*a:input array
length: number of elements in array a
min_value: the minimum value is returned here
max_value: the maximum value is returned here*/
void find_min_max(int a[], int length, int *min_value, int *max_value) {
    int i = 0;
    *max_value = MIN_INT;
    *min_value = MAX_INT;
    if (length % 2 == 1) {
        /*If there are odd number of elements, then initialize
        max_value and min_value with a[0]*/
        *max_value = *min_value = a[0];
        i = 1;
    }

    for (; i < length; i += 2) {
        if (a[i] > a[i+1]) {
            if (a[i] > *max_value)
                *max_value = a[i];
            if (a[i+1] < *min_value)
                *min_value = a[i+1];
        } else {
            if (a[i] < *min_value)
                *min_value = a[i];
            if (a[i+1] > *max_value)
                *max_value = a[i+1];
        }
    }
}
```

3. Find the first occurrence of a number in a sorted array

Consider the sorted array A = {10, 10, 20, 20, 30, 30, 30}. If we are asked to return the first occurrence of 30, then we return the index 4. If we are asked to return the first occurrence of a number not present in the array such as 15, then we return -1.

We can do this using modified binary search in O(logn). In normal binary search, we stop as soon as we find the element being searched. In the modified binary search, we continue the binary search if we find the element but the found element is not the first occurrence of the element in the array. The code is given below

```
/*
a: array being searched
n: number of elements in array
x: element being searched
Return value: first position of x in a, if x is absent -1 is returned
*/
int find_first(int a[], int n, int x)
{
    int start, end, mid;

    start = 0;
    end = n - 1;

    while (start <= end) {
        mid = (start + end) / 2;

        if (a[mid] == x) {
                if (mid == 0 || a[mid - 1] != x)
                    return mid;
                else
                    end = mid - 1;

        } else if (a[mid] > x) {
                end = mid - 1;
        } else {
                start = mid + 1;
        }
    }
    return -1;
}
```

4. Find the first element larger than k in a sorted array

Consider the sorted array A = {10, 20, 20, 30, 40, 50}. The first element larger than 25 is 30. In normal binary search, we search for a particular element and stop when we find the element. When we are trying to find the first element larger than k, k may not even exist in the array. So we instead use a modified form of binary search where we keep track of the first element larger than k that we have encountered so far as we search the array. The time complexity is O(logn). The code is given below

```
/*
a: sorted array containing elements in non-decreasing order
length: number of elements in the array
k: we are searching for the number immediately above k
Returns: the number immediately greater than k in the array if it exists,
         MAX_INT otherwise
*/
int find_next_higher(int a[], int length, int k)
{
    int low, high, mid, result;

    low = 0;
    high = length - 1;

    result = MAX_INT;
    while (low <= high) {
        mid = (low + high) / 2;

        if (a[mid] > k) {
                result = a[mid]; /*update the result and continue*/
                high = mid - 1;
        } else {
                low = mid + 1;
        }
    }

    return result;
}
```

5. Consider the sorted array of strings A= {"", "apple", "", "", "ball", "cat", "", "dog", "", "", "", "egg", ""}. The array has empty strings interspersed in it. How will you efficiently search for strings in such an array?

We can use binary search to search the array of sorted strings. However since the array has empty strings in it, suppose we hit an empty string during binary search, we won't know how to continue the search. To solve this problem we slightly modify the binary search and use the following strategy:

1. Binary search will occur between indexes low and high. If A[high] is an empty string, then we go on decrementing high until A[high] is a non-empty string. (Suppose we don't find a non-empty string and we reach A[low], then all elements between low and high are empty strings. So we simply return indicating the search string was not found.)

2. We then find the mid element between low and high. If A[mid] is a non-empty string, then we proceed with the usual binary search. If A[mid] however is an empty string, then we go on incrementing mid until A[mid] is a non-empty string. Since A[high] already has a non-empty string, we will surely find a non-empty string when we keep incrementing mid.

```
/*
strings: sorted array of strings in which some of the strings can be empty ("")
num_strings: number of strings present (including empty strings)
x: string to be searched
Returns: index of x in the array strings if found, -1 otherwise
*/
int search(char *strings[], int num_strings, char *x)
{
    int mid, result;
    int low = 0;
    int high = num_strings - 1;

    while (low <= high) {
        /*If we hit an empty string at position high, then keep decreasing
        high until we get a non-empty string*/
        while (low <= high && strcmp(strings[high], "") == 0) {
            --high;
        }

        /*If we have only empty strings between low and high, then return
        not found*/
        if (low > high)
            return -1;
        mid = (low + high) / 2;

        /*If we get an empty element at mid, then keep incrementing mid.
```

```
        We are guaranteed to find a non-empty string since strings[high]
        is non-empty*/
        while (strcmp(strings[mid], "") == 0)
                mid = mid + 1;

        /*Compare the mid element with the element being searched*/
        result = strcmp(strings[mid], x);

        if (result == 0) {
                return mid;
        } else if (result < 0) {
                low = mid + 1;
        } else {
                high = mid - 1;
        }
    }
    return -1;
}
```

Note that we can use this approach for any sorted array that is interspersed with elements that can be skipped. So if we are given an array of positive integers interspersed with -1, then we can use the same strategy.

6. How will you search for an element in a sorted array of unknown length?

If we don't know the length of an array, we may access an element outside the array bounds. In this case an exception is raised. We should catch the exception and continue the search. We use the following approach to search an element:

1. First we find the upper bound on the length of the array using exponential search. So say an array has 20 elements in it and we don't know its length beforehand. We first check element at position 0, followed by position 1, position 2, position 4, position 8, position 16 and position 32. When we access position 32, we will be outside the array and an exception is raised. So we know that the upper bound on length is 32 and the actual array length must be less than 32.

2. Once we know the upper bound, we use normal binary search to find the element. While doing binary search, we may still try to access an element outside the array bounds. In such a case, we again catch the exception, reduce the index range being searched and continue the search.

```
/* Helper function that performs binary search on an array of unknown length
a: vector which should be searched
x: element which we are trying to find
low: start position of region in array for searching
high: end position of region in array for searching
*/
int binary_search(vector<int>& a, int x, int low, int high)
{
    int value, mid;

    while (low <= high) {
        try {
            mid = (low + high) / 2;

            /*Use a.at(mid) instead of a[mid] since at
            function throws an exception if mid crosses the bounds*/
            value = a.at(mid);

            if (value == x)
                    return mid;
            else if (value > x)
                    high = mid - 1;
            else
                    low = mid + 1;
        }
        catch(exception& e) {
            /*mid has crossed the boundary of the array. So reduce
```

```
                    the search region to (low, mid - 1)*/
                    high = mid - 1;
        }

    }

    return -1;
}


/* Main function for performing search on array whose length is not known
a: input vector
x: item to be searched
Returns: if x is found, position of x is returned, otherwise -1 is returned
*/
int search(vector<int>& a, int x)
{
    int value, low, high;

    /*Perform exponential search to first find upper bound. Start with
    high = 0 and then increase high to 1, 2, 4, 8, 16 and so on*/
    low = high = 0;
    while (1) {
        try {
                /*Use a.at(high) instead of a[high] since at
                function throws an exception if high crosses bounds*/
                value = a.at(high);

                if (value == x)
                        return high; /*We found the element x*/
                else if (value > x)
                        break;/*We found the range (low, high) to search*/

                low = high + 1;

                if (high == 0)
                        high = 1;
                else
                        high = high * 2;
        }
        catch (exception& e) {
                /*We have crossed the boundary of the array. So we have
                found the upper bound for high. */
                break;
        }
    }

    /*Perform binary search in range(low, high). Note that high may still be
    outside the array bounds*/
    return binary_search(a, x, low, high);
}
```

7. Given a two dimensional matrix M in which each row contains 0's and 1's in sorted order, find the row with the maximum number of 1's

Suppose the matrix below is provided, then we should return that row 2 has the maximum number of 1's. If the matrix doesn't have any 1's, then we should return -1.

row 0	0	0	0	1	1
row 1	0	0	0	0	0
row 2	0	1	1	1	1

The algorithm is as follows:

1.) Find the first location of 1 in each row. To find the first location of 1, we use the find_first function described earlier on page 194. Then subtract the first location of 1 from the total number of columns to get the number of 1's in each row. For instance, in row 0 of above matrix, the first 1 is present at index 3 and the total number of columns is 5. So the total number of 1's = 5 – 3 = 2.

2.) Now that we know the number of 1's in each row, we can easily find the row with the most 1's

If there are n columns, we can find the first 1 in a row and thereby the number of 1's in a row in O(logn). Since there are m rows, the complexity of the algorithm is O(mlogn).

```
/*
a: array where each row is sorted and has only 0's and 1's
nrows: number of rows in the array
ncols: number of columns in the array (ncols is equal to NUM_COLS)
Returns: row number that has most ones, if no row has 1's then return -1
*/
int find_row_with_most_ones(int a[][NUM_COLS], int nrows, int ncols)
{
    int i, first_one_index;
    int cur_num_ones, max_num_ones;
    int max_row;

    max_row = -1;
    max_num_ones = 0;

    for (i = 0; i < nrows; ++i) {
        /*Find the position of the first 1 in the row*/
        first_one_index = find_first(a[i], ncols, 1);

        /*Compute number of 1's in row based on position of the first 1*/
        if (first_one_index == -1)
                cur_num_ones = 0; /*there are no 1's in the row*/
        else
                cur_num_ones = ncols - first_one_index;

        if (cur_num_ones > max_num_ones) {
                max_num_ones = cur_num_ones;
                max_row = i;
        }
    }

    return max_row;
}
```

8. Given a matrix in which the elements in any row or column are in sorted order, efficiently find if an element k is present in the matrix.

Let the elements in the array be sorted in non-decreasing order in each row and column. To solve the problem, we start from the rightmost top corner of the array and apply the following logic to solve the problem in O(m+n)

- If element in matrix is less than the searched value, then go to the row below
- If element in matrix is greater than the searched value, then go to the previous column

Let us take an example. Consider the following matrix M, which is sorted in non-decreasing order along both rows and columns and we have to find 72 in it.

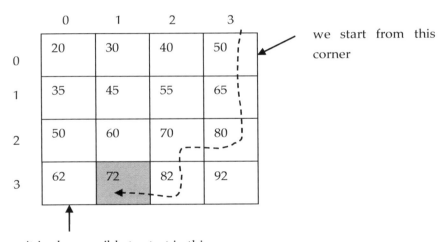

we start from this corner

it is also possible to start in this corner

In our case, we start with M[0][3] and compare with 72.

- M[0][3] = 50 which is less than 72. So we go to the row below
- M[1][3] = 65 which is less than 72. So we go to the row below
- M[2][3] = 80 which is greater than 72. So we go to the previous column
- M[2][2] = 70 which is less than 72. So we go to the row below
- M[3][2] = 82 which is greater than 72. So we go to the previous column
- M[3][1] = 72 which matches our search key and we have found the element

```
/*
m: matrix to be searched
NUM_COLS: number of columns in the matrix
num_rows: number of rows in the matrix
x: element to search
Return value: 1 if element is present, 0 otherwise
*/
int search_matrix(int m[][NUM_COLS],  int num_rows, int x)
{
    int i, j;
    int is_found;

    i = 0;
    j = NUM_COLS - 1;
    is_found = 0;
    while (i < num_rows && j >= 0) {
        if (m[i][j] == x) {
                is_found = 1;
                break;
        } else if (m[i][j] < x) {
                ++i;    /*go to the row below*/
        } else {
                --j;    /*go to the previous column*/
        }
    }

    return is_found;
}
```

Note that it is also possible to search for the value from the opposite corner (the bottom leftmost corner). In this case, the logic we should use to search is

- If element in matrix is less than the searched value, then go to the next column
- If element in matrix is greater than the searched value, then go to the row above

9. The elements of an array first continually increase in value and then continually decrease in value. All elements in the array are unique. Find the maximum element in the array.

Let the size of the array be N. To solve the problem we first initialize start to 0 and end to N-1. Then

1. Find the middle element in the array between start and end.

2. If the middle element is greater than the previous element and also greater than the next element, then we have found the maximum element in the array. Otherwise modify the search range indexes (start and end) and repeat the process.

Consider array A = {1, 4, 9, 16, 25, 36, 5, 0}

(start, end)	middle	A[middle]	Compare A[middle] with neighbors and take action
(0, 7)	3	16	9 < 16 < 25. The maximum element should be after 16. So start = middle + 1 = 4, end = 7
(4, 7)	5	36	25 < 36 > 16. Since 36 is greater than previous and next element, the maximum element is 36

The time complexity of this approach is O(logn).

```
/*
a: array where elements first increase and then decrease
n: number of elements in the array, n > 0
Return value: maximum element in the array
*/
int find_max(int a[], int n)
{
    int start = 0, end = n-1, mid, max_element = MIN_INT;

    while (start <= end) {
        /*If only one element is left, then it is the max element*/
        if (start == end)      {
                max_element = a[start];
                break;
        }

        /*If two elements are left, find the maximum of the two*/
        if (start + 1 == end) {
                max_element = a[start];
                if (a[start+1] > max_element)
                        max_element = a[start+1];
                break;
        }

        /*If there are more than two elements left, then inspect the
        middle element between start and end */
        mid = (start+end)/2;

        /*If middle element is greater than previous element and also
        greater than the next element, then it is the maximum element*/
        if (a[mid - 1] < a[mid] && a[mid] > a[mid + 1]) {
                max_element = a[mid];
                break;
        }

        /*We have not yet been able to find the max. So modify the range
        in which the search should proceed in the next iteration */
        if (a[mid - 1] < a[mid] && a[mid] < a[mid + 1]) {
                start = mid + 1;
        } else {
                end = mid - 1;
        }
    }
    return max_element;
}
```

10.

A sorted array has been rotated an unknown number of times. Find the maximum element in the array and the number of times the array has been rotated. All elements in the array are unique

Consider the array A = {10, 20, 30, 40, 50} with unique elements that is sorted in ascending order. When we rotate the array, we end up with two sequences of numbers in ascending order. For instance, if we rotate A two times to the right, we get A~Rotated~ = {40, 50, 10, 20, 30}. So the two ascending order sequences are {40, 50} and {10, 20, 30}. Similarly if we rotate A 4 times to the right we get A~Rotated~ = {20, 30, 40, 50, 10} in which case the ascending order sequences are {20, 30, 40, 50} and {10}. Note that any number in the first sequence is always greater than any number of the second sequence. The maximum element will be the last element of the first sequence. Sometimes the maximum element in the array is also referred to as pivot element.

We use binary search to locate the largest element. When we choose the middle element in the range (start, end), there are three possibilities:

1. the middle element is greater than the next element. In this case, the middle element is the largest element in the sequence

2. the middle element is present in the first sequence. In this case the middle element will always be > than the ending element because ending element is present in the second sequence and elements in the first sequence are always greater than elements in the second sequence. For instance consider, A~Rotated~ = {20, 30, 40, 50, 10}. Middle element is 40 which is greater than 10. In this case, the maximum element will lie between the middle element and the last element.

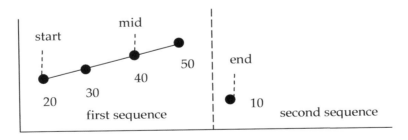

3. the middle element is present in the second sequence. In this case the middle element will always be < than the ending element since the second sequence has elements in ascending order. In this case we can ignore the range (middle, end) and search the range (start, middle – 1). For instance, consider $A_{Rotated}$ = {40, 50, 10, 20, 30}. The middle element is 10 which lies in the second sequence. So we can ignore (middle, end) which is {10, 20, 30} and search only (start, middle – 1) which is {40, 50} in the next iteration

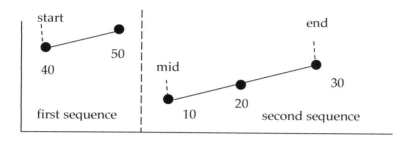

Based on these observations, given an array of size N, to solve the problem we first initialize start to 0 and end to N-1. Then

- Find the middle element in the array between start and end.
    - If the middle element is greater than next element, middle element is the largest element
    - If middle element is greater than the last element, then repeat the search in the range (middle, end).
    - Otherwise repeat the search in the range (start, middle – 1).

We put in one more optimization to the code. If a[start] < a[end], then we have found the exact starting and ending locations of the first sequence. In this case, we stop searching any further and return the last element a[end] as the maximum element. Note that this condition will also cover the case where the array has had 0 rotations (no shift has been performed on the array)

```
/*
a: array that has been sorted and rotated. There should NOT be any duplicates
n: number of elements in the array. Should be > 0
Return value: maximum element in the array
*/
int find_max(int a[], int n)
{
    int start, end, mid;

    assert(n > 0);
    start = 0;
    end = n - 1;

    while (a[start] > a[end]) {
        mid = (start + end) / 2;

        if (mid < n - 1 && a[mid] > a[mid + 1])
                return a[mid];

        if (a[mid] > a[end]) {
                start = mid;    /*max is in the region (mid, end)*/
        } else {
                end = mid - 1; /*max is in the region (start, mid - 1)*/
        }
    }

    return a[end];
}
```

In some cases, we may be asked to find the number of times the array has been rotated. In this case, (index of the maximum element in the array + 1) gives the number of rotations. For instance, if A = {10, 20, 30, 40, 50} is rotated twice, we get {40, 50, 10, 20, 30}. The maximum element 50 is present at position 1 in the rotated array. So the number of times the array has been rotated = 1+1 = 2.

Note that this solution will work only if the array has unique elements in it. If there are duplicates, for instance {2, 2, 3, 3, 1, 1, 2, 2, 2}, then the above solution will give the wrong result. If there are duplicates then we can perform a linear search.

11.

A sorted array has been rotated an unknown number of times. Search if a particular value is present in the array. All elements in the array are unique.

Consider the array A = {10, 20, 30, 40, 50} with unique elements that is sorted in ascending order. When we rotate the array, we end up with two sequences of numbers in ascending order. For instance, if we rotate A two times to the right, we get $A_{Rotated}$ = {40, 50, 10, 20, 30}. So the two ascending order sequences are {40, 50} and {10, 20, 30}. Similarly if we rotate A 4 times to the right we get $A_{Rotated}$ = {20, 30, 40, 50, 10} in which case the ascending order sequences are {20, 30, 40, 50} and {10}. Note that any number in the first sequence is always greater than any number of the second sequence.

We use binary search to locate a particular element X. When we choose the middle element during binary search, if A[mid] is equal to X then we have found the element we are looking for. Otherwise there are two possibilities:

1. Mid is in first sequence	2. Mid is in second sequence
$A_{Rotated}$ = (20, 30, 40, 50), (10)	$A_{Rotated}$ = (40, 50), (10, 20, 30)
mid	mid
Region (start, mid) is perfectly sorted in ascending order and is used to decide	Region (mid, end) is perfectly sorted in ascending order and is used to decide

1.) Here the middle element lies in the first ascending order sequence of the rotated array. So A[start] <= A[mid]. We are guaranteed that all elements in the region (start, mid) are perfectly sorted. So we use this region for taking a decision. So if the search element lies between A[start] and A[mid], then search (start, mid - 1) in the next iteration else search (mid +1, end) in the next iteration

2.) Here the middle element lies in the second ascending order sequence. So A[start] > A[mid]. We are guaranteed that all elements in the region (mid, end) are perfectly sorted. So we use this region for taking a decision. If the search element lies between A[mid] and A[end], then search (mid + 1, end) in the next iteration else search (start, mid -1)

209

```
/*
a: array that has been sorted and rotated. there should not be any duplicates
n: number of elements in the array, n > 0
x: element to be searched in the array
Return value: location of the element in array if found, -1 if not found
*/
int find_element(int a[], int n, int x)
{
    int start = 0, end = n - 1, mid;

    while (start <= end) {
        mid = (start+end)/2;

        if (x == a[mid]) {
                return mid;
        }

        /*Check which portion of the array has elements in sorted order*/
        if (a[start] <= a[mid]) {
                /*
                The lower portion (start, mid) is still sorted even after
                rotations. So use this portion for taking decisions
                */
                if (a[start] <= x && x < a[mid])
                        end = mid - 1; /*search in region (start, mid-1)*/
                else
                        start = mid + 1; /*search in region (mid+1, end)*/
        } else {
                /*
                The upper portion (mid, end) is sorted even after
                rotations. So use this portion for taking decisions
                */
                if (a[mid] < x && x <= a[end])
                        start = mid + 1; /*search in region (mid+1, end)*/
                else
                        end = mid - 1; /*search in region (start, mid-1)*/
        }
    }

    return -1;
}
```

Note that the above solution can't be applied to an array with duplicates. For instance, the above solution will not be able to find 2 in the array {3, 3, 2, 2, 3, 3, 3, 3, 3}. If there are duplicates, then we can perform linear search.

12. Find the largest k numbers out of a list of a trillion unsorted numbers

Since we have to find only the largest k numbers, we don't need to sort all the elements of the list. We can use a simple technique where-in the largest number in the list is found in each iteration and is marked so that it is not used in the subsequent iterations. If N is the size of the list we can find the k largest numbers in k iterations and the maximum number of operations needed is k*N. However there are better methods to solve the problem.

The preferable way to solve the problem is to use a min-heap of size k. Notice that to find the largest k numbers, min-heap is used and not max-heap. Using the first k numbers in the list, construct a min-heap. The root will contain the smallest element among the first k elements. Then compare the (k+1)th element in the list with root. If the (k+1)th element is greater than the root of the min-heap, then remove the root from the heap and add the (k+1)th element to the heap. Continue this procedure for all the remaining elements in the list. So at each stage if the next element in the list is greater than the smallest of our top k numbers, the smallest element is removed from the heap and the next element is added to the heap. This way we store only the largest k elements in the heap.

For instance, suppose we have to find the 5 largest numbers in the list of size 1 trillion. Let the list consist of the elements {80, 90, 60, 40, 20, 50, 10, ...}

We construct a min-heap using the first 5 numbers to get the following heap.

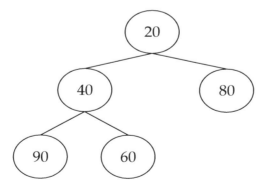

The next element is 50 which is greater than the root of the heap (20). So 20 is first removed from the heap and 50 is added in its place. The heap is then re-adjusted using the heapify procedure to form the heap shown below

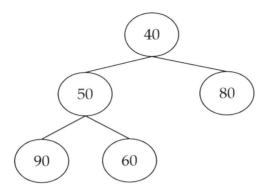

The next element is 10. 10 can't be added to the heap since it is smaller than the root of the heap (40).

Removing the root and adding 1 element to the heap of size k has a time complexity of O(logk). So worst case complexity for N elements is O(Nlogk).

Suppose instead of finding the largest k numbers, we are asked to find the smallest k numbers, then we can use a similar procedure using a max-heap instead of a min-heap.

```
/* Helper function to perform heapify
heap: min heap.  Maximum number of elements in heap is k
pos: position of the heap that may need to be fixed
heap_size: current number of nodes in the heap
*/
void heapify(int heap[], int pos, int heap_size)
{
    int left = 2 * pos;
    int right = (2 * pos) + 1;
    int ix_of_smallest = pos;

    /*Find which of the three are the smallest: heap[pos] OR left child
    OR right child*/
    if (left < heap_size && heap[pos] > heap[left])
        ix_of_smallest = left;
    if (right < heap_size && heap[ix_of_smallest] > heap[right])
        ix_of_smallest = right;

    if (ix_of_smallest != pos) {
        /*
        If pos doesn't contain the smallest value,
```

```
                then swap the smallest value into pos
                */
                int temp = heap[pos];
                heap[pos] = heap[ix_of_smallest];
                heap[ix_of_smallest] = temp;

                /*Recursively re-adjust the heap*/
                heapify(heap, ix_of_smallest, heap_size);
        }
}

/*Main function to find the k largest elements
a: array in which we have to find the k largest elements
n: number of elements in the array
k: the number of largest elements that we need to find
heap: the k largest elements will be stored in the heap and returned
*/
void find_k_largest(int a[], int n, int k, int heap[])
{
    int i;

    /*Store the first k elements of the array in the heap*/
    for (i = 0; i < k; ++i)
        heap[i] = a[i];

    /*Construct the initial min-heap*/
    for (i = k - 1; i >= 0; --i)
        heapify(heap, i, k);

    for (i = k; i < n; ++i) {
        /*The root of the heap will have the smallest item in the heap
        If current item in array is greater than root of the heap, then
        place current item into root of the heap and readjust the heap
        */
        if (a[i] > heap[0]) {
                heap[0] = a[i];
                heapify(heap, 0, k);
        }
    }
}
```

Suppose we are asked to find the k largest/smallest elements in a stream, we can use the same technique.

13. Given an array, find the maximum element for each window of size k

In the brute force approach, we look at all possible windows of size k and compute the maximum element for each window separately. If n is the size of the array, then there are (n − k + 1) windows of size k. To find the maximum in one window, we need k operations. So the total time complexity is O(k * (n-k+1)). We can do much better by using a double ended queue (also called dequeue or deque) wherein we can insert and remove elements at both ends of the queue.

The **indexes** of the elements of the array that are relevant for the neighboring windows are stored in the dequeue. The index of the maximum element for the current window will always be at the front of the dequeue. The maximum size of the dequeue at any point of time is equal to the length of the window k.

Consider the array A = {20, 40, 70, 60, 30, 40, 50} with a window size of 4. While processing the array, when we pick the element 70, 70 is greater than all the elements **before** it in the current window. So we no longer need to store 20 and 40 in the dequeue and we can discard them.

The solution is as follows:

1. From the front of the dequeue, remove all indexes that are outside the current window

2. Pick the next element (also called chosen element) in the array. Remove all the indexes from the rear of the dequeue if the elements corresponding to the indexes are <= the chosen element.

3. Store the index of the chosen element in the dequeue

4. If we have processed at least k items in the array, then output the element corresponding to the index at the front of the dequeue as the maximum for the current window

The operations of the dequeue are shown for array A = {20, 40, 70, 60, 30, 40, 50} and k = 4

1. Pick 20 and store its index

2. Pick 40 and store its index

3. Pick 70. Remove index of 40 and 20 since 70 > 40 and 70 > 20. Store index of 70

4. Pick 60 and store its index

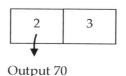

Output 70

5. Pick 30 and store index of 30

Output 70

6. Pick 40 and store its index

Output 70

7. 70 is out of the window. So remove its index.
Pick 50. Remove index of 30 and 40 since 50 > 30
and 50 > 40. Store index of 50

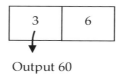

Output 60

```
/*
a: array for which we have to find the maximum in every window of size k
n: number of elements in the array
k: size of the window
dq: double ended queue that stores array indices
max: array that contains the result (maximum in every window of size k)
*/
void find_window_max(int a[], int n, int k, deque<int>& dq, int max[])
{
    int i, pos;

    pos = 0;
    for (i = 0; i < n ; ++i) {
        /*Remove the elements outside the current window from
        front of dequeue*/
        while (!dq.empty() && (dq.front() + k <= i))
                dq.pop_front();

        /*Remove all elements that are smaller than or equal to current
        element from the rear of the dequeue */
        while (!dq.empty() && a[i] >= a[dq.back()] )
                dq.pop_back();

        /*Push the index of current element into the end of the dequeue*/
        dq.push_back(i);

        if (i >= k-1) {
                /*Front of dequeue has index of maximum element
                for the current window*/
                max[pos] = a[dq.front()];
                ++pos;
        }
    }
}
```

14. Find the median in a stream of data

When we have a stream of data, the entire data will not be available immediately. Each time the next member in the stream will be available to us, we will have to recompute the median of the stream.

If the data is sorted, then the median is the middle element. So we can sort the stream each time a new member of the stream is available. If we perform merge sort, the complexity of one sort is O(nlogn) and we have to perform n such sorts. So the total complexity will be O(n²logn). We can do better using insertion sort. When a new member of stream is available, we add the new item into a sorted array and find the median. The time complexity of insertion sort is O(n²).

We can efficiently solve the problem using heaps in O(nlogn) (n items will be added to the heap and adding each item to heap has a time complexity of O(logn)). We will be using O(n) additional space. The idea is to maintain a max_heap for storing the smaller half of the elements in the stream and a min_heap for storing the larger half of the elements in the stream. The median of the stream will be stored in the root of the heaps. So let us say that the stream of data we have seen so far is 1, 5, 3, 6, 8, 2, then the two heaps that we construct will be as shown below

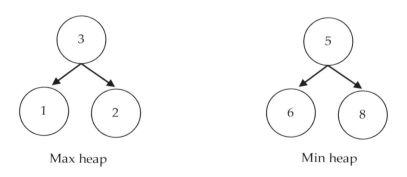

Max heap   Min heap

The smaller half of the numbers are {1, 2, 3} and they are stored in the max_heap. The larger half of the numbers are {5, 6, 8} and they are stored in the min_heap. Since the heaps are equal in size, the median of the stream is the average of the roots of the heaps ((3 + 5)/ 2 = 4).

217

To construct the heaps in this manner, we do the following

1. If the min_heap is empty, then we add the new item in the stream to the min_heap

2. If the min_heap is not empty, then if the new item in the stream is greater than the root of the min_heap, we will add the new item to the min_heap otherwise we will add it to the max_heap.

So min_heap takes the larger elements and max_heap takes the smaller elements. Note that one heap can grow much faster than the other. But our intention is to keep half the elements in each heap. To achieve this, whenever the size of one heap exceeds the size of the other heap by more than one element, we remove the root of the heap with more elements and add it to the heap with fewer elements. So the difference between the number of elements in the two heaps will never exceed 1.

To find the median at any time we do the following

1. If the two heaps are of equal size, then the total number of elements in the stream are even. We calculate the median as the average of the roots of the two heaps

2. If one heap has 1 more element than the other heap, then root of the heap having more elements is the median of the stream.

```
/*
min_heap: priority queue for storing larger half of numbers in the stream
max_heap: priority queue for storing smaller half of numbers in the stream
cur_value: value of the current item in the stream
Return value: Median of the stream
*/
int get_median(priority_queue<int, vector<int>, greater<int> >& min_heap,
        priority_queue<int, vector<int>, less<int> >& max_heap,
        int cur_value)
{
    /*If min_heap is empty, add the current value to min_heap.
    If min_heap is non-empty, the top of min_heap will contain the smallest
    among the larger half of numbers in the stream. So if current value is
    larger than the top of min_heap, then add it to min_heap otherwise add
    it to max_heap
    */
    if (min_heap.empty())
        min_heap.push(cur_value);
    else if (cur_value >= min_heap.top())
        min_heap.push(cur_value);
    else
        max_heap.push(cur_value);


    /*If min_heap has more than 1 element than the max_heap, move the top
    of min_heap into the max_heap and vice versa. */
    if (min_heap.size() > max_heap.size() + 1) {
        max_heap.push(min_heap.top());
        min_heap.pop();
    } else if (max_heap.size() > min_heap.size() + 1) {
        min_heap.push(max_heap.top());
        max_heap.pop();
    }

    int median;

    /*If both heaps are of the same size, then the median will be the
    average of the top element in the two heaps. Otherwise the median is
    the top of the heap with more elements
    */
    if (min_heap.size() == max_heap.size()) {
        median = (min_heap.top() + max_heap.top()) / 2;
    } else if (min_heap.size() > max_heap.size()) {
        median = min_heap.top();
    } else {
        median = max_heap.top();
    }

    return median;
}
```

2.2 Sorting

1. Re-arrange the elements in an array like a wave so that the values of the array alternately increase and decrease. The elements in the array are unique. For instance, if A = {50, 10, 20, 30, 40}, after re-arranging A can be {10, 30, 20, 50, 40} wherein the value of consecutive elements alternately increases and decreases

---

This problem can be solved in O(nlogn) without additional memory as follows:

1. First sort the entire array in ascending order. So {50, 10, 20, 30, 40} becomes {10, 20, 30, 40, 50}

2. Then starting from index 1 in the array, swap the neighboring elements. So {10, 20, 30, 40, 50} becomes {10, 30, 20, 50, 40}

```
/*
a: array that has to be sorted so that the values in it alternatively increase
    and decrease. The elements should be unique
length: number of elements in the array. should be >= 1
*/
void wave_sort(int a[], int length)
{
    int i, temp;

    /*Sort the elements in ascending order*/
    qsort(a, length, sizeof(int), cmp_function);

    /*Swap the neighboring elements*/
    for (i = 1; i < length - 1; i += 2) {
        temp = a[i];
        a[i] = a[i+1];
        a[i+1] = temp;
    }
}
```

2. Given a small array of size n having n sorted elements and a big array of size m+n having m sorted elements at the beginning of the big array, merge the two arrays and store them in the big array.

There is just enough free space in the big array to accommodate the elements of the small array. The two sorted arrays can be merged in O(m+n). The trick is to start filling up the big array from the end where the free space is present. The code for this is given below

```
/*
a: array of size m+n which has m elements at beginning and n spaces at end
b: array of size n with n elements
m: number of elements in array a
n: number of elements in array b
*/
void merge_arrays(int a[], int b[], int m, int n)
{
    int i, j, fill_pos;

    i = m - 1;
    j = n - 1;
    fill_pos = m + n - 1; /*Start filling from the rear of the array*/

    while (i >= 0 && j >= 0) {
        if (a[i] > b[j]) {
            a[fill_pos--] = a[i--];
        } else {
            a[fill_pos--] = b[j--];
        }
    }

    /*Fill up the remaining elements of array a if any*/
    while (i >= 0)
        a[fill_pos--] = a[i--];

    /*Fill up the remaining elements of array b if any*/
    while (j >= 0)
        a[fill_pos--] = b[j--];

}
```

3. Given m sorted arrays each of which has a size n, merge the arrays in sorted order into a single array of size m*n

To efficiently solve the problem we use a heap which has a maximum size of m (number of sorted arrays). If the arrays are sorted in non-decreasing order, then we maintain a min heap otherwise we maintain a max heap. The algorithm is as follows

1. Pick the first element from each array, add it to the heap and construct the heap using the heapify function

2. Add the topmost element in the heap to the result array. Then replace the topmost element of the heap with the next element from the same array as the topmost element. Re-adjust the heap using the heapify function. Suppose all elements in the same array are over, then add MAX_INT for non-decreasing order (MIN_INT for non-increasing order) into the root of the heap and re-adjust the heap using heapify. Repeat this step until all elements in all the arrays are processed.

Inserting an element into a heap of size m takes O(logm). Since we have n*m elements, the time complexity of this approach is O(nm * logm).

The code for merging k sorted lists is given below. The code for the heapify function has been described on page 212

```
/*
arrays: the arrays to be merged. arrays[0] has the first array, arrays[1] has
        the second array and so on
n: number of elements in each array
k: number of arrays
result: the merged results are passed back in this array
*/
void merge_k_sorted_arrays(int arrays[][MAX_NUM_ELEMENTS], int n, int k,
             int *result)
{
    struct node *heap = (struct node*) calloc(k, sizeof(struct node));
    int *arr_pos = (int*) calloc(k, sizeof(int));
    int i, pos, res_index, array_no;

    /*Store the first element in each array into the heap*/
    for (i = 0; i < k; ++i) {
       heap[i].value = arrays[i][0];
       heap[i].array_no = i;
       arr_pos[i] = 1;
    }

    /*Construct the initial heap using the heapify procedure*/
```

```
    for (i = k - 1; i >= 0; --i)
        heapify(heap, i, k);

    /*
    Process the remaining elements in the arrays. When all elements in the
    arrays have been processed, MAX_INT will be present at root of heap
    */
    res_index = 0;
    while (heap[0].value != MAX_INT) {
        /*
        root of the heap will have the lowest value. So store
        it into the result
        */
        result[res_index++] = heap[0].value;

        array_no = heap[0].array_no;
        pos = arr_pos[array_no];

        /*
        If the root belongs to array x, then replace the root with
        the next element in array x
        */
        if (pos >= n) {
                /*If we have exhausted all elements in the array,
                then insert MAX_INT into the heap*/
                heap[0].value = MAX_INT;
                heap[0].array_no = array_no;
        } else {
                heap[0].value = arrays[array_no][pos];
                heap[0].array_no = array_no;
        }

        /*Re-adjust the heap after replacing the root*/
        heapify(heap, 0, k);

        arr_pos[array_no]++;
    }

    free(arr_pos);
    free(heap);
}
```

4. Given a linked list where the nodes can have the values 0 or 1 or 2, sort it in a single pass. For instance 2->1->0->0->2->0>1 should be sorted as 0->0->0->1->1->2->2

To sort the linked list in a single pass, we make use of the fact that there are only 3 possible values for the nodes in the linked list. So as we traverse the linked list, we can remove the nodes from the original linked list and append them into 3 separate linked lists based on the value of the nodes. At the end we can merge the 3 linked lists. The procedure we can use to solve the problem is as follows:

1. Maintain the head and tail pointers for linked list-0 (will contain nodes with value 0), linked list-1 (will contain nodes with value 1) and linked list-2 (will contain nodes with value 2)

2. As we traverse through the original linked list, remove each node from the original linked list and add it to linked list-0 or linked list-1 or linked list-2 based on the value of the node.

3. At the end connect the tail of linked list-0 to the head of linked list-1 and the tail of linked list-1 to the head of linked list-2

The function used to add a node to a linked list is given below

```
/*
head: array of head pointers of the separated lists
tail: array of tail pointers of the separated lists
cur_node: current node being processed
i: data value of the node
*/
void add_node(struct node *head[], struct node *tail[],
        struct node *cur_node, int i)
{
    cur_node->next = head[i];
    head[i] = cur_node;
    if (!tail[i])
        tail[i] = cur_node;

}
```

The main function to sort the list is given below

```
/*first_node: first node in list to be sorted
num_distinct_values: number of distinct values in the nodes
Return value: head of the sorted list
*/
struct node * sort_list(struct node *first_node, int num_distinct_values)
{
    struct node **head, **tail;
    struct node *result = NULL, *cur_node, *next_node, *last_element;
    int i;

    if (!first_node)
        return NULL;

    head = (struct node**) calloc(num_distinct_values, sizeof(struct node*));
    tail = (struct node**) calloc(num_distinct_values, sizeof(struct node*));

    for (i = 0; i < num_distinct_values; ++i) {
        head[i] = NULL;
        tail[i] = NULL;
    }

    /*Partition the list into separate lists, (0-list, 1-list, 2-list)
    based on the data in the node*/
    cur_node = first_node;
    while (cur_node) {
        next_node = cur_node->next;
        add_node(head, tail, cur_node, cur_node->data);
        cur_node = next_node;
    }

    /*Connect the tail of first linked list with head of second linked list
    and so on*/
    result = head[0];
    last_element = tail[0];
    for (i = 1; i < num_distinct_values; ++i) {
        if (!result)
                result = head[i];

        /*Link last element of previous list with head of current list*/
        if (last_element)
                last_element->next = head[i];

        /*update the last element to the tail of current list*/
        if (tail[i])
                last_element = tail[i];
    }

    free(head);
    free(tail);

    return result;
}
```

5. Sort a linked list

To sort a linked list, we use the following recursive technique

- Traverse until the middle of the linked list and divide the linked list into two smaller linked lists.
- Recursively sort the two smaller linked lists
- Now merge the two sorted smaller linked lists into a single linked list

The procedure is shown in the diagram below:

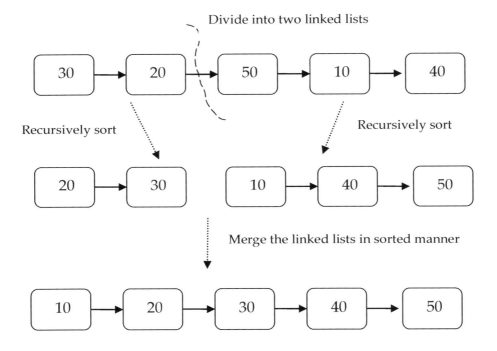

The source code for the merge sort is shown below. We are reusing the function for merging two sorted linked lists that has been described in page 24. One important point to note is that when we recursively divide the linked list and reach a single node, we have to make the next pointer of the node NULL in order to disconnect it from the original linked list and form a separate linked list that contains only that single node.

```
/*
first_node: head of the list to be sorted
num_elements: number of elements in the list
Return value: head of the merged and sorted list
*/
struct node * sort_list(struct node *first_node, int num_elements)
{
    struct node *list1, *list2, *cur_node;
    int i, count1, count2;

    if (num_elements == 0)
        return NULL;
    /*
    If there is only a single node in the list, then disconnect next
    and return the node as the result without any further recursive calls
    */
    if (num_elements == 1) {
        first_node->next = NULL;
        return first_node;
    }

    /*
    Divide the list into two lists. list1 has count1 elements and
    list2 has count2 elements
    */
    list1 = first_node;
    count1 = num_elements / 2;

    cur_node = first_node;
    for (i = 0; i < count1; ++i)
        cur_node = cur_node->next;

    list2 = cur_node;
    count2 = num_elements - count1;

    /*Call sort_list recursively on list1 and list2*/
    list1 = sort_list(list1, count1);
    list2 = sort_list(list2, count2);

    /*
    list1 and list2 are now sorted. So merge the two lists into a single
    sorted list and return its head node
    */
    return merge_lists(list1, list2);
}
```

6. Given an unsorted array A and a pivot element in the array, re-arrange the elements so that elements less than pivot occur first, followed by elements equal to pivot followed by elements greater than pivot.

When we perform quicksort, we pick a pivot and move all the elements that are < than pivot to one side and all elements that are > than pivot to the other side. But the problem is that if there are multiple elements with the same value of the pivot, then these elements are not guaranteed to be next to each other. So for instance consider the array = {5, 5, 2, 30, 10, 5}. If we pick the pivot value of 5 and perform quicksort then after the first set of operations we end up with {2, 5, 5, 30, 10, 5}. Note that all the 5's are not grouped together. So default quicksort is not efficient in dealing with duplicates. In fact the worst case for quicksort is $O(n^2)$ and occurs when there are all identical values in the array. If quicksort is modified to store all values of the pivot together, quicksort can be speeded up. So if we rearrange the array as {2, 5, 5, 5, 30, 10} in the first pass of modified quicksort, then we can skip all the consecutive 5's and sort the remaining regions {2} and {30, 10}.

Dijkstra suggested the modification to quicksort to speed it up. He posed the Dutch National Flag Problem and used the solution of the problem to speed up quicksort. The Dutch National Flag has 3 colors: red, white and blue. So he asked if there was a way to rearrange a random bunch of red, white and blue balls so that all the red balls appear first, followed by white balls followed by blue balls. He came up with a O(n) solution that doesn't use extra space. If we map the red balls to elements less than the pivot, white balls to elements equal to the pivot and blue balls to elements greater than the pivot, we end up with the same problem we are trying to solve. So we can apply Dijkstra's solution to our problem as well.

In Dijkstra's solution, we maintain two markers: a left marker (initialized to 0) and a right marker initialized to n-1 where n is the number of elements in A. The current position i in A is initialized to 0. We pick A[i] as the pivot. As the algorithm runs we maintain the elements in the following manner

- All elements that are less than pivot are stored from A[0] to A[left – 1]
- All elements equal to the pivot are stored from A[left] to A[current position - 1]
- All elements that still need to be processed will be in the region A[current position] to A[right]
- All elements that are greater than pivot are stored from A[right + 1] to A[n-1]

The code for solving the problem is given below:

```
/*
a: input array that has to be sorted.
length: number of elements in the array
pivot_value: after sorting, all elements smaller than pivot will lie to the
left of the pivot and all values that are greater than pivot will lie to the
right of the pivot. If there are many pivot values, then they will occur
together in the middle
*/
void dutch_sort(int a[], int length, int pivot_value)
{
    int cur_pos, left_pos, right_pos;
    int temp;

    cur_pos = 0;
    left_pos = 0;
    right_pos = length - 1;

    while (cur_pos <= right_pos) {
        if (a[cur_pos] < pivot_value) {
                /*swap a[left_pos], a[cur_pos]*/
                temp = a[left_pos];
                a[left_pos] = a[cur_pos];
                a[cur_pos] = temp;

                ++left_pos;    /*Advance the left fill location*/
                ++cur_pos;     /*Process the next element*/

        } else if (a[cur_pos] > pivot_value) {
                /*swap a[cur_pos], a[right_pos];*/
                temp = a[cur_pos];
                a[cur_pos] = a[right_pos];
                a[right_pos] = temp;

                /*Advance the right fill location. Since we have newly
                brought in an element from right_pos to cur_pos, we have
                to process the new element. So don't advance cur_pos*/
                --right_pos;

        } else {
                ++cur_pos; /*Process the next element*/
        }
    }
}
```

Suppose an array consists of random numbers and we need to re-arrange it so that we first have negative numbers followed by 0, followed by positive numbers, then we can use the same strategy.

7. Find the kth smallest element in an array

We can solve the problem by completely sorting the array and then finding the kth element in the sorted array. However for just finding one element, sorting the entire array is expensive.

We can solve the problem using a heap of k elements. As we process the elements in the array, we will maintain the k smallest elements in the heap. The problem with this approach is that if k is large, then we will need a large amount of space. So even though we need to find only one element, we will have to allocate space for k elements.

The other approach is to use quick sort. In each iteration of quicksort, we will pick a pivot and move all the elements that are smaller than the pivot to the left of the pivot and move all the elements greater than the pivot to the right of the pivot. Let the region on which the current iteration of quicksort has operated on be (left_index, right_index). Then based on the location of the pivot, we do the following

1. If the index of the pivot at the end of the quick-sort iteration matches with k, then we have found the kth smallest element.

2. If the index of the pivot is less than k, then we reduce the region to be searched in the next iteration to (index of pivot + 1, right_index)

3. If the location of the pivot is greater than k, then we reduce the region to be searched in the next iteration to (left_index, index of pivot – 1)

The worst case time complexity is O(n^2). However in practice, the algorithm is expected to run in linear time O(n) and the space complexity is O(1).

```
/* Helper function for finding the kth smallest element
 * This function, picks a pivot and arranges all numbers smaller than pivot to
 * the left of the pivot and all numbers greater than pivot to the right of pivot
 * a: array on which the partition operation should be performed
 * left: index of the starting element of the partition in the array
 * right: index of the ending element of the partition in the array
 * Return value: index of the pivot element of the partition
 */
int partition(int a[], int left, int right)
{
    int i, j, pivot;
    int num_elements = right - left + 1;
    int rand_pos = left + (rand() % num_elements);
```

```
/*pick a random element and swap it with the last element*/
swap(&a[rand_pos], &a[right]);

/*The last element is treated as the pivot*/
pivot = a[right];

i = left;
for (j = left; j <= right - 1; ++j) {
   if (a[j] <= pivot) {
         /*If i is not equal to j, then a[i] has a value
         greater than pivot and a[j] has a value less than
         pivot. So swap a[i] and a[j]*/
         if (i != j)
               swap(&a[i], &a[j]);
         ++i;
   }
}

/*Swap a[i] and the pivot that is at a[right]*/
swap(&a[i], &a[right]);

return i; /*the pivot is now at i. So return i*/
}


/*Finds the kth smallest element in an array
a: array in which the kth smallest element should be found
length: number of elements in the array
k: value of k (can range from 0 to length - 1)
Returns: the kth smallest element in the array
*/
int find_kth_smallest(int a[], int length, int k)
{
   int left = 0;
   int right = length - 1;

   while (k >= left && k <= right) {
      int pivot_pos = partition(a, left, right);

      if (pivot_pos == k)
            return a[pivot_pos];
      else if (pivot_pos < k) {
            left = pivot_pos + 1;
      } else {
            right = pivot_pos - 1;
      }
   }

   return MAX_INT; /*incorrect k value was specified*/
}
```

8. Sort an array which is almost sorted. An almost sorted array is one in which each element is at most k positions away from its position in the fully sorted array. For instance, the array {3, 2, 1, 5, 4} is almost sorted and k = 2 since the maximum distance an element has to be moved to get the fully sorted array in ascending order is 2.

To sort an almost sorted array where an element is at most k positions from its position in the sorted array, we will make use of a heap of size k+1. To sort in non-decreasing order, we will make use of a min_heap. We apply the following steps:

1. Store the first k elements in the array into the min_heap. Initialize write_pos to 0. write_pos is used to write the sorted values back into the array.

2. Add the next element in the array into the min_heap. The root of the min_heap will now contain the smallest element in the current window of size k+1. Remove the root and store the value of the root into the location write_pos in the array. Increment the write_pos

3. Repeat step 2 for all the remaining elements in the array

4. Once we have finished processing the array, the heap will still be containing elements in it. So go on removing the root from the heap and adding it to the array until the heap becomes completely empty. The array will now be completely sorted.

```
/*
a: almost sorted array that should be fully sorted
length: number of elements in the array
k: max distance that any element should be moved so that array becomes sorted
*/
void sort_almost_sorted_array(int a[], int length, int k)
{
    priority_queue <int, vector<int>, greater<int> > min_heap;

    int read_pos = 0, write_pos = 0;

    /*Fill in the first k values into the min_heap. If length is less than k
    then we have to fill in only length number of elements */
    for (read_pos = 0; read_pos < min(k, length); ++read_pos) {
        min_heap.push(a[read_pos]);
    }

    /*Add the element a[read_pos] to the heap and then pop out a value.
    Value popped from heap will contain the next smallest value. Add the
    value popped from the heap back into the array at the write position*/
    while (read_pos < length) {
        min_heap.push(a[read_pos]);
        a[write_pos] = min_heap.top();
```

```
            min_heap.pop();

            read_pos++;
            write_pos++;
    }

    /*Pop out the remaining elements in the heap and store them back
    into the array*/
    while (!min_heap.empty()) {
        a[write_pos] = min_heap.top();
        min_heap.pop();

        ++write_pos;
    }
}
```

9. Sort an array of words so that the anagrams are grouped together. For instance, if the words are {"tar", "phone", "rat"}, after sorting we should get {"tar", "rat", "phone"} (since "tar" and "rat" are anagrams, they are grouped together)

We will maintain a structure called the AnagramHelper as shown below

```
struct AnagramHelper
{
    char *word;
    int index;
};
```

Let the original array passed by user consist of {"tar", "phone", "rat"}

1. First copy the words and their index locations in the original array into an AnagramHelper array. So the AnagramHelper array will look like

word	"tar"	"phone"	"rat"
index	0	1	2

2. Sort each word in the AnagramHelper in the non-decreasing order of the characters in the word. After the sort, the AnagramHelper array will look like

word	"art"	"ehnop"	"art"
index	0	1	2

3. Now sort all the words in the AnagramHelper array. After the sort, the AnagramHelper array will be as shown below. Note that when we swap elements during sorting, both word and index will be moved together.

word	"art"	"art"	"ehnop"
index	0	2	1

Now the words in the AnagramHelper array have been modified ("rat" has become "art"). To get back the original word, we will use the index. The index will give us the location of the actual word in the original array. So if we lookup original_array[2] we will get "rat" and so we conclude that the second "art" is actually "rat".

234

4. We now have to move the words in the original_array so that anagrams occur together. If we use the AnagramHelper and directly write to the original_array, then we will overwrite contents in the original_array leading to an incorrect result. So we instead use a scratchpad array and fill it up using the information in the AnagramHelper array. So the scratchpad is filled up as shown below

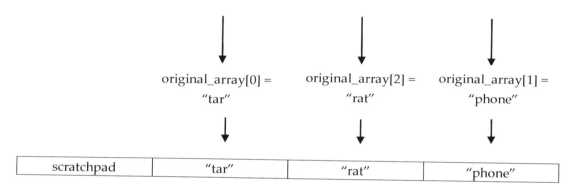

word	"art"	"art"	"ehnop"
index	0	2	1

original_array[0] = "tar"   original_array[2] = "rat"   original_array[1] = "phone"

scratchpad	"tar"	"rat"	"phone"

5. Finally we copy the contents of the scratchpad into the original_array. So original_array will now have {"tar", "rat", "phone"}

The code for sorting the anagrams together is given below:

```
/*Helper function for comparing characters. It is used during quicksort*/
int char_cmp_function(const void *p1, const void *p2) {
    char *x = (char*)p1;
    char *y = (char*)p2;

    if (*x < *y)
        return -1;
    else if (*x == *y)
        return 0;
    else
        return 1;
}

/*Sorts the characters in a string*/
void sort_word(char buffer[], int length) {
    qsort(buffer, length, sizeof(char), char_cmp_function);
}
/*Helper function for comparing words. It is used during quicksort*/
int helper_cmp_function(const void *p1, const void *p2)
{
```

```
    struct AnagramHelper *x = (struct AnagramHelper*)p1;
    struct AnagramHelper *y = (struct AnagramHelper*)p2;

    return strcmp(x->word, y->word);
}

/*Sorts the anagram helper array based on the words in it*/
void sort_anagram_helper(struct AnagramHelper helper[], int num_words)
{
    qsort(helper, num_words, sizeof(struct AnagramHelper),
            helper_cmp_function);
}

/*
word_list: list of words that should be sorted so that the anagrams occur
together
num_words: Number of elements in the word_list
*/
void anagram_sort(char *word_list[], int num_words)
{
    struct AnagramHelper *helper = (struct AnagramHelper*) calloc(num_words,
                                    sizeof(struct AnagramHelper));

    int i, length;
    char **scratchpad;

    for (i = 0; i < num_words; ++i) {
        length = strlen(word_list[i]);

        /*Allocate memory for the word in the helper and copy
        the original word into it. Add 1 to length for '\0' character*/
        helper[i].word = (char*) calloc(1, length + 1);
        strcpy(helper[i].word, word_list[i]);

        /*First sort the characters of the word in the helper*/
        sort_word(helper[i].word, length);

        /*Store the original index of the word in the helper*/
        helper[i].index = i;
    }

    /*Sort all the words in the helper*/
    sort_anagram_helper(helper, num_words);

    /*We need to move the words in word_list based on the indexes in the
    helper. We can't directly move the char pointers in the words array.
    First we will copy the char pointers into a scratchpad array
    based on the indexes in the helper and then copy the scratchpad
    array into the word_list array.
    */
    scratchpad = (char**) calloc(num_words, sizeof(char *));


    for (i = 0; i < num_words; ++i) {
        int index = helper[i].index;
        scratchpad[i] = word_list[index];
```

236

```
    }

    for (i = 0; i < num_words; ++i) {
        word_list[i] = scratchpad[i];
    }

    free(scratchpad);
    free(helper);
}
```

3. Algorithms

Some of the popular algorithm techniques used for solving problems are divide and conquer, greedy approach and dynamic programming.

In the divide and conquer approach, the main problem is broken into sub-problems recursively until the sub-problem can be easily solved. The solutions for the sub-problems are collected and used to find the solution for the main problem. Some of the problems where divide and conquer approach is used are: binary search, merge sort and Strassen's matrix multiplication.

In the greedy approach, at each stage of the algorithm, the local optimum is chosen hoping that this will result in the globally optimum solution. Some of the problems where the greedy approach is used are: the fractional knapsack problem, Huffman coding, finding minimum spanning trees and finding the shortest path from a single source (Dijkstra's algorithm)

The dynamic programming approach breaks the main problem into sub-problems that can be easily solved such that overlapping sub-problems are computed only once. Some of the problems where the dynamic programming approach is used are: the 0/1 knapsack problem, computing edit distance between two strings and longest common subsequence.

While solving algorithmic problems, sometimes we will have to make use of our knowledge of data structures. The other tools we can use for algorithmic problems include sorting, binary search, recursion and back tracking.

3.1 Greedy Algorithms

1. Given a set of stock prices over a period of time, find the maximum profit possible by buying and selling the stocks. For instance, if the stock prices are 100, 90, 200, 20, 70, 150, 10 and 40, then the maximum profit = 150 − 20 = 130

If we use a brute force approach, then we will compare every pair of numbers to find the maximum profit possible. This requires $O(n^2)$ operations. However using the greedy approach we can solve the problem in $O(n)$. The main idea of the greedy approach is that it is sufficient to maintain the minimum stock price that we have encountered so far as we traverse the stock prices.

The procedure is as follows: as we traverse the stock price list, subtract the minimum stock price seen so far from the current stock price to figure out the profit. If the profit is greater than the maximum profit so far, then update the maximum profit.

The working of the algorithm on the stock prices {100, 90, 200, 20, 70, 150, 10, 40} is given below. The minimum stock price is initialized to the first element 100. The max profit is initialized to 0. We start from the second stock price onwards.

Index	Current stock price	Minimum stock price so far	Current Profit	Max profit
1	90	100	90 − 100 = -10	0
2	200	90	200 − 90 = 110	110
3	20	90	20 − 90 = -70	110
4	70	20	70 − 20 = 50	110

239

5	150	20	$150 - 20 = 130$	130
6	10	20	$10 - 20 = -10$	130
7	40	10	$40 - 10 = 30$	130

```
/*
stock_price: array of stock price values
n: number of elements in the array
Return value: maximum profit possible
*/
int find_max_profit(int stock_price[], int n)
{
    int i, min_stock_price, cur_profit, max_profit;

    max_profit = 0;
    if (n <= 1)
        return max_profit;

    min_stock_price = stock_price[0];

    for (i = 1; i < n; ++i) {

        cur_profit = stock_price[i] - min_stock_price;

        if (cur_profit > max_profit)
                max_profit = cur_profit;

        if (stock_price[i] < min_stock_price)
                min_stock_price = stock_price[i];
    }

    return max_profit;
}
```

2. Given the start time and end time of N activities, find the maximum number of activities that can be performed (Activity Selection problem)

We can find the maximum number of activities using the greedy approach as indicated below

1. Sort the activities based on their end times so that an activity with a smaller end time is placed before an activity with a larger end time.

2. Traverse through the sorted list and choose the activities that can be completed without any conflicts (the start and end time of a chosen activity should not overlap with the start and end time of another chosen activity)

```
/*Function for comparing two elements. This function used while sorting*/
int cmp_function(const void *p1, const void *p2)
{
    struct activity *x = (struct activity *)p1;
    struct activity *y = (struct activity *)p2;

    if (x->end_time < y->end_time)
        return -1;
    else if (x->end_time == y->end_time)
        return 0;
    else
        return 1;
}


void sort(struct activity a[], int length)
{
    qsort(a, length, sizeof(struct activity), cmp_function);
}


/*
a: array of activities, where each activity has a start time and end time
num_activities: number of elements in the array. Should be >= 1
selected: the indexes of the selected activities
Return value: Maximum number of activities that can be performed
*/
int activity_selection(struct activity a[],  int num_activities, int selected[])
{
    int i, count, cur_time;

    /*Sort the activities in non-decreasing order of their end time*/
    sort(a, num_activities);

    /*Keep a track of the current time as we process the activities*/
```

```
cur_time = 0;
count = 0;
for (i = 0; i < num_activities; ++i) {
    /*Pick the activity whose start time is on or after current time*/
    if (a[i].start_time >= cur_time) {
            selected[count] = i;
            count++;

            /*Update the current time to the end time of the activity*/
            cur_time = a[i].end_time;
    }
}

    return count;
}
```

Note that if instead of start time and end time, we are given start time and duration of each activity, then we must compute the end time (end time = start time + duration) and then apply the above algorithm

3. Given the arrival time and the departure time of N trains, find the minimum number of platforms needed to accommodate the trains

---

To find the minimal number of platforms needed for N trains, we do the following

1. Sort the arrival time of the N trains so that an earlier arrival time is placed before a later arrival time

2. Sort the departure time of the N trains so that an earlier departure time is placed before a later departure time. Note that we independently sort the arrival time and the departure time of the trains.

3. Traverse through the arrival time and departure time of the trains as indicated below

- If the current arrival time is less than the current departure time, then we need an extra platform for the incoming train. So increment the number of platforms needed and advance to the next arrival time.
- If the current arrival time is equal to the current departure time, then we don't need an extra platform. So simply advance to the next arrival time and next departure time
- If the current departure time is less than the current arrival time, then a platform will be freed up. So decrement the number of platforms needed and advance to the next departure time.

As we do this, keep track of the maximum number of platforms needed at any given time. This will give us the minimum number of platforms needed to accommodate the trains.

```
/*
arrival: array containing the arrival time of the trains
departure: array containing the departure time of the trains
n: length of arrays. Both arrays should have same length
Return value: minimum number of train platforms needed
*/
int find_min_platforms(int arrival[], int departure[], int n)
{
    int cur_num_platforms, min_num_platforms;
    int i, j;

    if (n == 0)
        return 0;

    /*Sort arrival and departure time independently in non-decreasing order*/
```

```
    sort(arrival, n);
    sort(departure, n);

    cur_num_platforms = min_num_platforms = 1;
    i = 1; /*i is used for traversing arrival*/
    j = 0; /*j is used for traversing departure*/

    while (i < n && j < n) {
        if (arrival[i] < departure[j]) {
                /*A new train is coming in before a train departs. So
                we need an extra platform*/
                cur_num_platforms++;
                if (cur_num_platforms > min_num_platforms)
                        min_num_platforms = cur_num_platforms;
                ++i;
        } else if (arrival[i] == departure[j]) {
                /*A train arrives at the same time as a departing train.
                So we don't need an extra platform*/
                ++i;
                ++j;
        } else {
                /*A train departs before the new train arrives. So a
                platform is freed up*/
                cur_num_platforms--;
                j++;
        }
    }

    return min_num_platforms;
}
```

4. There are N gas stations around a circular path. Each gas station i has a finite amount of fuel gas[i] in it. The fuel tank of the car has an unlimited size. The sum of the fuel available at all the gas stations is sufficient for the driver to complete the journey on the circular path. Note however that an individual gas station might not have enough gas to reach the next gas station. Find out if the driver can finish one complete circular trip in the car using the fuel available in the gas stations

It is always possible to find a circular trip around the N gas stations if the sum of the fuel in all the stations is >= to the fuel needed for the whole trip irrespective of the distribution of the fuel in the individual gas stations. We can find the starting station in $O(n^2)$ using the brute force approach: start from each of the N station and check if it is possible to complete the journey around all gas stations. However there is a faster $O(n)$ solution. Let gas[i] be the gas available at station i. Let distance[i] be the distance between the ith station and $(i+1)^{th}$ station. The algorithm is as follows:

1. Starting from the first gas station, fill up all the gas available in the current gas station and proceed to the next station. On reaching each station, before refueling the car, compute the gas present in the car tank. Allow for negative amount of gas in the car tank

2. The station where the gas available in the tank before refueling is the least, is the station from where to start the journey.

To illustrate the algorithm, consider the following diagram

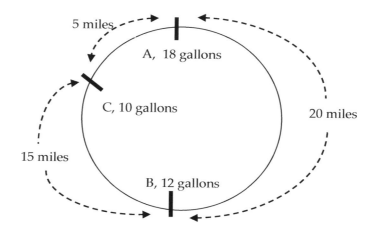

Let us start from gas station A. The initial amount of fuel in the tank is 0. The table below shows the sequence of events. Note that we allow the amount of gas in the fuel tank to become negative. Let the mileage be 1 mile per gallon.

Journey	Fuel in tank after filling up from starting gas station	Distance to next gas station	Fuel needed to reach next station = distance / mileage	Fuel left in tank after reaching next station
A -> B	18 gallons	20 miles	20 / 1 = 20 gallons	18-20 = -2 gallons
B -> C	-2 + 12 = 10 gallons	15 miles	15 / 1 = 15 gallons	10–15 = **-5 gallons**
C-> A	-5 + 10 = 5	5 miles	5 / 1 = 5 gallons	5 - 5 = 0 gallons

When we reach station C, before we refuel at station C, we have the lowest amount of gas in the entire trip (-5 gallons). So suppose we start the journey from gas station C, the amount of gas in the car will never fall below the lowest amount of gas. We will always have sufficient amount of gas or surplus gas in the fuel tank. Think of it this way: by starting from station C, we start with 0 gas in the car. Since the lowest amount of gas occurs when we reach station C, we are assured that the amount of gas when we reach other stations will always be >= 0.

```
/*
gas: the amount of gas available at each gas station. The total gas in all
    stations should be sufficient to complete the circular trip
distance: distance[i] has the distance between gas station i and i+1
num_stations: number of gas stations. Should be >= 1
mileage: how much distance can the car travel for 1 unit of gas consumed
Return value: station from where to start so that we don't run out of fuel and
    complete the circular trip around all stations
*/
int find_starting_gas_station(int gas[], int distance[], int num_stations, int
mileage)
{
    int i, starting_station;
    int least_gas, gas_required, gas_in_tank;

    /*Station from where to start the journey so that we don't run out of fuel*/
    starting_station = 0;

    least_gas = 0; /*Tracks the least amount of gas in fuel tank*/
    gas_in_tank = 0; /*Tracks how much fuel is currently present in fuel tank*/
    for (i = 0; i < num_stations; ++i) {
        gas_required = distance[i] / mileage;

        /*At station i, we fill up gas[i] and then as we drive, we consume
        gas_required to reach the destination station = (i+1) % num_stations */
```

```
        gas_in_tank += gas[i] - gas_required;
        if (gas_in_tank < least_gas) {
                least_gas = gas_in_tank;
                /*The starting station is the station where we have
                the least amount of gas in the tank just before we fill up*/
                starting_station = (i+1) % num_stations;
        }
    }

    return starting_station;
}
```

3.2 Dynamic Programming

1. Find the maximum continuous sum in an array

An array can have positive and negative elements in it. We have to find a subset of contiguous elements in the array whose sum is the maximum. Let the maximum continuous sum be represented as MCS

In the brute force approach, we pick an element and then go on adding its right neighbors one by one to find the maximum contiguous sum starting at that element. We then repeat the process for all elements in the array to find the MCS across all elements. The time complexity of the brute force approach is $O(n^2)$.

However it is possible to find the MCS in $O(n)$ time using Kadane's algorithm. This algorithm works for all cases (including the case where all the elements are negative). We maintain the variable max_local which will store the sum of the neighboring elements in the current window. The algorithm is described below:

1. Choose the first element and initialize max_local to the first element.

2. Traverse through the remaining elements. If the result of adding max_local to the current element is greater than current element, then add the current element to max_local and keep continuing the window. If however the result of adding max_local to the current element is less than the current element, then start a fresh window that starts at the current element and initialize max_local to the current element.

3. The maximum value of max_local across all elements will be the MCS of the array.

Let A = {4, -9, 5, 6 , 1} . max_local is initialized to 4. The remaining calculations are shown in the table below

i	max_local	A[i]	A[i] + max_local	Action max_local = max(A[i], A[i] + max_local)
1	4	-9	-5	max_local = max(-9, -5) = -5
2	-5	5	0	max_local = max(5, 0) = 5
3	5	6	11	max_local = max(6, 11) = 11
4	11	1	12	max_local = max(1, 12) = 12

The maximum value of max_local is 12. So the MCS is 12.

```
/*
a: the array of numbers for which the MCS should be found,
length: number of elements. Should >= 1
mcs_start_pos: the starting array index of the MCS is returned here
mcs_end_pos: the ending array index of the MCS is returned here
Return value: Maximum continuous sum of the elements
*/
int kadane_mcs(int a[], int length, int *mcs_start_pos, int *mcs_end_pos) {
    int i, max_local, max_global;
    int cur_start_pos;

    *mcs_start_pos = *mcs_end_pos = 0;
    cur_start_pos = 0; /*store the start position of the current window*/

    max_local = max_global = a[0];

    /*Traverse from the second element onwards*/
    for (i = 1; i < length; ++i) {
        max_local = max(a[i], a[i] + max_local);
        if (max_local == a[i])
                cur_start_pos = i; /*start a new window here*/

        /*Find the global maximum*/
        if (max_local > max_global) {
                max_global = max_local;
                *mcs_start_pos = cur_start_pos;
                *mcs_end_pos = i;
        }
    }

    return max_global;
}
```

2. Given a set of coin denominations, find the change for a given amount using the least number of coins. For instance, suppose the coin denominations are 4¢, 5¢ and 7¢, then to get 13¢ using the least number of coins, we need to pick two 4¢ coins and one 5¢ coin.

Let us say that coin denominations are 1¢, 5¢ and 25¢. We can use a greedy approach as follows - Pick the maximum possible number of coins with the highest denomination and then the maximum possible number of coins with the next highest denomination and so on. So if we have to pick the change for 58¢, we pick two 25¢, then one 5¢ and finally three 1¢. So we use a total of 6 coins. Greedy approach produces the optimal result for this set of coin denominations. However, given any arbitrary set of coin denominations, the greedy approach will fail for many cases. For instance let the denominations be 1¢, 3¢, 4¢ and 5¢. If we use the greedy approach to get 7¢, we use one 5¢ and two 1¢ thereby requiring three coins. However the optimal solution needs only two coins (one 3¢ and one 4¢).

To solve the problem for any possible coin denominations, we use dynamic programming. We first solve the minimum number of coins needed for the amount of 1¢, then for the amount of 2¢ and so on until we reach the required amount. To compute the minimum number of coins for a higher amount, we make use of the already computed minimum number of coins for lower amounts. The formula used is:

1. If amount = 0, min_num_coins(0) = 0

2. If amount > 0, min_num_coins(amount) = minimum of { 1 + min_num_coins(amount - denomination)} for all denominations which are less than or equal to the amount

For instance, let the denominations be 1¢, 3¢, 4¢ and 5¢. Using the formula above, min_num_coins[0¢] = 0 coins. The table below shows how the calculation is done for min_num_coins for 1¢, 2¢ and 3¢.

Amount	Denominations that are <= amount	1 + min_num_coins(amount - denomination)	min_num_coins
1¢	1¢	(1 + min_num_coins(1¢ - 1¢)} = 1 + min_num_coins(0¢) = 1 + 0 = 1	min(1) = 1
2¢	1¢	(1 + min_num_coins(2¢ - 1¢) = 1 + min_num_coins(1¢) = 1 + 1 = 2	min(2) = 2

Amount	Denominations that are <= amount	1 + min_num_coins(amount - denomination)	min_num_coins
3¢	1¢, 3¢	(1 + min_num_coins(3¢ - 1¢) = 1 + min_num_coins(2¢) = 1 + 2 = 3 (1 + min_num_coins(3¢ - 3¢) = 1 + min_num_coins(0) = 1 + 0 = 1	min(3, 1) = 1

So min_num_coins(1¢) = 1, min_num_coins(2¢) = 2 and min_num_coins(3¢) = 1. Similarly we find that min_num_coins(4¢) = 1 and min_num_coins(5¢) = 1. The calculations for 6¢ and 7¢ are shown below

Amount	Denominations that are <= amount	1 + min_num_coins(amount - denomination)	min_num_coins
6¢	1¢, 3¢, 4¢, 5¢	(1 + min_num_coins(6¢ - 1¢) = 1 + min_num_coins(5¢) = 1 + 1 = 2 (1 + min_num_coins(6¢ - 3¢) = 1 + min_num_coins(3¢) = 1 + 1 = 2 (1 + min_num_coins(6¢ - 4¢) = 1 + min_num_coins(2¢) = 1 + 2 = 3 (1 + min_num_coins(6¢ - 5¢) = 1 + min_num_coins(1¢) = 1 + 1 = 2	min(2, 2, 3, 2) = 2
7¢	1¢, 3¢, 4¢, 5¢	(1 + min_num_coins(7¢ - 1¢) = 1 + min_num_coins(6¢) = 1 + 2 = 3 (1 + min_num_coins(7¢ - 3¢) = 1 + min_num_coins(4¢) = 1 + 1 = 2 (1 + min_num_coins(7¢ - 4¢) = 1 + min_num_coins(3¢) = 1 + 1 = 2 (1 + min_num_coins(7¢ - 5¢) = 1 + min_num_coins(2¢) = 1 + 2 = 3	min(3, 2, 2, 3) = 2

So the minimum number of coins for 7¢ is 2 coins. If the final amount is m and there are n denominations, the time complexity of this approach is O(mn).

```
/*
denom: array having the coin denominations. Should have at least 1 element
num_denom: number of denominations
final_amount: amount for which change has to be obtained
Return value: Minimum number of coins needed to represent final_amount
*/
int find_min_coins(int denom[], int num_denom, int final_amount)
{
    /*Array for storing the minimum number of coins for an amount*/
    int *min_num_coins = (int*) malloc( (final_amount+1) * sizeof(int));

    /*Array for storing the coin denomination chosen for an amount*/
    int *chosen_denom = (int*) malloc( (final_amount+1) * sizeof(int));
    int i, cur_amt, smaller_amt, result;

    min_num_coins[0] = 0;
    for (cur_amt = 1; cur_amt <= final_amount; cur_amt++) {
        min_num_coins[cur_amt] = MAX_INT_VALUE;
        for (i = 0; i < num_denom; ++i) {
                if (denom[i] <= cur_amt) {

                        smaller_amt = cur_amt - denom[i];

                        if (1 + min_num_coins[smaller_amt] <
                                    min_num_coins[cur_amt]) {
                                min_num_coins[cur_amt] =
                                        1 + min_num_coins[smaller_amt];
                                chosen_denom[cur_amt] = denom[i];
                        }
                }
        }
    }

    result = min_num_coins[final_amount];
    printf("Minimum number of coins = %d\n", result);

    /*print the chosen denominations to get the final amount*/
    cur_amt = final_amount;
    while (cur_amt > 0) {
        printf("%d ", chosen_denom[cur_amt]);
        cur_amt = cur_amt - chosen_denom[cur_amt];
    }
    printf(" = %d\n", final_amount);

    free(min_num_coins);
    free(chosen_denom);
    return result;
}
```

3. Find the longest increasing subsequence in an unsorted array of numbers

Consider the sequence A = {30, 40, 20, 70, 10}. The longest increasing subsequence is {30, 40, 70}. Here we are considering a strictly increasing longest subsequence and so a number can be present only once in the longest increasing subsequence even if it occurs several times in the original sequence. To solve the problem, we use dynamic programming as follows:

1.) We make use of an array called seq_length where seq_length[i] stores the length of the longest increasing subsequence ending at the position i. For instance seq_length[3] stores the length of longest subsequence from 0th to 3rd position, i.e. for the region {30, 40, 20, 70} in the above example. We initialize seq_length array with 1 at each position since each number itself forms a sequence of size 1 by itself.

2. We then compute the seq_length[i] from position 1 onwards using the formula:

seq_length[i] = 1 + max(seq_length[j]) where j < i and A[j] < A[i]

position	value	calculation	seq_length
0	30		seq_length [0] = 1
1	40	1 +seq_length[0] = 1+1 = 2	seq_length [1] = 2
2	20	can't consider seq_length[0] since A[0] > A[2] can't consider seq_length[1] since A[1] > A[2]	seq_length [2] = 1
3	70	1 + seq_length[0] = 1 + 1 = 2 1 + seq_length[1] = 1 + 2 = 3 1 + seq_length[2] = 1 + 1 = 2	seq_length [3] = 3
4	10	can't consider seq_length[0] since A[0] > A[4], can't consider seq_length [1] since A[1] > A[4] can't consider seq_length [2] since A[2] > A[4] can't consider seq_length [3] since A[3] > A[4]	seq_length [4] = 1

3. Once we have computed sequence lengths for all positions, then the maximum value in the seq_length array gives the length of the longest increasing subsequence. In our example, the maximum value in the seq_length array is 3. So length of longest increasing subsequence is 3.

The time complexity of this approach is O(n²).

```
/*
a: array in which we need to find the longest increasing sequence
n: number of elements in the array. Should be >= 1
lis: the longest increasing sequence is returned in this array
Return value: length of the longest increasing sequence
*/
int find_lis(int a[], int n, int lis[])
{
    /*seq_length stores length of LIS for each position of array a*/
    int *seq_length = (int*) calloc(n, sizeof(int));

    /*prev_ix stores the index of previous element in the LIS sequence*/
    int *prev_ix = (int*) calloc(n, sizeof(int));

    int i, j, lis_length, lis_end;

    /*Each element by itself forms a sequence of length 1*/
    for (i = 0; i < n; ++i)
        seq_length[i] = 1;

    /*Find the LIS for each position in array a*/
    for (i = 1; i < n; ++i) {
        for (j = 0; j < i; ++j) {
            if ( a[j] < a[i] && seq_length[i] < seq_length[j] + 1 ) {
                seq_length[i] = seq_length[j] + 1;
                prev_ix[i] = j;
            }
        }
    }

    /*The longest LIS amongst all positions of array a will be the LIS
    for the whole array*/
    lis_length = 1;
    lis_end = 0;
    for (i = 1; i < n; ++i) {
        if (lis_length < seq_length[i]) {
            lis_length = seq_length[i];
            lis_end = i;
        }
    }

    /*Use the prev_ix array to reconstruct the LIS for the whole array
    lis_end has the index of the last element in the LIS for whole array*/
    j = lis_end;
    for (i = lis_length - 1; i >= 0; --i) {
        lis[i] = a[j];
        j = prev_ix[j];
    }

    free(seq_length);
    free(prev_ix);

    return lis_length;
}
```

4. Find the least number of dice throws needed to complete the snake and ladders game

---

To find the least number of dice throws, we use the following dynamic programming technique:

1. Initialize the least number of throws needed to reach the positions 1-6 on the board as 1 since we can reach these positions with a single dice throw of a 6-sided dice

2. For any remaining position, we can either reach it from

- any of the previous 6 positions with one dice throw. If there is a snake at a previous position, then we ignore that cell while calculating the least number of throws for the current position
- or we can reach it by a ladder if present from some previous position. If there is a ladder from position I to position P, and we need N throws to reach I, then we can reach P also in N throws.

So we use the formula below to calculate the least number of throws for positions greater than 6.

least_throws[pos] = Minimum of

1. least_throws[prev_pos] + 1

   where prev_pos refers to the positions from (pos – 1) to (pos – 6) that don't have a snake in them

2. least_throws[i], if there is a ladder from i to pos, where i < pos

3. The least number of throws to reach the final position of the board gives the least number of throws needed to complete the game.

```
/*is_snake: if there is a snake at position 20, then is_snake[20] is set to 1
ladder: if there is a ladder from position 30 to 44, then ladder[44] = 30.
    if there is no ladder at location 90 then ladder[90] = -1
predecessor: this array has the previous board position from where we came to
    current position with least number of dice throws. If predecessor[100]
    = 95, then we reached 100 from 95. It is computed and returned.
Return value: least number of throws to reach the final position on the board
*/
int find_least_throws(int is_snake[], int ladder[], int predecessor[])
{
    /*for a particular position pos on the board, least_throws[pos] will store
    the least number of dice throws required to reach the position*/
    int least_throws[MAX_POSITIONS_ON_BOARD + 1];
    int min_throws, i;
    int pos, prev_pos, ladder_start_pos;

    /*Positions from 1 to 6 can be reached from a single dice throw*/
    for (pos = 1; pos <= 6; pos++) {
        least_throws[pos] = 1;
        predecessor[pos] = 0;
    }

    for (pos = 7; pos <= MAX_POSITIONS_ON_BOARD; ++pos) {
        min_throws = MAX_POSITIONS_ON_BOARD;

        /*Find how many dice throws are needed to reach pos from any of
        the 6 previous cells*/
        for (i = 1; i <= 6; ++i) {
            prev_pos = pos - i;

            if (is_snake[prev_pos])
                continue;

            /*Pick the minimum throws needed from the 6 previous cells*/
            if (least_throws[prev_pos] + 1 < min_throws) {
                min_throws = least_throws[prev_pos] + 1;
                predecessor[pos] = prev_pos;
            }
        }

        /*Suppose we are at pos = 14 and ladder[14] = 4, then there is a ladder
        from 4 to 14. So number of dice throws needed to reach 14 = number of
        dice throws needed to reach position 4*/
        ladder_start_pos = ladder[pos];
        if (ladder_start_pos != -1) {
            if (least_throws[ladder_start_pos] < min_throws) {
                min_throws = least_throws[ladder_start_pos];
                predecessor[pos] = ladder_start_pos;
            }
        }

        least_throws[pos] = min_throws;
    }
    return least_throws[MAX_POSITIONS_ON_BOARD];
}
```

5. A thief wants to steal from houses that are arranged in a line. The thief knows the value of the valuables in each house. If the thief steals from one house, then the owner of the house will alert the immediate left and right neighbors and the thief can't steal from the immediately neighboring houses. What is the maximum loot that the thief can steal?

We use dynamic programming to solve this problem. Let value[i] store the net worth of valuables in the ith house. Let max_loot[i] store the sum of values of the houses that the thief has stolen up to the ith house. When a thief encounters a house, he has only two choices: either he can steal from the house or he can skip the house.

Then we can use the following formula to compute the max_loot for each house

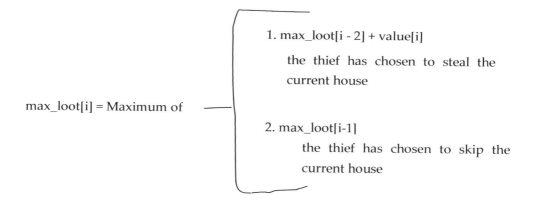

max_loot[i] = Maximum of

1. max_loot[i - 2] + value[i]

   the thief has chosen to steal the current house

2. max_loot[i-1]

   the thief has chosen to skip the current house

The max_loot of the last house gives the maximum loot that the thief can steal from all the houses.

It is not necessary to maintain a complete array for storing max_loot. The max_loot of the two previous houses is sufficient to calculate the max_loot of the current house.

```c
/*
house_value: value that the thief can steal from each house
n: number of houses
Return value: maximum loot value that the thief can steal from all the houses
*/
int find_max_loot(int house_value[], int n)
{
    int i;
    int cur_val, val1, val2;

    if (n == 0)
        return 0;

    if (n == 1)
        return house_value[0];

    if (n == 2)
        return max(house_value[0], house_value[1]);

    /*
    val1 has the max loot until the previous house,
    val2 has the max loot until the second previous house
    */
    val1 = max(house_value[0], house_value[1]);
    val2 = house_value[0];

    for (i = 2; i < n; ++i) {
        /*cur_val stores the maximum loot until the current house (ith house)*/
        cur_val = max(val2 + house_value[i], val1);

        /*val2 now takes the value of val1 and val1 takes the current value*/
        val2 = val1;
        val1 = cur_val;
    }

    return cur_val;
}
```

6. Given an array A, where A[i] indicates the maximum number of positions we can jump from location i, find the minimum number of jumps needed to reach the end of the array from the beginning of the array.

Let the given array be A = {3, 5, 2, 2, 1, 1, 0}. This means that from A[0], the maximum number of locations we can jump is 3. So in a single jump from A[0], we can choose to land at A[1] or A[2] or A[3]. The minimum number of jumps needed to reach the end of the array in this example is 2: We can jump from A[0] to A[1] and then jump from A[1] to A[6].

To solve the problem, we make use of dynamic programming. Let min_jumps[i] indicate the minimum number of jumps needed to reach location i. We calculate min_jumps[i] = Min { min_jumps[j] + 1} where j < i and j + A[j] >= i

So to figure out the minimum number of jumps to reach location i, we are looking at all the previous locations (j < i). We can jump from location j to location i only if j + A[j] is >= i. Since we start at the array beginning, min_jumps[0] = 0. min_jumps [last location in the array] gives the minimum number of jumps needed to reach the end of the array

```
/*a: a[i] contains the maximum number of locations we can jump from position i
n: number of elements in the array. Should be >= 1
Return value: minimum number of jumps needed to reach the end of the array*/
int find_min_jumps(int a[], int n)
{
    int i, j, result;
    int *min_jumps = (int *) calloc(n, sizeof(int));

    for (i = 1; i < n; ++i) {
        min_jumps[i] = MAX_INT;
        /*Compute the minimum number of jumps to reach location i by looking
        at the previous locations 0 to i - 1*/
        for (j = 0; j < i; ++j) {
                if (j + a[j] >= i && min_jumps[j] + 1 < min_jumps[i]) {
                        min_jumps[i] = min_jumps[j] + 1;
                }
        }
    }

    result = min_jumps[n-1];
    free(min_jumps);
    return result;
}
```

7.

If the number of nodes in a binary search tree (BST) is N, find the number of unique binary search trees that can be constructed with the N nodes.

If there is only one node in the BST, then only one unique BST can be constructed. If there are two nodes in the BST, then two unique BSTs can be constructed as shown below.

If there are more than 2 nodes in the BST, we make use of dynamic programming to solve the problem. Let num_bst[i] indicate the number of BSTs we can form with i nodes. num_bst[1] = 1 and num_bst[2] = 2. If there are N nodes, then one of the nodes will be the root. We can then distribute the remaining N-1 nodes between the left sub-tree and the right sub-tree. So we can have 0 nodes in the left sub-tree and N-1 nodes in the right sub-tree OR we can have 1 node in the left sub-tree and N-2 nodes in the right sub-tree ….. OR we can have N-1 nodes in the left sub-tree and 0 nodes in the right sub-tree. So if there are x nodes in the left sub-tree, there are N – 1 – x nodes in the right sub-tree.

Now note that left sub-tree of a binary search tree is also a binary search tree by itself. Similarly the right sub-tree of a binary search tree is also a binary search tree by itself. So if there are x nodes in the left sub-tree, num_bst[x] will give the number of ways we can arrange the x nodes in the left sub-tree and num_bst[N – 1 –x] will give the number of ways we can arrange the remaining N – 1 –x nodes in the right sub-tree. So the total number of ways we can arrange the nodes is num_bst[x] * num_bst[N – 1 – x].

If there are 0 nodes in the left sub-tree (x = 0), then remaining N-1 nodes will be in right sub-tree and the number of ways we can arrange the nodes = num_bst[N – 1]. So for the formula num_bst[x] * num_bst[N-1-x] to work for x = 0, we assume num_bst[0] = 1.

The formula for total number of BSTs is then given by

$$num\_bst[N] = \sum num\_bst[x] * num\_bst[N – 1 – x], \text{ where x can range from 0 to N-1}$$

Let us take an example. If N = 3, then

num_bst[3] = (num_bst[0] * num_bst[2]) + (num_bst[1] * num_bst[1]) + (num_bst[2] * num_bst[0])

num_bst[3] = (1 * 2) + (1 * 1) + (2 * 1) = 5

```
/*
n: total number of nodes in the binary search tree
Return value: Number of unique binary search trees that can be constructed with
n nodes
*/
int find_num_unique_bst(int n)
{
    int *num_bst;
    int i, left_sub_tree_size, right_sub_tree_size;
    int result;

    if (n <= 2)
        return n;

    num_bst = (int *) calloc(n+1, sizeof(int));

    num_bst[0] = 1;    /*We are making this 1 to simplify the calculation*/
    num_bst[1] = 1;
    num_bst[2] = 2;

    for (i = 3; i <= n; ++i) {
        /*the left sub-tree size can vary from 0 to i-1
        (one node has to be reserved for root)*/
        for (left_sub_tree_size = 0; left_sub_tree_size < i;
                    ++left_sub_tree_size) {
            /*Subtract the left subtree size and the root node to
            get right subtree size*/
            right_sub_tree_size = i - 1 - left_sub_tree_size;

            num_bst[i] += num_bst[left_sub_tree_size] *
                                num_bst[right_sub_tree_size];
        }
    }

    result = num_bst[n];
    free(num_bst);
    return result;
}
```

8. We are given a rod of length L and a price list p, where p[i] indicates the price of a piece of the rod of length i. The rod can be sold as a single piece or by cutting into multiple pieces. Find the maximum value that can be obtained for the rod.

Consider the following price list p for the rod of length 5.

Length	0	1	2	3	4	5
Price	0	3	8	5	6	7

The best value that we can get is by cutting the rod into three pieces of length 2, 2 and 1. The value will be 8 + 8 + 3 = 19.

We can solve this problem using dynamic programming. We will construct a best_value array and store in it the best value that we can get for each length. To compute the best_value for the current length, we will break the rod into two pieces. The length of the first piece is i and this piece will not be broken down further. The remainder piece will have a length of (current length – i) and can be sub-divided. So the value for i can range from 1 to current length.

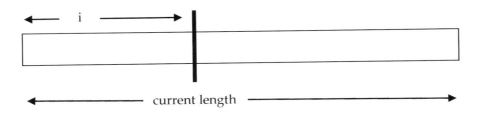

So best_value[current length] = max (price[i] + best_value[current length – i]) where i can range from 1 to current length.

If L is the total length of the rod, then best_value[L] will give the maximum value that we can obtain from the rod.

```
/*
price: price[i] gives the price of a rod of length i. price[0] is 0
max_length: the total length of the rod given to us. Should be >= 1
Return value: the best value that can be fetched from the rod
*/
int cut_rod(int price[], int max_length)
{
    /*Initialize best_value to 0*/
    int *best_value = (int*) calloc(max_length + 1, sizeof(int));

    /*first_cut[i] will indicate the length of the first piece when we cut
    the rod of length i. This is needed to print out where we should cut
    so that we get the best value*/
    int *first_cut = (int*) calloc(max_length + 1, sizeof(int));
    int i, cur_length, result;

    for (cur_length = 1; cur_length <= max_length; ++cur_length) {
        /*We are cutting a rod whose length is cur_length
        The length of the first piece after the cut can range from
        1 to cur_length*/
        for (i = 1; i <= cur_length; ++i) {
            if (price[i] + best_value[cur_length - i] >
                        best_value[cur_length]) {
                best_value[cur_length] = price[i] +
                                best_value[cur_length - i];
                first_cut[cur_length] = i;
            }
        }
    }

    print_pieces(first_cut, max_length);

    result = best_value[max_length];
    free(first_cut);
    free(best_value);

    return result;
}

/*Helper function for printing out the sizes of the individual pieces*/
void print_pieces(int first_cut[], int max_length)
{
    int cur_length;

    printf("The rod piece lengths are : ");

    cur_length = max_length;
    while (cur_length > 0 && first_cut[cur_length] > 0) {
        printf("%d ", first_cut[cur_length]);
        cur_length = cur_length - first_cut[cur_length];
    }

    printf("\n");
}
```

9.

Find the maximum sum sub-matrix in a 2D matrix. For instance, in the matrix

-10	20	30
-20	70	-10
10	-80	-60

the maximum
sum sub-matrix is

20	30
70	-10

and the maximum sum is $20 + 30 + 70 - 10 = 110$

The time complexity of the maximum sub-matrix sum problem can be reduced to $O(n^3)$ by using the Kadane algorithm which we have already described in page 249.

Kadane's algorithm gives the maximum continuous sum in a 1-D array in $O(n)$. To use Kadane's algorithm on a 2-D matrix, we sum up the elements in neighboring columns and store the result in a 1-D array. Kadane's algorithm is then applied on the 1-D array. Let us work out the procedure with an example.

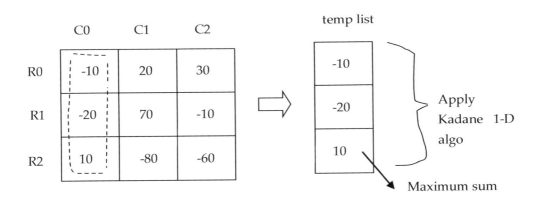

1. First we fix the start column to C0 and end column to C0. A 1-D temp array whose size is equal to the number of rows in the 2-D matrix is initialized to 0. The contents of column C0 are then added to the temp array and Kadane algorithm is applied on the 1-D temp array. In this example, we get the result from Kadane algorithm that 10 is the

maximum sum. This corresponds to row R2. Remember that our start column was C0, end column was C0. So the current maximum sum sub-matrix is the cell (R2, C0).

2. Then we keep start column at C0 and move end column to C1. The contents of column C1 are added to the temp array and Kadane algorithm is applied on the 1-D temp array. We get the result from Kadane algorithm that 60 (10 + 50) is the maximum sum. This corresponds to the rows R0, R1. The sum 60 is greater than the previous maximum of 10 and so 60 becomes the maximum submatrix sum and we update the current maximum sum sub-matrix to the region from cell (R0, C0) to the cell (R1, C1)

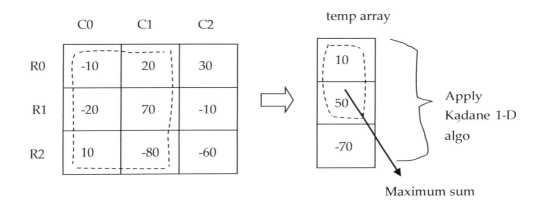

3. We then keep the start column at C0 and move the end column to C2 and add the contents of C2 to the temp array. Kadane algorithm is applied to the temp array and we update the maximum sum sub-matrix if we get a higher value

4. We then change the start column to C1. When we change the start column, we re-initialize the temp array to 0. The end column is fixed at C1 and the above procedure is applied. Then the end column is moved to C2 and the same procedure is repeated.

5. Finally we change the start column to C2, reinitialize the temp array to 0, fix the end column to C2 and repeat the procedure to get the final result.

The code for finding the maximum sum sub-matrix is given below. We are reusing the Kadane algorithm explained in page 249

```
/*
matrix: non-empty input matrix for which we have to find the maximum sum
n_rows: number of rows in the matrix
n_cols: number of columns in the matrix
Return value: the sum of elements in the max sum sub-matrix in the input matrix
*/
int find_max_sum_matrix(int matrix[][MAX_NUM_COLS], int n_rows, int n_cols)
{
    int left_col, right_col, i, cur_sum, max_sum, start, end;

    /*create a temporary 1-D array which stores the result of column additions*/
    int *a = (int*) malloc(n_rows * sizeof(int));

    max_sum = MIN_INT;
    for (left_col = 0; left_col < n_cols; ++left_col) {
        /*We have chosen a left column. Initialize the temp array to 0*/
        for (i = 0; i < n_rows; ++i)
                a[i] = 0;

        /*Iterate through the right side columns which are >= left column*/
        for (right_col = left_col; right_col < n_cols; ++right_col) {

                /*Add elements in the current right column to temp array*/
                for (i = 0; i < n_rows; ++i)
                        a[i] += matrix[i][right_col];

                /*Find the maximum continuous sum of the 1-D array using
                kadane algo. The start and end indices returned by kadane
                algo will correspond to the start row and end row of the
                2-D matrix*/
                cur_sum = kadane_mcs(a, n_rows, &start, &end);

                if (cur_sum > max_sum) {
                        max_sum = cur_sum;

                        /*The maximum sum sub-matrix is bounded between
                        col1 = left_col, col2 = right_col, row1 = start
                        row2 = end*/
                }
        }
    }

    free(a);

    return max_sum;
}
```

10. Given a 2-D matrix with m rows and n columns, find the minimum cost path to reach the destination cell (m-1, n-1) starting from the source cell (0, 0). From any cell, the allowed moves are: right, down and diagonal

Consider the matrix A shown below. The minimum cost path is 5 ->2 ->3->1. The cost of the path is 5 + 2 + 3 + 1 = 11.

To calculate the minimum cost path, we will use another 2-D matrix of the same dimensions called the cost matrix. The entries in the cost matrix are filled up in the following manner

1. cost[0][0] = A[0][0]

2. All cells in row 0 can be reached only by moving right from the starting cell (0, 0). So the cost reaching j^{th} cell in row 0 is cost[0][j] = cost[0][j-1] + A[0][j]

3. All cells in column 0 can be reached only by moving down from the starting cell (0, 0). So the cost of reaching the ith cell in column 0 is cost[i][0] = cost[i-1][0] + A[i][0]

4. The remaining cells can be reached by traversing down or right or diagonally from a preceding cell. So for the remaining cells, the minimum cost for reaching the cell is cost[i][j] = A[i][j] + min(cost[i-1][j], cost[i][j-1], cost[i-1][j-1])

	0	1	2
0	5	5+3 = 8	8+1 = 9
1	5 + 2 = 7		
2	7 + 9 = 16		

Cost matrix after computing
row 0 and column 0

	0	1	2
0	5	8	9
1	7	11	13
2	16	10	12

Final cost matrix

So in this example, cost[1][1] = 6 + min(5, 7, 8) = 6 + 5 = 11

If there are m rows and n columns, cost[m-1][n-1] will store the result. So in this example, cost[2][2] stores the cost of the minimum path which in this case is 12.

```
/*
a: non-empty 2-D matrix in which we have to find the minimum cost path
num_rows, num_cols: Number of rows and number of columns in the matrix
Return value: cost of the minimum path from (0, 0) to (num_rows-1, num_cols-1)
*/
int find_min_path(int a[][MAX_NUM_COLS], int num_rows, int num_cols) {
    int i, j;
    int cost[MAX_NUM_ROWS][MAX_NUM_COLS];

    cost[0][0] = a[0][0];

    for (i = 1; i < num_rows; ++i)
        cost[i][0] = cost[i-1][0] + a[i][0];

    for (j = 1; j < num_cols; ++j)
        cost[0][j] = cost[0][j-1] + a[0][j];

    for (i = 1; i < num_rows; ++i) {
        for (j = 1; j < num_cols; ++j) {
            cost[i][j] = a[i][j] +
                    min(cost[i-1][j], cost[i][j-1], cost[i-1][j-1]);
        }
    }

    return cost[num_rows - 1][num_cols - 1];
}
```

11. The strength of an egg can be found by dropping it from a floor in a building. For instance, if the egg doesn't break when dropped from floor 1, 2 and 3 but breaks when it is dropped from floor 4, then its strength is 3. Given N identical eggs and K floors in the building, find the minimum number of throws needed to find the strength of the egg.

We have to minimize the number of trials needed to find the strength of the egg. Let num_throws(N, K) represent the minimum number of throws needed to find the strength of the egg if we are given N eggs and K floors. Suppose we drop an egg from floor X, then there are two possibilities:

1. The egg breaks. In this case we are left with N-1 eggs and we have to find the strength of the egg in the X-1 floors. The number of throws needed will be 1 + num_throws(N-1, X-1). We have added 1 since we just used up 1 throw.

2. The egg doesn't break. In this case, we still have N eggs. We will have to try out the floors above floor X. There are K – X floors above floor X. The number of throws needed will be 1 + num_throws(N, K – X). We have added 1 since we just used up 1 throw.

We have to account for the worst case of the two possibilities since we don't know beforehand what we are going to encounter. So the number of throws needed from floor X is max(1 + num_throws (N-1, X-1), 1 + num_throws(N, K – X))

Now when we drop an egg, we have to intelligently pick which floor to drop from next. So given all K floors, each time we drop an egg, we need to pick the floor that needs the least number of throws. So

num_throws(N, K) = min (max(1 + num_throws (N-1, X-1), 1 + num_throws(N, K – X))
for all values of X from X = 1 to X = K)

To solve the problem, we make use of dynamic programming. If there is only 1 egg and there are K floors, then we need at least K throws to find the strength of the egg. If there are N eggs and only 1 floor, then we can perform only 1 throw. These details are filled up in the dynamic programming table below

floors

eggs \ floors	0	1	2	3	4	5
0						
1		1	2	3	4	5
2		1				
3		1				
4		1				

Minimum number of throws needed

The remaining cells are filled up using the formula

$$\text{num\_throws}(N, K) = \min (\ \max(1 + \text{num\_throws}\ (N\text{-}1, X\text{-}1),\ 1 + \text{num\_throws}(N, K - X)\ )$$
$$\text{for all values of } X \text{ from } X = 1 \text{ to } X = K)$$

At the end, the dynamic programming table will contain the result. Each cell in the table indicates the minimum number of throws needed for a particular number of eggs and a particular number of floors.

```
/*
num_eggs: total number of identical eggs available. should be >= 1
num_floors: total number of floors available. should be >= 1
Return value: minimum number of throws with which we can find egg strength
*/
int find_min_egg_drops(int num_eggs, int num_floors)
{
    int min_throws[MAX_NUM_EGGS+1][MAX_NUM_FLOORS+1];
    int cur_egg, cur_floor, floor_iter;


    /*If there is only 1 floor, we need only 1 throw*/
    for (cur_egg = 1; cur_egg <= num_eggs; ++cur_egg)
        min_throws[cur_egg][1] = 1;
```

```
/*If there is only 1 egg and k floors, we need k throws*/
for (cur_floor = 1; cur_floor <= num_floors; ++cur_floor)
    min_throws[1][cur_floor] = cur_floor;


for (cur_egg = 2; cur_egg <= num_eggs; ++cur_egg) {
    for (cur_floor = 2; cur_floor <= num_floors; ++cur_floor) {
            min_throws[cur_egg][cur_floor] = MAX_INT;

            for (floor_iter = 1; floor_iter <= cur_floor; ++floor_iter) {
                    /*Find the number of throws needed from floor_iter*/
                    int num_throws = max(
                            1 + min_throws[cur_egg - 1][floor_iter - 1],
                            1 + min_throws[cur_egg][cur_floor - floor_iter]);

                    if (min_throws[cur_egg][cur_floor] > num_throws)
                            min_throws[cur_egg][cur_floor] = num_throws;


            }
    }
}

return min_throws[num_eggs][num_floors];
}
```

12.

Given a dictionary of words, find if a string can be broken into the words in the dictionary. For instance, if the dictionary contains the words "play", "now", "will" and "i", then the string "nowiwillplay" can be broken into the words in the dictionary

To solve the problem, we make use of dynamic programming. We maintain an array is_break_possible. If the substring from position 0 to position i of the original string can be broken into words of the dictionary, then is_break_possible[i] will be set to true. Let the string be "nowiwillplay".

1. We will generate all the prefixes of the string namely "n", "no", "now", "nowi", "nowiw", "nowiwi", "nowiwil", "nowiwill", etc. and check if each prefix is present in the dictionary. If the prefix ending at position i is present in the dictionary, then is_break_possible[i] will be true. In this case, since "now" is present in the dictionary and the prefix "now" ends at position 2 in the original string, is_break_possible[2] will be true.

2. If is_break_possible[i] is true, we will check all the substrings that start from position i+1 if they are in the dictionary. If the substring starting at position i+1 and ending at position j is present in the dictionary, then we will make is_break_possible[j] true. Since is_break_possible[2] is true, we will check the substrings starting at position 3 of the original string, namely "i", "iw", "iwi", "iwil" and "iwill", etc. Only "i" is present in the dictionary. "i" ends at position 3 in the original string. So we will set is_break_possible[3] to true.

We apply steps 1 and 2 for the input string. At the end, if is_break_possible is set to true for the position of the last character in the input string, then we can say that the string can be broken into words in the dictionary. The position of the last character in the string "nowiwillplay" is 10. Since is_break_possible[10] is true, we conclude that it is possible to break the string into words in the dictionary.

Note that if the input word is "now", then the above algorithm will return true. If we want to return true only for the truly compound input words that can be broken into two or more dictionary words, then we add an additional check that the starting position of the word corresponding to the last character in the input string should not be 0. The code below returns true for words that can be broken into two or more dictionary words.

```
/*
str1: string that we need to check if it can be broken
dictionary: permitted words are stored in the dictionary
Return value: true if we can break str1 into words in the dictionary
*/
bool word_break(const string& str1, unordered_set<string>& dictionary)
{
    int i, j, substring_length;
    int length = str1.size();

    if (length == 0)
        return false;

    /*if we can break the string from 0 to pos, then is_break_possible[pos]
    will be true*/
    bool *is_break_possible = new bool[length];

    /*if the substring from position i to position j of the original string
    is a word in dictionary, then word_start[j] will be i*/
    int *word_start = new int[length];

    for (i = 0; i < length; ++i) {
        is_break_possible[i] = false;
        word_start[i] = -1;
    }

    for (i = 0; i < length; ++i) {
        /*Check if the substring from 0 to i is in the dictionary*/
        substring_length = i+1;
        if (!is_break_possible[i]
        && check_dictionary(str1.substr(0, substring_length),
                    dictionary)) {
            is_break_possible[i] = true;
            word_start[i] = 0;
        }


        /*If we can break the substring upto i into dictionary words,
        then check if all substrings starting from i+1 can be broken
        into dictionary words */
        if (is_break_possible[i]) {
            substring_length = 1;
            for (j = i + 1; j < length; ++j) {
                if (!is_break_possible[j]
                && check_dictionary(str1.substr(i+1,
                    substring_length), dictionary)) {
                    /*We can form a word from i+1 to j*/
                    is_break_possible[j] = true;
                    word_start[j] = i+1;
                }
                substring_length++;
            }
        }
    }
}
```

```
    /*
    If is_break_possible[length-1] is true, then entire string can be
    broken into dictionary words. If the word_start[length-1] is 0, then
    it means the entire input word is present in the dictionary. But we
    want a compound word that has 2 or more dictionary words in it.
    So modify the result condition to check word_start[length-1] != 0
    */
    bool result = is_break_possible[length-1] && word_start[length-1] != 0;

    if (result)
        print_result(str1, word_start);

    delete [] is_break_possible;
    delete [] word_start;

    return result;
}

/* Helper function to print the words present in the string
str1: input string
word_start: if the substring from position i to position j of the original
    string is a word in dictionary, then word_start[j] will be i
*/
void print_result(const string& str1, int word_start[])
{
    int pos = str1.size() - 1;
    while (pos >= 0) {
        /*The current word ends at pos in the input string and
        starts at word_start[pos] */
        int substring_length = pos - word_start[pos] + 1;
        cout << .str1.substr(word_start[pos], substring_length) << " ";
        pos = word_start[pos] - 1;
    }
}
```

13. Given a set of 3 dimensional boxes where length, breadth and height are specified, find the height of the tallest stack of boxes that can be constructed. Box B can be stacked on top of Box A only if the length **and** breadth of the base of Box B is **strictly smaller** than Box A. For each box, multiple instances of the box are available.

The length and breadth of the box will form the base of the box. Without loss of generality, we will pick the dimension with the greater value as length and the other dimension as breadth

Suppose we are given only one box A with the dimensions (10, 20, 30). Then there are 3 possible orientations of the box: A1 (height = 10, length = 30, breadth = 20), A2 (height = 20, length = 30, breadth = 10) and A3 (height = 30, length= 20, breadth = 10). Note that the problem states that multiple instances of the box are available. So we can pick all 3 possible orientations for the same box and check if one or more of them are feasible while constructing the stack of boxes. To construct the tallest stack, we place A1 at the bottom and then A3 on top of A1. Note that we can't place A2 on top of A1, since length of A2 (30) is not smaller than length of A1 (30). The height of the tallest stack = 10 + 30 = 40.

In general, given N boxes, to solve the problem we make use of dynamic programming.

1. For each box, generate all the 3 possible orientations and store them in an array. So if there are N boxes input, the array will store 3*N boxes. From now on we will be dealing with these 3*N boxes.

2. Sort the array so that boxes with larger base area are arranged earlier than those with smaller base area

3. Let best_height[i] be the height of the tallest stack built by placing box i on top of the stack. Initialize best_height[i] to the height of box i.

4. Use the formula below to update the best_height

best_height[i] = { Max(best_height[j] + height of box i} where j < i and length of box i < length of box j and breadth of box i < breadth of box j

So we are basically looking at boxes with larger area on top of whom box i can be placed

5. The maximum value in best_height array gives the height of the tallest stack of boxes.

```
/*
a: array of boxes of different dimensions. Should contain at least one box
num_input_boxes: number of boxes in the array. Should be >= 1
Result: maximum height of the stack of boxes that can be constructed.
Assumption is that multiple instances of each box are available
*/
int max_stack_height(struct Box a[], int num_input_boxes) {
    struct Box *boxes = (struct Box*) calloc(3 * num_input_boxes,
                                      sizeof(struct Box));
    int *best_height = (int *) calloc(3 * num_input_boxes, sizeof(int));
    int i, j, num_boxes, result;

    /*For each box, all 3 orientations are possible. Length will always be
    greater than breadth */
    for (i = 0; i < num_input_boxes; ++i) {
        boxes[3*i].height = a[i].height;
        boxes[3*i].length = max(a[i].length, a[i].breadth);
        boxes[3*i].breadth = min(a[i].length, a[i].breadth);

        boxes[3*i + 1].height  = a[i].length;
        boxes[3*i + 1].length  = max(a[i].breadth, a[i].height);
        boxes[3*i + 1].breadth = min(a[i].breadth, a[i].height);

        boxes[3*i + 2].height  = a[i].breadth;
        boxes[3*i + 2].length  = max(a[i].length, a[i].height);
        boxes[3*i + 2].breadth = min(a[i].length, a[i].height);
    }

    num_boxes = 3 * num_input_boxes;

    /*Sort the boxes so that the boxes with larger base area appear first*/
    sort(boxes, num_boxes);

    for (i = 0; i < num_boxes; ++i) {
        best_height[i] = boxes[i].height;
    }

    for (i = 1; i < num_boxes; ++i) {
        for (j = 0; j < i; ++j) {
            /*We can place box i on box j, only if base of box i
            is smaller than the base of box j*/
            if (boxes[i].length < boxes[j].length
            && boxes[i].breadth < boxes[j].breadth) {
                if (best_height[i] <
                best_height[j] + boxes[i].height) {
                    best_height[i] = best_height[j] +
                                          boxes[i].height;
                }
            }
        }
    }
}
```

```
    /*Find the stack with the maximum height*/
    result = best_height[0];
    for (i = 1; i < num_boxes; ++i) {
        if (best_height[i] > result)
                result = best_height[i];
    }

    free(best_height);
    free(boxes);

    return result;
}

void sort(struct Box a[], int num_elements)
{
    qsort(a, num_elements, sizeof(struct Box), cmp_function);
}

int cmp_function(const void *p1, const void *p2)
{
    struct Box *box1 = (struct Box *)p1;
    struct Box *box2 = (struct Box *)p2;

    /*Higher area boxes should be stored first after sorting*/
    return (box2->length * box2->breadth) - (box1->length * box1->breadth);
}
```

3.3 Miscellaneous Algorithms

1. There are n nuts and n bolts of distinct sizes in a box. For each bolt there is a matching nut and vice versa. We are allowed to compare only a nut with a bolt. Comparison of a nut with another nut or a bolt with another bolt is not allowed. Find the matching pairs of nuts and bolts.

If we are allowed to compare a nut with another nut or a bolt with another bolt, then we can solve the problem in O(nlogn) by sorting. We can sort all the nuts independently and all the bolts independently to find the matching pair of nuts and bolts. However direct comparison is not allowed.

In the brute force approach, we can pick a bolt and compare it with all the nuts until we find the matching nut and repeat this process for all the bolts. The time complexity will be O(n²).

There is a better approach that has an average time complexity of O(nlogn) similar to the quicksort algorithm. Let the bolts be stored in the array B and the nuts be stored in the array N. The procedure is as follows:

1.) Pick a bolt at random. This bolt acts as the pivot in quicksort. Compare the pivot bolt with each nut and partition the nuts into three groups: group N1 which has nuts smaller than the pivot bolt, group N2 which has the nut that exactly matches the pivot bolt and group N3 which has nuts that are larger than the pivot bolt.

2.) Pick the nut that exactly matched the pivot bolt. Now make this nut as the pivot nut. Compare the pivot nut with each bolt and partition the bolts into three groups: group B1 which has the bolts smaller than the pivot nut, group B2 which has the pivot bolt which matches the pivot nut and group B3 which has the bolts that are larger than the pivot nut.

3.) Recursively repeat steps 1 and 2 for the partitions N1 and B1. Then recursively repeat the steps 1 and 2 for the partitions N2 and B2.

At the end, we will have sorted the nuts and bolts without directly comparing a nut to a nut and a bolt to a bolt and we will know the matching pairs.

2. Place N queens on a chess board so that they can't attack each other

N queens on the chess board will be in non-attacking positions if:

1. Each row has only 1 queen.

2. Each column has only 1 queen

3. None of the queens are in the same diagonal.

To find the non-attacking positions of the queens, we make use of recursion and back-tracking. In each row, we place a queen in a cell which is not attacking with the other queens placed so far and then move to the next row. Suppose we can't place the queen in any of the cells in the current row, then we back-track to the previous row and pick the next possible cell for the queen in the previous row.

To keep the storage requirements small, we will maintain an array col_for_row that stores the positions of the queens. If we place a queen at cell (row = i, column = j), then col_for_row[i] = j.

Consider two cells (x1, y1) and (x2, y2). The two cells are in the same diagonal if the absolute difference between their rows is equal to the absolute difference between their columns. So if abs(x2 − x1) is equal to abs(y2 − y1), then the cells are diagonal.

```
/*
Helper function which checks if it is possible to place queen in cur_row
at position col_for_row[cur_row]
cur_row: Row in which the current queen should be placed
col_for_row: col_for_row[i] gives column in which queen of the ith row is placed
Return value: 1 if queen can be placed at col_for_row[cur_row], 0 otherwise
*/
int check_placement(int cur_row, int col_for_row[])
{
    int i, row_diff, col_diff;

    /*Check if the queens placed in the rows before the current row conflict
```

```
                    with the queen placed in current row*/
        for (i = 0; i < cur_row; ++i) {
            /*Check if two queens are present in the same column*/
            if (col_for_row[i] == col_for_row[cur_row])
                    return 0;

            /*Check if two queens are in the same diagonal*/
            col_diff = abs(col_for_row[cur_row] - col_for_row[i]);
            row_diff = cur_row - i;
            if (row_diff == col_diff)
                    return 0;

        }

        return 1;
}

/*
Main function for arranging the queens
cur_row: current row in which the queen should be placed
N: the number of cells in 1 row of the chess board
col_for_row: col_for_row[i] is used for storing the column of the ith row queen
*/
void arrange_queens(int cur_row, int N, int col_for_row[])
{
    int i;

    if (cur_row == N) {
        /*We have found a successful arrangement. So print it*/
        for (i = 0; i < N; ++i) {
                printf("(Row = %d, Col = %d) \n", i, col_for_row[i]);
        }
        printf("_____\n");

        return; /*Terminate the recursion*/
    }

    /*Try out different columns in the current row*/
    for (i = 0; i < N; ++i) {
        col_for_row[cur_row] = i;
        if (check_placement(cur_row, col_for_row)) {
                /*The placement of queens looks good so far.
                Go to the next row*/
                arrange_queens(cur_row + 1, N, col_for_row);
        }
    }

}
```

3. Given an equation in which only numbers are specified, fill in the operators + and – to get the required result. For instance, if equation without operators is 10 __ 20 __ 50 = 40, then we should fill in the operators as 10 – 20 + 50 = 40.

We use recursion and backtracking to solve the problem. The numbers of the equation will be stored in an array. We generate all possible combinations of operators between the numbers and check if we get the right hand side value of the equation.

```
/* Helper function that evaluates the numbers and operators
a: array of numbers
n: how many elements are present in array a. Should be >= 1
operators: array of operators (+, -) to be applied on numbers
*/
int evaluate(int a[], int n, char operators[])
{
    int i, result = a[0];

    for (i = 1; i < n; ++i) {
        if (operators[i-1] == '+')
                result += a[i];
        else
                result -= a[i];
    }

    return result;
}

/*
a: array of numbers
n: how many elements are present in array a. Should be >= 1
rhs: right hand side of the equation
operators: array for storing the operators to be applied on the numbers
num_operators: number of operators that have been filled so far
Return value: 1 if we can obtain the rhs by placing operators between numbers
*/
int fill_operators(int a[], int n, int rhs, char operators[], int num_operators)
{
    int is_possible, result;

    if (num_operators == n - 1) {
        /*We have filled in all the operators. So evaluate the result and
        terminate the recursion*/
        result = evaluate(a, n, operators);
        if (result == rhs)
                return 1;
        else
                return 0;
    }

    /*Fill in + as the next operator and try out*/
    operators[num_operators] = '+';
```

```
    is_possible = fill_operators(a, n, rhs, operators, num_operators + 1);
    if (is_possible)
        return 1;

    /*Fill in - as the next operator and try out*/
    operators[num_operators] = '-';
    is_possible = fill_operators(a, n, rhs, operators, num_operators + 1);

    return is_possible;
}
```

4. Implement a Sudoku solver

The Sudoku grid is a square of size 9 * 9. The rules of Sudoku are as follows:

1. Each cell contains a number from 1 to 9

2. A number should not be repeated in the same row or the same column

3. The grid is further sub-divided into squares of 3*3 called boxes. A number should also not be repeated in the same box.

In the Sudoku puzzle, the puzzle writer fills up some of the cells with numbers and we have to fill up the remaining cells. To solve Sudoku, we make use of recursion and back-tracking. Given a cell, we recursively try out all possible numbers that can be filled up in the cell. So we fill a cell with a possible number and then move to the next cell. Suppose we hit a dead-end at a cell and can't fill it with any number, then we back-track to the previous cell, try out the next possible number in the previous cell and proceed. To distinguish between the cells filled up by the puzzle writer and the other cells, we initialize the other cells with -1.

```
 /* Helper function which checks if it is possible to place a number in a cell
grid: the 2-D sudoku matrix
row_nr: row number of the cell we are checking
col_nr: column number of the cell we are checking
num: the number which we want to place in the cell
Returns: 1 if we can place num in the cell, 0 otherwise
*/
int can_fill_cell(int grid[][NUM_COLS], int row_nr, int col_nr, int num)
{
    int i, j;
    int region_start_row, region_start_col;

    /*Ensure that the number is not present in any row of requested column*/
    for (i = 0; i < NUM_ROWS; ++i)
       if (grid[i][col_nr] == num)
             return 0;

    /*Ensure that the number is not present in any column of requested row*/
    for (j = 0; j < NUM_COLS; ++j)
       if (grid[row_nr][j] == num)
             return 0;

    /*Ensure that the number is not present in the 3*3 box it belongs to*/
    region_start_row = (row_nr / 3) * 3;
    region_start_col = (col_nr / 3) * 3;
```

```
    for (i = region_start_row; i < region_start_row + 3; ++i)
        for (j = region_start_col; j < region_start_col + 3; ++j)
            if (grid[i][j] == num)
                    return 0;

    return 1;
}

/*Main function for solving the sudoku puzzle
grid: the 2-D sudoku matrix
row_nr: row number of the current cell being processed
col_nr: column number of the current cell being processed
*/
void solve_sudoku(int grid[][NUM_COLS], int row_nr, int col_nr)
{
    int next_row, next_col, num;

    if (row_nr >= NUM_ROWS) {
        /*We have found a solution. print the grid and
        terminate the recursion*/
        print_grid(grid, 1);
        return;
    }

    /*Pre-compute the row and column of the next cell*/
    next_row = row_nr;
    next_col = col_nr + 1;
    if (next_col >= NUM_COLS) {
        next_col = 0;
        next_row = row_nr + 1;
    }

    if (grid[row_nr][col_nr] == -1) {
        /*The puzzle writer has not assigned a number to this cell.
        So try assigning numbers 1-9 to the cell*/
        for (num = 1; num <= 9; ++num) {
                if (can_fill_cell(grid, row_nr, col_nr, num)) {
                        grid[row_nr][col_nr] = num;
                        solve_sudoku(grid, next_row, next_col);
                }
        }
        /*Once we are done trying all numbers from 1-9, assign the cell
        back to -1 to indicate puzzle writer has not assigned a number
        to the cell*/
        grid[row_nr][col_nr] = -1;

    } else {
        /*The puzzle writer has already assigned a value to the cell.
        So proceed to the next cell*/
        solve_sudoku(grid, next_row, next_col);
    }
}
```

5. Find the longest compound word in a given list of words. For instance, in the list {box, big, toybox, toy, bigbox, bigtoybox}, the longest compound word is bigtoybox

We have already solved the problem of breaking a compound word into simple words in page 273. To find the longest compound word, we again make use of this algorithm as described below:

1. Take each word in the list and add it into an unordered_set called dictionary. So the dictionary consists only of the words in the given list

2. Sort the words in the list in the descending (non-increasing) order of length so that longer words appear first.

3. Pick each word in the sorted list and check if the word can be broken into two or more simple words in the dictionary using the word_break algorithm in page 273. If yes, then we have found the longest compound word.

```
bool compare(string a, string b) {
        return (a.length() > b.length());/*Longer string should come first*/
}

/*words: the input list of words
Return value: pointer to the longest compound word if it exists, NULL otherwise
*/
string* find_longest_compound_word(vector<string>& words)
{
    unordered_set<string> dictionary;

    /*Store the input words in the dictionary*/
    auto it = words.begin();
    for (it = words.begin(); it != words.end(); ++it) {
        dictionary.emplace(*it);
    }
    /*Sort the words so that the longest word appears first*/
    sort(words.begin(), words.end(), compare);

    /*Starting from the longest word, check if the word can be broken
    into two or more words present in the dictionary. If yes, then we
    have found the longest compound word*/
    for (it = words.begin(); it != words.end(); ++it) {
        if (word_break(*it, dictionary))
                return &(*it);
    }
    /*There is no compound word in the input*/
    return NULL;
}
```

6. A person has travelled from city A to city B by transiting through one or more cities. Each ticket indicates the start city and the end city for each leg of the journey. However the tickets have been jumbled up. Reconstruct the travel path taken by the person using the jumbled tickets. There are no cycles in the path. For instance, if the tickets are [Tokyo -> Beijing], [LA -> San Francisco], [Hawaii -> Tokyo] and [San Francisco -> Hawaii], then the travel path is LA -> San Francisco -> Hawaii -> Tokyo -> Beijing.

To solve the problem, we need to do two things:

1. Given the current city, we quickly need to find the next city that the person is going to visit. For this purpose, we make use of a hash table called next_hop. The next_hop will store the current city as the key and the next city as the value. So if the person travels from Tokyo to Beijing, Tokyo will be the key and Beijing will be the corresponding value.

2. We need to find the starting city of the journey. For this, we make use of a set called destinations. If a person travels from city A to city B, then city B will be stored in destinations. To find the starting city, we check all cities in the destinations set and the city which is not present in it will be the starting city (since there are no cycles in the journey).

So using the destinations set, we find the starting city and then using the next hop hash table, we go on finding the next city of the journey and reconstruct the travel path of the person.

```
/*
tickets: 2-D array which stores the information about the tickets bought.
    ticket[i][0] stores the starting city of the ith ticket
    ticket[i][1] stores the destination city of the ith ticket
    There should be no loop in the trip
num_tickets: number of tickets. Should be >= 1
Return value: vector containing the names of cities in the order of travel
*/
vector<string>* reconstruct_trip(string tickets[][2], int num_tickets)
{
    unordered_map<string, string> next_hop;
    unordered_set<string> destinations;
    int i;

    /*Store the starting city (key) and destination city (value) in next_hop
    hash table. Store the destination cities in the destinations set*/
    for (i = 0; i < num_tickets; ++i) {
        next_hop.emplace(tickets[i][0], tickets[i][1]);
        destinations.emplace(tickets[i][1]);
```

```
    }

    /*Search the starting city of each ticket in the destinations set
    Only the first city of the entire trip will NOT be in destinations*/
    int start_index = -1;
    for (i = 0; i < num_tickets; ++i) {
        auto found = destinations.find(tickets[i][0]);
        if (found == destinations.end()) {
                /*We didn't find the city in the destinations set.
                So this must be the first city of the entire trip*/
                start_index = i;
                break;
        }
    }

    if (start_index == -1)
        return NULL;

    vector<string> *result = new vector<string>();

    /*push the first city of entire trip into the result*/
    result->push_back(tickets[start_index][0]);

    /*Search for the first city of the entire trip in the hash table*/
    auto it = next_hop.find(tickets[start_index][0]);

    while (it != next_hop.end()) {
        /*Store the destination city in the result*/
        result->push_back(it->second);

        /*make the destination city as the next starting city and
        search for it in the hash table*/
        it = next_hop.find(it->second);
    }

    return result;
}
```

7. A 2-dimensional matrix consists of 0's and 1's. An island is defined as a contiguous occurrence of 1's that are adjacent to each other. Find the number of islands in the matrix

If there are two adjacent cells (left-right neighbors, top-down neighbors, diagonally adjacent neighbors) with a value 1, then the two cells belong to the same island. In the matrix below there are 3 islands. The cells A0, B1, C0, D0 and E0 form one island. The cells A3, B3, C3 and B4 form one island. The cell E3 forms the remaining island.

	0	1	2	3	4
A	1	0	0	1	0
B	0	1	0	1	1
C	1	0	0	1	0
D	1	0	0	0	0
E	1	0	0	1	0

To find the number of islands, we make use of recursion. Once we find a cell whose value is 1, we start with the neighbors of this cell and recursively visit all cells that are reachable from this cell. To prevent from going into loops, we keep track if a cell has been visited or not and once a cell has been visited, we don't visit it again.

A similar problem is the flood fill problem. The color at each pixel of an image is stored in a 2 dimensional matrix. Given the starting pixel and the new color, we have to change the color of all adjacent pixels that have the same color as the starting pixel. So if the starting pixel A[2][3] is red and the new color is blue, then we have to recursively find all red cells that are reachable from A[2][3] and change their color to blue.

In some cases, diagonal neighbors may not be considered as adjacent. It is better to clarify this with the interviewer.

```
/*
Helper function that indicates if we can enter the cell or not
*/
int can_enter_cell(int matrix[][MAX_NUM_COLS], int is_visited[][MAX_NUM_COLS],
        int cur_row, int cur_col, int n_rows, int n_cols)
{
    /*If we are outside the bounds of the matrix or
    if the cell is already visited or if the value in cell is 0
    then we shouldn't enter the cell */
    if (cur_row < 0 || cur_row >= n_rows
        || cur_col < 0 || cur_col >= n_cols
        || is_visited[cur_row][cur_col]
        || matrix[cur_row][cur_col] == 0) {
        return 0;
    }

    return 1;
}


/* Helper function to count the number of islands of 1's
matrix: 2-D matrix consisting of 0's and 1's
is_visited: if cell (i, j) has been visited, is_visited[i][j] is set to 1
cur_row: row of the current cell being processed
cur_col: column of the current cell being processed
n_rows: number of rows in the matrix
n_cols: number of columns in the matrix
*/
void expand_search(int matrix[][MAX_NUM_COLS], int is_visited[][MAX_NUM_COLS],
    int cur_row, int cur_col, int n_rows, int n_cols)
{
    int i, j;

    is_visited[cur_row][cur_col] = 1;

    /*For the current cell, find out if we can continue the island of 1's
    with its neighbors. Each cell has 8 neighbors. The rows
    of neighbors will vary from cur_row - 1 to cur_row + 1
    The columns of the neighbors will vary from cur_col - 1
    to cur_col + 1*/
    for (i = -1; i <= 1; ++i) {
        for (j = -1; j <= 1; ++j) {
            int is_safe_cell = can_enter_cell(matrix, is_visited,
                            cur_row+i, cur_col+j, n_rows, n_cols);

            if (is_safe_cell) {
                expand_search(matrix, is_visited, cur_row+i,
                            cur_col+j, n_rows, n_cols);
            }
        }
    }
}
```

```
/* Main function to find the number of islands of 1's
matrix: 2-D matrix consisting of 0's and 1's. Should not be empty
n_rows: number of rows in the matrix. Should be >= 1
n_cols: number of columns in the matrix. Should be >= 1
*/
int find_islands(int matrix[][MAX_NUM_COLS], int n_rows, int n_cols)
{
    int is_visited[MAX_NUM_ROWS][MAX_NUM_COLS];
    int i, j, count;

    /*Initially all cells are not yet visited*/
    for (i = 0; i < n_rows; ++i)
        for (j = 0; j < n_cols; ++j)
                is_visited[i][j] = 0;

    /*Search all the cells in matrix that are not yet visited*/
    count = 0;
    for (i = 0; i < n_rows; ++i) {
        for (j = 0; j < n_cols; ++j) {
                if (matrix[i][j] && !is_visited[i][j]) {
                        /*We have found an island. Now expand the island
                        in all directions*/
                        expand_search(matrix, is_visited, i, j,
                                        n_rows, n_cols);
                        ++count;
                }
        }
    }
    return count;
}
```

8. Find the number of inversions in an array. If i < j and A[i] > A[j], then this constitutes an inversion.

We can use the brute force technique to find the number of inversions by comparing every pair of elements in the array. This can be done in $O(n^2)$. We can improve the time complexity to $O(nlogn)$ using the divide and conquer technique. We perform merge sort on the array and as we sort the array we calculate the number of inversions in it.

Let merge_sort(A, x, y) be the function that sorts the array A between index x and y and returns the number of inversions between indices x and y. Let merge(A, x, y, z) be the function that merges two sorted regions (x, y) and (y+1, z) in array A and returns the number of inversions between the two regions. Then we can recursively calculate the number of inversions between index low and index high as: number of inversions = merge_sort(A, low, mid) + merge_sort(A, mid+1, high) + merge(A, low, mid, high), where mid = (low + high) / 2

We need to now figure out how to calculate the number of inversions we encounter when we merge two sorted regions in the array. Let us say that we are merging region-1 (A[2] to A[5]) with region-2 (A[6] to A[7]). Index i is used to access region-1 and index j is used to access region-2.

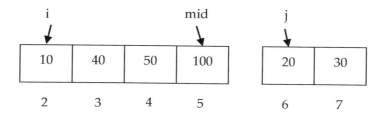

Initially i= 2 and j = 6. Since A[i] is smaller than A[j] and the two regions are sorted, we are sure that A[i] will be smaller than all elements after j in region-2. So we will not have any inversions in this case. We will then advance i to the next index

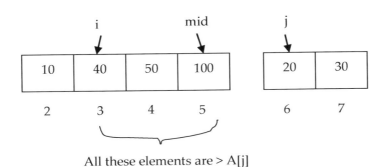

All these elements are > A[j]

Now i = 3 and j = 6. A[i] is greater than A[j]. Since region-1 is sorted, all elements in A from i onwards up to mid will be greater than A[j] and so these form inversions. The total number of elements from index i to index mid is mid + 1 − i. In this case mid = 5. So the total number of inversions = 5 + 1 − 3 = 3. The inversions are (40, 20), (50, 20) and (100, 20).

So while merging two sorted regions, each time we encounter an element at index i in the first region which is higher than the element at index j in the second region, we add mid + 1 − i to the number of inversions.

```
/*Helper function that merges two sorted regions
a: array where a[left] to a[mid] is sorted and a[mid+1] to a[right] is sorted
    We now need to merge these two regions
temp: temporary array used for sorting
Return value: Number of inversions
*/
int merge(int a[], int temp[], int left, int mid, int right)
{
    int i, j, k;
    int num_inversions = 0;

    i = left;
    j = mid + 1;
    k = left;

    while (i <= mid && j <= right) {
        if (a[i] <= a[j]) {
            temp[k++] = a[i++];
        } else {
            temp[k++] = a[j++];
            num_inversions += mid + 1 - i;
        }
    }

    /*Handle any pending entries in first region*/
    while (i <= mid)
        temp[k++] = a[i++];
```

```
        /*Handle any pending entries in second region*/
        while (j <= right)
            temp[k++] = a[j++];

        /*Restore the values from temp into a*/
        for (i = left; i <= right; ++i)
            a[i] = temp[i];

        return num_inversions;
}

/* Helper function that performs merge sort
a: array that should be sorted
temp: temporary array used for sorting
left: first index of the region in the array to be sorted
right: last index of the region in the array to be sorted
Return value: Number of inversions
*/
int merge_sort(int a[], int temp[], int left, int right)
{
    int num_inversions, mid;

    if (left >= right)
        return 0;

    mid = (left + right) / 2;

    num_inversions = merge_sort(a, temp, left, mid);

    num_inversions += merge_sort(a, temp, mid + 1, right);

    num_inversions += merge(a, temp, left, mid, right);

    return num_inversions;
}


/*
a: array of numbers
num_elements: number of elements in the array. Should be >= 1
Return value: number of inversions
*/
int find_inversions(int a[], int num_elements)
{
    int num_inversions;

    int *temp = (int*) calloc(num_elements, sizeof(int));

    num_inversions =  merge_sort(a, temp, 0, num_elements - 1);

    free(temp);

    return num_inversions;
}
```

9. Calculate the maximum amount of water that can be trapped in a histogram

Consider the histogram below. The water that can be stored in the histogram is shaded.

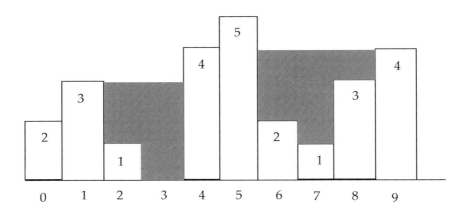

To efficiently find the amount of water that can be trapped in the histogram, we make use of the technique below and solve the problem in O(n).

1. We maintain two additional arrays: left_max and right_max

2. Traverse from the left of the histogram to the right and for each index i, store the height of the tallest bar encountered so far in left_max[i]. So left_max[i] will store the tallest bar in the region (0, i). Note that the height of the ith bar is also considered while computing left_max[i]

3. Traverse from the right of the histogram to the left and for each index i, store the height of the tallest bar encountered so far in right_max[i]. So right_max[i] will store the tallest bar in the region (i, n-1) where n is the total number of histogram bars. Note that the height of the ith bar is also considered while computing right_max[i]

The amount of water that can be stored above the ith bar in the histogram = min(left_max[i], right_max[i]) – height of the ith bar. The sum of the amount of water over each bar will give the total amount of water that can be trapped in the histogram

The table below gives the calculation for the amount of water that can be stored above each bar in the histogram

index i	left_max[i]	right_max[i]	min(left_max[i], right_max[i]	height of ith bar	Amount of water
0	2	5	2	2	$2-2=0$
1	3	5	3	3	$3-3=0$
2	3	5	3	1	$3-1=2$
3	3	5	3	0	$3-0=3$
4	4	5	4	4	$4-4=0$
5	5	5	5	5	$5-5=0$
6	5	4	4	2	$4-2=2$
7	5	4	4	1	$4-1=3$
8	5	4	4	3	$4-3=1$
9	5	4	4	4	$4-4=0$

The total amount of water that can be stored $= 2 + 3 + 2 + 3 + 1 = 11$

```
/*
histogram: histogram[i] contains the height of the bar at location i
n: number of bars in the histogram. Should be >= 1
Return value: amount of water that can be trapped by the histogram
*/
int water_trap(int histogram[], int n)
{
    int i, total_water, smaller_max;
    int *left_max = (int *) calloc(n, sizeof(int));
    int *right_max = (int *) calloc(n, sizeof(int));

    /*The left max of bar i is the height of the tallest bar in the
    region (0, i). Note that region (0, i) includes 0 and i*/
    left_max[0] = histogram[0];
    for (i = 1; i < n; ++i) {
        left_max[i] = max(left_max[i-1], histogram[i]);
    }

    /*The right max of bar i is the height of the tallest bar in the
    region (i, n-1). Note that region (i, n-1) includes i and n-1*/
    total_water = 0;
    right_max[n-1] = histogram[n-1];
    for (i = n - 2; i >= 0; --i) {
        /*Compute the right max and simultaneously calculate the
        amount of water that can be trapped*/
        right_max[i] = max(right_max[i+1], histogram[i]);

        smaller_max = min(left_max[i], right_max[i]);
```

```
        /*calculate the amount of water that can be stored
        on top of the histogram bar i*/
        total_water += smaller_max - histogram[i];
    }

    free(left_max);
    free(right_max);

    return total_water;
}
```

10. Calculate the area of the largest rectangle possible in a histogram

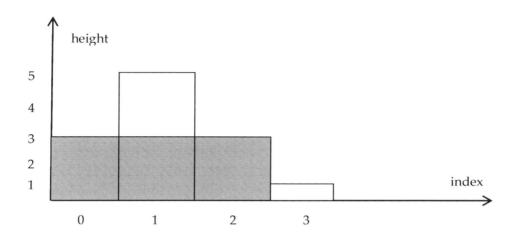

The largest possible rectangle in the histogram above has been shaded. The area of the largest rectangle is 9. To find the area of the largest rectangle in O(n) we make use of two stacks: one stack for storing the height of a histogram bar and another stack for storing the index of the histogram bar. We pick up each bar in the histogram and perform the following steps:

1. If the height of the current bar is > than the topmost element in the height stack, then push the height of the current bar into the height stack and push the index of the current bar into the index stack

2. If the height of the current bar is equal to the topmost element in the height stack, then do nothing

3. If the height of the current bar is < than the topmost element in the height stack, then keep popping the elements from the height stack and index stack until the height of the current bar becomes >= the topmost element in height stack. For each popped bar, compute the area of rectangle from the popped bar to the current bar. The length of the rectangle = (index of current bar – index of popped bar). The breadth of rectangle = height of the popped bar. Finally push the height of the current bar into the height stack and index of the last popped element into the index stack (not the index of the current bar). This is because all the popped bars are taller than the current bar and we can form a rectangle from current bar to the last popped element where the height of rectangle is

equal to the height of the current bar. For instance, for the histogram shown in the diagram, we perform the following steps

1. Push height and index of first bar

| 3 | height stack

| 0 | index stack

2. Height of 2nd bar (5) is > top of stack(3). So push height and index of 2nd bar

| 5 |
| 3 | height stack

| 1 |
| 0 | index stack

3. Height of 3rd bar (3) is < top of stack(5). So pop the height and index stack until top of stack is <= height of current bar. The height of the popped element (5) and the difference in index of popped element from current bar (2 − 1 = 1) is used to calculate the area of rectangle (**5 * 1 = 5**)

| 3 | height stack

| 0 | index stack

4. Height of 4th bar (1) is < top of stack(3). So pop the height and index stack until top of stack is <= height of current bar. The height of the popped element is 3. Current bar index - popped bar index = 3 − 0 = 3. So the area of rectangle (**3 * 3 = 9**). Then push the height of current bar (1) onto height stack and last popped index (0) onto the index stack

| 1 | height stack

| 0 | index stack

So area of rectangle is 9

At the end we have to empty out the contents of the stack. We have processed a total of 4 bars. The height in the height stack is 1. The numbers of bars processed – index in the index stack = 4 – 0 = 4. The area of the rectangle that can be formed = 4 * 1 = 4.

The area of the largest rectangle that can be formed = max (5, 9, 4) = 9.

```
/*histo_height: histo_height[i] has height of ith bar
n: number of bars in the histogram. Should be >= 1
Return value: returns the area of the largest rectangle in the histogram
*/
int find_max_area(int histo_height[], int n)
{
    int i, area, popped_index, popped_height, max_area = 0;
    stack<int> height_stack; /*used for storing the height of the bars*/
    stack<int> index_stack; /*used for storing the index of the bars*/

    for (i = 0; i < n; ++i) {
        if ( height_stack.empty() || histo_height[i] > height_stack.top() ) {
                /*push height and index of current bar*/
                height_stack.push(histo_height[i]);
                index_stack.push(i);

        } else if (histo_height[i] < height_stack.top()) {

                while (!height_stack.empty() &&
                histo_height[i] < height_stack.top()) {
                        /* keep popping from index and height stacks*/
                        popped_index = index_stack.top();
                        index_stack.pop();
                        popped_height = height_stack.top();
                        height_stack.pop();

                        /* calculate the area from popped bar to the
                        current bar.
                        Area = popped height * difference of index of
                        current bar and popped bar*/
                        area =  popped_height * (i - popped_index);

                        if (area > max_area)
                                max_area = area;
                }

                /*push height of the current bar into the height stack */
                height_stack.push(histo_height[i]);


                /*push the LAST POPPED INDEX into the index stack,
                since we can form a rectangle from the LAST POPPED INDEX
                to the current bar (where the height of the rectangle is
                height of current bar)*/
                index_stack.push(popped_index);
        }
    }
```

```
/*Process the remaining elements in the stacks*/
while (!height_stack.empty() ) {
    popped_index = index_stack.top();
    index_stack.pop();
    area = height_stack.top() * (n - popped_index);
    height_stack.pop();

    if (area > max_area)
            max_area = area;
}

return max_area;
}
```

11.

Evaluate a mathematical expression consisting of +, -, *, /, parenthesis and integers. For instance, when we evaluate (150 – 100) * 10 + 100 we should return the value 600.

To solve the problem, we make use of two stacks: an operator_stack for storing the operators +, -, *, /, (,) and a num_stack for storing the integers.

First we will define the compute operation as follows:

1. Pop the operator from the operator_stack

2. First pop the topmost element in num_stack into value2 and then pop the topmost element from the num_stack into value1

3. Apply the operator on value1 and value2. Then push the result onto the num_stack.

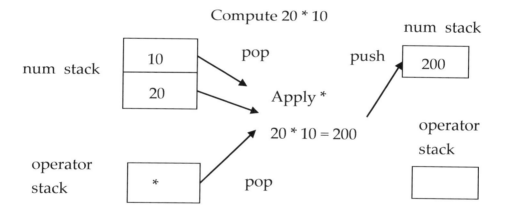

The mathematical expression will be stored in a string. To evaluate the expression, we parse the string and as we obtain tokens which may be operators or integers, we do the following:

1. If the current token is an integer, we push the integer onto the num_stack

2. If the current token is '(', then we push it onto the operator_stack

3. If the current token is ')', then we go on computing values using the num_stack and operator_stack until we get the '(' operator in the operator_stack. We then pop out '(' as we no longer need it.

4. If the current token is '+', '-', '*', '/', then as long as the operator on top of the operator_stack has a higher precedence than the current token, we go on computing values using the num_stack and operator_stack. Then we push the current token onto the operator_stack. The operators * and / have higher precedence than + and − as shown in the table below.

Operator	Precedence
*, /	2
+, -	1

5. After parsing the expression, if the operator_stack is not empty, then we go on computing values using the operator_stack and num_stack until the operator_stack becomes empty.

6. The top of the num_stack will contain the result.

```
/* Helper function that picks the operator from the top of operator stack
and applies them on the two values at the top of the num_stack. The result
will then be pushed back onto the num_stack */
void compute(stack<int>& num_stack, stack<char>& operator_stack) {
    int value1, value2;
    char c;

    c = operator_stack.top();
    operator_stack.pop();

    /*Since stack is LIFO we will first pop value2 and then pop value1 */
    value2 = num_stack.top();
    num_stack.pop();

    value1 = num_stack.top();
    num_stack.pop();

    if (c == '+')
        num_stack.push(value1 + value2);
    else if (c == '-')
        num_stack.push(value1 - value2);
    else if (c == '*')
        num_stack.push(value1 * value2);
    else if (c == '/')
        num_stack.push(value1 / value2);

}
/* Helper function to check priority of operators
stack_operator: operator that is at the top of the operator stack
exp_operator: operator that is currently being examined in the expression
Return value: true if the operator in the stack is higher priority than operator
being examined in the expression
```

```
*/
bool is_higher_precedence(char stack_operator, char exp_operator)
{
    if ((stack_operator == '*' || stack_operator == '/') &&
        (exp_operator == '+' || exp_operator == '-'))
        return true;

    return false;
}


/*
expression: string containing the expression to be evaluated
Return value: the integer result value obtained by evaluating the expression
*/
int evaluate_expression(const string& expression)
{
    stack<int> num_stack;
    stack<char> operator_stack;
    int i, cur_value;
    int length = expression.length();
    char temp_str[MAX_STR_LEN];

    i = 0;
    while (i < length) {
        /*Skip the white space characters*/
        if (expression[i] == ' ' || expression[i] == '\t'
        || expression[i] == '\n') {
                ++i;
                continue;
        }

        /*If we encounter an integer, then parse out the digits in it*/
        if (expression[i] >= '0' && expression[i] <= '9') {
                int pos = 0;
                while (i < length && expression[i] >= '0'
                && expression[i] <= '9') {
                        temp_str[pos++] = expression[i];
                        ++i;
                }
                temp_str[pos] = '\0';
                cur_value = atoi(temp_str);
                num_stack.push(cur_value);

        } else if (expression[i] == '(') {
                operator_stack.push(expression[i]);
                ++i;
```

```
        } else if (expression[i] == ')') {
                /*Until we encounter '(', process the two stacks*/
                while (operator_stack.top() != '(') {
                        compute(num_stack, operator_stack);
                }
                operator_stack.pop(); /*pop out '('*/
                ++i;
        } else if (expression[i] == '+' || expression[i] == '-' ||
                expression[i] == '*' || expression[i] == '/') {
                /*
                As long as the operator in the stack is of higher priority
                than the current token in expression, keep processing the
                two stacks
                */
                while (!operator_stack.empty()
                && is_higher_precedence(operator_stack.top(), expression[i])) {
                        compute(num_stack, operator_stack);
                }
                operator_stack.push(expression[i]);
                ++i;
        }

    }

    /*If there are still operators in the operator stack, then process them*/
    while (!operator_stack.empty())
        compute(num_stack, operator_stack);

    /*The result will be present at the top of the num_stack*/
    return num_stack.top();
}
```

12. Find the number of connected components in an undirected graph

In the graph below, there are two connected components in it. The nodes (0, 1, 2, 3) form one connected component and the nodes (4, 5, 6) form the other connected component.

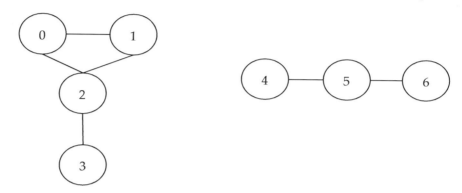

To simplify the implementation, the nodes in the graph will be represented by integers. For each node in the graph, we will keep a track of its neighboring nodes as shown in the table below:

Node	Adjacent nodes
0	1, 2
1	0, 2
2	0, 1, 3
3	2

To find the number of connected components, we will perform a depth first search on the graph as indicated below.

1. Initially all nodes will be marked as not visited.

2. Start with a node that has not been visited, and recursively traverse the node's neighbors and their neighbors and so on using depth first search. Once we traverse a node, it will be marked as visited. After we have finished traversing all nodes that are reachable from the starting node, we increment the number of connected components

3. Repeat step 2 until all the nodes in the graph have been visited.

```
/* Helper function that performs depth first search on the graph
cur_node: the node that we are searching
adjacency_table: an array of vectors. If there is an edge between node 0 and
        node 5, then adjacency_table[0] is a vector which will store 5 in it.
is_visited: this array indicates if a node has already been visited or not
num_nodes: total number of nodes in the graph
*/
void dfs(int cur_node, vector<int> adjacency_table[], bool is_visited[], int
num_nodes)
{
    unsigned int j;
    vector<int>& neighbors = adjacency_table[cur_node];

    is_visited[cur_node] = true;

    /*Go through all the neighbors of the current node*/
    for (j = 0; j < neighbors.size(); ++j) {
        int cur_neighbor = neighbors[j];

        /*If the current neighbor has not been visited, then recursively
        call dfs on it*/
        if (!is_visited[cur_neighbor])
                dfs(cur_neighbor, adjacency_table, is_visited, num_nodes);
    }
}

/*Main function to compute number of connected components in an undirected graph
adjacency_table: an array of vectors. If there is an edge between node 0 and
        node 5, then adjacency_table[0] is a vector which will store 5 in it.
num_nodes: total number of nodes in the graph
Return value: number of connected components in the graph
*/
int connected_components(vector<int> adjacency_table[], int num_nodes)
{
    bool *is_visited = new bool[num_nodes];
    int i, count;

    for (i = 0; i < num_nodes; ++i)
        is_visited[i] = false;

    /*Traverse through all the nodes in the graph and perform Depth First
    Search. Each time we perform DFS on a node that has not been visited
    so far, increment the number of connected components*/
    count = 0;
    for (i = 0; i < num_nodes; ++i) {
        if (!is_visited[i]) {
                dfs(i, adjacency_table, is_visited, num_nodes);
                ++count;
        }
    }

    delete [] is_visited;
    return count;
}
```

13. Find if a directed graph has a cycle

Suppose we are given an undirected graph and asked to find a cycle in it, then all we need to do is the following

1. Initialize all nodes in the graph as unvisited.

2. Pick a node that has not been visited and recursively traverse its neighbors and their neighbors and so on using depth first search. Once we traverse a node, we will mark it as visited.

3. Repeat step 2 until all the nodes in the graph are visited.

While traversing the graph, if we encounter a node that has already been visited, then there is a cycle in the undirected graph.

We can't apply the same procedure for a directed graph. Consider the diagram below:

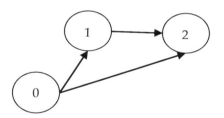

Suppose we start from node 0 and apply DFS. We first traverse the edge from node 0 to node 1. Then from node 1 we reach node 2. So nodes 0, 1 and 2 have been visited. Then we traverse the edge from 0 to 2. But node 2 has already been visited. Since we encounter a node that we have already visited, we conclude that there is a cycle in the directed graph. However this is incorrect since there is no directed cycle in this directed graph. If we had an edge from node 2 to node 0 instead of an edge from node 0 to node 2, then the graph has a directed cycle in it.

To overcome this problem, instead of just maintaining two states whether the node has been visited or not, we maintain 3 states that are identified using colors

- White: the node has not yet been processed
- Gray: the node is currently being processed. This means that the node's neighbors and their neighbors and so on are still being expanded
- Black: the node has been completely processed. This means that all the nodes that are reachable from this node have been traversed

During depth first search, if we encounter a node whose color is already gray, then it means that there is a cycle in the directed graph.

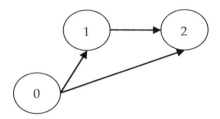

Using this approach, let us traverse the above directed graph. Initially all nodes are white. When we start with node 0, we change the color of 0 to gray. From 0 we move to 1. So node 1 now becomes gray. From 1 we reach 2. The color of 2 becomes gray. From 2 we try to traverse further. But there are no nodes reachable from 2. So we have finished processing node 2 and change its color to black. Then we check if we can reach another node from node 1. There are no new nodes that we can reach from node 1. So we change color of 1 to black and come back to node 0. From node 0 we can reach node 2. The color of node 2 is black. If color of 2 was still grey, then it means that there is a loop in the graph. In this case, since color of 2 is black, there is no loop in the graph.

To simplify the implementation, the nodes in the graph will be represented by integers. For each node in the graph, we will be storing its neighboring nodes as shown in the table below:

Node	Adjacent nodes
0	1, 2
1	2

```
/* Helper function that performs depth first search on the graph
cur_node: the current node that we are searching
adjacency_table: an array of vectors. If there is an edge from node 0 to
    node 5, then adjacency_table[0] is a vector which stores 5 in it
color: this array indicates the color assigned to the nodes
num_nodes: total number of nodes in the graph
Return value: true if cycle exists in directed graph, false otherwise
*/
bool dfs(int cur_node, vector<int> adjacency_table[], int color[], int
num_nodes)
{
    bool does_cycle_exist = false;
    unsigned int j;
    vector<int>& neighbors = adjacency_table[cur_node];

    /*Assign the gray color to the node indicating that we have
    started processing this node*/
    color[cur_node] = GRAY;

    for (j = 0; j < neighbors.size(); ++j) {
        int cur_neighbor = neighbors[j];

        /*If we find a neighboring node with the gray color, then we
        have found a loop*/
        if (color[cur_neighbor] == GRAY) {
                return true;
        }

        /*If the neighboring node has a white color, then perform
        DFS on it*/
        if (color[cur_neighbor] == WHITE) {
                does_cycle_exist = dfs(cur_neighbor, adjacency_table,
                                       color, num_nodes);
                if (does_cycle_exist)
                        return true;
        }
    }

    /*Assign the node the black color to indicate that we have finished
    processing it*/
    color[cur_node] = BLACK;
    return false;
}
```

```
/* Main function that checks if cycle is present or not
adjacency_table: an array of vectors. If there is an edge from node 0
    to node 5, then adjacency_table[0] is a vector which stores 5 in it
num_nodes: total number of nodes in the graph
Return value: true if cycle is present in directed graph, false otherwise
*/
bool is_cycle_present(vector<int> adjacency_table[], int num_nodes)
{
    int *color = new int[num_nodes];
    int i;
    bool does_cycle_exist = false;

    /*Assign the white color to all the nodes to indicate that we have
    not started processing the nodes*/
    for (i = 0; i < num_nodes; ++i)
        color[i] = WHITE;

    /*Go through all the nodes in the graph and perform DFS on the nodes
    whose color is white*/
    for (i = 0; i < num_nodes; ++i) {
        if (color[i] == WHITE) {
            does_cycle_exist = dfs(i, adjacency_table, color,
                                   num_nodes);
            if (does_cycle_exist)
                    break;
        }
    }

    delete [] color;
    return does_cycle_exist;
}
```

14. Given an alien dictionary comprising of a few **words** in sorted order, find out the sorted order of occurrence of **characters** in the alien language

Let the sorted words in the alien dictionary be "aba", "abb", "abd", "ac", "ad" and "pq". The first step is to compare adjacent words and look at the first mis-matching character. (Note that it is not necessary to compare all possible word pairs. Just comparing neighboring words is sufficient.). So when we compare "aba" and "abb", the two words mismatch at the last character. Add a directed edge in a graph from the mismatching character of the first word to the mismatching character of the second word. So we will add an edge from a to b. This procedure is shown below

Word 1	Word 2	First Mismatching char in word 1	First Mismatching char in word 2	Action
"aba"	"abb"	'a'	'b'	Add edge a -> b
"abb"	"abd"	'b'	'd'	Add edge b -> d
"abd"	"ac"	'b'	'c'	Add edge b -> c
"ac"	"ad"	'c'	'd'	Add edge c->d
"ad"	"pq"	'a'	'p'	Add edge a->p

The graph would look like this

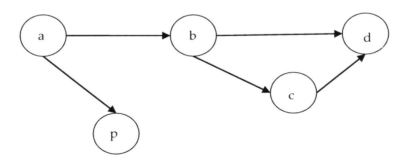

To represent the graph, we will use the adjacency information. So for each node, we will store the adjacent nodes as shown in the table

Node	Adjacent nodes
a	b, p
b	d, c
c	d

Then we perform topological sort on the graph with the help of a stack. In topological sorting, we first push all the adjacent nodes of the current node recursively onto the stack and then push the current node onto the stack. A node will be pushed onto the stack only once. So if we encounter the same node again while traversing the graph, we will not process it. Then at the end, when we pop out the contents of the stack, we will get the order of characters in the alien language. Note that topological sort is different from depth first search (in DFS, we first push the node to the stack and then push all its children to the stack recursively).

Let us say that, we start processing from node 'a'. Its adjacent nodes are 'b' and 'p'. Before placing 'b' on the stack, we first check its adjacent nodes 'd' and 'c'. 'd' has no adjacent nodes and so is pushed on to the stack. We then check the adjacent nodes of 'c'. Since 'd' is adjacent to 'c' and 'd' is already on the stack, we don't process 'd' again. Then we place 'c' on to the stack. Then we place 'b' onto the stack since all the nodes reachable from 'b' have been processed. Then we place 'p' on the stack. Finally we place 'a' on the stack. So the stack will look like this.

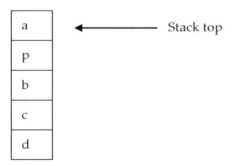

When we pop out the characters in the stack, we will get 'a', 'p', 'b', 'c', 'd'. This is the order of characters in the alien language. Note that 'p' comes ahead of 'b', 'c' and 'd'. From the words in the alien dictionary, we don't know the relationship between 'p' and 'b', 'c', 'd'. In such a case, topological sort will give us one possible order of characters that is consistent with the information available. Also note that although we started the topological sort with 'a', it is possible to start topological sort with any node in the graph.

```
/* Helper function for performing topological sorting
cur_char: current character that we are processing
adjacency_table: an array of vectors. if there is an edge from 'a' to 'b' then
adjacency_table['a'] contains a vector which will store b
is_visited: indicates if a character has already been visited or not
s: stack for storing the result of the topological sort
*/
void topological_sort_helper(char cur_char, vector<char> adjacency_table[],
             bool is_visited[], stack<char>& s) {
    unsigned int i;

    if (is_visited[(int)cur_char])
        return;

    /*make is_visited to true here so that we don't run into loops*/
    is_visited[(int)cur_char] = true;


    /*Process all the characters that are neighbors of the current
    character (ie  adjacent to current character) in the graph*/
    vector<char>& neighbor_list = adjacency_table[(int)cur_char];
    for (i = 0; i < neighbor_list.size(); ++i) {
        char neighbor_char = neighbor_list[i];

        if (!is_visited[(int)neighbor_char])
            topological_sort_helper(neighbor_char, adjacency_table,
                                    is_visited, s);

    }

    /*Push the current character onto the stack only after all the
    characters reachable from it have been recursively added to the stack*/
    s.push(cur_char);
}

/*Function that performs topological sorting
adjacency_table: an array of vectors. if there is an edge from 'a' to 'b' then
adjacency_table['a'] contains a vector which will store b
*/
void topological_sort(vector<char> adjacency_table[])
{
    bool is_visited[MAX_NUM_CHARACTERS];
    stack<char> s;
    int i;

    for (i = 0; i < MAX_NUM_CHARACTERS; ++i)
        is_visited[i] = false;

    /*Process all the characters*/
    for (i = 0; i < MAX_NUM_CHARACTERS; ++i) {
        if (adjacency_table[i].size())
            topological_sort_helper(i, adjacency_table, is_visited, s);
    }

    /*Pop out the contents of the stack to get the result of topological sort
```

```
    This is the order of characters in the alien language*/
    while (!s.empty()) {
        char cur_char = s.top();
        cout << cur_char << endl;
        s.pop();
    }

}


/*Main function to find the order of characters in an alien language
words: the words present in the dictionary
num_words: number of words in the dictionary
*/
void get_alphabet_order(const char *words[], int num_words)
{
    /*For each character in the language we maintain a vector*/
    vector<char> adjacency_table[MAX_NUM_CHARACTERS];
    int i;

    /*Go through the consecutive pairs of words in dictionary*/
    for (i = 0; i < num_words - 1; ++i) {
        const char *word1 = words[i];
        const char *word2 = words[i+1];
        int pos = 0;

        while (word1[pos] && word2[pos]) {
                /*Find first mismatching position between the two words*/
                if (word1[pos] != word2[pos]) {
                        char first = word1[pos];
                        char second = word2[pos];

                        /*In the graph, we have an edge from first char
                        to second char. Fetch the vector for first char
                        and store the second char in the vector, since
                        second character is adjacent to first char
                        */
                        adjacency_table[(int)first].push_back(second);
                        break;
                }
                pos++;
        }
    }

    /*Perform the topological sort*/
    topological_sort(adjacency_table);
}
```

314

15. Given a beginning word and an ending word, find out if there is a sequence of words in a dictionary using which we can transform the beginning word to the ending word by changing only one character at a time. For instance, we can transform the beginning word 'bell' to the ending word 'walk' using the following word sequence: bell -> ball -> tall -> talk -> walk

---

To solve the problem, we perform breadth first search. We make use of

- a queue for storing the words generated while performing the search,
- an unordered_set called visited which stores the words visited until now so that we don't go into loops while doing the search
- an unordered_map called reverse_path which stores the mapping from a word with its previous word. So if we generate the word ball from bell (bell -> ball), then we store ball as the key and bell as the value in the map (ball -> bell). This is needed to generate the word transformation sequence at the end

The procedure for solving the problem is:

1. Store the beginning word in the queue

2. Pick the current word from the front of the queue. If the current word is the same as the ending word, then we have found a successful word sequence to transform the words. Use the reverse_path to print out the word sequence.

If the current word at the front of the queue is not the same as the ending word, then generate all possible words that can be obtained by changing a single character in the current word. So if the current word is bell, we will generate *ell (from aell to zell), b*ll (from ball to bzll), be*l (from beal to bezl) and bel* (bela to belz). If the generated word is present in the dictionary and the generated word has not been visited so far, then add the generated word to the queue.

3. Repeat step 2, until we find the ending word or the queue becomes empty (in which case the word transformation is not possible)

```
/*
begin_word: starting word in the word transformation
end_word: ending word in the word transformation
dictionary: contains the permitted words that can be used in the transformation
Result: list that contains the sequence of words if word transformation is
    possible, NULL if word transformation is not possible
*/
list<string>* transform_word(string& begin_word, string& end_word,
              unordered_set<string>& dictionary)
{
    queue<string> q;
    unordered_set<string> visited;   /*words that have already been visited*/

    /*If we can transform word a to word b, then we store b -> a mapping
    in the reverse_path. b is the key and a is the value*/
    unordered_map<string, string> reverse_path;
    char char_array[MAX_WORD_LENGTH];
    unsigned int i;


    q.push(begin_word);
    visited.insert(begin_word);

    while (!q.empty()) {
        /*Get the word at the beginning of the queue*/
        string cur_word = q.front();
        q.pop();

        /*If the current word matches the ending word, we have found
        the word transformation. Store the sequence of transformation
        in the result list*/
        if (cur_word.compare(end_word) == 0) {
                list<string> *result = new list<string>();
                result->push_front(cur_word);

                /*Find previous word from where we reached the current
                word and add the previous word to the result list*/
                auto it = reverse_path.find(cur_word);
                while (it != reverse_path.end()) {
                        result->push_front(it->second);
                        it = reverse_path.find(it->second);
                }

                return result;
        }


        /*Look at all possible words that can be generated from the
        current word by changing a single character*/
        for (i = 0; i < cur_word.length(); ++i) {
                strcpy(char_array, cur_word.c_str());

                /*Generate new word by changing the character at
                position i*/
                for (char c = 'a'; c <= 'z'; ++c) {
```

```
                    char_array[i] = c;
                    string new_word = string(char_array);

                    auto it_in_dictionary = dictionary.find(new_word);
                    auto it_in_visited = visited.find(new_word);

                    /*If new word is present in dictionary and has not
                    been visited so far, then add it to the queue*/
                    if (it_in_dictionary != dictionary.end() &&
                            it_in_visited == visited.end() ) {
                        q.push(new_word);
                        visited.insert(new_word);

                        /*Store information that we reached
                        new_word from cur_word*/
                        reverse_path.emplace(new_word, cur_word);
                    }

                }
            }

        }

    return NULL; /*transformation is not possible*/
}
```

4. Math

In this section, we will cover math topics such as arithmetic, random numbers, probability and co-ordinate geometry.

A small note about random numbers: the best method to generate random numbers is to make use of a physical process that is random (it is difficult to say if a physical process is truly random!). Computers generate pseudo-random numbers. One of the techniques used is the Linear Congruential Generator where

$X_{n+1} = (AX_n + C) \bmod M$

where X_{n+1} is the $(n+1)^{th}$ random number and X_n is the nth random number.

A, C and M are constants whose values are pre-decided.

To obtain a good random number generator, C and M should be relatively prime. The seed specified during random number generation determines the value of X_0

1. Find the Greatest Common Divisor of two numbers

The Greatest Common Divisor (GCD) of two numbers a and b is the largest number that divides a and b without leaving a remainder. For instance, the GCD of 12 and 20 is 4. It is also called Greatest Common Factor, Highest Common Factor, etc. To find the GCD we use Euclid's algorithm which is as follows:

gcd(a, 0) = a

gcd(a, b) = gcd(b, a mod b)

So, suppose we have to calculate gcd(12, 20) then we get

gcd(12, 20) = gcd(20, 12 mod 20) = gcd(20, 12)

gcd(20, 12) = gcd(12, 20 mod 12) = gcd(12, 8)

gcd(12, 8) = gcd(8, 12 mod 8) = gcd(8, 4)

gcd(8, 4) = gcd(4, 8 mod 4) = gcd(4, 0) = 4

```
/*
a, b: Two integers. a may be greater than, equal to or less than b
Return value: Greatest common divisor
*/
int gcd(int a, int b)
{
    if (b == 0)
        return a;

    /*Find the GCD of b and the remainder of a/b*/
    return gcd(b, a%b);
}
```

Variation: We may be asked to find the Least Common Multiple (LCM) of a and b. For instance, LCM of (20, 12) = 60. In this case, we first find the GCD of a and b and use the formula LCM(a, b) = a * b / GCD(a, b). So LCM(20, 12) = 20 * 12 / 4 = 60

2. Swap two variables without using a temporary variable

There are two ways to solve this problem. The first uses XOR and the second uses addition and subtraction. The XOR technique can be used for swapping any two variables whereas the addition and subtraction technique can only be used for numbers. The two techniques are described below:

Steps for the XOR procedure	Example: let x initially have the value a and y have the value b
x = x ^ y;	x = x ^ y = a ^ b
y = x ^ y;	y = x ^ y = (a ^ b) ^ b = a
x = x ^ y;	x = x ^ y = (a ^ b) ^ a = b;
	So x has b and y has a at the end

Steps for the addition, subtraction procedure	let x initially have the value a and y have the value b
x = x + y;	x = x + y = a + b
y = x - y;	y = x - y = (a + b) - b = a
x = x - y;	x = x - y = (a + b) - a = b;
	So x has b and y has a at the end

3. An unsorted array contains all integers from 1 to N except one integer. All the elements in the array are unique. Find the missing integer in O(n) time and O(1) space. For instance in the array {5, 1, 3, 2}, the missing element is 4.

All integers from 1 to N are present in the array except one integer. To find the missing integer we do the following

1. Calculate the expected_sum of integers from 1 to N. We know that the sum of integers from 1 to N is given by the formula $N * (N+1) / 2$

2. Calculate the total_sum of the N-1 elements in the array.

3. The difference between expected_sum and the total_sum will give the missing element.

So if N = 5, and array is {5, 1, 3, 2}, then expected sum = $5 (5 + 1) / 2 = 15$. The total sum of elements in the array = $5 + 1 + 3 + 2 = 11$. So missing number = $15 - 11 = 4$.

```
/*
a: array of unique numbers. A number can have a value between 1 to n.
n: maximum value that can be stored in array. array has n-1 elements
Return value: missing element in the array
*/
int find_missing(int a[], int n)
{
    int i, total_sum, expected_sum;
    int missing_num;

    /*Since 1 element is missing, there are only n-1 elements in the array*/
    total_sum = 0;
    for (i = 0; i < n - 1; ++i) {
        total_sum += a[i];
    }

    expected_sum = n * (n+1) / 2;

    missing_num = expected_sum - total_sum;

    return missing_num;
}
```

4. An unsorted array contains all integers from 1 to N except two integers. All the elements in the array are unique. Find the missing integers in O(n) time and O(1) space. For instance in the array {5, 1, 3}, the missing elements are 2 and 4.

Since there are two missing numbers, we need two equations to solve the problem. Let the missing numbers be a and b.

1. Add up all the elements in the array and store the result in actual_normal_sum. Add up the squares of all elements in the array and store the result in actual_square_sum.

2. The sum of the first N numbers is given by the formula $N * (N+1) / 2$. Store this in expected_normal_sum.

actual_normal_sum + a + b = expected_normal_sum

So a+b = expected_normal_sum − actual_normal_sum

3. The sum of the squares of the first N numbers is given by the formula $N * (N+1) * (2N + 1) / 6$. Store this in expected_square_sum.

actual_square_sum + a^2 + b^2 = expected_square_sum

So a^2 + b^2 = expected_square_sum - actual_square_sum

4. Calculate 2ab using the formula $2ab = (a+b)^2 − (a^2 + b^2)$

We can calculate 2ab since we know a+b and $(a^2 + b^2)$

5. Calculate a-b. We know that $(a − b)^2 = a^2 + b^2 − 2ab$.

So $(a − b) = sqrt(a^2 + b^2 − 2ab)$

We know $(a^2 + b^2)$ and we know 2ab. So we can calculate a − b.

6. Now we have a + b and a − b.

So we can calculate a as a = ((a + b) + (a − b))/ 2

Using the value of a and (a+b), we can calculate b as b = (a + b) - a

```
/*
values: array of unique numbers. A number can have a value between 1 to n
n: maximum value in the array is n. array has n-2 elements
result: the missing elements in the array are returned here
*/
void find_missing(int values[], int n, int result[])
{
    int i, actual_normal_sum, expected_normal_sum;
    int actual_square_sum, expected_square_sum;
    int a_plus_b, a_minus_b, two_a_b, a_square_plus_b_square;
    int a, b;

    /*Since 2 elements are missing, there are only n-2 elements in array*/
    actual_normal_sum = 0;
    actual_square_sum = 0;
    for (i = 0; i < n - 2; ++i) {
        actual_normal_sum += values[i];
        actual_square_sum += values[i] * values[i];
    }

    expected_normal_sum = n * (n+1) / 2;
    expected_square_sum = n * (n+1) * (2*n + 1) / 6;

    a_plus_b = expected_normal_sum - actual_normal_sum;
    a_square_plus_b_square = (expected_square_sum - actual_square_sum);
    two_a_b =  ((a_plus_b * a_plus_b) - a_square_plus_b_square);
    a_minus_b = (int) sqrt(a_square_plus_b_square - two_a_b);

    a = (a_plus_b + a_minus_b) / 2;
    b = (a_plus_b - a);

    result[0] = a;
    result[1] = b;
}
```

5. Generate all the prime numbers that are less than or equal to N

To generate all prime numbers <= N, we make use of the sieve of Eratosthenes where we do the following

1. We generate the numbers from 2 to N and for each number X, we mark all multiples of X up to N to indicate that these multiples can't be primes

2. If a number is not a multiple of any of the numbers preceding it, then it is a prime

We skip 0 and 1 as they are not considered to be prime. 2 is the first prime number. Then all multiples of 2 up to N are marked to indicate that these multiples can't be primes. The next number is 3. Since 3 is not a multiple of any number before it (note that we have skipped 1 and so we ignore the fact that 3 is a multiple of 1), 3 is a prime. We then mark all multiples of 3. The next number is 4. Since 4 has been marked to be a multiple, it can't be prime. We then mark all the multiples of 4 and this process continues until N.

```c
/*sets the bit at position pos to 1 in the bitmap*/
void set_bit(unsigned char bitmap[], int pos)
{
    int byte_pos = pos / 8;
    int bit_pos = pos % 8;

    bitmap[byte_pos] |= 1u << bit_pos;
}

/*Returns the bit at position pos in the bitmap*/
int get_bit(unsigned char bitmap[], int pos)
{
    int byte_pos = pos / 8;
    int bit_pos = pos % 8;

    if (bitmap[byte_pos] & (1u << bit_pos) )
        return 1;
    else
        return 0;
}
```

```c
/*
n: Upto what number the primes should be generated
*/
void generate_primes(int n)
{
    int i, j;
    int total_num_bytes = 1 + (n / 8);

    /*is_multiple_bmp will be initialized with zeroes since we have not yet
    identified the multiples*/
    unsigned char *is_multiple_bmp = (unsigned char*) calloc(1,
                                                    total_num_bytes);

    /*We don't consider 0 and 1 as prime. Start from 2*/
    for (i = 2; i <= n; ++i) {
        if (get_bit(is_multiple_bmp, i))
                continue; /*i is a multiple, so it can't be prime*/

        printf("%d is prime\n", i);

        /*Mark all multiples of i (2i, 3i, 4i, etc) starting from 2*i */
        for (j = 2*i; j <= n; j += i) {
                set_bit(is_multiple_bmp, j);
        }
    }

    free(is_multiple_bmp);
}
```

6. Compute x^y efficiently

We can compute x^y by multiplying x for y times. This will require y multiplications. However there is a faster method to compute x^y. The procedure is as follows:

1. Initialize result to 1. Let the position of the most significant bit in y be z

2. Compute x to the power of powers of 2 until the 2^zth power. (x, x^2, x^4, x^8, x^{16}, etc.). This can be achieved by doubling the value of x every time.

3. If bit i is set in y, then multiply the 2^ith power of x with the result.

For instance, if we have to evaluate 3^{22}, we do the following

$$22 = 1\,0\,1\,1\,0 \text{ in binary}$$

$$3^{16} \quad 3^4 \quad 3^2 \qquad \text{Result} = 3^{16} \times 3^4 \times 3^2$$

So we need 3 multiplications to get the result. We have to also compute the powers of 3 which are 3^{16}, 3^8, 3^4, 3^2. So we need 4 multiplications. So the total number of multiplications needed to compute 3^{22} is 3+4 = 7 which is less than the 22 multiplications needed by the naïve solution. The source code is given below:

```
/*x, y: two integers, x > 0, y >= 0
Return value: x multiplied with itself y times*/
int power(int x, int y) {
    int result = 1;
    while (y) {
        /*look at the least significant bit of y*/
        if ((y & 1) == 1)
            result = result * x;
        y = y >> 1;/*shift out the least significant bit of y*/
        x = x * x;
    }
    return result;
}
```

7. Suppose you are given a random number generator that generates numbers uniformly in the range 1 to 5. How will you generate numbers uniformly in the range 1 to 7?

Let us say that we are provided with the rand5() function that generates values uniformly from 1 to 5. We can generate values uniformly from 0 to 4 by subtracting 1 from the result of rand5(). Now using rand5() we can uniformly generate numbers in the range 0 to 24 using the following formula

$$(rand5() - 1) + 5 * (rand5() - 1)$$

Now to generate numbers uniformly from 1 to 7, we use rejection sampling. If the above formula generates a random number in the range 0 to 20, we accept the number. If the formula generates a number in the range 21 to 24, then we reject the number and re-try the formula until we get a number in the range 0 to 20. We then find the remainder when the number in range 0 to 20 is divided with 7. The remainder will be uniformly distributed in the range 0 to 6. We then add 1 to the remainder to get the result which will be uniformly distributed in the range 1-7.

The rejection sampling in this case can be visualized with a 5 * 5 grid, wherein if we throw a dart and the dart randomly lands on a cell, the number in the grid is accepted for some cells and rejected for others.

	0	1	2	3	4
0	0	1	2	3	4
1	5	6	0	1	2
2	3	4	5	6	0
3	1	2	3	4	5
4	6	reject	reject	reject	reject

```
int rand7() {
    int result;
    while(1) {
        result = (rand5() - 1) + (5 * (rand5() - 1) );
        if (result <= 20)
                break;
    }
    result = 1 + (result % 7);
    return result;
}
```

8. Suppose you are given a random number generator that generates numbers uniformly in the range 1 to 7. How will you generate numbers uniformly in the range 1 to 5?

Let's say that rand7() generates values in the range 1 to 7. The instinctive answer to generate random values from 1 to 5 is $1 + ((rand7() - 1) \% 5)$. However this produces a wrong result.

rand7()	$1 + ((rand7() - 1) \% 5)$
1	1
2	2
3	3
4	4
5	5
6	1
7	2

As can be seen from the table, 1 and 2 are generated twice whereas 3, 4 and 5 are generated only once. So this can't be a uniform distribution. To get the correct result, we once again use rejection sampling. If rand7() produces a value greater than 5, we reject the sample and call rand7() again. The code is given below

```
int rand5()
{
    int result;

    while(1) {
        result = rand7();
        if (result <= 5)
            break;

    }

    return result;
}
```

9. How would you "perfectly" shuffle a deck of cards?

A deck of cards consists of 52 cards. There are 52! possible orderings of cards in the deck. When a perfect shuffle is done, there is an equal likelihood for one of the 52! possible orderings to occur. A simple approach to shuffle a deck of cards is to swap the ith card with a randomly chosen card. The code for this approach is

```
for (i = 0; i <= 51; ++i) {
    rand_num = get_random_number(0, 51);
    /* swap the ith card with a randomly chosen card */
    temp = cards[i];
    cards[i] = cards[rand_num];
    cards[rand_num] = temp;
}
```

While the above approach shuffles the cards, it does not produce a perfect shuffle. For a perfect shuffle, all cards should be shuffled equal number of times. However with the approach above, some cards are shuffled more times than others. To see this, consider a deck consisting of three cards A, B, C in that order.

In the first iteration we swap the first card with a random card (the random card position may be the same as the first card).

So [A, B, C] can give [A, B, C], [B, A, C] and [C, B, A]

In the second iteration, we swap the second card with a random card. So the set of states after the second iteration are

[A, B, C] can give [A, B, C], [B, A, C] and [A, C, B]

[B, A, C] can give [B, A, C], [A, B, C] and [B, C, A]

[C, B, A] can give [C, B, A], [B, C, A] and [C, A, B]

In the third iteration, we swap the third card with a random card. The set of states after the 3rd iteration are

[A, B, C] can give [A, B, C], [C, B, A] and [A, C, B]

[B, A, C] can give [B, A, C], [C, A, B] and [B, C, A]

[A, C, B] can give [A, C, B], [B, C, A] and [A, B, C]

[B, A, C] can give [B, A, C], [C, A, B] and [B, C, A]

[A, B, C] can give [A, B, C], [C, B, A] and [A, C, B]

[B, C, A] can give [B, C, A], [A, C, B] and [B, A, C]

[C, B, A] can give [C, B, A], [A, B, C] and [C, A, B]

[B, C, A] can give [B, C, A], [A, C, B] and [B, A, C]

[C, A, B] can give [C, A, B], [B, A, C] and [C, B, A]

We now count the number of outcomes for each ordering after the third iteration

[A, B, C] = 4. [A, C, B] = 5. [B, A, C] = 5. [B, C, A] = 5. [C, A, B] = 4. [C, B, A] = 4

So some outcomes are more likely than others. The problem becomes more severe when the deck contains more cards. To overcome this problem, Fish-Yates proposed a solution that was popularized by Knuth (sometimes the solution is also called Knuth shuffle). The idea used here is that in the first iteration, we pick a random card X out of 52 cards and swap it with the 51st card in the deck (last card in the deck, since the 0th card is the first card according to our convention). The card X continues to stay at the end of the deck and is not shuffled further. In the next iteration, we pick a random card Y out of 51 cards and swap it with the 50th card in the deck. The card Y continues to stay at its new position(50th position) and is not shuffled further. This process repeats. The code for this is given below

```
for (i = 51; i >= 0; --i) {
    rand_num = get_random_number(0, i);
    temp = cards[i];
    cards[i] = cards[rand_num];
    cards[rand_num] = temp;
}
```

Let the deck consist of 5 cards and the ordering of the cards be A, B, C, D, E. The table shows how the Knuth shuffle works

Iteration	Random number range	Chosen random number	Arrangement before swap	Arrangement after swap
1	0-4	2	A, B, **C**, D, **E**	A,B, **E**, D, **C**
2	0-3	0	**A**, B, E, **D**, C	**D**, B, E, **A**, C
3	0-2	1	D, **B**, **E**, A, C	D, **E**, **B**, A, C
4	0-1	0	**D**, **E**, B, A, C	**E**, **D**, B, A, C

10.

Given an array with n values, pick m (m < n) random values from it such that each element has an equal probability of being chosen

We could generate m random indexes from 0 to n-1 and pick the items at the random indices. The problem with this approach is that we may generate the same random index multiple times. But we want each element to have an equal probability of being chosen. So to solve the problem, we have to prevent choosing an already chosen element. We can do this as follows:

1. Initialize the last index that we can choose to n-1.

2. Pick a random position rand_index between 0 to last index and store the element at rand_index in the result. Then swap the element at rand_index with the element at last index. Then decrement the last index by 1. Repeat step 2 to get all the m values.

This way all the chosen values get moved to the end of the array and never get chosen again. Note that since we move elements around, the original array will get modified. To avoid this, we will create another copy of the array and work with the copy instead of the original.

```
/*Returns a random number between low and high, low and high are inclusive*/
int get_random_number(int low, int high)
{
    int random_num = low + rand() % (high - low + 1);
    return random_num;
}
```

```
/*
a: input array of unsorted numbers
n: number of elements in array a
k: number of random values to pick
result: the k random values will be stored in result
*/
void pick_random_values(int a[], int n, int k, int result[])
{
    int j, rand_index, last_index;

    /*We will need to rearrange the elements in array a. Since the user
    may expect array a to remain unchanged, we are allocating memory
    for another array b and copying elements of a into b*/
    int *b = (int*) calloc(n, sizeof(int));

    for (j = 0; j < n; ++j)
        b[j] = a[j];

    j = 0;
    last_index = n-1;
    while (j < k) {
        /*Pick a random position from 0 to last_index*/
        rand_index = get_random_number(0, last_index);

        /*Store b[rand_index] in the result*/
        result[j] = b[rand_index];

        /*Let's say original value at b[rand_index] is x.
        b[rand_index] is now overwritten with b[last_index].
        So we cannot choose x again in the next iterations*/
        b[rand_index] = b[last_index];

        --last_index;
        ++j;
    }

    free(b);
}
```

11. You are given an unfair coin where the probability of getting one outcome (say heads) is more than the other (tails). What strategy will you use to ensure that the outcome of the biased coin is fair?

Let the probability of turning up heads be p. Then probability of turning up tails is 1-p. A fair coin will have an equal likelihood of turning up heads and tails. So p = 1-p = 0.5. In a biased coin, the likelihood of turning up heads and tails is different. So p is not equal to 1-p. To make the biased coin fair, we will have to use the biased coin to produce two events that have an equal likelihood of occurrence. Let the biased coin be tossed twice. The probabilities of the resulting outcomes is given below

Outcome	Probability
(Heads, Heads)	p*p
(Heads, Tails)	p*(1-p)
(Tails, Heads)	(1-p)*p
(Tails, Tails)	(1-p)*(1-p)

We notice that the probability of (Heads, Tails) is equal to the probability of (Tails, Heads). So if we consider (Heads, Tails) as one event and (Tails, Heads) as the other event, then they will have an equal probability of occurrence. The events (Heads, Heads) and (Tails, Tails) can be ignored. So the strategy to use so that the biased coin becomes fair is to toss the biased coin twice and do the following:

1. If the coin shows up (Heads, Tails) or (Tails, Heads), then take the result into account. (Heads, Tails) will represent one event (say actual Heads) and (Tails, Heads) will represent the other event (say actual Tails).

2. If the coin shows up (Tails, Tails) or (Heads, Heads) then ignore it and retry.

```
/*Returns 0 with a probability of 0.5 and 1 with a probability of 0.5 */
int toss_fair_coin() {
    while (1) {
        int x = toss_unfair_coin();
        int y = toss_unfair_coin();
        if (x == 0 && y == 1)
                return 0;
        else if (x == 1 && y == 0)
                return 1;
    }
}
```

12. You are given a function that generates either 0 or 1 with an equal likelihood. Using this function, generate numbers that are uniformly distributed in the range (a, b)

The number of possible outcomes (num_outcomes) that we have to produce is $b - a + 1$. Our approach will be to first generate a random number in the range (0 to num_outcomes − 1) and then add a to the generated random number so that it lies in the range (a, b)

The given function generates 0 and 1 with equal probability. We can call the given function i times and get i random bits. We can then concatenate these i bits. The largest number that we can form by concatenating i bits is $2^i - 1$. So we can generate a uniform distribution from (0 to $2^i - 1$) by concatenating i random bits. To generate a uniform distribution from (0 to num_outcomes − 1), we do the following:

1. Find the closest i value so that $2^i >=$ num_outcomes. For instance, if num_outcomes is 10, then nearest i is 4 ($2^4 > 10$)

2. Construct the random number using i random bits. If the random number < num_outcomes, then accept the random number. If the random number >= num_outcomes then reject the random number and try again (rejection sampling)

Now that we have a random number in the range (0, num_outcomes − 1), we add a to it to get a random number in the range (a, b)

```
/*Returns number x where a <= x <= b and x is uniformly distributed*/
int get_random_num(int a, int b) {
    int i, rand_num;
    int num_outcomes = b - a + 1;

    while (1) {
        rand_num = 0;
        i = 0;
        while ( (1 << i) < num_outcomes) {
            /*Append the random binary digit to the end*/
            rand_num = (rand_num << 1) | binary_rand();
            ++i;
        }

        if (rand_num < num_outcomes)
            break;
        /*If rand_num >= num_outcomes, we try again*/
    }
    return rand_num + a;
}
```

13. Implement a function to calculate the square root of a number

One of the simplest techniques to calculate the square root of a number is to use binary search. Let us say that we have to find the square root of a positive number N, where N > 1. We know that the square root lies between 1 and N. We find the mid point M between 1 and N. We then compute M^2. If M^2 is greater than N, then we have to search for the square root in the region (1, M). If M^2 is less than N, then we have to search in the region (M, N). This process is repeated until we reach a mid point value with the required accuracy.

```
/*n: number >= 0 whose square root has to be computed
accuracy: how accurate should the result be
Return value: square root of n */
double compute_sqrt(int n, double accuracy)  {
    double low = 1.0, mid = 1.0, high = n * 1.0;
    double square, difference;

    if (n == 0)
        return 0.0;

    if (n == 1)
        return 1.0;

    while (low < high) {
        mid = (low + high) / 2;
        square = mid * mid;

        /*Find absolute difference between (mid * mid) and n*/
        difference =  square - n;
        if (difference < 0)
            difference = difference * -1;

        /*If the absolute difference is within the required accuracy
        then mid contains the square root. So break out of the loop*/
        if (difference < accuracy)
            break;

        if (square > n)
            high = mid;
        else
            low = mid;

    }
    return mid; /*Return the square root*/
}
```

14.

There is a staircase with N steps. A person can climb up either one step at a time or two steps at a time. Find out the number of ways the person can climb the staircase

Suppose there is only 1 step. The person can climb it only in 1 way.

Suppose there are 2 steps. There are 2 ways to climb them: the person either climbed to step 1 and then climbed to step 2 or he directly climbed to step 2.

Let us say that the number of steps is N. He can reach the Nth step either from step N-1 or from step N-2 only (since he can climb up only one or two steps at a time). So the number of ways he can reach step N = number of ways he can reach $(N - 1)^{th}$ step + number of ways he can reach step N-2.

Let climb_steps(N) represent the number of ways a person can reach step N, then, climb_steps(1) = 1, climb_steps(2) = 2 and

climb_steps(N) = climb_steps(N-1) + climb_steps(N-2) when N > 2

Note that this gives us a sequence similar to the Fibonacci sequence where the current value is the sum of the two previous values. In the Fibonacci sequence, the first two numbers of the series are 1, 1 whereas here the first two numbers are 1 and 2.

The recursive solution to solve the problem is given below

```
/*
n: number of steps. n >= 1
Returns: the number of ways to climb the steps using recursion
*/
int climb_steps_r(int n)
{
    if (n <= 2)
        return n;

    return climb_steps_r(n-1) + climb_steps_r(n-2);
}
```

The non-recursive solution to the problem is given below

```
/*
n: number of steps. n >= 1
Returns: the number of ways to climb the steps
*/
int climb_steps(int n)
{
    int i, x, y;

    /*Directly return the value for the first two fibonacci numbers*/
    if (n <= 2)
        return n;

    x = 1;
    y = 2;
    for (i = 3; i <=n; ++i) {
        int temp = x + y;
        x = y;
        y = temp;
    }

    return y;
}
```

15. Find if two lines intersect

It is easy to figure out if two lines intersect if we consider the two lines in the slope-intercept form (Every line can be written in the form y = mx+c where m is the slope and c is the y-intercept). Two lines intersect if they have different slopes. Two lines will not intersect if they have the same slope but different y-intercepts. One boundary condition is what happens if we are given the same two lines (where-in the slopes and y-intercepts of the two lines are equal). In this case, we will consider that the lines intersect each other

```c
/*
slope1: slope of the first line
c1: y-intercept of the first line
slope2: slope of the second line
c2: y-intercept of the second line
Return value: 1 if the lines intersect, 0 otherwise
*/
int do_lines_intersect(double slope1, double c1, double slope2, double c2)
{
    double epsilon = 0.0001;
    int intersect = 0;

    if (abs(slope1 - slope2) < epsilon) {
        /*Both lines have the same slope. Check the y-intercept*/
        if (abs(c1 - c2) < epsilon) {
            /*The y-intercepts are the same.
            So both lines are the same lines.
            We consider such lines to intersect with each other*/
            intersect = 1;
        } else {
            /*The lines are parallel and not coincident on each other
            So these lines will not intersect*/
            intersect = 0;
        }
    } else {
        /*The two lines have different slopes. They will intersect*/
        intersect = 1;
    }

    return intersect;
}
```

16. Find out if two rectangles overlap

It is easier to check if two rectangles don't overlap. Let each rectangle be specified by two points – its upper left corner (we will call this point left) and its lower right corner (we will call this point right). Each point has an x co-ordinate and a y co-ordinate.

Two rectangles will not overlap if any one of the two conditions below is satisfied:

- one of the rectangles lies completely to the right or left of the other

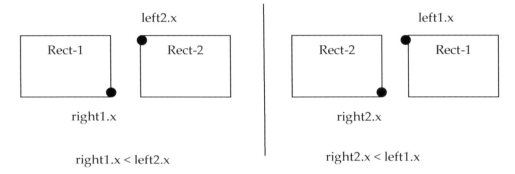

- one of the rectangles lies completely above or below the other

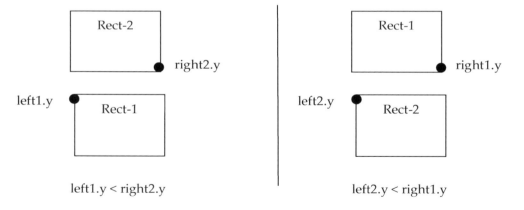

The code for checking if two rectangles overlap or not is given below

```
/*
left1: upper left corner of rectangle 1
right1: lower right corner of rectangle 1
left2: upper left corner of rectangle 2
right2: lower right corner of rectangle 2
Return value: 1 if the rectangles overlap, 0 otherwise
*/
int do_rectangles_overlap(struct point left1, struct point right1,
             struct point left2, struct point right2)
{
    /*one rectangle lies completely to the right or left of the other*/
    if (right1.x < left2.x || right2.x < left1.x)
        return 0;

    /*one rectangle lies completely above or below the other*/
    if (left1.y < right2.y || left2.y < right1.y)
        return 0;

    /*the rectangles overlap*/
    return 1;
}
```

17. Find the area of overlap between two rectangles

First we find if the rectangles overlap or not. If the rectangles don't overlap, then the area of overlap is 0. If the rectangles overlap, then the overlapping region will also be a rectangle. In this case, we find the co-ordinates of the upper left corner of the overlap and the lower right corner of the overlap. Using these two corners, we find the length and breadth of the rectangular overlap and then compute area of overlap = length * breadth.

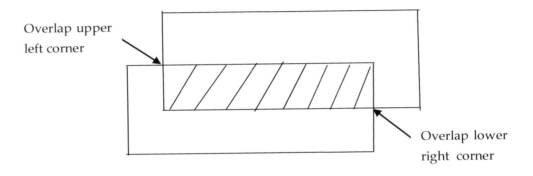

Overlap upper left corner

Overlap lower right corner

The code to find the area of overlap is given below:

```
/*
left1: upper left corner of rectangle 1
right1: lower right corner of rectangle 1
left2: upper left corner of rectangle 2
right2: lower right corner of rectangle 2
Return value: area of overlap of the two rectangles
*/
int find_overlap_area(struct point left1, struct point right1,
              struct point left2, struct point right2)
{
    struct point result_left, result_right;
    int area;

    /*one rectangle lies completely to the right or left of the other*/
    if (right1.x < left2.x || right2.x < left1.x)
        return 0;

    /*one rectangle lies completely above or below the other*/
    if (left1.y < right2.y || left2.y < right1.y)
        return 0;
```

```
    /*the rectangles overlap*/
    result_left.x = max(left1.x, left2.x);
    result_left.y = min(left1.y, left2.y);
    result_right.x = min(right1.x, right2.x);
    result_right.y = max(right1.y, right2.y);

    area = (result_right.x - result_left.x)
            * (result_left.y - result_right.y);

    return area;
}
```

18. How can you encode all possible orderings of a deck of cards using only 32 bytes (256 bits)?

A deck of cards has 52 cards. Each card has one of 4 possible symbols (diamond, clubs, heart, spades) and one of 13 possible values (Ace, 2, 3, 4, 5, 6, 7, 8, 9, 10, King, Queen, Jack). We can encode the 4 symbols using 2 bits and encode the 13 values using 4 bits. So each card needs 2+4 = 6 bits. To encode an ordering of 52 cards we need 52 * 6 = 312 bits. However we are provided only 256 bits.

To achieve this we use the following approach. As before we initially assign a 6 bit code for each card. We pick the first 20 cards in the deck and encode each card with 6 bits. So we need 20 * 6 = 120 bits. Next we are left with 32 cards remaining in the deck. Since we have already observed the first 20 cards which can no longer occur in the remaining deck, 5 bits is sufficient to encode the 32 cards in the remaining deck. So we assign a new 5 bit code for the remaining 32 cards and use 5 bits to encode the next 16 cards. We need 16 * 5 = 80 bits. Now we are left with 16 cards in the deck for which 4 bits are sufficient. We can encode the next 8 cards using 4 bits. We need 8 * 4 = 32 bits. Now we are left with 8 cards for which 3 bits are sufficient. We encode the next 4 cards with 3 bits. We need 4*3 = 12 bits. Now we are left with 4 cards for which 2 bits are sufficient. We encode the next 2 cards with 2 bits. We need 2*2 = 4 bits. Now we are left with 2 cards for which 1 bit is sufficient. We encode the next card with 1 bit. We need 1*1 = 1 bit. We are left with the last card. Since we know all the other 51 cards in the deck, we can automatically determine the last card and we don't need to encode this card.

So the total number of bits required = 120 + 80 + 32 + 12 + 4 + 1 = 249 bits which solves the problem.

19. Three ants are initially located at the 3 corners of an equilateral triangle. Each ant picks a direction randomly and begins to move along the edges of the triangle. All the ants move with the same speed. What is the probability that two or more ants collide with each other?

It is easier to first find out the probability that the ants don't collide with each other and then use this information to find the probability that any two ants collide.

Each ant can pick either the clock-wise direction or the anti-clock wise direction to move along the edges of the triangle. Since the ant picks the direction randomly, the probability that an ant moves in the clockwise direction is 0.5 and the probability that it moves in the anti-clockwise direction is 0.5.

The ants will not collide if all the ants decide to move in the clockwise direction or if all the ants move in the anti-clockwise direction.

The probability that all the 3 ants move in clockwise direction = 0.5 * 0.5 * 0.5 = 0.125

The probability that all the 3 ants move in anti-clockwise direction = 0.5 * 0.5 * 0.5 = 0.125

So probability that all ants move in either clockwise or anti-clockwise direction = 0.125 + 0.125 = 0.25

So the probability that no ant collides with any other ant is 0.25

The probability that two or more ants collide with each other = 1 − 0.25 = 0.75

20. If a stick breaks randomly into three pieces, what is the probability that you can form a triangle from the pieces?

To form a triangle, the sum of any two sides should be greater than the other side.

Let the length of the stick be L. Let the stick be broken at the points X and Y. Let the 3 pieces be a, b and c.

If the cuts are formed on the same half of the stick, then one side will always be larger than the sum of the other two sides as shown in Scenario-1 and Scenario-2 below.

Scenario-1: the two cuts are present in the left half of the stick

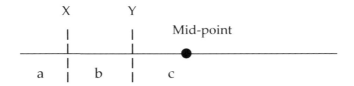

Since c > 0.5L and (a+b) < 0.5L, c > (a+b) and we can't form a triangle. The likelihood of forming the cut X on the left half of the stick = 0.5. Similarly the likelihood of forming the cut Y on the left half of stick = 0.5. So the likelihood of forming cut X and Y on the left half of the stick = 0.5 * 0.5 = 0.25

Scenario-2: the two cuts are present in the right half of the stick

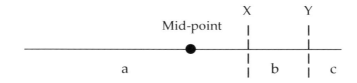

Since a > 0.5L and (b+c) < 0.5L, a > (b+c) and we can't form a triangle.

Similarly the likelihood of forming cut X and Y on the right half of the stick as shown in the diagram above = 0.5 * 0.5 = 0.25

So the two cuts have to be on different halves of the stick to form a triangle.

If the cuts are formed on different halves of the stick, then if cut X is formed in the first quarter of the stick and Y is formed in the last quarter of the stick, then again we can't form a triangle as shown in the diagram.

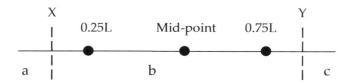

a < 0.25L, c < 0.25L. So b > 0.5L. Since b > (a+c) we can't form the triangle. The likelihood of cut X in the first quarter of the stick = 0.25. The likelihood of cut Y in the last quarter of the stick = 0.25. The likelihood of cut X in the first quarter and cut Y in the last quarter = 0.25 * 0.25 = 0.125

Similarly if cut X is formed in the last quarter and cut Y is formed in the first quarter as shown in the diagram, we can't form the triangle.

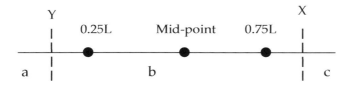

The likelihood of cut X in the last quarter and cut Y in the first quarter = 0.25 * 0.25 = 0.125

So the total likelihood that we can't form a triangle = 0.25 + 0.25 + 0.125 + 0.125 = 0.75

The likelihood that we can form a triangle = 1 - 0.75 = 0.25

5. Design

Data hiding

The data members of a class are made private and not exposed to the client. This prevents the client from trying to use the data members directly. So even if the data members change in the future, the client code will be unaffected.

Encapsulation

Encapsulation restricts the access to the members of an object. It includes data hiding and other types of hiding like an abstract class hiding the derived classes.

Abstraction

Abstraction is an idea or concept that is not associated with any particular implementation.

Interfaces

Interfaces describe the capabilities of a class without indicating how the capabilities are implemented.

Polymorphism

Polymorphism means a particular entity has several different forms. In programming languages, polymorphism indicates the same entity behaving in different ways. Some of the types of polymorphisms are

- ✓ ad-hoc polymorphism: function overloading and operator overloading are examples of ad-hoc polymorphism
- ✓ parametric polymorphism: templates are examples of parametric polymorphism
- ✓ subtype polymorphism: a base class pointer can be used to call a derived class function depending on the type of the derived class object pointed by the base class pointer

<u>Relation between classes</u>

The diagram below shows the classification of the relations between classes

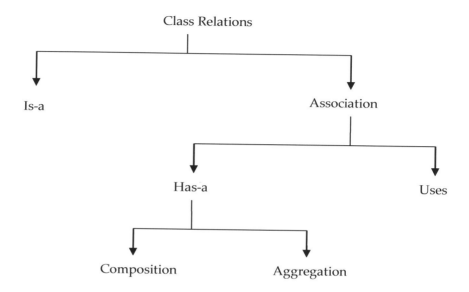

The relation between classes are broadly classified into two types:

- ✓ "Is-a": One class "is-a" kind of another class. For instance, parrot "is-a" bird. Inheritance can be used in this case.
- ✓ Association

Association has two further subtypes

- ✓ "Has-a" association: One class contains another class
- ✓ "uses" association: One class uses another class. For instance the class Car uses the class GasStation

"Has-a" has two further sub-types

- ✓ Composition – The contained class is an integral part of the containing class. For instance, tire is an integral part of a car. So a car is composed of a tire
- ✓ Aggregation – The contained class and container class can exist independently. For instance, class Car and class Passenger can exist independently. So the class Car aggregates class Passenger

Prefer Composition to inheritance

Composition is preferred to inheritance in many cases. Inheritance should be used only where there is a genuine "is-a" relationship. Let us say that the fly function is common to the class Airplane and the class Bird. The class Airplane has already implemented the fly function and the Bird class is now being developed. To reuse the fly functionality of the Airplane class, if we try to inherit the Bird class from the Airplane class it will result in a bad design because Bird is not an Airplane. A better design would be to have a separate class implement the fly functionality and let the Airplane and Bird classes contain this class that implements the fly functionality

UML Diagrams

Consider the C++ class

```
class A
{
    public:
        int x;
        int f1();
    protected:
        int y;
        int f2();
    private:
        int z;
        int f3();
};
```

In the UML diagram as shown below, the name of the class is first mentioned, followed by the data members followed by the function members. The public members are represented with + symbol, the protected members with # symbol and the private members with – symbol.

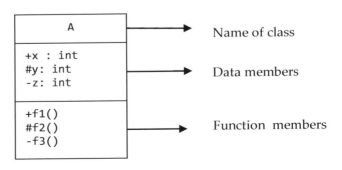

The UML diagram for class Parrot "is-a" class Bird is given below

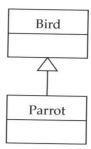

The UML diagram for class Car "has-a" class Tire (composition) is given below

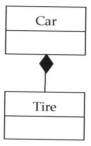

The UML diagram for class Car aggregates class Passenger (aggregation) is given below

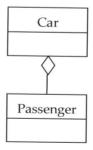

The UML diagram for class Car uses class Gas Station is given below

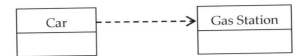

1. Design a book library

When interviewers ask a design problem, they may be interested in the class diagram or the code or both. It is good to ask the interviewers what they are interested in and proceed along those lines. For this design problem, we will give the class diagram. For the remaining design problems we will give the code. A possible design of a book library is shown below:

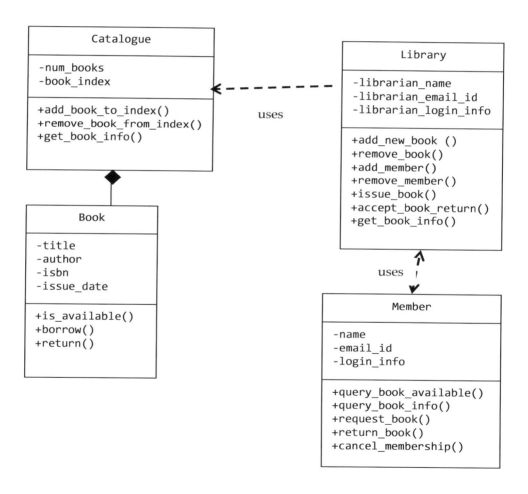

2. Design a parking lot

A parking lot consists of two main classes: the Vehicle class and the ParkingLot class.

Vehicle class is the abstract base class consisting of pure virtual functions. Different types of vehicles such as Car, Truck, MotorBike etc. will be derived from the Vehicle class and implement the pure virtual functions.

The Slot class maintains the information about every parking slot such as the location of the slot, the vehicle currently present in the slot, etc. The ParkingLot class is a composition of many objects of the Slot class.

```
class Vehicle
{
    private:
    VehicleId m_id;
    VehicleType m_type;
    Size m_size;

    public:

    Vehicle(VehicleId& id, VehicleType& type, Size& size) { }
    ~Vehicle() { }

    virtual VehicleId getVehicleRegistrationId() = 0;
    virtual VehicleType getVehicleType() = 0;
    virtual Size getVehicleSize() = 0;
    virtual bool doesVehicleFit(Size& parkingSlotSize) = 0;
};


class Car: Vehicle
{
    /*
    Car is derived from Vehicle class and implements the pure virtual
    functions of the Vehicle class
    */
};
```

```
class Slot
{
    int unique_slot_num;
    Location location;
    Vehicle *v;
    Time startTime;
};

class ParkingLot
{
    public:

    Slot* assignSlot(Vehicle *v) {
        /*Assigns a parking slot to the vehicle*/
    }

    Slot* reserveSlot(Time& from, Time& to, Vehicle *v) {
        /*Reserves a parking slot to the vehicle for the time specified*/
    }

    double computeParkingFare(Slot *s) {
        /*Computes the parking fare for a particular parking slot*/
    }

    int vacateSlot(Slot *s) {
        /*Vehicle has vacated the slot. So the slot will be freed up*/
    }

    Location getLocation(Slot *s) {
        /*Returns the physical location of the parking slot*/
    }

    int getNumFreeSlots() {
        /*Returns the number of free parking slots available right now*/
    }

    bool isFull() {
        /*Indicates whether parking lot is full or not*/
    }
};
```

3. Design an elevator

Each elevator maintains its current state. The state information includes the current floor in which the elevator is present, whether the door is open or shut, etc. The design for an elevator class is shown below:

```
class Elevator {
    private:
    int numFloors;
    int floorHeight;
    State currentState;

    public:
    Elevator(int numFloors, int floorHeight) {
        /*Initializes the elevator indicating how many floors
        are in the building and the height of each floor*/
    }
    ~Elevator() { }

    Button& getUserInput() {
        /*Returns the data about the button the user has pressed*/
    }

    bool isWeightSafe() {
        /*Indicates if weight of all passengers in lift is within
        the safe limits or not*/
    }

    int closeDoor() {
        /*closes the doors of the lift*/
    }

    int openDoor() {
        /*Opens the door of the lift*/
    }

    int goToFloor(int floorNumber) {
        /*Performs actions needed to go to the floor the user has requested*/
    }
    int powerFailure() {
        /*Performs the actions needed during a power failure*/
    }
    int emergencyProcedure() {
        /*Performs the actions needed during an emergency*/
    }
    State getState() {
        /*Returns the current state of the lift*/
    }
};
```

4. Design a hotel reservation system

A hotel reservation system consists of two main classes: the Room class and the BookingSystem class.

Room class is the abstract base class consisting of pure virtual functions. Different types of rooms such as Normal-Room, Queen-Room, Deluxe-Room etc. will derive from the Room class and implement the pure virtual functions.

The BookingSystem class is a composition of many objects of the Room class.

```
class Room {
    private:
    int roomId;
    RoomType type;
    Size size;
    int roomNumber;
    int numBeds;

    Room() { }

    ~Room() { }

    /*Reserves a room for a particular customer for the indicated duration*/
    virtual int reserveRoom(Time& from, Time& to, Customer *c) = 0;

    /*Frees up a room and makes it available for being booked*/
    virtual int freeRoom() = 0;

    /*Checks if a particular room is occupied or free*/
    virtual bool isOccupied() = 0;
};


class NormalRoom: Room
{
    /*
    NormalRoom is derived from Room class and implements the pure virtual
    functions of the Room class
    */
};
```

```
class BookingSystem {

    BookingSystem() { }

    ~BookingSystem() { }

    int checkAvailability(RoomType& type, Time& from, Time& to) {
        /*Checks if a room of the required type is available*/
    }

    Reservation* bookRoom(RoomType& type, Time& from, Time& to, Customer *c) {
        /*Reserves a room of required type and returns the reservation*/
    }

    int cancelRoom(Reservation *reservation) {
        /*Cancels a reservation*/
    }

    int checkOut(Room *room) {
        /*Performs the actions during checkout (such as calculating the bill)
        and then frees up the room*/
    }

    double getRunningBillAmount(Room *room) {
        /*Returns the current bill amount for the room*/
    }
};
```

5. Design a chess game

The chess game can be implemented using the ChessPiece class and the Chess class. ChessPiece is the abstract base class consisting of pure virtual functions. Each type of chess piece such as the King, Queen, Pawn, etc. will derive from the ChessPiece class and implement the virtual functions. The Chess class is a composition of the chess pieces. The main function of the Chess class is to move a chess piece from one location of the board to another.

```
class ChessPiece
{
    bool isWhite;
    bool isActive;
    Position currentPosition;
    ChessPieceType type;

    public:
    /*Checks if the piece can be moved to position p*/
    virtual bool validateMove(Position *p) = 0;

    /*Moves the piece to the position p*/
    virtual int move(Position *p) = 0;
};


class King: public ChessPiece
{
    /*
    King is derived from ChessPiece class and implements the pure virtual
    functions of the ChessPiece class
    */
};


class Chess {

    private:
    ChessPiece * grid[8][8]; /*8 * 8 grid for storing the chess pieces*/

    public:
    Chess() {
        //Create all the pieces at their initial position
    }

    ~Chess() {
    }
```

```
    int move(ChessPiece *piece1, Position *pos1, ChessPiece *piece2 = NULL,
            Position *pos2 = NULL) {
        //Moves a chess piece to a particular position. If we castle the
        //king, we will have to move two pieces in a single move. So we
        //have another set of arguments whose default value is NULL
    }

    bool isCheckMate() {
    }

};
```

6. Design a vending machine

The main classes in a vending machine are the Item class and the VendingMachine class. The Item class is used for representing the items dispensed by the vending machine. Item class is an abstract base class with pure virtual functions. Derived classes such as Beverage class or Candy class will implement the pure virtual functions of the Item class. The VendingMachine class is a composition of Items. A vending-code is associated with each item and corresponds to the buttons that the user has to press on the vending machine to get the item.

```
class Item {
    private:
    int productId;
    int vendingCode;
    double price;
    int quantity;

    public:
    Item() { }
    ~Item() { }

    virtual void setPrice(double newPrice) = 0;
    virtual void setQuantity(int newQuantity) = 0;

    virtual double getPrice() = 0;
    virtual int getQuantity() = 0;

};

class Beverage: public Item
{
    /*
    Beverage is derived from Item class and implements the pure virtual
    functions of the Item class
    */
};
```

```
class VendingMachine
{
    private:
    vector<Item*> items;

    public:
    VendingMachine() { }

    ~VendingMachine() { }


    int addNewItem(Item *item) {
        /*Adds a new item to the vending machine*/
    }


    int loadMachine(Item *item, int count) {
        /*Loads a certain number of units of the item into the
        vending machine*/
    }


    int updatePrice(Item *item, int newPrice) {
        /*Updates the price of the item*/
    }

    int setVendingCode(Item *item, int vendingCode) {
        /*Changes the vending code for an item*/
    }


    int getCount(int vendingCode) {
        /*Gets the number of units available for the item given the
        vending code*/
    }

    int getPrice(int vendingCode) {
        /*Gets the price of the item given the vending code*/
    }

    int purchase(int vendingCode) {
        /*Performs the actions when user presses the button to purchase
        an item*/
    }

    int removeItem(Item *item) {
        /*Removes an item from the vending machine*/
    }

};
```

7. Implement a singleton class

A singleton class is a class where at most only one object of the class can exist at a given time. To achieve this, we maintain a static member pointer (m_instance in the code below) to the instance of the class. The constructor is made private. The user can get the pointer to the instance using a static function called getInstance()

When the user calls getInstance(), if m_instance is NULL, then the object is created using the private constructor. Then the pointer to the created object is stored in m_instance and the pointer is returned to the user. If m_instance is not NULL when the user calls getInstance(), then m_instance is returned back to the user.

```
class Singleton
{
    public:

    //Function for getting the pointer to the single instance
    static Singleton* getInstance();

    //Function for freeing the single instance
    static void freeInstance();

    private:

    //Private constructor
    Singleton(int size);

    //Private assignment operator
    Singleton& operator = (Singleton&);

    //Private destructor
    ~Singleton();

    //Pointer to the single instance of Singleton.
    //The pointer is declared static
    static Singleton *m_instance;

    //Data members in Singleton
    char *buf;
};
```

```
Singleton::Singleton(int size)
{
    buf = new char[size];
}

Singleton::~Singleton()
{
    delete [] buf;
}

Singleton* Singleton::getInstance()
{
    //If the instance hasn't been created, then create it
    if (!m_instance)
        m_instance = new Singleton(MAX_BUF_SIZE);

    return m_instance;
}

void Singleton::freeInstance()
{
    if (m_instance)
        delete m_instance;
}

//Initialize the static member of Singleton
Singleton* Singleton::m_instance = NULL;
```

8. Implement a factory class

Sometimes the creation of the object should be hidden from the user. In such a case, we use a factory class. The user calls a function of the factory class to create the object. This function will in turn call the constructor of the object and create the object.

In the example below, the user should not know how the Circle/Square object is created. The Factory class provides the getShape method to the user to create the Circle/Square and hides how the objects are created from the user.

```
class Shape {
    public:
    virtual void draw() = 0;

};

class Circle: public Shape {
    public:
    void draw() {
        cout << "Drawing Circle" << endl;
    }
};

class Square: public Shape {
    public:
    void draw() {
        cout << "Drawing Square" << endl;
    }
};

class Factory {
    public:
    Shape * getShape(string str1) {
        if (str1.compare("Circle") == 0) {
                return new Circle();
        } else if (str1.compare("Square") == 0) {
                return new Square();
        }
        return NULL;
    }
};
```

9. Implement an adapter design pattern

Sometimes the user wants to use a class but the interface of the class is incompatible with what the user expects. The adapter design pattern converts the interface of a class so that the interface becomes compatible with the client. For instance, the client wants to use the Celsius class which reports the temperature in Celsius but the client expects the temperature to be reported in Fahrenheit. In this case, we use the adapter design pattern. The Fahrenheit class gets the temperature from the Celsius class, converts it to Fahrenheit and gives back the temperature in Fahrenheit to the user.

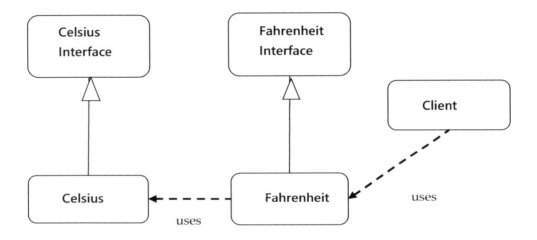

```
class  CelsiusInterface {

    public:
    virtual  double  getCelsius()  =  0;

};

class Celsius: public CelsiusInterface
{
    private:
    double  temperature;

    public:

    Celsius()  {temperature  =  10;  }
```

```
      double getCelsius() {
          return temperature;
      }
};


class FahrenheitInterface
{
    public:
    virtual double getFahrenheit() = 0;
};


class Fahrenheit : public FahrenheitInterface
{
    private:
    Celsius *celsiusObj;

    public:
    Fahrenheit() {
        celsiusObj = new Celsius();
    }

    double getFahrenheit() {
        double temperature = celsiusObj->getCelsius();
        temperature = (temperature * 9 / 5) + 32;
        return temperature;
    }
};
```

10. Implement the decorator design pattern

Decorator pattern is used when we need to modify the behavior of a particular object of a class without affecting the behavior of the other objects of the class.

For instance, let's say that we are in a donut shop where simple donuts are made by default. We can translate this into OOP by having an interface called Donut and the SimpleDonut class that implements the Donut interface. Now let's say that one of the customers in the shop wants to have a chocolate spread on a simple donut. In this case, the behavior of only one simple donut object needs to be modified. To achieve this, we use the DonutDecorator class. The ChocolateDonut is derived from the DonutDecorator. The user creates a ChocolateDonut object and the simple donut object is passed to the constructor of ChocolateDonut and stored in the DonutDecorator. Now if we want to get the price of the ChocolateDonut, we use the simple donut object to get its original price, then add the extra price for the chocolate spread and return the final amount to the user.

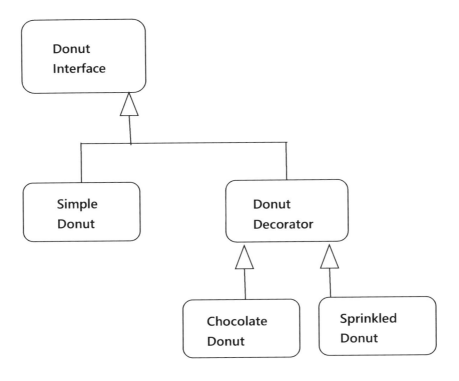

```cpp
class  Donut {
    public:
    virtual  double getPrice() = 0;
};

class SimpleDonut: public Donut
{
    public:
    double getPrice() {
        return 0.5;
    }
};

class DonutDecorator : public Donut
{
    private:
    Donut *plainObj;

    public:
    DonutDecorator(Donut *obj) {
        /*The simple donut object is stored in the donut decorator*/
        plainObj = obj;
    }

    double getPrice() {
        return plainObj->getPrice();
    }
};

class DonutWithChocolate : public DonutDecorator {
    public:
    DonutWithChocolate (Donut *obj): DonutDecorator(obj) {

    }

    double getPrice() {
        /*Get the price of the simple donut object and then
        add price for the chocolate spread*/
        return DonutDecorator::getPrice() + 0.3;
    }
};


void test() {
    Donut *simple = new SimpleDonut();

    /*We are changing the behavior of the simple donut object using the
    donut decorator*/
    DonutDecorator *withChocolate = new DonutWithChocolate(simple);
    double price = withChocolate->getPrice();
    cout << "Price of chocolate donut is " << price << endl;
}
```

The price of the chocolate donut returned is 0.5 + 0.3 = 0.8

6. Programming Language C

Storage Classes in C

	Visibility	Lifetime	Initial value	Storage
Automatic	block	block	uninitialized	stack segment
Static	block	entire program	0	data segment
External	file	entire program	0	data segment
Register	block	block	uninitialized	Processor registers

The register keyword is a request to the compiler to store the variable in a register to improve performance. If the compiler can't store the variable in the register, the compiler treats is as an automatic variable.

Constants

Let's say that the constant 52 is used in the C program. By default the data type of the constant is int (if the value of the constant is big and can't be stored in an int, then the next higher integer data type such as long is used).

52L or 52l is a constant with data type explicitly declared as long

52U or 52u is a constant with data type explicitly declared as unsigned

Expression evaluation

While evaluating an expression with values of two different types, the value having the "lower" data type is first converted to the "higher" data type and then the expression is evaluated. The order of the data types is double > float > long > int

If an expression has an int and an unsigned int, the int value is first converted to unsigned int.

Sizeof operator

The sizeof operator evaluates the size of the operand in bytes at compile time (except for variable length arrays whose sizes are computed at run time). When sizeof operator is applied on an array, the entire size of the array in bytes is returned.

The value returned by sizeof operator is of the type size_t. size_t is an unsigned integer type. size_t can safely store a pointer. So on 32-bit systems size_t is 32 bits and on 64-bit systems size_t is 64 bits.

Bitwise operators

Operator	Function
!	Bitwise not operator
|	Bitwise or
&	Bitwise and
~	Bitwise xor
>>	Right shift
<<	Left shift

When a right shift operator is applied on an unsigned integer, the vacated bits at the most significant portion of the integer are set to 0. When a right shift operator is applied

371

to a signed integer, the vacated bits at the most significant portion of the integer are set to the sign bit.

Memory management

Dynamic memory is allocated from the heap. The malloc and calloc functions are used to obtain memory from the heap. calloc in addition to allocating memory, also sets all the bytes in the allocated memory to zero. The free function is used to return memory back to the heap. A memory leak occurs if an allocated block of memory is not freed. A dangling pointer points to a memory that has not been allocated or to a memory that has already been freed.

Pointers

Pointer arithmetic: The following arithmetic operations are permitted on a pointer

- ✓ Increment and Decrement: Increment operator ++ increments the pointer to point to the next item in the array. The decrement pointer – decrements the pointer to point to the previous member in the array
- ✓ Addition: An integer can be added to a pointer. For instance the statement p = p+3; makes point to the third element from the current element. It is not possible to add two pointers.
- ✓ Subtraction: An integer can be subtracted from a pointer. It is also possible to subtract two pointers of the same type

If a is an array, then a[i] and i[a] mean the same. If a is an array then, address of a is equal to a (&a and a have the same value).

To easily identify the difference between char const * and char * const, read the declaration backwards (from right to left).   WoW

char const * ptr; /* indicates ptr is a pointer to constant char */

char * const ptr; /* indicates ptr is a constant pointer to a character */

*ptr++ will return the item that pointer points to and then increment the pointer. This is because although * and ++ have the same precedence, right associativity is used. So ++ is applied first on ptr and not on *ptr.

372

Function pointers

Let us say that we have the function sum. We want a function pointer to point to sum. This is shown in the code below:

typedef int (* fptr) (int a, int b); //declares the function pointer type

int sum(int a, int b);

fptr f1 = ∑ // variable f1 is assigned the address of the function sum

C++

Function overloading

Functions can have the same name but different arguments. Either the number of arguments or the type of the arguments must be different. Functions can't be overloaded based on the return type. For instance:

int f(int a);

int f(int a, int b);

int f(float a);

Passing by reference, Return by reference

Arguments can be passed to functions by reference. By passing by reference, a function argument in the calling function can be modified by the called function.

Return by reference is also possible in C++. Operator chaining can be achieved by returning by reference. For instance, by returning by reference in the assignment operator, it is possible to chain the assignment operators as a=b=c;

Classes

Classes contain data and functions. The access types in a class are

- ✓ public – accessible from anywhere

✓ protected – accessible from the class to which the member belongs to and all classes derived from it

✓ private – accessible only from the class to which the member belongs to

C++ structures can also contain data and functions. The difference between a C++ class and a C++ structure is that the default access type of a class is private whereas the default access type of a structure is public.

Friends

Friends of a class can access the private members of the class. A function or a class can be declared as a friend of the class. For instance

```
class A
{
    friend void f ();
    friend class B;
    //Other declarations
};
```
class B and function f() can access the private members of class A

Static Members

Classes can have static data and static functions. There will be only one instance of the static data member shared by all the objects of the class. Static data members have to be explicitly defined. Static functions can operate only on static data members and can't operate on non-static data members of a class.

Constructors

When an object is created, the constructor of the object is called. Constructors don't have a return type. If an error occurs in a constructor, the program can be informed about the error using function arguments (passed by reference or passed by pointer) or by throwing an exception.

The default constructor takes no arguments. The copy constructor takes the object of the same class as an argument. The compiler provides default implementation for the default constructor and copy constructor in case the programmer hasn't implemented them.

Destructors

When an object is destroyed, the destructor of the object is called. Destructors also don't have a return type. In addition, destructors also don't have any function arguments. If an error occurs in a destructor, the program can be informed about this by throwing an exception. The compiler provides default implementation for the destructor in case the programmer hasn't implemented it.

Operator overloading

Operators such as = (assignment operator), *, ->, ||, && etc. can be overloaded. The operator overloading rules are

- ✓ Only existing C++ operators can be overloaded. New operators can't be introduced
- ✓ The operators ., .*, :: and ?: can't be overloaded
- ✓ The number of arguments and precedence of operators can't be changed

Assignment Operator

The compiler provides the default implementation for the assignment operator in case the programmer hasn't implemented it. The scenarios when the assignment operator is invoked and when the constructor is invoked are shown below

```
A object1, object2; // Default constructor is invoked
A object3(object1); //Copy constructor
object2 = object3; //Assignment operator is invoked
f (object1); //Since object1 is passed by value to the function f, copy
constructor is invoked
```

operator ->

Consider the expression x->a, where -> is overloaded on object x.

This expression will be treated as (x.operator->())->a. Notice that -> is evaluated twice.

Function call operator

The function call operator is operator (). It can take different number of arguments of different types. Example:

```
class A
{
        bool operator() (int a, int b);
        void operator() (float a);
        //Other declarations
};
A object1;
```

```
object1(x, y); //will be called as object1.()(x, y). So function bool operator()
(int a, int b) is called.
```

By using a function call operator, it appears as though the object is a function pointer. Classes that have a function call operator are called function objects (sometimes also called functors).

Inheritance

A derived class (subclass) can inherit from the base class (superclass). The derived class can access the protected and public members of the base class. When an object of a derived class is instantiated, the derived class constructor is first called followed by the base class constructor. When an object of a derived class is destroyed, the base class destructor is first called followed by the derived class destructor.

Function overriding

If the base class and the derived class have the same function which takes the same arguments, then when the function is invoked on the derived class object, the derived class function will be called. The function of the base class is overridden by the function of the derived class.

Virtual functions

When the virtual keyword is used for a function, the compiler delays the linking of the function to run-time (dynamic binding). At run-time, the function is called based on the type of the object the pointer points to. For instance:

```
class A
{
    virtual void f();
};
class B: A
{
    virtual void f();
};

A *ptr1 = new A();
A *ptr2 = new B(); //Base class pointer can store derived class pointer
ptr1->f(); // this will call A::f()
ptr2->f(); //this will call B::f() since ptr2 points to object of class B at run
time
```

Pure virtual functions have no implementation. The declaration of a pure virtual function is

```
class A
{
    virtual void f() = 0;
};
```

Virtual functions are implemented using virtual tables (vtables)

Abstract classes

An abstract class is a class that can't be instantiated. If a class consists of at least one pure virtual function, then it can't be instantiated and hence is abstract. Ideally abstract classes contain only pure virtual functions and no data members. They are used to define the interface. The classes deriving from the abstract class will have the implementation for the functions. This helps in separating the interface from the implementation

Templates

Example of a function template that swaps two variables is

```
template<typename T> void swap(T x, T y)
{
    T temp = x;
    x = y;
    y = temp;
}
```

Example of a class template is

```
Template<typename T> class A
{
    private:
        T *m_ptr;
    //other declarations
};
```

Casting

1. dynamic_cast - it is used to perform safe casting of pointers in a class hierarchy at run time. The following safe castings can be done using dynamic casting

   ✓ convert a derived class pointer to a base class pointer (upcasting)

377

    ✓   convert a base class pointer to a derived class pointer if the object pointed to by the base class is of the derived class type. For instance if class B is derived from class A, then it is possible to do the following

```
class A* ptr1 = new B();
class B* ptr2 = dynamic_cast<class B*> ptr1; //ok
```

However the following is not allowed

```
class A* ptr1 = new A();
class B* ptr2 = dynamic_cast<class B*> ptr1; // results in an error
```

Run-time type information should be enabled for dynamic_cast to work.

2. static_cast - the casting of pointers is done at compile time. Using static_cast it is possible to

    ✓   cast class pointers of one type to another type anywhere in the class hierarchy.

    ✓   perform implicit conversions. Implicit conversions are conversion which are automatically done without requiring a cast operator. For instance casting an int to float etc.

    ✓   perform conversions between classes using constructors or operator functions

static_cast can't remove constness. static_cast also can't perform pointer to non-pointer conversions (and vice versa)

3. const_cast - Casting is done at compile time. const_cast can be used to remove constness or volatileness of an object

4. reinterpret_cast - Casting is done at compile time. Any type can be converted to any other type using reinterpret_cast.

1. What happens when you execute the following block of code?

```
{
    unsigned int i;

    for (i = 10; i >= 0; --i) {
        printf("%d\n", i);
    }
}
```

The program goes into an infinite loop. This is because i is declared as an unsigned integer. In the for loop, i takes values from 10 to 0. After the processing the loop with i taking the value 0, i is then decremented. Decrementing an unsigned integer whose value is 0 will result in i taking the value 4,294,967,295. So the for loop continues instead of stopping.

To solve the problem i should be declared as a signed integer. Decrementing a signed integer whose value is 0 will give -1 and the for loop will terminate

2. Find the problem in the code below to print the values from 0 to n-1

```
void print_values(unsigned int n){
    int i;

    for (i = 0; i <= n - 1 ; ++i)    {
        printf("%d\n", i);
    }
}
```

The problem occurs if the function print_values is called with n = 0.

Consider the expression i <= n – 1 in the for loop. According to the rules for expression evaluation, if we have a signed integer and unsigned integer in an expression, then the signed integer is converted to an unsigned integer for comparison. Since n is an unsigned

379

integer, the sub-expression n – 1 is an unsigned integer. We now have to compare i which is a signed integer with an n -1 which is an unsigned integer. So using the rules for expression evaluation, i is converted to an unsigned integer and compared with n - 1.

Now if n is passed as 0 to the function, then since n-1 is unsigned, n-1 will take the value 4,294,967,295 which is the maximum unsigned integer. The value of i is converted to an unsigned integer and compared with n - 1. But since n – 1 has the value of the maximum unsigned integer, no matter ever be the value of i, the expression i <= n – 1 will always evaluate to true. So the loop will continue infinitely.

3. Is there any portability problem with the declaration below?

```
char x;
```

We normally expect that the declaration char x is equivalent to the declaration signed char x. However this is not always the case. "The C Programming Language" book by Kernighan & Ritchie states that "Whether plain chars are signed or unsigned is machine-dependent, but printable characters are always positive." So if we declare char x, then the variable x can be treated as a signed char in some platforms whereas it can be treated as an unsigned char in some platforms. This can create portability problems. For instance, consider the code below

```
{
    char x = 0;
    --x;
    /* Further processing*/
}
```

The variable x is initialized to 0 and then decremented. If x is treated as an unsigned char on the platform, then x will have the value of 255. If x is treated as a signed char x on the platform, then x will have the value of -1. Clearly this poses a portability problem.

To overcome this problem, it is always better to avoid plain char declaration and explicitly declare the variable either as signed char or as unsigned char.

little endian: "little end" (LSB) stored first (at lowest address)
big endian: "big end" (MSB) stored first (at lowest address)

6.1 C

4. Find the problem in the code written to extract the least significant byte from a 32 bit integer   int = 0x AABBCCDD;

```
                                        0  1  2  3
                                BIG:   AA BB CC DD
unsigned char extract_lsb(int a) {
    unsigned char *ptr  = (unsigned char*) &a;  LITTLE DD CC BB AA
    return ptr[0];
}
```

The code is not portable. It will work on little endian machines since the least significant byte is stored in the lower memory address on little endian machines. However the code will not work on big endian machines since the most significant byte is stored in the lower memory address on big endian machines

One way to solve the problem is to use bit wise operators. The function can be rewritten as

```
unsigned char extract_lsb(unsigned int a)
{
    return a & 0xFF;
}
```

☆ interesting. review this

5. What value is printed when the following code is executed?

```
{
    unsigned int i = 0;
    i = i++;
    printf("i = %d\n", i);
}
```

The result is unspecified by the C Standard. The actual result will depend on the implementation of the compiler and so the result can vary in different platforms.

The reason for the unspecified behavior is that the value of the same variable is being changed more than once within the same statement. So in the statement i = i++ the postfix operator and the assignment operator are trying to change value of i. Since the behavior of such statements is unspecified, these type of statements should be avoided.

In the above explanation I have used the term "statement" to simplify the discussion. The more precise way of describing is that a variable's value can change only once between two sequence points. Some the sequence points in the C language are

- the end of a full expression (includes statements terminated by semi-colon)
- the comma operator
- logical && and logical || operators

The presence of a sequence point forces the evaluation of the preceding expression to conclude. So for instance if we have the statements

```
i++;
i += 10;
```

Then the semi-colon at the end of i++ forces i++ to be evaluated completely before proceeding to the next statement.

The statement i = i++ is sandwiched between two sequence points and the value of i changes more than once. So the result is unspecified.

6. What value is printed when the following code is executed?

```
{
    int a = 1, b = 2, c = 0;
    c = a+++b;
    printf("%d\n", c);
}
```

The value printed is 3.

The expression c = a+++b can either evaluated as c = a + (++b) or as (a++) + b. Which of the two evaluations is picked is determined by the tokenizer. The tokenizer performs lexical analysis on the code and breaks it into tokens. The tokenizer uses a greedy strategy and assigns the maximum number of characters possible to a token (also referred to as maximal munch rule).

In the expression c = a+++b, the obvious tokens are a, b and c. While scanning +++, the tokenizer reads the first + symbol. Since it is greedy, it does not immediately form the token and reads the next symbol which is also a +. The tokenizer realizes that it can form the ++ token with the first two symbols. It then reads the third symbol which is also +. But +++ is not a valid token. So +++ is tokenized as ++ and +. So the expression is tokenized as c = a ++ + b and so the expression is evaluated as c = (a++) + b. If a = 1 and b = 2, then c = 1 + 2 = 3.

7. Do you see any problem with the following function that is used to calculate the midpoint of two numbers?

```
unsigned int calc_middle(unsigned int low, unsigned int high)
{
    unsigned int mid = (low + high) / 2;
    return mid;
}
```

The above function will work in most cases. But there is one subtle problem with it. In case we are trying to compute the middle of very large numbers, then the value (low + high) can overflow leading to an incorrect result.

A better way to calculate the middle to overcome the overflow problem is to write the function as

```
unsigned int calc_middle(unsigned int low, unsigned int high)
{
    unsigned int mid = low + ((high - low) / 2);
    return mid;
}
```

8. What is wrong with the following code block?

```
{
    int i;
    double x = 0.0;

    for (i = 0; i < 10; ++i)
        x = x + 0.1;

    if (x == 1.0) {
        printf("result matches expected value\n");
    } else {
        printf("result doesn't match expected value\n");
    }
}
```

Floating point calculations are not exact. Due to limited precision, floating point calculations will incur truncation errors. So floating point numbers should never be exactly compared with each other using the $==$ or $!=$ operators.

In the code above, the floating point number x is exactly compared with 1.0 using $==$ which is incorrect. In fact when the above code is executed, the output is **result doesn't match expected value**. The reason is that on adding 0.1 in the for loop for 10 iterations, x takes the value of 0.99999 and not 1.0 due to truncation. So the comparison will fail.

To solve the problem, we should compare if the absolute difference between the result and the expected value is within the required accuracy as shown below

```
if (fabs(x - 1.0) < 0.0001) {
    printf("result matches expected value\n");
} else {
    printf("result doesn't match expected value\n");
}
```

fabs gives the absolute value of a floating point number and 0.0001 is required accuracy.

9. What value is printed on executing the following code?

```
int x = 10;

int main()
{
    int x = x;
    printf("x = %d\n", x);
    return 0;
}
```

Garbage value is printed.

There is a global variable with name x and also a local variable with the same name x. Inside the main function, the moment the local variable x is defined, the global variable is no longer visible. So in the statement int x = x, the local variable is assigned to itself and not to the global variable. Since the local variable x has a random value when it is defined, the same random value is assigned to itself. So garbage value is printed on the screen.

10. When should a variable be declared as volatile? Can a variable be defined as const and volatile?

The volatile keyword prevents the compiler from applying optimizations to the variable. For instance, consider the main program that has the following code

```
status = 1;
while (status){
    /*Processing Code*/
}
```

The compiler can figure out that in the main program, status value is always 1. So the compiler can optimize the code not to check the value of status every time in the loop resulting in an infinite while loop. However the status can be set to 0 in an Interrupt Service Routine. This will have no effect, if the compiler has optimized the code to run the while loop infinitely. To prevent this from happening, the volatile keyword should be used while declaring the variable status.

A similar situation can happen when a global variable is shared between two threads. So it is better to declare global variables shared between threads as volatile.

Volatile should also be used for memory mapped registers. For instance, reg_p is a variable that stores the address of the memory mapped register. Let us say that the contents of the register have to be polled. The code may be written as

```
while (*reg_p == 0) {
    /*Processing code*/
}
```
Again the compiler figures out that the memory pointed to by reg_p does not change anywhere in the program. So it may optimize this code to prevent checking the value of *reg_p every time in the loop resulting in an infinite loop.

However the value of the register may be changed asynchronously by the hardware which won't be noticed due to the compiler optimization. To solve the problem, we have to declare reg_p as a pointer to volatile memory as shown

uint32_t volatile * reg_p;

volatile indicates that a variable may be modified. const indicates that the variable can't be modified. But there are cases where a variable may be declared as const and volatile. For instance, consider a shared buffer to which a producer thread writes into and a consumer thread reads from. The consumer thread will declare the buffer as a const because the consumer should only read from the buffer and not write to the buffer. The consumer thread will declare the buffer as volatile because the buffer can be modified by the producer thread and the compiler should not optimize the access to the buffer from the consumer thread.

11. What is the size of the following structure on a 32-bit machine?

```
struct X
{
    char a;
    int b;
    short c;
};
```

32-bit processors can fetch an entire word (4 contiguous bytes) in a single cycle, if the address is a multiple of 4 bytes. Compilers try to make use of this and align the structure members so that they can be fetched in fewer cycles.

Let a variable var of struct X start at the address 0xf000. If the compiler packs the data members, then var.a would start at the address 0xf000 and occupy 1 byte. var.b needs 4 bytes. So var.b would start at 0xf001 and end at 0xf004. var.c would start at address 0xf005 and occupy 2 bytes. Now var.b spans across two 32 bit words 0xf000 and 0xf004. So to fetch var.b two cycles would be needed. This results in lower performance.

To avoid this problem, compilers generally pad the structure members with empty space so that they are aligned. Members of type char can start on any address since they occupy only 1 byte. Members of the type short occupy 2 bytes and are aligned to start on addresses that are multiples of 2. Members of the type int occupy 4 bytes and are aligned to start on addresses that are multiples of 4. Also the size of the entire structure will be made a multiple of 4 bytes.

So var.a would start at address 0xf000 and occupy 1 byte. The next member var.b is an int. The nearest multiple of 4 bytes is 0xf004. So var.b starts at 0xf004 and ends at 0xf007 occupying 4 bytes. Empty space is padded from 0xf001 to 0xf003. var.c can then start at 0xf008 and end at 0xf009. Since the entire structure should be a multiple of 4 bytes, two more spaces are padded at the end. So the entire structure will take up 12 bytes.

The space taken up by the structure can be reduced without any negative impact on performance by re-arranging the members of the structure. First we can place all the character members, followed by all the short members followed by all the integer members. So if the structure is defined as

```
struct X
{
    char a;
    short c;
    int b;
};
```
var.a would start at 0xf000. Empty space would be padded at 0xf001. var.b would start at 0xf002 and end at 0xf003. var.c would start at 0xf004 and end at 0xf007. So this would require only 8 bytes.

12. What value is printed when the following code is executed?

```
{
    int i = 0, s = 0;
    s = sizeof(i++);
    printf("i = %d\n", i);
}
```

The value of i that is printed is 0 and not 1. This is because sizeof operator is applied during compile time only. So the expression i++ is not evaluated during run-time. So the value of i is unmodified at run-time and continues to be 0.

13. What is the sizeof the string in the following code?

```
{
    char string[] = "abcde";
    printf("Size of string = %d\n", sizeof(string));
}
```

The size of the string array in bytes is reported as 6.

The sizeof operator takes into the entire size of the string array. This includes '\0' character also (the strlen function on the other hand doesn't include '\0' character). So the size is reported as 6.

14. Implement a macro to find the size of a variable and size of a type without making use of the sizeof operator

The default sizeof operator returns a value of type size_t. size_t is an unsigned integer. The number of bits for size_t depends on the number of bits needed to represent a pointer on the system. On a 32-bit system where pointers are 32-bits long, size_t will take 32 bits. On a 64-bit system where pointers are 64 bits long, size_t will take 64 bits.

The macro to find the size of a variable is given below

#define sizeof_var(var) ((size_t)(&(var)+1)- (size_t)(&(var)))

var is the variable. &(var) gives the address of the variable. The data type of &(var) is pointer to the variable. &(var)+1 gives the address of the next contiguous variable to the same type as var due to pointer arithmetic

So in the macro we are finding the difference between the address of the next contiguous variable with the address of the current variable. This will give us the size of the variable

The macro to find the size of a type is given below

#define sizeof_type(type) (size_t) (((type*)0) + 1)

type indicates the data type whose size we wish to find. For instance let the type be int. The macro will expand as

(((int*)0) + 1)

((int*)0) will be treated as an integer pointer pointing to address 0. The type of ((int*)0) is integer pointer

((type*)0) + 1 will add 1 to an integer pointer. Again due to pointer arithmetic, this will give the address of the next integer. Since we are finding the address of the integer immediately after the integer at address 0, we are in effect finding the size of the integer.

15. What is wrong with the following macro?

#define SQUARE(a) a * a

The arguments of the macro have not been enclosed in parenthesis. So the macro may not be evaluated correctly. For instance, if the user uses the macro as SQUARE(2+3). The user expects the result to be 25. However the result returned is 11. This is because the macro is expanded as

2+3*2+3 = 2 + 6 + 3 = 11 (* has higher precedence than + and so 3*2 will be evaluated first)

So the correct way to write the macro is

```
#define SQUARE(a) ((a) *(a))
```

16. What happens when the following code is executed?

```
#define B x
#define A B
{
    int x = 10;
    printf("%d\n", A);
}
```

The answer output is 10.

The pre-processor can substitute a macro more than once. So the term A in the print statement is first substituted to B. The pre-processor then substitutes B as x. So the final output is 10.

It is important to note that the moment the pre-processor notices that the macro substitution has become recursive it stops any further substitution. For instance if we have the following code

```
{
    int X = 10;

    #define X   (4 + X)

    printf("%d\n", X);
}
```

The pre-processor first substitutes X in the print statement with 4+X. Now it doesn't again replace X in the 4+X otherwise it will enter into an infinite loop. So it stops there. The final output of the above code will be 14.

17. Define a macro to find byte offset of a given field in a structure.

Let the macro be offsetof(s, m) where s is structure type and m is the name of the member in the structure. For instance if we have a structure of type

```
struct A
{
    int x;
    int y;
};
```

To find the offset of member y in structure A, the macro is invoked as offsetof(A, y). The macro is defined as follows:

#define offsetof(s, m) ((size_t) (&((s *)0)->m))

18. Do you see any problem with the following macro for calculating the minimum of two values?

```
#define MIN(x, y) ( (x) < (y) ? (x) : (y))
```

In spite of using parenthesis for all the arguments in the macro, there can still be problems depending on how the user invokes it. Suppose the user invokes the macro as

```
z = MIN(a++, foo(b));
```

On substituting the macro, gets expanded as ((a++) < foo(b) ? (a++) : foo(b)). So a++ gets evaluated twice although the user wanted a to be incremented only once. Also the function foo is called twice but the user wanted the function to be called only once. So there can be unwanted side-effects when macros are used. So considering this, it is safer to use inline functions where ever possible.

19. What is the value of ptr after executing the following code?

```
{
    int *ptr1 = (int*)0x100, *ptr2 = (int*)0x108;
    printf("Difference = %d \n", ptr2 - ptr1);
}
```

The pointers ptr1 and ptr2 point to integers. Assuming a 32-bit machine, the size of each integer is 4 bytes. The subtraction of the pointers to integers will give the number of integers present between the two pointers.

So the result = (0x108 – 0x100)/ sizeof(integer) = 8/4 = 2

Similarly don't forget that when the following piece of code is executed,

```
{
    int *ptr = NULL;
    ptr++;
}
```

ptr will have the value 4 and not 1.

20. What values are printed when the following code is executed?

```
{
    int numbers[] = {10, 20, 30, 40, 50};
    int *ptr = numbers;
    int x , y, z;

    x = *ptr++;
    y = *++ptr;
    z = ++*ptr;

    printf("x = %d, y = %d, z = %d, *ptr = %d\n\n", x, y, z, *ptr);
}
```

The result is x = 10, y = 30, z = 31 and *ptr is 31.

Consider the expression x = *ptr++ . Although * and ++ have the same precedence, right associativity is used. So ++ is applied on ptr and not on *ptr. So x takes on the value of ptr which is 10. Then ptr++ is applied and ptr now points to 20.

Consider the expression y = *++ptr . First ptr is incremented to the next position. So ptr now points to 30. Then the * operator is applied. So y takes the value 30.

Consider the expression y = ++*ptr . The ++ prefix operator is applied on *ptr. *ptr is 30. Applying the ++ operator on *ptr modifies 30 to 31. So z takes the value 31.

ptr is pointing to the third item in the array which is 31. So *ptr has the value 31.

21. What is wrong with the following code?

```
{
    char *ptr = "CODE";
    ptr[0] = 'N';
    printf("%s\n", ptr);
}
```

Executing the code results in a segmentation fault. The reason is that the string "CODE" is allocated in the data segment as a constant. When we try to modify the constant string "CODE" using the statement ptr[0] = 'N', it results in an access violation resulting in a crash.

To fix the problem, we have to allocate a separate string on the stack or heap and use it. For instance the following code will work

```
{
    char str[] = "CODE";
    char *ptr = str;
    ptr[0] = 'N';
    printf("%s\n", ptr);
}
```

Here str is a separate string that is allocated on the stack. The string "CODE" in the data segment is copied into str on the stack and then operated upon.

22. What is wrong with the following code?

```
int* compute_sum(int *set1, int *set2, int n){
    int result[MAX_NUM_ITEMS];
    int i;

    assert(MAX_NUM_ITEMS <= n);
    for (i = 0; i < n; ++i) {
        result[i] = set1[i] + set2[i];
    }
    return result;
}
```

Since result is an auto variable, it is allocated on the stack. When compute_sum function completes, the pointer to the stack variable is returned. However, when other functions are called, the result variable will be overwritten on the stack and contains garbage. So pointers to automatic variables should not be returned. To solve the problem, the result should be allocated on the heap.

23. Is there anything wrong with the following code to left shift an array by one position

```
{
    unsigned char buf[5] = { 100, 101, 102, 103, 104};
    memcpy(&buf[0], &buf[1], 4);
}
```

For the function memcpy, the source and destination areas should be non-overlapping. In case the source and destination overlap, then the operation of memcpy is unpredictable. In the code above, the source is from &buf[0] to &buf[3] and destination is from &buf[1] to &buf[4]. So the locations &buf[1] to &buf[3] are overlapping between the source and destination. When overlapping source and destination are passed to memcpy, the result is unpredictable. To overcome this problem memmove function should be used in case the source and destination overlap.

24.

In many embedded systems, a custom memory allocator is used instead of malloc. Why is this done?

When malloc allocates memory, it stores the size of the block allocated in the bytes just before the allocated memory. This helps free to figure out how much of memory to free when the memory block is freed. So the total number of bytes used up to allocate a memory block = number of bytes required for storing the size of the block + number of bytes for the actual block of memory.

On 32-bit Linux systems 8 bytes are used up for storing the size of the block. If the size of the block is large, the additional 8 bytes overhead is insignificant. However if many small blocks have to be allocated, then an additional 8 byte overhead becomes significant. In many cases, the small blocks have the same size. In such cases, it is possible to do away with the 8 byte overhead by having a custom memory allocator.

When a custom allocator is initialized, the size of the blocks is specified. The custom allocator is specific for this particular block size. The custom allocator acquires a big chunk of memory from malloc. Then when memory for the blocks is requested using the custom allocator, the custom allocator assigns the memory from the big chunk of memory it has. When the blocks are freed using the custom allocator, the custom allocator know how much to free since all blocks have the same size and the size has been specified while initializing the custom allocator. At the end of the program, the customer allocator releases the memory using system free.

25. Why are strcpy and strncpy functions considered unsafe?

strcpy can result in buffer overflow security problems. strcpy copies the source string into the destination without checking if we are exceeding the size of the destination string. So the memory locations next to the destination string can be overwritten with malicious data to suit an attacker.

strncpy function limits the number of characters that can be copied to the destination. But strncpy doesn't always place the string termination character in the destination. This can also lead to security problems.

strlcpy is the preferred function for copying strings. It restricts the number of characters that can be copied to the destination and also null terminates the destination string.

26. What happens when the following code is executed?

```
int main()
{
    return main();
}
```

Since the main function calls itself recursively and there is no condition for the termination of the recursive calls, the program will run out of space in the stack segment.

27. Find out if a machine is little endian or big endian

In a little endian system, the least significant byte is stored in the lower address whereas in a big endian system, the most significant byte is stored in the lower address. The code to check if a machine is little endian or big endian is given below

```
int is_little_endian(void)
{
    int is_little_endian;
    int i = 1;
    char *ptr = (char*)&i;

    if (*ptr == 1) {
        is_little_endian = 1;
    }
    else {
        is_little_endian = 0;
    }

    return is_little_endian;
}
```

28. Find the direction of growth of stack

The code to find the direction of growth of stack is given below

```
void function2( int* ptr) {
    int y;
    if (&y > ptr) {
        printf("Stack grows from lower address to higher address\n");
    }
    else {
        printf("Stack grows from higher address to lower address\n");
    }
}

void function1(void) {
    int x;
    function2(&x);
}


int main() {
    function1();
    return 0;
}
```

$1.$ Is there anything wrong with the copy constructor in the class below?

```
class A
{
public:
    A() : x(0)  { }

    A(A obj) : x(obj.x) { }

private:
    int x;
};
```

In the code above, the argument to the copy constructor is passed by value. In this case, when the copy constructor is invoked, then to create the argument to the copy constructor, the same copy constructor should be invoked again. This creates the infinite recursion problem. So the compiler foresees this problem and flags an error on detecting an argument passed by value to a copy constructor.

To solve the problem, the argument to the copy constructor should be passed by reference and not by value as shown below.

```
A(A& obj) : x(obj.x) { }
```

2. Consider the following class

```
class A
{
public:
    A(A& obj): x(obj.x) { }
private:
    int x;
};
```

What happens when an object of A is defined as?

```
A object;
```

The compiler reports an error indicating that the default constructor for class A is not available.

When we define the variable object, since we are not passing any arguments to the constructor, the compiler looks for the default constructor. The default constructor is provided automatically only if the user has not defined any other constructor. In this case, since the user has already provided the copy constructor, the system generated default constructor is no longer available and so the compiler reports an error.

To solve the problem, the default constructor should be defined.

3. Class A has been declared as shown below and object1 of class A is instantiated

```
class A {
public:
    A(int value) : y(value), x(y) { }
private:
    int x;
    int y;

};

A object1(99);
```

What are the values of object1.x and object1.y after initialization?

---

object1.x will have garbage value and object1.y will have the value 99.

The reason for this is that irrespective of the order in which the members are listed in the initialization list, the members are initialized in the order in which they are listed in the class declaration. So although y(value) comes ahead of x(y) in the initialization list, x is initialized first followed by y since in the class declaration x is declared first. When x is initialized, y still has not yet been initialized. So x will end up having a garbage value

C++ compilers don't follow the order of declarations in the initialization list to avoid overhead. C++ compilers call the destructors of the class members in the opposite order of the constructors. Now if constructors are to be called based on the initialization list, the initialization order must be stored and the destructors have to be called in opposite order. To avoid this overhead, C++ compilers simply call the constructors in the order of members listed in the class declaration

So it is always better to ensure that the order of members listed in the initialization list matches the order of the members in the class declaration to avoid confusion

4. Can constructors be private?

Yes, constructors can be private. Sometimes we want to prevent the user from directly accessing the constructor. In this case we make the constructor private. Once a constructor is made private, it can still be accessed from friend functions and from member functions of the class.

Suppose we don't want the user to call the constructor of class A which takes no arguments. Then we make this constructor private and don't implement it.

```
class A
{
    /*Other declarations*/
    private:
    A ();

};
```

In case the user tries to create an object of class A without passing arguments from non-friend functions, then the compiler will return an error since the class A constructor is private.

In case the user tries to create an object of class A without passing arguments from friend functions, the linker will give an error since the constructor has not been implemented

One practical scenario where constructor is made private is in a singleton class. A singleton class can have at most only one instance of an object of that class. So to avoid the user from creating multiple objects of the singleton class, the constructors are made private. The object of the singleton class is created using a static member function of the class.

5. Can destructors be private?

Yes, destructors can be private.

If a class has a private destructor, then in non-friend and non-member functions it is not possible to directly declare a variable of the class. This is because when the variable goes out of scope, it has to be destroyed but the destructor can't be called because it is private. It is also not possible to call delete on a pointer to an object of a class whose destructor is private from non-friend and non-member functions.

A private destructor can still be accessed from friend functions and member functions of the class.

In singleton class (a class where at most only one instance of the object can exist at a given time), it is useful to use private destructors although it is not mandatory. Let us say we have two pointers p1 and p2 which point to the object of the singleton class. It is possible to accidentally try to first delete p1 and then somewhere else in the code delete p2. The deletion of p1 will be successful. However deletion of p2 will fail since there is only one instance of the class which has already been deleted. To avoid this error, the destructors can be made private. A separate static member function can be provided for deleting the singleton object. The private destructor can be accessed from the static member function. By doing this the likelihood of the user trying to free up the pointer to a singleton object is comparatively less.

6. Overload the $\ll$ operator to print the objects of the following class

```
class ComplexNum {
public:
    ComplexNum (int x , int y) : real(x), imaginary(y) { }
private:
    int real;
    int imaginary;
};
```

The $\ll$ operator must have access to the private data members of the class in order to print them. So we have to declare the operator function as a friend of the class.

When we print using cout, we have to pass the object of type ostream by reference and return the ostream by reference. Returning by reference allows us to print multiple objects by chaining the $\ll$ operator. For instance cout $\ll$ a $\ll$ b will print two variables. So the declaration of the friend function inside the class is

```
friend ostream& operator << (ostream &out, ComplexNum& num);  // declare this
inside class
```

The function definition is given below

```
ostream& operator << (ostream &out, ComplexNum& num)
{
    out << "Real = "<<num.real<<" Imaginary = "<<num.imaginary<<endl;
    return out;
}
```

7. What are the possible ways in which an object of class Metre can be assigned to an object of class Feet?

```
class Metre {
public:
    Metre(double var) : m(var) { }
private:
    double m;
};
class Feet {
public:
    Feet(double var):f(var) { }
private:
    double f;
};
```

The object of class Metro can be converted to class Feet using two approaches

a.) Using operator Feet in the Metre class

```
Metre::operator Feet()
{
        Feet temp(m * 3.28);
        return temp;
}
```

b.) Using constructor in class Feet

```
Feet::Feet(Metre& obj)
{
    f = obj.m * 3.28;
}
```

Note that only one of the two approaches should be used. If both these approaches are used then the compiler will indicate that the conversion is ambiguous.

8. What is the use of the explicit keyword in C++?

C++ can perform implicit type conversions. In places where we don't want implicit type conversions, we use the explicit keyword to force the user to explicitly specify the type conversion.

For instance consider the code

```
class A
{
public:
    A(int x): m_value(x) { }
private:
    int m_value;
};

void compute (A obja)
{
    /*process obja*/
}
```

It is possible to call the compute function by passing an integer variable as shown in the block of code

```
{
    int i = 10;
    compute(i);
}
```

This is because the compiler can use the constructor of A that takes the integer parameter to convert an integer to an object of class A. To prevent this implicit conversion, we can declare the constructor explicit as shown below

```
explicit A(int x): m_value(x) { }
```

Now if the user simply calls compute(i) it will result in a compiler error. The user is forced to explicitly specify the type conversion from integer to class A as compute((A) i)

9. Implement the prefix and postfix operators for the following class

```
class A
{
public:
    A(int var) : x(var) { }
private:
    int x;
};
```

Both prefix and postfix operators make use the same symbol ++. In order to distinguish the two operators, prefix operator takes no argument, whereas the postfix operator takes an additional argument that is not used.

The prefix operator is given below

```
A& A::operator ++()
{
    ++x;
    return *this; // return by reference
}
```

The postfix operator is given below

```
A A::operator ++(int unused)
{
    //create a temporary variable that has the value before the increment
    //call the copy constructor and pass *this
    A temp(*this);

        x++;

    // return by value. can't return by reference as temp is stored on stack
    return temp;
}
```

Note that in the prefix operator we can return by reference whereas in the postfix operator we are forced to return by value.

10.

Class A has two operations add and subtract. How will you define a function pointer to the add and subtract member functions?

```
class A
{
public:
    A() : x(0) { }
    int add(int var) { return x += var; }
    int subtract(int var) { return x -= var; }
private:
    int x;
};
```

It is possible to have function pointers to member functions. The declaration of the function pointer is

```
typedef int (A::*compute)(int) ;
```

A function pointer variable is defined as shown

```
compute fptr = &A::add;
```

The add function is invoked as shown

```
result = (obj.*fptr)(10);
```

Since fptr is a function pointer, we can change it to the subtract function and invoke it

```
fptr = &A::subtract;
result = (obj.*fptr)(5);
```

11.

What are the main differences between new and malloc? What are the main differences between delete and free?

Differences between new and malloc

- new allocates memory and calls the constructor of the class. Malloc only allocates the memory but does not call the constructor

- new returns the pointer of the type requested whereas malloc returns a void pointer

- new is an operator whereas malloc is a function

- If new operator fails, an exception is thrown. malloc doesn't throw an exception if malloc fails

The difference between delete and free is that delete calls the destructor and releases the memory whereas free only releases the memory.

12. What happens if the following code is executed?

```
int *ptr = new int [1];
delete ptr;
```

The result is undefined. The program may crash or may have unpredictable behavior.

This is because when new [] is used to allocate memory, delete [] should be used for deallocating the memory. This holds good even if we are allocating memory only for a single member. Similarly when new is used for allocating memory only delete should be used for de-allocating the memory.

13. Write the copy constructor and assignment operator for the following class

```
class A {
    public:
    A(const A&);
    A& operator= (A&);
    private:
    char *buf; /*Dynamically allocated memory*/
};
```

The class has dynamically allocated memory. So if we use the default copy constructor, it will do a shallow copy. So we create an object as shown below

A object2 = A(object1);

object1.buf and object2.buf will point to the same memory. However this is not what we want. A deep copy should be done instead of a shallow copy. So new memory should be allocated for buf of object2 and the contents of string object1.buf should be copied into the new string object2.buf

If we use the default operator = and assign object2 = object1, then the original object2.buf is replaced by object1.buf. This will cause a memory leak since the pointer pointing to the original object2.buf is overwritten and hence lost.

So the default copy constructor and operator = should not be used here. The correct implementation of copy constructor and assignment operator are given below

```
A::A(const A& source) {
    int newLength = strlen(source->buf) + 1;

    buf = new char[newLength];

    strcpy(buf, rhs->buf);

}
```

```
A& A::operator=(const A& rhs){

    /*In case of self assignment, return*/
    if (this == &rhs)
        return *this;

    delete [] buf;

    int newLength = strlen(rhs->buf)+1;

    buf = new char[newLength];

    strcpy(buf, rhs->buf);

    return *this
}
```

For the operator= the user can self assign a variable as shown below

object1 = object1;

If we don't check for self assignment in the code then the code will fail. This is because rhs and *this both refer to object1. So we will first free up object1.buf. When we try to find the length of the string(object1->buf), the code will fail since object1.buf has already been freed.

14. What is the difference between the new operator and operator new?

The new operator dynamically allocates memory and calls the constructor of the object. In the code below the new operator is used

int *ptr = new int[100];

To dynamically allocate memory, the new operator internally makes use of operator new. C++ provides a default operator new. The signature of operator new is shown below (operator new is overloaded and has many signatures. One of the signatures is shown below)

void *operator new(size_t numBytes) throw(bad_alloc);

The default operator can be invoked using the code below:

::operator new(numBytes)

The default operator new can be overridden in a class by having a custom implementation of operator new. Sometimes it is more efficient if memory is allocated using a custom allocator instead of the default allocator. In such cases, a custom operator new can be implemented. If a custom operator new is implemented then custom operator delete should also be developed. The signature of operator delete is

void * operator delete(void * ptr) throw();

operator new[] and operator delete[] are different from operator new and operator delete.

Custom operator new[] and custom operator delete[] can also be implemented for a class that will override the default operator new[] and default operator delete[].

15. Why should return by reference be avoided for dynamically allocated memory?

Consider the following code below:

```
A& A::operator +( A& obj1, A& obj2)
{
    A *result = new A;

    //Compute the sum

    //Return the dynamically allocated memory by reference.
    return *result;
}
```

No problem in the code so far since we are returning the memory allocated on the heap and not on the stack. The function would be invoked in the code below.

A& p = q + r;

To free up the memory allocated on the heap, we have to do the following

delete &p;

Still no problem in the code. However it is highly likely that the programmer will forget to delete the memory on a return by reference object. Even if the programmer remembers to free the memory, if the expression is complex then there will be temporary unnamed objects whose memory can't be freed by the programmer resulting in a memory leak. For instance, consider the expression

A& p = q + r + s;

The result of q + r will be stored in a temporary unnamed variable which the programmer can't access leading to a memory leak. So it is good practice to avoid returning dynamically allocated memory by reference.

16. What is an Auto pointer (Smart pointer) class?

Using normal pointers, we can end up with problems such as dangling pointers and memory leaks. Auto pointers automatically avoid these problems.

An auto pointer is an object which behaves syntactically like a normal pointer. To behave like normal pointers, the auto pointer implements the dereference operator (operator *) and the indirection operator (operator ->).

There are different types of auto pointers. In many implementations, the auto pointer uses reference counting. When an auto pointer is made to point to a block of memory, the reference count for the block of memory is incremented. When an auto pointer no longer points to a block of memory, the reference count for the block of memory is decremented. If the reference count for the block of memory becomes 0, then the block of memory is automatically freed.

17.

Suppose we have a base class and a derived class. What is the order in which constructors and destructors are called for a derived class object?

The order of calling constructors is as follows:

- first base class constructor is executed
- next derived class constructor is executed

The order of calling the destructors is opposite to the constructors and is as follows:

- first the derived class destructor is called
- next the base class destructor is called

18. Suppose two classes A and B are declared as shown below

```
class A {
public:
    int f1() {cout<<"In f1\n";}
private:
    int x;
};

class B :  A {
private:
    int y;
};
```

Is there anything wrong with the code below?

```
{
    B object;
    object.f1();
}
```

The compiler reports an error that function f1 can't be accessed.

The reason is that in the code when class B inherits from class A, the access control has not been specified. The default inheritance access control is private. So although function f1 is public in class A, it becomes private for objects of class B. So f1 can't be accessed outside class A for objects of class B.

19. In the code below which function is called - A::compute or B::compute

```
class A {
public:
    int compute(int x);
};
class B : public A {
public:
    int compute(float x);
};

B object;
object.compute(9);
```

The compute function of class B (B::compute) is called.

object.compute(9) calls the compute function with an integer argument 9. It may look as though the base class function A::compute will be called since its argument is an integer which exactly matches the type of argument 9. However this is not the case

When a derived class implements a function which has the same name as one or more functions in the base class, all the base class functions with that name are hidden. So when object.compute(9) is called, only a function with name compute of the class B can be called and not of the base class. So B::compute(float x) is called and the argument 9 is converted to a float.

The compute function of class A is declared as public and can still be accessed from class B. But to do this the user has to explicitly call the function as shown in the code below

object.A::compute(9);

20. Why is use of multiple inheritance generally avoided?

Multiple inheritance is generally avoided. Although C++ allows multiple inheritance, some languages like Java don't support multiple inheritance of concrete classes. The main reasons for avoiding multiple inheritance are:

- Multiple inheritance can be misused (single inheritance itself has been misused frequently by programmers) and can complicate the design. Instead of inheriting multiple classes, it is often possible to use composition.

- New kinds of design problems are encountered with multiple inheritance. For instance, the diamond problem is encountered if class B and class C are derived from class A and class D inherits class B and class C. In C++, class B and class C each inherit a copy of the parent class A. So there are now two copies of the base class A in class D (via class B and via class C). So accessing base class members from class D becomes ambiguous. The problem can be solved if class B and class C virtually inherit from class A in which case, only a single copy of class A is maintained.

- It is difficult to support multiple inheritance in a programming language. For instance, in most programming languages, the offset at which a data member of the class is stored is fixed. If a class inherits from two parent classes A and B, the compiler has to decide whether to store class A data members first or class B members first. The compiler should still ensure that whatever data order is chosen, virtual functions of C can be accessed polymorphically from the base class pointers of A and B which is not easy if the data layout is fixed.

21. Can constructors be virtual?

The keyword virtual can't be used for a constructor. The keyword virtual delays the binding of the function call with the actual function implementation to run-time. By using the virtual keyword, we can invoke a virtual function on a pointer to an object without knowing the exact type of the object at compile time. However the exact type of the object must be known to create the object itself. So constructors can't be virtual.

22. Can destructors be virtual?

Yes, destructors can be virtual. In fact it is a good programming practice to declare destructors virtual. Otherwise we can end up with nasty problems. For instance, let us say that class B derives from class A. The destructors of class A and class B are non-virtual. It is possible that we can have the following code in the program

```
A *ptr = new B;
/*
code that operates on ptr
*/

delete ptr;
```

Now ptr is of type class A and contains an object of the derived class B. When we try to delete a derived class object through a base class pointer and the destructor of the base class is non-virtual, then the behavior of the program is not clearly defined. In some C++ implementations, since ptr is of type class A and the destructor of A is not virtual, only the destructor of A will be called on deleting ptr. So if we have an object of class B in a pointer of class A, the destructor of B will not be called resulting in a potential memory leak. To solve the problem the destructors should be declared virtual so that the correct destructor is called based on the type of the object residing in the base class pointer.

23.

Can a virtual function be inlined? Can a virtual function be static? Can a virtual function be private?

A virtual function can be declared as an inline function. It is left up to the compiler whether the function will be inlined or not. While it appears counter-intuitive that a virtual function which is decided at run time can be inlined, the compiler may sometimes be able to inline the virtual function.

For instance, consider the code

```
class A {
public:
    inline virtual int get();
private:
    int x;
};

class B : public A {
public:
    inline virtual int get();
private:
    int y;
};

B objectB;
objectB.get();
```

Since we are calling the get function on an object and not a pointer, the compiler knows that B::get() should always be called here and the compiler can inline the function call. If we have the following code

```
A* ptr = new B();
ptr->get();
delete ptr;
```

The compiler can figure out that ptr will always have an object of class B and can inline the function. The compiler will not try to do a complex analysis of the type of object a pointer will hold. If it is easy for the compiler to figure out that only one type of object is held in the pointer, then the compiler can inline the virtual function.

Virtual functions can't be declared as static since the virtual function called depends on the specific object on which it is invoked. Static functions on the other hand can be invoked on a class without requiring a specific object. The compiler reports an error if a virtual function is declared static.

418

Virtual functions can be private. In most of the designs used, the base class is abstract and has pure-virtual functions that are public as shown below

```
class A {
public:
    virtual int compute(int x) = 0;
};
```

An alternate design is to have concrete public functions in the base class that make use of private virtual functions as shown below

```
class A {
public:
    int compute(int x);

private:
    virtual int do_compute(int x) = 0;
}
```

The compute function will make use of the do_compute function. The do_compute function is pure virtual and the correct do_compute function will be called based on the type of the object in the base class pointer. The advantage of this is that any pre-processing and post-processing for the compute function can take occur at a single place - in the base class compute function and doesn't have to be duplicated in all the derived classes. In such cases, virtual functions can be made private.

24. Consider the following classes A and B

```
class A
{
public:
    virtual int compute() {cout<<"Inside A::compute"<<endl;}
};

class B : public A
{
public:
    virtual int compute() {cout<<"Inside B::compute"<<endl;}
};
```

What is the output when the following code is executed?

```
{
    B obj_b;
    A& obj_a = obj_b;
    obj_a.compute();
}
```

In this case the function B::compute() is called.

Although we are not calling the compute function by a pointer, the derived class function is called. This is because obj_a is a reference and virtual table lookup is performed for references also. Since the virtual function table has the compute function of class B, B::compute is called.

25. What is the size of the following class on a 32-bit machine?

```
class A
{
public:
    virtual int compute();
private:
    int x;
};
```

The size of the class is 8 bytes.

Normally we expect the size of the class A to be the size of the int which is 4 bytes on a 32-bit machine. However the class has a virtual function. So an object of the class must maintain a pointer to the virtual table. This consumes an additional 4 bytes resulting in a total of 8 bytes being needed for an object of the class.

26. Consider the classes A, B, C as shown below

```
class A {
public:
    virtual void compute() = 0;
};

class B : public A {
public:
    void compute() {cout<<"Inside B::compute\n";}
};

class C: public B {
public:
    void compute() {cout<<"Inside C::compute\n";}
};
```

In the code below which compute function is called?

```
B *ptr = new C;
ptr->compute();
```

The function C::compute() function of class C is called.

Once a function is declared as virtual in the base class, then the corresponding functions in the derived class will be virtual even if they are not declared as virtual. So the compute function is virtual in class B and class C even though we have not explicitly declared them as virtual. So in the code above, the compute function of class C is called.

27. Consider the classes A and B.

```
class A {
public:
    virtual int compute(int x) { }
};
class B : public A {
public:
    virtual int compute(double x) { }
};
```

In the code below which function is called - A::compute or B::compute

```
A *ptr = new B();
ptr->compute(9);
ptr->compute(9.99);
```

In both cases A::compute is called. The answer looks counter-intuitive because we expect the derived class function to be called when using a base class pointer. However, in this case the base class function is called.

The reason for this behavior is because only the functions that have been declared as virtual in the base class can be invoked from the base class pointer. The virtual table for the object of class B will have function pointers to the virtual functions compute(int x) and compute(double x). The function pointer for compute(int x) points to A::compute(int x) and the function pointer for compute(double x) points to B::compute(double x).

When the address of the object of class B is assigned to a pointer of the base class A, then only the function pointer to compute(int x) is visible to the base class pointer. So even when an argument of type double is passed, since the function pointer to compute(double x) is not visible to the base class pointer, the argument is converted to an int and the function pointer to compute(int x) is used. The function pointer to compute(int x) points to A::compute(int x). So A::compute(int x) is called.

28. Consider the classes A and B below

```
class A  {
public:
    virtual void compute() {cout<<"Inside A::compute\n";}
};

class B : public A {
public:
    void compute() {cout<<"Inside B::compute\n";}
};
```

Suppose we have the following code

```
A *ptr = new B;
```

Can we access the compute function of class A using ptr?

It is possible to access the compute function of class A using ptr by explicitly invoking it. The syntax is ptr->A::compute();

29. When is extern "C" used?

The C++ compiler supports function overloading. So it is possible to have function1(int x) and function1(int x, int y). To distinguish between the two functions which have the same name but different arguments, the C++ compiler mangles the name of the function.

So function1(int x) becomes function1@aaaaa for instance and function1(int x, int y) becomes function1@bbbbb.

The mangling of function names is done for all functions by the C++ compiler irrespective of whether the function is overloaded or not. A C compiler on the other hand does not support function overloading and hence does not mangle the name of the function.

If the library obtained by using a C++ compiler is given to a user who has a C compiler, then we have a problem. The C++ compiler would have mangled the names of the functions. When the user tries to link to the functions in the library, the C compiler will search for the unmangled names. So the functions won't be found by the C compiler in the library.

To solve this problem extern "C" is used. extern "C" indicates to the C++ compiler not to mangle the names of the functions. So the library created using the C++ compiler can be linked by using a C compiler

The typical usage of extern "C" is

```
#ifdef __cplusplus
extern "C"
{
#endif

// Declare the functions that need to have C linkage


#ifdef __cplusplus
}
#endif
```

7. Computer Science Concepts

Scheduling

The scheduler decides which thread to execute. The different types of scheduling are first come first serve, round-robin, priority based, etc. When the scheduler picks a new thread to execute, a context switch is performed. Context switch involves the following actions

- ✓ save the context (register values, etc.) of the currently executing thread
- ✓ place the current thread in the queue
- ✓ pick the next thread to execute from the queue
- ✓ load the context of the new thread and execute it

Inter-Process Communication

Processes can communicate with one another using the following

- ✓ Pipes: one-way channel of communication between processes mainly used to connect the output of one process to the input of another process
- ✓ Message queues: queue for storing messages sent to a process or thread
- ✓ Semaphores: synchronization element that is mainly used for controlling access to a shared resource by multiple threads or processes
- ✓ Shared memory: memory that can be accessed by multiple processes
- ✓ Signals: an asynchronous notification about an event sent to a process or a thread
- ✓ Sockets: end-points in a computer network that are used for communicating across the network

Deadlocks

A deadlock occurs when two or more sequences of code execution are waiting for each other to finish. The necessary conditions for a deadlock are

- ✓ At least one resource can't be shared by all the processes

✓ At least one process has acquired some resources and is waiting to acquire another resource

✓ Resources can't be preempted

✓ The processes are circularly waiting for resources (example: Process P0 is waiting for resources of process P1 and P1 is waiting for resources of P0)

Deadlock prevention schemes try to make sure that at least one of these necessary conditions doesn't hold good.

Segmentation

In segmentation, the logical memory is partitioned into segments that have variable lengths. To access a particular address, the user specifies the segment number and the offset within the segment.

Paging

In paging, the logical memory is broken into fixed sized blocks called pages. The physical memory is also partitioned into fixed sized frames. Page tables maintain the mapping between the logical memory and physical memory. TLB (Translation Lookaside Buffer) is a cache that stores the page table.

Virtual Memory

Virtual memory is a technique which enables execution of processes that can't be completely be stored in physical memory. Logical memory is divided into pages. The pages that are currently in use are stored in physical memory. The unused pages that can't fit into physical memory are stored on the disk. When a page that is not present in physical memory is accessed (a page fault), an unused page is swapped out from physical memory to the disk and the page stored on the disk is swapped into physical memory.

Belady's anomaly states that the number of page faults can increase with increase in number of pages stored in physical memory

Least Recently Used (LRU) is one of the most commonly used page replacement algorithm, where-in the least recently used page is replaced to make space for the incoming page.

Thrashing occurs when too many page faults occur and the process spends more time on paging than actually executing

Miscellaneous

Watch dog timers are used to detect if a system has become unresponsive. Watchdog timer is initialized to a value and allowed to count down to zero. If the system is operating correctly, then watch dog timer is reinitialized before the timer reaches 0. If the system becomes unresponsive due to a deadlock, then the watchdog timer doesn't get reinitialized and eventually the timer becomes 0. When a watchdog timer reaches 0, the typical action taken is to reboot the system

DMA (Direct Memory Access) allows hardware to directly access physical memory without the intervention of the processor

Interrupt is an asynchronous signal to the processor that an important event has occurred. The processor suspends the current activity, executes the appropriate interrupt service routine and then resumes the suspended activity

1. What are the differences between a process and a thread?

Process and thread are sequences of code execution. A process can consist of one or more threads. Different threads in a process share the same address space whereas different processes running on a system have separate address spaces.

2. What are the differences between a mutex and a semaphore?

The primary function of a mutex is mutual exclusion. The mutex allows only a single thread to access a resource at a given time. A mutex has only two states - locked state and unlocked state.

The primary function of a semaphore is signaling. For instance, a thread can signal to another thread that a particular activity is complete using a semaphore. Semaphores are not restricted to just two states and have a count associated with them.

All the actions of a mutex can be performed using a semaphore but the reverse is not true.

3. What is the difference between a reentrant function and a thread safe function?

A reentrant function can be interrupted in the middle of its execution and then be safely resumed from its previous state. The interruption is usually caused by an interrupt service routine or a function call. The conditions for a function to be reentrant are

- A reentrant function should not have global data or static data
- A reentrant function should not modify its own code
- A reentrant function should not call non-reentrant functions

A thread-safe function can be called safely by multiple threads and maintains data concurrency even when accessed simultaneously by multiple threads.

A function can be thread-safe and still non-reentrant. For instance, consider a function that uses a lock on the critical section to ensure that it is thread-safe. Now suppose this function is used as an interrupt service routine. When the function is executing the critical section, another interrupt occurs and invokes the same function. The first instance of the function is suspended and the second instance of the function is invoked. However the second instance of the function can't complete as it can't enter the critical section since the first instance of the function has already acquired a lock on it. So this function is thread-safe but non-reentrant.

4. What are the main differences between kernel mode and user mode?

In the kernel mode, the code that is executed has complete and unrestricted access to CPU instructions, memory locations and underlying hardware. There is no protection offered in the kernel mode. So crashes in the kernel mode are catastrophic and will halt the entire system. Only the most basic functions of the OS which need to be carefully executed and the drivers which directly interact with the hardware are run in the kernel mode.

In the user mode, the code that is executed cannot directly access the underlying hardware. The code also can't access unallocated memory. Protection is offered in the user mode. So if a crash occurs in the user mode, then the system terminates execution of the offending process and recovers so that other user-mode processes can continue to be executed. Most of the programs developed by users run in user mode.

5. What are the main differences between a real time OS and a non-real time OS?

The primary goal of a real time OS is to provide deterministic execution time guarantees and to run fast. So the following differences are observed between a real time and non-real time OS

- a real time OS generally has no virtual memory
- a real time OS generally has no memory protection (mechanism to prevent a thread or task from accessing unallocated memory) and there is only a single mode in which the OS runs. A non-real time OS has memory protection and has a separate user mode and kernel mode.
- a real time OS generally has no dynamic linking

6. When are spin locks used?

When a thread uses a spin lock, it waits in a while loop until the lock is acquired. The thread does not go to a sleep state if the lock is currently unavailable. So the thread uses up CPU cycles as it waits on the lock. So this waiting is also called busy waiting.

Spin locks are efficient if the time needed to execute the critical section is smaller than the time taken to switch the context.

Consider a multi-core system where thread-A is executing on core-1 and thread-B is executing on core-2. Thread-A has successfully acquired the lock, while thread-B is waiting on the same lock. Let us say that the context switching time is 50 micro seconds and the time to execute the critical section is 20 micro seconds. If a normal lock was used, thread-B would be pre-empted and some other thread-C would be executed on core-2 after 50 micro seconds since the OS has to switch the context from thread-B to thread-C. However if a spin lock is used, after 20 micro seconds, thread-B can start executing on core-2 thereby saving 30 micro seconds.

Spin locks are also used in interrupt service routines since interrupt service routines can't go to a wait state (ISRs have to be processed immediately).

7. What is Priority Inversion?

Priority inversion is the scenario where a lower priority task is processed even though a higher priority task is waiting to be executed, thereby indirectly inverting the priorities of the tasks.

Consider 3 tasks L, M and H. L has lowest priority, M has medium priority and H has highest priority. Tasks L and H need to access a common resource R.

Initially task L is executing and locks the resource R. Then task H starts and tries to acquire R. Since L has already acquired the resource, H has to wait. Then task M starts. Since task M has higher priority than L, it pre-empts L. Now task M will continue until it is finished even though there is a higher priority task H. This is because task H can't run until L releases the resource and L can't run until M finishes. If the task H is starved due to priority inversion, then it can result in a serious system malfunction. This is what happened on the Mars Pathfinder. The high priority task was starved, causing the watch dog timer to reset the entire system.

To solve this issue, priority inheritance is used. When a high priority task waits on a resource held by a low priority task, the low priority task is temporarily assigned the priority of the high priority task until it releases the resource.

So in the example above if we used priority inversion, task L will get the priority of task H until it releases the resource. So task M can't pre-empt task L. Once task L releases the resource, it will get back its original priority. Then since task H is the highest priority task and it can acquire the resource released by L, task H will be scheduled next.

8. What is a race condition?

Race condition is a condition where the output of a system depends on the order in which events occur in the system. If the sequence in which the events occur is not how the programmer intended them to occur, then it can result in a bug. The problem with race conditions is that they are hard to reproduce and debug.

For instance, consider a multi-threaded system in which there are two threads and each thread tries to read the same shared variable, and then increments the value by 1.

If the order in which the events occur is as shown in the table below, then there is no problem

Thread-1	Thread-2	Value of shared variable
Read		1
Increment and write		1 + 1 = 2
	Read	2
	Increment and write	2 + 1 = 3

However if the order of execution of the two threads is as shown below, then there is a clear problem since the increment of the shared variable does not occur correctly.

Thread-1	Thread-2	Value of shared variable
Read		1
	Read	1
Increment and write		1 + 1 = 2
	Increment and write	1 + 1 = 2

To prevent race conditions from occurring, the critical section where a shared variable is operated upon should be protected using a synchronization construct such as a mutex or a semaphore, so that only one thread can be active in the critical section.

9. What is the difference between a DBMS (Database Management System) and a Relational DBMS?

In a DBMS, data is generally stored in files. It is not possible to apply normalization on the database. Example of a DBMS is an xml file.

In a Relational DBMS, the data is stored in a tabular form using the relational model. Since data is stored as tables, it is possible to apply normalization to the relational database. Example of a relational DBMS is mysql.

10. Describe the ACID properties in a database management system?

Each transaction in a database management system should follow the ACID properties: Atomicity, Consistency, Isolation and Durability

Atomicity: Each transaction may involve multiple operations in it. Atomicity indicates that every transaction should be treated as an atomic unit. Either all the operations in the transaction are completed or none of the operations are performed. For instance, if A wants to transfer $50 to B, then this transaction has two operations: debit A's account by $50 and credit B's account by $50. Atomicity indicates that we are not allowed to do only one operation. Either both the operations are done or none of them are done.

Consistency: If the database is consistent before the transaction, then it should remain consistent after the transaction is complete. For instance, suppose there is a request for buying 2 books but there is only one book in the warehouse, then the number of books in the database should not become negative.

Isolation: When there are concurrent transactions taking place in a database management system, the transactions should be isolated from one another. Each transaction is unaware of the other concurrent transactions.

Durability: Once a transaction is complete and the user has been notified about the success of the transaction, then the result of the transaction should persist and should not be lost. For instance, if a transaction is complete but before writing the result to the disk if the power is lost, then the results should be written to the disk once the power is back.

11. In SQL, what is the difference between inner join and outer join?

The join operation combines two tables into a single table. One of the fields in one table is used to find matching records in the other table. For instance, consider the Price table and the Quantity table below

ID	Price
A	$5
B	$2
C	$8

ID	Quantity
B	3
C	7
D	6

The join operation will be based on the key field ID which is common to both tables

Inner join will select the records where the joined keys are present in both the tables. So we get

ID	Price	Quantity
B	$2	3
C	$8	7

Left outer join will select all the records from the first table and those records from the second table that match the joined key. So we get

ID	Price	Quantity
A	$5	NULL
B	$2	3
C	$8	7

Right outer join will select all the records from the second table and those records from the first table that match the joined key. So we get

ID	Price	Quantity
B	$2	3
C	$8	7
D	NULL	6

Full outer join will select all the records from the first table and the second table.

ID	Price	Quantity
A	$5	NULL
B	$2	3
C	$8	7
D	NULL	6

12. What is denormalization?

Data normalization is the process of removing redundancy in a relational database. Denormalization is the opposite process wherein redundancy is introduced into a database in order to improve its performance.

When data normalization is done, the database is divided into multiple tables. When a query on the database is issued, data from two or more tables may have to be joined to get the result. This can slow down the performance. There are two ways in which redundancy can be introduced to speed up the performance:

1. Store multiple copies of each table on the disk - This keeps the design of the table free from redundancy. The database management system has to ensure that multiple copies are kept consistent

2. Have redundancy in the logical data design – This complicates the database design.

13. Differentiate between OSI model and TCP/IP model?

OSI is a theoretical model proposed by the International Organization for Standardization (ISO). It consists of 7 layers. The interfaces and services in the model are clearly defined.

TCP/IP is the protocol suite which is practically used for communicating on the internet. It consists of 4 layers. The interfaces and services are not clearly separated in TCP/IP.

The layers of OSI and TCP/IP are given below

Application
Presentation
Session
Transport
Network
Data link
Physical

Application
Transport
Network
Network interface

13. What is circuit switching and packet switching?

In circuit switching, a static communication channel is established between the sender and the receiver. The communication channel is a dedicated channel that is used exclusively by the sender and receiver. The order of intermediate nodes in the communication channel is pre-established and doesn't change. The advantage of circuit switching is reliability while the disadvantage is low utilization of the communication channel.

In packet switching, the data to be transferred is divided into packets and sent across the network. The exact route which the packets will take is determined dynamically. Each packet can take a different path and the packets can arrive out of order. The advantage of packet switching is that the effective utilization of the communication channel increases.

15. Describe the TCP 3-way handshake?

If A wants to establish a TCP connection with B, then A first sends a TCP packet with the SYN (Synchronize) bit set to 1 in the TCP header. Let the sequence number in the TCP header of this packet be X.

When B receives the packet, B sends a response with SYN and ACK (Acknowledgement) bits set to 1. The sequence number in this packet is initialized to Y and the acknowledgement number is set to X+1.

On receiving the packet sent by B, A sends the response with ACK bit set to 1. The sequence number of this packet will be X+1 and the acknowledgement number will be Y+1.

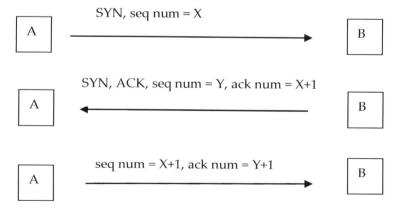

16. What is the difference between TCP and UDP?

The differences between TCP and UDP are

1. Connection: TCP is a connection oriented protocol that first establishes a connection between sender and receiver. UDP is a connectionless protocol where the packet is sent across the network without first establishing a connection

2. Reliability: As long as the connection is active, it is the responsibility of TCP to make sure that a transmitted packet is received by the receiver. If a packet is lost and the sender doesn't get back an acknowledgement for a packet, then the sender resends the packet. In UDP, since there is no acknowledgement sent for a received packet, the sender has no information if the packet was received at the destination

3. Ordering of packets: The TCP header consists of sequence numbers. So if the packets arrive out of order, TCP can rearrange the data packets so that the upper layer receives packets in the order in which they were sent. The UDP header doesn't consist of sequence numbers. So UDP can't guarantee that the data packets will be delivered in the order in which they were sent. If ordering of data packets is needed, then the application layer should take care of it.

4. Flow control: Flow control is performed in TCP. If the sender is fast and the receiver is slow, then flow control limits the rate at which data is sent by the sender. UDP has no flow control.

So UDP is a light weight protocol compared to TCP. Example of protocols that use TCP are HTTP, FTP and SMTP. Examples of protocols that use UDP are DNS (Domain Name System) and TFTP (Trivial File Transfer Protocol)

17. What is the difference between IPv4 and IPv6?

The differences between IPv4 and IPv6 are:

1. Address: An IPv4 address is 32 bit long whereas an IPv6 address is 128 bit long

2. Header length: The IPv4 header is 20 bytes long whereas an IPv6 header is 40 bytes long

3. Checksum: Checksum is present in the IPv4 header whereas the checksum is absent in the IPv6 header

4. Internet Protocol Security (IPsec): IPsec is optional in IPv4 whereas it is mandatory in IPv6

5. Fragmentation: Fragmentation is done by the host and routers in IPv4 whereas fragmentation is done only by the host in IPv6.

18. What are the sequence of events that occur when you type a URL in a browser?

The URL is first sent to a Domain Name Server. The DNS lookup happens over UDP. The DNS server returns the IP address corresponding to the URL.

The browser then makes a HTTP request to the server to get the web page. The HTTP request is sent via TCP. The IP address returned by the DNS server is filled into the destination address of the IP header. TCP will establish a 3 way handshake with the webserver. The webserver will then respond to the HTTP request with a HTTP response. The browser will parse the information sent by the web server and display it. Unless the connection is a persistent one, the webserver will close the HTTP session. The TCP connection between the browser and the webserver is closed using the four way handshake.

8. Puzzles

In most interviews, the interviewer asks puzzles to get an idea of the general problem solving skills of the candidate.

In this section, we will cover the following topics

1. Arithmetic puzzles
2. Measurement puzzles
3. Probability puzzles
4. Lateral thinking puzzles
5. Logic puzzles
6. Classic puzzles

8.1 Arithmetic Puzzles

1. In a certain type of sugar syrup, 99% of the weight of the sugar syrup is made of water while the remaining 1% is made of sugar. 100 pounds of sugar syrup is exposed to the sun and some of the water evaporates. The sugar syrup is now composed of 98% water. How much of water has evaporated?

It looks like 1 pound of water has evaporated, but this is not the right answer.

Initially we have 99 pounds of water and 1 pound of sugar in the sugar syrup. After the water evaporates, there is 98% of water and 2% of sugar. The amount of sugar remains constant after evaporation. So even after evaporation, there is still 1 pound of sugar in the sugar syrup.

Now 1 pound is 2% of the sugar syrup

So how many pounds (x) is 100% of sugar syrup

x = 100/2 = 50 pounds

So the final weight of the sugar syrup is 50 pounds. Of this, 1 pound is sugar. So only 49 pounds of water is present after evaporation. Before evaporation, we had 99 pounds of water. So the amount of water that has evaporated is 99 - 49 = **50 pounds**.

2. A car travels a distance of 60 miles from city A to city B at an average speed of 30 mph. How fast should the car travel on the return leg from city B back to city A so that the average speed for the entire journey is 60 mph?

At first glance it looks as if the car should be driven at a speed of 90 mph on the return journey so that the average speed for the entire journey is 60 mph. However this is not the case.

In the first leg of the journey, the car travels 60 miles at 30 mph. So the total time taken for the first leg of the journey = 60/30 = 2 hours.

For the return leg of the journey, the car travels 60 miles. Let the speed in the return journey be S and the time taken be T.

For the entire journey (from A to B and then back from B to A), the total distance covered = 60 + 60 = 120 miles. The total time for the entire journey = 2 + T

Average speed = total distance / total time

So average speed for entire journey = 120 / (2 + T)

Since average speed for entire journey must be 60 mph, 60 = 120 / (2+T)

If we solve this equation, we get T = 0. This means that the car should travel the 60 miles on the return leg within 0 time which implies that the car should travel at infinite speed! This is obviously not possible. So **it is not possible to achieve an average speed of 60 mph on the return journey.**

3. How many squares are there in a chessboard?

A chess board has 8 rows and 8 columns. Starting at any row and column we can form a square of size 1*1. Since there are 8 rows and 8 columns, the number of squares of size 1 are 8 * 8 = 64.

To form a square of size 2*2, we can't start from the last row and last column. For instance a 2*2 square can start in row 7 and extend into row 8, but it can't start at row 8 itself. So the number of 2*2 squares we can form = 7 * 7 = 49.

Similarly to form a square of size 3*3, we can't start from the last two rows and last two columns. So the number of 3*3 squares we can form = 6 * 6 = 36.

Using this reasoning, we can compute the total number of squares on the board as (8*8) + (7*7) + (6*6) + (5*5) + (4*4) + (3*3) + (2*2) + (1*1) = 64 + 49 + 36 + 25 + 16 + 9 + 4 + 1 = **204**

4. How many rectangles are there in a chessboard?

A chess board has 8 rows and 8 columns. To have 8 rows, there should be 9 horizontal lines (H1 to H9) and to have 8 columns, there should be 9 vertical lines (V1 to V9).

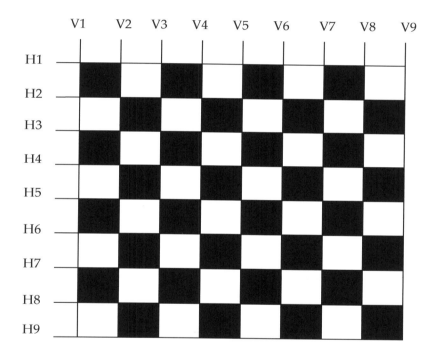

To form a unique rectangle, we can pick any 2 horizontal lines and any 2 vertical lines. For instance the intersection of the lines H1, H2, V3, and V7 forms one unique rectangle. The number of ways in which we can pick 2 horizontal lines out of 9 lines is $^9C_2$. The number of ways in which we can pick 2 vertical lines out of 9 lines is $^9C_2$. So the total number of rectangles = $^9C_2 * ^9C_2 = 36 * 36 = $ **1296**.

5. A small cube measures 1 * 1 * 1. 1000 such small cubes are used to make a single large cube that measures 10 * 10 * 10. The large cube is completely dipped in blue paint. How many of the small cubes have paint on them?

Each face of the cube measures 10 * 10. So there are 100 smaller cubes on each face. When a face is dipped in paint all the 100 smaller cubes get painted. Since there are 6 faces on a cube it looks like 6 * 100 = 600 cubes are painted. However this is not the correct answer since some of the cubes have been counted multiple times and have to be subtracted to arrive at the correct answer.

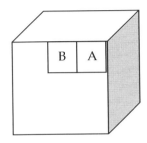

Consider the small cube (labeled A in the diagram) at the corner of the large cube. It gets counted 3 times since it is common to 3 faces. Ideally we should count it only once. So we should subtract 2 cubes for every corner cube. There are totally 8 corners in a cube. So we should subtract 2 * 8 = 16 cubes.

Consider the small non-corner cubes (labeled B in the diagram) that are at an edge of the large cube. There are 8 such small cubes at each edge (10 cubes along edge – 2 corner cubes = 8). These cubes are counted twice but they should have been counted only once. So we should subtract 8 cubes for each edge. There are totally 12 edges in a cube. So we should subtract 12 * 8 = 96 cubes.

So the total number of cubes that are painted = 600 - (16 + 96) = **488**

In general, if we have an N * N * N cube, then the number of non-unique smaller cubes = $6N^2$
Number of cubes to be subtracted at the corners = 8 corners * 2 per corner = 16 (this is independent of N). Number of cubes to be subtracted at the edges other than corners = 12 edges * (N-2) per edge = 12 * (N-2)

So the number of unique cubes that are painted = $6N^2 - (12(N-2) + 16) = 6N^2 - 12N + 8$

$6.$ Find the angle between the hour hand and minute hand in a clock at any given time

Let the angles of the hour and minute hands be calculated from the 12 o' clock position.

The minute hand moves 360° in 60 minutes. So the number of degrees it moves in 1 minute = 360/60 = 6°. If the time is M minutes in the clock, then the angle made by the minute hand from the 12 o' clock position is $\theta_M = 6 * M$

The hour hand moves 360° in 12 hours. So the number of degrees the hour hand moves in 1 hour = 360/12 = 30°. The number of minutes in 12 hours = 60*12 = 720. So the hour hand moves 360° in 720 minutes. So the number of degrees it moves in 1 minute is 360/720 = 0.5° per minutes. If the time is H hours and M minutes in the clock, then the angle made by the hour hand from the 12 o' clock position is $\theta_H = 30H + 0.5M$

The absolute difference between θ_H and θ_M will give the angle between the hour hand and minute hand

= absolute_value(30H + 0.5M - 6M) = **absolute_value(30H - 5.5M)**

So if the time is 3:30, then the angle between the two hands = absolute_value(30*3 - 5.5 * 30) = 75°.

$7.$ How many times will the hour hand and minute hand of a clock be exactly aligned in a day?

The minute hand is faster than the hour hand. The minute hand overtakes the hour hand many times in a day. Each time the minute hand overtakes the hour hand, the angle between them will be zero (0° and 360° are equivalent) and they will be exactly aligned. So to solve the problem, we need to find the number of times the minute hand overtakes the hour hand.

For each hour, the hour hand moves 360/12 = 30° whereas the minute hand moves 360°. So for each hour, the minute hand is ahead of the hour hand by 360 - 30 = 330°.

Over a 24 hour period, the minute hand will be ahead of the hour hand by 330 * 24 = 7920°

If the angle between the hour hand and minute hand is 360° - then there is 1 overtake

If the angle between hour hand and minute hand is 7920°- then how many overtakes (x)?

x = 7920 / 360 = 22

So the minute hand overtakes the hour hand 22 times in a day. So the hour hand and minute hand will be exactly aligned **22 times** in a day.

To calculate the exact time when the hour hand and minute hand are aligned, we use the formula derived in the previous problem: the angle between the hour hand and the minute hand = absolute_value(30H - 5.5M).

When the hour and minute hand are exactly aligned, the angle between them will be zero. So 30H - 5.5M = 0

M = 30 H / 5.5

Using this formula, for a particular hour H, we can calculate the minute M when the hands are exactly aligned as shown in the table below

Hour	Minute
0	0
1	5.45
2	10.91
3	16.36
4	21.82
5	27.27
6	32.73
7	38.18
8	43.64
9	49.09
10	54.54
11	60

Note that 11:60 is the same as 0:0

8. There are 100 players in a knockout tennis tournament where each loser is immediately eliminated and the winner advances to the next round. How many matches should be played to determine the final winner?

The easy way to solve the problem is to use the following argument: at the end of the tournament there will be only 1 winner and the remaining 99 players have to be eliminated. In each match, exactly 1 player is eliminated. So **99 matches** have to be played to eliminate 99 players and determine the final winner. In general if there are N players, then N-1 matches will be needed

9. There is a rectangular floor with size m*n. Square tiles have to be laid on the floor without breaking any tile so that the entire floor is covered. Find the maximum size of the square tile with which this is possible.

The total area of the floor is m*n. Let the length of one side of the square tile be k. Then the area of a single tile is k^2.

Let the number of tiles needed to fill the room be t.

Then, $t * k^2 = m * n$. So $t = m * n / k^2 = m * n / (k * k)$

Since the tiles should not be broken, the number of tiles t should be an integer. This implies that k should be a factor of m and k should also be a factor of n. So **the maximum possible size of the square tile is equal to the greatest common factor of m and n**.

10. There are N people in a room. Two people shake hands only if they know each other. Prove that there are at least two people with the same number of handshakes

---

If a person does not know anyone then he will make no handshakes. If a person knows everyone else in the room then he will make N-1 handshakes. So the number of handshakes that a person can make is in the range 0 to N-1. So there are a total of N possibilities.

Now, if a person does not shake hands with anybody, then no person can shake hands with everybody in the room since one person didn't participate in the handshakes at all.

Similarly if a person shakes hands with everybody in the room, then no person can have 0 handshakes since everybody has participated in at least one hand shake.

So 0 handshakes and N-1 handshakes are mutually exclusive. Only one of them can occur and never both. So the number of possible handshakes a person can make is either in the range (1, N-1) or in the range (0, N-2). So that is a total of N-1 possibilities in either case.

There are N people and N-1 possible number of handshakes. So there are more people than the possible number of handshakes. Using the pigeon-hole principle, we infer that at least two of the people should have the same number of handshakes.

8.2 Measurement Puzzles

1. How will you get 4 gallons of water using a 3 gallon jug and a 5 gallon jug?

Fill the 3 gallon jug completely

Pour water from the 3 gallon jug completely into the 5 gallon jug. The 5 gallon jug now has 3 gallons of water.

Fill the 3 gallon jug completely

Pour water from the 3 gallon jug into the 5 gallon jug until the 5 gallon jug is full. So the 3 gallon jug now has 1 gallon of water.

Empty the 5 gallon jug completely

Pour the 1 gallon of water from the 3 gallon jug to the 5 gallon jug. The 5 gallon jug now has 1 gallon of water

Fill the 3 gallon jug completely

Pour the water completely from 3 gallon jug into the 5 gallon jug. The 5 gallon jug now has 4 gallons of water.

2. How will you get 6 gallons of water using a 7 gallon jug and a 4 gallon jug?

Fill the 7 gallon jug completely.

Fill the 4 gallon jug completely from 7 gallon jug. The 7 gallon jug now has 3 gallons of water.

Empty the 4 gallon jug

Fill the 4 gallon jug using the remaining 3 gallons of water in the 7 gallon jug. The 4 gallon jug now has 3 gallons and the 7 gallon jug is empty.

Fill up the 7 gallon jug completely.

Pour the water from the 7 gallon jug into the 4 gallon jug until the 4 gallon jug fills up. The 4 gallon jug already had 3 gallons in it and so it can only accept another one gallon. So 6 gallons remain in the 7 gallon jug.

3. How will you get 6 gallons of water using a 4 gallon jug and a 9 gallon jug?

Fill the 9 gallon jug completely.

Fill the 4 gallon jug completely from 9 gallon jug. The 9 gallon jug now has 5 gallons of water.

Empty the 4 gallon jug

Fill the 4 gallon jug completely using the remaining 5 gallons of water in the 9 gallon jug. The 9 gallon jug now has 1 gallon of water in it.

Empty the 4 gallon jug

Fill the 4 gallon jug using the remaining 1 gallon of water in the 9 gallon jug. The 4 gallon jug now has 1 gallon and the 9 gallon jug is empty.

Fill up the 9 gallon jug completely.

Pour the water from the 9 gallon jug to the 4 gallon jug until the 4 gallon jug fills up. The 4 gallon jug already had 1 gallon in it and so it can accept another 3 gallons. So 6 gallons remain in the 9 gallon jug.

4. There is a small jug with capacity x gallons and another bigger jug with capacity y gallons. x and y are co-prime. How will you get exactly 1 gallon of water using these two jugs?

Two numbers are co-primes if the only common factor between the two numbers is 1. For instance, 3 and 8 are co-prime.

If two numbers x and y are co-prime, we are guaranteed that there is some multiple of x which when divided by y leaves a remainder of 1 (this is called the multiplicative inverse property of co-primes under modulo operation). For instance, consider 33 which is a multiple of three. 33 on dividing by 8 gives a remainder of 1.

So to measure 1 gallon, we have to use the following technique

- Find the multiple M of x which when divided by y leaves a remainder of 1.

- Transfer a total of M gallons of water from the small jug to the big jug, x gallons at a time. If the big jug becomes full at any point, then discard the water in the big jug and keep continuing.

At the end, 1 gallon of water will be left in the large jug.

5. There are two sandglasses: one measuring 7 minutes and the other measuring 11 minutes. An egg needs 15 minutes to boil. Using just these two sandglasses, accurately measure 15 minutes and boil the egg.

First start the 7 minute sandglass and the 11 minute sandglass simultaneously.

When the 7 minute sandglass runs out, start boiling the egg.

When the 11 minute sandglass runs out, the egg would have boiled for 11-7 = 4 minutes.

Reverse the 11 minute sandglass and start it. When the 11 minute sandglass runs out, stop boiling the egg. The egg would have boiled for a total of 4+11 minutes = 15 minutes.

6. Using a 7 minute sandglass and a 4 minute sandglass, how can you measure 9 minutes?

First start the 7 minute sandglass and the 4 minute sandglass simultaneously. The measurement of 9 minutes duration starts as soon as both sandglasses are started

At 4 minutes, the 4 minute sandglass runs out. So reverse the 4 minute sandglass.

At 7 minutes, the 7 minute sandglass runs out. So reverse the 7 minute sandglass.

At 8 minutes, the 4 minute sandglass runs out again. Now 1 minute has passed since the 7 minute sandglass has been reversed. Reverse the 7 minute sandglass.

At 9 minutes, the 7 minute sandglass runs out since it had only 1 minute of sand left in it.

So this way 9 minutes can be measured using the 7 minute and 4 minute sandglasses.

7. There are two ropes. Each rope takes one hour to burn completely. The ropes burn non-uniformly. So the length of the ropes burnt can't be used to find the time elapsed. How will you time 45 minutes using the two ropes?

Start burning the first rope by lighting a fire at both ends of the first rope. At the same time, light a fire at one end of the second rope.

Since the fire is started from both ends of the first rope, the two flames will meet after 30 minutes (note that the point where the flames meet need not be the center of the rope as the ropes burn non-uniformly).

When the two flames in the first rope meet, the first rope will be completely burnt. The second rope will still need another 30 minutes to burn completely. Now start a flame at the other end of the second rope. The two flames on the second rope will meet after 15 minutes.

When the two flames on the second rope meet, a total of 30 + 15 = 45 minutes would have elapsed.

8. There are 8 marbles. One of the marbles weighs heavier than the other marbles. All the remaining 7 marbles have the same weight. You are given a weighing pan balance. Find the heavier marble using minimum number of weighings

We need only 2 steps to find the heavier marble.

Step 1: Place 3 marbles on the left side of the scale and 3 marbles on the right side of the scale.

If the scale indicates that the marbles on one of the side are heavier, then

Step 2: Discard the 3 marbles from the lighter side of the scale and pick the 3 marbles from the heavier side of the scale. Reinitialize the scale. Place one of the marbles on the left side of the scale and another marble on the right side. If the scale indicates that one of them is heavier, then this is the heaviest marble. If the scale indicates that both are of the same weight, then the third marble which has not been used is the heaviest marble.

If the scale indicates that marbles on both sides are of the same weight, then

> Step 2: Discard all the 6 marbles from the scale. Reinitialize the scale. Two marbles remain. Place one of the marbles on the left pan and the other on the right pan. The scale will indicate the heaviest marble.

9. There are 10 boxes of oranges. Each box can contain either all good oranges or all bad oranges. One of the boxes contains bad oranges. The remaining 9 boxes contain good oranges. Each good orange weighs 1 pound while a bad orange weighs 0.9 pounds. You are given a digital weighing machine. How will you find the box which has bad oranges with just a single weighing?

It is possible to find the box with bad oranges using the digital weighing machine only once. Pick one orange from the first box, two oranges from the second box, ... n oranges from the nth box. Place all of them on the weighing machine and find the weight W.

There are a total of 1+2+3 ... +10 = 55 oranges. If all oranges were good the total weight should be 55 pounds. However since one of the boxes has bad oranges that are lighter, the weight will be less than 55 pounds.

If the weight W is 54.9, then there is exactly one bad orange in 55 oranges because a bad orange is lighter by 0.1 pound. Since the only box from which we picked only a single orange is the first box, the first box must have the bad orange.

Similarly if the weight is 54.8, then there are exactly two bad oranges in the 55 oranges. Since the box from which we picked exactly two oranges is the second box, the second box must have the bad oranges.

Using this reasoning we have the results below

Weight	Bad orange box number
54.9	1
54.8	2
54.7	3
54.6	4
54.5	5
54.4	6
54.3	7

54.2	8
54.1	9
54	10

10. There are 3 boxes of oranges. Each box can contain either all good oranges or all bad oranges. Any of the boxes can contain bad oranges. So the number of boxes that contain bad oranges can be 0 or 1 or 2 or 3. A good orange weighs 1 pound while a bad orange weighs 0.9 pounds. You are given a digital weighing machine. How will you find which boxes have bad oranges with just a single weighing?

It is possible to find the boxes with bad oranges using the digital weighing machine only once. Pick one orange from the first box, two oranges from the second box and four oranges from the third box (in general 2^{n-1} oranges from the nth box). Place the chosen oranges on the weighing machine and find the weight.

Based on the weight obtained, we can make the following inference

Weight	Inference
7	All the boxes have good oranges (1*1 + 2*1 + 4*1).
6.9	1st box has bad oranges (1*0.9 + 2*1 + 4*1).
6.8	2nd box has bad oranges (1*1 + 2*0.9 + 4*1).
6.7	1st and 2nd box have bad oranges (1*0.9 + 2*0.9 + 4*1)
6.6	3rd box has the bad oranges (1*1 + 2*1 + 4*0.9)
6.5	3rd box and 1st box have bad oranges (1*0.9 + 2*1 + 4*0.9)
6.4	3rd box and 2nd box have bad oranges (1*1 + 2*0.9 + 4*0.9)
6.3	All boxes have bad oranges (1*0.9 + 2*0.9 + 4*0.9)

11. A company has to sort boxes into the following four weight categories: 1-25 pounds, 26-50 pounds, 51-75 pounds and 76-100 pounds. A scale will be provided to weigh a box. If the weight of the box is within the range of the scale, then a bulb will glow otherwise the bulb will not glow. You can choose the range of the scale. For instance if you choose a scale 20-40 and weight of the box is 38, then the light will glow. Each scale is expensive. What is the minimum number of scales that you will need to sort the boxes?

The minimum number of scales required is **2**. The range of weights of the scales will be 1-50 pounds and 26-75 pounds. Weigh each box in both the scales and do the following

If the 1-50 pound scale glows and the 26-75 pound scale is off, then the weight of the box is 1-25 pounds

If the 1-50 pound scale glows and the 26-75 pound scale glows, then the weight of the box is 26-50 pounds

If the 1-50 pound scale is off and the 26-75 pound scale glows, then the weight of the box is 51-75 pounds

If the 1-50 pound scale is off and the 26-75 pound scale is off, then the weight of the box is 76-100 pounds

12. You are given a weighing pan balance and asked to purchase weights to measure any whole number up to 100 pounds. What is the least number of weights that you need to purchase?

The answer that an interview candidate is likely to give is that 7 weights are needed, the weights being: 1 pound, 2 pounds, 4 pounds, 8 pounds, 16 pounds, 32 pounds and 64 pounds. However this answer is wrong.

The least number of weights required is **5**, the weights are: 1 pound, 3 pounds, 9 pounds, 27 pounds and 81 pounds (powers of 3). Any number from 1 to 100 can be represented using a combination of addition and subtraction of these weights. For instance, the number 25 can be represented as 27 + 1 - 3. So to measure if an object weighs 25 pounds,

27 pounds and 1 pound is placed in one pan while the object and 3 pounds is placed in the other pan.

8.3 Probability Puzzles

1. It is night and the lights are not working in your room. The drawer has socks of three different colors - black, white and grey. How many socks do you have to remove from the drawers to be absolutely sure that you have a matching pair of socks?

Let us say that you remove two socks from the drawers. In the worst case both socks can be of different colors and you can't be sure of having a matching pair.

Let us say that you remove three socks from the drawers. In the worst case, all the three socks have different colors and you can't be sure of having a matching pair of socks. So in the worst case you will have 1 black socks, 1 white socks and 1 grey socks. Now when you pick up the fourth socks from the drawer, its color is either black or white or grey. So it has to match with any one of the socks that you already have. So to be absolutely sure that you have a matching socks pair, the least number of socks to pick up is **4**.

In general, the problem can be solved using the pigeon hole principle. If there are N unique item types, and N+1 items are chosen, then there will be at least one type which has two chosen items. For instance if a bag contains 50 red balls, 25 green balls, 34 blue balls and 48 yellow balls then there are 4 unique item types (red, green, blue and yellow). So to be absolutely sure to pick two balls of the same color, N+1 = 4+1 = 5 balls have to be picked.

2. A bag contains a single marble that is either white or black. A new white marble is added to the bag and the bag is shaken. Then a marble is removed from the bag and it happens to be white. What is the probability that the remaining marble in the bag is also white?

It may initially look as though the answer is 0.5, but this answer is not correct.

Let marble P be inside the bag. Its color may be black or white. Let the white marble Q be added to the bag. A white marble is removed from the bag. So there are a total of three possibilities by which a white marble can be removed from the bag as shown in the diagrams below

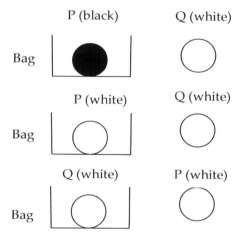

Out of these 3 possibilities, the bag has a white marble in two of the scenarios. So the probability of having a white marble in the bag is **2/3**.

3. Initially bag A has 10 red marbles and bag B has 10 blue marbles. Three marbles are randomly picked from bag A and added to bag B. Then 3 marbles are randomly picked from bag B and added to bag A. Which bag contains more marbles of the other color? (which of the two is greater - the number of blue marbles in bag A OR the number of red marbles in bag B)

Initially 3 red marbles are removed from bag A and added to bag B. Bag A now has 7 red marbles. Bag B now has 10 blue marbles and 3 red marbles.

Now 3 marbles are removed from bag B and added to A. The manner in which this can be done and the effect on the bags is shown in the table

Action	Effect on bag A	Effect on bag B
Remove 3 blue marbles from B and add to A	7 red, 3 blue	7 blue, 3 red
Remove 2 blue marbles and 1 red marble from B and add to A	8 red, 2 blue	8 blue, 2 red
Remove 1 blue marble and 2 red marbles from B and add to A	9 red, 1 blue	9 blue, 1 red
Remove 3 red marbles from B and add to A	10 red	10 blue

So there are four possibilities and in each of the four possibilities, the number of blue marbles in bag A is equal to the number of red marbles in bag B. So at the end, both bags contain the same number of marbles of the other color.

4. There are 50 red marbles and 50 blue marbles. You are allowed to place all the marbles in two jars in whatever manner you want. One of the jars will then be randomly selected and given to you from which you have to pick a marble randomly. If you pick a blue marble you win. How should you arrange the marbles in the jars to maximize your chances of winning?

To maximize the chances of winning, place 1 blue marble in the first jar and place the remaining marbles (49 blue marbles and 50 red marbles) in the second jar.

The likelihood of selecting the first jar is 0.5. Once the first jar is selected, the likelihood of choosing a blue marble is 1 since there is only a single blue marble in the jar. So the likelihood of selecting the first jar and choosing the blue marble = 0.5 * 1 = 0.5

The likelihood of selecting the second jar is 0.5. Once the second jar is selected, the likelihood of choosing a blue marble = number of blue marbles / total number of marbles = 49 / (49+50) = 49/99. The likelihood of selecting the second jar and choosing the blue marble = 0.5 * 49 / 99 = 0.247

The overall likelihood of choosing the blue marble = 0.5 + 0.247 = **0.747**

5. You are given two dice. The first dice is a normal dice while the second dice has no numbers on it. How will you mark numbers on the second dice so that when both dice are thrown, the sum of the results of the two dice is uniformly distributed between 1 and 12?

Suppose we get a six on the second dice, then when the first dice generates numbers from 1 to 6, the sum of the results of the first two dice will be in the range 7 to 12.

Suppose we get a zero on the second dice, then when the first dice generates numbers from 1 to 6, the sum of the results of the first two dice will be in the range 1 to 6.

To ensure that there is an equal likelihood of generating numbers from 1 to 12, the second dice should have an equal number of zeroes and sixes. So three faces of the second dice should be marked with 0 and the remaining three faces of the second dice should be marked with 6.

6. You are participating in a game show where you are shown 3 doors. Behind one of the doors is a treasure. When you have decided which door to pick, the game show host opens another door which you have not chosen and shows that there is nothing behind. Now there are two doors left and behind one of them is a treasure - either the one you have picked or the one you haven't picked. You are allowed to change your original decision. What should you do?

The answer to this problem is counter-intuitive. It looks as though there is an equal likelihood that the treasure is behind any of the two doors. But this is not the case.

To have a deeper understanding, let us first modify the problem. Suppose there are 100 doors shown and there is treasure only behind one of the doors. When you choose a door there is a 1/100 chance that the treasure is behind that door. There is 99/100 chance that the treasure is behind some other door.

Now the game show host opens 98 of the doors and shows you that there is no treasure behind any of the 98 doors. Now the probability that there is treasure behind the door you have chosen continues to be 1/100. The probability that the treasure is present in the remaining doors continues to be 99/100. But only one of the remaining doors is unopened. So the probability of the treasure in the remaining unopened door which you didn't choose is 99/100. So if you are allowed to switch the doors, you should.

Similarly, when there are 3 doors and you choose 1 of the doors, the probability of treasure behind the door is 1/3. When the game show host opens one of the doors, then the probability that the treasure is behind the unopened door which you have not chosen is 2/3. So if you are allowed to switch the doors, you should.

7. There are 50 people in a room. Your friend offers a bet. If all persons in the room have different birthdays, then your friend will pay you $100. If any two people in the room share the same birthday, then you have to pay your friend $100. Will you accept the bet?

The likelihood that any two persons share the same birthday is 1/365. The likelihood that any two people have different birthdays is 364/365.

In the room of 50 people, the number of pairs of people present is $^{50}C_2 = 1225$.

The probability that a pair of people have different birthdays is 364/365

So the probability that all the 1225 pairs have different birthdays is $(364/365)^{1225} = 0.035$.

So the probability that any of the 1225 pairs have the same birthday = 1 - 0.035 = 0.965.

So there is a very high likelihood that any two people share the same birthday. So **you should not take the bet**.

If the number of persons in the room is 23, then the likelihood of two people sharing the same birthday is 0.4995. If there are more than 23 people, then the likelihood of two people sharing the same birthday increases to more than 0.5. So you can accept the bet only if there are up to 23 people in the room.

8. In a particular country, people only want boy children. So if a family gets a boy child, the family stops having kids. If they get a girl child, then they continue to have kids until they get a boy. What is the ratio of boys to girls in this country? Assume that there is an equal likelihood of getting a boy or a girl.

Surprisingly the ratio of number of boys to number of girls is equal (1:1) in that country.

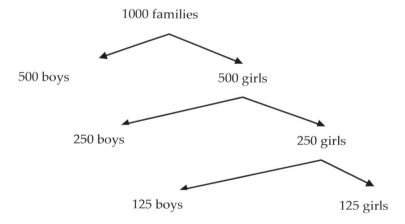

1000 families

500 boys   500 girls

250 boys   250 girls

125 boys   125 girls

Let us say that there are 1000 families in the country. 500 of the families will have the first kid as a boy and 500 of them will have the first kid as a girl. So at this stage there are 500 boys and 500 girls. So the number of boys and girls are equal.

Next the 500 families that had a girl child will have a second child. In 250 of the families the second child will be a boy and in 250 of the families the second child will be a girl. This is shown in the diagram. So at this stage there are 500 + 250 = 750 boys. The number of girls = 500 + 250 = 750. So there are equal number of boys and girls.

Next the 250 families that had two girl children will have a third child. In 125 of the families, the third child will be a boy and in 125 of the families the third child will be a girl. This is shown in the diagram below.

So at this stage there are 500 + 250 + 125 = 875 boys. The number of girls = 500 + 250 + 125 = 875. So there are equal number of boys and girls.

We observe that at each stage, there are equal number of boys and girls and this will continue in further stages. So **the proportion of boys to girls will be 1:1**.

9. 100 airline travelers are waiting in line to board a plane that has 100 seats. Each traveler has been assigned a specific seat number on the plane. The first traveler in the line has lost his boarding pass and will pick one of the 100 seats at random to sit. The remaining travelers will sit in the seat assigned to them if it is free. But if the seat assigned to them is already occupied, then they will choose a random free seat. What is the probability that the last traveler to board the plane will sit in his proper seat?

Let the travelers in the line be labeled from T1 to T100. Let the probability that the traveler Ti will **not** sit in his seat be P(i).

The first traveler T1 has lost his boarding pass and will choose a seat at random.

The next passenger T2 will not sit in his seat, if T1 sits in T2's seat. T1 has a 1/100 chance of choosing T2's seat. So

P(2) = 1/100

T3 will not sit in his seat, if T1 sits in T3's seat or if T2 sits in T3's seat. T1 has a 1/100 chance of choosing T3's seat.

P(3) = 1/100 + probability that T2 sits in T3's seat.

P(3) = 1/100 + probability that T2 doesn't sit on his seat * probability that T2 chooses seat of T3

By definition, probability that T2 doesn't sit on his seat is P(2). When T2 chooses, there are 99 seats available. So the probability that T2 chooses the seat of T3 is 1/99.

P(3) = 1/100 + P(2) * (1/99)

P(3) = 1/100 + (1/100) * (1/99)

P(3) = 1/100 (1 + 1/99)

P(3) = 1/99

T4 will not sit in his seat, if T1 sits in T4's seat or if T2 sits in T4's seat or if T3 sits on T4's seat. T1 has a 1/100 chance of choosing T4's seat.

P(4) = 1/100 + probability that T2 sits in T4's seat + probability that T3 sits in T4's seat

P(3) = 1/100 + (probability that T2 doesn't sit on his seat * probability that T2 chooses seat of T3) + (probability that T3 doesn't sit on his seat * probability that T3 chooses seat of T4)

By definition, probability that T2 doesn't sit on his seat is P(2). When T2 chooses, there are 99 seats available. So the probability that T2 chooses the seat of T4 is 1/99.

By definition, probability that T3 doesn't sit on his seat is P(3). When T3 chooses, there are 98 seats available. So the probability that T3 chooses the seat of T4 is 1/98.

P(4) = 1/100 + P(2) * (1/99) + P(3) * (1/98)

P(4) = 1/100 + (1/100) * (1/99) + (1/99) * (1/98)

P(4) = 1/98

We observe that P(2) is 1/100. P(3) is 1/99. P(4) is 1/98. Extending this we get P(100) = 1/2

So the probability that the 100th traveler does **not** sit on the seat assigned to him is 1/2.

So the probability that the 100th traveler sits on the seat assigned to him = 1 - 1/2 = 1/2

10.

What is the probability that two dogs in the world have the same number of hair?

To solve the problem, we can use the pigeon hole principle which states that if n items have to be put into m pigeon holes and n > m, then at least one pigeon hole will have more than one item.

Let the number of dogs in the world be N. Let the maximum number of hair that a dog can have be H. If the number of dogs in the world is greater than the maximum number of hair on a dog, then applying the pigeon hole principle we are guaranteed to have two dogs with the same number of hair. The problem does not indicate the values for N and H. So we will have to guess here if N > H or not.

If we do some searching on the internet for the values for N and H, some sources indicate that the number of dogs is about 400 million and the average number of hair on a dog is about 1.5 million. So N > H and applying the pigeon hole principle the probability that two dogs share the same number of hair is **1**.

8.4 Lateral Thinking Puzzles

1. Cut a round cake into 8 equal pieces with three knife cuts

There are two ways to do it.

First method: Cut the cake into 4 equal parts with two cuts as indicated by the dashed lines in the diagram. Then make the third cut horizontally along the middle of the height of the cake so that the cake is divided into 4 pieces above and 4 pieces below.

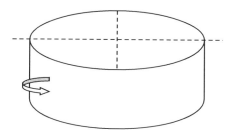

Second method: Cut the cake into 4 equal parts with two cuts. Then stack all the 4 pieces on top of each other and make the 3rd cut so that the 4 pieces get cut into 8 pieces.

2. Given a crescent moon shape, cut it into 6 parts using 2 straight lines

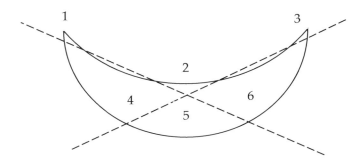

3. There are two cubes on a person's desk using which the person shows the current day of the month from 01 to 31. What numbers are present on the faces on the cubes?

We will have to represent the dates 11 and 22. So both cubes must have a 1 and a 2 on them.

We will also have to represent the dates 01 to 09. So 0 has to be paired with nine numbers. If we put 0 on one of the cubes, then we can pair this 0 with six numbers on the other cube. However we want 0 to be paired with nine numbers. This is possible only if 0 is present on both the cubes.

Let the two cubes be A and B. We have the following

A - 0, 1, 2

B - 0, 1, 2

There are a total of six positions still available - 3 on each cube. But we have to represent seven numbers still (3, 4, 5, 6, 7, 8, 9). To achieve this we have to do a little out of the box thinking and use the fact that 6 can be converted to 9 by inverting the cube. So it is sufficient to represent only one of them. So the cubes will be as follows:

A - 0, 1, 2, 3, 4, 5

B - 0, 1, 2, 6, 7, 8

4. There are 10 trees. How do you arrange them in a garden so that there are 5 rows, each row having 4 trees?

The trees should be placed on the dots shown in the diagram below. In this way we end up with 5 rows (ACFH, ADGJ, BCDE, BFIJ, EGIH), each having 4 trees

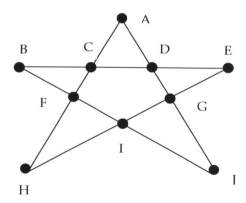

5. Arrange 9 trees in a garden so that there are 10 rows, each row having 3 trees

The trees are placed at the dotted points A, B, C, D, E, F, G, H and I as shown in the diagram below

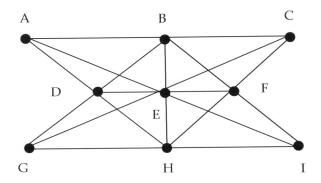

The 10 rows of trees are ABC, DEF, GHI, ADH, BDG, BFI, CFH, BEH, AEI and CEG

6. Can 4 trees on a farm be equidistant from each other?

If the farm is completely flat then this is not possible. However this is possible in 3 dimensions - the trees should be at the corners of a regular tetrahedron. So 3 trees on the farm form an equilateral triangle on the flat portion of the farm and the 4th tree is on an elevated portion at the middle of the equilateral triangle.

7. An ant is sitting at one corner of the cube and wants to go to the opposite corner of the cube. What is the shortest path that the ant can take?

The first answer that comes to mind is to take the diagonal path from A to C (or to F or to H) and then reach G from there. However this is not the correct answer. Let us say that the size of one edge of the cube is x. The ant is sitting at the corner A and wants to move to corner G. The shortest path for the ant is to take the path from A to P (P is the midpoint of BC) and then move from P to G.

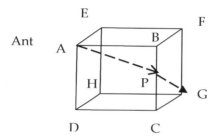

Using Pythagoras theorem, length of $AP^2 = AB^2 + BP^2$ (AB = x, BP = x/2)

So length of $AP = \sqrt{x^2 + \frac{x^2}{4}} = 1.12\ x$

Similarly the length of $PG^2 = CG^2 + PC^2$ (CG = x, PC = x/2)

So length of $PG = \sqrt{x^2 + \frac{x^2}{4}} = 1.12\ x$

So the total length of the shortest path = length of AP + length of PG = 1.12x + 1.12x = **2.24x**

8. An old man has three daughters. One day his intelligent friend visited him and asked the ages of his daughters. The old man replied that the product of their ages is 36. The friend couldn't figure out the ages and asked the old man for another clue. The old man replied that the sum of their ages was equal to his door number. The friend couldn't still figure out the ages and asked for another clue. The old man replied that only his youngest daughter had blue eyes. The friend immediately gave the correct answer. What are the ages of the old man's daughters?

Initially it looks like we can't figure out the ages of the daughters. The actual door number is not indicated in the problem. There are 3 unknown ages and we can construct only a single equation out of them. However if we consider all possible solutions to the problem and then go on filtering them out based on the old man's clues we can arrive at the correct answer.

The first clue indicates that the product of the ages of the 3 daughters is equal to 36. So let us find all possible groups of 3 numbers which when multiplied give 36. These are given below

Possible ages
(1, 1, 36)
(1, 2, 18)
(1, 3, 12)
(1, 4, 9)
(1, 6, 6)
(2, 2, 9)
(2, 3, 6)
(3, 3, 4)

The second clue indicates the sum of the ages. So let us find the sum of all the groups

Possible ages	Sum
(1, 1, 36)	38
(1, 2, 18)	21
(1, 3, 12)	16
(1, 4, 9)	14
(1, 6, 6)	13
(2, 2, 9)	13
(2, 3, 6)	11
(3, 3, 4)	10

Now in 6 of the cases the sum is unique. So if it was any of the 6 cases, then when the old man indicated the sum of the ages, the friend would have immediately been able to tell the ages of the daughters. But the friend couldn't find the ages based on the second clue. So this means that the door number had multiple answers associated with it. The only sum that has multiple answers is 13. So the door number must have been 13. So the ages of the daughters may be (1, 6, 6) or (2, 2, 9).

The third clue indicates that only his youngest daughter has blue eyes. The possible answers are (1, 6, 6) and (2, 2, 9). We have to assume here that if two daughters are of the same age, then they are twins. So if only the youngest daughter has blue eyes, then the youngest daughter and second youngest daughter are not twins and so they should have different ages. The only solution that satisfies this is (1, 6, 6). So the ages of the old man's daughters are 1, 6 and 6.

9. There are 3 light bulbs inside a room. Outside the room there are 3 switches to those bulbs. The room is locked and has no windows. You are allowed to manipulate the switches before entering the room. Once you enter the room, you can't manipulate the switches. How will you find the switch for each bulb?

Put on the first switch for a few minutes. Then turn off the first switch and turn on the middle switch and go into the room. The middle switch is for the bulb which is glowing. Touch the remaining two bulbs and identify the bulb which is hot. The first switch is for the bulb which is hot but not glowing. The last switch is for the bulb which is neither hot nor glowing.

10. A sheikh tells his sons to race their camels to a distant city. The one whose camel is slower wins the race and inherits the fortune of the sheikh. The two brothers wander aimlessly in the desert until they reach an old man whom they ask for guidance. Upon hearing the advice of the old man, the two brothers run towards the camels and race to the city. What does the old man tell them?

The old man asks the two brothers to switch their camels. So now brother A has brother B's camel and vice versa. If A rides as fast as he can on B's camel and reaches the city first, then A's own camel will reach the city in second place and A will inherit the fortune. So the two brothers race the swapped camels and try to reach the city as soon as possible.

8.5 Logic Puzzles

1. There are three boxes, one containing only oranges, one containing only apples, and one containing both apples and oranges. However, EVERY box has been incorrectly labeled. You are allowed to pick only one fruit from any one of the boxes and then correctly label all the boxes. How will you do it?

Pick a fruit from the box labeled as Apples + Oranges. Since EVERY box is incorrectly labeled, the box labeled Apples + Oranges can't have both apples and oranges. It can have either apples or oranges.

Suppose the fruit that we picked from the box labeled Apples + Oranges is an apple, then

- the box labeled Apples + Oranges contains only apples
- the box labeled Oranges can't contain only oranges since each box is labeled incorrectly. It can't contain only apples since we have already found the box having only apples. So box labeled Oranges contains apples and oranges.
- the box labeled Apples should then be containing only oranges

Suppose the fruit that we picked from the box labeled Apples + Oranges is an orange, then

- the box labeled Apples + Oranges contains only oranges
- the box labeled Apples can't contain only apples since each box is labeled incorrectly. It can't contain only oranges since we have already found the box having only oranges. So box labeled Apples contains apples and oranges.
- the box labeled Oranges should then be containing only apples

2. There are two chests, a gold chest and a silver chest. Only one of the two chests has a treasure in it while the other chest is empty. The silver chest has the following inscription: "This chest is empty". The gold chest has the following inscription: "Only one of the two inscriptions is true". You are allowed to open only one chest. Which chest would you open?

Suppose the statement on the gold chest is correct, then the statement on the silver chest should be false since the gold chest states that only one of the inscriptions is true. So the silver chest is not empty and contains the treasure.

Suppose the statement on the gold chest is false, then there are two possibilities.

1. The statements on both the chests are false. So the silver chest is not empty and contains the treasure.

2. The statements on both the chests are true. However this is a contradiction, since we initially assumed that the statement on the gold chest is false and ended up with the conclusion that the statement on the gold chest is true. So we can discard this scenario.

So in all the valid scenarios, the silver chest has the treasure. So we can conclude that the silver chest has the treasure.

3. There are 3 chests - a silver chest, a gold chest and a bronze chest. The silver chest has the inscription "Treasure is in this Chest". The gold chest has the inscription "Treasure is not in this Chest". The bronze chest has the inscription "Treasure is not in the Gold Chest".

At least one of the inscriptions is true, and at least one of the inscriptions is false. You can open only one chest. Which one will you open?

We first note that the statements on the gold chest and the bronze chest are identical and just worded differently. So either the gold chest and bronze chest statements are both true or the gold chest and bronze chest statements are both false. We can't have gold chest statement true and bronze chest statement false since this will lead to a contradiction. Similarly we can't have the gold chest statement false and bronze chest statement true.

To solve this problem, let us form a truth table with all possibilities.

Silver chest	Gold chest	Bronze chest	Inference
T	T	T	not possible since the problem states at least one statement is false but here all statements are true
T	T	F	not possible since there is a contradiction between gold chest and bronze chest
T	F	T	not possible since there is a contradiction between gold chest and bronze chest
T	F	F	this indicates treasure is in the silver chest and that treasure is in the gold chest. But only one chest has the treasure. So this is not possible
F	T	T	**possible.** this indicates the treasure is in bronze chest
F	T	F	not possible since there is a contradiction between gold chest and bronze chest
F	F	T	not possible since there is a contradiction between gold chest and bronze chest
F	F	F	not possible since the problem states at least one statement is true but here all statements are false

So the treasure is in the bronze chest.

4. There are 100 statements written on a sheet of paper. The first statement says "At most 0 of these 100 statements are true". The second statement says "At most 1 of these statements are true". The nth statement says "At most (n-1) of these statements are true." The last statement says "At most 99 of these statements are true". So how many of these 100 statements are actually true?

Let us first look at a smaller case where there are 4 statements. Let the exact number of true statements be N.

Statement A: "At most 0 of the 4 statements are true" (indicates $N \le 0$)

Statement B: "At most 1 of the 4 statements are true" (indicates $N \le 1$)

Statement C: "At most 2 of the 4 statements are true" (indicates $N \le 2$)

Statement D: "At most 3 of the 4 statements are true" (indicates $N \le 3$)

Number of true statements (N)	True statements	Inference
N = 0	A ($N \le 0$), B ($N \le 1$), C ($N \le 2$), D ($N \le 3$)	4 statements – A, B, C, D are true. But we assumed that 0 statements are true. So this is a contradiction
N = 1	B ($N \le 1$), C ($N \le 2$), D ($N \le 3$)	3 statements - B, C, D are true. But we assumed that exactly 1 statement is true. So this is a contradiction
N = 2	C ($N \le 2$), D ($N \le 3$)	2 statements – C and D are true. We also assumed that exactly 2 statements are true. So this is **possible**
N = 3	D ($N \le 3$)	1 statement – D is true. But we assumed that exactly 3 statements are true. So this is a contradiction
N = 4	N > 3	All the 4 statements – A, B, C and D are false. But we assumed that all 4 statements are true. So this is a contradiction

So the only possible scenario when there is no contradiction is when exactly 2 out of the 4 statements are true. So if we have 4 statements, then exactly half of them (the last two statements) can be true. Extending this to 100 statements, exactly 50 statements (the last 50 statements) can be true without any contradictions.

5. Bob is lost in a forest and comes across a fork in the path: one way leads to a safe village while the other leads to hungry cannibals. There are two brothers present at that location. One of the brothers is always honest and the other always lies. Bob doesn't know which brother is honest and which brother lies. Bob can only ask a single question. What question should Bob ask?

Suppose Bob asks the question "which is the safe path?", the honest brother will point to the safe path while the lying brother will point to the cannibals. Since the two answers are different and since Bob does not know who the honest brother is, Bob has no way of figuring out the correct path. To solve this problem, Bob should ask a question so that both brothers give the same answer. One way to do this is to ask the honest brother what answer the lying brother will give and ask the lying brother what answer the honest brother will give. So Bob should ask the question "According to your brother, which path leads to the cannibals?".

If the question "which path leads to the cannibals?" is asked to the lying brother, the lying brother will indicate the safe path. So if Bob asks the honest brother "According to your brother, which path leads to the cannibals?", the honest brother will indicate the safe path.

If the question "which path leads to the cannibals?" is asked to the honest brother, the honest brother will indicate the path to the cannibals. So if Bob asks the lying brother "According to your brother, which path leads to the cannibals", the lying brother has to give the answer opposite to that of the honest brother. So the lying brother also indicates the safe path. So both brothers indicate the safe path and Bob can safely proceed in that direction.

6. Bob is lost in a forest and comes across a fork in the path: one way leads to a safe village while the other leads to hungry cannibals. There is a man present at that location but Bob doesn't know if he is honest or if he lies. Bob can only ask a single question. What question should Bob ask?

Since Bob doesn't know if the man is honest or if he always lies, Bob should ask a question for which an honest man and a lying man will give the same answer. To achieve this Bob should make use of the fact that lying on a lie will result in the truth. So Bob should ask the question "If I were to ask you which is the safe path, what would you indicate?"

Suppose the man is honest. The honest man will indicate the safe path when asked the question.

Suppose the man lies. If Bob asks the lying man the question "which is the safe path?", then the lying man would indicate the path to the cannibals. So if the man lies, the truthful answer to the question "If I were to ask you which is the safe path, what would you indicate?" is "the path to the cannibals". However the lying person always gives false answers. So when the lying man is asked "If I were to ask you which is the safe path, what would you indicate?" the lying man will indicate the opposite path – the safe path. So this way the lying person is forced to lie on a lie resulting him answering truthfully and indicating the safe path.

In both cases, if a man is honest or if he is lying, the safe path is always indicated. So Bob can safely take the direction indicated by the man

7. A box contains 3 black hats and 2 white hats. Three men A, B, and C pick one hat each from the box and place it on their heads. Each person does not know the color of the hat he is wearing. A can see the hats worn by B and C. B can see the hat worn by C. C can't see any hats. A is asked if he knows the color of the hat he is wearing. A replies no. B is asked if he knows the color of the hat he is wearing. B replies no. C is asked if he knows the color of the hat he is wearing, C replies yes and correctly tells the color of his hat. What is the color of C's hat?

Suppose B and C are wearing white hats. Since there are only two white hats, A will know that he is wearing a black hat. But A does not know the color of the hat he is wearing. So B and C should be wearing one of the following combinations

B	C
Black	White
White	Black
Black	Black

Now there are 3 possibilities. Consider the first possibility. Suppose C is wearing a white hat, then B can only be wearing a black hat. So when B sees C wearing a white hat, B will know for sure that B is wearing a black hat. However, B does not know the color of the hat that B is wearing. So this rules out the first possibility.

In the second and third possibilities, C wears a black hat and B could be wearing a white or black hat. Both the possibilities fit with the case where B knows the color of C's hat but can't figure out the color of B's own hat. In both possibilities C is wearing a black hat. So C should be wearing a black hat.

8.6 Classic Puzzles

1. Four men want to cross a bridge at night. Since it is night, the men need to carry a flashlight while crossing the bridge but there is only one flashlight. The bridge is strong enough only for 2 men to cross at a time. If 2 men simultaneously cross the bridge, they will move at the speed of the slower man. The first person takes 1 minute to cross the bridge, the second person takes 2 minutes, the third person takes 5 minutes and the fourth person takes 10 minutes. What is the least time that they need to cross the bridge?

Let the persons be labeled A (1 minute), B (2 minutes), C (5 minutes) and D (10 minutes)

Since there is only one flashlight, after two men cross the bridge, one of the men has to return back with the flashlight. One strategy is to make the fastest man A to return with the flashlight each time. With this approach, we can do the following

A and B cross the bridge in 2 minutes

A returns back in 1 minute

A and C cross the bridge in 5 minutes

A returns back in 1 minute

A and D cross the bridge in 10 minutes

So the total time taken is 2 + 1 + 5 + 1 + 10 = 19 minutes

However there is a better strategy which can reduce the time to 17 minutes. The idea is to make the slowest two persons cross the bridge together and on the return journey have a faster person return. With this approach we can do the following

A and B cross the bridge in 2 minutes

A returns back in 1 minute

C and D cross the bridge in 10 minutes (the two slowest persons are grouped together)

B returns back in 2 minutes (B who is already at the other end of the bridge is faster than C and D and returns back)

A and B cross the bridge in 2 minutes

The total time taken is 2 + 1 + 10 + 2 + 2 = 17 minutes

So the shortest time taken is **17** minutes

2. There are 3 missionaries and 3 cannibals who want to cross the river using a boat. The boat can carry a maximum of 2 people. If the cannibals outnumber the missionaries on any river bank, then the cannibals will eat the missionaries on that river bank. How will the missionaries cross the river without being eaten by the cannibals?

Let M represent a missionary and C represent a cannibal. The missionaries and cannibals have to move from bank A to bank B. Then the sequence of actions that should be taken are shown in the table

Trip Nr	Travel	Starting Bank (A)	Ending Bank (B)
Initial		3M, 3C	
1	1M, 1C move from A to B	2M, 2C	1M, 1C
2	1M moves from B to A	3M, 2C	1C
3	2C move from A to B	3M	3C
4	1C moves from B to A	3M, 1C	2C
5	2M move from A to B	1M, 1C	2M, 2C

6	1M, 1C move from B to A	2M, 2C	1M, 1C
7	2M move from A to B	2C	3M, 1C
8	1C move from B to A	3C	3M
9	2C move from A to B	1C	3M, 2C
10	1C moves from B to A	2C	3M, 1C
11	2C move from A to B		3M, 3C

So finally the 3 missionaries and the 3 cannibals are present on bank B.

3. How will three people find their average salary without revealing their individual salaries to each other?

Let the 3 persons be A, B and C.

A first picks a random number which is known only to A.

A then adds his salary to the random number and passes on the result to B (C should not get to know the value passed on from A to B).

B then adds his salary and passes on the result only to C (A should not get to know the value passed on from B to C)

C then adds his salary and passes on the result back to A. (B should not get to know the value passed from C to A)

A then subtracts the random number from the result to get the sum of the salaries of the 3 people. Dividing the sum of salaries by 3 will give the average salary.

4. A king has organized a party in 24 hours. 13 barrels of wine are going to be used for the party. However the king has come to know that one of the 13 barrels contains a poison. Consuming even a drop of wine from the poisoned barrel can make a person very sick. It takes about 24 hours for the poison to act. The king decides to use the prisoners to taste the wine and determine which barrel contains the poison. What is the least number of prisoners required?

The least number of prisoners required is **4**.

Let the Barrels be labeled B1 to B13. Let P1, P2, P3 and P4 be the four prisoners. The table below gives the barrels from which each prisoner will drink

	P1	P2	P3	P4
B1	0	0	0	0
B2	0	0	0	1
B3	0	0	1	0
B4	0	0	1	1
B5	0	1	0	0
B6	0	1	0	1
B7	0	1	1	0
B8	0	1	1	1
B9	1	0	0	0
B10	1	0	0	1
B11	1	0	1	0
B12	1	0	1	1
B13	1	1	0	0

None of the prisoners drink from barrel B1. So if none of the prisoners fall sick, then the poison is in B1

Only prisoner P4 drinks from barrel B2. So if only P4 falls sick, then the poison is in B2.

Only prisoner P3 drinks from barrel B3. So if only P3 falls sick, then the poison is in B3.

Only prisoners P3 and P4 drink from barrel B4. If only P3 and P4 fall sick, then the poison is in B4.

This technique can be extended to all the barrels.

5. A worker is going to work under you for 7 days. Each day the worker should be paid 1/7th portion of a silver bar. How will you pay the worker if you are allowed to cut the silver bar at two places only?

If we were permitted to cut the silver bar at 6 places, then we could have got 7 equal pieces. Each day we could pay one piece to the worker. However we are allowed to cut the silver bar at two places only.

To solve the problem, cut the silver bar at two places so that we have 3 pieces with lengths 1/7, 2/7 and 4/7. On the first day, give the worker the 1/7 piece. So the worker now has 1/7 portion of the silver bar.

On the second day, take back the 1/7 piece from the worker and give him the 2/7 piece. So the worker now has 2/7 portion of the silver bar

On the third day, give the worker the 1/7 piece. So worker now has 2/7 + 1/7 = 3/7 portion of the silver bar

On the fourth day, take back the 1/7 and 2/7 pieces from the worker and give him the 4/7 piece. So the worker now has 4/7 portion of the silver bar.

On the fifth day, give the worker the 1/7 piece. So the worker now has 4/7 + 1/7 = 5/7 portion of the silver bar.

On the sixth day, take back the 1/7 piece from the worker and give him the 2/7 piece. So the worker now has 4/7 + 2/7 = 6/7 portion of the silver bar.

On the seventh day, give the 1/7 piece to the worker. Now the worker has the entire silver bar with him.

6. There are many coins on the table of which 10 of the coins have heads facing up while the remaining have tails facing up. A blindfolded person has to split the coins into two groups such that each group has the same number of coins with heads facing up. The person does not know the total number of coins present and the person has no way of finding out which side of the coin is facing up. How can this be done?

Pick any 10 coins and form one group. The remaining coins form the other group. In the group having 10 coins, flip all the 10 coins to the opposite side. Now the number of heads is equal in both the groups.

To see how this solution works let us first take a specific case of 50 coins where 10 coins have heads facing up and 40 coins have tails facing up. Now pick any 10 coins and form a group. Let us say that there are 4 heads in this group. The remaining group will have 40 coins out of which there are 10 - 4 = 6 heads (since the total number of coins with heads facing up = 10)

	G1	G2
Heads	4	6
Tails	6	34

When we flip all the coins in the first group to the opposite side, we get the following

	G1	G2
Heads	6	6
Tails	4	34

So there are equal number of heads in both groups.

To see that this solution works in general, let the total number of coins be N with 10 coins having heads facing up. We form a group of 10 coins of which let us say x coins have heads. The remaining 10-x coins will have tails.

The total number of coins in the second group is N - 10 since the first group has 10 coins. The number of coins with heads in the second group will be 10-x since the total number of heads is 10 of which x heads are in the first group. The number of tails in the second group = total number of coins in second group - number of heads in second group = (N – 10) - (10-x) = N-20+x

	G1	G2
Heads	x	10-x
Tails	10-x	N-20+x

When we flip the coins in the first group, we get the following

	G1	G2
Heads	10-x	10-x
Tails	x	N-20+x

So the number of heads is the same in the two groups.

7. Alice has to take exactly one pill of type A and one pill of type B every day. On one day, Alice opens the A pill container and drops one pill on her hand. Then she opens the B pill container and accidentally drops two pills on her hand. The A pill and B pill look exactly identical and their weight is also the same. Now Alice doesn't know which pill on her hand is the type A pill and which pill is the type B pill. How will Alice ensure that she takes the correct dosage of the pills without wasting any pills?

Alice has two pills of type B and one pill of type A but she doesn't know which is which. To solve the problem, Alice drops one more pill of type A onto her hand. She now has 2 pills of type A and 2 pills of type B. She then breaks each pill into exactly two halves. The upper half of each pill is collected into one group and the lower half of each pill is collected into another group.

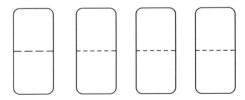

The upper half group will have some permutation of   0.5A, 0.5A, 0.5B and 0.5B. So totally we have 1 pill of type A and 1 pill of type B in the group. Alice can take the pills in the upper half group today. Similarly the lower half group will also totally have 1 pill of type A and 1 pill of type B. She can take the pills in the lower half group tomorrow.

8. Consider a game where coins have to be placed on a circular table. All coins are of the same size. There are two players: you and your friend. Each person takes turns placing a coin on the table. The last person to place a coin on the table wins. What strategy would you use to always win the game?

To always win the game, you should play first and place the coin at the center of the circular table. From then on, whenever your friend places a coin on the table, you should choose the diametrically opposite position to place your coin as shown in the diagram. If your friend has found a position, you are assured to find the position diametrically opposite to it to be vacant. So you will always place the last coin on the table

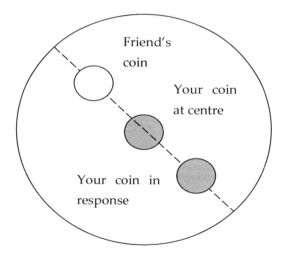

9.

You and your friend play a game of calling out numbers with the following rules: A player starts the game by calling out a number between 1 and 10. The next player should then call out a number that exceeds the previous player's number by at least 1 and no more than 10. The first person to call out 50 is the winner. What strategy would you use to win the game?

Generalize the strategy for any value N that the winner calls out in the end.

To solve this problem, let us work backwards. Suppose you call 39, then your friend is forced to choose a number between 40 and 49. You can then choose 50 and win. So your friend has no chance to win the game if you choose 39.

If you choose 28, then your friend is forced to choose a number from 29 to 38 and you can choose 39 which will result in you winning the game. So you can always win if you choose 28.

If you choose 17, then your friend is forced to choose a number from 18 to 27 and you can choose 28 which will result in you winning the game. So you can always win if you choose 17.

If you choose 6, then your friend is forced to choose a number from 7 to 16 and you can choose 17 which will result in you winning the game. So you can always win if you choose 6.

So to win the game you should be the first person to call out the number and you should call out 6.

The key to this game is that if you have chosen the number X, and your friend chooses X+A, then you can choose the number X+A+B where B is 11 - A. So if you chose X previously, then no matter what your friend chooses, you can always choose X+11 in your next turn.

Suppose we have to develop a general strategy for any value of N that the winner calls out in the end. Then we have to do the following:

➤ Find the remainder when N is divided by 11

➤ If the remainder is non-zero, then your strategy is to start first and pick the remainder of N /11 as your first number (So if N is 50, the remainder of 50/11 is 6.

So you should pick 6 as the starting number). Then when it is your turn to pick a number, you have to add 11 to your previous number (So the next numbers you will choose are 6+11 = 17, 17+11 = 28 and so on).

➤ If the remainder is 0, then your strategy is to allow your friend to start first. Then for each of your turn, you should choose the next multiple of 11. (So first pick 11, then 22 and so on)

10. To share a cake fairly between two people, one person cuts the cake and the other chooses. Three people want to fairly share a cake using this principle. How can they do it?

Let us say that three people A, B and C want to fairly share the cake using this principle. Then they have to do the following.

- A and B divide the cake equally amongst themselves where one of them cuts the cake and the other chooses. A now has half the cake and B has the other half of the cake.

- A then divides his share of the cake into three pieces and C chooses one piece. A is forced to cut fairly so that the three pieces are equal otherwise C will choose the larger piece.

- B also divides his share into three pieces and C chooses one piece. B is also forced to cut fairly so that the three pieces are equal otherwise C will choose the larger piece.

So A, B and C each now have 2 out of 6 equal pieces. So each has 1/3rd of the cake.

11. There is a cuboid cake from which someone has already cut out a small cuboid cake piece. How will you divide the remaining cake into two equal portions?

To solve this problem, the main idea we have to use is that any line passing through the center of a rectangle divides the rectangle into two portions of equal area. For instance in the diagram below, the line through the center divides the rectangle into two portions of equal area

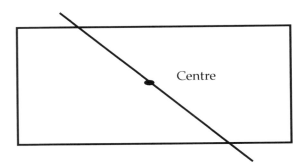

Now let us assume that the cake is flat and rectangular. Suppose a small rectangular portion is cut out of the cake and is missing from the cake and we have to divide the remaining cake into two equal partitions. We can achieve this if we can divide the original rectangular cake into two equal parts and the missing rectangular portion into two equal parts simultaneously. This way the missing portion and the remaining portion of the cake are equally shared by the two equal partitions.

Any line passing through the center of the original cake will divide the original cake into 2 equal parts. Any line passing through the center of the cut out rectangular portion will divide the missing portion into two equal parts. So to simultaneously achieve both, we need to pick the line that passes through the center of the original rectangle C1 and center of the cut out rectangle C2 as shown in the diagram below.

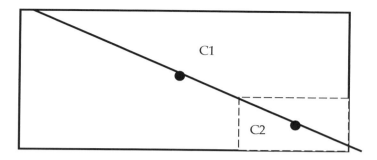

The same idea can be extended to 3 dimensions. So to divide the remaining cuboid cake into two equal parts, cut along the line joining the center of original cuboid cake and the center of the missing cuboid piece.

12. There are 25 racehorses and 5 race tracks. What is the least number of races needed to find out the top three fastest horses? Watches are not allowed to measure the time taken by the horses.

We can find out the fastest 3 horses in 7 races as described below.

Divide the horses into 5 groups, A, B, C, D and E. Each group has 5 horses. If a horse's rank in group A is N, then it is denoted as A-N. So the fastest horse in group A is represented as A-1.

Race each group of 5 horses. This requires 5 races. We then retain the 3 fastest horses in each race and discard the remaining horses. So we are left with A-1, B-1, C-1, D-1, E-1, A-2, B-2, C-2, D-2, E-2, A-3, B-3, C-3, D-3 and E-3.

In the 6ᵗʰ race, pick the fastest horse in each group and race them. So we will race A-1, B-1, C-1, D-1 and E-1. The horse that comes first in the race is the fastest horse among all the 25 horses.

For ease of understanding, let us assume that in the 6ᵗʰ race, A-1 comes first, B-1 comes second, C-1 comes third, D-1 comes fourth and E-1 comes fifth in the race. Then D-1 and E1 can be eliminated. Since D-2 and D-3 are slower than D1, D2 and D3 can also be eliminated. Since E-2 and E-3 are also slower than E1, E2 and E3 can also be removed.

Since A-1 is the fastest horse, only B-1 and B-2 may be present in the top 3. B-3 will definitely not be present in the top 3. So B-3 can be removed.

Similarly since A-1 is fastest and B-1 is second fastest, only C-1 may be present in the top 3. C-2 and C-3 will definitely not be present in the top 3. So C-2 and C-3 can be removed.

Now we are left with A-1, A-2, A-3, B-1, B-2 and C-1. We know that A-1 is the fastest. So in the 7th race, we race A-2, A-3, B-1, B-2 and C-1. The fastest horse in the 7th race will be the second fastest in the group of 25 horses. The second fastest horse in the 7th race will be the third fastest in the group of 25 horses.

13.

There are 100 people stranded on an island. A ship reaches the island and the captain of the ship decides to play a game. Each person will be made to wear a hat which is either red or blue. Each person does not know the color of the hat he is wearing. All the people are then made to stand in a line. A person can see the color of all the hats of the persons in front of him. The captain then will start asking each person to identify the color of his own hat starting from the person at the back of the line. If the person guesses the color correctly he will be saved otherwise he will have to stay on the island. What strategy can be used to save the maximum number of people?

The last person in the line counts the number of blue hats in front of him.

Scenario-1: If there are odd number of blue hats on the 99 people ahead of the last person, the last person shouts blue. Now the 99th person counts the number of blue hats on the 98 people ahead of him. After counting the blue hats, the table below can be used to find the color of the 99th person's hat.

Number of blue hats in the first 99 people	Number of blue hats in the first 98 people	Inference
Odd	Odd	99th person must be wearing red since the number of blue hats in the first 99 people should be odd
Odd	Even	99th person must be wearing blue since number of blue hats in the first 99 people should be odd

Scenario-2: If there are even number of blue hats on the 99 people ahead of the last person, the last person shouts red. Now the 99th person counts the number of blue hats on the 98 persons ahead of him. After counting the blue hats, the table below can be used to find the color of the 99th person's hat.

Number of blue hats in the first 99 people	Number of blue hats in the first 98 people	Inference
Even	Odd	99th person must be wearing blue since the number of blue hats in the first 99 people should be even
Even	Even	99th person must be wearing red since the number of blue hats in the first 99 people should be even

Now the remaining persons in the line can use similar logic to find the color of his hat using the table below. A = B + C + 1 if person X wears a blue hat. A = B + C if X wears a red hat

A: Number of blue hats in first 99 persons as indicated by 100th person	B: Number of blue hats called out from the previous persons, excluding 100th person	C: Number of blue hats in front of person X (excluding X)	The color of hat of person X
odd	odd	odd	B+C is even, A is odd. So X = blue
odd	odd	even	B+C is odd, A is odd. So X = red
odd	even	odd	B+C is odd, A is odd. So X = red
odd	even	even	B+C is even, A is odd. So X = blue
even	odd	odd	B+C is even, A is even. So X = red
even	odd	even	B+C is odd, A is even. So X = blue
even	even	odd	B+C is odd, A is even. So X = blue
even	even	even	B+C is even, A is even. So X = red

Using this strategy it is possible to definitely save the first 99 people in the line. The last person in the line has a 50% chance of correctly guessing the color of his hat.

14. A warden gives a challenge to 23 prisoners. Each day a random prisoner is chosen and brought to a room that has two switches. The prisoner has to choose one of the switches and then toggle the chosen switch. The prisoners will be kept isolated from each other at all times and so they can't communicate with each other. If a prisoner can correctly guess when all the prisoners have visited the switch room at least once, then they win their freedom. How can the prisoners achieve this?

Let the two switches in the room be called switch A and switch B. The prisoners will choose one of the prisoners to be the leader. The remaining 22 prisoners are referred to as helper prisoners.

Any helper prisoner can turn on switch A only once. Helper prisoners are never allowed to turn off switch A. Only the leader is allowed to turn off switch A. All the prisoners including the leader are allowed to turn on and turn off switch B any number of times. The strategy that the prisoners can use is as follows:

When a helper prisoner enters the room, if switch A is off and switch A has never been turned on by the prisoner, then he turns on switch A. Otherwise he presses switch B and toggles it.

When the leader prisoner enters the room, if switch A is on, he turns off switch A and keeps a track of the number of times he has turned off switch A. Otherwise he presses switch B and toggles it.

This way, for each helper prisoner, switch A is turned on exactly once and turned off exactly once. So when the leader has turned off switch A 22 times, once for each helper prisoner, then all prisoners have been to the switch room at least once.

15. A room has 100 doors. Initially all the doors are closed. The first person enters the room and toggles all the doors (toggling a door means that a closed door is opened and vice versa). Then a second person enters and toggles every 2nd door. Then a third person enters the room and toggles every 3rd door and so on. Find the final state of all the doors after 100 people enter the room.

The state of a door can be found based on the number of factors of the door number. If there are odd number of factors for the door number, the door will be open (opposite state of initial state). If there are even number of factors for the door number, the door will be closed (same state as initial state).

For instance, door 9 has three factors - 1, 3, 9. So the final state of door 9 will be open (opposite state of initial state). Door 10 has four factors - 1, 2, 5 and 10. So the final state of door 10 will be closed (same as initial state).

Only perfect squares like 1, 4, 9, etc. will have odd number of factors. The rest of the numbers will have even number of factors.

So at the end, the doors 1, 4, 9, 16, 25, 36, 49, 64, 81 and 100 will be open. The rest of the doors will be closed.

9. Personality

The HR round will consist of questions to check if the personality of the candidate and the attitude of the candidate are in line with the expectations of the company. Some of the frequently asked questions are listed below. For each of these questions, you will have to prepare your own answer based on your experiences at college and in the industry. It will be good if you can cite an example in your life while answering these questions.

1. Why should we hire you?

2. What is the most challenging task that you have done so far?

3. What was the most critical situation that you faced in any project and how did you handle it?

4. What are you most proud of yourself?

5. What are your strengths and weaknesses? How have you tried to overcome your weaknesses?

6. Give an instance where you were given negative feedback. How did you handle the situation?

7. How will you manage conflict with your manager or your colleague?

8. What are you not happy with in your current company? What did you do about it?

9. Explain the latest project that you are working on.

10. What software development model do you follow in your project? What are its pros and cons? Which software development model do you like and why?

11. Where do you see yourself in the organization a few years from now?

There are three more questions you should be prepared for. These require more careful thought.

1. Why are you leaving your current organization?

It is better not to talk about any personal disputes or differences of opinion you had with your colleagues or your manager. You can mention that you are looking for better career opportunities and that the skills that you possess would suit the role for which you are being interviewed for

2. Why have you been changing jobs frequently?

It is better not to change jobs too frequently. Each recruiting manager has his or her own criteria to decide on this issue. In case you have changed jobs too frequently you should prepare an answer for this. Again please be diplomatic while answering this question

3. What salary do you expect?

It is better to let the employer first make an offer and then you can negotiate. Sometimes employers will not make the offer. They may insist the candidate on indicating his or her expectation. In this case, do find out the average and maximum hike offered in the industry for your experience level. Mention that the market value of hike offered is x % and that you are willing to negotiate at the end of the technical rounds. Once you are through with all the rounds, if you have performed very well in the interview rounds, you can bargain hard and say that the hike you are asking for is worth it!

I hope you enjoyed reading the book. **If you liked the book, I request you to please give your review comments on Amazon.** All the best for your interviews!

Made in the USA
San Bernardino,
CA

The Miscellaneous Works of Tobias Smollett, M.D.

Drawn & Engraved by W.H.Lizars

ROBERT ANDERSON M.D.

Edinburgh Published by Stirling & Slade.

THE

MISCELLANEOUS WORKS

OF

TOBIAS SMOLLETT, M.D.

WITH

MEMOIRS

OF

HIS LIFE AND WRITINGS,

BY

ROBERT ANDERSON, M.D.

THE SIXTH EDITION, IN SIX VOLUMES.

VOLUME VI.

CONTAINING

THE EXPEDITION OF HUMPHRY CLINKER,

AND

ADVENTURES OF AN ATOM.

EDINBURGH:

PRINTED FOR STIRLING & SLADE, PETER HILL & CO., AND FAIRBAIRN
& ANDERSON, EDINBURGH; W. OTRIDGE, J. CUTHILL, LACKINGTON,
HARDING, HUGHES, MAVOR, & JONES, BALDWIN, CRADOCK, & JOY,
R. SCHOLEY, G. COWIE & CO., R. SAUNDERS, W. H. REID, G. MACKIE,
AND T. & J. ALLMAN, LONDON; WILSON & SONS, YORK; R. MILLIKEN
AND J. CUMMING, DUBLIN.

1820.

To Mr Henry Davies, Bookseller in London.

RESPECTED SIR,   *Abergavenny, Aug. 4.*

I HAVE received your esteemed favour of the 13th ultimo, whereby it appeareth, that you have perused those same letters, the which were delivered unto you by my friend the Reverend Mr Hugo Bhen; and I am pleased to find you think they may be printed with a good prospect of success: inasmuch as the objections you mention, I humbly conceive, are such as may be redargued, if not entirely removed. And, first, in the first place, as touching what prosecutions may arise from printing the private correspondence of persons still living, give me leave, with all due submission, to observe, that the letters in question were not written and sent under the seal of secrecy; that they have no tendency to the *mala fama* or prejudice of any person whatsoever; but rather to the information and edification of mankind: so that it becometh a sort of duty to promulgate them *in usum publicum*. Besides, I have consulted Mr Davy Higgins, an eminent attorney of this place, who after due inspection and consideration, declareth, that he doth not think the said letters contain any matter which will be held actionable in the eye of the law. Finally, if you and I should come to a right understanding, I do declare *in verba sacerdotis*, that, in case of any such prosecution, I will take the whole upon my own shoulders, even *quoad* fine and imprisonment, though I must confess I should not care to undergo flagellation: *Tam ad turpitudinem quam ad amaritudinem pœna spectans.*—Secondly, concerning the personal resentment of Mr Justice Lismahago, I may say, *non flocci facio.*—I would not willingly vilipend any Christian, if peradventure he deserveth that epithet: albeit I am much surprised that more care is not taken to exclude from the commission all such vagrant foreigners, as may be justly suspected of disaffection to our happy constitution in church and state.—God forbid that I should be so uncharitable, as to affirm positively that the said Lismahago is no better than a Jesuit in disguise; but this I will assert and maintain, *totis viribus*, that, from the day he qualified, he has never been once seen *intra templi parietes*, that is to say, within the parish church.

Thirdly, with respect to what passed at Mr Kendal's table, when the said Lismahago was so brutal in his reprehensions, I must inform you, my good Sir, that I was obliged to retire, not by fear arising from his minatory reproaches, which, as I said before, I value not a rush; but from the sudden effect produced by a barbel's row, which I had eaten at dinner, not knowing that the said row is at certain seasons violently cathartic, as Galen observeth in his chapter περι ιχθυς.

. Fourthly, and lastly, with reference to the manner in which I got possession of the letters, it is a circumstance which concerns my own conscience only: sufficeth it to say, I have fully satisfied the parties in whose custody they were; and by this time, I hope I have also satisfied you in such ways, that the last hand may be put to our agreement, and the work proceed with all convenient expedition. In which hope I rest,

Respected Sir,

Your very humble servant,

JONATHAN DUSTWICH.

P. S. I propose, *Deo volente*, to have the pleasure of seeing you in the great city towards All-hallow-tide, when I shall be glad to treat with you concerning a parcel of MS. sermons of a certain clergyman deceased; a cake of the right leaven for the present taste of the public. *Verbum sapienti*, &c.

J. D.

To the Reverend Mr Jonathan Dustwich, at ——

SIR,

I received yours in course of post, and shall be glad to treat
with you for the MS. which I have delivered to your friend Mr
Bhen; but can by means comply with the terms proposed.
Those things are so uncertain—Writing is all a lottery.—I have
been a loser by the works of the greatest men of the age.—I
could mention particulars, and name names; but don't chuse it.
—The taste of the town is so changeable. Then there have
been so many letters upon travels lately published.—What between Smollett's, Sharp's, Derrick's, Thickness's, Baltimore's,
and Barretti's, together with Shandy's Sentimental Travels, the
public seems to be cloyed with that kind of entertainment.—
Nevertheless, I will, if you please, run the risk of printing and
publishing, and you shall have half the profits of the impression.
—You need not take the trouble to bring up your sermons on
my account.—Nobody reads sermons but Methodists and Dis-
senters.—Besides, for my own part, I am quite a stranger to
that sort of reading; and the two persons, whose judgment I depended upon in these matters, are out of the way: one is gone
abroad, carpenter of a man of war; and the other has been silly
enough to abscond, in order to avoid a prosecution for blasphemy.—I'm a great loser by his going off.—He has left a ma-
nual of devotion half finished in my hands, after having received
money for the whole copy.—He was the soundest divine, and
had the most orthodox pen of all my people; and I never knew
his judgment fail, but in flying from his bread and butter on this
occasion.

By owning you was not put in bodily fear by Lismahago, you
preclude yourself from the benefit of a good plea, over and above
the advantage of binding him over. In the late war, I inserted
in my evening paper a paragraph that came by the post, reflecting upon the behaviour of a certain regiment in battle. An officer of said regiment came to my shop, and, in the presence of

my wife and journeymen, threatened to cut off my ears.—As I
exhibited marks of bodily fear more ways than one, to the conviction of the bystanders, I bound him over; my action lay, and
I recovered. As for flagellation, you have nothing to fear, and
nothing-to hope, on that head.—There has been but one printer
flogged at the cart-tail these thirty years; that was Charles
Watson; and he assured me it was no more than a flea-bite.
C—— S—— has been threatened several times by the House of
L——; but it came to nothing. If an information should be
moved for, and granted against you, as the editor of these letters,
I hope, you will have honesty and wit enough to appear and take
your trial.—If you should be sentenced to the pillory, your fortune is made.—As times go, that's a sure step to honour and preferment. I shall think myself happy, if I can lend you a lift;
and am, very sincerely,

Yours,

London, August 10.   HENRY DAVIES.

Please my kind service to your neighbour, my cousin Madoc.—
I have sent an almanack and court-calender, directed for him
at Mr Sutton's, bookseller in Gloucester, carriage paid, which
he will please to accept as a small token of my regard. My
wife, who is very fond of toasted cheese, presents her compliments to him, and begs to know if there's any of that kind
which he was so good as to send us last Christmas, to be sold
in London.

H. D.

EXPEDITION

HUMPHRY CLINKER.

―――――

TO DR LEWIS.

DOCTOR,

THE pills are good for nothing—I might as well swallow snow-balls to cool my reins—I have told you over and over, how hard I am to move; and, at this time of day, I ought to know something of my own constitution. Why will you be so positive? Prithee send me another prescription—I am as lame, and as much tortured in all my limbs, as if I was broke upon the wheel: indeed, I am equally distressed in mind and body—As if I had not plagues enough of my own, those children of my sister are left me for a perpetual source of vexation—What business have people to get children to plague their neighbours? A ridiculous incident that happened yesterday to my niece Liddy, has disordered me in such a manner, that I expect to be laid up with another fit of the gout.—Perhaps I may explain myself in my next. I shall set out to-morrow morning for the Hot-well at Bristol, where I am afraid I shall stay longer than I could wish. On the receipt of this, send Williams thither with my saddle-horse and the *demi-pique.* Tell Barns to thrash out the two old ricks, and send the corn to market, and sell it off to the poor at a shilling a bushel under market price.—I have received a snivelling letter from Griffin, offering to make a public submission, and pay costs. I want none of his submissions; neither will I pocket any of his money.—The fellow is a bad neighbour, and I desire to have nothing to do with him: but as he is purse-proud, he shall pay for his insolence: let him give five pounds to the poor of the parish, and I'll withdraw my action; and in the meantime you may tell Prig to stop proceedings.—Let Morgan's widow have the Alderney cow, and forty shillings to clothe her children: but don't say a syllable of the matter to any living soul—I'll make her pay when she is able. I desire you will lock up all my drawers, and keep the keys till meeting; and be sure you take the iron chest with my papers into your own custody—Forgive all this trouble from, dear Lewis, your affectionate

Gloucester, April 2.   M. BRAMBLE.

TO MRS GWYLLIM, HOUSEKEEPER AT BRAMBLETONHALL.

MRS GUYLLIM,

WHEN this cums to hand, be sure to pack up in the trunk-male that stands in my closet, to be sent me in the Bristol waggon, without loss of time, the following articles, vis. my rose-collard neglejay, with green robins, my yellow damask, and my black velvet suit, with the short hoop; my bloo quilted petticoat, my green manteel, my laced apron, my French commode, Macklin head and lappets, and the litel box with my jowls. Williams may bring over my bum-daffee, and the viol with the easings of Dr Hill's dock-water, and Chowder's lacksitiff. The poor creature has been terribly constuprated ever since we left huom. Pray take particular care of the house while the family is absent. Let there be a fire constantly kept in my brother's chamber and mine. The maids, having nothing to do, may be sat a-spinning. I desire you'll clap a pad-luck on the windseller, and let none of the men have excess to the strong bear—don't forget to have the gate shit every evening before dark.—The gardnir and hind may lie below in the landry, to partake the house, with the blunderbuss and the great dog; and I hope you'll have a watchful eye over the maids. I know that hussy, Mary Jones, loves to be rumping with the men. Let me know if Alderney's calf be

sould yet, and what he fought—if the ould goose be sitting;
and if the cobler has cut Dicky, and how the poor anemil
bore the operation.—No more at present, but rests, yours,

Glostar, April 2. TABITHA BRAMBLE.

TO MRS MARY JONES, AT BRAMBLETONHALL.

DEAR MOLLY,

Heaving this importunity, I send my love to you and
Saul, being in good health, and hoping to hear the same
from you; and that you and Saul will take my poor kitten
to bed with you this cold weather. We have been all in a
sad taking here at Glostar.—Miss Liddy had like to have
run away with a player-man, and young master and he
would adone themselves a mischief: but the 'squire applied
to the mare, and they were bound over.—Mistriss bid me
not speak a word of the matter to any christian soul—no
more I shall; for, we servints should see all, and say nothing—But, what was worse than all this, Chowder has had
the misfortune to be worried by a butcher's dog, and came
home in a terrible pickle—Mistriss was taken with the
asterisks, but they soon went off. The doctor was sent for
to Chowder, and he subscribed a repository, which did him
great service—thank God, he's now in a fair way to do well
—pray take care of my box and the pillyber, and put them
under your own bed; for, I do suppose Madam Gwyllim
will be a prying into my secrets, now my back is turned.
John Thomas is in good health, but sulky. The 'squire
gave away an ould coat to a poor man; and John says as
how 'tis robbing him of his parquisites.—I told him, by his
agreement, he was to receive no vails: but he says as how
there's a difference betwixt vails and parquisites; and so
there is for sartain. We are all going to the hot-well,
where I shall drink your health in a glass of water, being,
dear Molly, your humble servant to command,

Glostar, April 2. W. JENKINS.

TO SIR WATKIN PHILLIPS, BART. OF JESUS COLLEGE, OXON.

DEAR PHILLIPS,

As I have nothing more at heart than to convince you I am incapable of forgetting or neglecting the friendship I made at college, I now begin that correspondence by letters, which you and I agreed at parting to cultivate. I begin it sooner than I intended, that you may have it in your power to refute any idle reports which may be circulated to my prejudice at Oxford, touching a foolish quarrel, in which I have been involved on account of my sister, who had been some time settled here in a boarding-school. —When I came hither with my uncle and aunt, who are our guardians to fetch her away, I found her a fine tall girl of seventeen, with an agreeable person; but remarkably simple, and quite ignorant of the world. This disposition, and want of experience, had exposed her to the addresses of a person—I know not what to call him, who had seen her at a play; and, with a confidence and dexterity peculiar to himself, found means to be recommended to her acquaintance. It was by the greatest accident I intercepted one of his letters. As it was my duty to stifle this correspondence in its birth, I made it my business to find him out, and tell him very freely my sentiments of the matter. The spark did not like the style I used, and behaved with abundance of metal. Though his rank in life (which, by the by, I am ashamed to declare) did not entitle him to much deference, yet, as his behaviour was remarkably spirited, I admitted him to the privilege of a gentleman, and something might have happened, had we not been prevented. In short, the business took air, I know not how, and made abundance of noise—recourse was had to justice —I was obliged to give my word and honour, &c. and tomorrow morning we set out for Bristol wells, where I expect to hear from you by the return of the post. I have got into a family of originals, whom I may one day attempt to describe for your amusement. My aunt, Mrs Tabitha Bramble, is a maiden of forty-five, exceeding starched, vain, and ridiculous. My uncle is an odd kind of humourist, always on the fret, and so unpleasant in his manner, that, rather than be obliged to keep him company, I'd resign all claim to the inheritance of his estate. Indeed, his being tortured by the gout, may have soured his temper, and, perhaps, I may like him better on farther acquaintance : certain it is, all his servants and neighbours in the country are fond of him even to a degree of enthusiasm, the reason of which I cannot as yet comprehend. Remember me to Griffy Price, Gwyn, Mansel, Basset, and all the rest of my old Cambrian companions. Salute the bed-maker in my name—give my service to the cook, and pray take care of poor Ponto, for the sake of his old master, who is, and ever will be, dear Phillips, your affectionate friend, and humble servant,

Gloucester, April 2. JER. MELFORD.

TO MRS JERMYN, AT HER HOUSE IN GLOUCESTER.

DEAR MADAM,

HAVING no mother of my own, I hope you will give me leave to disburden my poor heart to you, who have always acted the part of a kind parent to me, ever since I was put under your care. Indeed, and indeed, my worthy gover-ness may believe me, when I assure her, that I never har-boured a thought that was otherwise than virtuous ; and, if God will give me grace, I shall never behave so as to cast a reflection on the care you have taken in my education. I confess I have given just cause of offence, by my want of prudence and experience. I ought not to have listened to what the young man said ; and it was my duty to have told you all that passed, but I was ashamed to mention it ; and then he behaved so modest and respectful, and seemed to be so melancholy and timorous, that I could not find in my heart to do any thing that should make him miserable and desperate. As for familiarities, I do declare, I never once allowed him the favour of a salute ; and as to the few letters that passed between us, they are all in my uncle's hands, and I hope they contain nothing contrary to innocence and honour. I am still persuaded that he is not what he appears to be: but time will discover—Meanwhile, I will endeavour to forget a connection, which is so displeasing to my family. I have cried without ceasing, and have not tasted any thing but tea, since I was hurried away from you; nor did I once close my eyes for three nights running. My aunt continues to chide me severely, when we are by ourselves; but I hope to soften her in time, by humility and submission. My uncle, who was so dreadfully passionate in the beginning, has been moved by my tears and distress, and is now all tenderness and compassion; and my brother is reconciled to me, on my promise to break off all correspondence with that unfortunate youth: but, notwithstanding all their indulgence, I shall have no peace of mind till I know my dear and ever honoured governess has forgiven her poor, disconsolate, forlorn, affectionate humble servant, till death,

Clifton, April 6.   LYDIA MELFORD.

TO MISS LÆTITIA WILLIS, AT GLOUCESTER.

MY DEAREST LETTY,

I AM in such a fright, lest this should not come safe to hand by the conveyance of Jarvis, the carrier, that I beg you will write me, on the receipt of it, directing to me, under cover, to Mrs Winifred Jenkins, my aunt's maid, who is a good girl, and has been so kind to me in my afflictions that I have made her my confidant; as for Jarvis, he was very shy of taking charge of my letter and the little parcel, because his sister Sally had like to have lost her place on my account: indeed I cannot blame the man for his caution; but I have made it worth his while. My dear companion and bed-fellow, it is a grievous addition to my other misfortunes, that I am deprived of your agreeable company and conversation, at a time when I need so much the comfort of your good humour and good sense; but, I hope, the friendship we contracted at the boarding-school will last for life—I doubt not but, on my side, it will daily increase and improve, as I gain experience, and learn to know the value of a true

friend...O, my dear Letty! what shall I say about poor
Mr Wilson? I have promised to break off all correspondence, and, if possible, to forget him: but, alas! I begin to
perceive that it will not be in my power. As it is by no
means proper that the picture should remain in my hands,
lest it should be the occasion of more mischief, I have sent
it to you by this opportunity, begging you will either keep
it safe till better times, or return it to Mr Wilson himself,
who, I suppose, will make it his business to see you at the
usual place. If he should be low-spirited at my sending
back his picture, you may tell him I have no occasion for
a picture, while the original continues engraved on my ——
but, no; I would not have you tell him that neither; because there must be an end of our correspondence—I wish
he may forget me for the sake of his own peace; and yet,
if he should, he must be a barbarous —— But 'tis impossible,—poor Wilson cannot be false and inconstant. I beseech him not to write to me, nor attempt to see me for some
time; for, considering the resentment and passionate temper
of my brother Jery, such an attempt might be attended with
consequences which would make us all miserable for life—
let us trust to time and the chapter of accidents; or rather
to that Providence which will not fail, sooner or later, to
reward those that walk in the paths of honour and virtue—
I would offer my love to the young ladies, but it is not fit
that any of them should know you have received this letter.
If we go to Bath, I shall send you my simple remarks upon
that famous centre of polite amusement, and every other
place we may chance to visit; and I flatter myself that my
dear Miss Willis will be punctual in answering the letters
of her affectionate

Clifton, April 6.   LYDIA MELFORD.

TO DR LEWIS.

DEAR LEWIS,

I HAVE followed your directions with some success, and might
have been upon my legs by this time, had the weather per-

mitted me to use my saddle-horse. I rode out upon the
Downs last Tuesday, in the forenoon, when the sky as far
as the visible horizon, was without a cloud; but, before I
had gone a full mile, I was overtaken instantaneously by a
storm of rain, that wet me to the skin in three minutes—
whence it came the devil knows; but it has laid me up (I
suppose) for one fortnight. It makes me sick to hear people
talk of the fine air upon Clifton downs; how can the air be
either agreeable or salutary, where the demon of vapours
descends in a perpetual drizzle? My confinement is the more
intolerable, as I am surrounded with domestic vexations.
My niece has had a dangerous fit of illness, occasioned by
that cursed incident at Gloucester, which I mentioned in my
last. She is a poor good-natured simpleton, as soft as butter, and as easily melted—not that she's a fool—the girl's
parts are not despicable, and her education has not been
neglected; that is to say, she can write and spell, and speak
French, and play upon the harpsichord; that she dances
finely, has a good figure, and is very well inclined; but
she's deficient in spirit, and so susceptible—and so tender
forsooth!—truly, she has got a languishing eye, and reads
romances. Then there's her brother, Squire Jery, a pert
jackanapes, full of college petulance and self-conceit; proud
as a German count, and as hot and hasty as a Welch mountaineer. As for that fantastical animal my sister Tabby,
you are no stranger to her qualifications. I vow to God,
she is sometimes so intolerable, that I almost think she's
the devil incarnate, come to torment me for my sins; and
yet I am conscious of no sin that ought to entail such family
plagues upon me—why the devil should I not shake off these
torments at once? I an't married to Tabby, thank heaven!
nor did I beget the other two: let them choose another guardian: for my part, I an't in a condition to take care of myself, much less to superintend the conduct of giddy-headed
boys and girls. You earnestly desire to know the particulars of our adventure at Gloucester, which are briefly these,
and I hope they will go no farther:—Liddy had been so long
cooped up in a boarding-school, which, next to a nunnery,

is the worst kind of seminary that ever was contrived for
young women, that she became as inflammable as touch-
wood; and, going to a play in holiday-time—'sdeath, I'm
ashamed to tell you! she fell in love with one of the
actors—a handsome young fellow, that goes by the name
of Wilson. The rascal soon perceived the impression
he had made, and managed matters so as to see her at a
house where she went to drink tea with her governess.
This was the beginning of a correspondence, which they
kept up by means of a jade of a milliner, who made and
dressed caps for the girls at the boarding-school. When
we arrived at Gloucester, Liddy came to stay at lodgings
with her aunt, and Wilson bribed the maid to deliver a letter into her own hands; but it seems Jery had already acquired so much credit with the maid (by what means he best
knows), that she carried the letter to him, and so the whole
plot was discovered. The rash boy, without saying a word
of the matter to me, went immediately in search of Wilson;
and, I suppose, treated him with insolence enough. The
theatrical hero was too far gone in romance to brook such
usage: he replied in blank verse, and a formal challenge
ensued. They agreed to meet early next morning, and to
decide the dispute with sword and pistol. I heard nothing
at all of the affair, till Mr Morley came to my bedside in
the morning, and told me he was afraid my nephew was
going to fight, as he had been overheard talking very loud
and vehement with Wilson, at the young man's lodgings the
night before, and afterwards went and bought powder and ball
at a shop in the neighbourhood. I got up immediately, and
upon inquiry, found he was just gone out. I begged Morley to knock up the mayor, that he might interpose as a
magistrate; and, in the meantime, I hobbled after the
squire, whom I saw at a distance, walking at a great pace
toward the city gate—in spite of all my efforts, I could not
come up till our two combatants had taken their ground,
and were priming their pistols. An old house luckily screen-
ed me from their view; so that I rushed upon them at once
before I was perceived. They were both confounded, and

attempted to make their escape different ways ; but Morley
coming up with constables at that instant, took Wilson into
custody, and Jery followed him quietly to the mayor's
house.   All this time I was ignorant of what had passed the
preceding day ; and neither of the parties would discover a
tittle of the matter.   The mayor observed, that it was great
presumption in Wilson, who was a stroller, to proceed to
such extremities with a gentleman of family and fortune ;
and threatened to commit him on the vagrant act.   The young
fellow bustled up with great spirit, declaring he was a
gentleman, and would be treated as such ; but he refused to
explain himself farther.   The master of the company being
sent for, and examined touching the said Wilson, said the
young man had engaged with him at Birmingham about six
months ago, but never would take his salary ; that he had
behaved so well in his private character, as to acquire the
respect and good-will of all his acquaintance ; and that the
public owned his merit as an actor was altogether extraordinary.   After all, I fancy he will turn out to be a run-away
'prentice from London.   The manager offered to bail him
for any sum, provided he would give his word and honour
that he would keep the peace ; but the young gentleman
was on his high ropes, and would by no means lay himself
under any restrictions : on the other hand, Hopeful was
equally obstinate ; till at length the mayor declared, that,
if they both refused to be bound over, he would immediately
commit Wilson, as a vagrant, to hard labour.   I own I was
much pleased with Jery's behaviour on this occasion ; he
said, that, rather than Mr Wilson should be treated in
such an ignominious manner, he would give his word and
honour to prosecute the affair no farther while they remained
at Gloucester.   Wilson thanked him for his generous manner of proceeding, and was discharged.   On our return to
our lodgings, my nephew explained the whole mystery ; and
I own I was exceedingly incensed.   Liddy being questioned
on the subject, and very severely reproached by that wild
cat my sister Tabby, first swooned away, then dissolving
into a flood of tears, confessed all the particulars of the cor-

respondence; at the same time giving up three letters, which were all she had received from her admirer. 'The last, which Jery intercepted, I send you inclosed; and when you have read it, I dare say you won't wonder at the progress the writer had made in the heart of a simple girl utterly unacquainted with the characters of mankind. Thinking it was high time to remove her from such a dangerous connection, I carried her off the very next day to Bristol; but the poor creature was so frightened and fluttered by our threats and expostulations, that she fell sick the fourth day after our arrival at Clifton, and continued so ill for a whole week, that her life was despaired of. It was not till yesterday that Dr Rigge declared her out of danger. You cannot imagine what I have suffered, partly from the indiscretion of this poor child, but much more from the fear of losing her entirely. This air is intolerably cold, and the place quite solitary. I never go down to the well, without returning low spirited; for there I meet with half a dozen poor emaciated creatures, with ghastly looks, in the last stage of a consumption, who have made shift to linger through the winter like so many exotic plants languishing in a hot-house; but in all appearance will drop into their graves before the sun has warmth enough to mitigate the rigour of this ungenial spring. · If you think the Bath water will be of any service to me, I will go thither as soon as my niece can bear the motion of the coach. Tell Barns I am obliged to him for his advice, but don't choose to follow it. If Davies voluntarily offers to give up the farm, the other shall have it; but I will not begin at this time of day to distress my tenants because they are unfortunate, and cannot make regular payments. I wonder that Barns should think me capable of such oppression. As for Higgins, the fellow is a notorious poacher, to be sure, and an impudent rascal, to set his snares in my own paddock; but I suppose he thought he had some right, especially in my absence, to partake of what nature seems to have intended for common use : you may threaten him in my name as much as you please; and, if he repeats the offence, let me know it before you have re-

course to justice—I know you are a great sportsman, and
oblige many of your friends. I need not tell you to make
use of my grounds; but it may be necessary to hint, that I'm
more afraid of my fowling-piece than of my game. When
you can spare two or three brace of partridges, send them
over by the stage-coach: and tell Gwyllim that she forgot
to pack up my flannels and wide shoes in the trunk-mail—
I shall trouble you as usual, from time to time, till at last,
I suppose, you will be tired of corresponding with your assured friend,

Clifton, April 17.   M. BRAMBLE.

TO MISS LYDIA MELFORD.

MISS WILLIS has pronounced my doom—you are going
away, dear Miss Melford,—you are going to be removed I
know not whither! what shall I do? which way shall I turn
for consolation? I know not what I say—all night long have
I been tossed in a sea of doubts and fears, uncertainty, and
distraction, without being able to connect my thoughts,
much less to form any consistent plan of conduct—I was
even tempted to wish that I had never seen you; or that
you had been less amiable, or less compassionate to your
poor Wilson; and yet it would be detestable ingratitude in
me to form such a wish, considering how much I am indebted to your goodness, and the ineffable pleasure I have
derived from your indulgence and approbation—Good God;
I never heard your name mentioned without emotion! the
most distant prospect of being admitted to your company,
filled my whole soul with a kind of pleasing alarm! as the
time approached, my heart beat with redoubled force, and
every nerve thrilled with a transport of expectation; but,
when I found myself actually in your presence—when I
heard you speak—when I saw you smile—when I beheld
your charming eyes turned favourably upon me, my breast
was filled with such tumults of delight, as wholly deprived
me of the power of utterance, and wrapt me in a delirium of
joy! Encouraged by your sweetness of temper and affability,

I ventured to describe the feelings of my heart—even then
you did not check my presumption—you pitied my sufferings, and gave me leave to hope ;—you put a favourable,
perhaps too favourable a construction, on my appearance
—Certain it is, I am no player in love—I speak the language
of my own heart, and have no prompter but nature. Yet
there is something in this heart, which I have not yet disclosed—I flattered myself—But, I will not, I must not proceed—Dear Miss Liddy ! for Heaven's sake contrive, if possible, some means of letting me speak to you before you
leave Gloucester; otherwise I know not what will—But I
begin to rave again—I will endeavour to bear this trial with
fortitude—while I am capable of reflecting upon your tenderness and truth, I surely have no cause to despair—yet I
am strangely affected. The sun seems to deny me light—a
cloud hangs over me, and there is a dreadful weight upon
my spirits ! While you stay in this place, I shall continually hover about your lodgings, as the parted soul is said to
linger about the grave where its mortal consort lies—I know,
if it is in your power, you will task your humanity—your
compassion—shall I add, your affection? in order to assuage the almost intolerable disquiet that torments the heart
of your afflicted

Gloucester, March 31.   WILSON.

TO SIR WATKIN PHILLIPS, OF JESUS COLLEGE, OXON.

DEAR PHILLIPS,   *Hot-Well, April* 18.

I give Mansel credit for his invention, in propagating the
report, that I had a quarrel with a mountebank's Merry
Andrew at Gloucester: but I have too much respect for
every appendage of wit, to quarrel even with the lowest
buffoonery ; and therefore I hope Mansel and I shall always
be good friends. I cannot, however, approve of his drowning my poor dog Ponto, on purpose to convert Ovid's
pleonasm into a punning epitaph—*deerant quoque littora
Ponto :* for that he threw him into the Isis, when it was so
high and impetuous, with no other view than to kill the

fleas, is an excuse that will not hold water: but I leave poor
Ponto to his fate, and hope Providence will take care to accommodate Mansel with a drier death.

As there is nothing that can be called company at the well,
I am here in a state of absolute rustication : this, however,
gives me leisure to observe the singularities in my uncle's
character, which seems to have interested your curiosity.
The truth is, his disposition and mine, which, like oil and
vinegar, repelled one another at first, have now begun to
mix, by dint of being beat up together. I was once apt to
believe him a complete cynic, and that nothing but the necessity of his occasions could compel him to get within the
pale of society—I am now of another opinion; I think his
peevishness arises partly from bodily pain, and partly from
a natural excess of mental sensibility; for, I suppose, the
mind, as well as the body, is, in some cases, endowed with
a morbid excess of sensation.

I was t'other day much diverted with a conversation that
passed in the pump-room, betwixt him and the famous Dr
L——n, who is come to ply at the well for patients. My uncle
was complaining of the stink, occasioned by the vast quantity
of mud and slime, which the river leaves at low ebb under
the windows of the pump-room. He observed, that the ex-
halations arising from such a nuisance, could not but be prejudicial to the weak lungs of many consumptive patients who
came to drink the water. The doctor, overhearing this remark, made up to him, and assured him he was mistaken. He
said, people in general were so misled by vulgar prejudices,
that philosophy was hardly sufficient to undeceive them.
Then, hemming thrice, he assumed a most ridiculous solemnity of aspect, and entered into a learned investigation
of the nature of stink. He observed, that stink or stench,
meant no more than a strong impression on the olfactory
nerves, and might be applied to substances of the most opposite qualities; that in the Dutch language, *stinken* signified
the most agreeable perfume, as well as the most fetid odour,
as appears in Van Vloudel's translation of Horace, in that
beautiful ode, *Quis malta gracilis*, &c. The words *liquidis*

perfusus odóribus, he translates, *van civet et moschata ge-
stinken ;* that individuals differed *toto cœla* in their opinion of
smells, which indeed was altogether as arbitrary as the opinion of beauty ; that the French were pleased with the putrid
effluvia of animal food, and so were the Hottentots in Africa,
and the savages in Greenland ; and that the negroes on the
coast of Senegal would not touch fish till it was rotten ; strong
presumptions in favour of what is generally called *stink*, as
those nations are in a state of nature, undebauched by luxury,
unseduced by whim and caprice; that he had reason to believe the stercoraceous flavour, condemned by prejudice as
a stink, was, in fact, most agreeable to the organs of smelling ; for that very person who pretended to nauseate the
smell of another's excrations, snuffed up his own with particular complacency; for the truth of which, he appealed
to all the ladies and gentlemen then present : he said, the
inhabitants of Madrid and Edinburgh found particular satisfaction in breathing their own atmosphere, which was
always impregnated with stercoraceous effluvia : that the
learned Dr B——, in his Treatise on the four digestions,
explains in what manner the volatile effluvia from the intestines stimulate and promote the operations of the animal
economy : he affirmed, the last grand duke of Tuscany,
of the Medicis family, who refined upon sensuality with the
spirit of a philosopher, was so delighted with that odour,
that he caused the essence of odour to be extracted, and
used it as the most delicious perfume : that he himself (the
doctor), when he happened to be low-spirited, or fatigued ·
with business, found immediate relief, and uncommon satisfaction, from hanging over the stale contents of a close stool,
while his servant stirred it about under his nose ; nor was
this effect to be wondered at, when we consider that this
substance abounds with the self-same volatile salts that are
so greedily smelled to by the most delicate invalids, after
they have been extracted and sublimed by the chemists.
By this time the company began to hold their noses ; but
the doctor, without taking the least notice of this signal,
proceeded to shew, that many fetid substances were not only

agreeable but salutary; such as assafœtida and other medi-
cinal gums, resins, roots, and vegetables, over and above
burnt feathers, tan-pits, candle-snuffs, &c.   In short he
used many learned arguments to persuade his audience out
of their senses; and from *stench* made a transition to *filth*,
which he affirmed was also a mistaken idea, inasmuch as
objects so called were no other than certain modifications of
matter, consisting of the same principles that enter into the
composition of all created essences, whatever they may be:
that, in the filthiest production of nature, a philosopher considered nothing but the earth, water, salt, and air, of which
it was compounded: that, for his own part, he had no more
objection to drinking the dirtiest ditch-water, than he had
to a glass of water from the hot-well, provided he was assured there was nothing poisonous in the concrete.   Then
addressing himself to my uncle,—' Sir,' said he, ' you seem
to be of a dropsical habit, and probably will soon have a
confirmed ascites; if I should be present when you are tap-
ped, I will give you a convincing proof of what I assert, by
drinking, without hesitation, the water that comes out of
your abdomen.'   The ladies made wry faces at this declaration; and my uncle, changing colour, told him, he did
not desire any such proof of his philosophy.—' But I should
be glad to know,' said he, ' what makes you think I am of
a dropsical habit?'   ' Sir, I beg pardon,' replied the doctor,
' I perceive your ancles are swelled, and you seem to have
the *facies-leucophlegmatica.*   Perhaps, indeed, your disorder
may be *œdematous,* or gouty, or it may be the *lues venerea.*
If you have any reason to flatter yourself it is this last, sir,
I will undertake to cure you with three small pills, even if
the disease should have attained its utmost inveteracy.   Sir,
it is an arcanum, which I have discovered, and prepared
with infinite labour.   Sir, I have lately cured a woman in
Bristol—a common prostitute, sir, who had got all the worst
symptoms of the disorder; such as *nodi, tophi,* and *gum-
mutæ, verrucæ, cristæ, galli,* and a *serpiginous* erruption, or
rather a pocky itch all over her body.   By that time she
had taken the second pill, sir, by heaven! she was as smooth

as my hand ; and the third made her as sound and as fresh
as a new born infant.' ' Sir,' cried my uncle peevishly, ' I
have no reason to flatter myself that my disorder comes within the efficacy of your nostrum : but this patient you talk of
may not be so sound at bottom as you imagine. ' I can't
possibly be mistaken,' rejoined the philosopher, ' for I have
had communication with her three times—I always ascertain
my cures in that manner.' At this remark, all the ladies
retired to another corner of the room, and some of them began to spit—As to my uncle, though he was ruffled at first
by the doctor's saying he was dropsical, he could not help
smiling at this ridiculous confession ; and, I suppose, with
a view to punish this original, told him there was a wart
upon his nose, that looked a little suspicious.—' I don't
pretend to be a judge of these matters,' said he, ' but I understand that warts are often produced by the distemper ;
and that one upon your nose seems to have taken possession
of the very key-stone of the bridge, which I hope is in no
danger of falling.'. L——n seemed a little confounded at
this remark, and assured him it was nothing but a common
excrescence of the cuticula, but that the bones were all sound
below ; for the truth of this assertion, he appealed to the
touch, desiring he would feel the part. My uncle said it
was a matter of such delicacy to meddle with a gentleman's
nose, that he declined the office ; upon which the doctor,
turning to me, intreated me to do him that favour. I complied with his request, and handled it so roughly, that he
sneezed, and the tears ran down his cheeks, to the no small
entertainment of the company, and particularly of my uncle,
who burst out a laughing for the first time since I have been
with him ; and took notice that the part seemed to be very
tender. ' Sir,' cried the doctor, ' it is naturally a tender
part ; but to remove all possibility of doubt, I will take off
the wart this very night.'

So saying, he bowed with great solemnity all round, and
retired to his own lodgings, where he applied caustic to the
wart ; but it spread in such a manner, as to produce a considerable inflammation, attended with an enormous swelling ;

so that, when he next appeared, his whole face was over-shadowed by this tremendous nozzle; and the rueful eager-ness with which he explained this unlucky accident, was ludicrous beyond all description. I was much pleased with meeting the original of a character which you and I have often laughed at in description; and what surprises me very much, I find the features in the picture which has been drawn for him rather softened than overcharged.

As I have some thing else to say, and this letter is run to an unconscionable length, I shall now give you a little respite, and trouble you again by' the very first post. I wish you would take it in your head to retaliate these double strokes upon yours always.   J. MELFORD.

TO SIR WATKIN PHLILLIPS, OF JESUS COLLEGE, OXON.

DEAR KNIGHT,   *Hot-Well, April 20.*

I NOW sit down to execute the threat in the tail of my last. The truth is, I am big with the secret, and long to be deli-vered. It relates to my guardian, who, you know, is at pre-sent our principal object in view.

T'other day I thought I had detected him in such a state of frailty as would but ill become his years and character. There is a decent sort of a woman, not disagreeable in her person, that comes to the well, with a poor emaciated child, far gone in a consumption. I had caught my uncle's eyes several times directed to this person, with a very suspicious expression in them; and every time he saw himself observed, he hastily withdrew them, with evident marks of confusion. I resolved to watch him more narrowly, and saw him speak-ing to her privately in a corner of the walk. At length, go-ing down to the well one day, I met her half way up the hill to Clifton, and could not help suspecting she was going to our lodgings by appointment, as it was about one o'clock, the hour when my sister and I are generally at the pump-room. This notion exciting my curiosity, I returned by a back way, and got unperceived into my own chamber, which is contiguous to my uncle's apartment. Sure enough the woman was introduced, but not into his bed-chamber: he gave her audience in a parlour; so that I was obliged to shift my station to another room, where, however, there was a small chink in the partition, through which I could perceive what passed. My uncle, though a little lame, rose up when she came in, and, setting a chair for her, desired she would sit down : then he asked if she would take a dish of chocolate, which she declined, with much acknowledgment. After a short pause, he said, in a croaking tone of voice, which confounded me not a little,—' Madam, I am truly concerned for your misfortunes : and if this trifle can be of any service to you, I beg you will accept it without ceremony.' So saying, he put a bit of paper into her hand; which she opening with great trepidation, exclaimed, in an ecstacy,— 'Twenty pounds! O, sir!' and, sinking down on a settee, fainted away. Frightened at this fit, and, I suppose, afraid of calling for assistance, lest her situation should give rise to unfavourable conjectures, he ran about the room in distraction, making frightful grimaces; and, at length, had recollection enough to throw a little water in her face; by which application she was brought to herself: but then her feelings took another turn. She shed a flood of tears, and cried aloud,—' I know not who you are ; but sure—worthy sir !— generous sir !—the distress of me and my poor dying child— Oh! if the widow's prayers—if the orphan's tears of gratitude can aught avail—Gracious Providence !—Blessings ! shower down eternal blessings'—Here she was interrupted by my uncle, who muttered, in a voice still more and more discordant,—' For Heaven's sake, be quiet, madam—consider—the people of the house—'sdeath ! can't you—All this time she was struggling to throw herself on her knees, while he, seizing her by the wrists, endeavoured to seat her upon the settee, saying,—' Prithee—good now—hold your tongue' —At that instant, who should burst into the room but our aunt Tabby ! of all antiquated maidens the most diabolically capricious. Ever prying into other people's affairs, she had seen the woman enter, and followed her to the door, where she stood listening, but probably could hear nothing distinctly, except my uncle's last exclamation ; at which she

bounced into the parlour in a violent rage, that dyed the tip
of her nose with a purple hue. ' Fy upon you, Matt !' cried
she, ' what doings are these, to disgrace your own character, and disparage your family ?' Then snatching the bank-
note out of the stranger's hand, she went on,—' How now,
twenty pounds !—here is a temptation with a witness !—
Good woman, go about your business—Brother, brother, I
know not which most to admire, your concupissins, or your
extravagance !' ' Good God ?' exclaimed the poor woman,
' shall a worthy gentleman's character suffer for an action
that does honour to humanity ?' By this time, uncle's indignation was effectually roused : his face grew pale, his teeth
chattered, and his eyes flashed—' Sister,' cried he, in a voice
like thunder, ' I vow to God, your impertinence is exceedingly provoking.' With these words, he took her by the
hand, and, opening the door of communication, thrust her
into the chamber where I stood, so affected by the scene,
that the tears ran down my checks. Observing these marks
of emotion,—' I don't wonder,' said she, ' to see you concerned at the backslidings of so near a relation ; a man of his
years and infirmities ; these are fine doings, truly—This is a
rare example set by a guardian for the benefit of his pupils
—Monstrous ! incongruous ! sophistical !' I thought it was
but an act of justice to set her to rights, and therefore explained the mystery ; but she would not be undeceived.
' What !' said she, ' would you go for to offer for to arguefy
me out of my senses ?' Didn't I hear him whispering to her
to hold her tongue ? Didn't I see her in tears ? Didn't I see
him struggling to throw her upon the couch ? O filthy ! hideous ! abominable !—Child, child, talk not to me of charity—Who gives twenty pounds in charity ?—But you are
a stripling—You know nothing of the world—Besides, charity begins at home—Twenty pounds would buy me a complete suit of flowered silk, trimmings and all.' In short, I
quitted the room, my contempt for her, and my respect for
her brother, being increased in the same proportion. I have
since been informed, that the person whom my uncle so ge-
nerously relieved, is the widow of an ensign, who has no-

thing to depend upon but the pension of fifteen pounds a-year. The people of the well-house give her an excellent character. She lodges in a garret, and works very hard at plain work, to support her daughter, who is dying of a consumption. I must own, to my shame, I feel a strong inclination to follow my uncle's example, in relieving this poor widow; but, betwixt friends, I am afraid of being detected in a weakness that might entail the ridicule of the company upon, dear Phillips, yours always,   J. MELFORD.

Direct your next to me at Bath; and remember me to all our fellow Jesuits.

TO DR LEWIS.

Hot-Well, April 20.

I UNDERSTAND your hint. There are mysteries in physic as well as in religion, which we of the profane have no right to investigate. A man must not presume to use his reason, unless he has studied the categories, and can chop logic by mode and figure. Between friends, I think, every man of tolerable parts ought, at my time of day, to be both physician and lawyer, as far as his own constitution and property are concerned. For my own part, I have had an hospital these fourteen years within myself, and studied my own case with the most painful attention, consequently may be supposed to know something of the matter, although I have not taken regular courses of physiology, *et cætera, et cætera.* In short, I have for some time been of opinion (no offence, dear doctor), that the sum of all your medical discoveries amounts to this,—that the more you study, the less you know. I have read all that has been written on the hot wells; and what I can collect from the whole is, that the water contains nothing but a little salt, and calcareous earth, mixed in such inconsiderable proportion, as can have very little, if any, effect on the animal economy. This being the case, I think the man deserves to be fitted with a cap and bells, who, for such a paltry advantage as this spring affords, sacrifices his precious time, which might be employed in taking more effectual remedies, and exposes himself to the dirt, the stench,

the chilling blasts, and perpetual rains, that render this place
to me intolerable.   If these waters, from a small degree of
astringency, are of some service in the *diabetes*, *diarrhœa*,
and night sweats, when the secretions are too much increased, must not they do harm in the same proportion, where
the humours are obstructed, as in the asthma, scurvy, gout,
and dropsy ?—Now we talk of the dropsy, here is a strange
fantastical oddity, one of your brethren, who harangues
every day in the pump-room, as if he was hired to give lectures on all subjects whatsoever—I know not what to make of
him.   Sometimes he makes shrewd remarks, at other times
he talks like the greatest simpleton in nature.   He has read
a great deal, but without method or judgment, and digested
nothing.   He believes every thing he has read, especially if
it has any thing of the marvellous in it; and his conversation is a surprising hotch-potch of erudition and extravagance.   He told me t'other day, with great confidence, that
my case was dropsical, or, as he called it, *leucophlegmatic* :
a sure sign that his want of experience is equal to his presumption; for you know there is nothing analogous to the
dropsy in my disorder.   I wish those impertinent fellows,
with their rickety understandings, would keep their advice
for those who ask it—Dropsy, indeed ! Sure I have not lived
to the age of fifty-five, and had such experience of my own
disorder, and consulted you and other eminent physicians so
often and so long, to be undeceived by such a ———.   But,
without all doubt, the man is mad, and therefore what he
says is of no consequence.   I had yesterday a visit from
Higgens, who came hither under the terror of your threats,
and brought me in a present a brace of hares, which he
owned he took in my ground; and I could not persuade the
fellow that he did wrong, or that I would ever prosecute
him for poaching.   I must desire you will wink hard at the
practices of this rascallion, otherwise I shall be plagued with
his presents, which cost me more than they are worth.—If
I could wonder at any thing Fitzowen does, I should be surprised at his assurance, in desiring you to solicit my vote
for him at the next election for the county; for him, who

opposed me on the like occasion with the most illiberal competition. You may tell him civilly that I beg to be excused. Direct your next for me at Bath, whither I propose to
remove to-morrow, not only on my own account, but for the
sake of my niece Liddy, who is like to relapse. The poor
creature fell into a fit yesterday, while I was cheapening a
pair of spectacles with a Jew pedlar. I am afraid there is
something still lurking in that little heart of hers, which I
hope a change of objects will remove. Let me know what
you think of this half-witted doctor's impertinent, ridiculous,
and absurd, notion of my disorder. So far from being dropsical, I am as lank in the belly as a grey-hound ; and, by
measuring my ancle with a pack-thread, I find the swelling
subsides every day—From such doctors good Lord deliver
us!—I have not yet taken any lodgings in Bath, because
there we can be accommodated at a minute's warning, and
I shall choose for myself. I need not say your directions for
drinking and bathing will be agreeable to, dear Lewis, yours
ever,   MATT. BRAMBLE.

P. S. I forgot to tell you that my right ancle pits ; a
symptom, as I take it, of its being *oedematous*, not *leuco-
phlagmatic.*

TO MISS LÆTITIA WILLIS, AT GLOUCESTER.

MY DEAR LETTY,   *Hot-Well, April 21.*

I DID not intend to trouble you again till we should be settled
at Bath ; but having the occasion of Jarvis, I could not let it
slip, especially as I have something extraordinary to communicate. O, my dear companion ! what shall I tell you ? for
several days past there was a Jew-looking man that plied at
the wells with a box of spectacles, and he always eyed me so
earnestly, that I began to be very uneasy. At last he came
to our lodgings at Clifton, and lingered about the door, as
if he wanted to speak to somebody. I was seized with an
odd kind of fluttering, and begged Win to throw herself in
his way ; but the poor girl has weak nerves, and was afraid
of his beard. My uncle, having occasion for new glasses,
called him up stairs, and was trying a pair of spectacles,

when the man, advancing to me, said, in a whisper—O gracious! what d'ye think he said?—' I am Wilson!' His features struck me that very moment—it was Wilson sure
enough! but so disguised, that it would have been impossible to know him, if my heart had not assisted in the discovery.   I was so surprised, and so frightened, that I fainted
away, but soon recovered, and found myself supported by
him on the chair, while my uncle was running about the
room, with the spectacles on his nose, calling for help.   I
had no opportunity to speak to him, but our looks were sufficiently expressive.   He was paid for his glasses, and went
away.   Then I told Win who he was, and sent her after him
to the pump-room, where she spoke to him, and begged him
in my name to withdraw from the place, that he might not
incur the suspicion of my uncle or my brother, if he did not
want to see me die of terror and vexation.   The poor youth
declared, with tears in his eyes, that he had something extraordinary to communicate, and asked if she would deliver
a letter to me; but this she absolutely refused, by my order.
Finding her obstinate in her refusal, he desired she would
tell me that he was no longer a player, but a gentleman, in
which character he would very soon avow his passion for
me, without fear of censure or reproach.   Nay, he even discovered his name and family, which, to my great grief, the
simple girl forgot, in the confusion occasioned by her being
seen talking to him by my brother, who stopped her on the
road, and asked what business she had with that rascally
Jew.   She pretended she was cheapening a stay-book; but
was thrown into such a quandary, that she forgot the most
material part of the information; and, when she came home,
went into an hysteric fit of laughing.   This transaction happened three days ago, during which he has not appeared;
so that I suppose he is gone.   Dear Letty! you see how fortune takes pleasure in persecuting your poor friend.   If you
should see him at Gloucester—or if you have seen him, and
know his real name and family, pray keep me no longer in
suspense—And yet, if he is under no obligation to keep
himself longer concealed, and has a real affection for me, I

should hope he will, in a little time, declare himself to my relations.   Sure, if there is nothing unsuitable in the match, they won't be so cruel as to thwart my inclinations—O what happiness would then be my portion! I can't help indulging the thought, and pleasing my fancy with such agreeable ideas, which, after all, perhaps, will never be realized. But why should I despair? who knows what will happen?—We set out for Bath to-morrow, and I am almost sorry for it, as I begin to be in love with solitude, and this is a charming romantic place.   The air is so pure; the downs are so agreeable;—the furse in full blossom; the ground enamelled with daisies, and primroses, and cowslips; all the trees bursting into leaves, and the hedges already clothed with their vernal livery; the mountains covered with flocks of sheep, and tender bleating wanton lambkins playing, frisking, and skipping from side to side; the groves resound with the notes of the blackbird, thrush, and linnet: and all night long sweet Philomel pours forth her ravishingly delightful song. Then, for variety, we go down to the *nymph of Bristol spring*, where the company is assembled before dinner; so goodnatured, so free, so easy; and there we drink the water so clear, so pure, so mild, so charmingly maukish—There the sun is so cheerful and reviving, the weather so soft, the walk so agreeable, the prospect so amusing, and the ships and boats going up and down the river, close under the windows of the pump-room, afford such an enchanting variety of moving pictures, as require a much abler pen than mine to describe.   To make this place a perfect paradise to me, nothing is wanting but an agreeable companion and sincere friend, such as my dear Miss Willis hath been, and I hope still will be, to her ever faithful   LYDIA MELFORD.

Direct for me, still under cover, to Win, and Jarvis will take care to convey it safe.   Adieu.

TO SIR WATKIN PHILLIPS, OF JESUS COLLEGE, OXON.

DEAR PHILLIPS,   *Bath, April 24.*

You have, indeed, reason to be surprised, that I should have concealed my correspondence with Miss Blackerby

from you, to whom I disclosed all my other connections of
that nature ! but the truth is, I never dreamed of any such
commerce, till your last informed me, that it had produced
something which could not be much longer concealed.   It
is a lucky circumstance, however, that her reputation will
not suffer any detriment, but rather derive advantage from
the discovery ; which will prove, at least, that it is not
quite so rotten as most people imagined.   For my own part,
I declare to you, in all the sincerity of friendship, that, far
from having any amorous intercourse with the object in
question, I never had the least acquaintance with her person; but if she is really in the condition you describe, I
suspect Mansel to be at the bottom of the whole.   His visits
to that shrine were no secret; and this attachment, added
to some good offices, which you know he has done me since
I left *alma-mater*, give me a right to believe him capable
of saddling me with this scandal when my back was turned—Nevertheless, if my name can be of any service to him,
he is welcome to make use of it ; and, if the woman should
be abandoned enongh to swear his bantling to me, I must
beg the favour of you to compound with the parish : I shall
pay the penalty without repining; and you will be so good
as to draw upon me immediately for the sum required—On
this occasion, I act by the advice of my uncle, who says I
shall have good luck if I pass through life without being
obliged to make many more compositions of the same kind.
The old gentleman told me last night, with great good humour, that, betwixt the age of twenty and forty, he had
been obliged to provide for nine bastards, sworn to him by
women whom he never saw.——Mr Bramble's character, which
seems to interest you greatly, opens and improves upon me
every day.——His singularities afford a rich mine of entertainment ; his understanding, so far as I can judge, is well cultivated ; his observations on life are equally just, pertinent,
and uncommon.   He effects misanthropy, in order to conceal the sensibility of a heart which is tender even to a degree
of weakness.   This delicacy of feeling, or soreness of the
mind makes him timorous and fearful; but then he is afraid

of nothing so much as of dishonour; and although he is exceedingly cautious of giving offence, he will fire at the least hint of insolence or ill-breeding—Respectable as he is, upon the whole, I can't help being sometimes diverted by his little distresses; which provoke him to let fly the shafts of his satire, keen and penetrating as the arrows of Teucer—Our aunt Tabitha acts upon him as a perpetual grind-stone—She is, in all respects, a striking contrast to her brother—But I reserve her portrait for another occasion.

Three days ago we came hither from the hot-well, and took possession of the first floor of a lodging-house on the South parade; a situation which my uncle chose, for its being near the bath, and remote from the noise of carriages. He was scarce warm in the lodgings, when he called for his night-cap, his wide shoes, and flannel, and declared himself invested with the gout in his right foot; though, I believe, it had as yet reached no farther than his imagination. It was not long before he had reason to repent his premature declaration; for our aunt Tabitha found means to make such a clamour and confusion, before the flannels could be produced from the trunk, that one would have imagined the house was on fire. All this time, uncle sat boiling with impatience, biting his fingers, throwing up his eyes, and muttering ejaculations; at length he burst into a kind of convulsive laugh, after which he hummed a song; and, when the hurricane was over, exclaimed,—' Blessed be God for all things!' This, however, was but the beginning of his troubles. Mrs Tabitha's favourite dog Chowder, having paid his compliments to a female turn-spit, of his own species, in the kitchen, involved himself in a quarrel with no fewer than five rivals, who set upon him at once, and drove him up stairs to the dining-room door, with hideous noise: there our aunt and her woman, taking arms in his defence, joined the concert, which became truly diabolical. This fray being with difficulty suppressed, by the intervention of our own footman and the cook-maid of the house, the squire had just opened his mouth to expostulate with Tabby, when the town-waits, in the passage below,

struck up their music (if music it may be called) with such
a sudden burst of sound, as made him start and stare, with
marks of indignation and disquiet.   He had recollection
enough to send his servant with some money, to silence
those noisy intruders ; and they were immediately dismissed, though not without some opposition on the part of
Tabitha, who thought it but reasonable that he should have
more music for his money.   Scarce had he settled this knot-
ty point, when a strange kind of thumping and bouncing
was heard right over head, in the second story, so loud and
violent as to shake the whole building.   I own I was exceedingly provoked at this new alarm ; and before my uncle
had time to express himself on the subject, I ran up stairs,
to see what was the matter.   Finding the room-door open,
I entered without ceremony, and perceived an object,
which I cannot now recollect without laughing to excess—
It was a dancing-master, with his scholar, in the act of
teaching.   The master was blind of one eye, and lame of
one foot, and led about the room his pupil, who seemed to
be about the age of threescore, stooped mortally, was tall,
raw-boned, hard-favoured, with a woollen night-cap on his
head ; and he had stript off his coat, that he might be more
nimble in his motions.—Finding himself intruded upon by
a person he did not know, he forthwith girded himself with
a long iron sword, and, advancing to me, with a peremptory air, pronounced, in a true Hibernian accent,—' Mister
What-d'ye-callum, by my shoul and conscience I am very
glad to sea you, if you are after coming in the way of friendship ; and indeed, and indeed now, I believe you are my
friend sure enough, gra ; though I never had the honour
to sea your face before, my dear ; for because you come like
a friend without any ceremony, at all, at all—'   I told him
the nature of my visit would not admit of ceremony ; that I
was come to desire he would make less noise, as there was a
sick gentleman below, whom he had no right to disturb
with such preposterous doings.   ' Why, look ye now,
young gentleman,' replied this original,' ' perhaps upon
another occasion, I might shivilly request you to explain

the maining of that hard word, *prepasterous :* but there's a time for all things, honey—' So saying, he passed me with great agility, and running down stairs, found our footman at the dining-room door, of whom he demanded admittance, to pay his respects to the stranger. As the fellow did not think proper to refuse the request of such a formidable figure, he was immediately introduced, and addressed himself to my uncle in these words.—' Your humble servant, good sir,—I am not so *prepasterous,* as your son calls it, but I know the rules of shivility—I am a poor knight of Ireland, my name is Sir Ulic Mackilligut, of the county of Galway ; being your fellow-lodger I'm come to pay my respects, and to welcome you to the South parade, and to offer my best services to you, and your good lady, and your pretty daughter ; and even to the young gentleman your son, though he thinks me a *prepasterous* fellow.—You must know I am to have the honour to open a ball, next door, to-morrow, with Lady Macmanus ; and, being rusted in my dancing, I was refreshing my memory with a little exercise : but if I had known there was a sick person below, by C——t ! I would sooner have danced a horn-pipe upon my own head, than walk the softest minuet over yours.' My uncle, who was not a little startled at his first appearance, received his compliment with great complacency, insisted upon his being seated, thanked him for the honour of his visit, and reprimanded me for my abrupt expostulation with a gentleman of his rank and character. Thus tutored, I asked pardon of the knight, who, forthwith starting up, embraced me so close, that I could hardly breathe ; and assured me, he loved me as his own soul. At length, recollecting his night-cap, he pulled it off in some confusion ; and with his bald pate uncovered, made a thousand apologies to the ladies as he retired.

At that instant the abbey bells began to ring so loud, that we could not hear one another speak ; and this peal, as we afterwards learned, was for the honour of Mr Bullock, an eminent cowkeeper of Tottenham, who had just arrived at Bath, to drink the waters for indigestion. Mr Bramble

had not time to make his remarks upon the agreeable nature
of this serenade, before his ears were saluted with another
concert that interested him more nearly. Two negroes that
belonged to a Creole gentleman who lodged in the same
house, taking their station at a window in the stair-case,
about ten feet from our dining-room door, began to practise
upon the French horn : and, being in the very first rudiments
of execution, produced such discordant sounds, as might
have discomposed the organs of an ass. You may guess
what effect they had upon the irritable nerves of uncle ; who,
with the most admirable expression of splenetic surprise in
his countenance, sent his man to silence those dreadful blasts,
and desire the musicians to practise in some other place, as
they had no right to stand there and disturb all the lodgers
in the house. Those sable performers, far from taking the
hint, and withdrawing, treated the messenger with great insolence, bidding him carry his compliments to their master,
Colonel Rigworm, who would give him a proper answer,
and a good drubbing into the bargain : in the meantime
they continued their noise, and even endeavoured to make
it more disagreeable, laughing between whiles, at the thoughts
of being able to torment their betters with impunity. Our
squire, incensed at this additional insult, immediately dispatched the servant, with his compliments to Colonel Rigworm, requesting that he would order his blacks to be quiet,
as the noise they made was altogether intolerable. To this
message the Creole colonel replied, that his horns had a
right to sound on a common stair-case ; that there they
should play for his diversion ; and that those who did not
like the noise might look for lodgings elsewhere. Mr Bramble
no sooner received this reply, than his eyes began to glisten, his face grew pale, and his teeth chattered. After a
moment's pause, he slipt on his shoes, without speaking a
word, or seeming to feel any farther disturbance from the
gout in his toes. Then snatching his cane, he opened the
door, and proceeded to the place where the black trumpet-
ers were posted. There, without farther hesitation, he began to belabour them both ; and exerted himself with such

astonishing vigour and agility, that both their heads and horns were broken in a twinkling, and they ran howling down stairs to their master's parlour door. The 'squire following them half way, called aloud, that the colonel might hear him,—' Go, rascals, and tell your master what I have done; if he thinks himself injured, he knows where to come for satisfaction. As for you, this is but an earnest of what you shall receive, if ever you presume to blow a horn again here, while I stay in the house.' So saying, he retired to his apartment, in expectation of hearing from the West Indian; but the colonel prudently declined any farther prosecution of the dispute. My sister Liddy was frighted into a fit, from which she was no sooner recovered than Mrs Tabitha began a lecture upon patience; which her brother interrupted with a most significant grin, exclaiming,— ' True, sister, God increase my patience and your discretion. I wonder,' added he, ' what sort of sonata we are to expect from this overture, in which the devil that presides over horrid sounds hath given us such variations of discord. —The trampling of porters, the creaking and crashing of trunks, the snarling of curs, the scolding of women, the squeaking and squalling of fiddles and hautboys out of tune, the bouncing of the Irish baronet overhead, and the bursting, belching, and brattling, of the French horns in the passage, (not to mention the harmonious peal that still thunders from the abbey steeple), succeeding one another without interruption, like the different parts of the same concert, have given me such an idea of what a poor invalid has to expect in this temple, dedicated to silence and repose, that I shall certainly shift my quarters to-morrow, and endeavour to effectuate my retreat before Sir Ulric opens the ball with my Lady Macmanus, a conjunction that bodes me no good.' This intimation was by no means agreeable to Mrs Tabitha, whose ears were not quite so delicate as those of her brother. —She said it would be great folly to move from such agreeable lodgings, the moment they were comfortably settled. She wondered he should be such an enemy to music and mirth. She heard no noise but of his own making: it was impossible to manage a family in dumb show. He might harp as long as he pleased upon her scolding; but she never scolded except for his advantage; but he would never be satisfied, even thof she should sweat blood and water in his service. I have a great notion that our aunt, who is now declining into the most desperate state of celibacy, had formed some design upon the heart of Sir Ulic Mackilligut, which she feared might be frustrated by our abrupt departure from these lodgings. Her brother, eyeing her askance, —'Pardon me, sister,' said he, 'I should be a savage, indeed, were I insensible of my own felicity, in having such a mild, complaisant, good-humoured, and considerate companion and housekeeper; but as I have got a weak head, and my sense of hearing is painfully acute, before I have recourse to plugs of wool and cotton, I'll try whether I can't find another lodging, where I shall have more quiet and less music.' He accordingly dispatched his man upon this service; and next day he found a small house in Milsham-street, which he hires by the week. Here at least we enjoy convenience and quiet within doors, as much as Tabby's temper will allow; but the 'squire still complains of flying pains in the stomach and head, for which he bathes and drinks the waters. He is not so bad, however, but that he goes in person to the pump, and rooms, and the coffee houses, where he picks up continual food for ridicule and satire. If I can gleam any thing for your amusement, either from his observation or my own, you shall have it freely, though I am afraid it will poorly compensate the trouble of reading these tedious insipid letters of, dear Phillips, your always,   J. MELFORD.

TO DR LEWIS.

DEAR DOCTOR,   *Bath, April 23.*

IF I did not know that the exercise of your profession has habituated you to the hearing of complaints, I should make a conscience of troubling you with my correspondence, which may be truly called *the lamentations of Matthew Bramble.* Yet I cannot help thinking I have some right to discharge the overflowings of my spleen upon you, whose province it is to remove those disorders that occasioned it; and, let me tell you, it is no small alleviation of my grievances, that I have a sensible friend, to whom I can communicate my crusty humours, which, by retention, would grow intolerably acrimonious.

You must know, I find nothing but disappointment at Bath, which is so altered, that I can scarce believe it is the same place that I frequented about thirty years ago. Methinks I hear you say,—' Altered it is, without all doubt; but then it is altered for the better; a truth, which, perhaps, you would own without hesitation, if you yourself was not altered for the worse.' The reflection may, for aught I know, be just. The inconveniences which I overlooked in the heyday of health, will naturally strike with exaggerated impression on the irritable nerves of an invalid, surprised by premature old age, and shattered with long suffering—But, I believe, you will not deny that this place, which Nature and Providence seem to have intended as a resource from distemper and disquiet, is become the very centre of racket and dissipation. Instead of that peace, tranquillity, and ease, so necessary to those who labour under bad health, weak nerves, and irregular spirits; here we have nothing but noise, tumult, and hurry, with the fatigue and slavery of maintaining a ceremonial, more stiff, formal, and oppressive, than the etiquette of a German elector. A national hospital it may be; but one would imagine, that none but lunatics are admitted; and, truly, I will give you leave to call me so, if I stay much longer at Bath—But I shall take another opportunity to explain my sentiments at greater length on this subject—I was impatient to see the boasted improvements in architecture, for which the upper parts of the town have been so much celebrated, and t'other day I made a circuit of all the new buildings. The square, though irregular, is, on the whole, pretty well laid out, spacious, open, and airy; and, in my opinion, by far the most wholesome and agreeable situation in Bath, especially the upper side of it; but the avenues to it are mean, dirty,

dangerous, and indirect.   Its communication with the baths
is through the yard of an inn, where the poor trembling va-
letudinarian is carried in a chair, betwixt the heels of a
double row of horses, wincing under the curry-combs of
grooms and postillions, over and above the hazard of being
obstructed, or overturned by the carriages which are continually making their exit or their entrance.—I suppose, after
some chairmen shall have been maimed, and a few lives lost
by those accidents, the corporation will think, in earnest,
about providing a more safe and commodious passage.   The
circus is a pretty bauble ; contrived for show, and looks
like Vespasian's amphitheatre, turned outside in.   If we consider it in point of magnificence, the great number of small
doors belonging to the separate houses, the inconsiderable
height of the different orders, the affected ornaments of the
architrave, which are both childish and misplaced, and
the areas projecting into the street, surrounded with iron
rails, destroy a good part of its effect upon the eye ; and
perhaps we shall find it still more defective, if we view it in
the light of convenience.   The figure of each separate dwelling house, being the segment of a circle, must spoil the sym-
metry of the rooms, by contracting them towards the street
windows, and leaving a larger sweep in the space behind.
If, instead of the areas and iron rails, which seem to be
of very little use, there had been a corridore with arcades
all round, as in Covent-garden, the appearance of the
whole would have been more magnificent and striking ;
those arcades would have afforded an agreeable covered walk,
and sheltered the poor chairmen and their carriages from the
rain, which is here almost perpetual.   At present, the chairs
stand soaking in the open street, from morning to night, till
they become so many boxes of wet leather, for the benefit
of the gouty and rheumatic, who are transported in them
from place to place.   Indeed, this is a shocking inconvenience, that extends over the whole city ; and I am persuaded
it produces infinite mischief to the delicate and infirm : even
the close chairs contrived for the sick, by standing in the
open air, have their freese linings impregnated, like so many

sponges, with the moisture of the atmosphere; and those cases of cold vapour must give a charming check to the perspiration of a patient, piping hot from the bath, with all his pores wide open.

But, to return to the circus: it is inconvenient from its situation, at so great a distance from all the markets, baths, and places of public entertainment.—The only entrance to it, through Gay street, is so difficult, steep, and slippery, that, in wet weather, it must be exceedingly dangerous, both for those that ride in carriages, and those that walk a-foot; and when the street is covered with snow, as it was for fifteen days successively this very winter, I don't see how any individual could go either up or down, without the most imminent hazard of broken bones. In blowing weather, I am told, most of the houses on this hill are smothered with smoke, forced down the chimneys by the gusts of wind reverberated from the hill behind, which (I apprehend likewise) must render the atmosphere here more humid and unwholesome than it is in the square below; for the clouds, formed by the constant evaporation from the baths and rivers in the bottom, will, in their ascent this way, be first attract-ed and detained by the hill that rises close behind the circus, and load the air with a perpetual succession of vapours: this point, however, may be easily ascertained by means of an hygrometer, or a·paper of salt of tartar exposed to the action of the atmosphere. The same artist who planned the circus, has likewise projected a crescent; when that is finished, we shall probably have a star; and those who are living thirty years hence, may, perhaps, see all the signs of the zodiac exhibited in architecture at Bath. These, however fantastical, are still designs that denote some ingenu-ity and knowledge in the architect; but the rage of build-ing has laid hold on such a number of adventurers, that one sees new houses starting up in every outlet and every corner of Bath; contrived without judgment, executed without solidity, and stuck together with so little regard to plan and propriety, that the different lines of the new rows and build-ings interfere with, and intersect one another in every different angle of conjunction. They look like the wreck of streets and squares disjointed by an earthquake, which hath broken the ground into a variety of holes and hillocs; or, as if some Gothic devil had stuffed them altogether in a bag, and left them to stand higgledy-piggledy, just as chance directed. What sort of a monster Bath will become in a few years, with those growing excrescences, may be easily conceived: but the want of beauty and proportion is not the worst effect of these new mansions: they are built so slight, with the soft crumbling stone found in this neighbourhood, that I should never sleep quietly in one of them, when it blowed (as the sailors say) a capful of wind; and I am persuaded, that my hind, Roger Williams, or any man of equal strength, would be able to push his foot through the strongest part of their walls, without any great exertion of his muscles. All these absurdities arise from the general tide of luxury, which hath overspread the nation, and swept away all, even the very dregs of the people. Every upstart of fortune, harnessed in the trappings of the mode, presents himself at Bath, as in the very focus of observation—Clerks and factors from the East Indies, loaded with the spoil of plundered provinces; planters, negro-drivers, and hucksters, from our American plantations, enriched they know not how; agents, commissaries, and contractors, who have fattened, in two successive wars, on the blood of the nation; usurers, brokers, and jobbers of every kind; men of low birth, and no breeding, have found themselves suddenly translated into a state of affluence, unknown to former ages; and no wonder that their brains should be intoxicated with pride, vanity, and presumption. Knowing no other criterion of greatness, but the ostentation of wealth, they discharge their affluence without taste or conduct, through every channel of the most absurd extravagance; and all of them hurry to Bath, because here, without any farther qualification, they can mingle with the princes and nobles of the land. Even the wives and daughters of low tradesmen, who, like shovel-nosed sharks, prey upon the blubber of those uncouth whales of fortune, are infected with the same rage of displaying their

importance; and the slightest indisposition serves them for
a pretext to insist upon being conveyed to Bath, where they
may hobble country-dances and cotillions among lordlings,
squires, counsellors, and clergy. These delicate creatures
from Bedfordbury, Butcher-row, Crutched friars, and Bo-
tolph lane, cannot breathe in the gross air of the lower town,
or conform to the vulgar rules of a common lodging house;
the husband, therefore, must provide an entire house; or
elegant apartments in the new buildings. Such is the composition of what is called the fashionable company at Bath;
where a very inconsiderable proportion of genteel people are
lost in a mob of impudent plebeians, who have neither understanding nor judgment, nor the least idea of propriety
and decorum; and seem to enjoy nothing so much as an opportunity of insulting their betters.

Thus the number of people and the number of houses
continue to increase; and this will ever be the case, till the
streams that swell this irresistible torrent of folly and extravagance, shall either be exhausted, or turned into other
channels, by incidents and events which I do not pretend to
foresee. This, I own, is a subject on which I cannot write
with any degree of patience; for the mob is a monster I never
could abide, either in its head, tail, midriff, or members:
I detest the whole of it, as a mass of ignorance, presumption,
malice, and brutality; and in this term of reprobation, I
include, without respect of rank, station, or quality, all
those of both sexes who affect its manners, and court its society.

But I have written till my fingers are crampt; and my
nausea begins to return—By your advise, I sent to London
a few days ago for half a pound of gengseng; though I
doubt much whether that which comes from America is
equally efficacious with what is brought from the East Indies.
Some years ago, a friend of mine paid sixteen guineas for
two ounces of it; and in six months after, it was sold in the
same shop for five shillings the pound. In short, we live in
a vile world of fraud and sophistication; so that I know
nothing of equal value with the genuine friendship of a sen-

sible man ; a rare jewel ! which I cannot help thinking myself in possession of, while I repeat the old declaration, that
I am, as usual, dear Lewis, your affectionate

M. BRAMBLE.

After having been agitated in a short hurricane, on my
first arrival, I have taken a small house in Milsham street,
where I am tolerably well lodged, for five guineas a-week.
I was yesterday at the pump-room, and drank about a pint
of the water, which seems to agree with my stomach ; and
to-morrow morning I shall bath for the first time ; so that,
in a few posts, you may expect farther trouble.   Meanwhile,
I am glad to find that the inoculation has succeeded so well
with poor Joyce, and that her face will be but little marked
—If my friend Sir Thomas was a single man, I would not trust
such a handsome wench in his family ; but as I have recommended her, in a particular manner, to the protection of
Lady G——, who is one of the best women in the world,
she may go thither without hesitation, as soon as she is quite
recovered, and fit for service—let her mother have money
to provide her with necessaries, and she may ride behind
her brother on Bucks ; but you may lay strong injunctions
on Jack, to take particular care of the trusty old veteran,
who has faithfully earned his present ease by his past services.

TO MISS WILLIS, AT GLOUCESTER.

MY DEAREST COMPANION,   *Bath, April 26.*

THE pleasure I received from yours, which came to hand
yesterday, is not to be expressed.   Love and friendship are,
without doubt, charming passions ; which absence serves
only to heighten and improve.   Your kind present of the
garnet bracelets I shall keep as carefully as I preserve my
own life ; and I beg you will accept, in return, of my
heart-housewife, with the tortoise-shell memorandum book,
as a trifling pledge of my unalterable affection.

Bath is to me a new world—all is gaiety, good humour,
and diversion.   The eye is continually entertained with the
splendour of dress and equipage, and the ear with the sound

of coaches, chaises, chairs, and other carriages. *The merry
bells ring round*, from morn till night. Then we are wel-
comed by the city waits in our own lodgings: we have music
in the pump-room every morning, cotillions every forenoon in
the rooms, balls twice a-week, and concerts every other night,
besides private assemblies, and parties without number.
As soon as we were settled in lodgings, we were visited by
the master of the ceremonies; a pretty little gentleman, so
sweet, so fine, so civil, and polite, that in our country he
might pass for the prince of Wales; then he talks so charmingly, both in verse and prose, that you would be delighted
to hear him discourse; for you must know he is a great
writer, and has got five tragedies ready for the stage. He
did us the favour to dine with us, by my uncle's invitation;
and next day squired my aunt and me to every part of Bath,
which to be sure is an earthly paradise. The square, the
circus, and the parades, put you in mind of the sumptuous
palaces represented in prints and pictures; and the new
buildings, such as Prince's row, Harlequin's row, Bladud's
row, and twenty other rows, look like so many enchanted
castles, raised on hanging terraces.

At eight in the morning we go in dishabille to the pump-
room, which is crowded like a Welsh fair; and there you
see the highest quality and the lowest trades-folks, jostling
each other, without ceremony, hail fellow, well met. The
noise of the music playing in the gallery, the heat and flavour of such a crowd, and the hum and buz of their conversation, gave me the headach and vertigo the first day; but,
afterwards, all these things became familiar, and even agreeable. Right under the pump-room windows is the king's
bath; a huge cistern, where you see the patients up to their
necks in hot water. The ladies wear jackets and petticoats
of brown linen, with chip hats, in which they fix their
handkerchiefs to wipe the sweat from their faces; but, truly,
whether it is owing to the steam that surrounds them, or,
the heat of the water, or the nature of the dress, or to all
these causes together, they look so flushed, and so frightful,
that I always turn my eyes another way. My aunt, who

says every person of fashion should make her appearance in
the bath, as well as in the abbey church, contrived a cap
with cherry-coloured ribbons to suit her complexion, and
obliged Win to attend her yesterday morning in the water.
But, really, her eyes were so red, that they made mine
water as I viewed her from the pump-room; and as for poor
Win, who wore a hat trimmed with blue, what betwixt her
wan complexion and her fear, she looked like the ghost of
some pale maiden, who had drowned herself for love. When
she came out of the bath, she took assafœtida drops, and
was fluttered all day, so that we could hardly keep her from
going into hysterics: but her mistress says it will do her
good, and poor Win court'sies, with the tears in her eyes.
For my part, I content myself with drinking about half a
pint of the water every morning.

The pumper, with his wife and servant, attend in a
bar; and the glasses, of different sizes, stand ranged in order
before them, so you have nothing to do but to point at that
which you choose, and it is filled immediately, hot and
sparkling from the pump. It is the only hot water I could
ever drink without being sick. Far from having that effect,
it is rather agreeable to the taste, grateful to the stomach,
and reviving to the spirits. You cannot imagine what wonderful cures it performs. My uncle began with it the other
day; but he made wry faces in drinking, and I am afraid
he will leave it off. The first day we came to Bath he fell
into a violent passion, beat two black-a-moors, and I was
afraid he would have fought with their master; but the stranger proved a peaceable man. To be sure the gout had got
into his head, as my aunt observed; but, I believe, his passion drove it away, for he has been remarkably well ever
since. It is a thousand pities he should ever be troubled
with that ugly distemper; for, when he is free from pain,
he is the best-tempered man upon earth; so gentle, so
generous, so charitable, that every body loves him; and so
good to me, in particular, that I shall never be able to shew
the deep sense I have of his tenderness and affection.

Hard by the pump-room is a coffee-house for the ladies;

but my aunt says, young girls are not admitted, inasmuch
as the conversation turns upon politics, scandal, philosophy,
and other subjects above our capacity; but we are allowed
to accompany them to the booksellers shops, which are
charming places of resort, where we read novels, plays,
pamphlets, and newspapers, for so small a subscription as
a crown a quarter, and in these offices of intelligence (as my
brother calls them), all the reports of the day, and all the
private transactions of the bath, are first entered and discussed. From the bookseller's shop we make a tour through
the milliners and toymen, and commonly stop at Mr Gill's
the pastry-cook, to take a jelly, a tart, or a small bason of
vermicelli. There is, moreover, another place of entertainment on the other side of the water, opposite to the grove,
to which the company cross over in a boat. It is called
Spring gardens; a sweet retreat, laid out in walks, and
ponds, and parterres of flowers; and there is a long room
for breakfasting and dancing. As the situation is low and
damp, and the season has been remarkably wet, my uncle
won't suffer me to go thither, lest I should catch cold: but
my aunt says it is all a vulgar prejudice; and to be sure, a
great many gentlemen and ladies of Ireland frequent the
place, without seeming to be the worse for it. They say,
dancing at Spring gardens, when the air is moist, is recommended to them as an excellent cure for the rheumatism.
I have been twice at the play, where, notwithstanding the
excellence of the performers, the gaiety of the company,
and the decorations of the theatre, which are very fine, I
could not help reflecting, with a sigh, upon our poor homely
representations at Gloucester. But this in confidence to my
dear Willis. You know my heart, and will excuse its
weakness.

After all, the great scenes of entertainment at Bath are the
two public rooms, where the company meet alternately every
evening. They are spacious, lofty, and, when lighted up,
appear very striking. They are generally crowded with
well-dressed people, who drink tea in separate parties, play
at cards, walk, or sit and chat together, just as they are

disposed. Twice a-week there is a ball, the expense of
which is defrayed by a voluntary subscription among the
gentlemen; and every subscriber has three tickets. I was
there Friday last with my aunt, under the care of my brother, who is a subscriber; and Sir Ulic Mackilligut recommended his nephew, Captain O'Donaghan, to me as a partner; but Jery excused himself, by saying I had got the
headach; and indeed it was really so, though I can't imagine how he knew it. The place was so hot, and the smell so
different from what we are used to in the country, that I was
quite feverish when we came away. Aunt says it is the effect of a vulgar constitution, reared among woods and mountains; and that, as I become accustomed to genteel company, it will wear off. Sir Ulic was very complaisant, made
her a great many high-flown compliments, and, when we
retired, handed her with great ceremony to her chair. The
captain, I believe would have done me the same favour; but
my brother, seeing him advance, took me under his arm,
and wished him good night. The captain is a pretty man,
to be sure: tall and straight, and well made, with light
grey eyes, and a Roman nose; but there is a certain boldness in his look and manner that puts one out of countenance.
But I am afraid I have put you out of all patience with this
long unconnected scrawl; which I shall therefore conclude,
with assuring you, that neither Bath, nor London, nor all
the diversions of life, shall ever be able to efface the idea of
my dear Letty, from the heart of her ever affectionate

                                        LYDIA MELFORD.

TO MRS MARY JONES, AT BRAMBLETON-HALL.

DEAR MOLLY JONES.

HEAVING got a frank, I now return your fever, which I
received by Mr Higgins at the hot-well, together with the
stockings which his wife footed for me; but now they are
of no survice. No body wears such things in this place.——
O Molly! you that live in the country have no deception
of our doings at Bath. Here is such dressing, and fiddling,

and dancing, and gadding, and courting, and plotting—
O gracious ! If God had not given me a good stock of discretion, what a power of things might not I reveal, con-
saming old mistress, and young mistress ; Jews with beards
that were no Jews, but handsome christians, without a hair
upon their chin, strolling with spectacles, to get speech of
Miss Liddy. But she's a dear sweet soul, as innocent as
the child unborn. She has tould me all her inward thoughts,
and disclosed her passion for Mr Wilson ; and that's not
his name neither ; and thof he acted among the player-men,
he is meat for their masters ; and she has gi'en me her yellow trolopea, which Mrs Drab, the manty-maker, says will
look very well when it is scowered and smoaked with silfur—
You knows as how yellow fitts my fizzogmony. God he
knows what havoc I shall make among the mail sex, when
I make my first appearance in this killing collar, with a
full suit of gaze, as good as new, that I bought last Friday
of Madam Friponeau, the French mullaner.—Dear girl I
have seen all the fine shows of Bath ; the prades, the squires,
and the circlis, the crashit, the hotogon, and Bloody
buildings, and Harry King's row ; and I have been twice
in the bath with mistress, and na'r a smoak upon our backs,
hussy.—The first time I was mortally afraid, and flustered
all day, and afterwards made believe that I had got the hed-
dick : but mistress said, if I didn't go, I should take a dose
of bumtaffy ; and so remembering how it worked Mrs Gwyllim a pennorth, I chose rather to go again with her into the
bath, and then I met with an axident. I dropt my petticoat, and could not get it up from the bottom—But what
did that signify ?—they mought laff, but they could see nothing ; for I was up to the sin in water. To be sure, it threw
me into such a gumbustion, that I know not what I said, nor
what I did, nor how they got me out, and rapt me in a blanket
—Mrs Tabitha scolded a little when me got home ; but
she knows as I know what's what—Ah, Laud help you !—
There is Sir Yuri Micligut, of Balnaclinch, in the cunty
of Kalloway—I took down the name from his gentleman,
Mr O Frizzle, and he has got an estate of fifteen hundred

a-year—I am sure he is both rich and generous.—But you
nose, Molly, I am always famous for keeping secrets; and
so he was very safe in trusting me with his flegm for mistress,
which, to be sure is very honourable; for Mr O Frizzle
assures me, he values not her portion a brass varthing—And,
indeed, what's poor ten thousand pounds to a baron-knight
of his fortune? and, truly, I told Mr O Frizzle that was
all she had to trust to.—As for John Thomas, he's a
morass fellor—I vow I thought he would a fit with Mr O
Frizzle, because he axed me to dance with him at Spring-
garden—But God he knows I have no thoughts eyther of
wan or 'tother.

As for house news, the worst is, Chowder has fallen off
greatly from his stomick—He eats nothing but white meats,
and not much of that; and wheezes, and seems to be much
bloated. The doctors think he is threatened with a dropsy
—Parson Marrowfat, who has got the same disorder, finds
great benefit from the waters; but Chowder seems to like
them no better than the squire; and mistress says if his case
don't take a favourable turn, she will sartainly carry him to
Aberga'ny to drink goats' whey—To be sure, the poor
dear honymil is lost for want of axercise; for which reason
she intends to give him an airing once a-day upon the
downs, in a post-chaise. I have already made very creditable connections in this here place, where, to be sure, we
have the very squintasence of satiety—Mrs Patcher, my
Lady Kilmacullock's woman, and I, are sworn sisters. She has
shewn me all her secrets, and learned me to wash gaze, and
refresh rusty silks and bumbeseens, by boiling them with
winegar, chamberlaye, and stale beer. My short sack and
apron luck as good as new from the shop, and my pumpy-
door as fresh as a rose, by the help of turtle-water—But
this is all Greek and Latten to you, Molly. If we should
come to Aberga'ny, you'll be within a day's ride of us;
and then we shall see wan another, please God. If not, remember me in your prayers, as I shall do by you in mine;
and take care of my kitten, and give my kind sarvice to

Saul; and this is all at present, from your beloved friend
and sarvent,

Bath, April 26. WINIFRED JENKINS.

TO MRS GWYLLIM, HOUSEKEEPER, AT BRAMBLETONHALL.

I AM astonished that Dr Lewis should take upon him to
give away Alderney, without my privity and concurrants.
What signifies my brother's order?—My brother is little
better than noncompush. He would give away the shirt of
his back, and the teeth out of his head; nay, as for that
matter, he would have ruinated the family with his ridiculous charities, if it had not been for my four quarters. What
between his wilfulness and his waste, his trumps, and his
frenzy, I lead the life of an indented slave. Alderney gave
four gallons a-day ever since the calf was sent to market.
There is so much milk out of my dairy, and the press must
stand still:—but I won't loose a cheese-paring; and the
milk shall be made good, if the sarvants should go without
butter. If they must needs have butter let them make it of
sheeps milk; but then my wool will suffer for want of grace;
so that I must be a loser on all sides.—Well, patience is like
a stout Welsh poney; it bears a great deal, and trots a great
way, but it will tire at the long run.——Before its long,
perhaps I may shew Matt, that I was not born to be the
household drudge to my dying day. Gwyn rites from
Crickhowel, that the price of flannel is fallen three farthings
an ell; and that's another good penny out of my pocket.
When I go to market to sell, my commodity stinks; but
when I want to buy the commonest thing, the owner pricks
it up under my nose, and it can't be had for love nor money—I think every thing runs cross at Brambletonhall.—
You say the gander has broke the eggs, which is a phinu-
menon I don't understand; for, when the fox carried off
the old goose last year, he took her place, and hatched the
eggs, and partected the goslings like a tender parent.—
Then you tell me the thunder has soured two barrels of bear
in the seller. But how the thunder should get there, when

the seller was double locked, I 'can't comprehend. How-
somever, I wont have the bear thrown out till I see it with
mine own eyes. Perhaps it will recover—at least it will
serve for vinegar to the sarvants. You may leave off the
fires in my brother's chamber and mine, as it is unsartin
when we return. I hope Gwyllim, you'll take care there is
no waste; and have an eye to the maids and keep them to
their spinning. I think they may go very well without
bear in hot weather—it serves only to inflame the blood, and
set them agog after the men; water will make them fair,
and keep them cool and tamperit. Don't forget to put up
in the portmantle, that cums with Williams, along with my
riding-habit, hat, and feather, the vial of purl-water, and
the tinctur for my stomach; being as how I am much
troubled with flutterencies. This is all at present, from
yours,

Bath, April 26.   TABITHA BRAMBLE.

TO DR LEWIS.

DEAR DICK,

I HAVE done with the waters; therefore your advice comes
a day too late.—I grant that physic is no mystery of your
making. I know it is a mystery in its own nature, and, like
other mysteries, requires a strong gulp of faith to make it go
down.—Two days ago I went into the king's bath, by the
advice of our friend Ch——, in order to clear the strainer of
the skin, for the benefit of a free perspiration; and the first
object that saluted my eye was a child, full of scrofulous
ulcers, carried in the arms of one of the guides, under the
very noses of the bathers. I was so shocked at the sight,
that I retired immediately with indignation and disgust.—
Suppose the matter of those ulcers, floating in the water,
comes in contact with my skin, when the pores are all open,
I would ask you what must be the consequence?—Good
heavens, the very thought makes my blood run cold! We
know not what sores may be running into the water while
we are bathing, and what sort of matter we may thus imbibe;
the king's evil, the scurvy, the cancer, and the pox; and,

no doubt, the heat will render the *virus* the more volatile and penetrating. To purify myself from all such contamination, I went to the duke of Kingston's private bath, and there I was almost suffocated for want of free air, the place was so small, and the steam so trifling.

After all, if the intention is no more than to wash the skin, I am convinced that simple element is more effectual than any water impregnated with salt and iron; which being astringent, will certainly contract the pores, and leave a kind of crust upon the surface of the body. But I am now as much afraid of drinking as of bathing; for, after a long conversation with the doctor, about the construction of the pump and the cistern, it is very far from being clear with me, that the patients in the pump-room don't swallow the scourings of the bathers. I can't help suspecting, that there is, or may be, some regurgitation from the bath into the cistern of the pump. In that case, what a delicate beverage is every day quaffed by the drinkers, medicated with the sweat, and dirt, and dandriff, and the abominable discharges of various kinds, from twenty different diseased bodies, parboiling in the kettle below. In order to avoid this filthy composition I had recourse to the spring that supplies the private baths on the abbey green; but I at once perceived something extraordinary in the taste and smell; and, upon inquiry, I find, that the Roman baths in this quarter were found covered by an old burying-ground belonging to the abbey, through which, in all probability, the water drains in its passage; so that, as we drink the decoction of living bodies at the pump-room, we swallow the strainings of rotten bones and carcasses at the private bath.—I vow to God, the very idea turns my stomach!—Determined, as I am, against my farther use of the Bath waters, this consideration would give me little disturbance, if I could find any thing more pure, or less pernicious, to quench my thrist; but although the natural springs of excellent water are seen gushing spontaneous on every side from the hills that surround us, the inhabitants in general make use of well water, so impregnated with nitre, or alum, or some other villanous mineral, that

it is equally ungrateful to the taste, and mischievous to *t*
constitution. It must be owned, indeed, that here, in M*
sham street, we have a precarious and scanty supply fro*
the hill, which is collected in an open bason in the circu*
liable to be defiled with dead dogs, cats, rats, and every sp*
cies of nastiness, which the rascally populace may throw in*
to it from mere wantonness and brutality.

Well, there is no nation that drinks so hoggishly as th*
English.—What passes for wine among us is not the juice*
of the grape : it is an adulterous mixture, brewed up of nauseous ingredients, by dunces, who are bunglers in the art of
poison-making ; yet we and our forefathers are, and have
been, poisoned by this cursed drench, without taste or flavour.
The only genuine and wholesome beverage in England is
London porter, and Dorchester table-beer ; but as for your
ale and your gin, your cyder and your perry, and all the
trashy family of made wines, I detest them, as infernal compositions, contrived for the destruction of the human species.
But what have I to do with the human species ? Except a
very few friends, I care not if the whole was ——

Hark ye, Lewis, my misanthropy increases every day.—
The longer I live, I find the folly and the fraud of mankind
grow more and more intolerable.—I wish I had not come
from Brambletonhall : after having lived in solitude so long,
I cannot bear the hurry and impertinence of the multitude ;
besides, every thing is sophisticated in these crowded places.
Snares are laid for our lives in every thing we eat or drink ;
the very air we breathe is loaded with contagion. We cannot even sleep without risk of infection. I say infection—
This place is the rendezvous of the diseased—You won't
deny that many diseases are infectious ; even the consumption itself is highly infectious. When a person dies of it in
Italy, the bed and bedding are destroyed ; the other furniture
is exposed to the weather, and the apartment white-washed,
before it is occupied by any other living soul. You'll allow, that nothing receives infection sooner, or retains it
longer, than blankets, feather-beds, and matresses.—'Sdeath !
how do I know what miserable objects have been stewing in

the bed where I now lie!—I wonder, Dick, you did not put me in mind of sending for my own matresses.—But if I had not been an ass, I should not have needed a remembrancer. There is always some plaguy reflection that rises up in judgement against me, and ruffles my spirits—therefore, let us change the subject.

I have other reasons for abridging my stay at Bath.—You know sister Tabby's complexion—If Mrs Tabitha Bramble had been of any other race, I should certainly have looked upon her as the most———But the truth is, she has found means to interest my affection; or rather, she is beholden to the force of prejudice, commonly called the ties of blood. Well, this amiable maiden has actually commenced a flirting correspondence with an Irish baronet of sixty-five. His name is Sir Ulic Mackilligut. He is said to be much out at elbows; and, I believe, has received false intelligence with respect to her fortune. Be that as it may, the connection is exceedingly ridiculous, and begins already to excite whispers.—For my part, I have no intention to dispute her free agency; though I shall fall upon some expedient to undeceive her paramour as to the point which he has principally in view. But I don't think her conduct is a proper example for Liddy, who has also attracted the notice of some coxcombs in the rooms; and Jery tells me, he suspects a strapping fellow, the knight's nephew, of some design upon the girl's heart. I shall, therefore, keep a strict eye over her aunt and her, and even shift the scene, if I find the matter grow more serious.—You perceive what an agreeable task it must be, to a man of my kidney, to have the cure of such souls as these.—But, hold, you shall not have another peevish word (till the next occasion) from yours,

Bath, April 28.   MATT. BRAMBLE.

TO SIR WATKIN PHILLIPS, BART. OF JESUS COLLEGE, OXON.

DEAR KNIGHT,

I THINK those people are unreasonable, who complain that Bath is a contracted circle, in which the same dull scenes perpetually revolve, without variation.—I am, on the contrary, amazed to find so small a place so crowded with entertainment and variety. London itself can hardly exhibit one species of diversion to which we have not something analogous at Bath, over and above those singular advantages that are peculiar to the place. Here, for example, a man has daily opportunities of seeing the most remarkable characters of the community. He sees them in their natural attitudes and true colours, descended from their pedestals, and divested of their formal draperies, undisguised by art and affectation.—Here we have ministers of state, judges, generals, bishops, projectors, philosophers, wits, poets, players, *chemists, fiddlers,* and *buffoons.* If he makes any considerable stay in the place, he is sure of meeting with some particular friend whom he did not expect to see; and to me there is nothing more agreeable than such casual rencounters.—Another entertainment, peculiar to Bath, arises from the general mixtures of all degrees assembled in our public rooms, without distinction of rank or fortune. This is what my uncle reprobates as a monstrous jumble of heterogenous principles; a vile mob of noise and impertinence, without decency or subordination. But this chaos is to me a source of infinite amusement.

I was extremely diverted, last ball-night, to see the master of the ceremonies leading with great solemnity, to the upper end of the room, an antiquated abigail, dressed in her lady's cast clothes; whom he (I suppose) mistook for some countess just arrived at the bath. The ball was opened by a Scotch lord, with a mulatto heiress, from S^t. Christophers; and the gay Colonel Tinsel danced all the evening with the daughter of an eminent tinman from the borough of Southwark.—Yesterday morning, at the pump-room, I saw a broken-winded Wapping landlady squeeze through a circle of peers, to salute her brandy-merchant, who stood by the window, propp'd upon crutches; and a pralytic attorney of Shoe-lane, in shuffling up to the bar, kicked the shins of the chancellor of England, while his lordship, in a cut bob, drank a glass of water at the pump. I cannot account for my being

pleased with these incidents any other way than by saying
they are truly ridiculous in their own nature, and serve to
heighten the humour in the farce of life, which I am determined to enjoy as long as I can.

Those follies that move my uncle's spleen excite my laughter. He is as tender as a man without a skin, who cannot
bear the slightest touch without flinching. What tickles
another would give him torment; and yet he has what we
may call lucid intervals, when he is remarkably facetious.—
Indeed, I never knew a hypochondriac so apt to be infected
with good humour. He is the most risible misanthrope I
ever met with. A lucky joke, or any ludicrous incident,
will set him a-laughing immoderately even in one of his most
gloomy paroxysms; and when the laugh is over, he will
curse his own imbecility. In conversing with strangers, he
betrays no marks of disquiet—He is splenetic with his fami-
liars only; and not even with them, while they keep his attention employed; but, when his spirits are not exerted ex-
ternally, they seem to recoil, and prey upon himself. He
has renounced the waters with execration; but he begins to
find a more efficacious, and, certainly, a much more palatable remedy, in the pleasures of society. He has discovered
some old friends among the invalids of Bath; and, in particular, renewed his acquaintance with the celebrated James
Quin, who certainly did not come here to drink water. You
cannot doubt but that I had the strongest curiosity to know
this original; and it was gratified by Mr Bramble, who has
had him twice at our house to dinner.

So far as I am able to judge, Quin's character is rather
more respectable than it has been generally represented.
His bon mots are in every witling's mouth; but many of
them have a rank flavour, which one would be apt to think
was derived from a natural grossness of idea. I suspect,
however, that justice has not been done the author by the
collectors of those *Quiniana*, who have let the best of them
slip through their fingers, and only retained such as were
suited to the taste and organs of the multitude. How far he
may relax in his hours of jollity, I cannot pretend to say;

but his general conversation is conducted by the nicest rules of propriety; and Mr James Quin is certainly one of the best bred men in the kingdom. He is not only a most agreeable companion, but (as I am credibly informed) a very honest man; highly susceptible of friendship, warm, steady, and even generous, in his attachments; disdaining flattery, and incapable of meanness and dissimulation. Were I to judge, however, from Quin's eye alone, I should take him to be proud, insolent, and cruel. There is something remarkably severe and forbidding in his aspect; and I have been told he was ever disposed to insult his inferiors and dependents. Perhaps that report has influenced my opinion of his looks—You know we are the fools of prejudice. Howsoever that may be, I have as yet seen nothing but his favourable side; and my uncle, who frequently confers with him in a corner, declares he is one of the most sensible men he ever knew. He seems to have a reciprocal regard for old squaretoes, whom he calls by the familiar name of Matthew, and often reminds of their old tavern adventures: on the other hand, Matthew's eyes sparkle whenever Quin makes his appearance. Let him be never so jarring and discordant, Quin puts him in tune; and, like treble and bass in the same concert, they make excellent music together. T'other day, the conversation turning upon Shakspeare, I could not help saying, with some emotion, that I would give an hundred guineas to see Mr Quin act the part of Falstaff; upon which, turning to me with a smile,—' And I would give a thousand, young gentleman,' said he, ' that I could gratify your longing.' My uncle and he are perfectly agreed in their estimate of life, which, Quin says, would stink in his nostrils, if he did not steep it in claret.

I want to see this phenomenon in his cups; and have almost prevailed upon uncle to give him a small turtle at the Bear. In the meantime, I must entertain you with an incident that seems to confirm the judgment of those two cynic philosophers. I took the liberty to differ in opinion from Mr Bramble, when he observed, that the mixture of people in the entertainments of this place was destructive of

all order and urbanity; that it rendered the plebeians insufferably arrogant and troublesome, and vulgarized the deportment and sentiments of those who moved in the upper
spheres of life. He said, such a preposterous coalition would
bring us into contempt with all our neighbours; and was
worse in fact, than debasing the gold coin of the nation. I
argued, on the contrary, that those plebeians who discovered
such eagerness to imitate the dress and equipage of their superiors, would likewise, in time, adopt their maxims and
their manners, be polished by their conversation, and refined
by their example; but when I appealed to Mr Quin, and
asked if he did not think that such an unreserved mixture
would improve the whole mass?—'Yes,' said he, 'as a
plate of marmalade would improve a pan of sir-reverence.'

I owned I was not much conversant in high life, but I
had seen what were called polite assemblies in London and
elsewhere; that those of Bath seemed to be as decent as any;
and that, upon the whole, the individuals that composed it
would not be found deficient in good manners and decorum.
'But let us have recourse to experience,' said I—'Jack
Holder, who was intended for a parson, has succeeded to an
estate of two thousand a-year, by the death of his elder brother. He is now at the Bath, driving about in a phæton
and four, with French horns. He has treated with turtle and
claret at all the taverns in Bath and Bristol, till his guests
are gorged with good cheer: he has bought a dozen suits of
fine clothes, by the advice of the master of the ceremonies,
under whose tuition he has entered himself: he has lost some
hundreds at billiards to sharpers, and taken one of the
nymphs of Avon street into keeping; but, finding all these
channels insufficient to drain him of his current cash, his
counsellor has engaged him to give a general tea-drinking
to-morrow at Wiltshire's room. In order to give it the
more eclat, every table is to be furnished with sweetmeats
and nosegays, which, however, are not to be touched till
notice is given by the ringing of a bell, and then the ladies
may help themselves without restriction. This will be no
bad way of trying the company's breeding—'

' I will abide by that experiment,' cried my uncle, ' and
if I could find a place to stand secure without the vortex of
the tumult, which I know will ensue, I would certainly go
thither and enjoy the scene.' Quin proposed that we should
take our station in the music gallery, and we took his advice. Holder had got thither before us, with his horns per-
due; but we were admitted. The tea-drinking passed as
usual; and the company having risen from the tables, were
sauntering in groups, in expectation of the signal for attack,
when the bell beginning to ring, they flew with eagerness to
the dessert, and the whole place was instantly in commotion.
There was nothing but justling, scrambling, pulling, snatching, struggling, scolding, and screaming. The nosegays
were torn from one another's hands and bosoms; the glasses
and china went to wreck; the tables and floor were strewed
with comfits. Some cried, some swore, and the tropes and
figures of Billingsgate were used without reserve in all their
native zest and flavour; nor were those flowers of rhetoric un-
attended with significant gesticulation. Some snapped their
fingers, some forked them out, some clapped their hands,
and some their backsides; at length they fairly proceeded to
pulling caps, and every thing seemed to presage a general
battle, when Holder ordered his horns to sound a charge,
with a view to animate the combatants, and inflame the contest; but this manœuvre produced an effect quite contrary
to what he expected. It was a note of reproach that roused
them to an immediate sense of their disgraceful situation.
They were ashamed of their absurd deportment, and suddenly desisted. They gathered up their caps, ruffles, and
handkerchiefs; and great part of them retired in silent mortification.

Quin laughed at this adventure, but my uncle's delicacy
was hurt. He hung his head in manifest chagrin, and seemed to repine at the triumph of his judgment. Indeed his
victory was more complete than he imagined; for, as we
afterwards learned, the two amazons who signalized themselves most in the action, did not come from the purlieus of
Puddledock, but from the courtly neighbourhood of St.

James's palace. One was a baroness, and the other a wealthy knight's dowager. My uncle spoke not a word till we had made our retreat good to the coffee-house, where, taking off his hat, and wiping his forehead,—' I bless God,' said he, ' that Mrs Tabitha Bramble did not take the field to-day !' ' I would pit her for a cool hundred,' cried Quin, ' against the best shakebag of the whole main.' The truth is, nothing could have kept her at home but the accident of her having taken physic before she knew the nature of the entertainment. She has been for some days furbishing up an old suit of black velvet, to make her appearance as Sir Ulic's partner at the next ball.

I have much to say of this amiable kinswoman; but she has not been properly introduced to your acquaintance. She is remarkably civil to Mr Quin, of whose sarcastic humour she seems to stand in awe; but her caution is no match for her impertinence. ' Mr Gwynn,' said she the other day, ' I was once vastly entertained with your playing the ghost of Gimlet at Drury-lane, when you rose up through the stage, with a white face and red eyes, and spoke of *quails upon the frightful porcupine*. Do, pray, spout a little the ghost of Gimlet.' ' Madam,' said Quin, with a glance of ineffable disdain, ' the ghost of Gimlet is laid, never to rise again.' Insensible of this check, she proceeded.—' Well, to be sure, you looked and talked so like a real ghost—and then the cock crowed so natural—I wonder how you could teach him to crow so exact in the very nick of time; but I suppose he's game—An't he game, Mr Gwynn ?' ' Dunghill, madam.' ' Well, dunghill or not dunghill, he has got such a clear counter-tenor, that I wish I had such another at Brambletonhall, to wake the maids of a morning. Do you know where I could find one of his brood ?' ' Probably in the workhouse of St. Giles's parish, madam; but I protest I know not his particular mew.' My uncle, frying with vexation, cried,—' Good God, sister, how you talk ! I have told you twenty times that this gentleman's name is not Gwynn—' ' Hoity, toity, brother of mine,' she replied, ' no offence, I hope—Gwynn is an honourable name, of true

old British extraction—I thought the gentleman had been
come of Mrs Helen Gwynn, who was of his own profession;
and if so be that were the case, he might be of King Charles's
breed, and have royal blood in his veins—' 'No, madam,'
answered Quin, with great solemnity, ' my mother was not
a w—— of such distinction—True it is, I am sometimes
tempted to believe myself of royal descent; for my inclinations are often arbitrary—If I was an absolute prince at this
instant, I believe I should send for the head of your cook in
a charger—She has committed felony on the person of that
John Dory, which is mangled in a cruel manner, and even
presented without sauce—*O tempora! O mores!'*

This good-humoured sally turned the conversation into
a less disagreeable channel—But, lest you should think my
scribble as tedious as Mrs Tabby's clack, I shall not add
another word, but that I am, as usual, yours,

Bath, April 30.   J. MELFORD.

TO DR LEWIS.

DEAR LEWIS,

I RECEIVED your bill upon Wiltshire, which was punctually
honoured; but as I don't choose to keep so much cash by
me in a common lodging-house, I have deposited £250 in
the bank of Bath, and shall take their bills for it on London,
when I leave this place, where the season draws to an end—
You must know, that now being a-foot, I am resolved to
give Liddy a glimpse of London. She is one of the best
hearted creatures I ever knew, and gains upon my affection
every day.—As for Tabby, I have dropped such hints to
the Irish baronet, concerning her fortune, as, I make no
doubt, will cool the ardour of his addresses. Then her pride
will take the alarm; and the rancour of stale maidenhood
being chaffed, we shall hear nothing but slander and abuse
of Sir Ulic Mackilligut—This rupture, I forsee, will facilitate our departure from Bath; where, at present, Tabby
seems to enjoy herself with peculiar satisfaction. For my
part, I detest it so much, that I should not have been able to

stay so long in the place, if I had not discovered some old friends, whose conversation alleviates my disgust. Going to the coffee-house one forenoon, I could not help contemplating the company with equal surprise and compassion— We consisted of thirteen individuals; seven lamed by the gout, rheumatism, or palsy; three maimed by accident; and the rest either deaf or blind. One hobbled, another hopped, a third dragged his legs after him like a wounded snake, a fourth straddled betwixt a pair of long crutches, like the mummy of a felon hanging in chains; a fifth was bent into an horizontal position, like a mounted telescope, shoved in by a couple of chairmen; and a sixth was the bust of a man, set upright in a wheel machine, which the waiter moved from place to place.

Being struck with some of their faces, I consulted the subscription-book; and, perceiving the names of several old friends, began to consider the group with more attention. At length I discovered Rear-admiral Balderick, the companion of my youth, whom I had not seen since he was appointed lieutenant of the Severn. He was metamorphosed into an old man, with a wooden leg and a weather-beaten face; which appeared the more ancient from his grey locks, that were truly venerable.—Sitting down at the table where he was reading a newspaper, I gazed at him for some minutes, with a mixture of pleasure and regret, which made my heart gush with tenderness; then, taking him by the hand,—'Ah, Sam,' said I, forty years ago I little thought—' I was too much moved to proceed. 'An old friend, sure enough!' cried he, squeezing my hand, and surveying me eagerly through his glasses, 'I know the looming of the vessel, though she has been hard strained since we parted; but I can't heave up the name.'—The moment I told him who I was, he exclaimed,—'Ha! Matt, my old fellow-cruiser, still afloat!' and, starting up, hugged me in his arms. His transport, however, boded me no good; for, in saluting me, he thrust the spring of his spectacles into my eye, and, at the same time, set his wooden stump upon my gouty toe; an attack that made me shed tears in sad earnest.

After the hurry of our recognition was over, he pointed out two of our common friends in the room : the bust was what remained of Colonel Cockril, who had lost the use of his limbs in making an American campaign ; and the telescope proved to be my college chum, Sir Reginald Bentley, who, with his new title, and unexpected inheritance, commenced fox-hunter, without having served his apprenticeship to the mystery ; and, in consequence of following the hounds through a river, was seized with an inflammation in his bowels, which has contracted him into his present attitude.

Our former correspondence was forthwith renewed, with the most hearty expressions of mutual good-will ; and, as we had met so unexpectedly, we agreed to dine together that very day at the tavern. My friend Quin, being luckily unengaged, obliged us with his company ; and, truly, this was the most happy day I have passed these twenty years. You and I, Lewis, having been always together, never tasted friendship in this high goût, contracted from long absence. I cannot express the half of what I felt at this casual meeting of three or four companions, who had been so long separated, and so roughly treated by the storms of life. It was a renovation of youth'; a kind of resuscitation of the dead, that realised those interesting dreams in which we sometimes retrieve our ancient friends from the grave. Perhaps, my enjoyment was not the less pleasing for being mixed with a strain of melancholy, produced by the remembrance of past scenes, that conjured up the ideas of some endearing connections, which the hand of death has actually dissolved.

The spirits and good humour of the company seemed to triumph over the wreck of their constitutions. They had even philosophy enough to joke upon their own calamities ; such is the power of friendship, the sovereign cordial of life —I afterwards found, however, that they were not without their moments and even hours of disquiet. Each of them apart, in succeeding conferences, expatiated upon his own particular grievances ; and they were all malcontents at bottom—Over and above their personal disasters, they thought themselves unfortunate in the lottery of life. Balderick complained, that all the recompense he had received for his long and hard service was the half-pay of a rear-admiral. The colonel was mortified to see himself overtopped by upstart generals, some of whom he had once commanded; and, being a man of a liberal turn, could ill put up with a moderate annuity, for which he had sold his commission. As for the baronet, having run himself considerably in debt, on a contested election, he has been obliged to relinquish his seat in parliament, and his seat in the country at the same time, and put his estate to nurse: but his chagrin, which is the effect of his own misconduct, does not affect me half so much as that of the other two, who have acted honourable and distinguished parts on the great theatre, and are now reduced to lead a weary life in this stew-pan of idleness and insignificance. They have long left off using the waters, after having experienced their inefficacy. The diversions of the place they are not in a condition to enjoy. How then do they make shift to pass their time? In the forenoon they crawl out to the rooms or the coffee-house, where they take a hand at whist, or discant upon the General Advertiser; and their evenings they murder in private parties, among peevish invalids, and insipid old women—This is the case with a good number of individuals, whom nature seems to have intended for better purposes.

About a dozen years ago, many decent families, restricted to small fortunes, besides those that came hither on the score of health, were tempted to settle at Bath, where they could then live comfortably, and even make a genteel appearance at a small expense: but the madness of the times has made the place too hot for them, and they are now obliged to think of other migrations—some have already fled to the mountains of Wales, and others have retired to Exeter. Thither, no doubt, they will be followed by the flood of luxury and extravagance, which will drive them from place to place to the very Land's end; and there, I suppose, they will be obliged to ship themselves to some other country. Bath is become a mere sink of profligacy and extortion. Every ar-

ticle of house-keeping is raised to an enormous price; a circumstance no longer to be wondered at, when we know that
every petty retainer of fortune piques himself upon keeping
a table, and thinks 'tis for the honour of his character to
wink at the knavery of his servants, who are in a confederacy with the market-people, and of consequence pay whatever they demand.   Here is now a mushroom of opulence,
who pays a cook seventy guineas a-week for furnishing him
with one meal a-day.   This portentous frenzy is become so
contagious, that the very rabble and refuse of mankind are
infected.   I have known a negro-driver, from Jamaica, pay
over-night, to the master of one of the rooms, sixty-five
guineas for tea and coffee to the company, and leave Bath
next morning, in such obscurity, that not one of his guests
had the slightest idea of his person, or even made the least
inquiry about his name.   Incidents of this kind are frequent ;
and every day teems with fresh absurdities, which are too
gross to make a thinking man merry.   But I feel the spleen
creeping on me apace, and therefore will indulge you with
a cessation, that you may have no unnecessary cause to curse
your correspondence with, Dear Dick, yours ever.

Bath, May 5.   MATT. BRAMBLE.

TO MISS LÆTITIA WILLIS, AT GLOUCESTER.

MY DEAR LETTY,

I wrote you at great length by the post, the twenty-sixth
of last month, to which I refer you for an account of our
proceedings at Bath ; and I expect your answer with impatience.   But having this opportunity of a private hand, I
send you two dozen of Bath rings ; six of the best of which
I desire you will keep for yourself, and distribute the rest
among the young ladies, our common friends, as you shall
think proper—I don't know how you will approve of the
mottoes ; some of them are not much to my own liking ;
but I was obliged to take such as I could find ready manufactured—I am vexed that neither you nor I have received
any further information of a certain person—sure it can't be

wilful neglect!—O my dear Willis! I begin to be visited by strange fancies, and to have some melancholy doubts; which, however, it would be ungenerous to harbour without further inquiry.—My uncle, who has made me a present of a very fine set of garnets, talks of treating us with a jaunt to London, which, you may imagine, will be highly agreeable: but I like Bath so well, that I hope he wont think of leaving it till the season is quite over; and yet betwixt friends, something has happened to my aunt, which will probably shorten our stay in this place.

Yesterday, in the forenoon, she went by herself to a breakfasting in one of the rooms; and, in half an hour, returned in great agitation, having Chowder along with her in the chair. I believe some accident must have happened to that unlucky animal, which is the great source of all her troubles. Dear Letty! what a pity it is that a woman of her years and discretion should place her affection upon such an ugly ill-conditioned cur, that snarles and snaps at every body. I asked John Thomas, the footman who attended her, what was the matter? and he did nothing but grin. A famous dog doctor was sent for, and undertook to cure the patient, provided he might carry him home to his own house; but his mistress would not part with him out of her own sight—she ordered the cook to warm cloths, which she applied to his bowels with her own hand. She gave up all thoughts of going to the ball in the evening; and when Sir Ulic came to drink tea, refused to be seen; so that he went away to look for another partner. My brother Jery whistles and dances. My uncle sometimes shrugs up his shoulders, and sometimes bursts out a laughing. My aunt sobs and scolds by turns; and her woman, Win Jenkins, stares and wonders with a foolish face of curiosity; and for my part, I am as curious as she, but ashamed to ask questions.

Perhaps time will discover the mystery; for if it was any thing that happened in the rooms, it can't be long concealed—all I know is, that last night, at supper, Miss Bramble spoke very disdainfully of Sir Ulic Mackilligut, and asked

her brother if he intended to keep us sweltering all the summer at Bath?—' No, sister Tabitha,' said he, with an arch
smile, ' we shall retreat before the dog-days begin ; though
I make no doubt, that, with a little temperance and discretion, our constitutions might be kept cool enough all the
year, even at Bath.' As I don't know the meaning of this
insinuation, I won't pretend to make any remarks upon it
at present : hereafter, perhaps, I may be able to explain it
more to your satisfaction—in the meantime, I beg you will
be punctual in your correspondence, and continue to love
your ever faithful

Bath, May 6.   LYDIA MELFORD.

TO SIR WATKIN PHILLIPS, BART. OF JESUS COLLEGE, OXON.

So then Mrs Blackberby's affair has proved a false alarm,
and I have saved my money ? I wish, however, her declar-
tion had not been so premature ; for though my being
thought capable of making her a mother, might have given
me some credit, the reputation of an intrigue with such a
cracked pitcher does me no honour at all.   In my last I told
you I had hopes of seeing Quin in his hours of elevation at
the tavern, which is the temple of mirth and good fellowship, where, he, as priest of Comus, utters the inspirations
of wit and humour—I have had that satisfaction.   I have
dined with his club at the Three Tuns, and had the honour
to sit him out.   At half an hour past eight in the evening,
he was carried home with six good bottles of claret under
his belt ; and it being then Friday, he gave orders that he
should not be disturbed till Sunday at noon—You must not
imagine that this dose had any other effect upon his conversation, but that of making it more extravagantly entertaining—he had lost the use of his limbs, indeed, several hours
before we parted, but he retained all his other faculties in
perfection ; and as he gave vent to every whimsical idea as
it rose, I was really astonished at the brillancy of his thoughts,
and the force of his expression.   Quin is a real voluptuary
in the articles of eating and drinking ; and so confirmed an
epicure, in the common acceptation of the term, that he

cannot put up with ordinary fare. This is a point of such importance with him, that he always takes upon himself the charge of catering; and a man admitted to his mess is always sure of eating delicate victuals, and drinking excellent wine—he owns himself addicted to the delights of the stomach, and often jokes upon his own sensuality; but there is nothing selfish in this appetite—he finds that good cheer unites good company; exhilarates the spirits, opens the heart, banishes all restraint from conversation, and promotes the happiest purposes of social life. But Mr James Quin is not a subject to be discussed in the compass of one letter; I shall, therefore, at present, leave him to his repose, and call in another of a very different complexion.

You desire to have further acquaintance with the person of our aunt, and promise yourself much entertainment from her connection with Sir Ulic Mackilligut; but in this hope you are baulked already; that connection is dissolved. The Irish baronet is an old hound, that, finding her carrion, has quitted the scent. I have already told you, that Mrs Tabitha Bramble is a maiden of forty-five. In her person, she is tall, raw-boned, awkward, flat-chested, and stooping; her complexion is sallow and freckled; her eyes are not grey, but greenish, like those of a cat, and generally inflamed; her hair is of a sandy or rather dusty hue; her forehead low; her nose long, sharp, and towards the extremity, always red in cool weather; her lips skinny, her mouth extensive, her teeth straggling and loose, of various colours and conformation; and her long neck shrivelled into a thousand wrinkles—in her temper, she is proud, stiff, vain, imperious, prying, malicious, greedy, and uncharitable. In all likelihood, her natural austerity has been soured by disappointment in love; for her long celibacy is by no means owing to her dislike of matrimony: on the contrary, she has left no stone unturned, to avoid the reproachful epithet of old maid.

Before I was born, she had gone such lengths in the way of flirting with a recruiting officer, that her reputation was a little singed. She afterwards made advances to the curate of the parish, who dropped some distant hints about the next presentation to the living, which was in her brother's gift; but finding that was already promised to another, he flew off at a tangent; and Mrs Tabby, in revenge, found means to deprive him of his cure. Her next lover was a lieutenant of a man of war, a relation of the family, who did not understand the refinements of the passion, and expressed no aversion to grapple with cousin Tabby in the way of marriage; but before matters could be properly adjusted, he went out on a cruise, and was killed in an engagement with a French frigate. Our aunt, though baffled so often, did not yet despair—she laid all her snares for Dr Lewis, who is the *fides Achates* of my uncle. She even fell sick upon the occasion, and prevailed with Matt to interpose in her behalf with his friend; but the doctor being a shy cock, would not be caught with chaff, and flatly rejected the proposal: so that Mrs Tabitha was content to exert her patience once more, after having endeavoured in vain to effect a rupture betwixt the two rivals; and now she thinks proper to be very civil to Lewis, who is become necessary to her in the way of his profession.

These, however, are not the only efforts she has made towards a nearer conjunction with our sex. Her fortune was originally no more than a thousand pounds; but she gained an accession of five hundred, by the death of a sister, and the lieutenant left her three hundred in his will. These sums she has more than doubled, by living free of all expense, in her brother's house, and dealing in cheese and Welch flannel, the produce of his flocks and dairy. At present her capital is increased to about four thousand pounds; and her avarice seems to grow every day more and more rapacious; but even this is not so intolerable, as the perverseness of her nature, which keeps the whole family in disquiet and uproar. She is one of those geniuses who find some diabolical enjoyment in being dreaded and detested by their fellow-creatures.

I once told my uncle, I was surprised that a man of his disposition could bear such a domestic plague, when it could be so easily removed—The remark made him sore, because it seemed to tax him with want of resolution—Wrinkling up his nose, and drawing down his eye-brows,—'A young fellow,' said he, ' when he first thrusts his snout into the world, is apt to be surprised at many things which a man of experience knows to be ordinary and unavoidable—This precious aunt of yours is become insensibly a part of my constitution— Damn her, she's a *noli me tangere* in my flesh, which I cannot bear to be touched or tampered with.' I made no reply ; but shifted the conversation. He really has an affection for this original, which maintains its ground in defiance of common sense, and in despite of that contempt which he must certainly feel for her character and understanding. Nay, I am convinced, that she has likewise a most violent attachment to his person ; though her love never shews itself but in the shape of discontent ; and she persists in tormenting him out of sheer tenderness.—The only object within doors upon which she bestows any marks of affection, in the usual style, is her dog Chowder, a filthy cur from Newfoundland, which she had in a present from the wife of a skipper in Swansey.—One would imagine she had distinguished this beast with her favour on account of his ugliness and ill-nature ; if it was not, indeed, an instinctive sympathy between his disposition and her own. Certain it is, she caresses him without ceasing ; and even harasses the family in the service of this cursed animal, which, indeed, has proved the proximate cause of her breach with Sir Ulic Mackilligut.

You must know, she yesterday wanted to steal a march of poor Liddy, and went to breakfast in the room, without any other companion than her dog, in expectation of meeting with the baronet, who had agreed to dance with her in the evening—Chowder no sooner made his appearance in the room, than the master of the ceremonies, incensed at his presumption, ran up to drive him away, and threatened him with his foot ; but the other seemed to despise his authority, and, displaying a formidable case of long, white, sharp teeth, kept the puny monarch at bay.—While he stood under some trepidation, fronting his antagonist, and bawl.

ing to the waiter, Sir Ulic Mackilligut came to his assistance; and, seeming ignorant of the connection between this
intruder and his mistress, gave the former such a kick in the
jaws, as sent him howling to the door.—Mrs Tabitha, incensed at this outrage, ran after him, squalling in a tone
equally disagreeable; while the baronet followed her on one
side, making apologies for his mistake; and Derrick, on
the other, making remonstrances upon the rules and regulations of the place.

Far from being satisfied with the knight's excuses, she
said she was sure he was no gentleman; and when the master of the ceremonies offered to hand her into the chair, she
rapped him over the knuckles with her fan. My uncle's
footman being still at the door, she and Chowder got into
the same vehicle, and were carried off amidst the jokes of
the chairmen and other populace.—I had been riding out on
Clarkendown, and happened to enter just as the *fracas* was
over—The baronet coming up to me with an affected air
of chagrin, recounted the adventure; at which I laughed
heartily, and then his countenance cleared up. ' My dear
soul,' said he, ' when I saw a sort of a wild baist, snarling
with open mouth at the master of the ceremonies, like the
red cow going to devour Tom Thumb, I could not do less
than go to the assistance of the little man; but I never
dreamt the baist was one of Mrs Bramble's attendants—O!
if I had, he might have made his breakfast upon Derrick,
and welcome—but, you know, my dear friend, how natural it is for us Irishmen to blunder, and to take the wrong
sow by the ear—However, I will confess judgment, and cry
her mercy; and, 'tis to be hoped, a penitent sinner may be
forgiven.' I told him, that as the offence was not voluntary
on his side, it was to be hoped he would not find her implacable.

But, in truth, all this concern was dissembled. In his
approaches of gallantry to Mrs Tabitha, he had been misled by a mistake of at least six thousand pounds in the calculation of her fortune; and in this particular he was just
undeceived. He, therefore, seized the first opportunity of

incurring her displeasure decently, in such a manner as would certainly annihilate the correspondence ; and he could not have taken a more effectual method, than that of beating her dog. When he presented himself at our door, to pay his respects to the offended fair, he was refused admittance ; and given to understand, that he should never find her at home for the future. She was not so inaccessible to Derrick, who came to demand satisfaction for the insult she had offered to him, even in the verge of his own court. She knew it was convenient to be well with the master of the ceremonies, while she continued to frequent the rooms ; and, having heard he was a poet, began to be afraid of making her appearance in a ballad or lampoon. She therefore made excuses for what she had done, imputing it to the flutter of her spirits ; and subscribed handsomely for his poems : so that he was perfectly appeased, and overwhelmed her with a profusion of compliment. He even solicited a reconciliation with Chowder ; which, however, the latter declined ; and he declared, that if he could find a precedent in the annals of the Bath, which he would carefully examine for that purpose, her favourite should be admitted to the next public breakfasting.—But, I believe, she will not expose herself or him to the risk of a second disgrace.—Who will supply the place of Mackilligut in her affections, I cannot foresee ; but nothing in the shape of a man can come amiss. Though she is a violent church-woman, of the most intolerant zeal, I believe in my conscience she would have no objection, at present, to treat on the score of matrimony with an anabaptist, quaker, or Jew ; and even ratify the treaty at the expense of her own conversion. But, perhaps, I think too hardly of this kinswoman ; who, I must own, is very little beholden to the good opinion of yours,

Bath, May 6.   J. MELFORD.

TO DR LEWIS.

You ask me, why I don't take the air a-horseback, during this fine weather ?—In which of the avenues of this paradise would you have me take that exercise ? Shall I commit

myself to the high roads of London or Bristol, to be stifled
with dust, or pressed to death in the midst of post-chaises,
flying-machines, waggons, and coal horses; besides the
troops of fine gentlemen, that take to the highway, to shew
their horsemanship; and the coaches of fine ladies, who go
thither to shew their equipages? Shall I attempt the downs,
and fatigue myself to death in climbing up an eternal ascent,
without any hopes of reaching the summit?—Know, then,
I have made divers desperate leaps at those upper regions;
but always fell backward into this vapour-pit, exhausted
and dispirited by those ineffectual efforts; and here we poor
valetudinarians pant and struggle, like so many Chinese
gudgeons, gasping in the bottom of a punch-bowl. By
heaven, it is a kind of enchantment! If I do not speedily
break the spell, and escape, I may chance to give up the
ghost in this nauseous stew of corruption. It was but two
nights ago that I had like to have made my public exit, at
a minute's warning. One of my greatest weaknesses, is that
of suffering myself to be over-ruled by the opinion of people whose judgments I despise.—I own, with shame and confusion of face, that importunity of any kind I cannot resist.
This want of courage and constancy is an original flaw in
my nature, which you must have often observed with compassion, if not with contempt. I am afraid some of our
boasted virtues may be traced up to this defect.

  Without further preamble, I was persuaded to go to a
ball, on purpose to see Liddy dance a minuet with a young
petulant jackanapes, the only son of a wealthy undertaker from
London, whose mother lodges in our neighbourhood, and
has contracted an acquaintance with Tabby. I sat a couple
of long hours, half stifled, in the midst of a noisome crowd;
and could not help wondering, that so many hundreds of
those that rank as rational creatures, could find entertainment in seeing a succession of insipid animals, describing
the same dull figure for a whole evening, on an area not
much larger than a tailor's shop-board. If there had been
any beauty, grace, activity, magnificent dress, or variety
of any kind, howsoever absurd, to engage the attention, and

amuse the fancy, I should not have been surprised; but there was no such subject—it was a tiresome repetition of the same languid frivolous scene, performed by actors that seemed to sleep in all their motions. The continual swimming of those phantoms before my eyes, gave me a swimming of the head, which was also affected by the fouled air, circulating through such a number of rotten human bellows—I therefore retreated towards the door, and stood in the passage to the next room, talking to my friend Quin; when, an end being put to the minuets, the benches were removed to make way for the country dances, and the multitude rising at once, the whole atmosphere was put in commotion. Then, all of a sudden, came rushing upon me an Egyptian gale, so impregnated with pestilential vapours, that my nerves were overpowered, and I dropt senseless upon the floor.

You may easily conceive what a clamour and confusion this accident must have produced in such an assembly. I soon recovered, however, and found myself in an easy chair, supported by my own people. Sister Tabby, in her great tenderness, had put me to the torture, squeezing my head under her arm, and stuffing my nose with spirit of hartshorn, till the whole inside was excoriated. I no sooner got home, than I sent for Dr Ch——, who assured me I needed not be alarmed, for my swooning was entirely occasioned by an accidental impression of fetid effluvia upon nerves of uncommon sensibility. I know not how other people's nerves are constructed; but one would imagine they must be made of very coarse materials, to stand the shock of such a horrid assault.

It was, indeed, *a compound of villanous smells*, in which the most violent stinks and the most powerful perfumes contended for the mastery. Imagine to yourself a high exalted essence of mingled odours, arising from putrid gums, imposthumated lungs, sour flatulencies, rank arm-pits, sweating feet, running sores and issues; plasters, ointments, and embrocations, Hungary water, spirit of lavender, assafœtida drops, musk, hartshorn, and sal volatile; besides a thou-

sand frowsy steams, which I could not analyse. Such, O
Dick ! is the fragrant ether we breathe in the polite assemblies of Bath—Such is the atmosphere I have exchanged for
the pure elastic, animating air of the Welch mountains—
O Rus, quando te aspiciam !—I wonder what the devil possessed me—but few words are best : I have taken my resolution—you may well suppose I don't intend to entertain the
company with a second exhibition. I have promised, in an
evil hour, to proceed to London, and that promise shall be
performed ; but my stay in the metropolis shall be brief. I
have, for the benefit of my health, projected an expedition
to the north, which I hope, will afford some agreeable pastime. I have never travelled farther that way than Scarborough ; and, I think, it is a reproach upon me, as a British freeholder, to have lived so long without making an excursion to the other side of the Tweed. Besides, I have
some relations settled in Yorkshire, to whom it may not be
improper to introduce my nephew and his sister. At present I have nothing to add, but that Tabby is happily dis-
entangled from the Irish baronet ; and that I will not fail to
make you acquainted, from time to time, with the sequel of
our adventures ; a mark of consideration which, perhaps,
you would willingly dispense with in your humble servant,

Bath, May 8.   MATT. BRAMBLE.

TO SIR WATKIN PHILLIPS, BART. OF JESUS COLLEGE, OXON.

DEAR PHILLIPS,

A few days ago we were terribly alarmed by my uncle's
fainting at a ball—He has been ever since cursing his own
folly for going thither at the request of an impertinent woman. He declares he will sooner visit a house infected with
the plague, than trust himself in such a nauseous spittal for
the future ; for he swears the accident was occasioned by
the stench of the crowd ; and that he would never desire a
stronger proof of our being made of very gross materials,
than our having withstood the annoyance by which he was
so much discomposed. For my own part, I am very thank-

ful for the coarseness of my organs, being in no danger of
ever falling a sacrifice to the delicacy of my nose. Mr
Bramble is extravagantly delicate in all his sensations, both
of soul and body. I was informed by Dr Lewis, that he
once fought a duel with an officer of the horse guards, for
turning aside to the park wall on a necessary occasion, when
he was passing with a lady under his protection. His blood
rises at every instance of insolence and cruelty, even where
he himself is no way concerned; and ingratitude makes his
teeth chatter. On the other hand, the recital of a generous,
humane, or grateful action, never fails to draw from him
tears of approbation, which he is often greatly distressed to
conceal.

Yesterday one Paunceford gave tea on particular invitation.—This man, after having been long buffetted by adversity, went abroad; and fortune, resolving to make him amends
for her former coyness, set him all at once up to the very
ears in affluence. He has now emerged from obscurity, and
blazes out in all the tinsel of the times. I don't find that he
is charged with any practices that the law deems dishonest,
or that his wealth has made him arrogant or inaccessible;
on the contrary, he takes great pains to appear affable and
gracious.   But, they say, he is remarkable for shrinking
from his former friendships, which was generally too plain
and homespun, to appear amidst his present brilliant connections; and that he seems uneasy at sight of some old benefactors, whom a man of honour would take pleasure to acknowledge.—Be that as it may, he had so effectually engaged the company at Bath, that, when I went with my uncle
to the coffeehouse in the evening, there was not a soul in the
room but one person, seemingly in years, who sat by the fire,
reading one of the papers. Mr Bramble, taking his station
close by him,—' There is such a crowd and confusion of
chairs in the passage to Simpson's' said he, ' that we could
hardly get along.—I wish those minions of fortune would
fall upon more laudable ways of spending their money. I
suppose, sir, you like this kind of entertainment as little as
I do?' ' I can't say I have any great relish for such enter-

tainments,' answered the other, without taking his eyes off
the paper. ' Mr Serle,' resumed my uncle, ' I beg pardon
for interrupting you; but I can't resist the curiosity I have
to know if you received a card on this occasion ?'

The man seemed surprised at this address, and made some
pause, as doubtful what answer he should make. ' I know
my curiosity is impertinent,' added my uncle, ' but I have
a particular reason for asking the favour. ' If that be the
case,' replied Mr Serle, ' I shall gratify you without hesitation, by owning, that I have had no card. But, give me
leave, sir, to ask in my turn, what reason you think I have
to expect such an invitation from the gentleman who gives
tea ?' I have my own reasons,' cried Mr Bramble, with
some emotion, ' and am convinced more than ever, that this
Paunceford is a contemptible fellow.' ' Sir,' said the other,
laying down the paper, ' I have not the honour to know
you, but your discourse is a little mysterious, and seems to
require some explanation. The person you are pleased to
treat so cavalierly is a gentleman of some consequence in the
community; and for aught you know, I may also have my
particular reasons for defending his character——' ' If I
was not convinced of the contrary,' observed the other, ' I
should not have gone so far—' ' Let me tell you, sir,' said
the stranger, raising his voice, ' you have gone too far in
hazarding such reflections—.'

Here he was interrupted by my uncle; who asked, peevishly, if he was Don Quixote enough at this time of day, to
throw down his gauntlet as champion for a man who had
treated him with such ungrateful neglect ? ' For my part,'
added he, ' I shall never quarrel with you again upon this
subject; and what I have said now has been suggested as
much by my regard for you, as by my contempt of him—'
Mr Serle, then, pulling off his spectacles, eyed uncle very
earnestly, saying, in a mitigated tone, ' Surely I am much
obliged—ah, Mr Bramble! I now recollect your features,
though I have not seen you these many years.' ' We might
have been less strangers to one another,' answered the squire,
' if our correspondence had not been interrupted, in conse-

quence of a misunderstanding, occasioned by this very—
But no matter—Mr Serle, I esteem your character; and my
friendship, such as it is, you may freely command. ' The
offer is too agreeable to be declined,' said he : ' I embrace
it very cordially; and, as the first fruits of it, request that
you will change this subject, which, with me, is a matter of
peculiar delicacy.'

My uncle owned he was in the right, and the discourse
took a more general turn. Mr Serle passed the evening
with us at our lodgings; and appeared to be intelligent, and
even entertaining, but his disposition was rather of a melancholy hue. My uncle says he is a man of uncommon parts,
and unquestioned probity: that his fortune, which was originally small, has been greatly hurt by a romantic spirit of
generosity, which he has often displayed, even at the expense of his discretion, in favour of worthless individuals :
that he had rescued Paunceford from the lowest distress,
when he was bankrupt both in means and reputation : that
he had espoused his interests with a degree of enthusiasm,
broke with several friends, and even drawn his sword against
my uncle, who had particular reasons for questioning the
moral character of the said Paunceford : that, without Serle's
countenance and assistance, the other never could have embraced the opportunity, which has raised him to this pin-
nacle of wealth : that Paunceford, in the first transports of
his success, had written, from abroad, letters to different cor-
respondents, owning his obligations to Mr Serle, in the
warmest terms of acknowledgment, and declaring he considered himself only as a factor for the occasions of his best
friend : that, without doubt, he had made declarations of the
same nature to his benefactor himself, though this last was
always silent and reserved on the subject; but, for some years,
those tropes and figures of rhetoric had been disused : that
upon his return to England, he had been lavish in his caresses to Mr Serle, invited him to his house, and pressed
him to make it his own : that he had overwhelmed him with
general professions, and affected to express the warmest regard for him, in company of their common acquaintance;

so that every body believed his gratitude was as liberal as his fortune; and some went so far as to congratulate Mr Serle on both.

All this time Paunceford carefully and artfully avoided particular discussions with his old patron, who had too much spirit to drop the most distant hint of balancing the account of obligation: that, nevertheless, a man of his feelings could not but resent this shocking return for all his kindness; and, therefore, he withdrew himself from the connection, without coming to the least explanation, or speaking a syllable on the subject to any living soul; so that now their correspondence is reduced to a slight salute with the hat, when they chance to meet in any public place; an accident that rarely happens, for their walks lie different ways.   Mr Paunceford lives in a palace, feeds upon dainties, is arrayed in sumptuous apparel, appears in all the pomp of equipage, and passes his time among the nobles of the land.   Serle lodges in Stall street, up two pair of stairs backwards, walks a-foot in a Bath rug, eats for twelve shillings a-week, and drinks water, as a preservative against the gout and gravel. Mark the vicissitude.   Paunceford once resided in a garret; where he subsisted upon sheep's trotters and cowheel, from which commons he was translated to the table of Serle, that ever abounded with good cheer; until want of economy and retention reduced him to a slender annuity, in his decline of years, that scarce affords the bare necessaries of life.—Paunceford, however, does him the honour to speak of him still, with uncommon regard; and to declare what pleasure it would give him to contribute in any shape to his convenience: 'But you know,' he never fails to add, 'he's a shy kind of a man—And then such a perfect philosopher, that he looks upon all superfluities with the most sovereign contempt.'

Having given you this sketch of 'Squire Paunceford, I need not make any comment on his character, but leave it at the mercy of your own reflection; from which, I dare say, it will meet with as little quarter as it has found with, yours always,

Bath, May 10.   J. MELFORD.

TO MRS MARY JONES, AT BRAMBLETONHALL.

DEAR MOLLY,

WE are all upon the ving—Hey for London, girl!—Feeks! we have been long enough here; for we're all turned tipsy turvy—Mistress has excarded Sir Ulic for kicking of Chowder; and I have sent O Frizzle away, with a flea in his ear —I've shown him how little I minded his tinsy and his long tail—A fellor, who would think for to go for to offer to take up with a dirty trollep under my nose—I ketched him in the very fect, coming out of the house-maid's garret—but I have gi'en the dirty slut a siserary. O Molly! the sarvants at Bath are devils in garnet—they lite the candle at both ends— Here's nothing but ginketting, and wasting, and thieving, and tricking, and trigging; and then they are never content.—They won't suffer the squire and mistress to stay any longer, because they have been already above three weeks in the house, and they look for a couple of ginneys a-piece at our going away; and this is a parquisite they expect every month in the season, being as how no family has a right to stay longer than four weeks in the same lodgings; and so the cuck swears she will pin the dish-clout to mistress's tail, and the house-maid vows she'll put cow-itch in master's bed, if so be he don't discamp without furder ado—I don't blame them for making the most of their market, in the way of vails and parquisites; and I defy the devil to say I am a tail-carrier, or ever brought a poor sarvant into trouble—but then they oft to have some conscience, in vronging those that be sarvants like themselves—For you must no, Molly, I missed three quarters of blond lace, and a remnent of muslin, and my silver thimble, which was the gift of true love; they were all in my work basket, that I left upon the table in the sarvant's hall, when mistress's bell rung; but if they had been under lock and kay, 'twould have been all the same, for there are double kays to all the locks in Bath; and they say as how the very teeth an't safe in your head, if you sleep with your mouth open.—And so, says I to myself, *them things could not go without hands, and so I'll watch their waters*; and so I did with a vitness—for then it was I found Bett consarned with O Frizzle. And as the cuck had thrown her slush at me, because I had taken part with Chowder, when he fit with the turnspit, I resolved to make a clear kitchen, and throw some of her fat into the fire. I ketched the charewoman going out with her load in the morning, before she thought I was up, and brought her to mistress with her whole cargo—Marry, what do'st think she had got, in the name of God?—Her buckets were foaming full of our best beer, and her lap was stuffed with a cold tongue, part of a buttock of beef, half a turkey, and a swinging lump of butter, and the matter of ten moulded kandles, that had scarce ever been lit. The cuck brazened it out, and said, it was her rite to rummage the pantry, and she was ready for to go before the mare; that he had been her potticary many years, and would never think of hurting a poor sarvant, for giving away the scraps of the kitchen.—I went another way to work with Madam Betty, because she had been saucy, and called me skandelus names; and said O Frizzle could'nt abide me, and twenty other odorous false-hoods. I got a varrant from the mare, and her box being sarched by the constable, my things came out sure enuff; besides a full pound of vax kandles, and a nite-cap of mistress, that I could swear to on my cruperal oaf—Oh! then Madam Mopstick came upon her merrybones; and as the squire would'nt hare of a pursecution, she escaped a skewering; but the longest day she has to live, she'll remember your humble sarvant,

Bath, May 15.   WINIFRED JENKINS.

If the hind should come again, before we begone, pray send me the shift and apron, with the vite gallow manky shoes, which you'll find in my pillober.—Service to Saul.

TO SIR WATKIN PHILLIPS, BART. OF JESUS COLLEGE, OXON.

You are in the right, dear Phillips; I don't expect regular answers to every letter—I know a college life is too circumscribed to afford materials for such quick returns of communication. For my part, I am continually shifting the scene, and surrounded with new objects, some of which are striking enough. I shall therefore conclude my journal for your amusement; and though, in all appearance, it will not treat of very important or interesting particulars, it may prove, perhaps, not altogether uninstructive and unentertaining.

The music and entertainments of Bath are over for this season; and all the gay birds of passage have taken their flight to Bristol well, Tunbridge, Brighthelmstone, Scarborough, Harrowgate, &c. Not a soul is seen in this place, but a few broken-winded persons, waddling like so many crows along the north parade. There is always a great show of the clergy at Bath; none of your thin, punny, yellow hectic figures, exhausted with abstinence and hard study, labouring under the *morbi eruditorum;* but great overgrown dignitaries, and rectors, with rubicund noses and gouty ancles, or broad bloated faces, dragging along great swag bellies, the emblems of sloth and indigestion.——

Now we are upon the subject of parsons, I must tell you a ludicrous adventure, which was achieved the other day by Tom Eastgate, whom you may remember on the foundation of Queen's. He had been very assiduous to pin himself upon George Prankley, who was a gentleman commoner of Christ Church, knowing the said Prankley was heir to a considerable estate, and would have the advowson of a good living, the incumbent of which was very old and infirm. He studied his passions, and flattered them so effectually, as to become his companion and counsellor: and at last obtained of him a promise of the presentation, when the living should fall. Prankley, on his uncle's death, quitted Oxford, and made his first appearance in the fashionable world at London; from whence he came lately to Bath, where he has been exhibiting himself among the bucks and gamesters of the place. Eastgate followed him hither; but he should not have quitted him for a moment, at his first emerging into life. He ought to have known he was a fantastic, foolish, fickle fellow, who would forget his college attachments

the moment they ceased appealing to his senses.   Tom met
with a cold reception from his old friend ; and was, moreover, informed, that he had promised the living to another
man, who had a vote in the county, where he proposed to
offer himself a candidate at the next general election.   He
now remembered nothing of Eastgate, but the freedoms he
had used to take with him, while Tom had quietly stood his
butt, with an eye to the benefice ; and those freedoms he
began to repeat in common-place sarcasms on his person and
his cloth, which he uttered in the public coffee-house, for
the entertainment of the company.   But he was egregiously
mistaken in giving his own wit credit for that tameness of
Eastgate, which had been entirely owing to prudential considerations.   These being now removed, he retorted his repartee with interest, and found no great difficulty in turning
the laugh upon the aggressor, who, losing his temper, called
him names, and asked, *if he knew whom he talked to ?* After
much altercation, Prankley, shaking his cane, bid him hold
his tongue, otherwise he would dust his cassoc for him.
' I have no pretensions to such a valet,' said Tom, but if
you should do me that office, and overheat yourself, I have
here a good oaken towel at your service.'

Prankley was equally incensed and confounded at this
reply.   After a moment's pause, he took him aside towards
the window, and, pointing to the clump of firs on Clerken-
down, asked, in a whisper, if he had spirit enough to meet
him there, with a case of pistols, at six o'clock to-morrow
morning !   Eastgate answered in the affirmative ; and, with
a steady countenance, assured him, he would not fail to give
him the rendezvous at the hour he mentioned.   So saying,
he retired ; and the challenger staid some time in manifest
agitation.   In the morning, Eastgate, who knew his man,
and had taken his resolution, went to Prankley's lodgings,
and roused him by five o'clock.

The squire, in all probability, cursed his punctuality in
his heart, but he affected to talk big ; and having prepared
his artillery over-night, they crossed the water at the end of
the south parade.   In their progress up the hill, Prankley

often eyed the parson, in hopes of perceiving some reluctance in his countenance; but as no such marks appeared, he attempted to intimidate him by word of mouth. 'If these flints do their office,' said he, 'I'll do thy business in a few minutes.' 'I desire you will do your best,' replied the other; 'for my part, I come not here to trifle. Our lives are in the hands of God, and one of us already totters on the brink of eternity.' This remark seemed to make some impression upon the squire, who changed countenance, and, with a faltering accent, observed,—'That it ill became a clergyman to be concerned in quarrels and bloodshed.' 'Your insolence to me,' said Eastgate, 'I should have bore with patience, had you not cast the most infamous reflections upon my order, the honour of which I think myself in duty bound to maintain, even at the expense of my heart's blood; and surely it can be no crime to put out of the world a profligate wretch, without any sense of principle, morality, or religion.' 'Thou mayest take away my life,' cried Prankley, in great perturbation, 'but don't go to murder my character—What! hast got no conscience?' 'My conscience is perfectly quiet,' replied the other; 'and now, sir, we are upon the spot—Take your ground as near as you please; prime your pistol; and the Lord, of his infinite mercy, have compassion upon your miserable soul!'

This ejaculation he pronounced in a loud solemn tone, with his hat off, and his eyes lifted up; then drawing a large horse pistol, he presented, and put himself in a posture of action. Prankley took his distance, and endeavoured to prime; but his hand shook with such violence, that he found this operation impracticable. His antagonist, seeing how it was with him, offered his assistance, and advanced for that purpose; when the poor squire, exceedingly alarmed at what he had heard and seen, desired the action might be deferred till next day, as he had not settled his affairs. 'I ha'n't made my will,' said he; 'my sisters are not provided for; and I just now recollect an old promise, which my conscience tells me I ought to perform—I'll first convince thee that I'm not a wretch without principle, and then thou shalt have an opportunity to take my life, which thou seemest to thirst after so eagerly.'

Eastgate understood the hint, and told him, that one day should break no squares; adding,—' God forbid that I should be the means of hindering you from acting the part of an honest man, and a dutiful brother.' By virtue of this cessation, they returned peaceably together. Prankley forthwith made out the presentation of the living, and delivered it to Eastgate, telling him, at the same time, he had now settled his affairs, and was ready to attend him to the fir grove; but Tom declared he could not think of lifting his hand against the life of so great a benefactor—He did more: when they next met at the coffee-house, he asked pardon of Mr Prankley, if in his passion he had said any thing to give him offence; and the squire was so gracious as to forgive him with a cordial shake of the hand, declaring that he did not like to be at variance with an old college companion. Next day, however, he left Bath abruptly; and then Eastgate told me all these particulars, not a little pleased with the effects of his own sagacity, by which he has secured a living worth £160 per annum.

Of my uncle I have nothing at present to say; but that we set out to-morrow for London *en famille*. He and the ladies, with the maid and Chowder, in a coach; I and the man-servant a-horseback. The particulars of our journey you shall have in my next, provided no accident happens to prevent yours ever,

Bath, May 17.   J. MELFORD.

TO DR LEWIS.

DEAR DICK,

I SHALL to-morrow set out for London, where I have bespoke lodgings at Mrs Norton's in Golden square. Although I am no admirer of Bath, I shall leave it with regret; because I must part with some old friends, whom, in all probability, I shall never see again. In the course of coffee-house conversation, I had often heard very extraordinary encomiums passed on the performances of Mr T—, a gentleman residing in this place, who paints landscapes for his amusement. As I have no great confidence in the taste and judgment of coffee-house connoisseurs, and never received much pleasure from this branch of the art, those general praises made no impression at all on my curiosity; but, at the request of a particular friend, I went yesterday to see the pieces which had been so warmly commended—I must own I am no judge of painting, though very fond of pictures. I don't imagine that my senses would play me so false, as to betray me into admiration of any thing that was very bad; but, true it is, I have often overlooked capital beauties in pieces of extraordinary merit. If I am not totally devoid of taste, however, this young gentleman of Bath is the best landscape painter now living: I was struck with his performances in such a manner as I had never been by painting before. His trees not only have a richness of foliage, and warmth of colouring, which delights the view; but also a certain magnificence in the disposition, and spirit in the expression, which I cannot describe. His management of the *chiaro oscuro*, or light and shadow, especially gleams of sunshine, is altogether wonderful, both in the contrivance and execution; and he is so happy in his perspective, and marking his distances at sea, by a progressive series of ships, vessels, capes, and promontories, that I could not help thinking I had a distant view of thirty leagues upon the background of the picture. If there is any taste for ingenuity left in a degenerate age, fast sinking into barbarism, this artist, I apprehend, will make a capital figure, as soon as his works are known.

Two days ago, I was favoured with a visit by Mr Fitzowen: who, with great formality, solicited my vote and interest at the general election. I ought not to have been shocked at the confidence of this man; though it was remarkable, considering what had passed between him and me on a former occasion. These visits are mere matter of form, which a candidate makes to every elector, even to those, who, he knows, are engaged in the interest of his competitor, lest he should expose himself to the imputation of pride, at a

time when it is expected he should appear humble. Indeed,
I know nothing so abject as the behaviour of a man canvassing for a seat in parliament. This mean prostration (to
borough electors especially) has, I imagine, contributed in a
great measure to raise that spirit of insolence among the
vulgar, which, like the devil, will be found very difficult
to lay. Be that as it may, I was in some confusion at the
effrontery of Fitz-owen; but I soon recollected myself, and
told him, I had not yet determined for whom I should give
my vote, nor whether I should give it for any. The truth
is, I look upon both candidates in the same light; and should
think myself a traitor to the constitution of my country, if
I voted for either. If every elector would bring the same
consideration home to his conscience, we should not have
such reason to exclaim against the venality of p———ts.
But we are all a pack of venal and corrupted rascals; so lost
to all sense of honesty, and all tenderness of character, that,
in a little time, I am fully persuaded, nothing will be infamous but virtue and public spirit.

G. H———, who is really an enthusiast in patriotism, and
represented the capital in several successive parliaments, declared to me t'other day, with the tears in his eyes, that he
had lived above thirty years in the city of London, and
dealt in the way of commerce with all the citizens of note in
their turns; but that, as he should answer to God, he had
never, in the whole course of his life, found above three or
four whom he could call thoroughly honest; a declaration,
which was rather mortifying than surprising to me, who
have found so few men of worth in the course of my acquaintance, that they serve only as exceptions; which, in the
grammarian's phrase, confirm and prove a general canon.—
I know you will say, G. H——— saw imperfectly through the
mist of prejudice, and I am rankled by the spleen—Perhaps
you are partly in the right; for I have perceived that my
opinion of mankind, like mercury in the thermometer, rises
and falls according to the variations of the weather.

Pray settle accounts with Barnes; take what money of
mine is in his hands, and give him acquittance. If you

think Davis has stock or credit enough to do justice to the
farm, give him a discharge for the rent that is due: this
will animate his industry; for I know that nothing is so discouraging to a farmer, as the thoughts of being in arrears
with his landlord. He becomes dispirited, and neglects his
labour; and so the farm goes to wreck. Tabby has been
clamouring for some days about the lamb's skin, which
Williams the hind begged of me when he was last at Bath.
Prithee take it back, paying the fellow the full value of it,
that I may have some peace in my own house; and let him
keep his own counsel, if he means to keep his place.—O! I
shall never presume to despise or censure any poor man for
suffering himself to be henpecked; conscious how I myself
am obliged to truckle to a domestic demon; even though
(blessed be God) she is not yoked with me for life, in the
matrimonial waggon.—She has quarrelled with the servants
of the house about vails; and such intolerable scolding ensued on both sides, that I have been fain to appease the cook
and chambermaid by stealth. Can't you find some poor
gentleman of Wales, to take this precious commodity off
the hands of yours,

Bath, May 19. M. BRAMBLE.

TO DR LEWIS.

DOCTOR LEWIS,

GIVE me leaf to tell you, methinks you mought employ
your talons better, than to encourage servants to pillage their
masters—I find by Gwyllim, that Villiams has got my skin;
for which he is an impotent rascal. He has not only got my
skin, but, moreover, my butter-milk to fatten his pigs; and,
I suppose, the next thing he gets, will be my pad to carry
his daughter to church and fair: Roger gets this, and Roger
gets that; but I'd have you to know, I won't be rogered at
this rate by any ragmatical fellow in the kingdom—And I
am surprised, Doctor Lewis, you would offer to put my affairs in composition with the refuge and skim of the hearth.
I have toiled and moyled to a good purpus, for the advantage of Matt's family, if I can't safe as much owl as will

make me an under petticoat.   As for the butter milk, ne'er
a pig in the parish shall thrust his snout in it, with my
good-will.   There's a famous physician at the hot-well,
that prescribes it to his patience, when the case is consumptive ; and the Scots and Irish have begun to drink it already,
in such quantities, that there is not a drop left for the hogs
in the whole neighbourhood of Bristol.   I'll have our butter-
milk barelled up and sent twice a-week to Aberginny, where
it may be sold for a halfpenny the quart ; and so Roger
may carry his pigs to another market.—I hope, Doctor,
you will not go to put any more such plans in my brother's
head, to the prejudice of my pocket ; but rather give me
some raisins (which hitherto you have not done) to subscribe
myself your humble servant,

Bath, May 19.   TAB. BRAMBLE.

TO SIR WATKIN PHILLIPS, OF JESUS COLLEGE, OXON.

DEAR PHILLIPS,

WITHOUT waiting for your answer to my last, I proceed
to give you an account of our journey to London, which has
not been wholly barren of adventure.   Tuesday last, the
squire took his place in a hired coach-and-four, accompanied by his sister and mine, and Mrs Tabby's maid, Winifred Jenkins, whose province it was to support Chowder on
a cushion in her lap.   I could scarce refrain from laughing,
when I looked into the vehicle, and saw that animal sitting
opposite to my uncle, like any other passenger.   The squire,
ashamed of his situation, blushed to the eyes ; and, calling
to the postillions to drive on, pulled the glass up in my
face.   I, and his servant John Thomas, attended them on
horseback.

Nothing worth mentioning occurred, till we arrived on
the edge of Marlborough downs.   There one of the fore
horses fell, in going down hill at a round trot ; and the postillion behind, endeavouring to stop the carriage, pulled it
on one side into a deep rut, where it was fairly overturned.
I had rode on about two hundred yards before ; but, hear-

ing a loud scream, gallopped back and dismounted, to give
what assistance was in my power. When I looked into the
coach, I could see nothing distinctly, but the nether end of
Jenkins, who was kicking her heels, and squalling with great
vociferation. All of a sudden, my uncle thrust up his bare
pate, and bolted through the window, as nimble as a grass-
hopper, having made use of poor Win's posteriors as a step
to rise in his ascent—The man (who had likewise quitted his
horse) dragged this forlorn damsel, more dead than alive,
through the same opening. Then Mr Bramble, pulling
the door off its hinges with a jerk, laid hold on Liddy's arm,
and brought her to the light, very much frighted, but little
hurt. It fell to my share to deliver our aunt Tabitha, who
had lost her cap in the struggle ; and, being rather more
than half frantic with rage and terror, was no bad representation of one of the sister furies that guard the gates of hell—
She expressed no sort of concern for her brother, who ran
about in the cold, without his periwig, and worked with the
most astonishing agility, in helping to disentangle the horses
from the carriage : but she cried, in a tone of distraction,—
'Chowder ! Chowder ! my dear Chowder ! my poor Chowder is certainly killed.'

This was not the case—Chowder, after having tore my
uncle's leg in the confusion of the fall, had retreated under
the seat, and from thence the footman drew him by the neck ;
for which good office he bit his fingers to the bone. The
fellow, who is naturally surly, was so provoked at this assault, that he saluted his ribs with a hearty kick, exclaiming,—' Damn the nasty son of a b——, and them he belongs
to !' A benediction which was by no means lost upon the
implacable virago his mistress.—Her brother, however, prevailed upon her to retire into a peasant's house, near the
scene of action, where his head and hers were covered, and
poor Jenkins had a fit.—Our next care was to apply some
sticking plaster to the wound in his leg, which exhibited
the impression of Chowder's teeth ; but he never opened his
lips against the delinquent—Mrs Tabby, alarmed at this
scene—' You say nothing, Matt,' cried she, but I know

your mind—I know the spite you have to that poor unfortunate animal! I know you intend to take his life away!
' You are mistaken, upon my honour!' replied the squire,
with a sarcastic smile, ' I should be incapable of harbour-
ing any such cruel design against an object so amiable and
inoffensive; even if he had not the happiness to be your favourite.'

John Thomas was not so delicate. The fellow, whether
really alarmed for his life, or instigated by the desire of revenge, came in, and bluntly demanded that the dog should
be put to death; on the supposition, that, if ever he should
run mad hereafter, he, who had been bit by him would be
infected. My uncle calmly argued upon the absurdity of
his opinion, observing, that he himself was in the same predicament, and would certainly take the precaution he proposed, if he was not sure he ran no risk of infection. Nevertheless Thomas continued obstinate; and, at length, declared, that if the dog was not shot immediately, he himself
would be his executioner. This declaration opened the flood-
gates of Tabby's eloquence, which would have shamed the
first-rate oratress of Billingsgate. The footman retorted in the
same style; and the squire dismissed him from his service,
after having prevented me from giving him a good horse-
whipping for his insolence.

The coach being adjusted, another difficulty occurred—
Mrs Tabitha absolutely refused to enter it again, unless another driver could be found to take the place of the postillion; who, she affirmed, had overturned the carriage from
malice aforethought. After much dispute, the man resigned
his place to a shabby country fellow, who undertook to go
as far as Marlborough, where they could be better provided;
and at that place we arrived about one o'clock, without
farther impediment. Mrs Bramble, however, found new
matter of offence; which indeed she had a particular genius
for extracting at will from almost every incident in life.—
We had scarce entered the room at Marlborough, where we
staid to dine, when she exhibited a formal complaint against
the poor fellow who had superseded the postillion. She said

he was such a beggarly rascal, that he had ne'er a shirt to
his back; and had the impudence to shock her sight by
shewing his bare posteriors, for which act of indelicacy he
deserved to be set in the stocks. Mrs Winifred Jenkins
confirmed the assertion, with respect to his nakedness, observing, at the same time, that he had a skin as fair as ala-
baster.

'This is a heinous offence indeed,' cried my uncle; ' let
us hear what the fellow has to say in his own vindication.'
He was accordingly summoned, and made his appearance,
which was equally queer and pathetic.—He seemed to be
about twenty years of age, of a middling size, with bandy
legs, stooping shoulders, high forehead, sandy locks, pink-
ing eyes, flat nose, and long chin—but his complexion was
of a sickly yellow : his looks denoted famine ; and the rags
that he wore could hardly conceal what decency requires to
be covered. My uncle, having surveyed him attentively,
said, with an ironical expression in his countenance,—' An't
you ashamed, fellow, to ride postillion without a shirt to
cover your backside from the view of the ladies in the coach?'
'Yes, I am, an' please your noble honour,' answered the
man, ' but necessity has no law, as the saying is—And
more than that, it was an accident—my breeches cracked
behind after I had got into the saddle—' ' You're an impudent varlet,' cried Mrs Tabby, ' for presuming to ride
before persons of fashion without a shirt.—' ' I am so, an'
please your worthy ladyship,' said he, ' but I'm a poor
Wiltshire lad—I ha'n't a shirt in the world, that I can call
my own, nor a rag of clothes, an' please your ladyship, but
what you see—I have no friend nor relation upon earth to
help me out—I have had the fever and ague these six
months, and spent all I had in the world upon doctors, and
to keep soul and body together ; and, saving your ladyship's
good presence I ha'n't broke bread these four-and-twenty
hours.' .

Mrs Bramble, turning from him, said she had never seen
such a filthy tatterdemalion, and bid him begone ; observing,
that he would fill the room full of vermin. Her brother

darted a significant glance at her, as she retired with Liddy
into another apartment; and then asked the man if he was
known to any person in Marlborough?   When he answered,
that the landlord of the inn had known him from his infancy; mine host was immediately called, and, being interrogated on the subject, declared, that the young fellow's
name was Humphry Clinker: that he had been a love-be-
gotten babe, brought up in the workhouse, and put out
apprentice by the parish to a country blacksmith, who died
before the boy's time was out: that he had for sometime
worked under his ostler, as a helper and extra postillion, till
he was taken ill of the ague, which disabled him from getting his bread; that having sold or pawned every thing he
had in the world for his cure and subsistence he became so
miserable and shabby, that he disgraced the stable, and was
dismissed; but that he never heard any thing to the prejudice of his character in other respects.   ' So that the fellow
being sick and destitute,' said my uncle, ' you turned him
out to die in the streets.'   ' I pay the poor's rate,' replied
the other, ' and I have no right to maintain idle vagrants,
cither in sickness or health; besides, such a miserable object
would have brought discredit upon my house.'

'You perceive,' said the squire, turning to me, ' our
landlord is a christian of bowels—who shall presume to censure the morals of the age, when the very publicans exhibit
such examples of humanity?   Hark ye, Clinker, you are a
most notorious offender—you stand convicted of sickness,
hunger, wretchedness, and want—but, as it does not belong
to me to punish criminals, I will only take upon me the task
of giving you a word of advice—Get a shirt with all convenient dispatch, that your nakedness may not henceforward
give offence to travelling gentlewomen, especially maidens in
years.'

So saying, he put a guinea into the hand of the poor
fellow, who stood staring at him in silence, with his mouth
wide open, till the landlord pushed him out of the room.

In the afternoon, as our aunt stept into the coach, she
observed, with some marks of satisfaction, that the postillion,

who rode next to her, was not a shabby wretch like the raga-
muffin who had drove them into Marlborough. Indeed,
the difference was very conspicuous : this was a smart fellow,
with a narrow brimmed hat, with gold cording, a cut bob,
a decent blue jacket, leather breeches, and a clean linen
shirt, puffed above the waistband. When we arrived at
the castle on Spinhill, where we lay, this new postillion was
remarkably assiduous in bringing in the loose parcels; and
at length displayed the individual countenance of Humphry
Clinker, who had metamorphosed himself in this manner,
by relieving from pawn part of his own clothes, with the money he had received from Mr Bramble.

Howsoever pleased the rest of the company were with such
a favourable change in the appearance of this poor creature,
it soured on the stomach of Mrs Tabby, who had not yet
digested the affront of his naked skin.—She tossed her nose
in disdain, saying, she supposed her brother had taken him
into favour, because he had insulted her with his obscenity;
that a fool and his money were soon parted; but that if Matt
intended to take the fellow with him to London she would
not go a foot farther that way.—My uncle said nothing with
his tongue, though his looks were sufficiently expressive : and
next morning Clinker did not appear, so that we proceeded
without farther altercation to Salthill, where we proposed to
dine.—There, the first person that came to the side of the
coach, and began to adjust the footboard, was no other than
Humphry Clinker.—When I handed out Mrs Bramble, she
eyed him with a furious look, and passed into the house—
My uncle was embarrassed, and asked him peevishly what
had brought him hither ? The fellow said, his honour had
been so good to him, that he had not the heart to part with
him;—that he would follow him to the world's end, and
serve him all the days of his life without fee or reward.'

Mr Bramble did not know whether to chide or laugh at
this declaration.—He foresaw much contradiction on the side
of Tabby ; and, on the other hand, he could not but be
pleased with the gratitude of Clinker, as well as with the
simplicity of his character.—' Suppose I was inclined to take

you into my service,' said he, ' what are your qualifications?
what are you good for? ' An' please your honour,' answered this original, ' I can read and write, and do the business of the stable indifferent well—I can dress a horse and
shoe him, and bleed and rowl him ; and, as for the practice
of sow-gelding, I wont turn my back on e'er a he in the
county of Wilts—Then I can make hogs puddings and hob-
nails, mend kettles, and tin sauce-pans—' Here uncle burst
out a-laughing ; and inquired what other accomplishments
he was master of? ' I know something of single stick and
psalmody,' proceeded Clinker, ' I can play upon the Jew's
harp, sing Black-ey'd Susan, Arthur O'Bradley, and divers
other songs ; I can dance a Welsh jig, and Nancy Dawson ;
wrestle a fall with any lad of my inches, when I'm in heart ;
and, under correction, I can find a hare when your honour
wants a bit of game.' ' Foregad, thou art a complete fellow !' cried my uncle still laughing, ' I have a mind to take
thee into my family—Prithee, go and try if thou can'st make
peace with my sister—Thou hast given her much offence, by
shewing her thy naked tail.

Clinker, accordingly, followed us into the room, cap in
hand, where addressing himself to Mrs Tabitha,—' May it
please your ladyship's worship,' cried he, ' to pardon and
fogive my offences, and, with God's assistance, I shall take
care that my tail shall never rise up in judgment against me,
to offend your ladyship again—Do, pray, good, sweet, beautiful lady, take compassion on a poor sinner—God bless
your noble countenance, I am sure you are too handsome and
generous to bear malice—I will serve you on my bended
knees, by night and by day, by land and by water ; and all
for the love and pleasure of serving such an excellent lady.'

This compliment and humiliation had some effect upon
Tabby ; but she made no reply ; and Clinker, taking silence
for consent, gave his attendance at dinner. The fellow's
natural awkwardness, and the flutter of his spirits, were productive of repeated blunders in the course of his attendance.
At length, he spilt part of a custard upon her right shoulder ;
and, starting back, trode upon Chowder, who set up a dis-

mal howl—Poor Humphry was so disconcerted at this double
mistake, that he dropt the china dish, which broke into a
thousand pieces; then, falling down upon his knees, remained in that posture, gaping, with a most ludicrous aspect of
distress—Mrs Bramble flew to the dog, and, snatching him
in her arms, presented him to her brother, saying, 'This is
all a concerted scheme against this unfortunate animal,
whose only crime is its regard for me—Here it is; kill it at
once; and then you'll be satisfied.'

Clinker, hearing these words, and taking them in the literal acceptation, got up in some hurry, and, seizing a knife
from the sideboard, cried, 'Not here, an' please your ladyship—It will daub the room—Give him to me, and I'll carry
him into the ditch by the road-side—' To this proposal he
received no other answer, than a hearty box on the ear, that
made him stagger to the other side of the room. 'What!'
said she to her brother, 'am I to be affronted by every
mangy hound that you pick up in the highway? I insist
upon your sending this rascallion about his business immediately—' 'For God's sake, sister, compose yourself,' said
my uncle, 'and consider, that the poor fellow is innocent of
any intention to give you offence—' 'Innocent as the babe
unborn—' cried Humphry. 'I see it plainly,' exclaimed
this implacable maiden, 'he acts by your direction; and
you are resolved to support him in his impudence—This is
a bad return for all the services I have done you; for nursing
you in your sickness, managing your family, and keeping
you from ruining yourself by your own imprudence—But
now you shall part with that rascal or me, upon the spot,
without farther loss of time; and the world shall see whether
you have more regard for your own flesh and blood, or for a
beggarly foundling taken from the dunghill—'

Mr Bramble's eyes began to glisten, and his teeth to chatter. 'If stated fairly,' said he, raising his voice, 'the question is, whether I have spirit to shake off an intolerable yoke,
by one effort of resolution, or meanness enough to do an act
of cruelty and injustice, te gratify the rancour of a capricious
woman—Hark ye, Mrs Tabitha Bramble, I will now pro-

pose an alternative in my turn—Either discard your four-
footed favourite, or give me leave to bid you eternally adieu—
For I am determined that he and I shall live no longer under
the same roof; and now *to dinner with what appetite you may.*'
Thunderstruck at this declaration, she sat down in a corner ;
and, after a pause of some minutes, ' Sure I don't understand
you, Matt,' said she ! ' And yet I spoke in plain English'—
answered the squire, with a peremptory look.   ' Sir,' resumed this virago, effectually humbled, ' it is your prerogative
to command, and my duty to obey.   I can't dispose of the
dog in this place ; but if you'll allow him to go in the coach
to London, I give you my word, he shall never trouble you
again—'

Her brother, entirely disarmed by this mild reply, declared, she could ask him nothing in reason that he would refuse ; adding, ' I hope, sister, you have never found me deficient in natural affection.   Mrs Tabitha immediately rose,
and throwing her arms about his neck, kissed him on the
cheek : he returned her embrace with great emotion.   Liddy
sobbed ; Win Jenkins cackled ; Chowder capered ; and
Clinker skipped about, rubbing his hands, for joy of this
reconciliation.

Concord being thus restored, we finished our meal with
comfort ; and in the evening arrived at London, without having met with any other adventure. My aunt seems to be much
mended by the hint she received from her brother. She has
been graciously pleased to remove her displeasure from
Clinker, who is now retained as a footman, and, in a day or
two, will make his appearance in a new suit of livery ; but
as he is little acquainted with London, we have taken an occasional valet, whom I intend hereafter to hire as my own servant.   We lodge in Golden square, at the house of one Mrs
Norton, a decent sort of a woman, who takes great pains to
make us all easy. My uncle proposes to make a circuit of all
the remarkable scenes of this metropolis, for the entertainment
of his pupils ; but as both you and I are already acquainted
with most of those he will visit, and with some others he little
dreams of, I shall only communicate what will be in some

measure new to your observation. Remember me to our jesuitical friends, and believe me ever, dear knight, yours af-
fectionately,

London, May 24.   J. MELFORD.

TO DR LEWIS.

DEAR DOCTOR,

London is literally new to me; new in its streets, houses,
and even in its situation: as the Irishman said, ' London is
now gone out of town.' What I left open fields, producing
hay and corn, I now find covered with streets and squares,
and palaces and churches. I am credibly informed, that,
in the space of seven years, eleven thousand new houses have
been built in one quarter of Westminster, exclusive of what
is daily added to other parts of this unwieldy metropolis.
Pimlico and Knightsbridge are now almost joined to Chelsea
and Kensington; and, if this infatuation continues for half
a century, I suppose the whole county of Middlesex will be
covered with brick.

It must be allowed, indeed, for the credit of the present
age, that London and Westminster are much better paved
and lighted than they were formerly. The new streets are
spacious, regular, and airy, and the houses generally convenient. The bridge at Blackfriars is a noble monument of
taste and public spirit—I wonder how they stumbled upon a
work of such magnificence and utility. But, notwithstanding these improvements, the capital is become an overgrown
monster; which, like a dropsical head, will in time leave the
body and extremities without nourishment and support.
The absurdity will appear in its full force, when we consider,
that one sixth part of the natives of this whole extensive kingdom is crowded within the bills of mortality. What wonder that our villages are depopulated, and our farms in want
of day-labourers! The abolition of small farms is but one
cause of the decrease of population. Indeed, the incredible
increase of horses and black cattle, to answer the purposes of
luxury, requires a prodigious quantity of hay and grass,

which are raised and managed without much labour; but a
number of hands will always be wanted for the different
branches of agriculture, whether the farms be large or small.
—The tide of luxury has swept all the inhabitants from the
open country—The poorest squire, as well as the richest
peer, must have his house in town, and make a figure with
an extraordinary number of domestics.   The plough-boys,
cow-herds, and lower hinds, are debauched and seduced by
the appearance and discourse of those coxcombs in livery,
when they make their summer excursions.   They desert
their dirt and drudgery, and swarm up to London, in hopes
of getting into service, where they can live luxuriously, and
wear fine clothes, without being obliged to work; for idleness is natural to man.   Great numbers of these, being disappointed in their expectation, become thieves and sharpers;
and London, being an immense wilderness, in which there
is neither watch nor ward of any signification, nor any order
or police, affords them lurking-places as well as prey.

There are many causes that contribute to the daily increase
of this enormous mass; but they may be all resolved into the
grand source of luxury and corruption.   About five-and-
twenty years ago, very few even of the most opulent citizens
of London kept any equipage, or even any servants in livery.
Their tables produced nothing but plain boiled and roasted,
with a bottle of port and a tankard of beer.   At present,
every trader in any degree of credit, every broker and attorney, maintains a couple of footmen, a coachman, and
postillion.   He has his town-house and his country-house,
his coach and his post-chaise.   His wife and daughters appear in the richest stuffs, bespangled with diamonds.   They
frequent the court, the opera, the theatre, and the masque-
rade.   They hold assemblies at their own houses; they
make sumptuous entertainments, and treat with the richest
wines of Bourdeaux, Burgundy, and Champaigne.   The
substantial tradesman, who wont to pass his evenings at the
ale-house for four pence halfpenny, now spends three shillings at the tavern, while his wife keeps card-tables at home;
she must also have fine clothes, her chaise, or pad, with

country lodgings, and go three times a-week to public diversions. Every clerk, apprentice, and even waiter of a
tavern or coffee-house, maintains a gelding by himself or in
partnership, and assumes the air and apparel of a petit-
maitre. The gayest places of public entertainment are filled with fashionable figures, which, upon inquiry, will be
found to be journeymen tailors, serving-men, and abigails,
disguised like their betters.

In short, there is no distinction or subordination left. The
different departments of life are jumbled together—The hod-
carrier, the low mechanic, the tapster, · the publican, the
shop-keeper, the pettifogger, the citizen, and courtier, *all
tread upon the kibes of one another ;* actuated by the demons
of profligacy and licentiousness, they are seen everywhere,
rambling, riding, rolling, rushing, jostling, mixing, bouncing, cracking, and crashing, in one vile ferment of stupidity
and corruption—All is tumult and hurry. One would imagine they were impelled by some disorder of the brain, that
will not suffer them to be at rest. The foot-passengers run
along as if they were pursued by bailiffs ; the porters and
chairmen trot with their burdens. People, who keep their
own equipages, drive through the streets at full speed. Even
citizens, physicians, and apothecaries, glide in their chariots like lightning. The hackney-coachmen make their
horses smoke, and the pavement shakes under them ; and I
have actually seen a waggon pass through Piccadilly at the
hand-gallop. In a word, the whole nation seems to be
running out of their wits.

The diversions of the times are not ill-suited to the genius
of this incongruous monster, called *the public.*—Give it
noise, confusion, glare, and glitter, it has no idea of elegance and propriety.—What are the amusements at Ranelagh ? One half of the company are following one another's
tails, in an eternal circle, like so many blind asses in an
olive mill, where they can neither discourse, distinguish,
nor be distinguished ; while the other half are drinking hot
water, under the denomination of tea, till nine or ten o'clock
at night, to keep them awake for the rest of the evening.

As for the orchestra, the vocal music especially, it is well
for the performers that they cannot be heard distinctly.——
Vauxhall is a' composition of baubles, overcharged with
paltry ornaments, ill conceived, and poorly executed, without any unity of design, or propriety of disposition.   It is
an unnatural assemblage of objects, fantastically illuminated
in broken masses, seemingly contrived to dazzle the eyes and
divert the imagination of the vulgar.   Here a wooden lion,
there a stone statue ; in one place a range of things like
coffee-house boxes covered a-top, in another a parcel of ale-
house benches ; in a third, a puppet-show representation of
a tin cascade ; in a fourth, a gloomy cave of a circular
form, like a sepulchral vault, half-lighted ; in a fifth, a
scanty slip of grass-plot, that would not afford pasture sufficient for an ass's colt.   The walks, which nature seems to
have intended for solitude, shade, and silence, are filled with
crowds of noisy people, sucking up the nocturnal rheums of
an aguish climate ; and through these gay scenes a few
lamps glimmer like so many farthing candles.

When I see a number of well-dressed people, of both
sexes, sitting on the covered benches, exposed to the eyes
of the mob, and, which is worse, to the cold, raw, night air,
devouring sliced beef, and swilling port, and punch, and
cyder, I can't help compassionating their temerity, while I
despise their want of taste and decorum ; but, when they
course along those damp and gloomy walks, or crowd together upon the wet gravel, without any other cover than
the cope of heaven, listening to a song, which one half of
them cannot possibly hear, how can I help supposing they
are actually possessed by a spirit more absurd and pernicious
than any thing we meet with in the precincts of bedlam ?
In all probability, the proprietors of this, and other public
gardens of inferior note, in the skirts of the metropolis,
are, in some shape, connected with the faculty of physic,
and the company of undertakers ; for, considering that
eagerness in the pursuit of what is called pleasure, which
now predominates through every rank and denomination of
life, I am persuaded that more gouts, rheumatisms, catarrhs,

and consumptions, are caught in these nocturnal pastimes, *sub dio*, than from all the risks and accidents to which a life of toil and danger is exposed.

These, and other observations which I have made in this excursion, will shorten my stay in London, and send me back with a double relish to my solitude and mountains; but I shall return by a different route from that which brought me to town. I have seen some old friends, who constantly reside in this virtuous metropolis, but they are so changed in manners and disposition, that we hardly know or care for one another.—In our journey from Bath, my sister Tabby provoked me into a transport of passion; during which, like a man who has drank himself pot-valiant, I talked to her in such a style of authority and resolution, as produced a most blessed effect. She and her dog have been remarkably quiet and orderly ever since this expostulation. How long this agreeable calm will last, heaven above knows.—I flatter myself the exercise of travelling has been of service to my health; a circumstance which encourages me to proceed in my projected expedition to the north. But I must, in the meantime, for the benefit and amusement of my pupils, explore the depth of this chaos, this mishapen and monstrous capital, without head or tail, members or proportion.

Thomas was so insolent to my sister on the road, that I was obliged to turn him off abruptly, betwixt Chippenham and Marlborough, where our coach was overturned. The fellow was always sullen and selfish; but if he should return to the country, you may give him a character for honesty and sobriety; and provided he behaves with proper respect to the family, let him have a couple of guineas in the name of yours always.

London, May 29.   MATT. BRAMBLE.

TO MISS LÆTITIA WILLIS, AT GLOUCESTER.

MY DEAR LETTY,

INEXPRESSIBLE was the pleasure I received from yours of the 25th, which was last night put into my hands by Mrs

Brentwood, the milliner, from Gloucester.—I rejoice to
hear that my worthy governess is in good health, and still
more, that she no longer retains any displeasure towards her
poor Liddy.   I am sorry you have lost the society of the
agreeable Miss Vaughan; but, I hope, you won't have
cause much longer to regret the departure of your school-
companions, as I make no doubt but your parents will, in
a little time, bring you into the world, where you are so
well qualified to make a distinguished figure.   When that
is the case, I flatter myself you and I shall meet again, and
be happy together, and even improve the friendship which
we contracted in our tender years—This at least I can promise, it shall not be for the want of my utmost endeavours,
if our intimacy does not continue for life.

About five days ago we arrived in London, after an easy
journey from Bath; during which, however, we were overturned, and met with some other little incidents, which had
like to have occasioned a misunderstanding betwixt my uncle
and aunt: but now, thank God, they are happily reconciled; we live in harmony together, and every day make
parties to see the wonders of this vast metropolis, which,
however, I cannot pretend to describe; for I have not as
yet seen one hundredth part of its curiosities, and I am quite
in a maze of admiration.

The cities of London and Westminster are spread out to
an incredible extent.   The streets, squares, rows, lanes, and
alleys, are innumerable.   Palaces, public buildings, and
churches, rise in every quarter; and, among these last, S‘
Paul's appears with the most astonishing pre-eminence.
They say it is not so large as S‘ Peter's at Rome; but, for
my own part, I can have no idea of any earthly temple more
grand and magnificent.

But even these superb objects are not so striking as the
crowds of people that swarm in the streets.   I at first imagined, that some great assembly was just dismissed, and
wanted to stand aside till the multitude should pass; but
this human tide continues to flow without interruption or
abatement, from morn till night.   Then there is such an in-

finity of gay equipages, coaches, chariots, chaises, and other carriages, continually rolling and shifting before your eyes, that one's head grows giddy looking at them; and the imagination is quite confounded with splendour and variety. Nor is the prospect by water less grand and astonishing than that by land : you see three stupendous bridges, joining the opposite banks of a broad, deep, and rapid river ; so vast, so stately, so elegant, that they seem to be the work of the giants : betwixt them, the whole surface of the Thames is covered with small vessels, barges, boats, and wherries, passing to and fro; and below the three bridges, such a prodigious forest of masts, for miles together, that you would think all the ships in the universe were here assembled. All that you read of wealth and grandeur, in the Arabian nights entertainment, and the Persian tales, concerning Bagdad, Diarbekir, Damascus, Ispahan, and Samarkand, is here realized.

Ranelagh looks like the enchanted palace of a genii, adorned with the most exquisite performances of painting, carving, and gilding, enlightened with a thousand golden lamps, that emulate the noon-day sun; crowded with the great, the rich, the gay, the happy, and the fair ; glittering with cloth of gold and silver, lace, embroidery, and precious stones. While these exulting sons and daughters of felicity tread this round of pleasure, or regale in different parties, and separate lodges, with fine imperial tea and other delicious refreshments, their ears are entertained with the most ravishing delights of music, both instrumental and vocal. There I heard the famous Tenducci, a thing from Italy— It looks for all the world like a man, though they say it is not. The voice, to be sure, is neither man's nor woman's ; but it is more melodious than either ; and it warbled so divinely, that, while I listened, I really thought myself in paradise.

At nine o'clock in a charming moon-light evening, we embarked at Ranelagh, for Vauxhall, in a wherry, so light and slender, that we looked like so many fairies sailing in a

nut-shell. My uncle, being apprehensive of catching cold
upon the water, went round in the coach, and my aunt would
have accompanied him, but he would not suffer me to go by
water if she went by land ; and therefore she favoured us
with her company, as she perceived I had a curiosity to
make this agreeable voyage. After all, the vessel was sufficiently loaded ; for, besides the waterman, there was my bro-
thery Jery, and a friend of his, one Mr Barton, a country
gentleman, of a good fortune, who had dined at our house.
The pleasure of this little excursion was, however, damped, by my being sadly frighted at our landing; where
there was a terrible confusion of wherries, and a crowd
of people bawling, and swearing, and quarrelling; nay, a
parcel of ugly-looking fellows came running into the water,
and laid hold on our boat with great violence, to pull it
ashore; nor would they quit their hold, till my brother
struck one of them over the head with his cane. But this
flutter was fully recompensed by the pleasures of Vauxhall ;
which I no sooner entered, than I was dazzled and confounded with the variety of beauties that rushed all at once upon
my eye. Image to yourself, my dear Letty, a spacious garden, part laid out in delightful walks, bounded with high
hedges and trees, and paved with gravel; part exhibiting a
wonderful assemblage of the most picturesque and striking
objects, pavilions, lodges, groves, grottoes, lawns, temples,
and cascades ; porticoes, colonnades, and rotundas ; adorned
with pillars, statues, and painting ; the whole illuminated
with an infinite number of lamps, disposed in different
figures of suns, stars, and constellations ; the place crowded
with the gayest company, ranging through those blissful
shades, or supping, in different lodges, on cold collations,
enlivened with mirth, freedom, and good humour, and animated by an excellent band of music. Among the vocal
performers, I had the happiness to hear the celebrated Mrs
———, whose voice was so loud and so shrill, that it made
my head ache, through excess of pleasure.

In about half an hour after we arrived, we were joined by
my uncle, who did not seem to relish the place.—People of

experience and infirmity, my dear Letty, see with very different eyes from those that such as you and I make use of.—
Our evening's entertainment was interrupted by an unlucky
accident.   In one of the remotest walks, we were surprised
with a sudden shower, that set the whole company a-running,
and drove us in heaps, one upon another, into the rotunda;
where my uncle, finding himself wet, began to be very
peevish and urgent to be gone.   My brother went to look
for the coach, and found it with much difficulty; but as it
could not hold us all, Mr Barton staid behind.   It was some
time before the carriage could be brought up to the gate, in
the confusion, notwithstanding the utmost endeavours of our
new footman, Humphry Clinker, who lost his scratch periwig, and got a broken head in the scuffle.   The moment we
were seated, my aunt pulled off my uncle's shoes, and carefully wrapped his poor feet in her capuchin; then she gave
him a mouthful of cordial, which she always keeps in her
pocket, and his clothes were shifted as soon as we arrived at
our lodgings; so that, blessed be God, he escaped a severe
cold, of which he was in great terror.

As for Mr Barton, I must tell you in confidence, he was a
little particular; but, perhaps, I mistake his complaisance;
and I wish I may for his sake.   You know the condition of
my poor heart; which, in spite of hard usage—And yet I
ought not to complain; nor will I, till farther information.

Besides Ranelagh and Vauxhall, I have been at Mrs Cor-
nely's assembly, which, for the rooms, the company, the
dresses, and decorations, surpasses all description; but as I
have no great turn for card-playing, I have not yet entered
thoroughly into the spirit of the place: indeed I am still such
a country hoyden that I could hardly find patience to be put
in a condition to appear; yet I was not above six hours under
the hands of the hair-dresser, who stuffed my head with as
much black wool as would have made a quilted petticoat;
and, after all, it was the smallest head in the assembly, except my aunt's—She, to be sure, was so particular with her
rumpt gown and petticoat, her scanty curls, her lappet head,

deep triple ruffles, and high stays, that every body looked at
her with surprise ; some whispered, and some tittered ; and
Lady Griskin, by whom we were introduced, flatly told her
she was twenty good years behind the fashion.

Lady Griskin is a person of fashion, to whom we have the
honour to be related. She keeps a small rout at her own
house, never exceeding ten or a dozen card tables ; but these
are frequented by the best company in town. She has been
so obliging as to introduce my aunt and me to some of her
particular friends of quality, who treat us with the most familiar good humour : we have once dined with her, and she
takes the trouble to direct us in all our motions. I am so
happy as to have gained her good will to such a degree, that
she sometimes adjusts my cap with her own hands ; and she
has given me a kind invitation to stay with her all the winter. This, however, has been cruelly declined by my uncle,
who seems to be, I know not how, prejudiced against the
good lady ; for, whenever my aunt happens to speak in her
commendation, I observe that he makes wry faces, though
he says nothing—Perhaps, indeed, these grimaces may be
the effect of pain arising from the gout and rheumatism, with
which he is sadly distressed—To me, however, he is always
good-natured and generous, even beyond my wish. Since
we came hither, he has made me a present of a suit of clothes,
with trimmings and laces, which cost more money than I
shall mention ; and Jery, at his desire, has given me my mother's diamond drops, which are ordered to be set anew ; so
that it won't be his fault if I do not glitter among the stars
of the fourth or fifth magnitude. I wish my weak head may
not grow giddy in the midst of all this gallantry and dissipation ; though as yet I can safely declare, I could gladly
give up all these tumultuous pleasures for country solitude,
and a happy retreat with those we love ; among whom my
dear Willis will always possess the first place in the breast
of her ever affectionate

London, May 31.   LYDIA MELFORD.

TO SIR WATKIN PHILLIPS, BART. OF JESUS COLLEGE, OXON.

DEAR PHILLIPS,

I send you this letter, franked by our old friend Barton; who is as much altered as it was possible for a man of his kidney to be—Instead of the careless indolent sloven we knew at Oxford, I found him a busy talkative politician; a petit-maitre in his dress, and a ceremonious courtier in his manners. He has not gall enough in his constitution, to be inflamed with the rancour of party, so as to deal in scurrilous invectives; but, since he obtained a place, he is become a warm partisan of the ministry; and sees every thing through such an exaggerating medium, as to me, who am happily of no party, is altogether incomprehensible. Without all doubt, the fumes of faction not only disturb the faculty of reason, but also pervert the organs of sense; and I would lay an hundred guineas to ten, that, if Barton on one side, and the most conscientious patriot in the opposition on the other, were to draw, upon honour, the picture of the k—— or m——, you and I, who are still uninfected and unbiassed, would find both painters equally distant from the truth. One thing, however, must be allowed, for the honour of Barton, he never breaks out into illiberal abuse, far less endeavours, by infamous calumnies, to blast the moral character of any individual on the other side.

Ever since we came hither, he has been remarkably assiduous in his attention to our family; an attention which, in a man of his indolence and avocations, I should have thought altogether odd, and even unnatural, had not I perceived that my sister Liddy has made some impression upon his heart. I can't say that I have any objection to his trying his fortune in this pursuit. If an opulent estate, and a great stock of good nature, are sufficient qualifications in a husband, to render the marriage state happy for life, she may be happy with Barton; but, I imagine there is something else required, to engage and secure the affection of a woman of sense and delicacy—something which nature has denied our friend;

Liddy seems to be of the same opinion. When he addresses himself to her in discourse, she seems to listen with reluctance, and industriously avoids all particular communication; but in proportion to her coyness, our aunt is coming. Mrs Tabitha goes more than half way to meet his advances; she mistakes, or affects to mistake, the meaning of his courtesy, which is rather formal and fulsome; she returns his compliments with hyperbolical interest; she persecutes him with her civilities at table; she appeals to him for ever in conversation; she sighs, and flirts, and ogles; and, by her hideous affectation and impertinence, drives the poor courtier to the very extremity of his complaisance: in short, she seems to have undertaken the siege of Barton's heart, and carries on her approaches in such a desperate manner, that I don't know whether he will not be obliged to capitulate. In the meantime, his aversion to this inamorata, struggling with his acquired affability, and his natural fear of giving offence, throws him into a kind of distress which is extremely ridiculous.

Two days ago, he persuaded my uncle and me to accompany him to S^t. James's, where he undertook to make us acquainted with the persons of all the great men in the kingdom; and, indeed, there was a great assemblage of distinguished characters, for it was a high festival at court. Our conductor performed his promise with great punctuality. He pointed out almost every individual of both sexes, and generally introduced them to our notice with a flourish of panegyric. Seeing the king approach,—' There comes,' said he, ' the most amiable sovereign that ever swayed the sceptre of England; the *deliciæ humani generis;* Augustus in patronizing merit, Titus Vespasian in generosity, Trajan in beneficence, and Marcus Aurelius in philosophy.' ' A very honest, kind-hearted gentleman,' added my uncle; ' he's too good for the times. A king of England should have a spice of the devil in his composition.' Barton then turning to the duke of C————, proceeded,—' You know the duke; that illustrious hero, who trod rebellion under his feet, and secured us in possession of every thing we ought to

hold dear as Englishmen and christians. Mark what an
eye, how penetrating, yet pacific! what dignity in his mein!
what humanity in his aspect! Even malice must own that
he is one of the greatest officers in Christendom.' 'I think
he be,' said Mr Bramble; 'but who are these young gentlemen that stand beside him?' 'Those!' cried our friend,
'those are his royal nephews; the princes of the blood.
Sweet young princes! the sacred pledges of the protestant
line; so spirited, so sensible, so princely—' 'Yes, very sensible! very spirited!' said my uncle, interrupting him; 'but
see the queen! ha, there's the queen! there's the queen! let
me see—let me see—Where are my glasses?—Ha! there's
meaning in that eye—there's sentiment—there's expression.
Well, Mr Barton, what figure do you call next?' The
next person he pointed out was the favourite *yearl*, who
stood solitary by one of the windows.—' Behold yon northern star,' said he, '*shorn of his beams*—' 'What! the Caledonian luminary, that lately blazed so bright in our hemisphere! Methinks at present it glimmers through a fog, like
Saturn without his ring, bleak, and dim, and distant—Ha
there's the other great phenomenon, the grand pensionary,
that weather-cock of patriotism that veers about in every
point of the political compass, and still feels the wind of
popularity in his tail. He, too, like a portentous comet,
has risen again above the court horizon; but how long he
will continue to ascend, it is not easy to foretel, considering
his great eccentricity—Who are those two satellites that attend his motions?' When Barton told him their names—
' To their character,' said Mr Bramble, ' I am no stranger.
One of them, without a drop of red blood in his veins, has
a cold intoxicating vapour in his head, and rancour enough
in his heart to inoculate and affect a whole nation. The
other is (I hear) intended for a share in the ad———n, and
the pensionary vouches for his being duly qualified. The
only instance I ever heard of his sagacity, was his deserting
his former patron, when he found him declining in power,
and in disgrace with the people. Without principle, talent, or intelligence, he is ungracious as a hog, greedy as a

vulture, and thievish as a jackdaw; but, it must be owned,
he is no hypocrite.   He pretends to no virtue, and takes no
pains to disguise his character.   His ministry will be attended with one advantage; no man will be disappointed by
his breach of promise, as no mortal ever trusted to his word.
I wonder how Lord ——— first discovered this happy genius, and for what purpose Lord ——— has now adopted
him: but one would think, that as amber has a power to
attract dirt, and straws, and chaff, a minister is endued with
the same kind of faculty, *to lick up every knave and blockhead in his way*—'   His eulogium was interrupted by the
arrival of the old duke of N——, who, squeezing into the
circle with a busy face of importance, thrust his head into
every countenance, as if he had been in search of somebody,
to whom he wanted to impart something of great consequence.   My uncle, who had been formerly known to him,
bowed as he passed; and the duke seeing himself saluted so
respectfully by a well-dressed person, was not slow in returning the courtesy.   He even came up, and, taking him
cordially by the hand,—' My dear friend, Mr A——,' said
he, ' I am rejoiced to see you—How long have you been
come from abroad?—How did you leave our good friends
the Dutch?—The king of Prussia don't think of another
war, ah?—He's a great king! a great conqueror! a very
great conqueror!   Your Alexanders and Hanibals, were nothing at all to him, sir—corporols! drummers! dross! mere
trash—damn'd trash heh?'   His grace being by this time
out of breath, my uncle took the opportunity to tell him he
had not been out of England, that his name was Bramble,
and that he had the honour to sit in the last parliament but
one of the late king, as representative for the borough of
Dymkymraig.   ' Odso,' cried the duke, ' I remember you
perfectly well, my dear Mr Bramble—You was always a
good and loyal subject—a staunch friend to administration
—I made your brother an Irish bishop—'   ' Pardon me,
my lord,' said the squire, ' I once had a brother, but he was
a captain in the army—'   ' Ha!' said his grace, ' he was so
—he was indeed!   But who was the bishop then? Bishop

Blackberry—Sure it was Bishop Blackberry—Perhaps some
relation of yours—' 'Very likely, my lord,' replied my
uncle, 'the blackberry is the fruit of the bramble—But I
believe the bishop is not a berry of our bush'— 'No more
he is, no more he is, ha, ha, ha!' exclaimed the duke,
'there you give me a scratch, good Mr Bramble, ha, ha,
ha!—Well, I shall be glad to see you at Lincoln's-inn-fields
—You know the way—Times are altered. Though I have
lost the power, I retain the inclination—Your very humble
servant, good Mr Blackberry.' So saying, he shoved to
another corner of the room. 'What a fine old gentleman!'
cried Mr Barton, 'what spirits! what a memory! he never
forgets an old friend.' 'He does me too much honour,' observed our squire, 'to rank me among the number. Whilst
I sat in parliament, I never voted with the ministry but three
times, when my conscience told me they were in the right:
however, if he still keeps levee, I will carry my nephew thither, that he may see, and learn to avoid the scene; for I
think an English gentleman never appears to such disadvantage as at the levee of a minister.—Of his grace I shall
say nothing at present, but that for thirty years he was the
constant and common butt of ridicule and execration. He
was generally laughed at as an ape in politics, whose office
and influence served only to render his folly the more notorious; and the opposition cursed him as the indefatigable
drudge of a first mover, who was justly styled and stigmatised as the father of corruption: but this ridiculous ape,
this venal drudge, no sooner lost the places he was so ill
qualified to fill, and unfurled the banners of faction, than
he was metamorphosed into a pattern of public virtue; the
very people who reviled him before, now extolled him to
the skies, as a wise experienced statesman, chief pillar of the
protestant succession, and corner-stone of English liberty.
I should be glad to know how Mr Barton reconciles these
contradictions, without obliging us to resign all title to the
privilege of common sense.' 'My dear sir,' answered Barton, 'I don't pretend to justify the extravagancies of the
multitude, who, I suppose, were as wild in their former cen-

sure as in their present praise; but I shall be very glad to
attend you on Thursday next to his grace's levee, where, I
am afraid, we shall not be crowded with company; for, you
know, there's a wide difference between his present office of
president of the council, and his former post of first lord
commissioner of the treasury.'

This communicative friend having announced all the remarkable characters of both sexes that appeared at court,
we resolved to adjourn, and retired.   At the foot of the stair-
case there was a crowd of lacqueys and chairmen, and in the
midst of them stood Humphry Clinker, exalted upon a stool,
with his hat in one hand, and a paper in the other, in the
act of holding forth to the people.   Before we could inquire
into the meaning of this exhibition, he perceived his master,
thrust the paper into his pocket, descended from his elevation, bolted through the crowd, and brought up the carriage
to the gate.

My uncle said nothing till we were seated, when, after
having looked at me earnestly for some time, he burst out
a-laughing, and asked me if I knew upon what subject Clinker was holding forth to the mob? ' If,' said he, ' the fellow
is turned mountebank, I must turn him out of my service,
otherwise he'll make Merry Andrews of us all.'   I observed,
that, in all probability, he had studied physic under his
master, who was a farrier.

At dinner the squire asked him if he had ever practised
physic? ' Yes, an' please your honour,' said he, ' among
brute beasts; but I never meddle with rational creatures.'
' I know not whether you rank in that class the audience
you was haranguing in the court at St James's, but I should
be glad to know what kind of powders you was distributing,
and whether you had a good sale.'   ' Sale, sir!' cried Clinker, ' I hope I shall never be base enough to sell 'for gold and
silver what freely comes of God's grace.   I distributed nothing, an' like your honour, but a word of advice to my
fellows in servitude and sin.'   ' Advice! concerning what!'
' Concerning profane swearing, an' please your honour; so
horrid and shocking, that it made my hair stand on end.'

'Nay, if thou canst cure them of that disease, I shall think thee a wonderful doctor indeed.' 'Why not cure them, my good master? the hearts of these poor people are not so stubborn as your honour seems to think. Make them first sensible that you have nothing in view but their good, then they will listen with patience, and easily be convinced of the sin and folly of a practice that affords neither profit nor pleasure.' At this remark our uncle changed colour, and looked round the company, conscious that *his own withers were not altogether unwrung*. 'But, Clinker,' said he, 'if you should have eloquence enough to persuade the vulgar to resign those tropes and figures of rhetoric, there will be little or nothing left to distinguish their conversation from that of their betters.' 'But then, your honour knows, their conversation will be void of offence; and, at the day of judgment, there will be no distinction of persons.'

Humphry going down stairs to fetch up a bottle of wine, my uncle congratulated his sister upon having such a reformer in the family; when Mrs Tabitha declared he was a sober civilized fellow, very respectful, and very industrious; and she believed, a good christian into the bargain. One would think Clinker must really have some very extraordinary talent to ingratiate himself in this manner with a virago of her character, so fortified against him with prejudice and resentment; but the truth is, since the adventure of Salthill, Mrs Tabby seems to be entirely changed. She has left off scolding the servants, an exercise which was grown habitual, and even seemed necessary to her constitution, and is become so indifferent to Chowder, as to part with him in a present to Lady Griskin, who proposes to bring the breed of him into fashion. Her ladyship is the widow of Sir Timothy Griskin, a distant relation of our family. She enjoys a jointure of five hundred pounds a-year, and makes shift to spend three times that sum. Her character, before marriage, was a little equivocal, but at present she lives in the *bon ton*, keeps card-tables, gives private suppers to select friends, and is visited by persons of the first fashion.—She has been remarkably civil to us all, and cultivates my uncle with the

most particular regard; but the more she stroaks him, the
more his bristles seem to rise.—To her compliments he makes
very laconic and dry returns.—T'other day she sent us a
pottle of fine strawberries, which he did not receive without
signs of disgust, muttering from the Æneid, *Timeo Danaos
et dona ferentes.*—She has twice called for Liddy, of a forenoon, to take an airing in the coach; but Mrs Tabby was
always so alert (I suppose by his direction), that she never
could have the niece without the aunt's company.—I have
endeavoured to sound Squaretoes on this subject, but he
carefully avoids all explanation.

I have now, dear Phillips, filled a whole sheet; and, if
you have read it to an end, I dare say you are as tired as
your humble servant,

London, June 2.   J. MELFORD.

TO DR LEWIS.

YES, Doctor, I have seen the British museum; which is a
noble collection, and even stupendous, if we consider it was
made by a private man, a physician, who was obliged to
make his own fortune at the same time; but, great as the
collection is, it would appear more striking if it was arranged
in one spacious saloon, instead of being divided into different apartments, which it does not entirely fill. I could wish
the series of medals was connected, and the whole of the
animal, vegetable, and mineral kingdoms completed, by
adding to each, at the public expense, those articles that
are wanting. It would likewise be a great improvement,
with respect to the library, if the deficiencies were made up
by purchasing all the books of character that are not to be
found already in the collection. They might be classed in
centuries, according to the dates of their publication, and
catalogues printed of them and the manuscripts, for the information of those who want to consult or compile from such
authorities. I could also wish, for the honour of the nation,
that there was a complete apparatus for a course of mathematics, mechanics, and experimental philosophy; and a

good salary settled upon an able professor, who should give
regular lectures on these subjects.

But this is all idle speculation, which will never be reduced to practice.—Considering the temper of the times, it
is a wonder to see any institution whatsoever established for
the benefit of the public. The spirit of party is risen to a
kind of phrenzy, unknown to former ages, or rather degener-
ated to a total extinction of honesty and candour.—You
know I have observed, for some time, that the public papers are become the infamous vehicles of the most cruel and
perfidious defamation.—Every rancorous knave, every desperate incendiary, that can afford to spend half a crown or
three shillings, may skulk behind the press of a newsmonger,
and have a stab at the first character in the kingdom, without running the least hazard of detection or punishment.

I have made acquaintance with a Mr Barton, whom Jery
knew at Oxford; a good sort of a man, though most ridi-
culously warped in his political principles; but his partiality
is the less offensive, as it never appears in the style of scurrility and abuse. He is a member of parliament, and a retainer to the court; and his whole conversation turns upon
the virtues and perfections of the ministers who are his patrons. T'other day when he was bedaubing one of those
worthies with the most fulsome praise, I told him I had seen
the same nobleman characterized very differently in one of
the daily papers; indeed, so stigmatised, that if one half of
what was said of him was true, he must be not only unfit to
rule, but even unfit to live; that those impeachments had
been repeated again and again, with the addition of fresh
matter; and that, as he had taken no steps towards his own
vindication, I began to think there was some foundation for
the charge. 'And pray, sir,' said Mr Barton, 'what
steps would you have him take?—Suppose you should prosecute the publisher, who screens the anonymous accuser,
and bring him to the pillory for a libel; this is so far from
being counted a punishment *in terrorem*, that it will probably make his fortune. The multitude immediately take him
into their protection, as a martyr to the cause of defamation,

which, they have always espoused.—They pay his fine, they
contribute to the increase of his stock, his shop is crowded
with customers, and the sale of his paper rises in proportion
to the scandal it contains. All this time the prosecutor is
inveighed against as a tyrant and oppressor, for having
chosen to proceed by the way of information, which is deemed a grievance: but if he lays an action for damages, he
must prove the damage; and I leave you to judge, whether
a gentleman's character may not be brought into contempt,
and all his views in life blasted by calumny, without his
being able to specify the particulars of the damage he has
sustained.

‘ This spirit of defamation is a kind of heresy, that thrives
under persecution. *The liberty of the press*, is a term of
great efficacy; and, like that of the *Protestant religion*, has
often served the purposes of sedition.—A minister, therefore, must arm himself with patience, and bear those attacks
without repining.—Whatever mischief they may do in other
respects, they certainly contribute in one particular, to the
advantage of government; for those defamatory articles have
multiplied papers in such a manner, and augmented their
sale to such a degree, that the duty upon stamps and adver-
tisements has made a very considerable addition to the revenue.' Certain it is, a gentleman's honour is a very delicate
subject to be handled by a jury, composed of men who cannot be supposed remarkable either for sentiment or impartiality.—In such a case, indeed, the defendant is tried, not
only by his peers, but also by his party; and I really think,
that, of all patriots, he is the most resolute, who exposes
himself to such detraction for the sake of his country.—If,
from the ignorance or partiality of juries, a gentleman can
have no redress from law for being defamed in a pamphlet
or newspaper, I know but one other method of proceeding
against the publisher, which is attended with some risk,
but has been practised successfully, more than once, in my
remembrance.—A regiment of horse was represented, in one
of the newspapers, as having misbehaved at Dettingen; a
captain of that regiment broke the publisher's bones, telling

him, at the same time, if he went to law, he should certainly have the like salutation from every officer of the corps.. Governor ———— took the same satisfaction on the ribs of an author, who traduced him by name in a periodical paper.—I know a low fellow of the same class, who, being turned out of Venice for his impudence and scurrility, retired to Lugano, a town of the Grisons (a free people, God wot), where he found a printing-press, from whence he squirted his filth at some respectable characters in the republic which he had been obliged to abandon. Some of these, finding him out of the reach of legal chastisement, employed certain useful instruments, such as may be found in all countries, to give him the bastinado; which, being repeated more than once, effectually stopped the current of his abuse.

As for the liberty of the press, like every other privilege, it must be restrained within certain bounds; for if it is carried to a breach of law, religion, and charity, it becomes one of the greatest evils that every annoyed the community. If the lowest ruffian may stab your good name with impunity in England, will you be so uncandid as to exclaim against Italy for the practice of common assassination? To what purpose is our property secured, if our moral character is left defenceless?—People thus baited, grow desperate; and the despair of being able to preserve one's character untainted by such vermin, produces a total neglect of fame; so that one of the chief incitements to the practice of virtue is effectually destroyed.

Mr Barton's last consideration, respecting the stamp-duty, is equally wise and laudable with another maxim which has been long adopted by our financiers, namely, to connive at drunkenness, riot, and dissipation, because they enhance the receipt of the excise; not reflecting, that, in providing this temporary convenience, they are destroying the morals, health, and industry, of the people.—Notwithstanding my contempt for those who flatter a minister, I think there is something still more despicable in flattering a mob.—When I see a man of birth, education, and fortune, put himself

on a level with the dregs of the people, mingle with low mechanics, feed with them at the same board, and drink with
them in the same cup, flatter their prejudices, harangue in
praise of their virtues, expose themselves to the belchings of
their beer, the fumes of their tobacco, the grossness of their
familiarity, and the impertinence of their conversation, I
cannot help despising him, as a man guilty of the vilest
prostitution, in order to effect a purpose equally selfish and
illiberal.

I should renounce politics the more willingly if I could
find other topics of conversation discussed with more modesty and candour : but the demon of party seems to have
usurped every department of life.   Even the world of literature and taste is divided into the most virulent factions, which
revile, decry, and traduce the works of one another.   Yesterday I went to return an afternoon's visit to a gentleman of
my acquaintance, at whose house I found one of the authors of the present age, who has written with some success.
As I had read one or two of his performances, which gave
me pleasure, I was glad of this opportunity to know his person : but his discourse and deportment destroyed all the impressions which his writings had made in his favour.   He
took upon him to decide dogmatically upon every subject,
without deigning to shew the least cause for his differing
from the general opinions of mankind, as if it had been our
duty to acquiesce in the *ipse dixit* of this new Pythagoras.
He rejudged the characters of all the principal authors, who
had died within a century of the present time ; and in this
revision, paid no sort of regard to the reputation they had
acquired—Milton was harsh and prosaic ; Dryden, languid
and verbose ; Butler and Swift, without humour ; Congreve,
without wit ; and Pope, destitute of any sort of poetical merit.
—As for his contemporaries, he could not bear to hear one of
them mentioned with any degree of applause : they were all
dunces, pedants, plagiaries, quacks, and impostors ; and you
could not name a single performance, but what was tame,
stupid, and insipid.   It must be owned, that this writer had
nothing to charge his conscience with on the side of flattery ;

for, I understand, he was never known to praise one line
that was written even by those with whom he lived in terms
of good fellowship.   This arrogance and presumption, in
depreciating authors, for whose reputation the company may
be interested, is such an insult upon the understanding, as I
could not bear without wincing.

I desired to know his reasons for decrying some works
which had afforded me uncommon pleasure ; and as demonstration did not seem to be his talent, I dissented from
his opinion with great freedom.   Having been spoiled by
the deference and humility of his hearers, he did not bear
contradiction with much temper ; and the dispute might
have grown warm, had it not been interrupted by the entrance of a rival bard, at whose appearance he always quits
the place.——They are of different cabals, and have been at
open war these twenty years.——If the other was dogmatical,
this genius was declamatory ; he did not discourse, but
harangue ; and his orations were equally tedious and turgid.
He too pronounced *ex cathedra* upon the characters of his
contemporaries ; and though he scruples not to deal out praise
even lavishly, to the lowest reptile in Grub street, who
will either flatter him in private, or mount the public rostrum
as his panegyrist, he damns all the other writers of the age
with the utmost insolence and rancour.——One is a blunderbuss, as being a native of Ireland ; another a half-starved
louse of literature, from the banks of the Tweed ; a third,
an ass, because he enjoys a pension from government ; a
fourth the very angel of dulness, because he succeeded in
a species of writing in which this Aristarchus had failed ; a
fifth, who presumed to make strictures upon one of his performances, he holds as a bug in criticism, whose stench is
more offensive than his sting.——In short, except himself and
his myrmidons, there is not a man of learning or genius in
the three kingdoms.   As for the success of those who have
written without the pale of this confederacy, he imputes it
entirely to want of taste in the public, not considering, that
to the approbation of that very tasteless public, he himself
owes all the consequence he has in life.

Those originals are not fit for conversation.   If they would maintain the advantage they have gained by their writing, they should never appear but upon paper.   For my part, I am shocked to find a man have sublime ideas in his head, and nothing but illiberal sentiments in his heart.—The human soul will be generally found most defective in the article of candour.—I am inclined to think, no mind was ever wholly exempt from envy; which, perhaps, may have been implanted, as an instinct essential to our nature.   I am afraid we sometimes palliate this vice, under the spacious name of emulation.   I have known a person remarkably generous, humane, moderate, and apparently self-denying, who could not hear even a friend commended, without betraying marks of uneasiness; as if that commendation had implied an odious comparison to his prejudice, and every wreath of praise added to the other's character, was a garland plucked from his own temples.   This is a malignant species of jealousy, of which I stand acquitted in my own conscience.—Whether it is a vice, or an infirmity, I leave you to inquire.

There is another point, which I would much rather see determined; whether the world was always as contemptible as it appears to me at present?—If the morals of mankind have not contracted an extraordinary degree of depravity within these thirty years, then must I be infected with the common vice of old men, *difficilis, querulus, laudator temporis acti;* or, which is more probable, the impetuous pursuits and avocations of youth have formerly hindered me from observing those rotten parts of human nature, which now appear so offensively to my observation.

We have been at court and 'change, and every where; and every where we find food for spleen, and subject for ridicule.—My new servant, Humprey Clinker, turns out a great original; and Tabby is a changed creature—she has parted with Chowder; and does nothing but smile, like Malvolio in the play.—I'll be hanged if she is not acting a part which is not natural to her disposition, for some purpose which I have not yet discovered.

With respect to the characters of mankind, my curiosity is quite satisfied : I have done with the science of men, and must now endeavour to amuse myself with the novelty of *things.* I am, at present, by a violent effort of the mind, forced from my natural bias ; but this power ceasing to act, I shall return to my solitude with double velocity. Every thing I see, and hear, and feel, in the great reservoir of folly, knavery, and sophistication, contributes to enhance the value of a country life, in the sentiments of yours, al_ ways,

London, June 2. MATT. BRAMBLE.

TO MRS MARY JONES, AT BRAMBLETONHALL.

DEAR MOLLY JONES,

Lady Griskin's botler, Mr Crumb, having got Squire Bar-ton to frank me a kiver, I would not neglect to let you know how it is with me, and the rest of the family.

I could not rite by John Thomas, for because he went sway in a huff, at a minute's warning. He and Chowder could not agree, and so they fitt upon the road, and Chow-der bit his thumb, and he swore he would do him a mischief, and he spoke saucy to mistress, whereby the squire turned him off in gudgeon ; and by God's providence we picked up another footman, called Umphry Klinker ; a good sole as ever broke bread ; which shews, that a scalded cat may prove a good mouser ; and a hound be stanch, thof he has got narro hare on his buttocks ; but the proudest nose may be bro't baor to the grindstone by sickness and mis-fortunes.

O Molly ! what shall I say of London ! All the towns that ever I beheld in my born days are no more than Welch bar-rows and crumblecks to this wonderful sitty ! Even Bath it-self is but a fillitch, in the naam of God.—One would think there's no end of the streets, but the lands end. Then there's such a power of people, going hurry skurry ! Such a racket of coxes ! Such a noise and hali-balloo ! So many strange sites to be seen ! O gracious ! my poor Welch brain has been spinning like a top ever since I came hither! And I have seen the park, and the paleass of Saint Gimses, and the king's and the queen's magisterial pursing, and the sweet young princess, and the hillyfents, and pye blad ass, and all the rest of the royal family.

Last week I went with mistress to the tower, to see the crowns and wild beastis; and there was a monstracious lion, with teeth half a quarter long; and a gentleman bid me not go near him, if I wasn't a maid; being as how he would roar, and tear, and play the dickens.—Now I had no mind to go near him; for I cannot abide such dangerous honeymils, not I—But mistress would go; and the beast kept such a roaring and bouncing, that I tho't he would a broke his cage, and devoured us all; and the gentleman tittered forsooth; but I'll go to death upon it, I will, that my lady is as good a firchen as the child unborn; and therefore either the gentleman told a phib, or the lion oft to be set in the stocks for bearing false witness again his neighbour; for the commandment sayeth, *Thou shalt not bear false witness again thy neighbour.*

I was afterwards of a party at Sadler's wells, where I saw such tumbling and dancing upon ropes and wires, that I was frightened, and ready to go into a fit—I thought it was all enchantment; and believing myself bewitched, began for to cry.—You knows as how the witches in Wales fly upon broomsticks; but here was flying without any broomstick, or thing in the varsal world, and firing of pistols in the air, and blowing of trumpets, and swinging, and rolling of wheel-barrows upon a wire (God bliss us!) no thicker than a sewing thread; that, to be sure, they must deal with the devil.—A fine gentleman with a pig's tail, and a golden sord by his side, came to comfit me, and offered for to treat me with a pint of wind; but I would not stay; and so in going through the dark passage, he began to show his cloven futt, and went for to be rude; my fellow-servant Umphry Klinker bid him to be sivil, and he gave the young man a dowse in the chops; but, i'fackins, Mr Klinker wa'n't long in his debt—with a good oaken sapling he dusted his doublet, for all his golden cheese toaster; and, sipping me under his arm, carried me huom, I nose not how, being I was in such a flustration.—But, thank God! I'm now vaned from all such vanities; for what are all those rarities and vagaries to the glories that shall be revealed hereafter! O Molly! let not your poor heart be puffed up with vanity.

I had almost forgot to tell you, that I have had my hair cut and pippered, and singed, and bolstered, and buckled in the newest fashion, by a French freezer—*Parley vow Francey—Vee Madmansell*—I now carries my head higher than arrow private gentlewoman of Vales.—Last night, coming huom from the meeting, I was taken by lamp light for an iminent poulterer's daughter, a great beauty—But as I was saying, this is all vanity and vexation of spirit.—— The pleasures of London are no better than sower whey and stale cider, when compared to the joys of the New Gerusalem.

Dear Mary Jones! An' please God, when I return I'll bring you a new cap, with a turky-shell coom, and a pyehouse sermon, that was preached in the tabernacle; and I pray of all love, you will mind your vriting and your spelling; for, craving your pardon, Molly, it made me suet to disseyffer your last scrabble, which was delivered by the hind at Bath—O, voman! voman! if thou hadst but the least consumption of what pleasure we scullers have, when we can cunster the crabbidst buck off hand, and spell the ethnitch vords, without looking at the primmer. As for Mr Klinker, he is qualified to be clerk to a parish—But I'll say no more—Remember me to Saul—poor sole! it goes to my hart to think she don't yet know her letters.—But all in God's good time.—It shall go hard, but I will bring her the ABC in gingerbread; and that, you nose, will be learning to her taste.

Mistress says, we are going a long journey to the north; but go where we will, I shall ever be, dear Mary Jones, yours with true infection,

London, June 3.   WIN. JENKINS.

TO SIR WATKIN PHILLIPS, BART. OF JESUS COLLEGE, OXON.—

DEAR WAT,

I MENTIONED in my last, my uncle's design of going to the duke of N———'s levee, which design has been executed accordingly. His grace has been so long accustomed to this kind of homage, that, though the place he now fills does not imply the tenth part of the influence which he exerted in his former office, he has given his friends to understand, that they cannot oblige him in any thing more than in contributing to support the shadow of that power which he no longer retains in substance; and therefore he has still public days, on which they appear at his levee.

My uncle and I went thither with Mr Barton, who, being one of the duke's adherents, undertook to be our introducer. The room was pretty well filled with people, in a great variety of dress; but there was no more than one gown and cassoc, though I am told his grace had, while he was minister, preferred almost every individual that now filled the bench of bishops in the house of lords; but, in all probability, the gratitude of the clergy is like their charity, which shuns the light. Mr Barton was immediately accosted by a person well stricken in years, tall and raw-boned, with a hook nose, and an arch leer, that indicated at least as much cunning as sagacity. Our conductor saluted him by the name of Captain C———, and afterwards informed us he was a man of shrewd parts, whom the government occasionally employed in secret services; but I have had the history of him more at large from another quarter. He had been, many years ago, concerned in fraudulent practices, as a merchant in France; and, being convicted of some of them, was sent to the galleys, from whence he was delivered, by the interest of the late duke of Ormond, to whom he had recommended himself, in a letter, as his namesake and relation. He was, in the sequel, employed by our ministry, as a spy; and, in the war of 1740, traversed all Spain, as well as France, in the disguise of a capuchin, at the extreme hazard of his life, inasmuch as the court of Madrid had actually got scent of him, and given

orders to apprehend him at S^t. Sebastians, from whence he
had fortunately retired but a few hours before the order arrived.   This and other hair-breadth 'scapes he pleaded so
effectually as a merit with the English ministry, that they
allowed him a comfortable pension, which he now enjoys in
his old age.   He has still access to all the ministers, and is
said to be consulted by them on many subjects, as a man of
uncommon understanding, and great experience.   He is, in
fact, a fellow of some parts, and invincible assurance; and,
in his discourse, he assumes such an air of self-sufficiency, as
may very well impose upon some of the shallow politicians
who now labour at the helm of administration.   But, if he is
not belied, this is not the only imposture of which he is guilty.
—They say, he is at bottom not only a Roman catholic, but
really a priest; and, while he pretends to disclose to our state-
pilots all the springs that move the cabinet of Versailles, he
is actually picking up intelligence for the service of the
French minister.—Be that as it may, Captain C——
entered into conversation with us in the most familiar
manner, and treated the duke's character without any
ceremony.—' This wise-acre,' said he, ' is still a-bed; and,
I think, the best thing he can do is to sleep on till Christmas;
for, when he gets up, he does nothing but expose his own
folly.   Since Grenville was turned out, there has been no
minister in this nation worth the meal that whitened his periwig.—They are so ignorant, they scarce know a crab from a
cauliflower; and then they are such dunces, that there's no
making them comprehend the plainest proposition.   In the
beginning of the war, this poor half-witted creature told me,
in a great fright, that thirty thousand French had marched
from Acadia to Cape Breton.—' Where did they find transports,' said I ?   ' Transports,' said he!   ' I tell you they
marched by land—'   ' By land, to the island of Cape Breton !'   ' What ! is Cape Breton an island !'   ' Certainly.'
' Hah ! are you sure of that ?'   When I pointed it out on the
map, he examined it earnestly with his spectacles; then taking me in his arms, ' My dear C——,' cried he! ' you always bring us good news—Egad ! I'll go directly, and tell
the king that Cape Breton is an island—'

He seemed disposed to entertain us with more anecdotes of
this nature, at the expense of his grace, when he was interrupted by the arrival of the Algerine ambassador, a venerable Turk, with a long white beard, attended by his dragoman, or interpreter, and another officer of his household,
who had got no stockings to his legs.   Captain C————
immediately spoke with an air of authority to a servant in
waiting, bidding him go and tell the duke to rise, as there
was a great deal of company come, and, among others, the
ambassador from Algiers.—Then, turning to us, ' This poor
Turk,' said he, ' notwithstanding his grey beard, is a green
horn—He has been several years resident at London, and still
is ignorant of our political revolutions.   This visit is intended for the prime minister of England; but you'll see how
this wise duke will receive it as a mark of attachment to his
own person.'   Certain it is, the duke seemed eager to acknowledge the compliment—A door opening, he suddenly
bolted out, with a shaving cloth under his chin, his face
frothed up to the eyes with soap lather; and, running up to
the ambassador, grinned hideous in his face—' My dear Ma-
homet,' said he, ' God love your long beard; I hope the
day will make you a horse-tail at the next promotion, ha, ha,
ha!—Have but a moment's patience, and I'll send to you in
a twinkling.   So saying, he retreated into his den, leaving
the Turk in some confusion.   After a short pause, however,
he said somthing to his interpreter, the meaning of which I
had great curiosity to know, as he turned up his eyes while
he spoke, expressing astonishment mixed with devotion.—
We were gratified by means of the communicative Captain
C————, who conversed with the dragoman as an old acquaintance.   Ibrahim, the ambassador, who had mistaken
his grace for the minister's fool, was no sooner undeceived by
the interpreter, than he exclaimed to this effect—' Holy prophet! I don't wonder that this nation prospers, seeing it is
governed by the counsel of idiots; a species of men, whom
all good mussulmen revere as the organs of immediate inspiration!'   Ibrahim was favoured with a particular audience of
short duration; after which the duke conducted him to the

door, and then returned to diffuse his gracious looks among the crowd of his worshippers.

As Mr Barton advanced to present me to his grace, it was my fortune to attract his notice before I was announced. —He forthwith met me more than half way, and, seizing me by the hand, ' My dear Sir Francis!' cried he, ' this is so kind—I vow to Gad! I am so obliged—Such attention to a poor broken minister—Well—Pray when does your excellency set sail ?—For God's sake have a care of your health, and eat stewed prunes in the passage—Next to your own precious health, pray, my dear excellency, take care of the five nations, our good friends the five nations—the Torryrories, the Maccolmacks, the Out-o'the-ways, the Crickets, and the Kickshaws—Let 'em have plenty of blankets, and stinkubus, and vampum ; and your excellency won't fail to scour the kettle, and boil the chain, and bury the tree, and plant the hatchet— Ha, ha, ha!' When he had uttered this rhapsody, with his usual precipitation, Mr Barton gave him to understand, that I was neither Sir Francis, nor St. Francis ; but simply Mr Melford, nephew to Mr Bramble ; who, stepping forward, made his bow at the same time. ' Odso! no more it is Sir Francis,' said this wise statesman—' Mr Melford, I am glad to see you—I sent you an engineer to fortify your dock— Mr Bramble—your servant, Mr Bramble—How d'ye, good Mr Bramble! Your nephew is a pretty young fellow—Faith and troth a very pretty fellow? His father is my old friend. —How does he hold it? Still troubled with that damn'd disorder, ha ?' ' No my lord,' replied my uncle, ' all his troubles are over—He has been dead these fifteen years.' ' Dead! how—Yes, faith! now I remember : he is dead, sure enough. Well, and how—does the young gentleman stand for Haverfordwest ? or—a—what d'ye—My dear Mr Milfordhaven, I'll do you all the service in my power—I hope I have some credit left.' My uncle then gave him to understand that I was still a minor ; and that we had no intention to trouble him at present for any favour whatsoever—' I came hither with my nephew,' added he, ' to pay our respects to your grace ; and I may venture to say, that his views and mine

are at least as disinterested as those of any individual in this
assembly.' 'My dear Mr Brambleberry! you do me infinite honour—I shall always rejoice to see you and your
hopeful nephew, Mr Milfordhaven—My credit, such as it
is, you may command—I wish we had more friends of your
kidney.'

Then turning to Captain C——, 'Ha, C——!' said he,
'what news, C——? How does the world wag? ha!' 'The
world wags much after the old fashion, my lord,' answered
the captain: 'the politicians of London and Westminster
have begun again to wag their tongues against your grace;
and your short-lived popularity wags like a feather, which
the next puff of anti-ministerial calumny will blow away—'
'A pack of rascals,' cried the duke—'tories, jacobites, rebels; one half of them would wag their heels at Tyburn, if
they had their deserts.' So saying, he wheeled about; and,
going round the levee, spoke to every individual, with
the most courteous familiarity; but he scarce ever opened
his mouth, without making some blunder, in relation to the
person or business of the party with whom he conversed; so
that he really looked like a comedian hired to burlesque the
character of a minister. At length a person of a very pre-
possessing appearance coming in, his grace ran up, and
hugging him in his arms, with the appellation of 'My dear
Ch——s!' led him forthwith into an inner apartment, or
sanctum sanctorum of this political temple. 'That,' said
Captain C——, 'is my friend C— T—, almost the only
man of parts who has any concern in the present administration—Indeed, he would have no concern at all in the matter,
if the ministry did not find it absolutely necessary to make
use of his talents upon some particular occasions—As for the
common business of the nation, it is carried on in a constant
routine by the clerks of the different offices, otherwise the
wheels of government would be wholly stopt amidst the
abrupt succession of ministers, every one more ignorant than
his predecessor—I am thinking what a fine hovel we should
be in, if all the clerks of the treasury, of the secretaries, the
war-office, and the admiralty, should take it in their heads

to throw up their places, in imitation of the great pensioner.
But, to return to C— T—; he certainly knows more than all
the ministry and all the opposition, if their heads were laid
together, and talks like an angel on a vast variety of subjects.—He would really be a great man, if he had any consistency or stability of character.—Then, it must be owned,
he wants courage; otherwise he would never allow himself
to be cowed by the great political bully, for whose understanding he has justly a very great contempt. I have seen
him as much afraid of that overbearing Hector, as ever
school-boy was of his pedagogue; and yet this Hector, I
shrewdly suspect, is no more than a craven at bottom. Besides this defect, C— has 'another, which he is at too little
pains to hide—There's no faith to be given to his assertions,
and no trust to be put in his promises.—However, to give the
devil his due, he's very good-natured, and even friendly,
when close urged in the way of solicitation—As for principle, that's out of question. In a word, he is a wit and
an orator, extremely entertaining; and he shines very often
at the expense even of those ministers to whom he is a retainer. This is a mark of great imprudence, by which he
has made them all his enemies, whatever face they may put
upon the matter; and, sooner or later, he'll have cause to
wish he had been able to keep his own counsel—I have several times cautioned him on this subject; but 'tis all preaching to the desert—His vanity runs away with his discretion.'
I could not help thinking the captain himself might have
been the better for some hints of the same nature. His panegyric, excluding principle and veracity, puts me in mind
of a contest I once overheard, in the way of altercation, betwixt two apple-women, in Spring garden.—One of these
viragoes having hinted something to the prejudice of the
other's moral character, her antagonist, setting her hands in
her sides, replied, ' Speak out, hussey—I scorn your malice
—I own I'm both a whore and a thief; and what more have
you to say ?—Damn you, what more have you to say ? bating
that, which all the world knows, I challenge you to say black
is the white of my eye.' We did not wait for Mr T——'s

coming forth; but, after Captain C——— had characterized
all the originals in waiting, we adjourned to a coffee-house,
where we had buttered muffins and tea to breakfast, the said
captain still favouring us with his company—Nay, my uncle
was so diverted with his anecdotes, that he asked him to dinner, and treated him with a fine turbot, to which he did
ample justice. That same evening I spent at the tavern with
some friends, one of whom let me into C———'s character,
which Mr Bramble no sooner understood, than he expressed
some concern for the connection he had made, and resolved
to disengage himself from it, without ceremony.

We are become members of the society for the encouragement of the arts, and have assisted at some of their deliberations, which were conducted with equal spirit and sagacity.—My uncle is extremely fond of the institution, which
will certainly be productive of great advantages to the public, if, from its democratical form, it does not degenerate
into cabal and corruption.—You are already acquainted
with his aversion to the influence of the multitude, which
he affirms, is incompatible with excellence, and subversive
of order.—Indeed his detestation of the mob has been heightened by fear, ever since he fainted in the room at Bath: and
this apprehension has prevented him from going to the little theatre in the Hay-market, and other places of entertainment, to which, however, I have had the honour to attend the ladies.

It grates old squaretoes to reflect, that it is not in his
power to enjoy even the most elegant diversions of the capital, without the participation of the vulgar; for they now
thrust themselves into all assemblies, from a ridotto at S^t.
James's, to a hop at Rotherhithe.

I have lately seen our old acquaintance Dick Ivy, who
we imagined had died of dram-drinking; but he is lately
emerged from the Fleet, by means of a pamphlet which he
wrote and published against the government with some success. The sale of this performance enabled him to appear
in clean linen, and he is now going about soliciting subscrip-
tions for his poems; but his breeches are not yet in the most
decent order.

Dick certainly deserves some countenance for his intrepidity and perseverance—It is not in the power of disappointment, nor even of damnation, to drive him to despair. —After some unsuccessful essays in the way of poetry, he commenced brandy-merchant, and I believe his whole stock ran out through his own bowels; then he consorted with a milk-woman, who kept a cellar in Petty France: but he could not make his quarters good; he was dislodged and driven up stairs into the kennel by a corporal in the second regiment of foot-guards.—He was afterwards the laureat of Blackfriars, from whence there was a natural transition to the Fleet. As he had formerly miscarried in panegyric, he now turned his thoughts to satire, and really seems to have some talent for abuse. If he can hold out till the meeting of parliament, and be prepared for another charge in all probability Dick will mount the pillory, or obtain a pension, in either of which events his fortune will be made. Meanwhile he has acquired some degree of consideration with the respectable writers of the age; and as I have subscribed for his works, he did me the favour t'other night to introduce me to a society of those geniuses; but I found them exceedingly formal and reserved.—They seemed afraid, and jealous of one another, and sat in a state of mutual repulsion, like so many particles of vapour, each surrounded by its own electrified atmosphere. Dick, who has more vivacity than judgment, tried more than once to enliven the conversation; sometimes making an effort at wit, sometimes letting off a pun, and sometimes discharging a conundrum; nay, at length he started a dispute upon the hacknied comparison betwixt blank verse and rhyme, and the professors opened with great clamour; but, instead of keeping to the subject, they launched out into tedious dissertations on the poetry of the ancients; and one of them, who had been a schoolmaster, displayed his whole knowledge of prosody, gleaned from Disputer and Ruddiman. At last, I ventured to say, I did not see how the subject in question could be at all elucidated by the practice of the ancients, who certainly had neither blank verse nor rhyme in their

poems, which were measured by feet, whereas ours are reckoned by the number of syllables. This remark seemed to
give umbrage to the pedant, who forthwith involved himself in a cloud of Greek and Latin quotations, which nobody attempted to dispel.—A confused hum of insipid observations and comments ensued; and, upon the whole,
I never passed a duller evening in my life.—Yet, without all doubt, some of them were men of learning, wit,
and ingenuity. As they are afraid of making free with one
another, they. should bring each his butt, or whet-stone,
along with him, for the entertainment of the company.—
My uncle says he never desires to meet with more than one
wit at a time.—One wit, like a knuckle of ham in soup,
gives a zest and flavour to the dish; but more than one
serves only to spoil the pottage.—And now I'm afraid I
have given you an unconscionable mess without any flavour
at all: for which, I suppose, you will bestow your benedictions upon your friend and servant,

London, June 5.   J. MELFORD.

TO DR LEWIS.

DEAR LEWIS,

Your fable of the monkey and the pig is what the Italians
call *ben trovata*: but I shall not repeat it to my apothecary,
who is a proud Scotsman, very thin-skinned, and for
aught I know, may have his degree in his pocket.—A right
Scotsman has always two strings 'to his bow, and is *in
utrumque paratus.*—Certain it is I have not 'scaped a
scouring; but, I believe, by means of that scouring, I have
'scaped something worse, perhaps a tedious fit of the gout
or rheumatism; for my appetite began to flag, and I had
certain croakings in the bowels which boded me no good.—
Nay, I am not yet quite free of these remembrancers, which
warn me to be gone from this centre of infection.

What temptation can a man of my turn and temperament have, to live in a place where every corner teems with
fresh objects of detestation and disgust? What kind of
taste and organs must those people have, who really prefer

the adulterated enjoyments of the town to the genuine pleasures of a country retreat ?—Most people, I know, are originally seduced by vanity, ambition, and childish curiosity;
which cannot be gratified, but in the *busy haunts of men*:
but in the course of this gratification, their very organs of
sense are perverted, and they become habitually lost to
every relish of what is genuine and excellent in its own nature.

Shall I state the difference between my town grievances
and my country comforts?—At Brambletonhall, I have elbow room within doors, and breathe a clear, elastic, salutary,
air.—I enjoy refreshing sleep, which is never disturbed by
horrid noise, nor interrupted, but in a morning, by the
sweet twitter of the martlet at my window.—I drink the virgin lymph, pure and crystalline as it gushes from the rock,
or the sparkling beverage, home-brewed from malt of my
own making; or I indulge with cyder, which my own
orchard affords, or with claret of the best growth, imported
for my own use, by a correspondent on whose integrity I
can depend; my bread is sweet and nourishing, made from
my own wheat, ground in my own mill, and baked in
my own oven; my table is, in a great measure, furnished
from my own ground; my five-year old mutton, fed on
the fragrant herbage of the mountains, that might vie with
venison in juice and flavour; my delicious veal, fattened
with nothing but the mother's milk, that fills the dish
with gravy; my poultry from the barn-door, that never
knew confinement but when they were at roost; my rabbits panting from the warren; my game fresh from the
moors; my trout and salmon struggling from the stream;
oysters from their native banks; and herrings, with other
sea-fish, I can eat in four hours after they are taken.—
My sallads, roots, and pot-herbs, my own garden yields
in plenty and perfection, the produce of the natural soil,
prepared by moderate cultivation. The same soil affords
all the different fruits which England may call her own,
so that my dessert is every day fresh gathered from the
tree; my dairy flows with nectareous tides of milk and

cream, from whence we derive abundance of excellent butter, curds, and cheese ; and the refuse fattens my pigs that
are destined for hams and bacon.—I go to bed betimes, and
rise with the sun.—I make shift to pass the hours without
weariness or regret, and am not destitute of amusements within doors, when the weather will not permit me to go abroad
—I read, and chat, and play at billiards, cards, or back-
gammon.—Without doors, I superintend my farm, and execute plans of improvement, the effects of which I enjoy
with unspeakable delight.—Nor do I take less pleasure in
seeing my tenants thrive under my auspices, and the poor
live comfortably by the employment which I provide.—
You know I have one or two sensible friends, to whom I
can open all my heart ; a blessing which, perhaps, I might
have sought in vain among the crowded scenes of life.
There are a few others of more humble parts, whom I esteem
for their integrity ; and their conversation I find inoffensive,
though not very entertaining.   Finally, I live in the midst
of honest men, and trusty dependents, who, I flatter myself, have a disinterested attachment to my person.—You
yourself, my dear doctor, can vouch for the truth of these
assertions.

Now, mark the contrast at London—I am pent up in
frowsy lodgings, where there is not room enough to swing a
cat, and I breathe the steams of endless putrefaction ; and
these would, undoubtedly, produce a pestilence, if they
were not qualified by the gross acid of sea-coal, which is itself a pernicious nuisance to lungs of any delicacy of texture : but even this boasted corrector cannot prevent those
languid sallow looks, that distinguish the inhabitants of
London from those ruddy swains that lead a country life.—
I go to bed after midnight, jaded and restless from the dis-
sipations of the day.—I start every hour from my sleep, at
the horrid noise of the watchmen bawling the hour through
every street, and thundering at every door ; a set of useless
fellows, who serve no other purpose but that of disturbing
the repose of the inhabitants ; and, by five o'clock, I start
out of bed, in consequence of the still more dreadful alarm
made by the country carts, and noisy rustics bellowing green

pease under my window. If I would drink water I must quaff the maukish contents of an open aqueduct, exposed to all manner of defilement, or swallow that which comes from the river Thames, impregnated with all the filth of London and Westminster. Human excrement is the least offensive part of the concrete, which is composed of all the drugs, minerals, and poisons, used in mechanics and manufactures, enriched with the putrefying carcasses of beasts and men, and mixed with the scourings of all the wash-tubs, kennels, and common sewers within the bills of mortality.

This is the agreeable potation extolled by the Londoners as the finest water in the universe.—As to the intoxicating potion sold for wine, it is a vile, unpalatable, and pernicious sophistication, balderdashed with cyder, corn-spirit, and the juice of sloes. In an action at law, laid against a carman for having staved a cask of port, it appeared, from the evidence of the cooper, that there were not above five gallons of real wine in the whole pipe, which held above an hundred; and even that had been brewed and adulterated by the merchant at Oporto. The bread I eat in London is a deleterious paste, mixed up with chalk, alum, and bone-ashes, insipid to the taste, and destructive to the constitution. The good people are not ignorant of this adulteration; but they prefer it to wholesome bread, because it is whiter than the meal of corn. Thus they sacrifice their taste and their health, and the lives of their tender infants, to a most absurd gratification of a misjudging eye; and the miller or the baker is obliged to poison them and their families, in order to live by his profession. The same monstrous depravity appears in their veal, which is bleached by repeated bleedings, and other villanous arts, till there is not a drop of juice left in the body, and the poor animal is paralytic before it dies; so void of all taste, nourishment, and savour, that a man may dine as comfortably on a white fricassee of kid-skin gloves, or chip-hats from Leghorn.

As they have discharged the natural colour from their bread, their butchers meat, and poultry, their cutlets, ragouts, fricassees, and sauces of all kinds—so they insist up-

on having the complexion of their pot-herbs mended, even
at the hazard of their lives.   Perhaps, you will hardly believe they can be so mad as to boil their greens with brass
halfpence, in order to improve their colour ; and yet nothing is more true—Indeed, without this improvement in
the colour, they have no personal merit.   They are produced in an artificial soil, and taste of nothing but the dung-
hills from whence they spring.   My cabbage, cauliflower,
and 'sparagus, in the country, are so much superior in flavour to those that are sold in Covent-garden, as my heath
mutton is to that of S^t. James's market, which, in fact, is
neither lamb nor mutton, but something betwixt the two,
gorged in the rank fens of Lincoln and Essex, pale, coarse,
and frowsy.—As for the pork, it is an abominable carnivor-
ous animal, fed with horse flesh and distillers grains ; and
the poultry is all rotten, in consequence of a fever, occasioned by the infamous practice of sewing up the gut, that they
may be the sooner fattened in coops, in consequence of this
cruel retention.

Of the fish I need say nothing in this hot weather, but
that it comes sixty, seventy, fourscore, and a hundred miles
by land-carriage ; a circumstance sufficient, without any
comment, to turn a Dutchman's stomach, even if his nose
was not saluted in every alley with the sweet flavour of *fresh*
makeral, selling by retail.—This is not the season for oysters ; nevertheless, it may not be amiss to mention, that the
right Colchester are kept in slime pits, occasionally overflowed by the sea ; and that the green colour, so much admired by the voluptuaries of this metropolis, is occasioned
by the vitriolic scum, which rises on the surface of the stag-
nant and stinking water.   Our rabbits are bred and fed in
the poulterer's cellar, where they have neither air nor exercise ; consequently they must be firm in flesh, and delicious in flavour ;—and there is no game to be had for love
or money.

It must be owned, that Covent-garden affords some good
fruit ; which, however, is always engrossed by a few individuals of overgrown fortune, at an exorbitant price ; so

that little else than the refuse of the market falls to the share
of the community—and that is distributed by such filthy
hands, as I cannot look at without loathing. It was but
yesterday that I saw a dirty barrow-bunter in the street,
cleaning her dusty fruit with her own spittle; and who
knows but some fine lady of S^t. James's parish might admit
into her delicate mouth those very cherries, which had been
rolled and moistened between the filthy, and perhaps ulcerated chops of a S^t. Giles's huckster.—I need not dwell upon
the pallid contaminated mash which they call strawberries,
soiled and tossed by greasy paws through twenty baskets
crusted with dirt; and then presented with the worst milk,
thickened with the worst flour, into a bad likeness of cream:
but the milk itself should not pass unanalysed, the produce
of faded cabbage leaves and sour draff, lowered with hot
water, frothed with bruised snails, carried through the streets
in open pails, exposed to foul rinsings discharged from doors
and windows, spittle, snot, and tobacco quids, from foot-
passengers, overflowings from mud-carts, spatterings from
coach-wheels, dirt and trash chucked into it by roguish
boys for the joke's sake, the spewings of infants, who have
slabbered in the tin-measure, which is thrown back in that
condition among the milk, for the benefit of the next customer; and, finally, the vermin that drops from the rags
of the nasty drab that vends this precious mixture, under
the respectable denomination of milk-maid.

I shall conclude this catalogue of London dainties with
that table-beer, guiltless of hops and malt, vapid and nauseous, much fitter to facilitate the operation of a vomit, than
to quench thirst and promote digestion; the tallowy rancid
mass called butter, manufactured with candle-grease and
kitchen-stuff; and their fresh eggs, imported from France
and Scotland.—Now, all these enormities might be remedied
with a very little attention to the article of police, or civil
regulation; but the wise patriots of London have taken it
into their heads, that all regulation is inconsistent with
liberty; and that every man ought to live in his own way,
without restraint.—Nay, as there is not sense enough left

among them to be discomposed by the nuisances I have
mentioned, they may, for aught I care, wallow in the mire
of their own polution.

A companionable man will, undoubtedly, put up with
many inconveniencies, for the sake of enjoying agreeable
society.   A facetious friend of mine used to say, the wine
could not be bad where the company was agreeable; a
maxim which, however, ought to be taken *cum grano salis* :
but what is the society of London, that I should be tempted
for its sake to mortify my senses, and compound with such
uncleanness as my soul abhors ? All the people I see are too
much engrossed by schemes of interest or ambition, to have
any room left for sentiment or friendship.—Even in some of
my old acquaintance, those schemes and pursuits have ob-
literated all traces of our former connection.—Conversation
is reduced to party disputes and illiberal altercation—social
commerce to formal visits and card-playing.—If you pick
up a diverting original by accident, it may be dangerous to
amuse yourself with his oddities.—He is generally a tartar
at bottom—a sharper, a spy, or a lunatic.   Every person
you deal with endeavours to over-reach you in the way of
business.—You are preyed upon by idle mendicants, who
beg in the phrase of borrowing, and live upon the spoils of
the stranger.—Your tradesmen are without conscience, your
friends without affection, and your dependents without
fidelity.

My letter would swell into a treatise, were I to particular-
ize every cause of offence that fills up the measure of my
aversion to this and every other crowded city.—Thank heaven ! I am not so far sucked into the vortex, but that I can
disengage myself without any great effort of philosophy.—
From this wild uproar of knavery, folly, and impertinence,
I shall fly with double relish to the serenity of retirement,
the cordial effusions of unreserved friendship, the hospitality
and protection of the rural gods; in a word, the *jucunda
oblivia vitæ*, which Horace himself had not taste enough to
enjoy.

I have agreed for a good travelling coach-and-four at a

guineas a-day, for three months certain; and next week we
intend to begin our journey to the north, hoping still to be
with you by the latter end of October.—I shall continue to
write from every stage where we make any considerable halt,
as often as any thing occurs which I think can afford you
the least amusement. In the meantime, I must beg you
will superintend the economy of Barnes, with respect to my
hay and corn harvests; assured that my ground produces
nothing but what you may freely call your own.—On any
other terms I should be ashamed to subscribe myself your
invariable friend,

London, June 8.   MATT. BRAMBLE.

TO SIR WATKIN PHILLIPS, BART. OF JESUS COLLEGE, OXON.

DEAR PHILLIPS,

IN my last I mentioned my having spent an evening with a
society of authors, who seemed to be jealous and afraid of
one another. My uncle was not at all surprised to hear me
say I was disappointed in their conversation. 'A man may
be very entertaining and instructive upon paper,' said he,
'and exceedingly dull in common discourse. I have observed, that those who shine most in private company are
but secondary stars in the constellation of genius. A small
stock of ideas is more easily managed, and sooner displayed,
than a great quantity crowded together. There is very seldom any thing extraordinary in the appearance and address of a good writer; whereas, a dull author generally
distinguishes himself by some oddity or extravagance. For
this reason, I fancy that an assembly of Grubs must be very
diverting.'

My curiosity being excited by this hint, I consulted my
friend Dick Ivy, who undertook to gratify it the very next
day, which was Sunday last.—He carried me to dine with
S——, whom you and I have long known by his writings.
—He lives in the skirts of the town, and every Sunday his
house is open to all unfortunate brothers of the quill, whom
he treats with beef, pudding, and potatoes, port, punch,

and Calvert's entire butt-beer.—He has fixed upon the first
day of the week for the exercise of his hospitality, because
some of his guests could not enjoy it on any other, for reasons that I need not explain. I was civilly received, in a
plain yet decent habitation, which opened backwards into
a very pleasant garden kept in excellent order ; and, indeed,
I saw none of the outward signs of authorship, either in the
house or the landlord, who is one of those few writers of the
age that stand upon their own foundation, without patronage, and above dependence. If there was nothing characteristic in the entertainer, the company made ample amends
for his want of singularity.

At two in the afternoon, I found myself one of ten mess-
mates seated at table : and I question if the whole kingdom
could produce such another assemblage of originals. Among
their peculiarities, I do not mention those of dress, which
may be purely accidental. What struck me were oddities
originally produced by affectation, and afterwards confirmed by habit. One of them wore spectacles at dinner, and
another his hat flapped ; though (as Ivy told me) the first
was noted for having a seaman's eye, when a bailiff was in
the wind ; and the other was never known to labour under
any weakness or defect of vision, except about five years
ago, when he was complimented with a couple of black eyes
by a player, with whom he had quarrelled in his drink. A
third wore a laced stocking, and made use of crutches, because, once in his life, he had been laid up with a broken
leg, though no man could leap over a stick with more agility. A fourth had contracted such an antipathy to the country, that he insisted upon sitting with his back towards the
window that looked into the garden ; and when a dish of
cauliflower was set upon the table, he snuffed up volatile
salts to keep him from fainting : yet this delicate person was
the son of a cottager, born under a hedge, and had many
years run wild among asses on a common. A fifth affected
distraction—when spoke to, he always answered from the
purpose—sometimes he suddenly started up, and rapped
out a dreadful oath—sometimes he burst out a laughing—

then he folded his arms, and sighed—and then he hissed
like fifty serpents.

At first I really thought he was mad, and, as he sat near
me, began to be under some apprehensions for my own
safety, when our landlord, perceiving me alarmed, assured
me, aloud, that I had nothing to fear.—' The gentleman,'
said he, ' is trying to act a part for which he was by no means
qualified—if he had all the inclination in the world, it is not
in his power to be mad. His spirits are too flat to be kindled
into frenzy.' ' 'Tis no bad p-p-puff, how-ow-ever,' observed
a person in a tarnished laced coat, ' aff-ffected m-madness
w-will p-pass for w-wit, w-with nine-nine-teen out of t-twinty.'
'And affected stuttering for humour,' replied our landlord; ' though, God knows, there is no affinity between
them.' It seems this wag, after having made some abortive attempts in plain speaking, had recourse to this defect,
by means of which he frequently extorted the laugh of the
company, without the least expense of genius; and that imperfection, which he had at first counterfeited, was now become so habitual, that he could not lay it aside.

A certain winking genius, who wore yellow gloves at dinner, had, on his first introduction, taken such offence at
S——, because he looked and talked, and eat and drank,
like any other man, that he spoke contemptuously of his
understanding ever after, and never would repeat his visit,
until he had exhibited the following proof of his caprice.
Wat Wyvil, the poet, having made some unsuccessful advances towards an intimacy with S——, at last gave him to
understand, by a third person, that he had written a poem
in his praise, and a satire against his person; that, if he
would admit him to his house, the first should be immediately
sent to the press; but that, if he persisted in declining his
friendship, he would publish the same without delay. S——
replied, that he looked upon Wyvil's panegyric, as, in effect, a species of infamy, and would resent it accordingly
with a good cudgel; but if he published the satire, he might
deserve his compassion, and had nothing to fear from his
revenge. Wyvil, having considered the alternative, re-

solved to mortify S——, by printing the panegyric, for
which he received a sound drubbing. Then he swore the
peace against the aggressor, who, in order to avoid a prosecution at law, admitted him to his good graces. It was
the singularity in S——'s conduct on this occasion, that reconciled him to the yellow-gloved philosopher, who owned
he had some genius, and from that period cultivated his
acquaintance.

Curious to know upon what subjects the several talents
of my fellow-guests were employed, I applied to my communicative friend, Dick Ivy, who gave me to understand,
that most of them were, or had been, understrappers or journeymen to more creditable authors, for whom they translated, collated, and compiled, in the business of book-making;
and that all of them had, at different times, laboured in the
service of our landlord, though they had now set up for
themselves in various departments of literature. Not only
their talents, but also their nations and dialogues, were so
various, that our conversation resembled the confusion of
tongues at Babel.

We had the Irish brogue, the Scotch accent, and foreign
idiom, twanged off by the most discordant vociferation; for,
as they all spoke together, no man had any chance to be
heard, unless he could bawl louder than his fellows. It must
be owned, however, there was nothing pedantic in their discourse; they carefully avoided all learned disquisitions, and
endeavoured to be facetious; nor did their endeavours always
miscarry. Some droll repartee passed, and much laughter
was excited; and if any individual lost his temper so far as
to transgress the bounds of decorum, he was effectually checked by the master of the feast, who exerted a sort of paternal
authority over this irritable tribe.

The most learned philosopher of the whole collection,
who had been expelled the university for atheism, has made
great progress in a refutation of Lord Bolingbroke's meta-
physical works, which is said to be equally ingenious and
orthodox; but, in the meantime, he has been presented to
the grand jury as a public nuisance, for having blasphemed

in an ale-house on the Lord's day. The Scotsman gives
lectures on the pronunciation of the English language, which
he is now publishing by subscription.

The Irishman is a political writer, and goes by the name
of my Lord Potatoe. He wrote a pamphlet in vindication
of a minister, hoping his zeal would be rewarded with some
place or pension; but, finding himself neglected in that
quarter, he whispered about that the pamphlet was written
by the minister himself, and he published an answer to his
own production. In this he addressed the author under the
title of *your lordship*, with such solemnity, that the public
swallowed the deceit, and bought up the whole impression.
The wise politicians of the metropolis declared they were
both masterly performances, and chuckled over the flimsy
reveries of an ignorant garreteer, as the profound specula-
tions of a veteran statesman, acquainted with all the secrets
of the cabinet. The imposture was detected in the sequel,
and our Hibernian pamphleteer retains no part of his assumed importance but the bare title of *my lord*, and the upper
part of the table at the potatoe ordinary in Shoe lane.

Opposite to me sat a Piedmontese, who had obliged the
public with a humorous satire, entitled, *The balance of the
English poets ;* a performance which evinced the great modesty and taste of the author, and, in particular, his intimacy with the elegancies of the English language. The
sage, who laboured under the αλροφοϾα, or *horror of green
fields*, had just finished a treatise on practical agriculture,
though, in fact, he had never seen corn growing in his life,
and was so ignorant of grain, that our entertainer, in the
face of the whole company, made him own, that a plate of
hominy was the best rice-pudding he had ever ate.

The stutterer had almost finished his travels through Europe and part of Asia, without ever budging beyond the liberties of the king's bench, except in term time, with a tip-
staff for his companion ; and as for little Tim Cropdale, the
most facetious member of the whole society, he had happily
wound up the catastrophe of a virgin tragedy, from the exhibition of which he promised himself a large fund of profit

and reputation.   Tim had made shift to live many years by
writing novels, at the rate of five pounds a volume; but that
branch of business is now engrossed by female authors, who
publish merely for the propagation of virtue, with so much
ease, and spirit, and delicacy, and knowledge of the human
heart, and all in the serene tranquillity of high life, that the
reader is not only enchanted by their genius, but reformed
by their morality.

After dinner we adjourned into the garden, where, I observed, Mr S—— gave a short separate audience to every
individual, in a small remote filbert walk, from whence most
of them dropped off one after another, without further ceremony; but they were replaced by fresh recruits of the same
clan, who came to make an afternoon's visit; and, among
others, a spruce bookseller, called Birkin, who rode his own
gelding, and made his appearance in a pair of new jemmy
boots, with massy spurs of plate.   It was not without reason
that this midwife of the muses used to exercise a horseback,
for he was too fat to walk afoot; and he underwent some
sarcasms from Tim Cropdale, on his unwieldy size, and in-
aptitude for motion.   Birkin, who took umbrage at this poor
author's petulance, in presuming to joke upon a man so
much richer than himself, told him, he was not so unwieldy
but that he could move the Marshalsea court for a writ, and
even overtake him with it, if he did not very speedily come
and settle accounts with him, respecting the expense of publishing his last ode to the king of Prussia, of which he had
sold but three, and one of them was to Whitefield the methodist.   Tim affected to receive this intimation with good
humour, saying, he expected in a post or two, from Pots-
dam, a poem of thanks from his Prussian majesty, who
knew very well how to pay poets in their own coin; but, in
the meantime, he proposed that Mr Birkin and he should
run three times round the garden for a bowl of punch, to be
drank at Ashley's in the evening, and he would run boots
against stockings.   The bookseller, who valued himself upon
his mettle, was persuaded to accept the challenge, and he
forthwith resigned his boots to Cropdale, who, when he had

put them on, was no bad representation of Captain Pistol in the play.

Every thing being adjusted, they started together with great impetuosity, and, in the second round, Birkin had clearly the advantage, *larding the lean earth as he puff'd along.* Cropdale had no mind to contest the victory further, but, in a twinkling, disappeared through the back-door of the garden, which opened into a private lane that had communication with the high road. The spectators immediately began to holloo,—'Stole away!' and Birkin set off in pursuit of him with great eagerness; but he had not advanced twenty yards in the lane, when a thorn running into his foot, sent him hopping back into the garden, roaring with pain, and swearing with vexation. When he was delivered from this annoyance by the Scotsman, who had been bred to surgery, he looked about him wildly, exclaiming,—'Sure the fellow won't be such a rogue as to run clear away with my boots!' Our landlord having reconnoitred the shoes he had left, which indeed hardly deserved that name,—'Pray, said he, 'Mr Birkin, wa'n't your boots made of calf-skin?' 'Calf-skin or cow-skin,' replied the other, 'I'll find a slip of sheep-skin that will do his business.—I lost twenty pounds by his farce, which you persuaded me to buy. I am out of pocket five pounds by his damn'd ode; and now this pair of boots, bran new, cost me thirty shillings, as per receipt. But this affair of the boots is felony—transportation. I'll have the dog indicted at the Old Bailey—I will, Mr S——. I will be revenged, even though I should lose my debt in consequence of his conviction.'

Mr S—— said nothing at present, but accommodated him with a pair of shoes; then ordered his servant to rub him down, and comfort him with a glass of rum punch, which seemed in a great measure to cool the rage of his indignation. 'After all,' said our landlord, 'this is no more than a humbug in the way of wit, though it deserves a more respectable epithet, when considered as an effort of invention. Tim being, I suppose, out of credit with the cord-

wainer, fell upon this ingenious expedient to supply the
want of shoes, knowing that Mr Birkin, who loves humour,
would himself relish the joke upon a little recollection. Cropdale literally lives by his wit, which he has exercised upon
all his friends in their turns. He once borrowed my poney
for five or six days to go to Salisbury, and sold him in
Smithfield at his return. This was a joke of such a serious
nature, that, in the first transports of my passion, I had
some thoughts of prosecuting him for horse-stealing; and,
even when my resentment had in some measure subsided, as
he industriously avoided me, I vowed I would take satisfaction on his ribs with the first opportunity. One day, seeing
him at some distance in the street coming towards me, I began to prepare my cane for action, and walked in the shadow of a porter, that he might not perceive me soon enough
to make his escape; but, in the very instant I had lifted up
the instrument of correction, I found Tim Cropdale metamorphosed into a miserable blind wretch, feeling his way
with a long stick from post to post, and rolling about two
bald unlighted orbs instead of eyes. I was exceedingly
shocked at having so narrowly escaped the concern and disgrace that would have attended such a misapplication of
vengeance; but, next day, Tim prevailed upon a friend of
mine to come and solicit my forgiveness, and offer his note,
payable in six weeks, for the price of the poney. This gentleman gave me to understand, that the blind man was no
other than Cropdale, who, having seen me advancing, and
guessing my intent, had immediately converted himself into
the object aforesaid. I was so diverted at the ingenuity of
the evasion, that I agreed to pardon his offence, refusing his
note, however, that I might keep a prosecution for felony
hanging over his head, as a security for his future good behaviour; but Timothy would by no means trust himself in
my hands till the note was accepted. Then he made his
appearance at my door as a blind beggar, and imposed in
such a manner upon my man, who had been his old acquaintance and pot-companion, that the fellow threw the
door in his face, and even threatened to give him the basti-

nado. Hearing a noise in the hall, I went thither, and immediately recollecting the figure I had passed in the street,
accosted him by his own name, to the unspeakable astonishment of the footman.'

Birkin declared he loved a joke as well as another; but
asked if any of the company could tell where Mr Cropdale
lodged, that he might send him a proposal about restitution,
before the boots should be made away with. "I would willingly give him a pair of new shoes,' said he, ' and half a
guinea into the bargain, for the boots, which fitted me like
a glove, and I sha'n't be able to get the fellows of them, till
the good weather for riding is over.' The stuttering wit declared, that the only secret which Cropdale ever kept, was
the place of his lodgings; but he believed, that, during the
heats of summer, he commonly took his repose upon a bulk,
or indulged himself, in fresco, with one of the kennel-nymphs,
under the portico of S' Martin's church.—' Pox on him,'
cried the bookseller, ' he might as well have taken my whip
and spurs—In that case, he might have been tempted to steal
another horse, and then he would have rid to the devil of
course.'

After coffee I took my leave of Mr S——, with proper
acknowledgements of his civility, and was extremely well
pleased with the entertainment of the day, though not yet
satisfied with respect to the nature of this connection betwixt
a man of character in the literary world, and a parcel of
authorlings, who, in all probability, would never be able to
acquire any degree of reputation by their labours.   On this
head I interrogated my conductor, Dick Ivy, who answered
me to this effect : ' One would imagine S—— had some view
to his own interest, in giving countenance and assistance to
those people, whom he knows to be bad men, as well as bad
writers; but, if he has any such view, he will find himself
disappointed ; for if he is so vain as to imagine he can make
them subservient to his schemes of profit or ambition, they
are cunning enough to make him their property in the meantime. There is not one of the company you have seen to-
day, myself excepted, who does not owe him particular obli-

gations, One of them he bailed out of a spunging-house, and afterwards paid the debt—another he translated into his family, and clothed, when he was turned out half-naked from jail, in consequence of an act for the relief of insolvent debtors—a third, who was reduced to a woollen night-cap, and lived upon sheep's trotters, up three pair of stairs backward, in Butcher row, he took into present pay and free quarters, and enabled him to appear as a gentleman, without having the fear of sheriffs' officers before his eyes. Those who are in distress he supplies with money when he has it, and with his credit when he is out of cash. When they want business, he either finds employment for them in his own service, or recommends them to booksellers, to execute some project he has formed for their subsistence. They are always welcome to his table, which, though plain, is plentiful, and to his good offices, as far as they will go; and, when they see occasion, they make use of his name with the most petulant familiarity; nay, they do not even scruple to arrogate to themselves the merit of some of his performances, and have been known to sell their own lucubrations as the produce of his brain. The Scotsman you saw at dinner, once personated him at an alehouse in West Smithfield, and, in the character of S——, had his head broke by a cowkeeper, for having spoke disrespectfully of the christian religion; but he took the law of him in his own person, and the assailant was fain to give him ten pounds to withdraw his action.'

I observed, that all this appearance of liberality on the side of Mr S—— was easily accounted for, on the supposition that they flattered him in private, and engaged his adversaries in public; and yet I was astonished, when I recollected that I often had seen this writer virulently abused, in papers, poems, and pamphlets, and not a pen was drawn in his defence. 'But you will be more astonished,' said he, 'when I assure you those very guests, whom you saw at his table to-day, were the authors of great part of that abuse; and he himself is well aware of their particular favours, for they are all eager to detect and betray one another.' 'But this is doing the devil's work for nothing,' cried I—'What should induce them to revile their benefactor without provocation?' 'Envy,' answered Dick, 'is the general incitement; but they are galled by an additional scourge of provocation. S—— directs a literary journal, in which their productions are necessarily brought to trial; and though many of them have been treated with such lenity and favour as they little deserved, yet the slightest censure, such as perhaps could not be avoided, with any pretensions to candour and impartiality, has rankled in the hearts of those authors to such a degree, that they have taken immediate vengeance on the critic, in anonymous libels, letters, and lampoons. Indeed, all the writers of the age, good, bad, and indifferent, from the moment he assumed this office, became his enemies, either professed, or in petto, except those of his friends, who knew they had nothing to fear from his strictures; and he must be a wiser man than me, who can tell what advantage or satisfaction he derives from having brought such a nest of hornets about his ears.'

I owned that was a point which might deserve consideration; but still I expressed a desire to know his real motives for continuing his friendship to a set of rascals equally ungrateful and insignificant. He said, he did not pretend to assign any reasonable motive; that, if the truth must be told, the man was, in point of conduct, a most incorrigible fool; that, though he pretended to have a knack at hitting off characters, he blundered strangely in the distribution of his favours, which were generally bestowed on the most undeserving of those who had recourse to his assistance; that, indeed, this preference was not so much owing to a want of discernment, as to want of resolution; for he had not fortitude enough to resist the importunity even of the most worthless; and, as he did not know the value of money, there was very little merit in parting with it so easily; that his pride was gratified in seeing himself courted by such a number of literary dependants; that, probably, he delighted in hearing them expose and traduce one another; and, finally, from their information, he became acquainted with all the transactions of Grub street, which he had some thoughts of compiling, for the entertainment of the public.

I could not help suspecting, from Dick's discourse, that he had some particular grudge against S——, upon whose conduct he had put the worst construction it would bear; and, by dint of cross examination, I found he was not at all satisfied with the character which had been given in the review of his last performance, though it had been treated civilly, in consequence of the author's application to the critic. By all accounts, S—— is not without weakness and caprice; but he is certainly good humoured and civilised; nor do I find, that there is any thing overbearing, cruel, or implacable, in his disposition.

I have dwelt so long upon authors, that you will perhaps suspect I intend to enrol myself among the fraternity; but, if I were actually qualified for the profession, it is at best but a desperate resource against starving, as it affords no provision for old age and infirmity. Salmon, at the age of fourscore, is now in a garret, compiling matter, at a guinea a sheet, for a modern historian, who, in point of age, might be his grandchild; and Psalmonazar, after having drudged half a century in the literary mill, in all the simplicity and abstinence of an Asiatic, subsists upon the charity of a few booksellers, just sufficient to keep him from the parish.—I think Guy, who was himself a bookseller, ought to have appropriated one wing or ward of his hospital to the use of decayed authors; though, indeed, there is neither hospital, college, nor work-house, within the bills of mortality, large enough to contain the poor of this society, composed, as it is, from the refuse of every other profession.

I know not whether you will find any amusement in this account of an odd race of mortals, whose constitution had, I own, greatly interested the curiosity of yours,

London, June 10.   J. MELFORD.

TO MISS LÆTITIA WILLIS, AT GLOUCESTER.

MY DEAR LETTY,

THERE is something on my spirits, which I should not
venture to communicate by the post; but having the opportunity of Mrs Brentwood's return, I seize it eagerly, to disburden my poor heart, which is oppressed with fear and
vexation.—O Letty! what a miserable situation it is to be
without a friend to whom one can apply for counsel and consolation in distress! I hinted in my last, that one Mr Barton had been very particular in his civilities:—I can no
longer mistake his meaning.—He has formally professed
himself my admirer; and, after a thousand assiduities, perceiving I made but a cold return to his addresses, he had recourse to the mediation of Lady Griskin, who has acted the
part of a very warm advocate in his behalf.—But, my dear
Willis, her ladyship overacts her part—She not only expa-
tiates on the ample fortune, the great connections, and the
unblemished character of Mr Barton, but she takes the
trouble to catechise me; and, two days ago, peremptorily
told me that a girl of my age could not possibly resist so
many considerations, if her heart was not pre-engaged.

This insinuation threw me into such a flutter, that she
could not but observe my disorder; and, presuming upon the
discovery, insisted upon my making her the confidante of
my passion. But, although I had not such command of
myself as to conceal the emotion of my heart, I am not
such a child as to disclose its secrets to a person who would
certainly use them to its prejudice. I told her, it was no
wonder if I was out of countenance at her introducing a subject of conversation so unsuitable to my years and inexperience: that I believed Mr Barton was a very worthy gentleman, and I was much obliged to him for his good opinion;
but the affections were involuntary, and mine, in particular,
had as yet made no concessions in his favour. She shook
her head, with an air of distrust that made me tremble; and
observed, that, if my affections were free, they would submit

to the decision of prudence, especially when enforced by the
authority of those who had a right to direct my conduct.
This remark implied a design to interest my uncle or my
aunt, perhaps my brother, in behalf of Mr Barton's passion; and I am sadly afraid that my aunt is already gained
over. Yesterday, in the forenoon, he had been walking
with us in the park, and stopping in our return at a toy-shop,
he presented her with a very fine snuff-box, and me with a
gold etuis, which I resolutely refused, till she commanded
me to accept of it, on pain of her displeasure: nevertheless,
being still unsatisfied with respect to the propriety of receiving this toy, I signified my doubts to my brother, who said
he would consult my uncle on the subject, and seemed to
think Mr Barton had been rather premature in his presents.

What will be the result of this consultation, heaven knows;
but I am afraid it will produce an explanation with Mr
Barton, who will, no doubt, avow his passion, and solicit
their consent to a connection which my soul abhors; for, my
dearest Letty, it is not in my power to love Mr Barton, even
if my heart was untouched by any other tenderness: not that
there is any thing disagreeable about his person; but there is
a total want of that nameless charm which captivates and
controuls the enchanted spirit—at least he appears to me to
have this defect; but if he had all the engaging qualifications
which a man can possess, they would be excited in vain
against that constancy, which, I flatter myself, is the characteristic of my nature. No, my dear Willis, I may be
involved in fresh troubles, and I believe I shall, from the im-
portunities of this gentleman, and the violence of my relations; but my heart is incapable of change.

You know I put no faith in dreams; and yet I have been
much disturbed by one that visited me last night.—I thought
I was in a church, where a certain person, whom you know,
was on the point of being married to my aunt; that the
clergyman was Mr Barton, and that poor forlorn I stood
weeping in a corner, half naked, and without shoes or stockings. Now I know there is nothing so childish as to be
moved by those vain illusions; but, nevertheless, in spite of

all my reason, this hath made a strong impression upon my
mind, which begins to be very gloomy.   Indeed, I have another more substantial cause of affliction—I have some religious scruples, my dear friend, which lie heavy on my
conscience.—I was persuaded to go to the tabernacle, where
I heard a discourse that affected me deeply.   I have prayed
fervently to be enlightened, but as yet I am not sensible of
these inward motions, these operations of grace, which are
the signs of a regenerated spirit ; and therefore I begin to be
in terrible apprehensions about the state of my poor soul.
Some of our family have had very uncommon accessions,
particularly my aunt and Mrs Jenkins, who sometimes
speak as if they were really inspired ;—so that I am not like
to want for either exhortation or example, to purify my
thoughts, and recal them from the vanities of this world,
which, indeed, I would willingly resign, if it was in my
power ; but, to make this sacrifice, I must be enabled by
such assistance from above as hath not yet been indulged to
your unfortunate friend,

June 10.   LYDIA MELFORD.

TO SIR WATKIN PHILLIPS, BART. OF JESUS COLLEGE, OXON.

DEAR PHILLIPS,

THE moment I received your letter, I began to execute
your commission.—With the assistance of mine host at the
Bull and Gate, I discovered the place to which your fugi-
tive valet had retreated, and taxed him with his dishonesty.
The fellow was in manifest confusion at sight of me—but
he denied the charge with great confidence ; till I told him,
that, if he would give up the watch, which was a family-
piece, he might keep the money and the clothes and go to
the devil his own way, at his leisure ; but, if he rejected
this proposal, I would deliver him forthwith to the constable, whom I had provided for that purpose, and he would
carry him before the justice without farther delay.   After
some hesitation, he desired to speak with me in the next
room, where he produced the watch, with all its append-

ages; and I have delivered it to our landlord, to be sent you
by the first safe conveyance. So much for business.

I shall grow vain upon your saying you find entertainment in my letters, barren, as they certainly are, of incident
and importance; because your amusement must arise, not
from the matter, but from the manner, which you know is
all my own.—Animated, therefore, by the approbation of a
person whose nice taste and consummate judgment I can no
longer doubt, I will cheerfully proceed with our memoirs.—
As it is determined we shall set out next week for Yorkshire,
I went to-day, in the forenoon, with my uncle to see a
carriage belonging to a coachmaker in our neighbourhood.
Turning down a narrow lane, behind Long acre, we perceived a crowd of people standing at a door, which, it seems,
opened into a kind of methodist meeting, and were informed that a footman was then holding forth to the congregation
within. Curious to see this phenomenon, we squeezed into
the place with much difficulty; and who should this preacher be, but the identical Humphry Clinker! He had finished
his sermon, and given out a psalm, the first stave of which
he sung with peculiar grace.—But, if we were astonished
to see Clinker in the pulpit, we were altogether confounded
at finding all the females of our family among the audience.
There was Lady Griskin, Mrs Tabitha Bramble, Mrs Winifred Jenkins, my sister Liddy, and Mr Barton, and all of
them joined in the psalmody with strong marks of devotion.

I could hardly keep my gravity on this ludicrous occasion;
but old squaretoes was differently affected.—The first thing
that struck him was the presumption of his lacquey, whom
he commanded to come down, with such an air of authority, as Humphry did not think proper to disregard. He
descended immediately, and all the people were in commotion. Barton looked exceedingly sheepish, Lady Griskin
flirted her fan, Mrs Tabby groaned in spirit, Liddy changed countenance, and Mrs Jenkins sobbed as if her heart
was breaking. My uncle, with a sneer, asked pardon of
the ladies for having interrupted their devotions, saying, he
had particular business with the preacher, whom he ordered

to call a hackney-coach. This being immediately brought
up to the end of the lane, he handed Liddy into it, and my
aunt and I following him, we drove home, without taking
any farther notice of the rest of the company, who still remained in silent astonishment.

Mr Bramble, perceiving Liddy in great trepidation, assumed a milder aspect, bidding her to be under no concern,
for he was not at all displeased at any thing she had done.
—'I have no objection,' said he, ' to your being religiously inclined ; but I don't think my servant is a proper ghostly
director for a devotee of your sex and character.—If, in
fact (as I rather believe), your aunt is not the sole conduct-
ress of this machine——.' Mrs Tabitha made no answer,
but threw up the whites of her eyes, as if in the act of ejaculation.—Poor Liddy said she had no right to the title of a
devotee ; that she thought there was no harm in hearing a
pious discourse, even if it came from a footman, especially
as her aunt was present ; but that, if she had erred from
ignorance, she hoped he would excuse it, as she could
not bear the thoughts of living under his displeasure. The
old gentleman, pressing her hand, with a tender smile,
said she was a good girl, and that he did not believe her
capable of doing any thing that could give him the least
umbrage or disgust.

When we arrived at our lodgings, he commanded Mr
Clinker to attend him up stairs, and spoke to him in these
words.—' Since you are called upon by the spirit to preach
and to teach, it is high time to lay aside the livery of an
earthly master ; and, for my part, I am unworthy to have
an apostle in my service.' ' I hope,' said Humphry, ' I
have not failed in my duty to your honour—I should be a
vile wretch if I did, considering the misery from which your
charity and compassion relieved me—but having an inward
admonition of the spirit—' ' An admonition of the devil,'
cried the squire, in a passion. ' What admonition, you
blockhead ? What right has such a fellow as you to set up
for a reformer !' ' Begging your honour's pardon,' replied
Clinker, ' may not the new light of God's grace shine upon

the poor and ignorant in their humility, as well as upon the
wealthy and the philosopher in all his pride of human learning?' 'What you imagine to be the new light of grace,'
said his master,' I take to be a deceitful vapour, glimmering
through a crack in your upper story—In a word Mr Clinker, I will have no light in my family but what pays the
king's taxes, unless it be the light of reason, which you don't
pretend to follow.'

'Ah, sir!' cried Humphry, 'the light of reason is no
more, in comparison to the light I mean, than a farthing
candle to the sun at noon—.' 'Very true,'. said my uncle,
'the one will serve to shew you your way, and the other to
dazzle and confound your weak brain.—Hark ye, Clinker,
you are either an hypocritical knave, or a wrong-headed
enthusiast; and, in either case, unfit for my service.—If
you are a quack in sanctity and devotion, you will find it
an easy matter to impose upon silly women, and others of
crazed understanding, who will contribute lavishly for your
support.—If you are really seduced by the reveries of a disturbed imagination, the sooner you lose your senses entirely,
the better for yourself and the community. In that case some
charitable person might provide you with a dark room and
clean straw in Bedlam, where it would not be in your power
to infect others with your fanaticism; whereas, if you have
just reflection enough left to maintain the character of a
chosen vessel in the meetings of the godly, you and your
hearers will be misled by a Will-o'the-wisp, from one error
into another, till you are plunged into religious frenzy; and
then, perhaps, you will hang yourself in despair—' 'Which
the Lord of his infinite mercy, forbid!' exclaimed the affrighted Clinker. 'It is very possible I may be under the
temptation of the devil, who wants to wreck me on the rocks
of spiritual pride.—Your honour says I am either a knave or
a madman; now, as I'll assure your honour I am no knave,
it follows that I must be mad; therefore, I beseech your
honour, upon my knees, to take my case into consideration,
that means may be used for my recovery.'

The squire could not help smiling at the poor fellow's

simplicity, and promised to take care of him, provided he
would mind the business of his place, without running after
the new light of methodism: but Mrs Tabitha took offence
at his humility, which she interpreted into poorness of
spirit and worldly-mindedness—She upbraided him with the
want of courage to suffer for conscience-sake: she observed,
that if he should lose his place for bearing testimony of the
truth, Providence would not fail to find him another, perhaps more advantageous; and declaring, that it could not
be very agreeable to live in a family where an inquisition was
established, retired to another room in great agitation.

My uncle followed her with a significant look; then turning to the preacher,—'you hear what my sister says,—if
you cannot live with me upon such terms as I have prescribed, the vineyard of methodism lies before you, and she seems
very well disposed to reward your labour.' ' I would not
willingly give offence to any soul upon earth,' answered
Humphry; 'her ladyship has been very good to me ever
since we came to London; and surely she has a heart turned
for religious exercises, and both she and Lady Griskin sing
psalms and hymns like two cherubims: but, at the same
time, I am bound to love and obey your honour. It becometh not such a poor ignorant fellow as me to hold dispute
with a gentleman of rank and learning. As for the matter
of knowledge, I am no more than a beast in comparison to
your honour; therefore I submit, and, with God's grace, I
will follow you to the world's end, if you don't think me too
far gone to be out of confinement.'

His master promised to keep him for some time longer on
trial; then desired to know in what manner Lady Griskin
and Mr Barton came to join their religious society. He
told him, that her ladyship was the person who first carried
my aunt and sister to the tabernacle, whether he attended
them, and had his devotion kindled by Mr W———'s
preaching: that he was confirmed in this new way by the
preacher's sermons, which he had bought and studied with
great attention: that his discourse and prayers had brought
over Mrs Jenkins and the house-maid to the same way of

thinking; but as for Mr Barton, he had never seen him at
service before this day, when he came in company with
Lady Griskin.—Humphry moreover owned, that he had
been encouraged to mount the rostrum by the example and
success of a weaver, who was much followed as a powerful
minister: that, on his first trial, he found himself under
such strong impulsions, as made him believe he was certainly moved by the spirit; and that he had assisted in
Lady Griskin's, and several private houses, at exercises of
devotion.

Mr Bramble was no sooner informed that her ladyship
had acted as the *primum mobile* of this confederacy, than
he concluded she had only made use of Clinker as a tool,
subservient to the execution of some design, to the true secret of which he was an utter stranger.—He observed, that
her ladyship's brain was a perfect mill for projects; and that
she and Tabby had certainly engaged in some secret treaty,
the nature of which he could not comprehend. I told
him I thought it no difficult matter to perceive the
drift of Mrs Tabitha, which was to ensnare the heart
of Barton, and that in all likelihood my Lady Griskin acted
as her auxiliary; that this supposition would account for
their endeavours to convert him to methodism: an event
which would occasion a connection of souls that might be
easily improved into a matrimonial union.

My uncle seemed to be much diverted by the thoughts of
this scheme's succeeding; but I gave him to understand,
that Barton was pre-engaged: that he had the day before
made a present of an etuis to Liddy, which her aunt had
obliged her to receive, with a view, no doubt, to countenance her own accepting of a snuff-box at the same time:
that my sister having made me acquainted with this incident,
I had desired an explanation of Mr Barton, who declared
his intentions were honourable, and expressed his hope that
I would have no objections to his alliance; that I had thanked him for the honour he intended our family; but told him,
it would be necessary to consult her uncle and aunt, who
were her guardians; and their approbation being obtained,

I could have no objection to his proposal; though I was persuaded that no violence would be offered to my sister's inclinations, in a transaction that so nearly interested the happiness of her future life: that he had assured me, he should never think of availing himself of a guardian's authority, unless he could render his addresses agreeable to the young lady herself; and that he would immediately demand permission of Mr and Mrs Bramble to make Liddy a tender of his hand and fortune.

The squire was not insensible to the advantages of such a match, and declared he would promote it with all his influence; but when I took notice that there seemed to be an aversion on the side of Liddy, he said he would sound her on the subject; and, if her reluctance was such as would not be easily overcome, he would civilly decline the proposal of Mr Barton: for he thought, that, in the choice of a husband, a young woman ought not to sacrifice the feelings of her heart for any consideration upon earth.—' Liddy is not so desperate,' said he,' ' as to worship fortune at such an expense.' I take it for granted this whole affair will end in smoke; though there seems to be a storm brewing in the quarter of Mrs Tabby, who sat with all the sullen dignity of silence at dinner, seemingly pregnant with complaint and expostulation. As she has certainly marked Barton for her own prey, she cannot possibly favour his suit to Liddy, and therefore I expect something extraordinary will attend his declaring himself my sister's admirer. This declaration will certainly be made in form, as soon as the lover can pick up resolution enough to stand the brunt of Mrs Tabby's disappointment; for he is, without doubt, aware of her designs upon his person.—The particulars of the *denouement* you shall know in due season. Meanwhile, I am, always yours,

London, June 10.   J. MELFORD.

TO DR LEWIS.

DEAR LEWIS, '

THE deceitful calm was of short duration. I am plunged
again in a sea of vexation, and the complaints in my stomach
and bowels are returned; so that I suppose I shall be disabled from prosecuting the excursion I had planned.—
What the devil had I to do to come a plague hunting with
a leash of females in my train? Yesterday my precious sister,
(who, by-the-by, has been for some time a professed methodist) came into my apartment, attended by Mr Barton, and
desired an audience with a very stately air. ' Brother,'
said she, ' this gentleman has something to propose, which
I flatter myself will be the more acceptable, as it will rid you
of a troublesome companion.' Then Mr Barton proceeded
to this effect.—' I am, indeed, extremely ambitious of being
allied to your family, Mr Bramble, and I hope you will see
no cause to interpose your authority—' ' As for authority,'
said Tabby, interrupting him with some warmth, ' I know
of none that he has a right to use on this occasion.—If I pay
him the compliment of making him acquainted with the step
I intend to take, it is all he can expect in reason.—This is as
much as I believe he would do by me, if he intended to
change his own situation in life.—In a word, brother, I am
so sensible of Mr Barton's extraordinary merit, that I have
been prevailed upon to alter my resolution of living a single
life, and to put my happiness in his hands, by vesting him
with a legal title to my person and fortune, such as they are.
The business at present is to have the writings drawn; and I
shall be obliged to you, if you will recommend a lawyer to
me for that purpose.'

You may guess what an effect this overture had upon me,
who, from the information of my nephew, expected that Barton was to make a formal declaration of his passion for Liddy: I could not help gazing in silent astonishment, alternately at Tabby and her supposed admirer, which last hung
his head in the most awkward confusion for a few minutes

and then retired, on pretence of being suddenly seized with a vertigo. Mrs Tabitha affected much concern, and would have had him make use of a bed in the house; but he insisted upon going home, that he might have recourse to some drops, which he kept for such emergencies, and his inamorata acquiesced. In the meantime I was exceedingly puzzled at this adventure (though I suspected the truth), and did not know in what manner to demean myself towards Mrs Tabitha, when Jery came in and told me, he had just seen Mr Barton alight from his chariot at Lady Griskin's door. This incident seemed to threaten a visit from her ladyship, with which we were honoured accordingly, in less than half an hour. ' I find,' said she, ' there has been a match of cross-purposes among you, good folks; and I'm come to set you to rights.' So saying, she presented me with the following billet.—

' DEAR SIR,—I no sooner recollected myself from the extreme confusion I was thrown into by that unlucky mistake of your sister, than I thought it my duty to assure you, that my devoirs to Mrs Bramble never exceeded the bounds of ordinary civility, and that my heart is unalterably fixed upon Miss Liddy Melford, as I had the honour to declare to her brother, when he questioned me upon that subject. Lady Griskin has been so good as to charge herself, not only with the delivery of this note, but also with the task of undeceiving Mrs Bramble, for whom I have the most profound respect and veneration, though my affection being otherwise engaged, is no longer in the power of, sir, your very humble servant,   RALPH BARTON.'

Having cast my eyes over this billet, I told her ladyship that I would no longer retard the friendly office she had undertaken; and I and Jery forthwith retired into another room. There we soon perceived the conversation grow very warm betwixt the two ladies; and at length could distinctly hear certain terms of altercation, which we could no longer delay interrupting, with any regard to decorum. When we entered the scene of contention, we found Liddy had joined the disputants, and stood trembling betwixt them, as if she had been afraid they would have proceeded to something more practical than words.—Lady Griskin's face was like the full moon in a storm of wind, glaring, fiery, and portentous; while Tabby looked grim and ghastly, with an aspect breathing discord and dismay.—Our appearance put a stop to their mutual revilings; but her ladyship, turning to me,—'Cousin,' said she, 'I can't help saying I have met with a very ungrateful return from this lady, for the pains I have taken to serve her family.' 'My family is much obliged to your ladyship,' cried Tabby, with a kind of hysterical giggle, 'but we have no right to the good offices of such an honourable go-between.' 'But for all that, good Mrs Tabitha Bramble,' resumed the other, 'I shall be content with the reflection, that virtue is its own reward; and it shall not be my fault, if you continue to make yourself ridiculous.—Mr Bramble, who has no little interest of his own to serve, will, no doubt, contribute all in his power to promote a match betwixt Mr Barton and his niece, which will be equally honourable and advantageous; and, I dare say, Miss Liddy herself will have no objection to a measure so well calculated to make her happy in life.' 'I beg your ladyship's pardon,' exclaimed Liddy, with great vivacity; 'I have nothing but misery to expect from such a measure; and I hope my guardians will have too much compassion to barter my peace of mind for any consideration of interest or fortune.' 'Upon my word, Miss Liddy!' said she, 'you have profited by the example of your good aunt.—I comprehend your meaning, and will explain it when I have a better opportunity—In the meantime I shall take my leave—Madam, your most obedient, and devoted humble servant,' said she, advancing close up to my sister, and court'sying so low, that I thought she intended to squat herself down on the floor.—This salutation Tabby returned with equal solemnity; and the expression of the two faces, while they continued in this attitude, would be no bad subject for a pencil like that of the incomparable Hogarth, if any such should ever appear again in these times of dulness and degeneracy.

Jery accompanied her ladyship to her house, that he might have an opportunity to restore the etuis to Barton, and advise him to give up his suit, which was so disagreeable to his sister, against whom, however, he returned much irritated.—Lady Griskin had assured him, that Liddy's heart was pre-occupied; and immediately the idea of Wilson recurring to his imagination, his family pride took the alarm. —He denounced vengeance against that adventurer, and was disposed to be very peremptory with his sister; but I desired he would suppress his resentment, until I should have talked with her in private.

The poor girl, when I earnestly pressed her on this head, owned, with a flood of tears, that Wilson had actually come to the hot well at Bristol, and even introduced himself into our lodgings as a Jew pedlar; but that nothing had passed betwixt them, further than her begging him to withdraw immediately, if he had any regard for her peace of mind: that he had disappeared accordingly, after having attempted to prevail upon my sister's maid to deliver a letter, which, however, she refused to receive, though she had consented to carry a message, importing, that he was a gentleman of a good family, and that, in a very little time, he would avow his passion in that character.—She confessed, that, although he had not kept his word in this particular, he was not yet altogether indifferent to her affection; but solemnly promised, she would never carry on any correspondence with him, or any other admirer, for the future, without the privity and approbation of her brother and me.

By this declaration, she made her own peace with Jery; but the hot-headed boy is more than ever incensed against Wilson, whom he now considers as an impostor that harbours some infamous design upon the honour of his family. As for Barton, he was not a little mortified to find his present returned, and his addresses so unfavourably received; but he is not a man to be deeply affected by such disappointments; and I know not whether he is not as well pleased with being discarded by Liddy, as he would have been with a permission to prosecute his pretensions, at the risk of being every day exposed to the revenge or machinations of Tabby, who is not to be slighted with impunity.—I had

not much time to moralize on these occurrences; for the
house was visited by a constable and his gang, with a war-
rant from Justice Buzzard, to search the box of Humphry
Clinker, my footman, who was just apprehended as a highwayman.—This incident threw the whole family into confusion. My sister scolded the constable for presuming to
enter the lodgings of a gentleman on such an errand, without having first asked and obtained permission; her maid
was frightened into fits, and Liddy shed tears of compassion for the unfortunate Clinker, in whose box, however,
nothing was found to confirm the suspicion of robbery.

For my own part, I made no doubt of the fellow's being
mistaken for some other person, and I went directly to the
justice, in order to procure his discharge; but there I found
the matter much more serious than I expected—Poor Clinker stood trembling at the bar, surrounded by thief-takers;
and, at a little distance, a thick squat fellow, a postillion,
his accuser, who had seized him in the street, and swore
positively to his person, that the said Clinker had, on the
15th day of March last, on Blackheath, robbed a gentleman
in a post-chaise, which he (the postillion) drove. This deposition was sufficient to justify his commitment; and he
was sent accordingly to Clerkenwell prison, whither Jery
accompanied him in the coach, in order to recommend him
properly to the keeper, that he may want for no convenience
which the place affords.

The spectators, who assembled to see this highwayman,
were sagacious enough to discern something very villanous
in his aspect; which, begging their pardon, is the very
picture of simplicity; and the justice himself put a very unfavourable construction upon some of his answers, which,
he said, savoured of the ambiguity and equivocation of an
old offender: but, in my opinion, it would have been more
just and humane to impute them to the confusion into which
we may suppose a poor country lad to be thrown on such
an occasion. I am still persuaded he is innocent; and, in
this persuasion, I can do no less than use my utmost endeavours that he may not be oppressed.—I shall, to-morrow,

send my nephew to wait on the gentleman who was robbed, and beg he will have the humanity to go and see the prisoner; that, in case he should find him quite different from the person of the highwayman, he may bear testimony in his behalf.—Howsoever it may fare with Clinker, this cursed affair will be to me productive of intolerable chagrin.—I have already caught a dreadful cold, by rushing into the open air from the justice's parlour, where I had been stewing in the crowd; and though I should not be laid up with the gout, as I believe I shall, I must stay at London for some weeks, till this poor devil comes to his trial at Rochester; so that, in all probability, my northern expedition is blown up.

If you can find any thing in your philosophical budget, to console me in the midst of these distresses and apprehensions, pray let it be communicated to your unfortunate friend,

London, June 12.   MATT. BRAMBLE.

TO SIR WATKIN PHILLIPS, BART. OF JESUS COLLEGE, OXON.

DEAR WAT,

THE farce is finished, and another piece of a graver cast brought upon the stage.—Our aunt made a desperate attack upon Barton, who had no other way of saving himself, but by leaving her in possession of the field, and avowing his pretensions to Liddy, by whom he has been rejected in his turn. Lady Griskin acted as his advocate and agent on this occasion, with such zeal as embroiled her with Mrs Tabitha, and a high scene of altercation passed betwixt these two religionists, which might have come to action, had not my uncle interposed. They are, however, reconciled in consequence of an event which has involved us all in trouble and disquiet. You must know, the poor preacher, Humphry Clinker, is now exercising his ministry among the felons in Clerkenwell prison.—A postillion having sworn a robbery against him, no bail could be taken, and he was committed to gaol, notwithstanding all the remonstrances and interest my uncle could make in his behalf.

All things considered, the poor fellow cannot possibly be
guilty, and yet, I believe, he runs some risk of being hanged.—Upon his examination, he answered with such hesitation and reserve, as persuaded most of the people, who
crowded the place, that he was really a knave; and the justice's remarks confirmed their opinion. Exclusive of my
uncle and myself, there was only one person who seemed inclined to favour the culprit.—He was a young man, well
dressed, and, from the manner in which he cross-examined
the evidence, we took it for granted, that he was a student
in one of the inns of court.—He freely checked the justice
for some uncharitable inferences he made to the prejudice of
the prisoner, and even ventured to dispute with his worship
on certain points of law.

My uncle, provoked at the unconnected and dubious answers of Clinker, who seemed in danger of falling a sacrifice
to his simplicity, exclaimed,—' In the name of God, if you
are innocent, say so,—' No,' cried he, ' God forbid that I
should call myself innocent, while my conscience is burden-
ed with sin.' 'What then, you did commit this robbery,'
resumed his master. ' No, sure,' said he; ' blessed be the
Lord, I'm free of that guilt.'

Here the justice interposed, observing, that the man
seemed inclined to make a discovery by turning king's evidence, and desired the clerk to take his confession; upon
which Humphry declared, that he looked upon confession
to be a popish fraud, invented by the whore of Babylon.
The templar affirmed, that the poor fellow was *non compos*,
and exhorted the justice to discharge him as a lunatic.
' You know very well,' added he, ' that the robbery in
question was not committed by the prisoner.'

The thief-takers grinned at one another; and Mr Justice
Buzzard replied with great emotion,—' Mr Martin, I desire you will mind your own business; I shall convince you
one of these days that I understand mine.' In short, there
was no remedy; the mittimus was made out, and poor
Clinker sent to prison in a hackney-coach, guarded by the
constable, and accompanied by your humble servant. By

the way, I was not a little surprised to hear this retainer to justice bid the prisoner to keep up his spirits, for that he did not at all doubt but that he would get off for a few weeks confinement.—He said, his worship knew very well that Clinker was innocent of the fact, and that the real high-wayman, who robbed the chaise, was no other than that very individual Mr Martin, who had pleaded so strenuous-ly for honest Humphry.

Confounded at this information, I asked,—'Why then is he suffered to go about at his liberty, and this poor in-nocent fellow treated as a malefactor?' 'We have exact intelligence of all Mr Martin's transactions,' said he; 'but as yet there is no evidence sufficient for his conviction; and, as for this young man, the justice could do no less than commit him, as the postillion swore point blank to his iden-tity.' 'So, if this rascally postillion should persist in the falsity to which he has sworn,' said I, 'this innocent lad may be brought to the gallows.'

The constable observed, that he would have time enough to prepare for his trial, and might prove an *alibi*; or per-haps, Martin might be apprehended, and convicted for an-other fact, in which case, he might be prevailed upon to take this affair upon himself; or, finally, if these chances should fail, and the evidence stand good against Clinker, the jury might recommend him to mercy, in consideration of his youth, especially if this should appear to be the first fact of which he had been guilty.

Humphry owned he could not pretend to recollect where he had been on the day when the robbery was committed, much less prove a circumstance of that kind so far back as six months, though he knew he had been sick of the fever and ague, which, however, did not prevent him from go-ing about.—Then, turning up his eyes, he ejaculated,—'The Lord's will be done! if it be my fate to suffer, I hope I shall not disgrace the faith, of which, though unworthy, I make profession.'

When I expressed my surprise, that the accuser should persist in charging Clinker, without taking the least notice.

of the real robber, who stood before him, and to whom, indeed, Humphry bore not the least resemblance, the constable (who was himself a thief-taker) gave me to understand,
that Mr Martin was the best qualified for business of all the
gentlemen on the road he had ever known; that he had always acted on his own bottom, without partner or correspondent, and never went to work but when he was cool and
sober; that his courage and presence of mind never failed
him; that his address was genteel, and his behaviour void
of all cruelty and insolence; that he never encumbered himself with watches, or trinkets, nor even with bank-notes, but
always dealt for ready money, and that in the current coin
of the kingdom; and that he could disguise himself and his
horse in such a manner, that after the action, it was impossible to recognize either the one or the other.—' This
great man,' said he, ' has reigned paramount in all the
roads within fifty miles of London above fifteen months,
and has done more business in that time than all the rest of
the profession put together; for those who pass through his
hands are so delicately dealt with, that they have no desire
to give him the least disturbance; but, for all that, his race is
almost run.—He is now fluttering about justice, like a moth
about a candle.—There are so many lime-twigs laid in his
way, that I'll bet a cool hundred he swings before christmas.'

Shall I own to you, that this portrait, drawn by a ruffian, heightened by what I myself had observed in his deportment, has interested me warmly in the fate of poor Martin, whom nature seems to have intended for a useful and
honourable member of that community upon which he now
preys for subsistence! It seems he lived some time as a clerk
to a timber-merchant, whose daughter Martin having privately married, he was discarded, and his wife turned out of
doors. She did not long survive her marriage; and Martin, turning fortune-hunter, could not supply his occasions
any other way, than by taking to the road, in which he
has travelled hitherto with uncommon success.—He pays
his respects regularly to Mr Justice Buzzard, the thief-

catcher general of this metropolis, and sometimes they smoke
a pipe together very lovingly, when the conversation generally turns upon the nature of evidence.—The justice has
given him fair warning to take care of himself, and he has
received his caution in good part.—Hitherto he has baffled
all the vigilance, art, and activity of Buzzard and his
emissaries, with such conduct as would have done honour
to the genius of a Cæsar or a Turenne; but he has one
weakness, which has proved fatal to all the heroes of the
tribe, namely, an indiscreet devotion to the fair sex, and,
in all probability, he will be attacked on this defenceless
quarter.

Be that as it may, I saw the body of poor Clinker consigned to the gaoler of Clerkenwell, to whose indulgence I
recommended him so effectually, that he received him in
the most hospitable manner, though there was a necessity
for equipping him with a suit of irons, in which he made a
very rueful appearance. The poor creature seemed as much
affected by my uncle's kindness, as by his own misfortune.
When I assured him, that nothing should be left undone for
procuring his enlargement, and making his confinement easy
in the meantime, he fell down upon his knees, and kissing
my hand, which he bathed with his tears,—'O squire!'
cried he, sobbing, 'what shall I say?—I can't—no, I can't
speak—my poor heart is bursting with gratitude to you and
my dear—dear—generous—noble benefactor.'

I protest, the scene became so pathetic, that I was fain to
force myself away, and returned to my uncle, who sent me
in the afternoon with his compliments to one Mr Mead, the
person who had been robbed on Blackheath. As I did not find
him at home, I left a message, in consequence of which he
called at our lodgings this morning, and very humanely
agreed to visit the prisoner. By this time lady Griskin
had come to make her formal compliments of condolence to
Mrs Tabitha, on this domestic calamity; and that prudent
maiden, whose passion was now cooled, thought proper to
receive her ladyship so civilly, that a reconciliation immediately ensued. These two ladies resolved to comfort the

poor prisoner in their own persons, and Mr Mead and I squired them to Clerkenwell, my uncle being detained at home by some slight complaints in his stomach and bowels.

The turnkey, who received us at Clerkenwell, looked remarkably sullen; and when we inquired for Clinker,—' I don't care if the devil had him,' said he; ' here has been nothing but canting and praying since the fellow entered the place.—Rabbit him! the tap will be ruined—we han't sold a cask of beer, nor a dozen of wine, since he paid his garnish—the gentlemen get drunk with nothing but your damn'd religion.—For my part, I believe as how your man deals with the devil.—Two or three as bold hearts as ever took the air upon Hounslow, have been blubbering all night; and if the fellow an't speedily removed by habeas corpus, or otherwise, I'll be damn'd if there's a grain of true spirit left within these walls—we shan't have a soul to do credit to the place, or to make his exit like a true-born Englishman —damn my eyes! there will be nothing but sniveling in the cart—we shall all die like so many psalm-singing weavers.

In short, we found that Humphry was, at that very instant, haranguing the felons in the chapel; and that the gaoler's wife and daughter, together with my aunt's woman, Win Jenkins, and our house-maid, were among the audience, which we immediately joined. I never saw any thing so strongly picturesque as this congregation of felons clanking their chains, in the midst of whom stood orator Clinker, expatiating, in a transport of fervour, on the torments of hell, denounced in scripture against evil-doers, comprehending murderers, robbers, thieves, and whoremongers. The variety of attention exhibited in the faces of those ragamuffins, formed a group, that would not have disgraced the pencil of a Raphael. In one, it denoted admiration; in another, doubt; in a third, disdain; in a fourth, contempt; in a fifth, terror; in a sixth, derision; and in a seventh, indignation. As for Mrs Winifred Jenkins, she was in tears, overwhelmed with sorrow; but whether for her own sins, or the misfortune of Clinker, I cannot pretend to say. The other females seemed to listen with a mixture of wonder and devotion. The gaoler's wife declared he was a saint in trouble, saying, she wished from her heart there was such another good soul like him, in every gaol in England.

Mr Mead, having earnestly surveyed the preacher, declared his appearance was so different from that of the person who robbed him on Blackheath, that he could freely make oath he was not the man. But Humphry himself was by this time pretty well rid of all apprehensions of being hanged; for he had been the night before solemnly tried and acquitted by his fellow-prisoners, some of whom he had already converted to methodism. He now made proper acknowledgments for the honour of our visit, and was permitted to kiss the hands of the ladies, who assured him, he might depend upon their friendship and protection. Lady Griskin, in her great zeal, exhorted his fellow-prisoners to profit by the precious opportunity of having such a saint in bonds among them, and turn over a new leaf for the benefit of their poor souls; and, that her admonition might have the greater effect, she reinforced it with her bounty.

While she and Mrs Tabby returned in the coach with the two maid-servants, I waited on Mr Mead to the house of Justice Buzzard, who, having heard his declaration, said, his oath could be of no use at present, but that he would be a material evidence for the prisoner at his trial: so that there seems to be no remedy but patience for poor Clinker; and indeed the same virtue, or medicine, will be necessary for us all, the squire, in particular, who had set his heart upon his excursion to the northward.

While we were visiting honest Humphry in Clerkenwell prison, my uncle received a much more extraordinary visit at his own lodgings. Mr Martin, of whom I have made such honourable mention, desired permission to pay him his respects, and was admitted accordingly. He told him, that having observed him, at Mr Buzzard's, a good deal disturbed by what had happened to his servant, he had come to assure him he had nothing to apprehend for Clinker's life; for, if it was possible that any jury could find him guilty upon such evidence, he, Martin himself, would produce in

court a person whose deposition would bring him off as clear
as the sun at noon.—Sure the fellow would not be so romantic as take the robbery upon himself!—He said the postil-.
lion was an infamous fellow, who had been a dabbler in the
same profession, and saved his life at the Old Bailey by im-
peaching his companions ; that, being now reduced to great
poverty, he had made this desperate push, to swear away
the life of an innocent man, in hopes of having the reward
upon his conviction ; but that he would find himself miserably disappointed, for the justice and his myrmidons were
determined to admit of no interloper in this branch of business ; and that he did not at all doubt but that he would
find matter enough to stop the evidence himself before the
next gaol delivery.   He affirmed, that all these circumstances
were well known to the justice ; and that his severity to
Clinker was no other than a hint to his master to make him
a present in private, as an acknowledgment of his candour
and humanity.

   This hint, however, was so unpalatable to Mr Bramble,
that he declared with great warmth, he would rather confine himself for life to London, which he detested, than be
at liberty to leave it to-morrow, in consequence of encouraging corruption in a magistrate.   Hearing, however, how
favourable Mr Mead's report had been for the prisoner, he
resolved to take the advice of counsel in what manner to
proceed for his immediate enlargement.   I make no doubt
but in a day or two this troublesome business may be discussed : and in this hope we are preparing for our journey.
If our endeavours do not miscarry, we shall have taken the
field before you hear again from yours,

London, June 11.   J. MELFORD.

TO DR LEWIS.

THANK heaven ! dear Lewis, the clouds are dispersed ; and
I have now the clearest prospect of my summer campaign,
which I hope, I shall be able to begin to-morrow.   I took
the advice of counsel with respect to the case of Clinker, in
whose favour a lucky incident has intervened.—The fellow

who accused him has had his own battery turned upon himself. Two days ago, he was apprehended for a robbery on the highway, and committed on the evidence of an accomplice.—Clinker having moved for a writ of habeas corpus was brought before the lord-chief-justice, who, in consequence of an affidavit of the gentleman who had been robbed, importing that the said Clinker was not the person who stopped him on the highway, as well as in consideration of the postillion's character and present circumstances, was pleased to order that my servant should be admitted to bail ; and he has been discharged accordingly, to the unspeakable satisfaction of our whole family, to which he has recommended himself in an extraordinary manner, not only by his obliging deportment, but by his talents of preaching, praying, and singing psalms, which he has exercised with such effect, that even Tabby respects him as a chosen vessel. If there was any thing like affectation or hypocrisy in this excess of religion, I would not keep him in my service ; but so far as I can observe, the fellow's character is downright simplicity, warmed with a kind of enthusiasm, which renders him very susceptible of gratitude and attachment to his benefactors.

As he is an excellent horseman, and understands farriery, I have bought a stout gelding for his use, that he may attend us on the road, and have an eye to our cattle, in case the coachman should not mind his business. My nephew, who is to ride his own saddle-horse, has taken, upon trial, a servant just come from abroad with his former master, Sir William Strollop, who vouches for his honesty. The fellow, whose name is Dutton, seems to be a petit maitre.—He has got a smattering of French, bows, and grins, and shrugs, and takes snuff *a la mode de France*, but values himself chiefly upon his skill and dexterity in hair-dressing.—If I am not much deceived by appearance, he is, in all respects, the very contrast of Humphry Clinker.

My sister has made up matters with Lady Griskin, though, I must own, I should not have been sorry to see that connection entirely destroyed ; but Tabby is not of a

disposition to forgive Barton, who, I understand, is gone
to his seat in Berkshire for the summer season.   I cannot
help suspecting, that in the treaty of peace which has been
lately ratified betwixt those two females, it is stipulated,
that her ladyship shall use her best endeavours to provide
an agreeable help-mate for our sister Tabitha, who seems
to be quite desperate in her matrimonial designs.—Perhaps
the match-maker is to have a valuable consideration in the
way of brokerage, which she will most certainly deserve, if
she can find any man in his senses, who will yoke with Mrs
Bramble from motives of affection or interest.

I find my spirits and my health affect each other recipro-
cally—that is to say, every thing that discomposes my mind,
produces a correspondent disorder in my body; and my
bodily complaints are remarkably mitigated by those considerations that dissipate the clouds of mental chagrin.—The
imprisonment of Clinker brought on those symptoms which
I mentioned in my last, and now they are vanished at his
discharge.   It must be owned, indeed, I took some of the
tincture of ginseng, prepared according to your prescription,
and found it exceedingly grateful to the stomach; but the
pain and sickness continued to return, after short intervals,
till the anxiety of my mind was entirely removed, and then
I found myself perfectly at ease.   We have had fair weather these ten days, to the astonishment of the Londoners,
who think it portentous.   If you enjoy the same indulgence
in Wales, I hope Barnes has got my hay made, and safe
cocked, by this time.   As we shall be in motion for some
weeks, I cannot expect to hear from you as usual; but I
shall continue to write from every place at which we make
any halt, that you may know our track, in case it should
be necessary to communicate any thing to your assured
friend,

London, June 14.   MATT. BRAMBLE.

TO MRS MARY JONES, AT BRAMBLETONHALL.

DEAR MARY,

HAVING the occasion of my cousin Jenkins of Aberga'ny,
I send you, as a token, a turkey-shell-comb, a kiple of
yards of green ribbon, and a sarment upon the nothingness
of good works, which was preached in the tabernacle; and
you will also receive a horn-buck for Saul, whereby she may
learn her letters; for I am much consarned about the state
of her poor sole—and what are all the pursuits of this life to
the consarns of that immortal part?—what is life but a veil
of affliction? O Mary! the whole family have been in such
a constipation!—Mr Clinker has been in trouble, but the
gates of hell have not been able to prevail against him. His
virtue is like pour gold, seven times tried in the fire. He
was tuck up for a robbery, and had before Gustass Bushard,
who made his mittamouse; and the pore youth was sent to
prison upon the fals oaf of a willian, that wanted to sware
his life away for the looker of cain.

The squire did all in his power, but could not prevent
his being put in chains, and confined among common manu-
factors, where he stud like an innocent sheep in the midst
of wolves and tygers. Lord knows what mought have happened to this pyehouse young man, if master had not applied to Apias Korkus, who lives with the ould bailiff, and
is, they say, five hundred years ould (God bless us!), and a
congeror; but, if he be, sure I am he don't deal with the
devil, otherwise he would'nt have fought out Mr Clinker, as
he did, in spite of stone walls, iron bolts, and double locks,
that flew open at his command; for ould Scratch has not a
greater enemy upon hearth than Mr Clinker, who is indeed
a very powerful labourer in the Lord's vineyard. I do no
more than use the words of my good lady, who has got the
infectual calling; and I trust, that even myself, though
unworthy, shall find grease to be accepted.—Miss Liddy has
been touched to the quick, but is a little timorsome: how-
somever, I make no doubt, but she and all of us, will be

brought, by the endeavours of Mr Clinker, to produce blessed fruit of generation and repentance. As for master, and the young squire, they have as yet had narro glimpse of the new light. I doubt as how their hearts are hardened by worldly wisdom, which, as the pyebill saith is foolishness in the sight of God.

O Mary Jones, pray without seizing for grease to prepare you for the operations of this wonderful instrument, which I hope, will be exercised this winter upon you and others at Brambletonhall. To-morrow, we are to set out in a cox and four for Yorkshire; and, I believe, we shall travel that way far, and far, and farther than I can tell; but I shan't go so far as to forget my friends; and Mary Jones will always be remembered as one of them by her humble sarvant,

London, June 14.   WIN. JENKINS.

TO MRS GWYLLIM, HOUSEKEEPER, AT BRAMBLETONHALL.

MRS GWYLLIM,

I CAN'T help thinking it very strange, that I never had an answer to the letter I wrote you some weeks ago from Bath, concerning the sour bear, the gander, and the maids eating butter, which I won't allow to be wasted.—We are now going upon a long gurney to the north, whereby I desire you will redouble your care and circumflexion, that the family may be well managed in our absence; for you know you must render an accunt, not only to your earthly master, but also to him that is above; and if you are found a good and faithful sarvant, great will be your reward in haven. I hope there will be twenty stun of cheese ready for market by the time I get huom, and as much owl spun as will make half a dozen pair of blankets; and that the savings of the buttermilk will fetch me a good penny before martinmas, as the two pigs are to be fed for baking with birchmast and acrons.

I wrote to Doctor Lewis for the same porpuss, but he never had the good manners to take the least notice of my letter; for which reason I shall never favour him with another, though he beshits me on his bended knees. You will do well to keep a watchful eye over the hind Villiam's who is one of his amissories, and, I believe, no better than he should be at bottom. God forbid that I should lack christian charity; but charity begins at huom, and sure nothing can be a more charitable work than to rid the family of such vermin. I do suppose, that the brindled cow has been had to the parson's bull, that old Moll has had another litter of pigs, and that Dick has become a mighty mouser. Pray order every thing for the best, and be frugal, and keep the maids to their labour. If I had a private opportunity, I would send them some hymns to sing instead of profane ballads; but, as I can't, they and you must be contented with the prayers of your assured friend,

London, June 14.   T. BRAMBLE.

TO SIR WATKIN PHILLIPS, BART. OF JESUS COLLEGE, OXON.

DEAR PHILLIPS,

THE very day after I wrote my last, Clinker, was set at liberty—as Martin had foretold, the accuser was himself committed for a robbery, upon unquestionable evidence. He had been for some time in the snares of the thief-taking society; who, resenting his presumption in attempting to encroach upon their monopoly of impeachment, had him taken up and committed to Newgate, on the deposition of an accomplice, who has been admitted as evidence for the king. The postillion being upon record as an old offender, the chief-justice made no scruple of admitting Clinker to bail, when he perused the affidavit of Mr Mead, importing that the said Clinker was not the person that robbed him on Blackheath; and honest Humphry was discharged.—When he came home, he expressed great eagerness to pay his respects to his master: and here his elocution failed him, but his silence was pathetic; he fell down at his feet, and embraced his knees, shedding a flood of tears, which my uncle did not see without emotion.—He took snuff in some confusion; and, putting his hand in his pocket, gave him his blessing in something more substantial than words.—' Clinker,' said he, ' I am so well convinced, both of your honesty

and courage, that I am resolved to make you my lifeguard-
man on the highway.

He was accordingly provided with a case of pistols, and
a carabine to be slung across his shoulders; and every other
preparation being made, we set out last Thursday, at seven
in the morning; my uncle, with the three women in the
coach; Humphry, well mounted on a black gelding bought
for his use; myself ahorseback, attended by my new valet,
Mr Dutton, an exceeding coxcomb, fresh from his travels,
whom I have taken upon trial. The fellow wears a solitaire,
uses paint, and takes rappee with all the grimace of a French
marquis. At present, however, he is in a riding dress, jack
boots, leather breeches, a scarlet waistcoat, with gold binding, a laced hat, a hanger, a French posting whip in his
hand, and his hair *en queue.*

Before we had gone nine miles, my horse lost one of his
shoes: so that I was obliged to stop at Barnet, to have another, while the coach proceeded at an easy pace over the
common. About a mile short of Hatfield, the postillions,
stopping the carriage, gave notice to Clinker that there were
two suspicious fellows ahorseback, at the end of a lane who
seemed waiting to attack the coach. Humphry forthwith
apprised my uncle, declaring he would stand by him to the
last drop of his blood; and, unslinging his carabine, prepared for action. The squire had pistols in the pockets of
the coach, and resolved to make use of them directly; but
he was effectually prevented by his female companions, who
flung themselves about his neck, and screamed in concert.—
At that instant, who should come up, at a hand-gallop, but
Martin, the highwayman, who, advancing to the coach,
begged the ladies would compose themselves for a moment:
then desiring Clinker to follow him to the charge, he pulled
a pistol out of his bosom, and they rode up together to give
battle to the rogues, who, having fired at a great distance,
fled across the common. They were in pursuit of the fugi-
tives when I came up, not a little alarmed at the shrieks in
the coach, where I found my uncle in a violent rage, without his periwig, struggling to disentangle himself from Tab-

by and the other two, with swearing and great vociferation.
Before I had time to interpose, Martin and Clinker returned
from the pursuit, and the former paid his compliments with
great politeness, giving us to understand, that the fellows
had scampered off, and that he believed they were a couple
of raw 'prentices from London. He commended Clinker
for his courage, and said, if he would give him leave, he
would have the honour to accompany us as far as Stevenage,
where he had some business.

The 'squire, having recollected and adjusted himself, was
the first to laugh at his own situation; but it was not without difficulty that Tabby's arms could be untwisted from his
neck, Liddy's teeth chattered, and Jenkins was threatened
with a fit as usual. I had communicated to my uncle the
character of Martin, as it was described by the constable,
and he was much struck with its singularity.—He could not
suppose the fellow had any design upon our company, which
was so numerous and well armed; he therefore thanked him
for the service he had just done them, said he would be glad
of his company, and asked him to dine with us at Hatfield.
This invitation might not have been agreeable to the ladies,
had they known the real profession of our guest; but this
was a secret to all, except my uncle and myself.—Mrs Tabitha, however, would by no means consent to proceed with
a case of loaded pistols in the coach, and they were forthwith discharged in complaisance to her and the rest of the
women.

Being gratified in this particular, she became remarkably
good-humoured, and at dinner behaved in the most affable
manner to Mr Martin, with whose polite address, and agreeable conversation, she seemed to be much taken. After dinner, the landlord accosting me in the yard, asked, with a
significant look, if the gentleman that rode the sorrel belonged to our company?—I understood his meaning, but answered no; that he had come up with us on the common, and
helped us to drive away two fellows, that looked like high-
waymen.—He nodded three times distinctly, so much as to
say he knows his cue. Then he inquired, if one of those

men was mounted on a bay mare, and the other on a chesnut gelding, with a white streak down his forehead? and
being answered in the affirmative, he assured me, they had
robbed three post-chaises this very morning.—I inquired, in
my turn, if Mr Martin was of his acquaintance; and, nodding thrice again, he answered, that *he had seen the gentleman.*

Before we left Hatfield, my uncle, fixing his eyes on
Martin, with such expression as is more easily conceived
than described, asked, if he often travelled that road? and
he replied with a look which denoted his understanding the
question, that he very seldom did business in that part of the
country. In a word, this adventurer favoured us with his
company to the neighbourhood of Stevenage, where he took
his leave of the coach and me in very polite terms, and turned
off upon a cross-road that led to a village on the left. At
supper, Mrs Tabby was very full in the praise of Mr Martin's good sense and good breeding, and seemed to regret
that she had not a farther opportunity to make some experiment upon his affection. In the morning, my uncle was
not a little surprised to receive, from the waiter, a billet
couched in these words.—

' SIR,—I could easily perceive from your looks when I had the
honour to converse with you at Hatfield, that my character is not
unknown to you; and, I dare say, you won't think it strange,
that I should be glad to change my present way of life for any other
honest occupation, let it be ever so humble, that will afford me bread
in moderation, and sleep in safety. Perhaps you may think I flatter, when I say, that from the moment I was witness to your generous concern in the cause of your servant, I conceived a particular
esteem and veneration for your person; and yet what I say is true.
I should think myself happy, if I could be admitted into your protection and service as house-steward, clerk, butler, or bailiff, for
either of which places I think myself tolerably well qualified; and
sure I am, I should not be found deficient in gratitude and fidelity;
at the same time, I am very sensible how much you must deviate
from the common maxims of discretion, even in putting my professions to the trial; but I don't look upon you as a person that
thinks in the ordinary style; and the delicacy of my situation,
will, I know, justify this address to a heart warmed with beneficence

and compassion. Understanding you are going pretty far north, I shall take an opportunity to throw myself in your way again before you reach the borders of Scotland; and I hope, by that time you will have taken into consideration the truly distressful case of, honoured sir, your very humble and devoted servant,

EDWARD MARTIN.'

The squire having perused this letter, put it into my hand, without saying a syllable; and, when I had read it, we looked at each other in silence. From a certain sparkling in his eyes, I discovered there was more in his heart than he cared to express with his tongue, in favour of poor Martin; and this was precisely my own feeling, which he did not fail to discern, by the same means of communication. 'What shall we do,' said he, 'to save this poor sinner from the gallows, and make him a useful member of the commonwealth? and yet the proverb says,—"Save a thief from the gallows, and he'll cut your throat." I told him I really believed Martin was capable of giving the proverb the lie; and that I should heartily concur in any step he might take in favour of his solicitation. We mutually resolved to deliberate upon the subject, and in the meantime proceeded on our journey. The roads having been broke up by the heavy rains in the spring, were so rough, that, although we travelled very slowly, the jolting occasioned such pain to my uncle, that he was become exceedingly peevish when we arrived at this place, which lies about eight miles from the post road, between Wetherby and Boroughbridge.

Harrowgate water, so celebrated for its efficacy in the scurvy and other distempers, is supplied from a copious spring, in the hollow of a wild common, round which a good many houses have been built for the convenience of the drinkers, though few of them are inhabited. Most of the company lodge at some distance, in five separate inns, situated in different parts of the common, from whence they go every morning to the well, in their own carriages. The lodgers of each inn form a distinct society that eat together; and there is a commodious public room, where they break-

fast in dishabille, at separate tables, from eight o'clock till
eleven, as they chance or choose to come in.—Here also
they drink tea in the afternoon, and play at cards, or dance
in the evening. One custom, however, prevails, which I
look upon as a solecism in politeness. The ladies treat with
tea in their turns, and even girls of sixteen are not exempted from this shameful imposition. There is a public ball
by subscription every night at one of the houses, to which
all the company from the others are admitted by tickets;
and, indeed, Harrowgate treads upon the heels of Bath, in
the articles of gaiety and dissipation—with this difference,
however, that here we are more sociable and familiar. One
of the inns is already full up to the very garrets, having no
less than fifty lodgers, and as many servants. Our family
does not exceed thirty-six; and I should be sorry to see the
number augmented, as our accommodations won't admit of
much increase.

At present the company is more agreeable than one could
expect, from an accidental assemblage of persons, who are
utter strangers to one another.—There seems to be a general
disposition among us to maintain good fellowship, and promote the purposes of humanity, in favour of those who come
thither on the score of health. I see several faces which we
left at Bath, although the majority are of the northern
counties, and many come from Scotland for the benefit of
these waters.—In such a variety there must be some originals,
among whom Mrs Tabitha Bramble is not the most inconsiderable.—No place, where there is such an intercourse between the sexes, can be disagreeable to a lady of her views
and temperament.—She has had some warm disputes at table
with a lame parson from Northumberland, on the new birth,
and the insignificance of moral virtue; and her arguments
have been reinforced by an old Scots lawyer, in a tye-periwig, who, though he has lost his teeth, and the use of his
limbs, can still wag his tongue with great volubility. He
has paid her such fulsome compliments, upon her piety and
learning, as seems to have won her heart; and she, in her
turn, treats him with such attention, as indicates a design

upon his person; but, by all accounts, he is too much a
fox to be inveigled into any snare that she can lay for his
affection.

We do not propose to stay long at Harrowgate, though
at present it is our head-quarters, from whence we shall make
some excursions to visit two or three of our rich relations,
who are settled in this county. Pray remember me to all
our friends of Jesus, and allow me to be still yours affec-
tionately,

Harrowgate, June 23. J. MELFORD.

TO DR LEWIS.

DEAR DOCTOR.

Considering the tax we pay for turnpikes, the roads of
this country constitute a most intolerable grievance. Between Newark and Wetherby, I have suffered more from
jolting and swinging, than ever I felt in the whole course of
my life, although the carriage is remarkably commmodious
and well hung, and the postillions were very careful in driving. I am now safely housed at the new inn at Harrowgate, whither I came to satisfy my curiosity, rather than
with any view of advantage to my health; and truly, after
having considered all the parts and particulars of the place,
I cannot account for the concourse of people one finds here,
upon any other principle but that of caprice, which seems
to be the character of our nation.

Harrowgate is a wild common, bare and bleak, without
tree or shrub, or the least signs of cultivation; and the people who come to drink the water, are crowded together in
paltry inns, where the few tolerable rooms are monopolized
by the friends and favourites of the house, and all the rest
of the lodgers are obliged to put up with dirty holes, where
there is neither space, air, nor convenience. My apartment is about ten feet square; and when the folding-bed is
down, there is just room sufficient to pass between it and
the fire. One might expect, indeed, that there would be
no occasion for a fire at midsummer; but here the climate

is so backward, that an ash-tree, which our landlord has
planted before my window, is just beginning to put forth
its leaves: and I am fain to have my bed warmed every
night.

As for the water, which is said to have effected so many
surprising cures, I have drank it once, and the first draught
has cured me of all desire to repeat the medicine. Some
people say it smells of rotten eggs, and others compare it to
the scourings of a foul gun.—It is generally supposed to be
strongly impregnated with sulphur; and Dr Shaw, in his
book upon mineral waters, says, he has seen flakes of sulphur floating in the well—*Pace tanti viri.*—I for my part,
have never observed any thing like sulphur, either in or
about the well; neither do I find that any brimstone has
ever been extracted from the water. As for the smell, if I
may be allowed to judge from my own organs, it is exactly
that of bilge water; and the saline taste of it seems to declare that it is nothing else than salt water purified in the
bowels of the earth. I was obliged to hold my nose with one
hand, while I advanced the glass to my mouth with the
other; and after I had made shift to swallow it, my stomach
could hardly retain what it had received.—The only effects
it produced were sickness, griping, and insurmountable disgust.—I can hardly mention it without puking.—The world
is strangely misled by the affectation of singularity. I cannot
help suspecting that this water owes its reputation in a great
measure to its being so strikingly offensive.—On the same
kind of analogy, a German doctor has introduced hemlock
and other poisons, as specifics, into the *materia medica.* I am
persuaded, that all the cures ascribed to the Harrowgate water, would have been as efficaciously, and infinitely more
agreeably, performed by the internal and external use of
sea-water. Sure I am, this last is much less nauseous to the
taste and smell, and much more gentle in its operation as a
purge, as well as more extensive in its medical qualities.

Two days ago, we went across the country to visit Squire
Burdock, who married a first cousin of my father, an heiress, who brought him an estate of a thousand a-year. This

gentleman is a declared opponent of the ministry in parliament; and, having an opulent fortune, piques himself upon living in the country, and maintaining *old English hospitality.*—By the by, this is a phrase very much used by the English themselves, both in words and writing; but I never heard of it out of the island, except by way of irony and sarcasm. What the hospitality of our forefathers has been, I should be glad to see recorded rather in the memoirs of strangers who have visited our country, and were the proper objects and judges of such hospitality, than in the discourse and lucubrations of the modern English, who seem to describe it from theory and conjecture. Certain it is, we are generally looked upon by foreigners as a people totally destitute of this virtue; and I never was in any country abroad where I did not meet with persons of distinction, who complained of having been inhospitably used in Great Britain. A gentleman of France, Italy, or Germany, who has entertained and lodged an Englishman at his house, when he afterwards meets with his guest at London, is asked to dinner at the Saracen's head, the Turk's head, the Boar's head, or the Bear, eats raw beef and butter, drinks execrable port, and is allowed to pay his share of the reckoning.

But, to return from this digression, which my feeling for the honour of my country obliged me to make.—Our Yorkshire cousin has been a mighty fox-hunter *before the Lord;* but now he is too fat and unwieldy to leap ditches and five-bar gates; nevertheless, he still keeps a pack of hounds, which are well exercised, and his huntsman every night entertains him with the adventures of the day's chase, which he recites in a tone and terms that are extremely curious and significant. In the meantime, his broad brawn is scratched by one of his grooms.—This fellow, it seems, having no inclination to curry any beast out of the stable, was at great pains to scollop his nails in such a manner, that the blood followed at every stroke.—He was in hopes that he would be dismissed from this disagreeable office, but the event turned out contrary to his expectation.—His master declared he was the best scratcher in the family; and now he will not suffer any other servant to draw a nail upon his carcass.

The 'squire's lady is very proud, without being stiff or inaccessible.—She receives even her inferiors in point of fortune with a kind of arrogant civility; but then she thinks she has a right to treat them with the most ungracious freedoms of speech, and never fails to let them know she is sensible of her own superior affluence.—In a word, she speaks well of no living soul, and has not one single friend in the world.—Her husband hates her mortally; but although the brute is sometimes so very powerful in him, that he will have his own way, he generally truckles to her dominion, and dreads, like a school-boy, the lash of her tongue. On the other hand, she is afraid of provoking him too far, lest he should make some desperate effort to shake off her yoke. —she therefore acquiesces in the proofs he daily gives of his attachment to the liberty of an English freeholder, by saying and doing, at his own table, whatever gratifies the brutality of his disposition, or contributes to the ease of his person. The house, though large, is neither elegant nor comfortable.—It looks like a great inn, crowded with travellers, who dine at the landlord's ordinary, where there is a great profusion of victuals and drink; but mine host seems to be misplaced—and I would rather dine upon filberts with a hermit, than feed upon venison with a hog. The footmen might be aptly compared to the waiters of a tavern, if they were more serviceable, and less rapacious; but they are generally insolent and inattentive, and so greedy, that I think I can dine better, and for less expense, at the Star and Garter in Pall-mall, than at our cousin's castle in Yorkshire. The squire is not only accommodated with a wife, but he is also blessed with an only son, about two-and-twenty, just returned from Italy, a complete fiddler, and *dilletante*; and he slips no opportunity of manifesting the most perfect contempt for his own father.

When we arrived, there was a family of foreigners at the house, on a visit to this virtuoso, with whom they had been acquainted at the Spa: it was the count de Melville, with his lady, on their way to Scotland. Mr Burdock had met with an accident, in consequence of which both the count and I would have retired; but the young gentleman and his mother insisted upon our staying dinner, and their serenity seemed to be so little ruffled by what had happened, that we complied with their invitation. The squire had been brought home over-night in his post-chaise, so terribly be-laboured about the pate, that he seemed to be in a state of stupefaction, and had ever since remained speechless. A country apothecary, called Grieve, who lived in a neigh-bouring village, having been called to his assistance, had let him blood, and applied a poultice to his head, declar-ing that he had no fever, nor any other bad symptom, but the loss of speech, if he really had lost that faculty. But the young squire said this practitioner was an *ignorantaccio*, that there was a fracture in the *cranium*, and that there was a necessity for having him trepanned without loss of time. His mother espousing this opinion, had sent an ex-press to York for a surgeon to perform the operation, and he was already come, with his 'prentice and instruments. Having examined the patient's head, he began to prepare his dressings; though Grieve still retained his first opinion, that there was no fracture, and was the more confirmed in it, as the squire had passed the night in profound sleep, uninterrupted by any catching or convulsion. The York surgeon said he could not tell whether there was a fracture, until he should take off the scalp; but, at any rate, the operation might be of service, in giving vent to any blood that might be extravasated, either above or below the *dura mater*. The lady and her son were clear for trying the ex-periment; and Grieve was dismissed with some marks of contempt, which, perhaps, he owed to the plainness of his appearance. He seemed to be about the middle age, wore his own black hair without any sort of dressing; by his garb, one would have taken him for a quaker, but he had none of the stiffness of that sect; on the contrary, he was very submissive, respectful, and remarkably taciturn.

Leaving the ladies in an apartment by themselves, we ad-

journed to the patient's chamber, where the dressings and
instruments were displayed in order upon a pewter dish.
The operator, laying aside his coat and periwig, equipped himself with a night-cap, apron, and sleeves, while his
'prentice and footman, seizing the squire's head, began to
place it in a proper posture.—But mark what followed.—
The patient, bolting upright in the bed, collared each of
these assistants with the grasp of Hercules, exclaiming, in a
bellowing tone,—' I ha'nt lived so long in Yorkshire to be
trepanned by such vermin as you;' and, leaping on the
floor, put on his breeches quietly, to the astonishment of us
all.   The surgeon still insisted upon the operation, alleging
it was now plain that the brain was injured, and desiring the
servants to put him into bed again ; but nobody would venture to execute his orders, or even to interpose ; when the
squire turned him and his assistants out of doors, and threw
his apparatus out at the window.   Having thus asserted his
prerogative, and put on his clothes with the help of a valet,
the count, with my nephew and me, were introduced by
his son, and received with his usual style of rustic civility.
Then, turning to Signior Macaroni, with a sarcastic grin,
—' I tell thee what, Dick,' said he, ' a man's skull is not to
be bored every time his head is broken ; and I'll convince
thee and thy mother, that I know as many tricks as e'er an
old fox in the West Riding.'

We afterwards understood he had quarrelled at a public-
house with an exciseman, whom he challenged to a bout
at single stick, in which he had been worsted ; and that the
shame of this defeat had tied up his tongue.   As for madam,
she had shewn no concern for his disaster, and now heard
of his recovery without emotion.   She had taken some little
notice of my sister and niece, though rather with a view to
indulge her own petulance, than out of any sentiment of
regard to our family.—She said Liddy was a fright, and ordered her woman to adjust her head before dinner ; but she
would not meddle with Tabby, whose spirit, she soon perceived, was not to be irritated with impunity.   At table,
she acknowledged me so far as to say she had heard of my

father; though she hinted, that he had disobliged her family, by making a poor match in Wales. She was disagreeably familiar in her inquiries about our circumstances; and asked, if I intended to bring up my nephew to the law? I told her, that, as he had an independent fortune, he should follow no profession but that of a country gentleman; and that I was not without hopes of procuring for him a seat in parliament. 'Pray, cousin,' said she, 'what may his fortune be?' When I answered, that, with what I should be able to give him, he would have better than two thousand a-year; she replied, with a disdainful toss of her head, that it would be impossible for him to preserve his independence on such a paltry provision.

Not a little nettled at this arrogant remark, I told her, I had the honour to sit in parliament with her father, when he had little more than half that income; and I believed there was not a more independent and incorruptible member in the house. ' Ay, but times are changed,' cried the squire. 'Country gentlemen now-a-days live after another fashion. —My table alone stands me in a cool thousand a quarter, though I raise my own stock, import my own liquors, and have every thing at the first hand.—True it is, I keep open house, and receive all comers, for the honour of Old England.' ' If that be the case,' said I, ' 'tis a wonder you can maintain it at so small an expense; but every private gentleman is not expected to keep a caravansera for the accommodation of travellers.—Indeed, if every individual lived in the same style, you would not have such a number of guests at your table; of consequence your hospitality would not shine so bright for the glory of the West Riding.'—The young squire, tickled by this ironical observation, exclaimed,—' O che burla !' His mother eyed me in silence with a supercilious air; and the father of the feast, taking a bumper of October,—'My service to you, cousin Bramble,' said he; ' I have always heard there was something keen and biting in the air of the Welch mountains.'

I was much pleased with the count de Melvil, who is sensible, easy, and polite; and the countess is the most ami-

able woman I ever beheld.   In the afternoon they took leave
of their entertainers; and the young gentleman, mounting
his horse, undertook to conduct their coach through the
park, while one of the servants rode round to give notice
to the rest, whom they had left at a public house on the
road.   The moment their backs were turned, the censorious
demon took possession of our Yorkshire landlady and our
sister Tabitha.—The former observed, that the countess was
a good sort of a body, but totally ignorant of good breeding,
consequently awkward in her address.   The squire said, he
did not pretend to the breeding of any thing but colts; but
that the jade would be very handsome, if she was a little
more in flesh.   ' Handsome !' cried Tabby ; ' she has indeed
a pair of black eyes without any meaning; but then there is
not a good feature in her face.'   ' I know not what you call
good features in Wales, ' replied our landlord; ' but they'll
pass in Yorkshire.'   Then turning to Liddy, he added,—
' What say you, my pretty redstreak ?—what is your opinion of the countess ?'   ' I think,' cried Liddy, with great
emotion, ' she's an angel.'   Tabby chid her for talking with
such freedom in company, and the lady of the house said,
in a contemptuous tone, she supposed miss had been brought
up at some country boarding-school.

Our conversation was suddenly interrupted by the young
gentleman, who galloped into the yard all aghast, exclaiming that the coach was attacked by a great number of high-
waymen.   My nephew and I rushing out, found his own
and his servant's horse ready saddled in the stable, with pistols in the caps.   We mounted instantly, ordered Clinker
and Dutton to follow with all possible expedition; but notwithstanding all the speed we could make, the action was
over before we arrived, and the count with his lady safe
lodged at the house of Grieve, who had signalised himself
in a very remarkable manner on this occasion.   At the turning of a lane that led to the village where the count's servants remained, a couple of robbers a-horseback suddenly
appeared, with their pistols advanced; one kept the coachman in awe, and the other demanded the count's money,

while the young squire went off at full speed, without ever
casting a look behind. The count desiring the thief to withdraw his pistol, as the lady was in great terror, delivered
his purse without making the least resistance; but not satisfied with this booty, which was pretty considerable, the
rascal insisted upon rifling her of her ear-rings and necklace,
and the countess screamed with affright. Her husband, exasperated at the violence with which she was threatened,
wrested the pistol out of the fellow's hand, and, turning it
upon him, snapped it in his face; but the robber knowing
there was no charge in it, drew another from his bosom, and
in all probability would have killed him on the spot, had
not his life been saved by a wonderful interposition. Grieve,
the apothecary, chancing to pass that very instant, ran up
to the coach, and, with a crabstick, which was all the wea-
pon he had, brought the fellow to the ground with the first
blow; then seizing his pistol, presented it to his colleague,
who fired his piece at random, and fled without farther opposition. The other was secured by the assistance of the
count and the coachman; and his legs being tied under the
belly of his own horse, Grieve conducted him to the village,
whither also the carriage proceeded. It was with great difficulty the countess could be kept from swooning; but at
last she was happily conveyed to the house of the apothecary,
who went into the shop to prepare some drops for her, while
his wife and daughter administered to her in another apartment. I found the count standing in the kitchen with the
parson of the parish, and expressing much impatience to see
his protector, whom as yet he had scarce found time to thank
for the essential service he had done him and the countess.
The daughter passing at the same time with a glass of water,
monsieur de Melvil could not help taking notice of her
figure, which was strikingly engaging. 'Ay,' said the parson, 'she is the prettiest girl, and the best girl in all my parish; and if I could give my son an estate of ten thousand
a-year, he should have my consent to lay it at her feet. If
Mr Grieve had been as solicitous about getting money, as he
has been in performing all the duties of a primitive christian,

Fy would not have hung so long upon his hands.'   'What is
her name ?' said I.   'Sixteen years ago,' answered the vicar,
'I christened her by the name of Serafina Melvilia.'   'Ha!
what! how!' cried the count eagerly, 'sure you said Serafina Melvilia.'   'I did,' said he;   'Mr Grieve told me
those were the names of two noble persons abroad, to whom
he had been obliged for more than life.'

The count, without speaking another syllable, rushed into
the parlour crying,—' This is your god-daughter, my dear.'
Mrs Grieve, then seizing the countess by the hand, exclaimed, with great agitation,—'O madam !—O sir! I am
—I am your poor Elinor. This is my Serafina Melvilia.
O child! these are the count and countess of Melvil—the
generous—the glorious benefactors of thy once unhappy
parents.'

The countess rising from her seat, threw her arms about
the neck of the amiable Serafina, and clasped her to her
breast with great tenderness, while she herself was embraced
by the weeping mother. This moving scene was completed
by the entrance of Grieve himself, who, falling on his knees
before the count,—' Behold,' said he, 'a penitent, who at
length can look upon his patron without shrinking.'   'Ah,
Ferdinand!' cried he, raising and folding him in his arms,
' the play-fellow of my infancy—the companion of my
youth !—Is it to you then I am indebted for my life ?'   'Heaven has heard my prayer,' said the other, 'and given me
an opportunity to prove myself not altogether unworthy of
your clemency and protection.'   He then kissed the hand
of the countess, while monsieur de Melvil saluted his wife
and lovely daughter, and all of us were greatly affected by
this pathetic recognition.

In a word, Grieve was no other than Ferdinand Count
Fathom, whose adventures were printed many years ago.
Being a sincere convert to virtue, he had changed his name,
that he might elude the inquiries of the count, whose generous allowance he determined to forego, that he might have
no dependence but upon his own industry and moderation.
He had accordingly settled in this village as a practitioner

in surgery and physic, and for some years wrestled with all
the miseries of indigence; which, however, he and his wife
had borne with the most exemplary resignation. At length,
by dint of unwearied attention to the duties of his profession,
which he exercised with equal humanity and success, he
had acquired a tolerable share of business among the farmers and common people, which enabled him to live in a
decent manner. He had been scarce ever seen to smile; was
unaffectedly pious; and all the time he could spare from
the avocations of his employment, he spent in educating
his daughter and in studying for his own improvement. In
short, the adventurer Fathom was, under the name of Grieve,
universally respected among the commonalty of this district,
as a prodigy of learning and virtue. These particulars I
learned from the vicar, when we quitted the room, that they
might be under no restraint in their mutual effusions. I
make no doubt that Grieve will be pressed to leave off business, and reunite himself to the count's family; and as the
countess seemed extremely fond of his daughter, she will, in
all probability, insist upon Serafina's accompanying her to
Scotland.

Having paid our compliments to these noble persons, we
returned to the squire's, where we expected an invitation to
pass the night, which was wet and raw; but, it seems,
Squire Burdock's hospitality reached not so far for the honour of Yorkshire: we therefore departed in the evening,
and lay at an inn, where I caught cold.

In hope of riding it down before it could take fast hold on
my constitution, I resolved to visit another relation, one
Mr Pimpernel, who lived about a dozen miles from the
place where we lodged. Pimpernel, being the youngest of
four sons, was bred an attorney at Furnival's inn; but all
his elder brothers dying, he got himself called to the bar for
the honour of his family; and, soon after this preferment,
succeeded to his father's estate, which was very considerable.
He carried home with him all the knavish chicanery of the
lowest pettifogger, together with a wife whom he had purchased of a drayman for twenty pounds; and he soon found

means to obtain a *dedimus* as an acting justice of peace. He
is not only a sordid miser in his disposition, but his avarice
is mingled with a spirit of despotism, which is truly diabolical. He is a brutal husband, an unnatural parent, a harsh
master, an oppressive landlord, a litigious neighbour, and
a partial magistrate. Friends he has none ; and, in point of
hospitality and good breeding, our cousin Burdock is a
prince in comparison of this ungracious miscreant, whose
house is the lively representation of a gaol. Our reception
was suitable to the character I have sketched. Had it depended upon the wife, we should have been kindly treated.
She is really a good sort of a woman, in spite of her low original, and well respected in the county ; but she has not
interest enough in her own house to command a draught of
table-beer, far less to bestow any kind of education on her
children, who run about like ragged colts in a state of nature. Pox on him ! he is such a dirty fellow, that I have
not patience to prosecute the subject.

By that time we reached Harrowgate, I began to be visited by certain rheumatic symptoms. The Scotch lawyer,
Mr Micklewhimmen, recommended a hot bath of these waters so earnestly, that I was over-persuaded to try the experiment. He had used it often with success, and always staid
an hour in the bath, which was a tub filled with Harrowgate
water, heated for the purpose. If I could hardly bear the
smell of a single tumbler when cold, you may guess how my
nose was regaled by the steams arising from a hot bath of
the same fluid.—At night I was conducted into a dark hole
on the ground floor, where the tub smoked and stunk like
the pot of Acheron in one corner, and in another stood a dirty
bed, provided with thick blankets, in which I was to sweat,
after coming out of the bath. My heart seemed to die within me, when I entered this dismal bagnio, and found my brain
assaulted by such insufferable effluvia. I cursed Micklewhimmen, for not considering that my organs were formed
on this side of the Tweed ; but being ashamed to recoil upon the threshold, I submitted to the process.

After having endured all but real suffocation for above a

quarter of an hour in the tub, I was moved to the bed, and wrapped in blankets. · There I lay a full hour, panting with intolerable heat; but not the least moisture appearing on my skin, I was carried to my own chamber, and passed the night without closing an eye, in such a flutter of spirits as rendered me the most miserable wretch in being. I should certainly have run distracted, if the rarefaction of my blood, occasioned by that Stygian bath, had not burst the vessels, and produced a violent hemorrhage, which, though dreadful and alarming, removed the horrible disquiet. I lost two pounds of blood and more on this occasion, and find myself still weak and languid; but, I believe a little exercise will forward my recovery; and therefore I am resolved to set out to-morrow for York, in my way to Scarborough, where I propose to brace up my fibres by sea-bathing, which I know is one of your favourite specifics. There is, however, one disease, for which you have found as yet no specific, and that is old age, of which this tedious unconnected epistle is an infallible symptom. *What* therefore *cannot be cured must be endured*, by you, as well as by yours,

Harrowgate, June 26. MATT. BRAMBLE.

TO SIR WATKIN PHILLIPS, BART. OF JESUS COLLEGE, OXON.

DEAR KNIGHT,

The manner of living at Harrowgate was so agreeable to my disposition, that I left the place with some regret.—Our aunt Tabby would have probably made some objection to our departing so soon, had not an accident embroiled her with Mr Micklewhimmen, the Scots advocate, on whose heart she had been practising, from the second day after our arrival.—That original, though seemingly precluded from the use of his limbs, had turned his genius to good account. In short, by dint of groaning and whinning, he had excited the compassion of the company so effectually, that an old lady, who occupied the very best apartment in the house, gave it up for his ease and convenience. When his man led him into the long-room, all the females were immediately in com-

motion.—One set an elbow-chair; another shook up the
cushion; a third brought a stool; and a fourth a pillow, for
the accommodation of his feet.—Two ladies (of whom Tabby
was always one) supported him into the dining-room, and
placed him properly at the table; and his taste was indulged
with a succession of delicacies, culled by their fair hands.
All this attention he repaid with a profusion of compliments
and benedictions, which were not the less agreeable for being
delivered in the Scottish dialect.   As for Mrs Tabitha, his
respects were particularly addressed to her, and he did not
fail to mingle them with religious reflections, touching free
grace, knowing her bias to methodism; which he also professed upon a calvinistical model.

For my part, I could not help thinking this lawyer was
not such an invalid as he pretended to be.   I observed he eat
very heartily three times a-day; and though his bottle was
marked *stomachic tincture*, he had recourse to it so often,
and seemed to swallow it with such peculiar relish, that I
suspected it was not compounded in the apothecary's shop,
or the chemist's laboratory.   One day, while he was earnest
in discourse with Mrs Tabitha, and his servant had gone out
on some occasion or other, I dexterously exchanged the labels
and situation of his bottle and mine; and, having tasted his tincture, found it was excellent claret. I forthwith handed it about
to some of my neighbours, and it was quite emptied before
Mr Micklewhimmen had occasion to repeat his draught.   At
length, turning about, he took hold of my bottle instead of
his own, and, filling a large glass, drank to the health of Mrs
Tabitha.   It had scarce touched his lips, when he perceived the
change which had been put upon him, and was at first a little
out of countenance.—He seemed to retire within himself, in
order to deliberate, and in half a minute his resolution was
taken; addressing himself to our quarter, ' I give the gentleman credit for his wit,' said he; ' it was a gude practical
joke; but sometimes *hi joci in seria ducunt malo.*—I hope,
for his own sake, he has na drank all the liccor; for it was a
vara poorful infusion of jalap in Bourdeaux wine; and its
possible he may ha ta'en sic a dose as will produce a terrible
catastrophe in his ain booels.'

By far the greater part of the contents had fallen to the
share of a young clothier from Leeds, who had come to make
a figure at Harrowgate, and was, in effect, a great coxcomb
in his way.   It was with a view to laugh at his fellow guests,
as well as to mortify the lawyer, that he had emptied the
bottle, when it came to his turn, and he had laughed accordingly : but now his mirth gave way to his apprehension.
He began to spit, to make wry faces, and writhe himself into various contortions.—'Damn the stuff,' cried he, 'I thought
it had a villanous twang—pah ! he that would cozen a Scot,
mun get oop betimes, and take old Scratch for his counsellor.'
'In troth Mester what d'ye ca'um,' replied the lawyer, 'your
vit has run you into a filthy puddle—I'm truly consarned
for your waeful case.—The best advice I can give you in sic
a delemma, is to send an express to Rippon for Dr Waugh
without delay ; and, in the meantime, swallow all the oil and
butter you can find in the hoose, to defend your poor stomach and intestines from the villication of the particles of
the jalap, which is vara violent, even when taken in moderation.'

The poor clothier's torments had already begun . he retired, roaring with pain, to his own chamber ; the oil was swallowed, and the doctor sent for ; but before he arrived, the
miserable patient had made such discharges upwards and
downwards, that nothing remained to give him farther offence : and this double evacuation was produced by imagination alone ; for what he had drank was genuine wine of
Bourdeaux, which the lawyer had brought from Scotland,
for his own private use.   The clothier, finding the joke turn
out so expensive and disagreeable, quitted the house next
morning, leaving the triumph to Micklewhimmen, who enjoyed it internally, without any outward signs of exultation ;
on the contrary, he affected to pity the young man for what
he had suffered, and acquired fresh credit from this show of
moderation.

It was about the middle of the night which succeeded this
adventure, that the vent of the kitchen-chimney, being foul,
the soot took fire, and the alarm was given in a dreadful

manner. Every body leaped naked out of bed, and in a minute the whole house was filled with cries and confusion. There were two stairs in the house, and to these we naturally ran; but they were both so blocked up, by the people pressing one upon another, that it seemed impossible to pass without throwing down and trampling upon the women. In the midst of this anarchy, Mr Micklewhimmen, with a leathern portmanteau on his back, came running as nimbly as a buck along the passage; and Tabby, in her under petticoat, endeavouring to hook him under the arm, that she might escape through his protection, he very fairly pushed her down, crying, ' Na, na, gude faith, charity begins at hame!' Without paying the least respect to the shrieks and entreaties of his female friends, he charged through the midst of the crowd, overturning every thing that opposed him, and actually fought his way to the bottom of the stair-case.—By this time Clinker had found a ladder, by which he entered the window of my uncle's chamber, where our family was assembled, and proposed that we should make our exit successively by that conveyance. The squire exhorted his sister to begin the descent, but before she could resolve, her woman, Mrs Winifred Jenkins, in a transport of terror, threw herself out at the window upon the ladder, while Humphry dropped upon the ground, that he might receive her in her descent.—This maiden was just as she had started out of bed, the moon shone very bright, and a fresh breeze of wind blowing, none of Mrs Winifred's beauties could possibly escape the view of the fortunate Clinker, whose heart was not able to withstand the united force of so many charms; at least, I am much mistaken if he has not been her humble slave from that moment. He received her in his arms, and, giving her his coat to protect her from the weather, ascended again with admirable dexterity.

At that instant, the landlord of the house called out, with an audible voice, that the fire was extinguished, and the ladies had nothing farther to fear: this was a welcome note to the audience, and produced an immediate effect; the shrieking ceased, and a confused sound of expostulation ensued. I conducted Mrs Tabitha and my sister to their own chamber, where Liddy fainted away, but was soon brought to herself. Then I went to offer my service to the other ladies, who might want assistance. They were all scudding through the passage to their several apartments; and as the thoroughfare was lighted by two lamps, I had a pretty good observation of them in their transit; but, as most of them were naked to the smock, and all their heads shrouded in huge night-caps, I could not distinguish one face from another, though I recognized some of their voices. These were generally plaintive; some wept, some scolded, and some prayed.—I lifted up one poor old gentlewoman, who had been overturned and sore bruised by a multitude of feet; and this was also the case with the lame parson from Northumberland, whom Micklewhimmen had in his passage overthrown, though not with impunity; for the cripple, in falling, gave him such a good pelt in the head with his crutch, that the blood followed.

As for the lawyer, he waited below till the hurly-burly was over, and then stole softly to his own chamber, from whence he did not venture to make a second sally till eleven in the forenoon, when he was led into the public room by his own servant and another assistant, groaning most woefully, with a bloody napkin round his head. But things were greatly altered. The selfish brutality of his behaviour on the stairs had steeled their hearts against all his arts and address. Not a soul offered to accommodate him with a chair, cushion, or footstool; so that he was obliged to sit down on a hard wooden bench. In that position he looked around with a rueful aspect, and, bowing very low, said, in a whining tone, ' Your most humble servant, ladies—Fire is a dreadful calamity.' ' Fire purifies gold, and it tries friendship,' cried Mrs Tabitha, bridling. ' Yea, madam,' replied Micklewhimmen, ' and it trieth discretion also.' ' If discretion consists in forsaking a friend in adversity, you are eminently possessed of that virtue,' resumed our aunt. ' Na, madam,' rejoined the advocate, ' well I wot, I cannot claim any merit from the mode of my retreat.—Ye'll please to observe, ladies, there are twa independent principles that actuate our nature.

One is instinct, which we have in common with the brute creation, and the other is reason.   Noo, in certain great emergencies, when the faculty of reason is suspended, instinct taks the lead; and, when this predominates, having no affinity with reason, it pays no sort of regard to its convictions; it only operates for the preservation of the individual, and that by the most expeditious and effectual means: therefore, begging your pardon, ladies, I'm no accountable, *in foro conscientiæ*, for what I did, while under the influence of this irrisistible pooer.'

Here my uncle interposed,—' I should be glad to know,' said he ' whether it was instinct that prompted you to retreat with bag and baggage; for, I think, you had a portmanteau on your shoulder.'   The lawyer answered, without hesitation, ' Gif I might tell my mind freely, without incurring the suspicion of presumption, I should think it was something superior to either reason or instinct, which suggested that measure, and this on a twafald account: in the first place, the portmanteau contained the writings of a worthy nobleman's estate; and their being burnt would have occasioned a loss that could not be repaired: secondly, my good angel seems to have laid the portmantle on my shoulders, by way of defence, to sustain the violence of a most inhuman blow from the crutch of a reverend clergyman; which, even in spite of that medium, hath wounded me sorely, even unto the pericranium.' ' By your own doctrine,' cried the parson, who chanced to be present, ' I am not accountable for the blow, which was the effect of instinct.' ' I crave your pardon, reverend sir,' said the other, ' instinct never acts but for the preservation of the individual; but your preservation was out of the case—You had already received the damage; and therefore the blow must be imputed to revenge, which is a sinful passion, that ill becomes any christian, especially a protestant divine; and let me tell you, most reverend doctor, gin I had a mind to plea, the law would hauld my libel relevant.' ' Why, the damage is pretty equal on both sides,' cried the parson; ' your head is broken, and my crutch is snapped in the middle—Now, if you will repair the one, I will be at the expense of curing the other.'

This sally raised the laugh against Micklewhimmen, who began to look grave; when my uncle, in order to change the discourse, observed, that instinct had been very kind to him in another respect; for it had restored to him the use of his limbs, which, in his exit, he had moved with surprising agility.—He replied, that it was the nature of fear to brace up the nerves; and mentioned some surprising feats of strength and activity performed by persons under the impulse of terror; but he complained, that, in his own particular, the effects had ceased, when the cause was taken away.—The squire said he would lay a tea-drinking on his head, that he should dance a Scotch measure, without making a false step; and the advocate, grinning, called for the piper. A fiddler being at hand, this original started up, with his bloody napkin over his black tye-periwig, and acquitted himself in such a manner, as excited the mirth of the whole company; but he could not regain the good graces of Mrs Tabby, who did not understand the principle of instinct; and the lawyer did not think it worth his while to proceed to further demonstration.

From Harrowgate we came hither, by the way of York; and here we shall tarry some days, as my uncle and Tabitha are both resolved to make use of the waters. Scarborough, though a paltry town, is romantic, from its situation along a cliff that overhangs the sea.—The harbour is formed by a small elbow of land that runs out as a natural mole, directly opposite to the town; and on that side is the castle, which stands very high, of considerable extent, and, before the invention of gunpowder, was counted impregnable. At the other end of Scarborough are two public rooms, for the use of the company who resort to this place in the summer, to drink the waters, and bath in the sea; and the diversions are pretty much on the same footing here as at Bath. The Spa is a little way beyond the town, on this side, under a cliff, within a few paces of the sea; and thither the bathers go every morning in dishabille; but the descent is by a great number of steps, which invalids find very inconvenient. Betwixt the well and the harbour, the bathing machines are ranged along the beach, with all their proper utensils and attendants.—You have never seen one of these machines— Image to yourself a small, snug, wooden chamber, fixed upon a wheel-carriage, having a door at each end, and, on each side, a little window above, a bench below. The bather, ascending into this apartment by wooden steps, shuts himself in, and begins to undress; while the attendant yokes a horse to the end next the sea, and draws the carriage forwards, till the surface of the water is on a level with the floor of the dressing-room; then he moves and fixes the horse to the other end—The person within, being stripped, opens the door to the seaward, where he finds the guide ready, and plunges headlong into the water. After having bathed, he reascends into the apartment, by the steps which had been shifted for that purpose, and puts on his clothes at his leisure, while the carriage is drawn back again upon the dry land; so that he has nothing further to do, but to open the door, and come down as he went up: should he be so weak or ill as to require a servant to put off and on his clothes, there is room enough in the apartment for half a dozen people. The guides who attend the ladies in the water, are of their own sex; and they and the female bathers have a dress of flannel for the sea; nay, they are provided with other conveniencies for the support of decorum. A certain number of the machines are fitted with tilts, that project from the seaward ends of them, so as to screen the bathers from the view of all persons whatsoever.—The beach is admirably adapted for this practice, the descent being gently gradual, and the sand soft as velvet; but then the machines can be used only at a certain time of the tide, which varies every day; so that sometimes the bathers are obliged to rise very early in the morning—For my part, I love swimming as an exercise, and can enjoy it at all times of the tide, without the formality of an apparatus. You and I have often plunged together into the Isis; but the sea is a much more noble bath, for health as well as pleasure. You cannot conceive what a flow of spirits it gives, and how it braces every sinew of the human frame. Were I to enumerate half the diseases which are every day cured by sea-bathing, you might justly say you had received a treatise, instead of a letter, from your affectionate friend and servant,

Scarborough, July 1. J. MELFORD.

TO DR LEWIS.

I HAVE not found all the benefit I expected at Scarborough, where I have been these eight days.—From Harrowgate we came hither by the way of York, where we staid only one day, to visit the castle, the minster, and the assembly room. The first, which was heretofore a fortress, is now converted into a prison, and is the best, in all respects, I ever saw at home or abroad. It stands in a high situation, extremely well ventilated, and has a spacious area within the walls, for the health and convenience of all the prisoners, except those whom it is necessary to secure in close confinement. Even these last have all the comforts that the nature of their situation can admit of. Here the assises are held, in a range of buildings erected for that purpose.

As for the minster, I knew not how to distinguish it, except by its great size, and the height of its spire, from those other ancient churches in different parts of the kingdom, which used to be called monuments of Gothic architecture; but it is now agreed that this style is Saracen rather than Gothic, and, I suppose, it was first imported into England from Spain, great part of which was under the dominion of the Moors. Those British architects who adopted this style don't seem to have considered the propriety of their adoption. The climate of the country possessed by the Moors or Saracens, both in Africa and Spain, was so exceedingly hot and dry, that those who built places of worship for the multitude, employed their talents in contriving edifices that should be cool; and, for this purpose, nothing could be better adapted than those buildings, vast, narrow, dark, and lofty, impervious to the sun-beams, and having little communication with the scorched external atmosphere; but ever affording a refreshing coolness, like subterranean cellars in the heats of summer, or natural caverns in the bowels of huge mountains. But nothing could be more preposterous than to imitate such a mode of architecture in a country like England, where the climate is cold, and the air eternally loaded with vapours, and where, of consequence, the builder's intention should be to keep the people dry and warm. For my part, I never entered the abbey-church at Bath but once, and, the moment I stepped over the threshold, I found myself chilled to the very marrow of my bones. When we consider, that, in our churches in general, we breathe a gross stagnated air, surcharged with damps from vaults, tombs, and charnel-houses, may we not term them so many magazines of rheums, created for the benefit of the medical faculty; and safely aver, that more bodies are lost than souls saved by going to church, in the winter especially, which may be said to engross eight months in the year. I should be glad to know what offence it would give to tender consciences if the house of God was made more comfortable, or less dangerous to the health of valetudinarians; and whether it would not be an encouragement to piety, as well as the salvation of many lives, if the place of worship was well floored, wainscoted, warmed, and ventilated, and its area kept sacred from the pollution of the dead. The practice of burying in churches was the effect of ignorant superstition, influenced by knavish priests, who pretended that the devil could have no power over the defunct, if he was interred in holy ground; and this indeed is the only reason that can be given for consecrating all cemetries even at this day.

The external appearance of an old cathedral cannot be but displeasing to the eye of every man who has any idea of propriety or proportion, even though he may be ignorant of architecture as a science; and the long slender spire puts one in mind of a criminal impaled, with a sharp stake rising up through his shoulder. These towers, or steeples, were likewise borrowed from the Mahometans, who, having no bells, used such minarets, for the purpose of calling the people to prayers. They may be of farther use, however, for making observations and signals; but I would vote for their being distinct from the body of the church, because they serve only to make the pile more barbarous, or Saracenical.

There is nothing of this Arabic architecture in the assembly-room, which seems to me to have been built upon a design of Palladio, and might be converted into an elegant place of worship; but it is indifferently contrived for that sort of idolatry which is performed in it at present: the grandeur of the fane gives a diminutive effect to the little painted divinities that are adored in it, and the company, on a ball-night, must look like an assembly of fantastic fairies, revelling by moon-light among the columns of a Grecian temple.

Scarborough seems to be falling off in point of reputation. All these places (Bath excepted) have their vogue, and then the fashion changes. I am persuaded there are fifty spas in England as efficacious and salutary as that of Scarborough, though they have not yet risen to fame, and perhaps never will, unless some medical encomiast should find an interest in displaying their virtues to the public view. Be that as it may, recourse will always be had to this place for the convenience of sea-bathing, while this practice prevails; but it were to be wished they would make the beach more accessible to invalids.

I have here met with my old acquaintance, H——t, whom you have often heard me mention as one of the most original characters upon earth. I first knew him at Venice, and afterwards saw him in different parts of Italy, where he was well known by the nickname of Cavallo Bianco, from his appearing always mounted on a pale horse, like Death in the Revelations. You must remember the account I once gave you of a curious dispute he had at Constantinople with a couple of Turks in defence of the christian religion; a dispute from which he acquired the epithet of Demonstrator. The truth is, H——t owns no religion but that of nature; but, on this occasion, he was stimulated to shew his parts, for the honour of his country. Some years ago, being in the

Campidoglio at Rome, he made up to the bust of Jupiter, and, bowing very low, exclaimed, in the Italian language,— ' I hope, sir, if ever you get your head above water again, you will remember that I paid my respects to you in your adversity.' This sally was reported to the Cardinal Camerlengo, and by him laid before Pope Benedict XIV. who could not help laughing at the extravagance of the address, and said to the cardinal,—' Those English heretics think they have a right to go to the devil in their own way.'

Indeed H——t was the only Englishman I ever knew who had resolution enough to live his own way in the midst of foreigners; for, neither in dress, diet, customs, or conversation, did he deviate one tittle from the manner in which he had been brought up. About twelve years ago, he began a giro, or circuit, which he thus performed. At Naples, where he fixed his head-quarters, he embarked for Marseilles, from whence he travelled with a voiturin to Antibes. There he took his passage to Genoa and Lerici; from which last place he proceeded, by the way of Cambvatina, to Pisa, and Florence. After having halted some time in this metropolis, he set out with a vetturino for Rome, where he reposed himself a few weeks, and then continued his route to Naples, in order to wait for the next opportunity of embarkation. After having twelve times described this circle, he lately flew off at a tangent to visit some trees at his country-house in England, which he had planted above twenty years ago, after the plan of the double colonnade in the piazza of St. Peter's at Rome. He came hither to Scarborough to pay his respects to his noble friend and former pupil, the m—— of G——, and, forgetting that he is now turned of seventy, sacrificed so liberally to Bacchus, that next day he was seized with a fit of the apoplexy, which has a little impaired his memory; but he retains all the oddity of his character in perfection, and is going back to Italy by the way of Geneva, that he may have a conference with his friend Voltaire, about giving the last blow to the christian superstition. He intends to take shipping here for Holland or Hamburgh; for it is a matter of great indifference to him at what part of the continent he first lands.

When he was going abroad the last time, he took his
passage in a ship bound for Leghorn, and his baggage was
actually embarked. In going down the river by water, he
was, by mistake, put on board of another vessel under sail,
and, upon inquiry, understood she was bound to Petersburgh. 'Petersburgh—Petersburgh—' said he, 'I don't care
if I go along with you.' He forthwith struck a bargain with
the captain, bought a couple of shirts of the mate, and was
safe conveyed to the court of Muscovy, from whence he travelled by land to receive his baggage at Leghorn. He is now
more likely than ever to execute a whim of the same nature;
and I will hold any wager, that, as he cannot be supposed
to live much longer, according to the course of nature, his
exit will be as odd as his life has been extravagant.[*]

But, to return from one humorist to another—you must
know I have received benefit both from the chalybeate and
the sea, and would have used them longer, had not a most
ridiculous adventure, by making me the town-talk, obliged
me to leave the place; for I can't bear the thoughts of affording a spectacle to the multitude. Yesterday morning, at
six o'clock, I went down to the bathing-place, attended by
my servant Clinker, who waited on the beach as usual.—
The wind blowing from the north, and the weather being
hazy, the water proved so chill, that, when I rose from my
first plunge, I could not help sobbing and bawling out,
from the effects of the cold. Clinker, who heard my cry,
and saw me indistinctly a good way without the guide, buf-
feting the waves, took it for granted I was drowning, and

[*] This gentleman crossed the sea to France, visited and conferred with M.
de Voltaire at Fernay, resumed his old circuit at Genoa, and died in 1767,
at the house of Vanini in Florence. Being taken with a suppression of urine,
he resolved, in imitation of Pomponius Atticus, to take himself off by abstinence; and this resolution he executed like an ancient Roman. He saw company to the last, cracked his jokes, conversed freely, and entertained his guests
with music. On the third day of his fast he found himself entirely freed of
his complaint, but refused taking sustenance. He said, the most disagreeable
part of the voyage was past, and he should be a cursed fool indeed to put a-
bout ship when he was just entering the harbour. In these sentiments he persisted, without any marks of affectation, and thus finished his course with such
ease and serenity, as would have done honour to the firmest stoic of antiquity.

rushing into the sea, clothes and all, overturned the guide, in his hurry to save his master. I had swam out a few strokes, when, hearing a noise, I turned about, and saw Clinker, already up to his neck, advancing towards me, with all the wildness of terror in his aspect. Afraid he would get out of his depth, I made haste to meet him, when, all of a sudden, he seized me by one ear, and dragged me bellowing with pain upon the dry beach, to the astonishment of all the people, men, women, and children, there assembled.

I was so exasperated by the pain of my ear, and the disgrace of being exposed in such an attitude, that, in the first transport, I struck him down; then, running back into the sea, took shelter in the machine, where my clothes had been deposited. I soon recollected myself so far, as to do justice to the poor fellow, who, in great simplicity of heart, had acted from motives of fidelity and affection.—Opening the door of the machine, which was immediately drawn on shore, I saw him standing by the wheel, dropping like a waterwork, and trembling from head to foot, partly from cold, and partly from the dread of having offended his master.— I made my acknowledgments for the blow he had received, assured him I was not angry, and insisted upon his going home immediately, to shift his clothes; a command which he could hardly find in his heart to execute, so well disposed was he to furnish the mob with farther entertainment at my expense. Clinker's intention was laudable, without all doubt; but, nevertheless, I am a sufferer by his simplicity.—I have had a burning heat, and a strange bussing noise in that ear, ever since it was so roughly treated; and I cannot walk the street without being pointed at, as the monster that was hauled naked ashore upon the beach. Well, I affirm that folly is often more provoking than knavery, ay and more mischievous too; and whether a man had not better choose a sensible rogue, than an honest simpleton, for his servant, is no matter of doubt with yours,

Scarborough, July 4.   MATT. BRAMBLE.

TO SIR WATKIN PHILLIPS, BART. OF JESUS COLLEGE, OXON.

DEAR WAT,

WE made a precipitate retreat from Scarborough, owing to the excessive delicacy of our squire, who cannot bear the thoughts of being *prætereuntium digito monstratus.*

One morning, while he was bathing in the sea, his man Clinker took it in his head that his master was in danger of drowning; and, in this conceit, plunging into the water, he lugged him out naked on the beach, and almost pulled off his ear in the operation. You may guess how this achievement was relished by Mr Bramble, who is impatient, irascible, and has the most extravagant ideas of decency and decorum in the economy of his own person.—In the first ebulition of his choler, he knocked Clinker down with his fist; but he afterwards made him amends for this outrage; and, in order to avoid the further notice of the people, among whom this incident had made him remarkable, he resolved to leave Scarborough next day.

We set out accordingly over the muirs, by the way of Whitby, and began our journey betimes, in hopes of reaching Stockton that night; but in this hope we were disappointed.—In the afternoon, crossing a deep gutter, made by a torrent, the coach was so hard strained, that one of the irons which connect the frame snapt, and the leather sling on the same side cracked in the middle. The shock was so great, that my sister Liddy struck her head against Mrs Tabitha's nose with such violence that the blood flowed; and Win Jenkins was darted through a small window in that part of the carriage next the horses, where she stuck like a bawd in the pillory, till she was released by the hand of Mr Bramble. We were eight miles distant from any place where we could be supplied with chaises, and it was impossible to proceed with the coach, until the damage should be repaired.—In this dilemma, we discovered a blacksmith's forge on the edge of a small common, about half a mile from the scene of our disaster, and thither the postillions made shift to draw the carriage slowly, while the company walked a-foot; but we

found the blacksmith had been dead some days; and his
wife, who had been lately delivered, was deprived of her
senses, under the care of a nurse hired by the parish.   We
were exceedingly mortified at this disappointment, which,
however, was surmounted by the help of Humphry Clinker,
who is a surprising compound of genius and simplicity.
Finding the tools of the defunct, together with some coals
in the smithy, he unscrewed the damaged iron in a twinkling, and, kindling a fire, united the broken pieces with
equal dexterity and dispatch.   While he was at work upon
this operation, the poor woman in the straw, struck with
the well-known sound of the hammer and anvil, started up,
and, notwithstanding all the nurse's efforts, came running
into the smithy, where, throwing her arms about Clinker's
neck,—'ah, Jacob!' cried she, 'how could you leave me
in such a condition?'

This incident was too pathetic to occasion mirth—it brought
tears into the eyes of all present.   The poor widow was put
to bed again; and we did not leave the village without doing
something for her benefit.—Even Tabitha's charity was
awakened on this occasion.   As for the tender-hearted Humphry Clinker, he hammered the iron, and wept at the same
time.—But his ingenuity was not confined to his own province of farrier and blacksmith—it was necessary to join the
leather sling, which had been broke; and this service he
likewise performed, by means of a broken awl, which he
new-pointed and ground, a little hemp which he spun into
lingles, and a few tacks which he made for the purpose.
Upon the whole, we were in a condition to proceed in little
more than one hour; but even this delay obliged us to pass
the night at Gainsborough.   Next day we crossed the Tees at
Stockton, which is a neat agreeable town; and there we resolved to dine, with purpose to lie at Durham.

Whom should we meet in the yard, when we alighted,
but Martin the adventurer! Having handed out the ladies,
and conducted them into an apartment, where he paid his
compliments to Mrs Tabby, with his usual address, he
begged leave to speak to my uncle in another room; and

there, in some confusion, he made an apology for having taken the liberty to trouble him with a letter at Stevenage. He expressed his hope, that Mr Bramble had bestowed some consideration on his unhappy case, and repeated his desire of being taken into his service.

My uncle, calling me into the room, told him, that we were both very well inclined to rescue him from a way of life that was equally dangerous and dishonourable; and that he should have no scruple in trusting to his gratitude and fidelity, if he had any employment for him, which he thought would suit his qualifications and his circumstances; but that all the departments he had mentioned in his letter were filled up by persons of whose conduct he had no reason to complain; of consequence he could not, without injustice, deprive any one of them of his bread.—Nevertheless, he declared himself ready to assist him in any feasible project, either with his purse or credit.

Martin seemed deeply touched at this declaration.—The tear started in his eye, while he said, in a faltering accent—'Worthy sir—your generosity oppresses me—I never dreamed of troubling you for any pecuniary assistance—indeed I have no occasion—I have been so lucky at billiards and betting at different places, at Buxton, Harrowgate, Scarborough, and Newcastle races, that my stock in ready-money amounts to three hundred pounds, which I would willingly employ in prosecuting some honest scheme of life; but my friend Justice Buzzard has set so many springs for my life, that I am under the necessity of either retiring immediately to a remote part of the country, where I can enjoy the protection of some generous patron, or of quitting the kingdom altogether.—It is upon this alternative that I now beg leave to ask your advice.—I have had information of all your route since I had the honour to see you at Stevenage; and, supposing you would come this way from Scarborough, I came hither last night from Darlington to pay you my respects.'

'It would be no difficult matter to provide you with an asylum in the country,' replied my uncle; 'but a life of

indolence and obscurity would not suit with your active and
enterprising disposition.—I would therefore advise you to
try your fortune in the East Indies.—I will give you a letter
to a friend in London, who will recommend you to the directors, for a commission in the company's service; and if
that cannot be obtained, you will at least be received as a
volunteer—in which case you may pay for your passage,
and I shall undertake to procure you such credentials, that
you will not be long without a commission.'

Martin embraced the proposal with great eagerness; it
was therefore resolved that he should sell his horse, and take
a passage by sea for London, to execute the project without
delay.—In the meantime, he accompanied us to Durham,
where we took up our quarters for the night.—Here, being
furnished with letters from my uncle, he took his leave of
us, with strong symptoms of gratitude and attachment, and
set out for Sunderland, in order to embark in the first collier
bound for the river Thames. He had not been gone half an
hour, when we were joined by another character, which promised something extraordinary.—A tall meagre figure, answering, with his horse, the description of Don Quixote
mounted on Rozinante, appeared in the twilight at the inn
door, while my aunt and Liddy stood at a window in the
dining-room.—He wore a coat, the cloth of which had once
been scarlet, trimmed with Branderburgs, now totally deprived of their metal; and he had holster-caps and housing
of the same stuff and same antiquity. Perceiving ladies at
the window above, he endeavoured to dismount with the
most graceful air he could assume; but the ostler neglecting to hold the stirrup, when he wheeled off his right foot,
and stood with his whole weight on the other, the girth un-
fortunately gave way, the saddle turned, down came the ca-
valier to the ground, and his hat and periwig falling off,
displayed a head-piece of various colours, patched and plas-
tered in a woeful condition.—The ladies at the window
above shrieked with affright, on the supposition that the
stranger had received some notable damage in his fall; but
the greatest injury he had sustained, arose from the dishon-

our of his descent, aggravated by the disgrace of exposing
the condition of his cranium; for certain plebeians that
were about the door, laughed aloud, in the belief that the
captain had got either a scald head, or a broken head, both
equally opprobrious.

He forthwith leaped up in a fury, and snatching one of
his pistols, threatened to put the ostler to death, when another squall from the women checked his resentment. He
then bowed to the window, while he kissed the but-end of
his pistol, which he replaced, adjusted his wig in great confusion, and led his horse into the stable.—By this time I
had come to the door, and could not help gazing at the
strange figure that presented itself to my view.—He would
have measured above six feet in height, had he stood upright; but he stooped very much, was very narrow in the
shoulders, and very thick in the calves of the legs, which
were cased in black spatterdashes.—As for his thighs, they
were long and slender, like those of a grashopper; his face
was at least half a yard in length, brown and shrivelled,
with projecting cheek-bones, little grey eyes on the greenish
hue, a large hook nose, a pointed chin, a mouth from ear
to ear, very ill furnished with teeth, and a high narrow
forehead well furrowed with wrinkles. His horse was exactly in the style of its rider; a resurrection of dry bones, which
(as we afterwards learned) he valued exceedingly, as the
only present he had ever received in his life.

Having seen this favourite steed properly accommodated
in the stable, he sent up his compliments to the ladies, begging permission to thank them in person for the marks of
concern they had shewn at his disaster in the court-yard.—
As the squire said they could not decently decline his visit,
he was shewn up stairs, and paid his respects in the Scots
dialect, with much formality.—' Ladies,' said he, perhaps you may be scandaleezed at the appearance my head
made when it was uncovered by accident: but I can assure
you, the condition you saw it in is neither the effects of disease, nor of drunkenness; but an honest scar received in th
service of my country.' He then gave us to understand,

that, having been wounded at Ticonderago in America, a
party of Indians rifled him, scalped him, broke his skull
with the blow of a tomahawk, and left him for dead on the
field of battle; but that, being afterwards found with signs
of life, he had been cured in the French hospital, though
the loss of substance could not be repaired; so that the skull
was left naked in several places, and these he covered with
patches.

There is no hold by which an Englishman is sooner taken
than that of compassion.—We were immediately interested
in behalf of this veteran.—Even Tabby's heart was melted;
but our pity was warmed with indignation, when we learned,
that, in the course of two sanguinary wars, he had been
wounded, maimed, mutilated, taken, and enslaved, without
ever having attained a higher rank than that of lieutenant.
—My uncle's eyes gleamed, and his nether lip quivered,
while he exclaimed,—' I vow to God, sir, your case is a reproach to the service.—The injustice you have met with is
so flagrant'— ' I must crave your pardon, sir,' cried the
other, interrupting him, ' I complain of no injustice.—I
purchased an ensigncy thirty years ago; and, in the course
of service, rose to be a lieutenant, according to my senior-
ity.—' But in such a length of time,' resumed the squire,
' you must have seen a great many young officers put over
your head.—' ' Nevertheless,' said he, ' I have no cause
to murmur.—They bought their preferment with their money.—I had no money to carry to market—that was my
misfortune; but nobody was to blame.—' ' What! no
friend to advance a sum of money?' said Mr Bramble.
' Perhaps I might have borrowed money for the purchase of
a company,' answered the other; ' but that loan must have
been refunded; and I did not choose to encumber myself
with a debt of a thousand pounds, to be paid from an income
of ten shillings a-day.' ' So you have spent the best part of
your life,' cried Mr Bramble, ' your youth, your blood, and
your constitution, amidst the dangers, the difficulties, the
horrors, and hardships of war, for the consideration of three
or four shillings a-day—a consideration—' ' Sir,' replied

the Scot, with great warmth, 'you are the man that does me injustice, if you say or think I have been actuated by any such paltry consideration.—I am a gentleman; and entered the service as other gentlemen do, with such hopes and sentiments as honourable ambition inspires.—If I have not been lucky in the lottery of life, so neither do I think myself unfortunate.—I owe no man a farthing; I can always command a clean shirt, a mutton chop, and a truss of straw; and, when I die, I shall leave effects sufficient to defray the expense of my burial.'

My uncle assured him, he had no intention to give him the least offence, by the observations he had made; but, on the contrary, spoke from a sentiment of friendly regard to his interest.—The lieutenant thanked him with a stiffness of civility, which nettled our old gentleman, who perceived that his moderation was all affected; for, whatsoever his tongue might declare, his whole appearance denoted dissatisfaction.—In short, without pretending to judge of his military merit, I think I may affirm, that this Caledonian is a self-conceited pedant, awkward, rude, and disputacious.—He has had the benefit of a school education, seems to have read a good number of books, his memory is tenacious, and he pretends to speak several different languages; but he is so addicted to wrangling, that he will cavil at the clearest truths, and, in the pride of argumentation, attempt to reconcile contradictions.—Whether his address and qualifications are really of that stamp which is agreeable to the taste of our aunt Mrs Tabitha, or that indefatigable maiden is determined to shoot at every sort of game, certain it is, she has begun to practise upon the heart of the lieutenant, who favoured us with his company at supper.

I have many other things to say of this man of war, which I shall communicate in a post or two. Meanwhile, it is but reasonable that you should be indulged with some respite from those weary lucubrations of, yours,

Newcastle upon Tyne, July 10.   J. MELFORD.

TO SIR WATKIN PHILLIPS, BART. OF JESUS COLLEGE, OXON.

DEAR PHILLIPS,

In my last, I treated you with a high-flavoured dish, in the character of the Scots lieutenant, and I must present him once more for your entertainment. It was our fortune to feed upon him the best part of three days; and I do not doubt that he will start again in our way before we shall have finished our northern excursion. The day after our meeting with him at Durham proved so tempestuous, that we did not choose to proceed on our journey; and my uncle persuaded him to stay till the weather should clear up, giving him, at the same time, a general invitation to our mess. The man has certainly gathered a whole budget of shrewd observations, but he brings them forth in such an ungracious manner as would be extremely disgusting, if it was not marked by that characteristic oddity which never fails to attract the attention.—He and Mr Bramble discoursed, and even disputed, on different subjects in war, policy, the belles lettres, law, and metaphysics; and sometimes they were warmed into such altercation as seemed to threaten an abrupt dissolution of their society; but Mr Bramble set a guard over his own irascibility, the more vigilantly as the officer was his guest; and when, in spite of all his efforts, he began to wax warm, the other prudently cooled in the same proportion.

Mrs Tabitha chancing to accost her brother by the familiar diminutive of Matt, 'Pray, sir,' said the lieutenant, 'is your name Matthias?' You must know, it is one of our uncle's foibles to be ashamed of his name, Matthew, because it is puritanical; and this question chagrined him so much, that he answered,—'No, by G—d!' in a very abrupt tone of displeasure.—The Scot took umbrage at the manner of his reply, and bristling up,—'If I had known,' said he, 'that you did not care to tell your name, I should not have asked the question.—The leddy called you Matt, and I naturally thought it was Matthias;—perhaps it may be Methu-

-selah, or Metrodorus, or Metellus, or Mathurians, or Mal-
thinnus, or Matamorus, or ———.' 'No,' cried my uncle
laughing, 'it is neither of those captain.—My name is
Matthew Bramble, at your service. The truth is, I have a
foolish pique at the name of Matthew, because it savours of
those canting hypocrites, who in Cromwell's time, christened all their children by names taken from the scripture.'
'A foolish pique, indeed,' cried Mrs Tabby, 'and even
sinful, to fall out with your name because it is taken from
holy writ. I would have you to know, you was called after
great uncle Matthew ap Madoc ap Meredith, esquire, of
Llanwysthln, in Montgomeryshire, justice of the *quorum*,
and *crusty rustleorum*, a gentleman of great worth and property, descended in a straight line, by the female side, from
Llewellyn, prince of Wales.

This genealogical anecdote seemed to make some impression upon the North Briton, who bowed very low to the descendants of Llewellyn; and observed, that he himself had
the honour of a scriptural nomination. The lady expressing
a desire of knowing his address, he said, he designed himself
Lieutenant Obadiah Lismahago; and in order to assist her
memory, he presented her with a slip of paper inscribed with
these three words, which she repeated with great emphasis,
declaring it was one of the most noble and senorous names
she had ever heard. He observed, that Obadiah was an ad-
ventitious appellation, derived from his great-grandfather,
who had been one of the original covenanters; but Lismahago was the family surname, taken from a place in Scotland
so called. He likewise dropped some hints about the antiquity of his pedigree, adding, with a smile of self-denial,
*sed genus et proavos, et quæ non fecimus ipsi, viæ ea nostra
voco*, which quotation he explained, in deference to the ladies; and Mrs Tabitha did not fail to compliment him on
his modesty, in waving the merit of his ancestry; adding,
that it was the less necessary to him, as he had such a considerable fund of his own.—She now began to glue herself to
his favour, with the grossest adulation. She expatiated upon the antiquity and virtues of the Scottish nation, upon their

valour, probity, learning, and politeness: she even descended
to encomiums on his own personal address, his gallantry,
good sense, and erudition: she appealed to her brother, whether the captain was not the very image of our cousin Governor Griffith. She discovered a surprising eagerness to
know the particulars of his life, and asked a thousand questions concerning his achievements in war; all which Mr
Lismahago answered; with a sort of jesuitical reserve; affecting a reluctance to satisfy her curiosity, on a subject that
concerned his own exploits.

By dint of her interrogations, however, we learned, that
he and Ensign Murphy had made their escape from the
French hospital at Montreal, and taken to the woods, in hope
of reaching some English settlement; but, mistaking their
route they fell in with a party of Miamis, who carried them
away in captivity. The intention of these Indians was to
give one of them as an adopted son to a venerable sachem,
who had lost his own in the course of the war, and to sacrifice the other, according to the custom of the country. Murphy, as being the younger and handsomer of the two, was
designed to fill the place of the deceased, not only as the son
of the sachem, but as the spouse of a beautiful squaw, to
whom his predecessor had been betrothed; but, in passing
through the different wigwams, or villages, of the Miamis,
poor Murphy was so mangled by the women and children,
who have the privilege of torturing all prisoners in their passage, that, by the time they arrived at the place of the sachem's residence, he was rendered altogether unfit for the
purposes of marriage: it was determined, therefore, in the
assembly of the warriors, that Ensign Murphy should be
brought to the stake, and that the lady should be given to
Lieutenant Lismahago, who had likewise received his share
of torments, though they had not produced emasculation.—
A joint of one finger had been cut, or rather sawed off, with
a rusty knife; one of his great toes was crushed into a mash
betwixt two stones; some of his teeth were drawn or dug out
with a crooked nail; splintered reeds had been thrust up his
nostrils, and other tender parts; and the calves of his legs

had been blown up with mines of gunpowder, dug in the
flesh with the sharp point of the tomahawk.

The Indians themselves allowed that Murphy died with
great heroism, singing, as his death song, the *Drimmendoo*,
in concert with Mr Lismahago, who was present at the solemnity. After the warriors and the matrons had made a
hearty meal upon the muscular flesh, which they pared from
the victim, and had applied a great variety of tortures,
which he bore without flinching, an old lady, with a sharp
knife, scooped out one of his eyes, and put a burning coal
in the socket. The pain of this operation was so exquisite,
that he could not help bellowing, upon which the audience
raised a shout of exultation, and one of the warriors, stealing
behind him, gave him the *coup de grace* with a hatchet.

Lismahago's bride, the squaw Squinkinacoosta, distinguished herself on this occasion. She shewed a great supe-
riority of genius, in the tortures which she contrived and executed with her own hands: she vied with the stoutest warrior in eating the flesh of the sacrifice; and, after all the other
females were fuddled with dram-drinking, she was not so intoxicated but that she was able to play the game of the plat-
ter with the conjuring sachem, and afterwards go through
the ceremony of her own wedding, which was consummated
that same evening. The captain had lived very happily
with this accomplished squaw for two years, during which
she bore him a son, who is now the representative of his mother's tribe; but, at length, to his unspeakable grief, she had
died of a fever, occasioned by eating too much raw bear,
which they had killed in a hunting excursion.

By this time Mr Lismahago was elected sachem, acknowledged first warrior of the Badger tribe, and dignified with
the name or epithet of Occacanastaogsrora, which signifies
nimble as a weasel; but all these advantages and honours he
was obliged to resign, in consequence of being exchanged for
the orator of the community, who had been taken prisoner
by the Indians that were in alliance with the English. At
the peace, he had sold out upon half pay, and was returned to Britain, with a view to pass the rest of his life in his

own country, where he hoped to find some retreat, where his
slender finances would afford him a decent subsistence.—
Such are the outlines of Mr Lismahago's history, to which
Tabitha *did seriously incline her ear* ; indeed, she seemed to
be taken with the same charms that captivated the heart of
Desdemona, who loved the Moor *for the dangers he had
passed.*

The description of poor Murphy's sufferings, which threw
my sister Liddy into a swoon, extracted some sighs from the
breast of Mrs Tabby ; when she understood he had been rendered unfit for marriage, she began to spit, and ejaculated,
' Jesus, what cruel barbarians !' and she made wry faces at
the lady's nuptial repast ; but she was eagerly curious to
know the particulars of her marriage dress ; whether she
wore high-breasted stays or boddice, a rob of silk or velvet, and laces of Mechlin or minionette—she supposed, as
they were connected with the French, she used *rouge*, and
had her hair dressed in the Parisian fashion.   The captain
would have declined giving a categorical explanation of all
these particulars, observing, in general, that the Indians were
too tenacious of their own customs to adopt the modes of any
nation whatever : he said, moreover, that neither the simplicity of their manners, nor the commerce of their country,
would admit of those articles of luxury which are deemed
magnificence in Europe ; and that they were too virtuous and
sensible to encourage the introduction of any fashion which
might help to render them corrupt and effeminate. '

These observations served only to inflame her desire of
knowing the particulars about which she had inquired ; and,
with all his evasion, he could not help discovering the following particulars—That his princess had neither shoes,
stockings, shifts, nor any kind of linen—that her bridal dress
consisted of a petticoat of red baize, and a fringed blanket,
fastened about her shoulders with a copper skewer ; but of
ornaments she had great plenty—Her hair was curiously
plaited, and interwoven with bobbins of human bone—one
eye-lid was painted green, and the other yellow ; the cheeks
were blue, the lips white, the teeth red, and there was a black

list drawn down the middle of the forehead as far as the tip
of the nose—a couple of gaudy parot's feathers were stuck
through the division of the nostrils—there was a blue stone
set in the chin—her ear-rings consisted of two pieces of hick-
ery, of the size and shape of drumsticks—her legs and arms
were adorned with bracelets of wampum—her breast glitter-
ed with numerous strings of glass beads—she wore a curious
pouch, or pocket, of woven grass, elegantly painted with
various colours—about her neck was hung the fresh scalp of
a Mohawk warrior, whom her deceased lover had lately slain
in battle—and, finally, she was anointed from head to foot
with bear's grease, which set forth a most agreeable odour.

One would imagine that these paraphernalia would not
have been much admired by a modern fine lady; but Mrs
Tabitha was resolved to approve of all the captain's connections. She wished, indeed, the squaw had been better provided with linen; but she owned there was much taste and
fancy in her ornaments; she made no doubt, therefore, that
Madam Squinkinacoosta was a young lady of good sense and
rare accomplishments, and a good christian at bottom. Then
she asked whether his consort had been high-church, or low-
church, presbyterian, or anabaptist, or had been favoured
with any glimmering of the new light of the gospel? When
he confessed that she and the whole nation were utter strangers to the christian faith, she gazed at him with signs of
astonishment; and Humphry Clinker, who chanced to be
in the room, uttered a hollow groan.

After some pause—' In the name of God, Captain Lismahago,' cried she, ' what religion do they profess?' ' As to
religion, madam,' answered the lieutenant, ' it is among
those Indians a matter of great simplicity—they never heard
of any *alliance between church and state.* They, in general,
worship two contending principles; one the fountain of all
good, the other the source of evil. The common people
there, as in other countries, run into the absurdity of superstition; but sensible men pay adoration to a supreme
Being, who created and sustains the universe.' ' O ! what
pity,' exclaimed the pious Tabby, ' that some holy man has
not been inspired to go and convert these poor heathens !'

The lieutenant told her, that, while he resided among them, two French missionaries arrived, in order to convert them to the catholic religion; but when they talked of mysteries and revelations, which they could neither explain nor authenticate, and called in the evidence of miracles, which they believed upon hearsay; when they taught, that the supreme Creator of heaven and earth had allowed his only son, his own equal in power and glory, to enter the bowels of a woman, to be born as a human creature, to be insulted, flagellated, and even executed as a malefactor; when they pretended to create God himself, to swallow, digest, revive, and multiply him, *ad infinitum*, by the help of a little flour and water, the Indians were shocked at the impiety of their presumption. They were examined by the assembly of the sachems, who desired them to prove the divinity of their mission by some miracle.—They answered, that it was not in their power—' If you were really sent by heaven for our conversion,' said one of the sachems, ' you would certainly have some supernatural endowments, at least you would have the gift of tongues, in order to explain your doctrine to the different nations among which you are employed; but you are so ignorant of our language, that you cannot express yourselves even on the most trifling subjects.'

In a word, the assembly was convinced of their being cheats, and even suspected them of being spies:—they ordered them a bag of Indian corn a-piece, and appointed a guide to conduct them to the frontiers; but the missionaries having more zeal than discretion, refused to quit the vineyard.— They persisted in saying mass, in preaching, baptising, and squabbling with the conjurors, or priests of the country, till they had thrown the whole commnuity into confusion.— Then the assembly proceeded to try them as impious impostors, who represented the Almighty as a trifling, weak capricious being; and pretended to make, unmake, and reproduce him at pleasure: they were, therefore, convicted of blasphemy and sedition, and condemned to the stake, where they died singing *salve regina*, in a rapture of joy, for the crown of martyrdom which they had thus obtained.

In the course of this conversation, Lieutenant Lismahago dropt some hints, by which it appeared he himself was a free-thinker. Our aunt seemed to be startled at certain sarcasms he threw out against the creed of S^t. Athanasius.—He dwelt much upon the words, *reason, philosophy,* and *contradiction in terms*—he bid defiance to the eternity of hell-fire ; and even threw such squibs at the immortality of the soul, as singed a little the whiskers of Mrs Tabitha's faith ; for, by this time she began to look upon Lismahago as a prodigy of learning and sagacity.—In short, he could be no longer insensible to the advances she made towards his affection ; and, although there was something repulsive in his nature, he overcame it so far, as to make some return to her civilities. Perhaps, he thought it would be no bad scheme, in a superannuated lieutenant on half-pay, to effect a conjunction with an old maid, who, in all probability, had fortune enough to keep him easy and comfortable in the fag-end of his days.—An ogling correspondence forthwith commenced between this amiable pair of originals.—He began to sweeten the natural acidity of his discourse with the treacle of compliment and commendation. He from time to time offered her snuff, of which he himself took great quantities, and even made her a present of a purse of silk-grass, woven by the hands of the amiable Squinkinacoosta, who had used it as a shot-pouch in her hunting expeditions.

From Doncaster northwards, all the windows of all the inns are scrawled with doggerel rhymes, in abuse of the Scots nation ; and what surprised me very much, I did not perceive one line written in the way of recrimination. Curious to hear what Lismahago would say on this subject, I pointed out to him a very scurrilous epigram against his countrymen, which was engraved on one of the windows of the parlour where we sat—He read it with the most starched composure ; and when I asked his opinion of the poetry—' It is vara terse and vara poignant,' said he ; ' but, with the help of a wat dishclout, it might be rendered more clear and perspicuous—I marvel much that some modern wit has not published a collection of these essays, under the title of the *Gla-*

xier's triumph 'over Sawney the Scot—I'm persuaded it would be a vara agreeable offering to the patriots of London and Westminster.' When I expressed some surprise that the natives of Scotland, who travel this way, had not broke all the windows upon the road,—' With submission,' replied the lieutenant, ' that were but shallow policy—it would only serve to make the satire more cutting and severe ; and I think, it is much better to let it stand in the window, than have it presented in the reckoning.'

My uncle's jaws began to quiver with indignation—He said, the scribblers of such infamous stuff deserved to be scourged at the cart's tail for disgracing their country with such monuments of malice and stupidity—' These vermin,' said he ' do not consider that they are affording their fellow-subjects, whom they abuse, continual matter of self-gratulation, as well as the means of executing the most manly vengeance that can be taken for such low illiberal attacks. For my part, I admire the philosophic forbearance of the Scots, as much as I despise the insolence of those wretched libellers, which is a-kin to the arrogance of the village cock, who never crows but upon his own dunghill.'—The captain, with an affectation of candour, observed, that men of illiberal minds were produced in every soil; that, in supposing those were the sentiments of the English in general, he should pay too great a compliment to his own country, which was not of consequence enough to attract the envy of such a flourishing and powerful people.

Mrs Tabby broke forth again in praise of his moderation, and declared that Scotland was the soil which produced every virtue under Heaven. When Lismahago took his leave for the night, she asked her brother, if the captain was not the prettiest gentleman he had ever seen ; and whether there was not something wonderfully engaging in his aspect ?—Mr Bramble having eyed her for some time in silence,—' sister,' said he, ' the lieutenant is, for aught I know, an honest man, and a good officer—he has a considerable share of understanding, and a title to more encouragement than he seems to have met with in life; but I cannot, with a safe conscience, affirm, that he is the prettiest gentleman I ever saw; neither can I discern any engaging charm in his countenance, which, I vow to God, is, on the contrary, very hard-favoured and forbidding.'

I have endeavoured to ingratiate myself with this North Briton, who is really a curiosity: but he has been very shy of my conversation, ever since I laughed at his asserting that the English tongue was spoke with more propriety at Edinburgh than at London. Looking at me with a double squeeze of souring in his aspect,—' if the old definition be true,' said he, ' that risibility is the distinguishing characteristic of a rational creature, the English are the most distinguished for rationality of any people I ever knew.' I owned that the English were easily struck with any thing that appeared ludicrous, and apt to laugh accordingly; but it did not follow, that, because they were more given to laughter, they had more rationality than their neighbours; I said, such an inference would be an injury to the Scots, who were by no means defective in rationality, though generally supposed little subject to the impressions of humour.

The captain answered, that this supposition must have been deduced either from their conversation or their compositions, of which the English could not possibly judge with precision, as they did not understand the dialect used by the Scots in common discourse, as well as in their works of humour. When I desired to know what those works of humour were, he mentioned a considerable number of pieces, which he insisted were equal in point of humour to any thing extant in any language dead or living—He, in particular recommended a collection of detached poems, in two small volumes, entitled, *The Evergreen*, and the works of Allan Ramsay, which I intend to provide myself with at Edinburgh—He observed, that a North Briton is seen to a disadvantage in an English company, because he speaks in a dialect that they can't relish, and in a phraseology which they don't understand.—He, therefore, finds himself under a restraint which is a great enemy to wit and humour.— These are faculties which never appear in full lustre, but when the mind is perfectly at ease, and, as an excellent writer says, enjoys *her elbow-room*.

He proceeded to explain his assertion, that the English language was spoken with greater propriety at Edinburgh than in London. He said, what we generally called the Scottish dialect, was, in fact, true, genuine, old English, with a mixture of some French terms and idioms, adopted in a long intercourse betwixt the French and Scots nations; that the modern English, from affectation and false refinement, had weakened, and even corrupted their language, by throwing out the guttural sounds, altering the pronunciation and the quantity, and disusing many words and terms of great significance. In consequence of these innovations, the works of our best poets, such as Chaucer, Spenser, and even Shakspeare, were become, in many parts, unintelligible to the natives of South Britain; whereas the Scots, who retain the ancient language, understand them without the help of a glossary.—'For instance,' said he, 'how have your commentators been puzzled by the following expression in the *Tempest—He's gentle, and not fearful:* as if it was a paralogism to say, that, being *gentle*, he must of course be *courageous*; but the truth is, one of the original meanings, if not the sole meaning, of that word was, *noble, high-minded;* and to this day, a Scotswoman in the situation of the young lady in the *Tempest*, would express herself nearly in the same terms—Don't provoke him; for being gentle, that is, *high-spirited*, he won't tamely bear an insult. Spenser, in the very first stanza of his *Faery Queen*, says,

'A *gentle* knight was pricking on the plain;'

which knight, far from being *tame* and fearful, was so stout, that

'Nothing did he dread, but ever was ydrad.'

To prove that we had impaired the energy of our language by false refinement, he mentioned the following words, which, though widely different in signification, are pronounced exactly in the same manner—*wright, write, right, rite;* but, among the Scots, these words are as different in pronunciation, as they are in meaning and orthography; and this is the case with many others which he mentioned by way of illustration. He moreover took notice, that we had (for what reason he could never learn) altered the sound of our vowels from that which is retained by all the nations in Europe; an alteration which rendered the language extremely difficult to foreigners, and made it almost impracticable to lay down general rules for orthography and pronunciation. Besides, the vowels were no longer simple sounds in the mouth of an Englishman, who pronounced both *i* and *u* as diphthongs. Finally, he affirmed, that we mumbled our speech with our lips and teeth, and ran the words together without pause or distinction, in such a manner, that a foreigner, though he understood English tolerably well, was often obliged to have recourse to a Scotsman to explain what a native of England had said in his own language.

The truth of this remark was confirmed by Mr Bramble from his own experience; but he accounted for it on another principle. He said, the same observation would hold in all languages; that a Swiss talking French was more easily understood than a Parisian, by a foreigner who had not made himself master of the language; because every language had its peculiar recitative, and it would always require more pains, attention, and practice, to acquire both the words and the music, than to learn the words only; and yet nobody would deny, that the one was imperfect without the other; he, therefore, apprehended, that the Scotsman and the Swiss were better understood by learners, because they spoke the words only, without the music, which they could not rehearse. One would imagine this check might have damped the North Briton; but it served only to agitate his humour for disputation. He said, if every nation had its own recitative or music, the Scots had theirs; and the Scotsman who had not yet acquired the cadence of the English, would naturally use his own in speaking their language; therefore, if he was better understood than the native, his recitative must be more intelligible than that of the English; of consequence, the dialect of the Scots had an advantage over that of their fellow-subjects, and this was

another strong presumption that the modern English had
corrupted their language in the article of pronunciation.

The lieutenant was, by this time, become so polemical,
that every time he opened his mouth, out flew a paradox,
which he maintained with all the enthusiasm of altercation;
but all his paradoxes savoured strong of a partiality for his
own country.   He undertook to prove that poverty was a
blessing to a nation; that *oatmeal* was preferable to *wheat
flower;* and that the worship of Cloacina, in temples which
admitted both sexes, and every rank of votaries promiscuously, was a filthy species of idolatry that outraged every
idea of delicacy and decorum.   I did not so much wonder
at his broaching these doctrines, as at the arguments, equally whimsical and ingenious, which he adduced in support
of them.

In fine, Lieutenant Lismahago is a curiosity which I
have not yet sufficiently perused; and, therefore, I shall be
sorry when we lose his company, though, God knows,
there is nothing very amiable in his manner or disposition.
As he goes directly to the south-west division of Scotland,
and we proceed in the road to Berwick, we shall part to-
morrow at a place called Feltonbridge; and, I dare say,
this separation will be very grievous to our aunt Mrs Tabitha, unless she has received some flattering assurance of
his meeting her again.   If I fail in my purpose of entertaining with these unimportant occurrences, they will at least
serve as exercises of patience, for which you are indebted to
yours always,

Morpeth, July 13.   J. MELFORD.

TO DR LEWIS.

DEAR DOCTOR,

I HAVE now reached the northern extremity of England,
and see, close to my chamber window, the Tweed gliding
through the arches of that bridge which connects this sub-
urb to the town of Berwick.   Yorkshire you have seen, and
therefore I shall say nothing of that opulent province.   The

city of Durham appears like a confused heap of stones and brick, accumulated so as to cover a mountain, round which a river winds its brawling course. The streets are generally narrow, dark, and unpleasant, and many of them almost impassable in consequence of their declivity. The cathedral is a huge gloomy pile; but the clergy are well lodged. The bishop lives in a princely manner—the golden prebends keep plentiful tables—and, I am told, there is some good sociable company in the place; but the country, when viewed from the top of Gateshead Fell, which extends to Newcastle, exhibits the highest scene of cultivation that ever I beheld. As for Newcastle, it lies mostly in a bottom, on the banks of the Tyne, and makes an appearance still more disagreeable than that of Durham; but it is rendered populous and rich by industry and commerce; and the country lying on both sides the river, above the town, yields a delightful prospect of agriculture and plantation. Morpeth and Alnwick are neat pretty towns, and this last is famous for the castle which has belonged so many ages to the noble house of Porcy, earls of Northumberland. It is, doubtless, a large edifice, containing a great number of apartments, and stands in a commanding situation; but the strength of it seems to have consisted not so much in its site, or the manner in which it is fortified, as in the valour of its defendants.

Our adventures, since we left Scarborough, are scarce worth reciting; and yet I must make you acquainted with my sister Tabby's progress in husband-hunting. After her disappointments at Bath and London, she had actually begun to practise upon a certain adventurer, who was in fact a highwayman by profession; but he had been used to snares much more dangerous than any she could lay, and escaped accordingly.—Then she opened her batteries upon an old weather-beaten Scots lieutenant, called Lismahago, who joined us at Durham, and is, I think, one of the most singular personages I ever encountered. His manner is as harsh as his countenance; but his peculiar turn of thinking, and his pack of knowledge, made up of the remnants of rarities,

rendered his conversation desirable, in spite of his pedantry
and ungracious address. I have often met with a crab-
apple in a hedge, which I have been tempted to eat for its
flavour, even while I was disgusted by its austerity. The
spirit of contradiction is naturally so strong in Lismahago,
that I believe in my conscience he has rummaged, and read,
and studied with indefatigable attention, in order to qualify
himself to refute established maxims, and thus raise trophies
for the gratification of polemical pride. Such is the asperi-
ty of his self-conceit, that he will not even acquiesce in a
transient compliment made to his own individual in particular, or to his country in general.

When I observed that he must have read a vast number
of books to be able to discourse on such a variety of subjects,
he declared he had read little or nothing, and asked how he
should find books among the woods of America, where he
had spent the greatest part of his life. My nephew re-
marking, that the Scots in general were famous for their
learning, he denied the imputation, and defied him to prove
it from their works.—' The Scots,' said he, ' have a slight
tincture of letters, with which they make a parade among
people who are more illiterate than themselves; but they
may be said to float on the surface of science, and they have
made very small advances in the useful arts.' ' At least,'
cried Tabby, ' all the world allows that the Scots behaved
gloriously in fighting and conquering the savages of America.' ' I can assure you, madam, you have been misinform-
ed,' replied the lieutenant; in that continent the Scots did
nothing more than their duty, nor was there one corps in his
majesty's service that distinguished itself more than another.
—Those who affected to extol the Scots for superior merit,
were no friends to that nation.'

Though he himself made free with his countrymen, he
would not suffer any other person to glance a sarcasm at
them with impunity. One of the company chancing to
mention Lord B——'s inglorious peace, the lieutenant immediately took up the cudgels in his lordship's favour, and
argued very strenuously to prove that it was the most hon-

ourable and advantageous peace that England had ever made since the foundation of the monarchy. Nay, between friends, he offered such reasons on this subject, that I was really confounded, if not convinced.—He would not allow that the Scots abounded above their proportion in the army and navy of Great Britain, or that the English had any reason to say his countrymen had met with extraordinary encouragement in the service. ' When a South and North Briton,' said he, ' are competitors for a place or commission, which is in the disposal of an English minister, or an English general, it would be absurd to suppose that the preference will not be given to the native of England, who has so many advantages over his rival.—First and foremost, he has in his favour that laudable partiality, which, Mr Addison says, never fails to cleave to the heart of an Englishman; secondly, he has more powerful connections, and a greater share of parliamentary interest, by which those contests are generally decided; and, lastly, he has a greater command of money to smooth the way to his success. For my own part,' said he, ' I know no Scots officer who has risen in the army above the rank of a subaltern, without purchasing every degree of preferment either with money or recruits; but I know many gentlemen of that country, who, for want of money and interest, have grown grey in the rank of lieutenants; whereas very few instances of this ill fortune are to be found among the natives of South Britain. Not that I would insinuate that my countrymen have the least reason to complain. Preferment in the service, like success in any other branch of traffic, will naturally favour those who have the greatest stock of cash and credit, merit and capacity being supposed equal on all sides.'

But the most hardy of all this original's positions were these:—That commerce would, sooner or later, prove the ruin of every nation, where it flourishes to any extent—that the parliament was the rotten part of the British constitution —that the liberty of the press was a national evil—and that the boasted institution of juries, as managed in England, was productive of shameful perjury and flagrant injustice.

He observed, that traffic was an enemy to all the liberal passions of the soul, founded on the thirst of lucre, a sordid
disposition to take advantage of the necessities of our fellow-creatures.   He affirmed, the nature of commerce was
such, that it could not be fixed or perpetuated, but, having flowed to a certain height, would immediately begin to
ebb, and so continue till the channels should be left almost
dry ; but there was no instance of the tide's rising a second
time to any considerable influx in the same nation.   Meanwhile, the sudden affluence occasioned by trade, forced open
all the sluices of luxury, and overflowed the land with every
species of profligacy and corruption ; a total depravity of
manners would ensue, and this must be attended with bankruptcy and ruin.   He observed of the parliament, that the
practice of buying boroughs, and canvassing for votes, was
an avowed system of venality, already established on the
ruins of principle, integrity, faith, and good order ; in consequence of which, the elected, and the elector, and, in
short, the whole body of the people, were equally and universally contaminated and corrupted.   He affirmed, that, of
a parliament thus constituted, the crown would always have
influence enough to secure a great majority in its dependence, from the great number of posts, places, and pensions,
it had to bestow ; that such a parliament would, as it had
already done, lengthen the term of its sitting and authority,
whenever the prince should think it for his interest to continue the representatives ; for, without doubt, they had the
same right to protract their authority *ad infinitum*, as they
had to extend it from three to seven years.—With a parliament, therefore, dependent upon the crown, devoted to the
prince, and supported by a standing army, garbled and
modelled for the purpose, any king of England may, and
probably some ambitious sovereign will, totally overthrow
all the bulwarks of the constitution ; for it is not to be supposed that a prince of a high spirit will tamely submit to
be thwarted in all his measures, abused and insulted by a
populace of unbridled ferocity, when he has it in his power
to crush all opposition under his feet with the concurrence

of the legislature.   He said, he should always consider the
liberty of the press as a national evil, while it enabled the
vilest reptile to soil the lustre of the most shining merit, and
furnished the most infamous incendiary with the means of
disturbing the peace, and destroying the good order of the
community.   He owned, however, that, under due restrictions, it would be a valuable privilege; but affirmed, that,
at present, there was no law in England sufficient to restrain
it within proper bounds.

With respect to juries, he expressed himself to this effect.
—Juries are generally composed of illiterate plebians, apt
to be mistaken, easily misled, and open to sinister influence;
for if either of the parties to be tried can gain over one of the
twelve jurors, he has secured the verdict in his favour; the
juryman thus brought over, will, in despight of all evidence and conviction, generally hold out till his fellows are
fatigued, and harassed, and starved into concurrence; in
which case the verdict is unjust, and the jurors are all per-
jured;—but cases will often occur, when the jurors are really divided in opinion, and each side is convinced in opposition to the other; but no verdict will be received, unless
they are unanimous, and they are all bound, not only in
conscience, but by oath, to judge and declare according to
their conviction.   What then will be the consequence?
They must either starve in company, or one side must sacrifice their conscience to their convenience, and join in a
verdict which they believe to be false.—This absurdity is
avoided in Sweden, where a bare majority is sufficient; and
in Scotland, where two-thirds * of the jury are required to
concur in the verdict.

You must not imagine that all these deductions were
made on his part, without contradiction on mine.—No—
the truth is, I found myself piqued in point of honour, at
his pretending to be so much wiser than his neighbours.—
I questioned all his assertions, started innumerable objections, argued and wrangled with uncommon perseverance,
and grew very warm, and even violent in the debate.   Some-

* A mistake—a majority is sufficient in Scotland.

times he was puzzled, and once or twice, I think, fairly refuted; but from those falls he rose again, like Antæus, with
redoubled vigour, till at length I was tired, exhausted, and
really did not know how to proceed, when luckily he dropped a hint, by which he discovered he had been bred to the
law; a confession which enabled me to retire from the dispute with a good grace, as it could not be supposed that a
man like me, who had been bred to nothing, should be able
to cope with a veteran in his own profession. I believe,
however, that I shall for some time continue to chew the
cud of reflection upon many observations which this original
discharged.

Whether our sister Tabby was really struck with his conversation, or is resolved to throw at every thing she meets
in the shape of a man, till she can fasten the matrimonial
noose, certain it is, she has taken desperate strides towards
the affection of Lismahago, who cannot be said to have met
her half way, though he does not seem altogether insensible
to her civilities.—She insinuated more than once, how happy we should be to have his company through that part of
Scotland which we proposed to visit, till at length he plainly told us, that his road was totally different from that
which we intended to take; that, for his part, his company
would be of very little service to us in our progress, as he
was utterly unacquainted with the country, which he had
left in his early youth, consequently, he could neither direct us in our inquiries, nor introduce us to any family of
distinction. He said, he was stimulated by an irresistible
impulse to revisit the *paternus lar*, or *patria domus*, though
he expected little satisfaction, inasmuch as he understood
that his nephew, the present possessor, was but ill qualified to support the honour of the family.—He assured us,
however, as we designed to return by the west road, that
he would watch our motions, and endeavour to pay his respects to us at Dumfries. Accordingly he took his leave
of us at a place half way betwixt Morpeth and Alnwick,
and pranced away in great state, mounted on a tall, meagre,
raw-boned, shambling grey gelding, without e'er a tooth

in his head, the very counterpart of the rider; and, indeed, the appearance of the two was so picturesque, that I would give twenty guineas to have them tolerably represented on canvas.

Northumberland is a fine county, extending to the Tweed, which is a pleasant pastoral stream; but you will be surprised when I tell you that the English side of that river is neither so well cultivated nor so populous as the other. The farms are thinly scattered, the lands uninclosed, and scarce a gentleman's seat is to be seen in some miles from the Tweed; whereas the Scots are advanced in crowds to the very brink of the river; so that you may reckon above thirty good houses in the compass of a few miles, belonging to proprietors whose ancestors had fortified castles in the same situations; a circumstance that shews what dangerous neighbours the Scots must have formerly been to the northern counties of England.

Our domestic economy continues on the old footing. My sister Tabby still adheres to methodism, and had the benefit of a sermon at Wesley's meeting in Newcastle; but I believe the passion of love has in some measure abated the fervour of devotion, both in her and her woman Mrs Jenkins, about whose good graces there has been a violent contest betwixt my nephew's valet, Mr Dutton, and my man Humphry Clinker. Jery has been obliged to interpose his authority to keep the peace; and to him I have left the discussion of that important affair, which had like to have kindled the flames of discord in the family of, yours always,

Tweedmouth, July 15. MATT. BRAMBLE.

TO SIR WATKIN PHILLIPS, BART. AT OXON.

DEAR WAT,

In my two last you had so much of Lismahago, that I suppose you are glad he is gone off the stage for the present. I must now descend to domestic occurrences. Love, it seems, is resolved to assert his dominion over all the females of our family. After having practised upon poor Liddy's heart,

and played strange vagaries with our aunt Mrs Tabitha,
he began to run-riot in the affections of her woman, Mrs
Winifred Jenkins, whom I have had occasion to mention
more than once in the course of our memoirs. Nature intended Jenkins for something very different from the character of her mistress; yet custom and habit have effected a
wonderful resemblance betwixt them in many particulars.
Win, to be sure, is much younger, and more agreeable in
her person; she is likewise tender-hearted and benevolent,
qualities for which her mistress is by no means remarkable,
no more than she is for being of a timorous disposition, and
much subject to fits of the mother, which are the infirmities
of Win's constitution; but then she seems to have adopted
Mrs Tabby's manner with her cast clothes. She dresses and
endeavours to look like her mistress, although her own looks
are much more engaging. She enters into her schemes of
economy, learns her phrases, repeats her remarks, imitates
her style in scolding the inferior servants, and, finally, sub-
scribes implicitly to her system of devotion. This, indeed,
she found the more agreeable, as it was in a great measure
introduced and confirmed by the ministry of Clinker, with
whose personal merit she seems to have been struck ever
since he exhibited the pattern of his naked skin at Mar-
borough.

Nevertheless, though Humphry had this double hold
upon her inclinations, and exerted all his power to maintain
the conquest he had made, he found it impossible to guard
it on the side of vanity, where poor Win was as frail as any
female in the kingdom. In short, my rascal Dutton professed himself her admirer, and, by dint of his outlandish
qualifications, threw his rival Clinker out of the saddle of
her heart. Humphry may be compared to an English pudding, composed of good wholesome flour and suet, and Dutton to a syllabub or iced froth, which, though agreeable to
the taste, has nothing solid or substantial. The traitor not
only dazzled her with his second-hand finery, but he fawned,
and flattered, and cringed—he taught her to take rappee,
and presented her with a snuff-box of *papier mache*—he

supplied her with a powder for her teeth—he mended her
complexion, and he dressed her hair in the Paris fashion—
he undertook to be her French master and her dancing master, as well as friseur, and thus imperceptibly wound himself into her good graces. Clinker perceived the progress
he had made, and repined in secret. He attempted to open
her eyes in the way of exhortation, and, finding it produced
no effect, had recourse to prayer. At Newcastle, while he
attended Mrs Tabby to the methodist meeting, his rival accompanied Mrs Jenkins to the play. He was dressed in a
silk coat, made at Paris for his former master, with a tawdry
waistcoat of tarnished brocade; he wore his hair in a great
bag, with a huge solitaire; and a long sword dangled from
his thigh. The lady was all of a flutter with faded lustring,
washed gause, and ribbons three times refreshed; but she
was most remarkable for the frisure of her head, which rose,
like a pyramid, seven inches above the scalp; and her face
was primed and patched from the chin up to the eyes; nay,
the gallant himself had spared neither red nor white in improving the nature of his own complexion. In this attire,
they walked together through the high street to the theatre;
and as they passed for players, ready dressed for acting,
they reached it unmolested; but as it was still light when
they returned, and by that time the people had got information of their real character and condition, they hissed and
hooted all the way; and Mrs Jenkins was all bespattered
with dirt, as well as insulted with the opprobrious name of
painted Jezabel; so that her fright and mortification threw
her into an hysteric fit the moment she came home.

Clinker was so incensed at Dutton, whom he considered
as the cause of her disgrace, that he upbraided him severely
for having turned the poor young woman's brain. The
other affected to treat him with contempt; and, mistaking
his forbearance for want of courage, threatened to horse-
whip him into good manners. Humphry then came to me,
humbly begging I would give him leave to chastise my servant for his insolence—' He has challenged me to fight him
at sword's point,' said he; 'but I might as well challenge

him to make a horse-shoe or a plough-iron; for I know no
more of the one than he does of the other: besides, it doth
not become servants to use those weapons, or to claim the
privilege of gentlemen to kill one another, when they fall
out; moreover, I would not have his blood upon my conscience for ten thousand times the profit or satisfaction I
should get by his death; but if your honour won't be angry,
I'll engage to gee 'en a good drubbing, that, mayhap, will
do 'en service, and I'll take care it shall do 'en no harm.'
said, I had no objection to what he proposed, provided he
could manage matters so as not to be found the aggressor
in case Dutton should prosecute him for an assault and battery.

Thus licensed, he retired; and that same evening easi
provoked his rival to strike the first blow, which Clinker
returned with such interest, that he was obliged to call for
quarter, declaring, at the same time, that he would exac
severe and bloody satisfaction the moment we should pas
the border, when he could run him through the body with
out fear of the consequence. This scene passed in presenc
of Lieutenant Lismahago, who encouraged Clinker to hazar
a thrust of cold iron with his antagonist. 'Cold iron,' crie
Humphry, 'I shall never use against the life of any human
creature; but I am so far from being afraid of his cold iron,
that I shall use nothing in my defence but a good cudgel,
which shall always be at his service.' In the meantime, the
fair cause of this contest, Mrs Winifred Jenkins, seemed
overwhelmed with affliction, and Mr Clinker acted much
on the reserve, though he did not presume to find fault with
her conduct.

The dispute between the two rivals was soon brought to a
very unexpected issue. Among our fellow-lodgers at Berwick, was a couple from London, bound to Edinburgh, on
the voyage of matrimony. The female was the daughter
and heiress of a pawn-broker deceased, who had given her
guardians the slip, and put herself under the tuition of a tall
Hibernian, who had conducted her thus far in quest of a clergyman to unite them in marriage, without the formalities re-

quired by the law of England. I know not how the lover had behaved on the road, so as to decline in the favour of his inamorata; but, in all probability, Dutton perceived a coldness on her side, which encouraged him to whisper, it was a pity she should have cast her affections upon a tailor, which he affirmed the Irishman to be. This discovery completed her disgust, of which my man taking the advantage, began to recommend himself to her good graces; and the smooth-tongued rascal found no difficulty to insinuate himself into the place of her heart, from which the other had been discarded. Their resolution was immediately taken. In the morning, before day, while poor Teague lay snoring abed, his indefatigable rival ordered a post-chaise, and set out with the lady for Coldstream, a few miles up the Tweed, where there was a parson who dealt in this branch of commerce, and there they were noosed, before the Irishman ever dreamed of the matter. But when he got up at six o'clock, and found the bird was flown, he made such a noise as alarmed the whole house. One of the first persons he encountered was the postillion returned from Coldstream, where he had been witness to the marriage, and over and above a handsome gratuity, had received a bride's favour, which he now wore in his cap. When the forsaken lover understood they were actually married, and set out for London, and that Dutton had discovered to the lady that he (the Hibernian) was a tailor, he had like to have run distracted. He tore the ribbon from the fellow's cap, and beat it about his ears. He swore he would pursue him to the gates of hell, and ordered a post-chaise and four to be got ready as soon as possible; but recollecting that his finances would not admit of this way of travelling, he was obliged to countermand this order.

For my part, I knew nothing at all of what had happened, till the postillion brought me the keys of my trunk and portmanteau, which he had received from Dutton, who sent me his respects, hoping I would excuse him for his abrupt departure, as it was a step upon which his fortune depended. Before I had time to make my uncle acquainted with this event, the Irishman burst into my chamber, without any introduction, exclaiming,—' By my soul, your sarvant has robbed me of five thousand pounds, and I'll have satisfaction, if I should be hanged to-morrow !' When I asked him who he was,—' My name,' said he, ' is Master Macloughlin—but it should be Leighlin Oneale, for I am come from Ter-Owen the Great; and so I am as good a gentleman as any in Ireland: and that rogue, your sarvant, said I was a tailor, which was as big a lie as if he had called me the pope—I'm a man of fortune, and have spent all I had; and so being in distress, Mr Coshgrave, the fashioner in Suffolk street, tuck me out, and made me his own private shecretary. By the same token, I was the last he bailed; for his friends obliged him to tie himself up, that he would bail no more above ten pounds; for why, because as how he could not refuse any body that asked, and therefore, in time, would have robbed himself of his whole fortune, and, if he had lived long at that rate, must have died bankrupt very soon—and so I made my addresses to Miss Skinner, a young lady of five thousand pounds fortune, who agreed to take me for better nor worse; and, to be sure, this day would have put me in possession, if it had not been for that rogue, your sarvant, who came like a tief, and stole away my property, and made her believe I was a tailor, and that she was going to marry the ninth part of a man : but the devil burn my soul, if ever I catch him on the mountains of Tullogbobegly, if I don't shew him that I'm nine times as good a man as he, or e'er a bug of his country.

When he had rung out his first alarm, I told him I was sorry he had allowed himself to be so jockied; but it was no business of mine; and that the fellow who robbed him of his bride, had likewise robbed me of my servant.—' Didn't I tell you then,' cried he, ' that Rogue was his true christian name—Oh ! if I had but one fair trust with him upon the sod, I'd give him leave to brag all the rest of his life.'

My uncle hearing the noise, came in, and being informed of this adventure, began to comfort Mr Oneale for the lady's elopement; observing, that he seemed to have had a lucky

escape ; that it was better she should elope before, than after
marriage.—The Hibernian was of a very different opinion.
He said, ' If he had been once married, she might have
eloped as soon as she pleased ; he would have taken care that
she should not have carried her fortune along with her—
Ah !' said he, ' she's a Judas Iscariot, and has betrayed me
with a kiss ; and, like Judas, she carried the bag, and has
not left me money enough to bear my expenses back to London ; and so as I am come to this pass, and the rogue that
was the occasion of it has left you without a sarvant, you
may put me in his place ; and by Jasus, it is the best thing
you can do.'   I begged to be excused, declaring I could put
up with any inconvenience, rather than treat as a footman
the descendent of Ter-Owen the Great.   I advised him to
return to his friend Mr Cosgrave, and take his passage from
Newcastle by sea, towards which I made him a small present, and he retired, seemingly resigned to his evil fortune.
I have taken upon trial a Scotsman, called Archy M'Al-
pin, an old soldier, whose last master, a colonel, lately died
at Berwick.   The fellow is old and withered ; but he has
been recommended to me for his fidelity, by Mrs Humph-
reys, a very good sort of a woman, who keeps the inn at
Tweedmouth, and is much respected by all the travellers on
this road.

Clinker, without doubt, thinks himself happy in the removal of a dangerous rival, and he is too good a christian
to repine at Dutton's success.   Even Mrs Jenkins will have
reason to congratulate herself upon this event, when she
cooly reflects upon the matter ; for, howsoever she was forced from her poise for a season, by snares laid for her vanity,
Humphry is certainly the north star to which the needle of
her affection would have pointed at the long-run.   At present the same vanity is exceedingly mortified, upon finding
herself abandoned by her new admirer, in favour of another
inamorata.   She received the news with a violent burst of
laughter, which soon brought on a fit of crying, and this
gave the finishing blow to the patience of her mistress,
which had held out beyond all expectation.   She now open-

ed all those flood-gates of reprehension which had been shut
so long.   She not only reproached her with her levity and
indiscretion, but attacked her on the score of religion, declaring roundly, that she was in a state of apostacy and reprobation ; and, finally threatened to send her a-packing at this
extremity of the kingdom.   All the family intereeded for
poor Winifred, not even excepting her slighted swain,
Mr Clinker, who, on his knees, implored and obtained her
pardon.

There was, however, another consideration that gave Mrs
Tabitha some disturbance.   At Newcastle, the servants had
been informed by some wag, that there was nothing to eat in
Scotland but *oatmeal* and *sheep-heads ;* and Lieutenant Lismahago being consulted, what he said served rather to confirm than to refute the report.—Our aunt being apprised of
this circumstance, very gravely advised her brother to provide a sumpter-horse, with store of hams, tongues, bread,
biscuit, and other articles, for our subsistence, in the course
of our peregrination; and Mr Bramble as gravely replied,
that he would take the hint into consideration : but, finding
no such provision was made, she now revived the proposal,
observing, that there was a tolerable market at Berwick,
where we might be supplied ; and that my man's horse would
serve as a beast of burden.   The squire, shrugging up his
shoulders, eyed her askance, with a look of ineffable contempt ; and, after some pause—' Sister,' said he, ' I can
hardly persuade myself you are serious.'—She was so little
acquainted with the geography of the island, that she imagined we could not go to Scotland but by sea ; and, after we
had passed through the town of Berwick, when we told her
we were upon Scottish ground, she could hardly believe the
assertion : if the truth must be told, the South Britons in general are woefully ignorant in this particular.   What between
want of curiosity, and traditional sarcasms, the effect of ancient animosity, the people at the other end of the island
know as little of Scotland as of Japan.

If I had never been in Wales, I should have been more
struck with the manifest difference in appearance betwixt the

peasants and commonalty on the different sides of the Tweed. The boors of Northumberland are lusty fellows, fresh complexioned, cleanly, and well-clothed; but the labourers in Scotland are generally lank, lean, hard-featured, sallow, soiled, and shabby; and their little pinched blue caps have a beggarly effect. The cattle are much in the same style with their drivers, meagre, stunted, and ill-equipped. When I talked to my uncle on this subject, he said—' Though all the Scottish hinds would not bear to be compared with those of the rich countries of South Britain, they would stand very well in competition with the peasants of France, Italy, and Savoy—not to mention the mountaineers of Wales, and the redshanks of Ireland.'

We entered Scotland by a frightful moor of sixteen miles, which promises very little for the interior parts of the kingdom; but the prospect mended as we advanced. Passing through Dunbar, which is a neat little town, situated on the sea-side, we lay at a country inn, where our entertainment far exceeded our expectation; but for this we cannot give the Scots credit, as the landlord is a native of England. Yesterday we dined at Haddington, which has been a place of some consideration, but is now gone to decay; and in the evening arrived at this metropolis, of which I can say very little. It is very romantic, from its situation on the declivity of a hill, having a fortified castle at the top, and a royal palace at the bottom. The first thing that strikes the nose of a stranger shall be nameless; but what first strikes the eye is the unconscionable height of the houses, which generally rise to five, six, seven, and eight stories, and, in some places, as I am assured, to twelve. This manner of building, attended with numberless inconveniencies, must have been originally owing to want of room. Certain it is, the town seems to be full of people; but their looks, their language, and their customs are so different from ours, that I can hardly believe myself in Great Britain.

The inn at which we put up, if it may be so called, was so filthy and disagreeable in all respects, that my uncle began to fret, and his gouty symptoms to recur.—Recollecting,

however, that he had a letter of recommendation to one Mr
Mitchelson, a lawyer, he sent it by his servant, with a compliment, importing, that he would wait upon him next day
in person; but that gentleman visited us immediately, and
insisted upon our going to his own house, until he could
provide lodgings for our accommodation. We gladly accepted of his invitation, and repaired to his house, where we
were treated with equal elegance and hospitality, to the utter
confusion of our aunt, whose prejudices, though beginning
to give way, were not yet entirely removed. To-day, by
the assistance of our friend, we are settled in convenient lodgings, up four pair of stairs, in the High street, the fourth
story being, in this city, reckoned more genteel than the
first. The air is, in all probability, the better; but it requires good lungs to breathe it at this distance above the surface of the earth.—While I do remain above it, whether
higher or lower, provided I do breathe at all, I shall ever be,
dear Phillips, yours,

Edinburgh, July 18.   J. MELFORD.

TO DR LEWIS.

DEAR LEWIS,

That part of Scotland contiguous to Berwick, nature seems
to have intended as a barrier between two hostile nations. It
is a brown desart, of considerable extent, that produces nothing but heath and fern; and what rendered it the more
dreary when we passed, there was a thick fog that hindered
us from seeing above twenty yards from the carriage.—My
sister began to make wry faces, and use her smelling-bottle;
Liddy looked blank; and Mrs Jenkins dejected; but in a
few hours these clouds were dissipated; the sea appeared on
our right, and on the left the mountains retired a little, leaving an agreeable plain betwixt them and the beach; but,
what surprised us all, this plain, to the extent of several miles,
was covered with as fine wheat as ever I saw in the most fertile parts of South Britain. This plentiful crop is raised in
the open field, without any inclosure, or other manure than

the *alga marina*, or sea-weed, which abounds on this coast;
a circumstance which shews that the soil and climate are favourable, but that agriculture in this country is not yet
brought to that perfection which it has attained in England.
Inclosures would not only keep the grounds warm, and the
several fields distinct, but would also protect the crop from
the high winds, which are so frequent in this part of the
island.

Dunbar is well situated for trade, and has a curious bason,
where ships of small burthen may be perfectly secure; but
there is little appearance of business in the place.—From
thence, all the way to Edinburgh, there is a continual succession of fine seats belonging to noblemen and gentlemen;
and, as each is surrounded by its own park and plantation,
they produce a very pleasing effect in a country which lies
otherwise open and exposed.—At Dunbar there is a noble
park, with a lodge, belonging to the duke of Roxburgh,
where Oliver Cromwell had his head-quarters, when Leslie,
at the head of a Scots army, took possession of the mountains in the neighbourhood, and hampered him in such a
manner, that he would have been obliged to embark and get
away by sea, had not the fanaticism of the enemy forfeited
the advantage which they had obtained by their general's
conduct.—Their ministers, by exhortation, prayer, assurance, and prophecy, instigated them to go down and slay
the Philistines in Gilgal; and they quitted their ground accordingly, notwithstanding all that Leslie could do to restrain
the madness of their enthusiasm.—When Oliver saw them
in motion, he exclaimed—' Praised be the Lord, he hath delivered them into the hands of his servant!' and ordered his
troops to sing a psalm of thanksgiving, while they advanced
in order to the plain, where the Scots were routed with great
slaughter.

In the neighbourhood of Haddington there is a gentleman's house, in the building of which, and the improvements about it, he is said to have expended forty thousand
pounds: but I cannot say I was much pleased with either
the architecture or the situation, though it has in front a

pastoral stream, the banks of which are laid out in a very agreeable manner.—I intended to pay my respects to Lord Elibank, whom I had the honour to know at London many years ago. He lives in this part of Lothian, but was gone to the north on a visit.—You have often heard me mention this nobleman, whom I have long revered for his humanity and universal intelligence, over and above the entertainment arising from the originality of his character.—At Musselburgh, however, I had the good fortune to drink tea with my old friend Mr Cardonel; and at his house I met with Dr C——, the parson of the parish, whose humour and conversation inflamed me with a desire of being better acquainted with his person.—I am not at all surprised that these Scots make their way in every quarter of the globe.

This place is but four miles from Edinburgh, towards which we proceeded along the sea-shore, upon a firm bottom of smooth sand, which the tide had left uncovered in its retreat.—Edinburgh, from this avenue, is not seen to much advantage.—We had only an imperfect view of the castle and upper parts of the town, which varied incessantly, according to the inflections of the road, and exhibited the appearance of detached spires and turrets, belonging to some magnificent edifice in ruins.—The palace of Holyroodhouse stands on the left as you enter the Canongate.—This is a street continued from hence to the gate called the Netherbow, which is now taken away; so that there is no interruption for a long mile, from the bottom to the top of the hill, on which the castle stands in a most imperial situation.—Considering its fine pavement, its width, and the lofty houses on each side, this would be undoubtedly one of the noblest streets in Europe, if an ugly mass of mean buildings, called the Luckenbooths, had not thrust itself, by what accident I know not, into the middle of the way, like Middle row in Holborn. The city stands upon two hills, and the bottom between them; and, with all its defects, may very well pass for the capital of a moderate kingdom.—It is full of people; and continually resounds with the noise of coaches, and other carriages, for luxury as well as commerce. As

far as I can perceive, here is no want of provisions.—The
beef and mutton are as delicate here as in Wales; the sea
affords plenty of good fish; the bread is remarkably fine;
and the water is excellent, though I'm afraid not in sufficient
quantity to answer all the purposes of cleanliness and convenience; articles in which, it must be allowed, our fellow-
subjects are a little defective.—The water is brought in lead-
en pipes from a mountain in the neighbourhood, to a cistern
on the Castle hill, from whence it is distributed to public
conduits in different parts of the city. From these it is carried in barrels, on the backs of male and female porters, up
two, three, four, five, six, seven, and eight pair of stairs,
for the use of particular families.—Every storey is a complete
house occupied by a separate family; and the stair being
common to them all, is generally left in a very filthy condition; a man must tread with great circumspection to get
safe housed with unpolluted shoes.—Nothing can form a
stronger contrast than the difference betwixt the outside and
inside of the door; for the good women of this metropolis
are remarkably nice in the ornaments and propriety of their
apartments, as if they were resolved to transfer the imputation from the individual to the public.—You are no stranger
to their method of discharging all their impurities from their
windows, at a certain hour of the night, as the custom is in
Spain, Portugal, and some parts of France and Italy.—A
practice to which I can by no means be reconciled; for notwithstanding all the care that is taken by their scavengers to
remove this nuisance every morning by break of day, enough
still remains to offend the eyes, as well as the other organs,
of those whom use has not hardened against all delicacy of
sensation.

The inhabitants seem insensible to these impressions, and
are apt to imagine the disgust that we avow is little better
than affectation; but they ought to have some compassion
for strangers, who have not been used to this kind of suffer-
ance, and consider whether it may not be worth while to
take some pains to vindicate themselves from the reproach
that on this account they bear among their neighbours. As

to the surprising height of their houses, it is absurd in many respects; but, in one particular light, I cannot view it without horror; that is, the dreadful situation of all the families above in case the common stair-case should be rendered impassable by a fire in the lower storeys.—In order to prevent the shocking consequences that must attend such an accident, it would be a right measure to open doors of communication from one house to another on every storey, by which the people might fly from such a terrible visitation.   In all parts of the world we see the force of habit prevailing over all the dictates of convenience and sagacity.—All the people of business at Edinburgh, and even the genteel company, may be seen standing in crowds every day, from one to two in the afternoon, in the open street, at a place where formerly stood a market-cross, which (by the by) was a curious piece of Gothic architecture, still to be seen in Lord Somerville's garden in this neighbourhood.—I say, the people stand in the open street from the force of custom, rather than move a few yards to an exchange, that stands empty on one side, or to the Parliament close on the other, which is a noble square, adorned with a fine equestrian statue of king Charles II.—The company thus assembled are entertained with a variety of tunes, played upon a set of bells, fixed in a steeple hard by.—As these bells are well toned, and the musician who has a salary from the city for playing upon them with keys, is no bad performer, the entertainment is really agreeable, and very striking to the ears of a stranger.

The public inns at Edinburgh are still worse than those of London; but, by means of a worthy gentleman, to whom I was recommended, we have got decent lodgings in the house of a widow gentlewoman of the name Lockhart; and here I shall stay until I have seen every thing that is remarkable in and about this capital.   I now begin to feel the good effects of exercise.—I eat like a farmer, sleep from midnight till eight in the morning, without interruption, and enjoy a constant tide of spirits, equally distant from inanition and excess; but whatever ebbs and flows my constitution may

undergo, my heart will still declare that I am, dear Lewis,
your affectionate friend and servant,

Edinburgh, July 18. MATT. BRAMBLE.

TO MRS MARY JONES, AT BRAMBLETONHALL.

DEAR MARY,

THE squire has been so kind as to rap my bit of nonsense
under the kiver of his own sheet.—O Mary Jones! Mary
Jones! I have had trials and trembulation. God help me!
I have been a vixen and a griffin these many days.—Sattin
has had power to temp me in the shape of van Ditton, the
young squire's wally de shamble; but by God's grease he
did not purvail.—I thoft as how there was no arm in going
to a play at Newcastle, with my hair dressed in the Parish
fashion; and as for the trifle of paint, he said as how my
complexion wanted rouch, and so I let him put it on with
a little Spanish owl; but a mischievous mob of colliers, and
such promiscous ribble rabble, that could bare no smut but
their own, attacked us in the street, and called me *hoar* and
painted Issabel, and splashed my close, and spoiled me a complete set of blond lace triple ruffles, not a pin the worse for the
vare.—They cost me seven good sillings to Lady Griskin's
woman at London.

When I axed Mr Clinker what they meant by calling me
Issabel, he put the byebill into my hand, and I read of van
Issabel, a painted harlot, that vas thrown out of a vindore,
and the dogs came and licked her blood.—But I am no harlot; and, with God's blessing, no dog shall have my poor
blood to lick: mary, Heaven forbid, amen! As for Ditton,
after all his courting and his compliment, he stole away an
Irishman's bride, and took a French leave of me and his
master; but I vally not his going a farting; but I have
had hanger on his account.—Mistress scoulded like mad;
thof I have the comfit that all the family took my part, and
even Mr Clinker pleaded for me on his bended knee; thof,
God he knows, he had raisins enuff to complain; but he's a
good sole, abounding with christian meekness, and one day
will meet with his reward.

And now, dear Mary, we have got to Haddingborough, among the Scots, who are civil enuff for our money, thof I don't speak their lingo.—But they should not go for to impose upon foreigners; for the bills on their houses say, they have different *easemènts* to let; and behold there is nurra geaks in the whole kingdom, nor any thing for pore servants, but a barrel with a pair of tongs thrown across; and all the chairs in the family are emptied into this here barrel once a-day; and at ten o'clock at night the whole cargo is flung out at a back windose that looks into some street or lane, and the maid calls *gardy loo* to the passengers, which signifies, *Lord have mercy upon you !* and this is done every night in every house in Haddingborough; so you may guess, Mary Jones, what a sweet savour comes from such a number of profuming pans. But they say it is wholesome, and truly I believe it is ; for being in the vapours, and thinking of Issabel and Mr Clinker, I was going into a fit of astericks, when this fiff, saving your presence, took me by the nose so powerfully, that I sneesd three times, and found myself wonderfully refreshed ; and this to be sure is the raisin why there are no fits in Hadding-borough.

I was likewise made believe, that there was nothing to be had but *oat-meal* and *seeps heads* ; but if I hadn't been a fool, I mought have known there could be no *heads* without karcasses.—This very blessed day I dined upon a delicate leg of Velsh mutton and cully-flower ; and as for the oat-meal, I leave that to the servants of the country, which are pore drudges, many of them without shoes or stockings.—Mr Clinker tells me here is a great call of the gospel; but I wish, I wish some of our family be not fallen off from the rite way.—O, if I was given to tail-baring, I have my own secrets to discover.—There has been a deal of huggling and flurtation betwixt mistress and an old Scots officer called Kismycago. He looks for all the orld like the scarecrow that our gardner set up to frite away the sparrows; and what will come of it the Lord nows; but come what will, it shall never be said that I mentioned a syllabub of the matter.——Remember me kindly to Saul and the kitten.—I hope they got the horn-buck, and will put it to a good yuse, which is the constant prayer of, dear Molly, your loving friend,

Addingborough, July 18.   WIN. JENKINS.

TO SIR WATKIN PHILLIPS, BART. OF JESUS COLLEGE, OXON.

DEAR PHILLIPS,

If I stay much longer at Edinburgh, I shall be changed into a downright Caledonian.—My uncle observes, that I have already acquired something of the country accent. The people here are so social and attentive in their civilities to strangers, that I am insensibly sucked into the channel of their manners and customs, although they are in fact much more different from ours than you can imagine.—That difference, however, which struck me very much at my first arrival, I now hardly perceive, and my ear is perfectly reconciled to the Scots accent, which I find even agreeable in the mouth of a pretty woman.—It is a sort of Doric dialect, which gives an idea of amiable simplicity.—You cannot imagine how we have been carressed and feasted in the *good town of Edinburgh*, of which we are become free denizens and guild-brothers, by the special favour of the magistracy.

I had a whimsical commission from Bath, to a citizen of this metropolis.—Quin, understanding our intention to visit Edinburgh, pulled out a guinea, and desired the favour I would drink it at a tavern, with a particular friend and bottle-companion of his, one Mr R—— C——, a lawyer of this city.—I charged myself with the commission, and taking the guinea,—' You see,' said I, ' I have pocketed your bounty.' ' Yes,' replied Quin, laughing, ' and a headach into the bargain, if you drink fair.' I made use of this introduction to Mr C——, who received me with open arms, and gave me the rendezvous, according to the cartel. He had provided a company of jolly fellows, among whom I found myself extremely happy ; and did Mr C—— and

Quin all the justice in my power; but, alas! I was no more than a tyro among a troop of veterans, who had compassion upon my youth, and conveyed me home in the morning, by what means I know not.—Quin was mistaken, however, as to the headach; the claret was too good to treat me so roughly.

While Mr Bramble holds conferences with the graver literati of the place, and our females are entertained at visits by the Scots ladies, who are the best and kindest creatures upon earth, I pass my time among the bucks of Edinburgh; who, with a great share of spirit and vivacity, have a certain shrewdness and self-command that is not often found among their neighbours in the hey-day of youth and exultation.—Not a hint escapes a Scotsman that can be interpreted into offence by any individual in the company; and national reflections are never heard.—In this particular, I must own, we are both unjust and ungrateful to the Scots; for, as far as I am able to judge, they have a real esteem for the natives of South Britain; and never mention our country, but with expressions of regard. Nevertheless, they are far from being servile imitators of our modes and fashionable vices. All their customs and regulations of public and private economy, of business and diversion, are in their own style. This remarkably predominates in their looks, their dress and manner, their music, and even their cookery. Our 'squire declares, that he knows not another people upon earth, so strongly marked with a national character.—Now we are upon the article of cookery, I must own, some of their dishes are savoury, and even delicate; but I am not yet Scotsman enough to relish their singed sheep's head and haggis, which were provided, at our request, one day at Mr Mitchelson's, where we dined.—The first put me in mind of the history of Congo, in which I had read of negroes heads sold publicly in the markets; the last, being a mess of minced lights, livers, suet, oatmeal, onions, and pepper, inclosed in a sheep's stomach, had a very sudden effect upon mine, and the delicate Mrs Tabby changed colour; when the cause of our disgust was instantaneously removed at the nod of our entertainer. The Scots in general are attached to this composition, with a sort of national fondness, as well as to their oatmeal bread; which is presented at every table, in thin triangular cakes, baked upon a plate of iron, called a girdle; and these many of the natives, even in the higher ranks of life, prefer to wheaten bread, which they have here in perfection.—You know we used to vex poor Murray of Baliol college, by asking, if there was really no fruit but turnips in Scotland!—Sure enough, I have seen turnips make their appearance, not as a dessert, but by way of *hors d'œuvres*, or whets, as radishes are served up betwixt more substantial dishes in France and Italy; but it must be observed, that the turnips of this country are as much superior in sweetness, delicacy, and flavour, to those of England, as a musk-melon is to the stock of a common cabbage. They are small and conical, of a yellowish colour, with a very thin skin; and, over and above their agreeable taste, are valuable for their antiscorbutic quality.—As to the fruit now in season, such as cherries, gooseberries, and currants, there is no want of them at Edinburgh; and in the gardens of some gentlemen, who live in this neighbourhood, there is now a very favourable appearance of apricots, peaches, nectarines, and even grapes; nay, I have seen a very fine shew of pine apples within a few miles of this metropolis. Indeed, we have no reason to be surprised at these particulars, when we consider how little difference there is, in fact, betwixt this climate and that of London.

All the remarkable places in the city and its avenues, for ten miles round, we have visited much to our satisfaction. In the castle are some royal apartments, where the sovereign occasionally resided; and here are carefully preserved the regalia of the kingdom, consisting of a crown, said to be of great value; a sceptre, and a sword of state, adorned with jewels.—Of these symbols of sovereignty, the people are exceedingly jealous.—A report being spread, during the sitting of the union-parliament, that they were removed to London, such a tumult arose, that the lord-commissioner would have been torn in pieces, if he had not produced them for the satisfaction of the populace.

The palace of Holyroodhouse is an elegant piece of architecture, but sunk in an obscure, and, as I take it, unwholesome bottom, where one would imagine it had been placed
on purpose to be concealed.   The apartments are lofty, but
unfurnished ; and as for the pictures of the Scottish kings,
from Fergus I. to King William, they are paltry daubings,
mostly by the same hand, painted either from the imagination, or porters hired to sit for the purpose.   All the diversions of London we enjoy at Edinburgh in a small compass.
Here is a well-conducted concert, in which several gentlemen perform on different instruments.—The Scots are all
musicians.—Every man you meet plays on the flute, the
violin, or violoncello ; and there is one nobleman whose compositions are universally admired.—Our company of actors
is very tolerable ; and a subscription is now on foot for
building a new theatre ; but their assemblies please me above
all other public exhibitions.

We have been at the hunter's ball, where I was really
astonished to see such a number of fine women.—The English, who have never crossed the Tweed, imagine erroneously, that the Scots ladies are not remarkable for personal attractions ; but I can declare with a safe conscience I never
saw so many handsome females together as were assembled
on this occasion.   At the Leith races, the best company
comes hither from the remoter provinces ; so that, I suppose,
we had all the beauty of the kingdom concentered as it were
into one focus ; which was indeed so vehement, that my
heart could hardly resist its power.—Between friends, it has
sustained some damage from the bright eyes of the charming Miss R——n, whom I had the honour to dance with at
the ball.   The countess of Melvil attracted all eyes, and
the admiration of all present.—She was accompanied by the
agreeable Miss Grieve, who made many conquests ; nor did
my sister Liddy pass unnoticed in the assembly.—She is become a toast at Edinburgh, by the name of the Fair Cambrian, and has already been the occasion of much wine-shed ;
—but the poor girl met with an accident at the ball, which
has given us much disturbance.

A young gentleman, the express image of that rascal Wilson, went up to ask her to dance a minuet; and his sudden appearance shocked her so much, that she fainted away.—I call Wilson a rascal, because if he had been really a gentleman, with honourable intentions, he would have ere now appeared in his own character.—I must own, my blood boils with indignation when I think of that fellow's presumption; and heaven confound me if I don't—but I won't be so womanish as to rail—time will perhaps furnish occasion—thank God the cause of Liddy's disorder remains a secret. The lady-directress of the ball, thinking she was overcome by the heat of the place, had her conveyed to another room, where she soon recovered so well, as to return and join in the country dances, in which the Scots lasses acquit themselves with such spirit and agility, as put their partners to the height of their mettle.—I believe our aunt, Mrs Tabitha, had entertained hopes of being able to do some execution among the cavaliers at this assembly.—She had been several days in consultation with milliners and mantua-makers, preparing for the occasion, at which she made her appearance in a full suit of damask, so thick and heavy, that the sight of it alone, at this season of the year, was sufficient to draw drops of sweat from any man of ordinary imagination—She danced one minuet with our friend Mr Mitchelson, who favoured her so far, in the spirit of hospitality and politeness; and she was called out a second time by the young laird of Balymawhaple, who, coming in by accident, could not readily find any other partner; but as the first was a married man, and the second paid no particular homage to her charms, which were also overlooked by the rest of the company, she became dissatisfied and censorious.—At supper, she observed that the Scots gentlemen made a very good figure, when they were a little improved by travelling; and, therefore, it was pity they did not all take the benefit of going abroad.—She said the women were awkward masculine creatures; that, in dancing, they lifted their legs like so many colts; that they had no idea of graceful motion; and put on their clothes in a fright-

ful manner; but if the truth must be told, Tabby herself
was the most ridiculous figure, and the worst dressed of the
whole assembly.—The neglect of the male sex rendered her
malcontent and peevish; she now found fault with every
thing at Edinburgh, and teased her brother to leave the place,
when she was suddenly reconciled to it on a religious consideration.—There is a sect of fanatics, who have separated
themselves from the established kirk, under the name of
seceders.—They acknowledge no earthly head of the church,
reject lay patronage, and maintain the methodist doctrines
of the new birth, the new light, the efficacy of grace, the
insufficiency of works, and the operations of the spirit. Mrs
Tabitha, attended by Humphry Clinker, was introduced to
one of their conventicles, where they both received much
edification; and she has had the good fortune to become acquainted with a pious christian, called Mr Moffat, who is
very powerful in prayer, and often assists her in private exercises of devotion.

I never saw such a concourse of genteel company at any
races in England, as appeared on the course of Leith.—Hard
by, in the fields called the Links, the citizens of Edinburgh
divert themselves at a game called golf, in which they use
a curious kind of bats tipped with horn, and small elastic
balls of leather, stuffed with feathers, rather less than tennis-
balls, but of a much harder consistence.—This they strike
with such force and dexterity from one hole to another, that
they will fly to an incredible distance. Of this diversion the
Scots are so fond, that, when the weather will permit, you
may see a multitude of all ranks, from the senator of justice
to the lowest tradesman, mingled together in their shirts,
and following the balls with the utmost eagerness.—Among
others, I was shewn one particular set of golfers, the youngest
of whom was turned of fourscore.—They were all gentlemen
of independent fortunes, who had amused themselves with
this pastime for the best part of a century, without having
ever felt the least alarm from sickness or disgust; and they
never went to bed, without having each the best part of a
gallon of claret in his belly. Such uninterrupted exercise,

co-operating with the keen air from the sea, must, without all doubt, keep the appetite always on edge, and steel the constitution against all the common attacks of distemper.

The Leith races gave occasion to another entertainment of a very singular nature.—There is at Edinburgh a society or corporation of errand-boys called *cadies*, who ply in the streets at night with paper lanterns, and are very serviceable in carrying messages.—These fellows, though shabby in their appearance, and rudely familiar in their address, are wonderfully acute, and so noted for fidelity, that there is no instance of a cadie's having betrayed his trust.—Such is their intelligence, that they know not only every individual of the place, but also every stranger, by the time he has been four-and-twenty hours in Edinburgh; and no transaction, even the most private, can escape their notice. —They are particularly famous for their dexterity in executing one of the functions of Mercury; though, for my own part, I never employed them in this department of business.—Had I occasion for any service of this nature, my own man, Archy M'Alpine, is as well qualified as e'er a cadie in Edinburgh; and I am much mistaken, if he has not been heretofore of their fraternity. Be that as it may, they resolved to give a dinner and a ball at Leith, to which they formally invited all the young noblemen and gentlemen that were at the races; and this invitation was reinforced by an assurance, that all the celebrated ladies of pleasure would grace the entertainment with their company.—I received a card on this occasion, and went thither with half a dozen of my acquaintance.—In a large hall, the cloth was laid on a long range of tables joined together, and here the company seated themselves, to the number of about fourscore, lords and lairds, and other gentlemen, courtezans and cadies, mingled together, as the slaves and their masters were in the time of the Saturnalia in ancient Rome. The toastmaster, who sat at the upper end, was one Cadie Fraser, a veteran pimp, distinguished for his humour and sagacity, well known and much respected in his profession by all the guests, male and female, that were here as-

sembled.   He had bespoke the dinner and the wine : he had
taken care that all his brethren should appear in decent apparel and clean linen ; and he himself wore a periwig with
three tails, in honour of the festival.   I assure you the banquet was both elegant and plentiful, and seasoned with a
thousand sallies, that promoted a general spirit of mirth and
good humour.   After the dessert, Mr Fraser proposed the
following toasts, which I don't pretend to explain.—' The
best in Christendom'—' Gibb's contract'—' The Beggar's
bennison'—' King and kirk'—' Great Britain and Ireland.'
—Then, filling a bumper, and turning to me,—' Mester
Malford,' said he, ' may a' unkindness cease betwixt John
Bull and his sister Maggy.'   The next person he singled
out, was a nobleman who had been long abroad.   ' Ma
lord,' cried Fraser, ' here is a bumper to a' those noblemen who have virtue enough to spend their rents in their ain
coontray.'   He afterwards addressed himself to a member of
parliament in these words.—' Mester—I'm sure ye'll ha'
nae objection to my drinking, Disgrace and dool to ilka
Scot, that sells his conscience and his vote.'   He discharged a third sarcasm at a person very gaily dressed, who
had risen from small beginnings, and made a considerable
fortune at play.—Filling his glass, and calling him by name,
—' Lang life,' said he, ' to the wylie loon that gans a-
field with a toom poke at his lunzie, and comes hame with a
sackful o' siller.'   All these toasts being received with loud
bursts of applause, Mr Fraser called for pint glasses, and
filled his own to the brim : then standing up, and all his
brethren following his example,—' Ma lords and gentlemen,' cried he, ' here is a cup of thanks for the great and
undeserved honour you have done your poor errand-boys
this day.—So saying, he and they drank off their glasses in
a trice, and, quitting their seats, took their station each behind one of the other guests ; exclaiming—' Noo we're your
honour's cadies again.'

   The nobleman who had bore the first brunt of Mr Fraser's satire, objected to his abdication.   He said, as the
company was assembled by invitation from the cadies, he

xpected they were to be entertained at their expense. ' By
no means, my lord,' cried Fraser; ' I wad na be guilty of
sic presumption for the wide warld.—I never affronted a
gentleman since I was born; and sure, at this age, I won-
not offer an indignity to sic an honourable convention.'
' Well,' said his lordship, ' as you have expended some
wit, you have a right to save your money. You have given
me good counsel, and I take it in good part. As you have
voluntarily quitted your seat, I will take your place, with
the leave of the good company, and think myself happy to
be hailed, *Father of the feast*.' He was forthwith elected
into the chair, and complimented in a bumper on his new
character.

The claret continued to circulate without interruption, till
the glasses seemed to dance upon the table; and this, perhaps, was a hint to the ladies to call for music.—At eight
in the evening the ball began in another apartment: at midnight we went to supper; but it was broad day before I
found the way to my lodgings; and, no doubt, his lordship
had a swinging bill to discharge.

In short, I have lived so riotously for some weeks, that
my uncle begins to be alarmed on the score of my constitution, and very seriously observes, that all his own infirmities are owing to such excesses indulged in his youth.—Mrs
Tabitha says it would be more for the advantage of my soul
as well as body, if, instead of frequenting these scenes of debauchery, I would accompany Mr Moffat and her to hear
a sermon of the Reverend Mr M'Corkendale. Clinker often exhorts me with a groan, to take care of my precious
health; and even Archy M'Alpine, when he happens to
be overtaken (which is oftener the case than I could wish),
reads me a long lecture upon temperance and sobriety; and
is so very wise and sententious, that, if I could provide him
with a professor's chair, I would willingly give up the benefit of his admonitions and service together; for I was
tutor-sick at alma mater.

I am not, however, so much engrossed by the gaities of
Edinburgh, but that I find time to make parties in the fa-

mily way. We have not only seen all the villas and villages within ten miles of the capital, but we have also crossed the Frith, which is an arm of the sea seven miles broad, that divides Lothian from the shire, or, as the Scots call it, *the kingdom of Fife.* There is a number of large open sea boats that ply on this passage from Leith to Kinghorn, which is a borough on the other side. In one of these our whole family embarked three days ago, excepting my sister, who, being exceedingly fearful of the water, was left to the care of Mrs Mitchelson. We had an easy and quick passage into Fife, where we visited a number of poor towns on the sea-side, including S^t. Andrews, which is the skeleton of a venerable city; but we were much better pleased with some noble and elegant seats and castles, of which there is a great number in that part of Scotland. Yesterday we took boat again on our return to Leith, with a fair wind and agreeable weather; but we had not advanced half way, when the sky was suddenly overcast, and the wind changing, blew directly in our teeth; so that we were obliged to turn, or tack, the rest of the way. In a word, the gale increased to a storm of wind and rain, attended with such a fog, that we could not see the town of Leith, to which we were bound, nor even the castle of Edinburgh, notwithstanding its high situation. It is not to be doubted but that we were all alarmed on this occasion. And, at the same time, most of the passengers were seized with a nausea that produced violent retchings. My aunt desired her brother to order the boatmen to put back to Kinghorn, and this expedient he actually proposed; but they assured him there was no danger. Mrs Tabitha, finding them obstinate, began to scold, and insisted upon my uncle's exerting his authority as a justice of the peace. Sick and peevish as he was, he could not help laughing at this wise proposal, telling her, that his commission did not extend so far; and, if it did, he should let the people take their own way; for he thought it would be great presumption in him to direct them in the exercise of their own profession. Mrs Winifred Jenkins made a general clearance, with the assistance of Mr

Humphry Clinker, who joined her both in prayer and ejaculation. As he took it for granted that we should not be
long in this world, he offered some spiritual consolation to
Mrs. Tabitha, who rejected it with great disgust, bidding
him keep his sermons for those who had leisure to hear such
nonsense. My uncle sat, recollected in himself, without
speaking; my man Archy. had recourse to a brandy bottle,
with which he made so free, that I imagined he had sworn
to die of drinking any thing rather than sea-water; but the
brandy had no more effect upon him in the way of intoxication, than if it had been sea-water in good earnest. As
for myself, I was too much engrossed by the sickness at my
stomach, to think of any thing else.—Meanwhile the sea
swelled mountains high; the boat pitched with such violence, as if it had been going to pieces; the cordage rattled,
the wind roared, the lightning flashed, the thunder bellowed, and the rain descended in a deluge.—Every time the
vessel was put about, we shipped a sea that drenched us all
to the skin. When, by dint of turning, we thought to
have cleared the pier-head, we were driven to leeward, and
then the boatmen themselves began to fear that the tide
would fail before we should fetch up our lee-way: the next
trip, however, brought us into smooth water, and we were
safely landed on the quay about one o'clock in the afternoon. 'To be sure,' cried Tabby, when she found herself
on *terra firma*, 'we must all have perished, if we had not
been the particular care of Providence.' 'Yes,' replied
my uncle, 'but I am much of the honest Highlander's mind:
after he had made such a passage as this, his friend told
him he was much indebted to Providence. "Certainly,"
said Donald; "but, by my saul, mon, I'ese n'er trouble
Providence again, so long as the brig of Stirling stands."
You must know, the brig, or bridge of Stirling, stands
above twenty miles up the river Forth, of which this is the
outlet.—I don't find that our squire has suffered in his
health from this adventure; but poor Liddy is in a peak-
ing way.—I'm afraid this unfortunate girl is uneasy in her

mind; and this apprehension distracts me, for she is really
an amiable creature.

We shall set out to-morrow, or next day, for Stirling and
Glasgow: and we propose to penetrate a little way into the
Highlands, before we turn our course to the southward.—
In the meantime, commend me to all our friends round Car-
fax, and believe me to be ever yours,

Edinburgh, August 8.   J. MELFORD.

TO DR LEWIS.

I SHOULD be very ungrateful, dear Lewis, if I did not find
myself disposed to think and speak favourably of this people,
among whom I have met with more kindness, hospitality,
and rational entertainment, in a few weeks, than ever I received in any other country during the whole course of my
life.—Perhaps the gratitude excited by these benefits may interfere with the impartiality of my remarks; for a man is as
apt to be prepossessed by particular favours, as to be prejudiced by private motives of disgust. If I am partial, there
is at least some merit in my conversion from illiberal prejudices, which had grown up with my constitution.

The first impressions which an Englishman receives in this
country, will not contribute to the removal of his prejudices;
because he refers every thing he sees to a comparison with
the same articles in his own country; and this comparison
is unfavourable to Scotland in all its exteriors; such as the
face of the country, in respect to cultivation, the appearance of the bulk of the people, and the language of conversation in general.—I am not so far convinced by Mr Lismahago's arguments, but that I think the Scots would do
well, for their own sakes, to adopt the English idioms and
pronunciation; those of them especially who are resolved to
push their fortunes in South Britain.—I know, by experience, how easily an Englishman is influenced by the ear,
and how apt he is to laugh, when he hears his own language
spoken with a foreign or provincial accent.—I have known
a member of the house of commons speak with great energy

and precision, without being able to engage attention; because his observations were made in the Scots dialect,
which (no offence to Lieutenant Lismahago) certainly gives
a clownish air even to sentiments of the greatest dignity and
decorum. I have declared my opinion on this head to
some of the most sensible men of this country, observing, at
the same time, that if they would employ a few natives of
England to teach the pronunciation of our vernacular tongue,
in twenty years there would be no difference, in point of dialect, between the youth of Edinburgh and of London.

The civil regulations of this kingdom and metropolis are
taken from very different models than those in England, excepting in a few particular establishments, the necessary
consequences of the union. Their college of justice is a bench
of great dignity, filled with judges of character and ability.
I have heard some causes tried before this venerable tribunal; and was very much pleased with the pleadings of their
advocates, who are by no means deficient either in argument
or elocution. The Scottish legislation is founded, in a great
measure, on the civil law; consequently, their proceedings
vary from those of the English tribunals; but, I think, they
have the advantage of us in their method of examining witnesses apart, and in the constitution of their jury; by which
they certainly avoid the evil which I mentioned in my last
from Lismahago's observation.

The university of Edinburgh is supplied with excellent
professors in all the sciences; and the medical school, in particular, is famous all over Europe. The students of this
art have the best opportunity of learning it to perfection, in
all its branches, as there are different courses for the *theory
of medicine*, and the *practice of medicine*; for *anatomy, che-
mistry, botany*, and the *materia medica*, over and above those
of *mathematics* and *experimental philosophy*; and all these
are given by men of distinguished talents. What renders
this part of education still more complete, is the advantage
of attending the infirmary, which is the best instituted charitable foundation that I ever knew. Now we are talking of
charities, here are several hospitals, exceedingly well endow-

ed, and maintained under admirable regulations; and these are not only useful, but ornamental to the city. Among these, I shall only mention the general workhouse, in which all the poor, not otherwise provided for, are employed, according to their different abilities, with such judgment and effect, that they nearly maintain themselves by their labour, and there is not a beggar to be seen within the precincts of this metropolis. It was Glasgow that set the example of this establishment, about thirty years ago. Even the kirk of Scotland, so long reproached with fanaticism and canting, abounds at present with ministers celebrated for their learning, and respectable for their moderation. I have heard their sermons with equal astonishment and pleasure. The good people of Edinburgh no longer think dirt and cobwebs essential to the house of God. Some of their churches have admitted such ornaments as would have excited sedition, even in England, a little more than a century ago; and psalmody is here practised and taught by a professor from the cathedral of Durham. I should not be surprised, in a few years, to hear it accompanied with an organ.

Edinburgh is a hot-bed of genius. I have had the good fortune to be made acquainted with many authors of the first distinction; such as the two Humes, Robertson, Smith, Wallace, Blair, Ferguson, Wilkie, &c. and I have found them all as agreeable in conversation, as they are instructive and entertaining in their writings. These acquaintances I owe to the friendship of Dr Carlyle, who wants nothing but inclination to figure with the rest upon paper.—The magistracy of Edinburgh is changed every year by election, and seems to be very well adapted both for state and authority. The *lord provost* is equal in dignity to the *lord mayor of London*; and the *four bailies* are equivalent to the rank of aldermen. There is a *dean of guild*, who takes cognisance of mercantile affairs; a treasurer, a town-clerk; and the council is composed of deacons, one of whom is returned every year in rotation, as representative of every company of artificers or handicraftsmen. Though this city, from the nature of its situation, can never be made either very conveni-

ent or very cleanly, it has, nevertheless, an air of magnificence that commands respect.   The castle is an instance of
the sublime in site and architecture.   Its fortifications are
kept in good order, and there is always in it a garrison of
regular soldiers, which is relieved every year ; but it is incapable of sustaining a seige carried on according to the modern operations of war.   The Castle hill, which extends
from the outward gate to the upper end of the High street,
is used as a public walk for the citizens, and commands a
prospect, equally extensive and delightful, over the county
of Fife, on the other side of the Frith, and all along the sea-
coast, which is covered with a succession of towns, that
would seem to indicate a considerable share of commerce ;
but if the truth must be told, these towns have been falling
to decay ever since the union, by which the Scots were in
a great measure deprived of their trade with France.—The
palace of Holyroodhouse is a jewel in architecture, thrust into a hollow where it cannot be seen ; a situation which was
certainly not chosen by the ingenious architect, who must
have been confined to the site of the old palace, which was
a convent.—Edinburgh is considerably extended on the
south side, where there are divers little elegant squares, built
in the English manner ; and the citizens have planned some
improvements on the north, which, when put in execution,
will add greatly to the beauty and convenience of this capital.

    The sea-port is Leith, a flourishing town, about a mile
from the city, in the harbour of which I have seen above one
hundred ships lying all together.   You must know I had
the curiosity to cross the Frith in a passage-boat, and staid
two days in Fife, which is remarkably fruitful in corn, and
exhibits a surprising number of fine seats, elegantly built,
and magnificently furnished.   There is an incredible number of noble houses in every part of Scotland that I have
seen—Dalkeith, Pinkie, Yester, and Lord Hopetoun's, all
of them within four or five miles of Edinburgh, are princely
palaces, in every one of which a sovereign might reside at his
ease.   I suppose the Scots affect these monuments of gran-

dour. If I may be allowed to mingle censure with my remarks upon a people I revere, I must observe, that their weak
side seems to be vanity. I am afraid that even their hospitality is not quite free of ostentation. I think I have discovered among them uncommon pains taken to display their fine
linen, of which indeed they have great plenty, their furniture, plate, house-keeping, and variety of wines, in which
article, it must be owned, they are profuse, if not prodigal.
A burgher of Edinburgh, not content to vie with a citizen of
London who has ten times his fortune, must excel him in the
expense as well as elegance of his entertainments.

Though the villas of the Scots nobility and gentry have
generally an air of grandeur and state, I think their gardens
and parks are not comparable, to those of England; a circumstance the more remarkable, as I was told by the ingenious Mr. Philip Miller of Chelsea, that almost all the gar-
deners of South Britain were natives of Scotland. The verdure of this country is not equal to that of England. The
pleasure-grounds are, in my opinion, not so well laid out
according to the *genius loci*; nor are the lawns, and walks,
and hedges, kept in such delicate order. The trees are planted in prudish rows, which have not such an agreeable natural effect, as when they are thrown into irregular groups,
with intervening glades; and the firs, which they generally
raise around their houses, look dull and funeral in the summer season. I must confess, indeed, that they yield serviceable timber, and good shelter against the northern blasts;
that they grow and thrive in the most barren soil, and continually perspire a fine balsam of turpentine, which must
render the air very salutary and sanative to lungs of a tender texture.

Tabby and I have been both frightened in our return by
sea from the coast of Fife. She was afraid of drowning, and
I of catching cold, in consequence of being drenched with
sea-water; but my fears, as well as hers, have been happily
disappointed. She is now in perfect health; I wish I could
say the same of Liddy. Something uncommon is the matter with that poor child; her colour fades, her appetite fails,

and her spirits flag. She is become moping and melancholy, and is often found in tears. Her brother suspects internal uneasiness on account of Wilson, and denounces vengeance against that adventurer. She was, it seems, strongly affected at the ball, by the sudden appearance of one Mr Gordon, who strongly resembles the said Wilson; but I am rather suspicious that she caught cold by being overheated with dancing. I have consulted Dr Gregory, an eminent physician, of an amiable character, who advices the Highland air, and the use of goat-milk whey, which surely cannot have a bad effect upon a patient who was born and bred among the mountains of Wales. The doctor's opinion is the more agreeable, as we shall find those remedies in the very place which I proposed as the utmost extent of our expedition—I mean the borders of Argyll.

Mr Smollett, one of the judges of the commissary-court, which is now sitting, has very kindly insisted upon our lodging at his country-house, on the banks of Loch Lomond, about fourteen miles beyond Glasgow. For this last city we shall set out in two days, and take Stirling in our way, well provided with recommendations from our friends at Edinburgh, whom, I protest, I shall leave with much regret. I am so far from thinking it any hardship to live in this country, that, if I was obliged to lead a town-life, Edinburgh would certainly be the head-quarters of yours always,

Edinburgh, Aug. 8.   MATT. BRAMBLE.

TO SIR WATKIN PHILLIPS, BART. OF JESUS COLLEGE, OXON.

DEAR KNIGHT,

I AM now little short of the *ultima Thule*, if this appellation properly belongs to the Orkneys or Hebrides.—These last are now lying before me, to the amount of some hundreds, scattered up and down the Deucaledonian sea, affording the most picturesque and romantic prospect I ever beheld.—I write this letter in a gentleman's house, near the town of Inverary, which may be deemed the capital of the West Highlands, famous for nothing so much as for the

stately castle begun and actually covered in by the late duke
of Argyll, at a prodigious expense.—Whether it will ever
be completely finished is a question.

But, to take things in order.—We left Edinburgh ten
days ago—and the farther north we proceed, we find Mrs
Tabitha the less manageable; so that her inclinations are
not of the nature of the loadstone—they point not towards
the pole.   What made her leave Edinburgh with reluctance
at last, if we may believe her own assertions, was a dispute
which she left unfinished with Mr Moffat, touching the
eternity of hell torments.   That gentleman, as he advanced
in years, began to be sceptical on this head, till at length
he declared open war against the common acceptation of the
word *eternal.*   He is now persuaded that *eternal* signifies no
more than an indefinite number of years; and that the most
enormous sinner may be quit for *nine millions nine hundred
thousand nine hundred and ninety-nine years of hell fire;*
which term or period, as he very well observes, forms but
an inconsiderable drop, as it were, in the ocean of eternity.
—For this mitigation he contends, as a system agreeable to
the ideas of goodness and mercy which we annex to the Supreme Being.—Our aunt seemed willing to adopt this doctrine in favour of the wicked · but he hinted, that no person
whatever was so righteous as to be exempted entirely from
punishment in a future state; and that the most pious christian upon earth might think himself very happy to get off
for a fast of seven or eight thousand years in the midst of
fire and brimstone.   Mrs Tabitha revolted at this dogma,
which filled her at once with horror and indignation.—She
had recourse to the opinion of Humphry Clinker, who roundly declared it was the popish doctrine of purgatory, and
quoted scripture in defence of the *fire everlasting prepared
for the devil and his angels.*—The Reverend Mr M'Corkendale, and all the theologists and saints of that persuasion,
were consulted, and some of them had doubts about the matter, which doubts and scruples had begun to infect our aunt
when we took our departure from Edinburgh.

We passed through Linlithgow, where there was an elegant royal palace, which is now gone to decay, as well as the town itself.—This too is pretty much the case with Stirling, though it still boasts of a fine old castle, in which the kings of Scotland were wont to reside in their minority.— But Glasgow is the pride of Scotland, and indeed it might very well pass for an elegant and flourishing city in any part of Christendom. There we had the good fortune to be received into the house of Mr Moore, an eminent surgeon, to whom we were recommended by one of our friends at Edinburgh; and truly he could not have done us more essential service.—Mr Moore is a merry facetious companion, sensible and shrewd, with a considerable fund of humour; and his wife an agreeable woman, well-bred, kind and obliging. Kindness, which I take to be the essence of good nature and humanity, is the distinguishing characteristic of the Scots ladies in their own country.—Our landlord shewed us every thing, and introduced us to all the world at Glasgow, where, through his recommendation, we were complimented with the freedom of the town. Considering the trade and opulence of this place, it cannot but abound with gaiety and diversions.—Here is a great number of young fellows that rival the youth of the capital in spirit and expense; and I was soon convinced, that all the female beauties of Scotland were not assembled at the hunters' ball in Edinburgh.—The town of Glasgow flourishes in learning as well as in commerce. Here is an university, with professors in all the different branches of science, liberally endowed, and judiciously chosen.—It was vacation time when I passed, so that I could not entirely satisfy my curiosity; but their mode of education is certainly preferable to ours in some respects.—The students are not left to the private instruction of tutors, but taught in public schools or classes, each science by its particular professor or regent.

My uncle is in raptures with Glasgow.—He not only visited all the manufactures of the place, but made excursions all round, to Hamilton, Paisley, Renfrew, and every other place within a dozen miles, where there was any thing remarkable to be seen in art or nature. I believe the exercise

occasioned by these jaunts was of service to my sister Liddy,
whose appetite and spirits begin to revive.   Mrs Tabitha
displayed her attractions as usual, and actually believed she
had entangled one Mr M'Clellan, a rich inkle manufacturer,
in her snares ; but when matters came to an explanation, it
appeared that his attachment was altogether spiritual, founded upon an intercourse of devotion at the meeting of Mr
John Wesley, who, in the course of his evangelical mission,
had come hither in person.—At length we set out for the
banks of Loch Lomond, passing through the little borough
of Dumbarton, or (as my uncle will have it) Dunbritton,
where there is a castle more curious than any thing of the
kind I had ever seen.   It is honoured with a particular description by the elegant Buchanan, as an *arx inexpugnabilis ;*
and, indeed, it must have been impregnable by the ancient
manner of besieging.   It is a rock of considerable extent,
rising with a double top, in an angle formed by the conflu-
ence of two rivers, the Clyde and the Leven, perpendicular
and inaccessible on all sides, except in one place where the
entrance is fortified ; and there is no rising ground in the
neighbourhood from whence it could be damaged by any
kind of battery.   From Dumbarton the West Highlands appear in the form of huge dusky mountains, piled one over
another ; but this prospect is not at all surprising to a native
of Glamorgan.—We have fixed our head-quarters at Cameron, a very neat country-house, belonging to Commissary
Smollett, where we found every sort of accommodation we
could desire.—It is situated like a Druid's temple, in a grove
of oak, close by the side of Loch Lomond, which is a surprising body of pure transparent water, unfathomably deep
in many places, six or seven miles broad, four-and-twenty
miles in length, displaying above twenty green islands, co-
covered with wood, some of them cultivated for corn, and
many of them stocked with red deer.—They belong to different gentlemen, whose seats are scattered along the banks
of the lake, which are agreeably romantic beyond all conception.   My uncle and I have left the women at Cameron,
as Mrs Tabitha would by no means trust herself again upon

the water, and, to come hither it was necessary to cross a
small inlet of the sea in an open ferry-boat. This country
appears more and more wild and savage the farther we advance; and the people are as different from the Lowland
Scots, in their looks, garb, and language, as the mountaineers of Brecnock are from the inhabitants of Hereford-
shire.

When the Lowlanders want to drink a cheer-upping cup,
they go to the public house, called the change-house, and
call for a chopin of twopenny, which is a thin yeasty beverage, made of malt, not quite so strong as the table-beer of
England.—This is brought in a pewter stoup, shaped like
a skittle; from whence it is emptied into a quaff, that is, a
curious cup made of different pieces of wood, such as box
and ebony, cut into little staves, joined alternately, and secured with delicate hoops, having two ears or handles.—It
holds about a gill, is sometimes tipt round the mouth with
silver, and has a plate of the same metal at the bottom, with
the landlord's cypher engraved.—The Highlanders, on the
contrary, despise this liquor, and regale themselves with
whisky, a malt spirit, as strong as geneva, which they swallow in great quantities, without any sign of inebriation.—
They are used to it from their cradle, and find it an excellent preservative against the winter cold, which must be extreme on these mountains.—I am told that it is given with
great success to infants, as a cordial, in the confluent small-
pox, when the eruption seems to flag, and the symptoms
grow unfavourable.—The Highlanders are used to eat much
more animal food than falls to the share of their neighbours
in the low country.—They delight in hunting—have plenty
of deer and other game, with a great number of sheep, goats,
and black cattle, running wild, which they scruple not to
kill as venison, without being at much pains to ascertain
the property.

Inverary is but a poor town, though it stands immediately under the protection of the duke of Argyll, who is a
mighty prince in this part of Scotland. The peasants live
in wretched cabins, and seem very poor; but the gentlemen

are tolerably well lodged, and so loving to strangers, that a
man runs some risk of his life from their hospitality.—It
must be observed, that the poor Highlanders are now seen
to disadvantage.—They have been not only disarmed by
act of parliament, but also deprived of their ancient garb,
which was both graceful and convenient; and, what is a
greater hardship still, they are compelled to wear breeches—a
restraint which they cannot bear with any degree of patience:
indeed, the majority wear them, not in the proper place, but
on poles, or long staves, over their shoulders.—They are even
debarred the use of their stripped stuff, called tartan, which was
their own manufacture, prized by them above all the velvets,
brocades, and tissues of Europe and Asia.   They now lounge
along in loose great coats, of coarse russet, equally mean
and cumbersome, and betray manifest marks of dejection.—
Certain it is, the government could not have taken a more
effectual method to break their national spirit.

We have had princely sport in hunting the stag on these
mountains: these are the lonely hills of Morven, where Fin-
gal and his heroes enjoyed the same pastime.   I feel an enthusiastic pleasure when I survey the brown heath that Ossian wont to tread, and hear the wind whistle through the
bending grass.   When I enter our landlord's hall, I look for
the suspended harp of that divine bard, and listen in hopes
of hearing the aërial sound of his respected spirit.   The
poems of Ossian are in every mouth.   A famous antiquarian
of this country, the laird of M'Farlane, at whose house we
dined a few days ago, can repeat them all in the original
Gaelic, which has a great affinity to the Welch, not only in
the general sound, but also in a great number of radical
words: and I make no doubt but that they are both sprung
from the same origin.   I was not a little surprised, when
asking a Highlander one day, if he knew where we should
find any game? he replied,—'*Hu niel Sassenagh*,' which
signifies, *no English* ; the very same answer I should have
received from a Welchman, and almost in the same words.
The Highlanders have no other name for the people of the
low country but Sassenagh, or Saxons ; a strong presump-

tion that the Lowland Scots and the English are derived
from the same stock. The peasants of these hills strongly
resemble those of Wales in their looks, their manners, and
habitations; every thing I see, and hear, and feel, seems
Welch. The mountains, vales, and streams, the air and
climate, the beef, mutton, and game, are all Welch. It
must be owned, however, that this people are better provided than we are in some articles: they have plenty of red
deer and roebuck, which are fat and delicious at this season
of the year; their sea teems with amazing quantities of the
finest fish in the world; and they find means to procure very
good claret at a very small expense.

Our landlord is a man of consequence in this part of the
country; a cadet from the family of Argyll, and hereditary
captain of one of his castles. His name, in plain English,
is Dougal Campbell; but as there are a great number of the
same appellation, they are distinguished (like the Welch)
by patronymics; and as I have known an ancient Briton
called Madoc ap Morgan, ap-Jenkin, ap-Jones, our Highland chief designs himself Dou'l Mac-Amish, mac-'oul ich-
ian, signifying, Dougal, the son of James, the son of Dougal, the son of John. He has travelled in the course of his
education, and is disposed to make certain alterations in his
domestic economy; but he finds it impossible to abolish the
ancient customs of the family, some of which are ludicrous
enough. His piper, for example, who is an hereditary officer of the household, will not part with the least particle of
his privileges. He has a right to wear the kilt, or ancient
Highland dress, with the purse, pistol, and durk; a broad
yellow ribbon, fixed to the chanter-pipe, is thrown over his
shoulders, and trails along the ground, while he performs the
functions of his minstrelsy; and this, I suppose, is analogous
to the pennon, or flag, which was formerly carried before
every knight in battle. He plays before the laird every Sunday in his way to the kirk, which he circles three times, performing the family march, which implies defiance to all the
enemies of the clan; and every morning he plays a full hour
by the clock, in the great hall, marching backwards and for-

wards all the time, with a solemn pace, attended by the laird's
kinsmen, who seem much delighted with the music. In this
exercise, he indulges them with a number of pibrachs or airs,
suited to the different passions which he would either excite
or assuage.

Mr Campbell himself, who performs very well on the
violin, has an invincible antipathy to the sound of the Highland bagpipe, which sings in the nose with a most alarming
twang, and, indeed, is quite intolerable to ears of common
sensibility, when aggravated by the echo of a vaulted hall;
he therefore begged the piper would have some mercy upon
him, and dispense with this part of the morning service. A
consultation of the clan being held on this occasion, it was
unanimously agreed that the laird's request could not be
granted, without a dangerous encroachment upon the customs of the family. The piper declared, he could not give
up for a moment the privilege he derived from his ancestors;
nor would the laird's relations forego an entertainment which
they valued above all others. There was no remedy; Mr
Campbell, being obliged to acquiesce, is fain to stop his ears
with cotton, to fortify his head with three or four night-caps,
and every morning retire into the penetralia of his habitation,
in order to avoid this dismal annoyance. When the music
ceases, he produces himself at an open window that looks
into the court-yard, which is by this time filled with a
crowd of his vassals and dependents, who worship his first
appearance, by uncovering their heads, and bowing to the
earth with the most humble prostration. As all these people
have something to communicate in the way of proposal,
complaint, or petition, they wait patiently till the laird
comes forth, and, following him in his walks, are favoured
each with a short audience in his turn. Two days ago he
dispatched above an hundred different solicitors, in walking
with us to the house of a neighbouring gentleman, where we
dined by invitation. Our landlord's house-keeping is equally rough and hospitable, and savours much of the simplicity
of ancient times. The great hall, paved with flat stones, is
about forty-five feet by twenty-two, and serves not only for

a dining-room, but also for a bed-chamber to gentlemen-dependents and hangers-on of the family. At night, half a dozen occasional beds are ranged on each side along the wall. These are made of fresh heath, pulled up by the roots, and disposed in such a manner as to make a very agreeable couch, where they lie, without any other covering than the plaid. My uncle and I were indulged with separate chambers and down-beds, which we begged to exchange for a layer of heath; and, indeed, I never slept so much to my satisfaction. It was not only soft and elastic, but the plant, being in flower. diffused an agreeable fragrance, which is wonderfully refreshing and restorative.

Yesterday we were invited to the funeral of an old lady, the grandmother of a gentleman in this neighbourhood, and found ourselves in the midst of fifty people who were regaled with a sumptuous feast, accompanied by the music of a dozen pipers. In short, this meeting had all the air of a grand festival; and the guests did such honour to the entertainment, that many of them could not stand when they were reminded of the business on which we had met. The company forthwith taking horse, rode in a very irregular cavalcade to the place of interment, a church, at the distance of two long miles from the castle. On our arrival, however, we found we had committed a small oversight in leaving the corpse behind; so that we were obliged to wheel about, and met the old gentlewoman half way, carried upon poles by the nearest relations of her family, and attended by the *coronach*, composed of a multitude of old hags, who tore their hair, beat their breasts, and howled most hideously. At the grave, the orator, or *senachie*, pronounced the panegyric of the defunct, every period being confirmed by a yell of the *coronach*. The body was committed to the earth, the pipers playing a pibroch all the time, and all the company standing uncovered. The ceremony was closed with the discharge of pistols; then we returned to the castle, resumed the bottle, and by midnight there was not a sober person in the family, the females excepted. The squire and I were, with some difficulty, permitted to retire with the landlord in the evening; but our entertainer was a little chagrined at our retreat; and afterwards seemed to think it a disparagement to his family that not above an hundred gallons of whisky had been drank upon such a solemn occasion. This morning we got up by four, to hunt the roe-buck, and in half an hour found breakfast ready served in the hall. The hunters consisted of Sir George Colquhoun and me, as strangers (my uncle not choosing to be of the party), of the *laird in person, the laird's brother, the laird's brother's son, the laird's sister's son, the laird's father's brother's son,* and all their *foster brothers,* who are counted part of the family : but we were attended by an infinite number of *gaellys,* or ragged Highlanders, without shoes or stockings.

The following articles formed our morning's repast : one kit of boiled eggs ; a second, full of butter ; a third, full of cream ; an entire cheese, made of goat's milk ; a large earthen pot full of honey ; the best part of a ham ; a cold venison pasty ; a bushel of oat-meal, made in thin cakes and bannocks, with a small wheaten loaf in the middle for the strangers ; a large stone bottle full of whisky, another of brandy, and a kilderkin of ale. There was a ladle chained to the cream kit, with curious wooden bickers, to be filled from this reservoir. The spirits were drank out of a silver quaff, and the ale out of horns. Great justice was done to the collation by the guests in general ; one of them, in particular, ate above two dozen of hard eggs, with a proportionable quantity of bread, butter, and honey ; nor was one drop of liquor left upon the board. Finally, a large roll of tobacco was presented by way of dessert, and every individual took a comfortable quid, to prevent the bad effects of the morning air. We had a fine chase over the mountains after a roebuck, which we killed, and I got home time enough to drink tea with Mrs Campbell and our squire. To-morrow we shall set out on our return for Cameron. We propose to cross the frith of Clyde, and take the towns of Greenock and Port Glasgow in our way. This circuit being finished, we shall turn our faces to the south, and follow the sun with augmented velocity, in order to enjoy the rest of the autumn in Eng-

land, where Boreas is not quite so biting, as he begins already
to be on the tops of these northern hills. But our progress
from place to place shall continue to be specified in these
detached journals of, yours always,

Argyllshire, Sept. 3.   J. MELFORD.

TO DR LEWIS.

DEAR DICK,

About a fortnight is now elapsed since we left the capital
of Scotland, directing our course towards Stirling, where we
lay. The castle of this place is such another as that of Edinburgh, and affords a surprising prospect of the windings of
the river Forth, which are so extraordinary, that the distance
from hence to Alloa by land is but four miles, and by water
it is twenty-four. Alloa is a neat thriving town, that depends
in a great measure on the commerce of Glasgow, the merchants of which send hither tobacco and other articles, to be
deposited in warehouses for exportation from the Frith of
Forth. In our way hither we visited a flourishing iron-
work, where, instead of burning wood, they use coal, which
they have the art of clearing in such a manner as frees it
from the sulphur, that would otherwise render the metal too
brittle for working. Excellent coal is found in almost every
part of Scotland.

The soil of this district produces scarce any other grain
but oats and barley, perhaps because it is poorly cultivated,
and almost altogether uninclosed. The few inclosures they
have consist of paltry walls of loose stones gathered from the
fields, which indeed they cover, as if they had been scattered on purpose. When I expressed my surprise that the
peasants did not disencumber their grounds of these stones,
a gentleman, well acquainted with the theory as well as practice of farming, assured me, that the stones, far from being
prejudicial, were serviceable to the crop. This philosopher
had ordered a field of his own to be cleared, manured, and
sown with barley, and the produce was more scanty than
before. He caused the stones to be replaced, and next year

Vol. VI.   S

the crop was as good as ever. The stones were removed a second time, and the harvest failed; they were again brought back, and the ground retrieved its fertility. The same experiment has been tried in different parts of Scotland with the same success. Astonished at this information, I desired to know in what manner he accounted for this strange phenomenon; and he said, there were three ways in which the stones might be serviceable. They might possibly restrain an excess in the perspiration of the earth, analogous to colliquative sweats, by which the human body is sometimes wasted and consumed. They might act as so many fences to protect the tender blade from the piercing winds of the spring; or, by multiplying the reflection of the sun, they might increase the warmth, so as to mitigate the natural chillness of the soil and climate. But surely this excessive perspiration might be more effectually checked by different kinds of manure, such as ashes, lime, chalk, or marl, of which last it seems there are many pits in this kingdom. As for the warmth, it would be much more equally obtained by inclosures; one half of the ground which is now covered would be retrieved, the cultivation would require less labour, and the ploughs, harrows, and horses, would not suffer half the damage which they now sustain.

These north-western parts are by no means fertile in corn. The ground is naturally barren and moorish. The peasants are poorly lodged, meagre in their looks, mean in their apparel, and remarkably dirty. This last reproach they might easily wash off, by means of those lakes, rivers, and rivulets of pure water, with which they are so liberally supplied by nature. Agriculture cannot be expected to flourish where the farms are small, the leases short, and the husbandman begins upon a rack-rent, without a sufficient stock to answer the purposes of improvement. The granaries of Scotland are the banks of the Tweed, the counties of East and Mid Lothian, the Carse of Gowrie, in Perthshire, equal in fertility to any part of England, and some tracts in Aberdeenshire and Moray, where I am told the harvest is more early than in Northumberland, although they lie above two degrees farther north. I have a strong curiosity to visit many places beyond the Forth and the Tay, such as Perth, Dundee, Montrose, and Aberdeen, which are towns equally elegant and thriving; but the season is too far advanced to admit of this addition to my original plan.

I am so far happy as to have seen Glasgow, which, to the best of my recollection and judgment, is one of the prettiest towns in Europe; and without all doubt, it is one of the most flourishing in Great Britain. In short, it is a perfect bee-hive in point of industry. It stands partly on a gentle declivity; but the greatest part of it is in a plain, watered by the river Clyde. The streets are straight, open, airy, and well paved; and the houses lofty and well built, of hewn stone. At the upper end of the town, there is a venerable cathedral, that may be compared with York-minster or Westminster; and, about the middle of the descent from this to the cross, is the college, a respectable pile of building, with all manner of accommodation for the professors and students, including an elegant library, and an observatory well provided with astronomical instruments. The number of inhabitants is said to amount to thirty thousand; and marks of opulence and independency appear in every quarter of this commercial city, which, however, is not without its inconveniencies and defects. The water of their public pumps is generally hard and brackish, an imperfection the less excusable, as the river Clyde runs by their doors, in the lower part of the town; and there are rivulets and springs above the cathedral, sufficient to fill a large reservoir with excellent water, which might be thence distributed to all the different parts of the city. It is of more consequence to consult the health of the inhabitants in this article than to employ so much attention in beautifying their town with new streets, squares, and churches. Another defect, not so easily remedied, is the shallowness of the river, which will not float vessels of any burden within ten or twelve miles of the city; so that the merchants are obliged to load and unload their ships at Greenock and Port-

Glasgow, situated about fourteen miles nearer the mouth of the frith, where it is about two miles broad.

The people of Glasgow have a noble spirit of enterprise.—Mr Moore, a surgeon, to whom I was recommended from Edinburgh, introduced me to all the principal merchants of the place. Here I became acquainted with Mr Cochran, who may be styled one of the sages of this kingdom. He was first magistrate at the time of the last rebellion. I sat as member when he was examined in the house of commons; upon which occasion Mr P—— observed he had never heard such a sensible evidence given at that bar. I was also introduced to Dr John Gordon, a patriot of a truly Roman spirit, who is the father of the linen manufacture in this place, and was the great promoter of the city work-house, infirmary, and other works of public utility.—Had he lived in ancient Rome, he would have been honoured with a statue at the public expense. I moreover conversed with one Mr G——ss——d whom I take to be one of the greatest merchants in Europe. In the last war, he is said to have had at one time five-and-twenty ships, with their cargoes, his own property, and to have traded for above half a million sterling a-year. The last war was a fortunate period for the commerce of Glasgow.—The merchants, considering that their ships bound for America, launching out at once into the Atlantic by the north of Ireland, pursued a track very little frequented by privateers, resolved to ensure one another, and saved a very considerable sum by this resolution, as few or none of their ships were taken.—You must know I have a sort of national attachment to this part of Scotland. —The great church, dedicated to S^t. Mongah, the river Clyde, and, among other particulars, that smack of our Welch language and customs, contribute to flatter me with the notion, that these people are the descendants of the Britons, who once possessed this country. Without all question, this was a Cumbrian kingdom; its capital was Dumbarton (a corruption of Dunbritton), which still exists as a royal borough, at the influx of the Clyde and Leven, ten miles below Glasgow. The same neighbourhood gave birth to S^t. Patrick, the apostle of Ireland, at a place where there is still a church and village, which retain his name. Hard by are some vestiges of the famous Roman wall, built in the reign of Antonine, from the Clyde to the Forth, and fortified with castles to restrain the incursions of the Scots or Caledonians, who inhabited the West Highlands. In a line parallel to this wall, the merchants of Glasgow have determined to make a navigable canal betwixt the two friths, which will be of incredible advantage to their commerce, in transporting merchandise from one side of the island to the other.

From Glasgow we travelled along the Clyde, which is a delightful stream, adorned on both sides with villas, towns, and villages. Here is no want of groves, and meadows, and corn fields interspersed; but on this side of Glasgow, there is little other grain than oats and barley; the first are much better, the last much worse, than those of the same species in England. I wonder there is so little rye, which is a grain that will thrive in almost any soil; and it is still more surprising, that the cultivation of potatoes should be so much neglected in the Highlands, where the poor people have not meal enough to supply them with bread through the winter. On the other side of the river are the towns of Paisley and Renfrew. The first, from an inconsiderable village, is become one of the most flourishing places of the kingdom, enriched by the linen, cambric, flowered lawn, and silk manufactures. It was formerly noted for a rich monastery of the monks of Clugny, who wrote the famous *Scoti-Chronicon*, called *The black book of Paisley*. The old abbey still remains, converted into a dwelling-house, belonging to the earl of Dundonald. Renfrew is a pretty town on the banks of Clyde, capital of the shire, which was heretofore the patrimony of the Stuart family, and gave the title of baron to the king's eldest son, which is still assumed by the prince of Wales.

The Clyde we left a little on our left hand at Dunbritton, where it widens into an estuary or frith, being augmented by the influx of the Leven. On this spot stands the castle

formerly called Alcluyd, washed by these two rivers on all
sides, except a narrow isthmus, which at every spring-tide
is overflowed.   The whole is a great curiosity, from the
quality and form of the rock, as well as from the nature of
its situation.   We now crossed the water of Leven, which,
though nothing near so considerable as the Clyde, is much
more transparent, pastoral, and delightful.   This charming
stream is the outlet of Loch Lomond, and through a track
of four miles pursues its winding course, murmuring over a
bed of pebbles, till it joins the frith at Dunbritton.   A very
little above its source, on the lake, stands the house of
Cameron, belonging to Mr Smollett, so embosomed in an
oak wood, that we did not see it till we were within fifty
yards of the door.   I have seen the Lago di Gardi, Albano,
De Vico, Bolsena, and Geneva, and, upon my honour, I
prefer Loch Lomond to them all; a preference which is certainly owing to the verdant islands that seem to float upon
its surface, affording the most enchanting objects of repose
to the excursive view.   Nor are the banks destitute of beauties, which even partake of the sublime.   On this side they
display a sweet variety of woodland, corn-field, and pasture, with several agreeable villas emerging as it were out of
the lake, till, at some distance, the prospect terminates
in huge mountains, covered with heath, which being in the
bloom, affords a very rich covering of purple.   Every thing
here is romantic beyond imagination.   This country is justly styled the Arcadia of Scotland; and I don't doubt but it
may vie with Arcadia in every thing but climate.   I am sure
it excels it in verdure, wood, and water.   What say you
to a natural bason of pure water, near thirty miles long, and
in some places seven miles broad, and in many above an
hundred fathoms deep, having four-and-twenty habitable
islands, some of them stocked with deer, and all of them
covered with wood; containing immense quantities of delicious fish, salmon, pike, trout, perch, flownders, eels, and
powans, the last a delicate kind of fresh-water herring peculiar to this lake; and, finally, communicating with the
sea, by sending off the Leven, through which all those spe-

cies (except the powan) make their exit and entrance occasionally!

Inclosed I send you the copy of a little ode to this river, by Dr Smollett, who was born on the banks of it, within two miles of the place where I am now writing. It is at least picturesque and accurately descriptive, if it has no other merit.—There is an idea of truth, in an agreeable landscape taken from nature, which pleases me more than the gayest fiction which the most luxuriant fancy can display.

I have other remarks to make; but as my paper is full, I must reserve them till the next occasion. I shall only observe at present, that I am determined to penetrate at least forty miles into the Highlands, which now appear like a vast fantastic vision in the clouds, inviting the approach of yours always,

Cameron, Aug. 8.　　　　　　　　　MATT. BRAMBLE.

ODE TO LEVEN WATER.

On Leven's banks, while free to rove,
And tune the rural pipe to love,
I envied not the happiest swain
That ever trode th' Arcadian plain.
Pure stream! in whose transparent wave
My youthful limbs I wont to lave;
No torrents stain thy limpid source;
No rocks impede thy dimpling course,
That sweetly warbles o'er its bed,
With white, round, polish'd pebbles spread;
While, lightly pois'd, the scaly brood
In myriads cleave thy crystal flood;
The springing trout in speckled pride;
The salmon, monarch of the tide;
The ruthless pike, intent on war;
The silver eel, and mottled par *.
Devolving from thy parent lake,
A charming maze thy waters make,
By bow'rs of birch, and groves of pine,
And hedges flower'd with eglantine.
Still on thy banks so gayly green,
May num'rous herds and flocks be seen,
And lasses chanting o'er the pail,
And shepherds piping in the dale,
And ancient faith that knows no guile,
And industry embrown'd with toil,
And hearts resolv'd, and hands prepar'd,
The blessings they enjoy to guard.

* The par is a small fish, not unlike the smelt, which it rivals in delicacy and flavour.

TO.DR LEWIS.

DEAR DOCTOR.

IF I was disposed to be critical, I should say this house of Cameron is too near the lake, which approaches on one side to within six or seven yards of the window. It might have been placed on a higher site, which would have afforded a more extensive prospect and a drier atmosphere; but this imperfection is not chargeable on the present proprietor, who purchased it ready built, rather than be at the trouble of repairing his own family house of Bonhill, which stands two miles from hence on the Leven, so surrounded with plantation, that it used to be known by the name of the Mavis (or thrush) nest. About that house is a romantic glen or cleft of a mountain, covered with hanging woods, having at bottom a stream of fine water that forms a number of cascades in its descent to join the Leven; so that the scene is quite enchanting. A captain of a man of war who had made the circuit of the globe with Mr Anson, being conducted to this glen, exclaimed,—' Juan Fernandez, by God!'

Indeed, this country would be a perfect paradise, if it was not, like Wales, cursed with a weeping climate, owing to the same causes in both, the neighbourhood of high mountains, and a westerly situation exposed to the vapours of the Atlantic ocean. This air, however, notwithstanding its humidity, is so healthy, that the natives are scarce ever visited by any other disease than the small pox, and certain cutaneous evils which are the effects of dirty living, the great and general reproach of the commonalty of this kingdom. Here are a great many living monuments of longevity, and, among the rest a person whom I treat with singular respect, as a venerable Druid, who has lived near ninety years, without pain or sickness, among oaks of his own planting. He was once proprietor of these lands: but, being of a projecting spirit, some of his schemes miscarried, and he was obliged to part with his possession, which hath shifted hands two or three times since that period; but every succeeding proprietor hath done every thing in his power to make his old age easy and comfortable. He has a sufficiency to procure the necessaries of life; and he and his old woman reside in a small convenient farm-house, having a little garden, which he cultivates with his own hands. This ancient couple live in great health, peace, and harmony, and, knowing no wants, enjoying the perfection of content. Mr Smollett calls him the admiral, because he insists upon steering his pleasure-boat upon the lake; and he spends most of his time in ranging through the woods, which he declares he enjoys as much as if they were still his own property. I asked him the other day, if he was never sick? and he answered, yes; he had a slight fever the year before the Union. If he was not deaf, I should take much pleasure in his conversation; for he is very intelligent, and his memory is surprisingly retentive. These are the happy effects of temperance, exercise, and good-nature.—Notwithstanding all his innocence, however, he was the cause of great perturbation to my man Clinker, whose natural superstition has been much injured by the histories of witches, fairies, ghosts, and goblins, which he has heard in this country.—On the evening after our arrival, Humphry strolled into the wood in the course of his meditation, and all at once the admiral stood before him, under the shadow of a spreading oak. Though the fellow is far from being timorous in cases that are not supposed preternatural, he could not stand the sight of this apparition, but ran into the kitchen, with his hair standing on end, staring wildly, and deprived of utterance. Mrs Jenkins, seeing him in this condition, screamed aloud,—' Lord have mercy upon us, he has seen something!' Mrs Tabitha was alarmed, and the whole house in confusion. When he was recruited with a dram, I desired him to explain the meaning of all this agitation; and, with some reluctance, he owned he had seen a spirit in the shape of an old man, with a white beard, a black cap, and a plaid night-gown. He was undeceived by the admiral in person, who coming in at this juncture, appeared to be a creature of real flesh and blood.

Do you know how we fare in this Scots paradise? We make free with our landlord's mutton, which is excellent, his poultry-yard, his garden, his dairy, and his cellar, which are all well-stored. We have delicious salmon, pike, trout, perch, par, &c. at the door, for the taking. The frith of Clyde, on the other side of the hill, supplies us with mullet, red and grey, cod, mackerel, whiting, and a variety of sea-fish, included the finest herrings I ever tasted. We have sweet juicy beef, and tolerable veal, with delicate bread, from the little town of Dunbritton; and plenty of partridge, grouse, heathcock, and other game in presents.

We have been visited by all the gentlemen in the neighbourhood, and they have entertained us at their houses, not barely with hospitality, but with such marks of cordial affection, as one would wish to find among near relations, after an absence of many years.

I told you, in my last, I had projected an excursion to the Highlands, which project I have now happily executed, under the auspices of Sir George Colquhoun, a colonel in the Dutch service, who offered himself as our conductor on this occasion. Leaving our women at Cameron, to the care and inspection of Lady H— C——, we set out on horseback for Inverary, the county town of Argyll, and dined on the road with the Laird of Macfarlane, the greatest genealogist I ever knew in any country, and perfectly acquainted with all the antiquities of Scotland.

The duke of Argyll has an old castle at Inverary, where he resides when he is in Scotland; and hard by is the shell of a noble Gothic palace, built by the last duke, which, when finished, will be a great ornament to this part of the Highlands. As for Inverary, it is a place of very little importance.

This country is amazingly wild, especially towards the mountains, which are heaped upon the backs of one another, making a most stupendous appearance of savage nature, with hardly any signs of cultivation, or even of population. All is sublimity, silence, and solitude. The people live together in glens or bottoms, where they are sheltered from the cold and storms of winter; but there is a margin of plain ground spread along the sea-side, which is well in—

habited and improved by the arts of husbandry; and this I take to be one of the most agreeable tracts of the whole island; the sea not only keeps it warm, and supplies it with fish, but affords one of the most ravishing prospects in the whole world; I mean the appearance of the Hebrides, or Western islands, to the number of three hundred, scattered as far as the eye can reach, in the most agreeable confusion. As the soil and climate of the Highlands are but ill adapted to the cultivation of corn, the people apply themselves chiefly to the breeding and feeding of black cattle, which turn to good account. Those animals run wild all the winter, without any shelter or subsistence, but what they can find among the heath. When the snow lies so deep and hard, that they cannot penetrate to the roots of the grass, they make a diurnal progress, guided by a sure instinct, to the sea-side at low water, where they feed on the *alga marina*, and other plants that grow on the beach.

Perhaps this branch of husbandry, which requires very little attendance and labour, is one of the principal causes of that idleness and want of industry which distinguishes these mountaineers in their own country.—When they come forth into the world, they become as diligent and alert as any people upon earth. They are undoubtedly a very distinct species from their fellow-subjects of the Lowlands, against whom they indulge an ancient spirit of animosity; and this difference is very discernable even among persons of family and education. The Lowlanders are generally cool and circumspect, the Highlanders fiery and ferocious; but this violence of their passions serves only to inflame the zeal of their devotion to strangers, which is truly enthusiastic.

We proceeded about twenty miles beyond Inverary, to the house of a gentleman, a friend of our conductor, where we staid a few days, and were feasted in such a manner, that I began to dread the consequence to my constitution.

Notwithstanding the solitude that prevails among these mountains, there is no want of people in the Highlands. I am creditably informed, that the duke of Argyll can assemble five thousand men in arms, of his own clan and sur-

name, which is Campbell; and there is besides a tribe of the
same appellation, whose chief is the earl of Breadalbane.
The M'Donalds are as numerous, and remarkably warlike:
the Camerons, M'Leods, Frasers, Grants, M'Kenzies, M'-
Kays, M'Phersons, M'Intoshes, are powerful clans; so that,
if all the Highlanders, including the inhabitants of the isles,
were united, they could bring into the field an army of
forty thousand fighting men, capable of undertaking the
most dangerous enterprise.   We have lived to see four thousand of them, without discipline, throw the whole kingdom
of Great Britain into confusion.   They attacked and defeated two armies of regular troops, accustomed to service.   They
penetrated into the centre of England; and afterwards marched back with deliberation, in the face of two other armies,
through an enemy's country, where every precaution was
taken to cut off their retreat.   I know not any other people
in Europe, who, without the use or knowledge of arms, will
attack regular forces sword in hand, if their chief will head
them in battle.   When disciplined, they cannot fail of
being excellent soldiers.   They do not walk like the generality of mankind, but trot and bounce like deer, as if they
moved upon springs.   They greatly excel the Lowlanders
in all the exercises that require agility: they are incredibly abstemious, and patient of hunger and fatigue; so steeled against the weather, that, in travelling, even when the
ground is covered with snow, they never look for a house
or any other shelter but their plaid, in which they warp
themselves up, and go to sleep under the cope of heaven.
Such people, in quality of soldiers, must be invincible,
when the business is to perform quick marches in a difficult
country, to strike sudden strokes, beat up the enemy's quarters, harass their cavalry, and perform expeditions without
the formality of magazines, baggage, forage, and artillery.
The chieftainship of the Highlanders is a very dangerous
influence, operating at the extremity of the island, where
the eyes and hands of government cannot be supposed to see
and act with precision and vigour.   In order to break the
force of clanship, administration has always practised the

political maxim, *Divide et impera.* The legislature hath
not only disarmed these mountaineers, but also deprived
them of their ancient garb, which contributed in a great
measure to keep up their military spirit; and their slavish
tenures are all dissolved by act of parliament; so that they
are at present as free and independent of their chiefs as the
law can make them: but the original attachment still remains, and is founded on something prior to the *feudal
system*, about which the writers of this age have made such
a pother, as if it was a new discovery, like the *Copernican
system.* Every peculiarity of policy, custom, and even
temperament, is affectedly traced to this origin, as if the
feudal constitution had not been common to almost all the
natives of Europe. For my part, I expect to see the use of
trunk-hose and buttered ale ascribed to the influence of the
feudal system. The connection between the clans and their
chiefs is without all doubt *patriarchal.* It is founded on
hereditary regard and affection, cherished through a long
succession of ages. The clan consider the chief as their father, they bear his name, they believe themselves descended from his family, and they obey him as their lord, with
all the ardour of filial love and veneration; while he, on his
part, exerts a paternal authority, commanding, chastising,
rewarding, protecting, and maintaining, them as his own
children. If the legislature would entirely destroy this connection, it must compel the Highlanders to change their
habitation and their names. Even this experiment has
been formerly tried without success.—In the reign of James
VI. a battle was fought within a few short miles of this
place, between two clans, the M'Gregors and the Colqu-
houns, in which the latter were defeated: the laird of
M'Gregor made such a barbarous use of his victory, that
he was forfeited and outlawed by act of parliament: his
lands were given to the family of Montrose, and his clan
were obliged to change their name. They obeyed so far, as
to call themselves severally Campbell, Graham, or Drum-
mond, the surnames of the families of Argyll, Montrose,
and Perth, that they might enjoy the protection of those

houses; but they still added M'Gregor to their new appellation; and as their chief was deprived of his estate, they robbed and plundered for his subsistence.—Mr Cameron of Lochiel, the chief of that clan, whose father was attainted for having been concerned in the last rebellion, returning from France, in obedience to a proclamation and act of parliament passed at the beginning of the late war, paid a visit to his own country, and hired a farm in the neighbourhood of his father's house, which had been burnt to the ground. The clan, though ruined and scattered, no sooner heard of his arrival, than they flocked to him from all quarters, to welcome his return, and in a few days stocked his farm with seven hundred black cattle, which they had saved in the general wreck of their affairs: but their beloved chief, who was a promising youth, did not live to enjoy the fruits of their fidelity and attachment.

The most effectual method I know to weaken, and at length destroy this influence, is to employ the commonalty in such a manner as to give them a taste of property and independence.—In vain the government grants them advantageous leases on the forfeited estates, if they have no property to prosecute the means of improvement.—The sea is an inexhaustible fund of riches; but the fishery cannot be carried on without vessels, casks, salt, lines, nets, and other tackle. I conversed with a sensible man of this country, who from a real spirit of patriotism, had set up a fishery on the coast, and a manufactory of coarse linen, for the employment of the poor Highlanders. Cod is here in such plenty, that he told me he had seen seven hundred taken on one line, at one haul. It must be observed, however, that the line was of immense length, and had two thousand hooks, baited with mussels; but the fish was so superior to the cod caught on the bank of Newfoundland, that his correspondent at Lisbon sold them immediately at his own price, although Lent was just over when they arrived, and the people might be supposed quite cloyed with this kind of diet.—His linen manufacture was likewise in a prosperous way; when, the late war intervening, all his best hands were pressed into the service.

It cannot be expected, that the gentlemen of this country should execute commercial schemes to render their vassals independent; nor indeed are such schemes suited to their way of life and inclination: but a company of merchants might, with proper management, turn to good account a fishery established in this part of Scotland.—Our people have a strange itch to colonize America, when the uncultivated parts of our own island might be settled to greater advantage.

After having rambled through the mountains and glens of Argyll, we visited the adjacent islands of Isla, Jura, Mull, and Icolmkill. In the first we saw the remains of a castle, built in a lake, where M'Donald, lord or king of the isles, formerly resided. Jura is famous for having given birth to one M'Crain, who lived one hundred and eighty years in one house, and died in the reign of Charles the Second. Mull affords several bays, where there is safe anchorage; in one of which, the Florida, a ship of the Spanish armada, was blown up by one of Mr Smollett's ancestors. About forty years ago, John, duke of Argyll is said to have consulted the Spanish registers, by which it appeared that this ship had the military chest on board.—He employed experienced divers to examine the wreck, and they found the hull of the vessel still entire, but so covered with sand, that they could not make their way between decks: however, they picked up several pieces of plate that were scattered about in the bay, and a couple of fine brass cannon.

Icolmkill, or Iona, is a small island which St. Columba chose for his habitation.—It was respected for its sanctity, and college or seminary of ecclesiastics.—Part of its church is still standing, with the tombs of several Scottish, Irish, and Danish sovereigns, who were here interred.—These islanders are very bold and dexterous watermen, consequently the better adapted to the fishery; in their manners, they are less savage and impetuous than their countrymen on the continent; and they speak the Erse or Gaelic in its greatest purity.

Having sent round our horses by land, we embarked in

the district of Cowal for Greenock, which is a neat little
town, on the other side of the frith, with a curious harbour,
formed by three stone jetties, carried out a good way into
the sea.—New Port Glasgow is such another place, about
two miles higher up.—Both have a face of business and
plenty, and are supported entirely by the shipping of Glasgow, of which I counted sixty large vessels in these harbours.—Taking boat again at Newport, we were in less than
an hour landed on the other side, within two short miles of
our head-quarters, where we found our women in good
health and spirits. They had been, two days before, joined by Mr Smollett and his lady, to whom we have such
obligations as I cannot mention, even to you, without blush-
ing.

To-morrow we shall bid adieu to the Scots Arcadia, and
begin our progress to the southward, taking our way by
Lanark and Nithsdale, to the west borders of England. I
have received so much advantage and satisfaction from this
tour, that, if my health suffers no revolution in the winter,
I believe I shall be tempted to undertake another expedition
to the northern extremity of Caithness, unencumbered by
those impediments which now clog the heels of yours,

Cameron, Sept. 6.   MATT. BRAMBLE.

TO MISS LÆTITIA WILLIS, AT GLOUCESTER.

MY DEAR LETTY,

NEVER did poor prisoner long for deliverance more than I
have longed for an opportunity to disburden my cares into
your friendly bosom; and the occasion which now presents
itself is little else than miraculous.—Honest Saunders M'Av-
ley, the travelling Scotsman, who goes every year to Wales,
is now at Glasgow, buying goods, and coming to pay his
respects to our family, has undertaken to deliver this letter
into your own hand. We have been six weeks in Scotland, and seen the principal towns of the kingdom, where
we have been treated with great civility. The people are
very courteous; and the country being exceedingly roman-

tie, suits my turn and inclinations. I contracted some friendships at Edinburgh, which is a large and lofty city, full of
gay company; and, in particular, commenced an intimate
correspondence with one Miss R—t—n, an amiable young
lady of my own age, whose charms seemed to soften and
even to subdue, the stubborn heart of my brother Jery; but
he no sooner left the place, than he relapsed into his former
insensibility.—I feel, however, that this indifference is not
the family constitution.—I never admitted but one idea of
love, and that has taken such root in my heart, as to be
equally proof against all the pulls of discretion, and the frosts
of neglect.

Dear Letty! I had an alarming adventure at the hunters
ball in Edinburgh.—While I sat discoursing with a friend
in a corner, all at once the very image of Wilson stood before
me, dressed exactly as he was in the character of Aimwell!
—It was one Mr Gordon, whom I had not seen before.
Shocked at the sudden apparition, I fainted away, and threw
the whole assembly into confusion. However, the cause of
my disorder remained a secret to every body but my brother,
who was likewise struck with the resemblance, and scolded
after we came home. I am very sensible of Jery's affection,
and know he spoke as well with a view to my own interest
and happiness, as in regard to the honour of the family;
but I cannot bear to have my wounds probed severely. I
was not so much affected by the censure he passed upon my
own indiscretion, as with the reflection he made on the conduct of Wilson.—He observed, that if he was really the gentleman he pretended to be, and harboured nothing but honourable designs, he would have vindicated his pretensions in
the face of day. This remark made a deep impression upon
my mind.—I endeavoured to conceal my thoughts; and
this endeavour had a bad effect upon my health and spirits;
so it was thought necessary that I should go to the Highlands, and drink goat-milk whey.

We went accordingly to Loch Lomond, one of the most
enchanting spots in the whole world; and what with this
remedy, which I had every morning fresh from the moun-

tains, and the pure air, and cheerful company, I have re-covered my flesh and appetite; though there is something still at bottom, which it is not in the power of air, exercise, company, or medicine, to remove. These incidents would not touch me so nearly, if I had a sensible confidant to sympathise with my affliction, and comfort me with wholesome advice. I have nothing of this kind, except Win Jenkins, who is really a good.body in the main, but very ill qualified for such an office. The poor creature is weak in her nerves, as well as in her understanding; otherwise I might have known the true name and character of that unfortunate youth. —But why do I call him *unfortunate !*—perhaps the epithet is more applicable to me, for having listened to the false professions of——But hold—I have as yet no right, and sure I have no inclination, to believe any thing to the prejudice of his honour. In that reflection I shall still exert my patience. As for Mrs Jenkins, she herself is really an object of compassion.—Between vanity, methodism, and love, her head is almost turned. I should have more regard for her, however, if she had been more constant in the object of her affection; but, truly, she aimed at conquest, and flirted at the same time with my uncle's footman, Humphry Clinker, who is really a deserving young man, and one Dutton, my brother's valet-de-chambre, a debauched fellow, who, leaving Win in the lurch, ran away with another man's bride at Berwick.

My dear Willis, I am truly ashamed of my own sex.—We complain of advantages which the men take of our youth, inexperience, sensibility, and all that; but I have seen enough to believe, that our sex in general make it their business to ensnare the other; and for this purpose employ arts which are by no means to be justified. In point of constancy, they certainly have nothing to reproach the male part of the creation. My poor aunt, without any regard to her years and imperfections, has gone to market with her charms in every place where she thought she had the least chance to dispose of her person, which, however, hangs still heavy on her hands. I am afraid she has used even re-

ligion as a decoy, though it has not answered her expectation.—She has been praying, preaching, and catechising,
among the methodists, with whom this country abounds;
and pretends to have such manifestations and revelations, as
even Clinker himself can hardly believe, though the poor
fellow is half crazy with enthusiasm. As for Jenkins, she
affects to take all her mistress's reveries for gospel.—She has
also her heart-heavings and motions of the spirit; and, God
forgive me if I think uncharitably; but all this seems to me
to be-downright hypocrisy and deceit. Perhaps, indeed,
the poor girl imposes on herself.—She is generally in a flutter, and is much subject to vapours.—Since we came to
Scotland, she has seen apparitions, and pretends to prophecy.
If I could put faith in all these supernatural visitations, I
should think myself abandoned of grace; for I have neither
seen, heard, nor felt any thing of this nature, although I
endeavour to discharge the duties of religion with all the sincerity, zeal, and devotion, that is in the power of, dear
Letty, your ever affectionate

Glasgow, Sept. 7.   LYDIA MELFORD.

We are so far on our return to Brambletonhall; and I would
    fain hope we shall take Gloucester in our way; in which
    case I shall have the inexpressible pleasure of embracing
    my dear Willis.—Pray remember me to my worthy go-
    verness.

TO MRS MARY JONES, AT BRAMBLETONHALL.

DEAR MARY,

Sunders Macully, the Scotchman, who pushes directly
for Vails, has promised to give it you into your own hand,
and therefore I would not miss the opportunity to let you
now, as I am still in the land of the living; and yet I have
been on the brink of the other world since I sent you my last
letter. We went by sea to another kingdom, called Fife,
and, coming back, had like to have gone to pot in a storm.
What between the frite and sickness, I thought I should have

brought my heart up; even Mr Clinker was not his own
man for eight-and-forty hours after we got ashore.—It was
well for some folks that we 'scaped drownding; for mistress
was very frexious, and seemed but indifferently prepared for
a change; but, thank God, she was soon put in a better
frame by the private exaltations of the Reverend Mr Macro-
codile.—We afterwards churned to Starling and Grascow,
which are a kipple of handsome towns; and·then we went to
a gentleman's house at Loff Loming, which is a wonderful sea
of fresh water, with a power of hylands in the midst on't.—
They say as how it has got ne'er a bottom, and was made by a
musician—and, truly, I believe it; for it is not in the coarse of
nature.—It has got *waves without wind, fish without fins, and
a floating hyland;* and one of them is a crutch-yard, where
the dead are buried; and always before the person dies, a
bell rings of itself to give warning.

O Mary! this is the land of congyration—The bell knoll-
ed when we were there—I saw lights and heard lamentations.—The gentleman, our landlord, has got another house,
which he was fain to quit, on account of a mischievous
ghost, that would not suffer people to lie in their beds.
The fairies dwell in a hole of Kairmann, a mounting hard
by; and they steal away the good women that are in the
straw, if so be as how there a'n't a horse-shoe nailed to the
door.—And I was shown an old vitch, called Elspath Rin-
gavey, with a red petticoat, bleared eyes, and a mould of
gray bristles on her sin.—That she mought do me no harm,
I crossed her hand with a taster, and bid her tell my fortune,
and she told me such things—descriving Mr Clinker to a
hair—but it shall ne'er be said that I minchioned a word of
the matter —As I was troubled with fits, she advised me to
bathe in the loff, which was holy water; and so I went in the
morning to a private place, along with the house-maid, and
we bathed in our birth-day soot, after the fashion of the
country; and behold, whilst we dabbled in the loff, Sir
George Coon started up with a gun; but we clapt our hands
to our faces, and passed by him to the place where we had
left our smocks.—A civil gentleman would have turned his

head another way. My comfit is, he know not which was which; and, as the saying is, *all cats in the dark are grey.* While we staid at Loff Loming, he and our two 'squires went three or four days churning among the wild men of the mountings; a parcel of selvidges that lie in caves among the rocks, devour young children, and speak Velch, but the vords are different. Our ladies would not part with Mr Clinker, because he is so stout, and so pyehouse, that he fears neither man nor devils, if so be as they dont take him by surprise. Indeed, he was once so flurried by an operition, that he had like to have sounded. He made believe as if it had been the ould edmiral; but the ould edmiral could not have made his air to stand on end, and his teeth to shatter; but he said so in prudence, that the ladies mought not be affeard.—Mis Liddy has been puny, and like to go into a decline. I doubt her pore art is too tinder—but the got's fey has sat her on her legs again.—You nows got's fey is mother's milk to a Velchvoman.—As for mistress, blessed be God, she ails nothing.—Her stomach is good, and she improves in grease and godliness; but, for all that, she may have infections like other people; and, I believe, she wouldn't be sorry to be called *your ladyship,* whenever Sir George thinks proper to ax the question.—But, for my part, whatever I may see or hear, not a pratical shall ever pass the lips of, dear Molly, your loving friend,

Grasco, Sept. 7.   WIN. JENKINS.

Remember me, as usual, to Saul.—We are now coming home, though not the nearest road.—I do suppose I shall find the kitten a fine boar at my return.

TO SIR WATKIN PHILLIPS, BART. AT OXON.

DEAR KNIGHT,

ONCE more I tread upon English ground, which I like not the worse for the six weeks ramble I have made among the woods and mountains of Caledonia; no offence to the *land of cakes, where bannocks grow upon straw.* I never saw my uncle in such health and spirits as he now enjoys. Liddy is

perfectly recovered, and Mrs Tabitha has no reason to complain. Nevertheless, I believe, she was, till yesterday,
inclined to give the whole Scots nation to the devil, as a
pack of insensible brutes, upon whom her accomplishments
had been displayed in vain.—At every place where we halted did she mount the stage, and flourished her rusty arms,
without being able to make one conquest. One of her last
essays was against the heart of Sir George Colquhoun, with
whom she fought all the weapons more than twice over.
She was grave and gay by turns—she moralised and metho-
dised—she laughed, and romped, and danced, and sung, and
sighed, and ogled, and lisped, and fluttered, and flattered—
but all was preaching to the desert. The baronet, being a
well-bred man, carried his civilities as far as she could in
conscience expect, and, if evil tongues are to be believed,
some degrees farther; but he was too much a veteran in
gallantry, as well as in war, to fall into any ambuscade that
she could lay for his affection.—While we were absent in the
Highlands, she practised also upon the laird of Ladrish-
more, and even gave him the rendezvous in the wood of
Drumscailloch; but the laird had such a reverend care of his
own reputation, that he came attended with the parson of the
parish, and nothing passed but spiritual communications.—
After all these miscarriages, our aunt suddenly recollected
Lieutenant Lismahago, whom, ever since our first arrival at
Edinburgh, she seemed to have utterly forgot; but now she
expressed her hopes of seeing him at Dumfries, according to
his promise.

We set out from Glasgow by the way of Lanark, the
county town of Clydesdale, in the neighbourhood of which
the whole river Clyde, rushing down a steep rock, forms a
very noble and stupendous cascade. Next day we were
obliged to halt in a small borough, until the carriage which
had received some damage, should be repaired; and here we
met with an incident, which warmly interested the benevolent spirit of Mr Bramble. As we stood at the window of
an inn that fronted the public prison, a person arrived on
horseback, genteelly, though plainly, dressed in a blue frock,

with his own hair cut short, and a gold-laced hat upon his head. Alighting, and giving his horse to the landlord, he advanced to an old man who was at work in paving the street, and accosted him in these words—' This is hard work, for such an old man as you.'—So saying, he took the instrument out of his hand, and began to thump the pavement.— After a few strokes—' Have you never a son,' said he, ' to ease you of this labour?' ' Yes, an' please your honour,' replied the senior, ' I have three hopeful lads, but, at present they are out of the way.' ' Honour not me,' cried the stranger; ' it more becomes me to honour your grey hairs.— Where are those sons you talk of?' The ancient pavior said, his eldest son was a captain in the East Indies, and the youngest had lately inlisted as a soldier, in hopes of prospering like his brother. The gentleman desiring to know what was become of the second, he wiped his eyes, and owned he had taken upon him his old father's debts, for which he was now in the prison hard by.

The traveller made three quick steps towards the gaol— then turning short—' Tell me,' said he, ' has that unnatural captain sent you nothing to relieve your distresses?' ' Call him not unnatural,' replied the other; ' God's blessing be upon him! he sent me a great deal of money; but I made a bad use of it—I lost it by being security for a gentleman that was my landlord, and was stript of all I had in the world besides.' At that instant a young man, thrusting out his head and neck between two iron bars in the prison window, exclaimed, ' Father! father! if my brother William is in life, that's he.' ' I am! I am!' cried the stranger, clasping the old man in his arms, and shedding a flood of tears—' I am your son Willy, sure enough!'—Before the father, who was quite confounded, could make any return to this tenderness, a decent old woman, bolting out from the door of a poor habitation, cried, ' Where is my bairn? where is my dear Willy!'—The captain no sooner beheld her, than he quitted his father, and ran into her embrace.

I can assure you, my uncle, who saw and heard every thing that passed, was as much moved as any one of the parties concerned in this pathetic recognition.—He sobbed, and wept, and clapped his hands, and hallooed, and finally ran down into the street.—By this time, the captain had retired with his parents, and all the inhabitants of the place were assembled at the door.—Mr Bramble, nevertheless, pressed through the crowd, and, entering the house, ' Captain,' said he, ' I beg the favour of your acquaintance.—I would have travelled a hundred miles to see this affecting scene ; and I shall think myself happy, if you and your parents will dine with me at the public house.' The captain thanked him for his kind invitation, which, he said, he would accept with pleasure ; but, in the meantime, he could not think of eating or drinking, while his poor brother was in trouble.—He forthwith deposited a sum, equal to the debt, in the hands of the magistrate, who ventured to set his brother at liberty, without farther process ; and then the whole family repaired to the inn with my uncle, attended by the crowd, the individuals of which shook their townsman by the hand, while he returned their caresses, without the least sign of pride or affectation.

This honest favourite of fortune, whose name was Brown, told my uncle, that he had been bred a weaver, and, about eighteen years ago, had, from a spirit of idleness and dissipation, inlisted as a soldier in the service of the East India company ; that, in the course of duty, he had the good fortune to attract the notice and approbation of Lord Clive, who preferred him from one step to another, till he had attained the rank of captain and paymaster to the regiment, in which capacities he had honestly amassed above twelve thousand pounds, and, at the peace, resigned his commission.—He had sent several remittances to his father, who received the first only, consisting of one hundred pounds; the second had fallen into the hands of a bankrupt ; and the third had been consigned to a gentleman of Scotland, who died before it arrived, so that it still remained to be accounted for by his executors. He now presented the old man with fifty pounds for his present occasions, over and above bank-notes for one hundred, which he had deposited for his brother's release.—He brought along with him a deed ready executed, by which he settled a perpetuity of four-score pounds upon his parents, to be inherited by the other two sons after their decease. He promised to purchase a commission for his youngest brother; to take the other as his own partner in a manufacture which he intends to set up, to give employment and bread to the industrious; and to give five hundred pounds, by way of dower, to his sister, who had married a farmer in low circumstances.—Finally, he gave fifty pounds to the poor of the town where he was born, and feasted all the inhabitants without exception.

My uncle was so charmed with the character of Captain Brown, that he drank his health three times successively at dinner.—He said, he was proud of his acquaintance; that he was an honour to his country, and had in some measure redeemed human nature from the reproach of pride, selfishness, and ingratitude.—For my part, I was as much pleased with the modesty as with the filial virtue of this honest soldier, who assumed no merit from his success, and said very little of his own transactions, though the answers he made to our inquiries were equally sensible and laconic. Mrs Tabitha behaved very graciously to him, until she understood that he was going to make a tender of his hand to a person of low estate, who had been his sweetheart while he worked as a journeyman weaver.—Our aunt was no sooner made acquainted with this design, than she starched up her behaviour with a double portion of reserve; and, when the company broke up, she observed, with a toss of her nose, that Brown was a civil fellow enough, considering the lowness of his origin; but that fortune, though she had mended his circumstances, was incapable to raise his ideas, which were still humble and plebeian.

On the day that succeeded this adventure, we went some miles out of our road to see Drumlanrig, a seat belonging to the duke of Queensberry, which appears like a magnificent palace, erected by magic, in the midst of a wilderness. It is indeed a princely mansion, with suitable parks and plantations, rendered still more striking by the nakedness of

the surrounding country, which is one of the wildest tracts
in all Scotland.—This wilderness, however, is different from
that of the Highlands; for here the mountains, instead of
heath, are covered with a fine green sward, affording pasture to innumerable flocks of sheep.   But the fleeces of this
country, called Nithsdale, are not comparable to the wool
of Galloway, which is said to equal that of Salisbury plain.
Having passed the night at the castle of Drumlanrig, by invitation from the duke himself, who is one of the best men
that ever breathed, we prosecuted our journey to Dumfries,
a very elegant trading town near the borders of England,
where we found plenty of good provision and excellent
wine, at very reasonable prices, and the accommodation as
good in all respects as in any part of South Britain.—If I
was confined to Scotland for life, I would choose Dumfries
for the place of my residence.   Here we made inquiries about
Captain Lismahago, of whom hearing no tidings, we proceeded by the Solway frith to Carlisle.—You must know,
that the Solway sands, upon which travellers pass at low
water, are exceedingly dangerous, because, as the tide makes,
they become quick in different places, and the flood rushes
in so impetuously, that passengers are often overtaken by
the sea, and perish.

    In crossing these treacherous syrtes with a guide, we per-
ceived a drowned horse, which Humphry Clinker, after
due inspection, declared to be the very identical beast which
Mr Lismahago rode when he parted with us at Feltonbridge in Northumberland.   This information, which seemed to intimate that our friend the lieutenant had shared the
fate of his horse, affected us all, and above all our aunt
Tabitha, who shed salt tears, and obliged Clinker to pull a
few hairs out of the dead horse's tail, to be worn in a ring
as a remembrance of his master.   But her grief and ours
was not of long duration; for one of the first persons we saw
in Carlisle was the lieutenant *in propria persona* bargaining
with a horse-dealer for another steed, in the yard of the inn
where we alighted.—Mrs Bramble was the first that perceived him, and screamed as if she had been a ghost; and,

truly, at a proper time and place, he might very well have
passed for an inhabitant of another world; for he was more
meagre and grim than before. We received him the more
cordially for having supposed he had been drowned; and he
was not deficient in expressions of satisfaction at this
meeting.—He told us he had inquired for us at Dumfries,
and been informed by a travelling merchant from Glasgow,
that we had resolved to return by the way of Coldstream.
—He said, that, in passing the sands without a guide, his
horse had knocked up; and he himself must have perished,
if he had not been providentially relieved by a return post-
chaise.—He moreover gave us to understand, that his scheme
of settling in his own country having miscarried, he was so
far in his way to London, with a view to embark for North
America, where he intended to pass the rest of his days
among his old friends the Miamis, and amuse himself in finishing the education of the son he had by his beloved
Squinkinacoosta.

This project was by no means agreeable to our good aunt,
who expatiated upon the fatigues and dangers that would
attend such a long voyage by sea, and afterwards such a
tedious journey by land.—She enlarged particularly on the
risk he would run, with respect to the concerns of his precious soul, among savages who had not yet received the
glad tidings of salvation; and she hinted, that his aband-
oning Great Britain might, perhaps, prove fatal to the inclinations of some deserving person, whom he was qualified
to make happy for life. My uncle, who is really a Don
Quixote in generosity, understanding that Lismahago's
real reason for leaving Scotland was the impossibility of subsisting in it with any decency upon the wretched provision
of a subaltern's half pay, began to be warmly interested on
the side of compassion. He thought it very hard, that a
gentleman, who had served his country with honour, should
be driven by necessity to spend his old age among the refuse
of mankind, in such a remote part of the world.—He discoursed with me upon the subject, observing, that he would
willingly offer the lieutenant an asylum at Brambletonhall,

if he did not foresee that his singularities and humour of
contradiction would render him an intolerable house-mate,
though his conversation at some times might be both instructive and entertaining; but, as there seemed to be something particular in his attention to Mrs Tabitha, he and I
agreed in opinion, that this intercouse should be encouraged, and improved, if possible, into a matrimonial union;
in which case there would be a comfortable provision for
both; and they might be settled in a house of their own,
so that Mr Bramble should have no more of their company
than he desired.

In pursuance of this design, Lismahago has been invited
to pass the winter at Brambletonhall, as it will be time
enough to execute his American project in the spring.—He
has taken time to consider of this proposal; meanwhile, he
will keep us company as far as we travel in the road to
Bristol, where he has hopes of getting a passage for America.
I make no doubt but that he will postpone his voyage, and
prosecute his addresses to a happy consummation; and sure,
if it produces any fruit, it must be of a very peculiar flavour. As the weather continues favourable, I believe we
shall take the Peak of Derbyshire and Buxton Wells in our
way.—At any rate, from the first place where we make any
stay, you shall hear again from yours always,

Carlisle, Sept. 12.   J. MELFORD.

TO DR LEWIS.

DEAR DOCTOR,

THE peasantry of Scotland are certainly on a poor footing
all over the kingdom; and yet they look better, and are
better clothed, than those of the same rank in Burgundy,
and many other places of France and Italy; nay, I will
venture to say they are better fed, notwithstanding the
boasted wine of these foreign countries. The country people of North Britain live chiefly on oat-meal, and milk,
cheese, butter, and some garden stuff, with now and then
a pickled-herring, by way of delicacy; but flesh-meat they
seldom or never taste, nor any kind of strong liquor, except

twopenny, at times of uncommon festivity.—Their breakfast is a kind of hasty-pudding, of oat-meal, or pease-meal,
eaten with milk.   They have commonly pottage to dinner,
composed of cale or cole, leeks, barley, or bigg, and butter;
and this is reinforced with bread, and cheese made of skim-
med milk.   At night they sup on sowens or flummery of
oat-meal.—In a scarcity of oats they use the meal of barley
and pease, which is both nourishing and palatable.   Some
of them have potatoes; and you find parsnips in every peasant's garden.—They are clothed with a coarse kind of russet
set of their own making, which is both decent and warm.—
They dwell in poor huts, built of loose stones and turf,
without any mortar, having a fire-place or hearth in the
middle, generally made of an old mill-stone, and a hole at
top to let out the smoke.

These people, however, are content, and wonderfully sagacious.—All of them read the Bible, and are even qualified
to dispute upon the articles of their faith, which, in those
parts I have seen, is entirely presbyterian.   I am told, that
the inhabitants of Aberdeenshire are still more acute.—I once
knew a Scots gentleman at London, who had declared
war against this part of his country, and swore that the impudence and knavery of the Scots in that quarter had
brought a reproach upon the whole nation.

The river Clyde, above Glasgow, is quite pastoral, and
the banks of it are every where adorned with fine villas.
From the sea to its source, we may reckon the seats of many
families of the first rank, such as the duke of Argyll at Rose-
neath, the earl of Bute in the isle of that name, the earl of
Glencairn at Finlayston, Lord Blantyre at Areskine, the
duchess of Douglas at Bothwell, the duke of Hamilton at
Hamilton, the duke of Douglas at Douglas, and the earl of
Hyndford at Carmichael.   Hamilton is a noble palace,
magnificently furnished; and hard by is the village of that
name, one of the neatest little towns I have seen in any country.   The old castle of Douglas being burnt to the ground
by accident, the late duke resolved, as head of the first family in Scotland, to have the largest house in the kingdom,

and ordered a plan for this purpose; but there was only one
wing of it finished when he died. It is to be hoped that his
nephew, who is now in possession of his great fortune, will
complete the design of his predecessor.—Clydesdale is in general populous and rich, containing a great number of gentlemen, who are independent in their fortune; but it produces more cattle than corn.—This is also the case with
Tweeddale, through part of which we passed, and Nithsdale,
which is generally rough, wild, and mountainous. These
hills are covered with sheep; and this is the small delicious
mutton, so much preferable to that of the London market.
As their feeding costs so little, the sheep are not killed till
five years old, when their flesh, juices, and flavour, are in
perfection: but their fleeces are much damaged by the tar
with which they are smeared to preserve them from the rot
in winter, during which they run wild night and day, and
thousands are lost under huge wreaths of snow.—'Tis a pity
the farmers cannot contrive some means to shelter this useful
animal from the inclemencies of a rigorous climate, especially from the perpetual rains, which are more prejudicial than
the greatest extremity of cold weather.

On the little river Nith, is situated the castle of Drumlanrig, one of the noblest seats in Great Britain, belonging to
the duke of Queensberry, one of those few noblemen whose
goodness of heart does honour to human nature.—I shall
not pretend to enter into a description of this palace, which
is really an instance of the sublime in magnificence, as well
as in situation, and puts one in mind of the beautiful city of
Palmyra, rising like a vision in the midst of the wilderness.
His grace keeps open house, and lives with great splendour.
—He did us the honour to receive us with great courtesy,
and detain us all night, together with above twenty other
guests, with all their servants and horses, to a very considerable number.—The duchess was equally gracious, and
took our ladies under her immediate protection. The longer
I live, I see more reason to believe that prejudices of education are never wholly eradicated, even when they are discovered to be erroneous and absurd. Such habits of thinking,

as interest the grand passions, cleave to the human heart in
such a manner, that though an effort of reason may force
them from their hold for a moment, this violence no sooner
ceases, than they resume their grasp with an increased elas-
ticity and adhesion.

I am led into this reflection, by what passed at the duke's
table after supper. The conversation turned upon the vulgar notions of spirits and omens, that prevail among the
commonalty of North Britain, and all the company agreed,
that nothing could be more ridiculous. One gentleman,
however, told a remarkable story of himself, by way of speculation. ' Being on a party of hunting in the north,' said
he, ' I resolved to visit an old friend, whom I had not seen
for twenty years.—So long he had been retired and sequest-
rated from all his acquaintance, and lived in a moping melancholy way, much afflicted with lowness of spirits, occasioned by the death of his wife, whom he loved with uncommon affection. As he resided in a remote part of the
country, and we were five gentlemen, with as many servants,
we carried some provision with us from the next market
town, lest we should find him unprepared for our reception.
The roads being bad, we did not arrive at the house till two
o'clock in the afternoon; and were agreeably surprised to
find a very good dinner ready in the kitchen; and the cloth
laid with six covers. My friend himself appeared in his
best apparel at the gate, and received us with open arms,
telling me he had been expecting us these two hours.—Astonished at this declaration, I asked who had given him intelligence of our coming? and he smiled, without making any
other reply.—However, presuming upon our former intimacy, I afterwards insisted upon knowing; and he told me,
very gravely, he had seen me in a vision of the second sight.
—Nay, he called in the evidence of his steward, who solemnly declared, that his master had the day before apprised him
of my coming with four other strangers, and ordered him to
provide accordingly; in consequence of which intimation,
he had prepared the dinner which we were now eating; and
laid the covers according to the number foretold.' The in-

cident we all owned to be remarkable, and I endeavoured to account for it by natural means. I observed, that as the old gentleman was of a visionary turn, the casual idea, or remembrance of his old friend, might suggest those circumstances which accident had for once realised; but that in all probability he had seen many visions of the same kind, which were never verified. None of the company directly dissented from my opinion: but from the objections that were hinted, I could plainly perceive, that the majority were persuaded there was something more extraordinary in the case.

Another gentleman of the company, addressing himself to me,—' Without all doubt,' said he, ' a diseased imagination is very apt to produce visions; but we must find some other method to account for something of this kind, that happened within these eight days in my neighbourhood.—A gentleman of a good family, who cannot be deemed a visionary in any sense of the word, was, near his own gate, in the twilight, visited by his grandfather, who has been dead these fifteen years.—The spectre was mounted seemingly on the very horse he used to ride, with an angry and terrible countenance, and said something, which his grandson, in the confusion of his fear, could not understand. But this was not all: he lifted up a huge horse-whip, and applied it with great violence to his back and shoulders, on which I saw the impression with my own eyes. The apparition was afterwards seen by the sexton of the parish, hovering about the tomb where his body lies interred; as the man declared to several persons in the village, before he knew what had happened to the gentleman.—Nay, he actually came to me, as a justice of the peace, in order to make oath of these particulars, which, however, I declined administering. As for the grandson of the defunct, he is a sober, sensible, worldly-minded fellow, too intent upon schemes of interest to give into reveries. He would have willingly concealed the affair; but he bawled out in the first transport of his fear, and, running into the house, exposed his back and his sconce to the whole family; so that there was no denying it in the sequel.

It is now the common discourse of the country, that this appearance and behaviour of the old man's spirit, portends some great calamity to the family, and the good woman has actually taken to her bed in this apprehension.'

Though I did not pretend to explain this mystery, I said, I did not at all doubt, but it would one day appear to be a deception ; and, in all probability, a scheme executed by some enemy of the person who had sustained the assault : but still the gentleman insisted upon the clearness of the evidence, and the concurrence of testimony, by which two creditable witnesses, without having any communication one with another, affirmed the appearance of the same man, with whose person they were both well acquainted.

From Drumlanrig we pursued the course of the Nith to Dumfries, which stands several miles above the place where the river falls into the sea; and is, after Glasgow, the handsomest town I have seen in Scotland.—The inhabitants, indeed, seem to have proposed that city as their model ; not only in beautifying their town and regulating its police, but also in prosecuting their schemes of commerce and manufacture, by which they are grown rich and opulent.

We re-entered England by the way of Carlisle, where we accidentally met with our friend Lismahago, whom we had in vain inquired after at Dumfries and other places.—It would seem that the captain, like the prophets of old, is but little honoured in his own country, which he has now renounced for ever. He gave me the following particulars of his visit to his native soil.—In his way to the place of his nativity, he learned that his nephew had married the daughter of a bourgeois, who directed a weaving manufacture, and had gone into partnership with his father-in-law : chagrined with this information, he had arrived at the gate in the twilight, where he heard the sound of treddles in the great hall, which had exasperated him to such a degree, that he had like to have lost his senses ; while he was thus transported with indignation, his nephew chanced to come forth, when, being no longer master of his passion, he cried,—' Degenerate rascal : you have made my father's house a den of thieves ;' and at the same time chastised him with his horse-whip; then, riding round the adjoining village, he had vi-sited the burying-ground of his ancestors by moon-light; and, having paid his respects to their *manes* travelled all night to another part of the country.—Finding the head of his family in such a disgraceful situation, all his own friends dead or removed from the places of their former residence, and the expense of living increased to double of what it had been, when he first left his native country, he had bid it an eternal adieu, and was determined to seek for repose among the forests of America.

I was no longer at a loss to account for the apparition, which had been described at Drumlanrig; and when I re-peated the story to the lieutenant, he was much pleased to think his resentment had been so much more effectual than he intended; and he owned, he might at such an hour, and in such an equipage, very well pass for the ghost of his fa-ther, whom he was said greatly to resemble.—Between friends, I fancy Lismahago will find a retreat without going so far as the wigwams of the Miamis. My sister Tabby is making continual advances to him, in the way of affection; and, if I may trust to appearances, the captain is disposed to take opportunity by the forelock.—For my part, I intend to encourage this correspondence, and shall be glad to see them united.—In that case we shall find a way to settle them comfortably in our own neighbourhood. I, and my servants, will get rid of a very troublesome and tyrannic governante; and I shall have the benefit of Lismahago's conversation, without being obliged to take more of his company than I desire; for though an olia is a high-flavoured dish, I could not bear to dine upon it every day of my life.

I am much pleased with Manchester, which is one of the most agreeable and flourishing towns in Great Britain; and I perceive, that this is the place which hath animated the spirit, and suggested the chief manufactures, of Glasgow. We propose to visit Chatsworth, the Peak, and Buxton, from which last place we shall proceed directly homewards, though by easy journeys. If the season has been as favourable in Wales as in the north, your harvest is happily finished; and we have nothing left to think of but our October, of which let Barnes be properly reminded. You will find me much better in flesh than I was at our parting; and this short separation has given a new edge to those sentiments of friendship with which I always have been, and ever shall be, yours,

Manchester, Sept. 15.   MATT. BRAMBLE.

TO MRS GWYLLIM, HOUSEKEEPER, AT BRAMBLETONHALL.

MRS GWYLLIM,

IT has pleased Providence to bring us safe back to England, and partake us in many pearls by land and water, in particular, the *Devil's Harse-a-pike,* and *Hoyden's hole,* which hath got no bottom; and, as we are drawing huomwards, it may be proper to uprise you, that Brambletonhall may be in a condition to receive us, after this long jurney to the islands of Scotland. By the first of next month, you may begin to make constant fires in my brother's chamber and mine; and burn a fagget every day in the yellow damask room; have the tester and curtains dusted, and the feather-bed and matrosses well haired; because, perhaps, with the blessing of heaven, they may be yused on some occasion. Let the ould hogsheads be well skewered and seasoned for bear, as Mat is resolved to have his seller choak-fool.

If the house was mine, I would turn over a new leaf.—I don't see why the sarvants of Wales shouldn't drink fair water, and eat hot cakes and barley cale, as they do in Scotland, without troubling the botcher above once a quarter.—I hope you keep accunt of Roger's purseeding in reverence to the butter-milk. I expect my due when I come huom, without baiting an ass, I'll assure you.—As you must have layed a great many more eggs than would be eaten, I do suppose there is a power of turks, chickings, and gussling about the house; and a brave kargo of cheese ready for market; and that the owl has been sent to Crickhowel, saving what the maids spun in the family.

Pray let the whole house and furniture have a thorough
cleaning from top to bottom, for the honour of Wales; and
let Roger search into, and make a general clearance of, the
slit holes which the maids have in secret; for I know they
are much given to sloth and uncleanness. I hope you have
worked a reformation among them, as I exhorted you in my
last, and set their hearts upon better things than they can
find in junkitting and caterwauling with the fellows of the
country.

As for Win Jenkins, she has undergone a perfect meta-
murphysis, and is become a new creeter from the ammuni-
tion of Humphry Clinker, our new footman, a pious young
man, who has laboured exceedingly, that she might bring
forth fruits of repentance. I make no doubt but he will take
the same pains with that pert hussy Mary Jones, and all of
you; and that he may have power given to penetrate and
instill his goodness, even into your most inward parts, is the
fervent prayer of, your friend in the spirit,

Sept. 18.   TAB. BRAMBLE.

TO DR LEWIS.

DEAR LEWIS,

LISMAHAGO is more paradoxical than ever.—The late gulp
he had of his native air seems to have blown fresh spirits into all his polemical faculties. I congratulated him the other
day on the present flourishing state of his country, observing, that the Scots were now in a fair way to wipe off the
national reproach of poverty, and expressing my satisfaction
at the happy effects of the union, so conspicuous in the improvement of their agriculture, commerce, manufactures,
and manners. The lieutenant, screwing up his features into a look of dissent and disgust, commented on my remarks
to this effect.—' Those who reproach a nation for its poverty,
when it is not owing to the profligacy or vice of the people,
deserve no answer.—The Lacedemonians were poorer than
the Scots, when they took the lead among all the free states
of Greece, and were esteemed above them all for their valour
and their virtue. The most respectable heroes of ancient

Rome, such as Fabricius, Cincinnatus, and Regulus, were poorer than the poorest freeholder in Scotland; and there are at this day individuals in North Britain, one of whom can produce more gold and silver than the whole republic of Rome could raise at those times when their public virtue shone with unrivalled lustre; and poverty was so far from being a reproach, that it added fresh laurels to her fame, because it indicated a noble contempt of wealth, which was proof against all the arts of corruption. If poverty be a subject of reproach, it follows, that wealth is the object of esteem and veneration. In that case there are Jews and others in Amsterdam and London, enriched by usury, peculation, and different species of fraud and extortion, who are more estimable than the most virtuous and illustrious members of the community; an absurdity which no man in his senses will offer to maintain. Riches are certainly no proof of merit: nay, they are often (if not most commonly) acquired by persons of sordid minds and mean talents: nor do they give any intrinsic worth to the possessor; but, on the contrary, tend to pervert his understanding, and render his morals more depraved. But granting that poverty were really matter of reproach, it cannot be justly imputed to Scotland. No country is poor that can supply its inhabitants with the necessaries of life, and even afford articles for exportation. Scotland is rich in natural advantages: it produces every species of provision in abundance, vast herds of cattle, and flocks of sheep, with a great number of horses; prodigious quantities of wool and flax, with plenty of copse wood, and in some parts large forests of timber. The earth is still more rich below than above the surface. It yields inexhaustible stores of coal, free-stone, marble, lead, iron, copper, and silver, with some gold. The sea abounds with excellent fish, and salt to cure them for exportation; and there are creeks and harbours round the whole kingdom, for the convenience and security of navigation. The face of the country displays a surprising number of cities, towns, villas, and villages, swarming with people; and there seems to be no want of art, industry, government, and police.—Such a kingdom never can be called poor, in any sense of the word, though there may be many others more powerful and opulent. But the proper use of those advantages, and the present prosperity of the Scots, you seem to derive from the union of the two kingdoms.'

I said, I supposed he would not deny that the appearance of the country was much mended; that the people lived better, had more trade, and a greater quantity of money circulating since the union, than before. ' I may safely admit these premises,' answered the lieutenant, ' without subscribing to your inference. The difference you mention, I should take to be the natural progress of improvement.—Since that period, other nations such as the Swedes, the Danes, and in particular the French, have greatly increased in commerce, without any such cause assigned. Before the union, there was a remarkable spirit of trade among the Scots, as appeared in the case of their Darien company, in which they had embarked no less than four hundred thousand pounds sterling; and in the flourishing state of the maritime towns in Fife, and on the eastern coast, enriched by their trade with France, which failed in consequence of the union. The only solid commercial advantage reaped from that measure, was the privilege of trading to the English plantations; yet, excepting Glasgow and Dumfries, I don't know any other Scots towns concerned in that traffic. In other respects, I conceive, the Scots were losers by the union. They lost the independency of their state, the greatest prop of national spirit; they lost their parliament, and their courts of justice were subjected to the revision and supremacy of an English tribunal.

' Softly, captain,' cried I, ' you cannot be said to have lost your own parliament, while you are represented in that of Great Britain.' ' True,' said he, with a sarcastic grin, ' in debates of national competition, the sixteen peers and forty-five commoners of Scotland must make a formidable figure in the scale, against the whole English legislature.' ' Be that as it may,' I observed, ' while I had the honour to sit in the lower house, the Scots members had always

the majority on their side.' ' I understand you, sir,' said
he; ' they generally side with the majority ; so much the
worse for their constituents. But even this evil is not the
worst they have sustained by the union. Their trade has
been saddled with grievous impositions, and every article of
living severely taxed, to pay the interest of enormous debts,
contracted by the English, in support of measures and connections in which the Scots had no interest nor concern.'
I begged he would at least allow, that, by the union, the
Scots were admitted to all the privileges and immunities of
English subjects ; by which means multitudes of them were
provided for in the army or navy, and got fortunes in different parts of England and its dominions. ' All these,' said
he, ' become English subjects to all intents and purposes,
and are in a great measure lost to their mother country. The
spirit of rambling and adventure has been always peculiar to
the natives of Scotland. If they had not met with encouragement in England, they would have served and settled, as
formerly, in other countries, such as Muscovy, Sweden,
Denmark, Poland, Germany, France, Piedmont, and Italy,
in all which nations their descendants continue to flourish
even at this day.'

By this time my patience began to fail, and I exclaimed,
—' For God's sake, what has England got by this union,
which, you say, has been so productive of misfortune to
the Scots ?' ' Great and manifold are the advantages which
England derives from the union,' said Lismahago, in a
solemn tone : ' first and foremost, the settlement of the protestant succession, a point which the English ministry drove
with such eagerness, that no stone was left unturned to ca-
jole and bribe a few leading men, to cram the union down
the throats of the Scottish nation, who were surprisingly
averse to the expedient. They gained by it a considerable
addition of territory, extending their dominion to the sea on
all sides of the island, thereby shutting up all back-doors
against the enterprises of their enemies. They got an accession of above a million of useful subjects, constituting a
never-failing nursery of seamen, soldiers, labourers, and

mechanics; a most valuable acquisition to a trading country, exposed to foreign wars, and obliged to maintain a
number of settlements in all the four quarters of the globe.
In the course of seven years, during the last war, Scotland
furnished the English army and navy with seventy thousand
men, over and above those who migrated to their colonies,
or mingled with them at home in the civil departments of
life. This was a very considerable and seasonable supply
to a nation, whose people had been for many years decreas-
ing in number, and whose lands and manufactures were actually suffering for want of hands. I need not remind you
of the hacknied maxim, that, to a nation in such circumstances, a supply of industrious people is a supply of wealth;
nor repeat an observation, which is now received as an eternal truth, even among the English themselves, that the
Scots who settle in South Britain are remarkably sober, orderly, and industrious.'

I allowed the truth of this remark, adding, that, by their
industry, economy, and circumspection, many of them in
England, as well as in her colonies, amassed large fortunes,
with which they returned to their own country, and this was
so much lost to South Britain. 'Give me leave, sir,' said
he, 'to assure you, that in your fact you are mistaken, and
in your deduction erroneous.—Not one in two hundred that
leave Scotland ever returns to settle in his own country; and
the few that do return, carry thither nothing that can possibly diminish the stock of South Britain; for none of their
treasure stagnates in Scotland.—There is a continual circulation, like that of the blood in the human body, and England
is the heart, to which all the streams which it distributes
are refunded and returned; nay, in consequence of that
luxury, which our connection with England hath greatly
encouraged, if not introduced, all the produce of our lands,
and all the profits of our trade, are engrossed by the natives
of South Britain; for you will find that the exchange between the two kingdoms is always against Scotland, and
that she retains neither gold nor silver sufficient for her own
circulation. The Scots, not content with their own manu-

factures and produce, which would very well answer all necessary occasions, seem to vie with each other in purchasing superfluities from England, such as broad cloth, velvet, stuffs, silks, lace, furs, jewels, furniture of all sorts,
sugar, rum, tea, chocolate, and coffee; in a word, not
only every mode of the most extravagant luxury, but even
many articles of convenience, which they might find as
good, and much cheaper, in their own country. For all
these particulars, England, I conceive, may touch about
one million sterling a-year.—I don't pretend to make an exact calculation; perhaps it may be something less, and
perhaps a great deal more.—The annual revenue arising
from all the private estates of Scotland cannot fall short of a
million sterling; and I should imagine their trade will
amount to as much more. I know, the linen manufacture
alone returns near half a million, exclusive of the home
consumption of that article. If, therefore, North Britain
pays a balance of a million annually to England, I insist
upon it, that country is more valuable to her, in the way
of commerce, than any colony in her possession, over and
above the other advantages which I have specified; therefore, they are no friends either to England or to truth, who
affect to depreciate the northern part of the united kingdom.'

I must own, I was at first a little nettled to find myself
schooled in so many particulars.—Though I did not receive
all his assertions as gospel, I was not prepared to refute
them; and I cannot help now acquiescing in his remarks,
so far as to think, that the contempt for Scotland, which
prevails too much on this side of the Tweed, is founded on
prejudice and error.—After some recollection,—' Well,
captain,' said I, ' you have argued stoutly for the importance of your own country: for my part, I have such a regard for our fellow-subjects of North Britain, that I should
be glad to see the day when your peasants can afford to give
all their oats to their cattle, hogs, and poultry, and indulge
themselves with good wheaten loaves, instead of such poor,
unpalatable, and inflammatory diet.' Here again I brought

myself into a premunire with the disputatious Caledonian.
He said, he hoped he should never see the common people
lifted out of that sphere for which they were intended by
nature and the course of things; that they might have some
reason to complain of their bread, if it were mixed, like
that of Norway, with saw-dust and fish-bones: but that
oat-meal was, he apprehended, as nourishing and salutary
as wheat-flour, and the Scots in general thought it at least
as savoury.—He affirmed, that a mouse, which, in the article of self-preservation, might be supposed to act from infallible instinct, would always prefer oats to wheat, as appeared from experience; for in a place where there was a
parcel of each, that animal had never begun to feed upon
the latter till all the oats were consumed. For their nutri-
tive quality, he appealed to the hale robust constitutions of
the people, who lived chiefly upon oat-meal: and, instead
of being inflammatory he asserted, that it was cooling,
subacid, balsamic, and mucilaginous; insomuch, that, in
all inflammatory distempers, recourse was had to water-
gruel, and flummery made of oatmeal.

'At least,' said I, 'give me leave to wish them such a
degree of commerce as may enable them to follow their own
inclinations.' 'Heaven forbid!' cried this philosopher.
'Woe be to that nation where the multitude is at liberty to
follow their own inclinations! Commerce is undoubtedly a
blessing, while restrained within its proper channels; but a
glut of wealth brings along with it a glut of evils: it brings
false taste, false appetite, false wants, profusion, venality,
contempt of order, engendering a spirit of licentiousness,
insolence, and faction, that keeps the community in continual ferment, and in time destroys all the distinctions of
civil society; so that universal anarchy and uproar must
ensue. Will any sensible man affirm, that the national advantages of opulence are to be sought on these terms? No,
sure:—but I am one of those who think, that, by proper
regulations, commerce may produce every national benefit,
without the alloy of such concomitant evils.'

So much for the dogmata of my friend Lismahago, whom

I describe the more circumstantially, as I firmly believe he will set up his rest in Monmouthshire. Yesterday, while I was alone with him, he asked, in some confusion, if I should have any objection to the success of a gentleman and a soldier, provided he should be so fortunate as to engage my sister's affection? I answered, without hesitation, that my sister was old enough to judge for herself; and that I should be very far from disapproving any resolution she might take in his favour. His eyes sparkled at this declaration. He declared, he should think himself the happiest man on earth to be connected with my family; and that he should never be weary of giving me proofs of his gratitude and attachment. I suppose Tabby and he are already agreed, in which case we shall have a wedding at Brambletonhall, and you shall give away the bride. It is the least thing you can do, by way of atonement for your former cruelty to that poor love-sick maiden, who has been so long a thorn in the side of, yours,

Sept. 20. MATT. BRAMBLE.

We have been at Buxton; but, as I did not much relish either the company or the accommodations, and had no occasion for the water, we staid but two nights in the place.

TO SIR WATKIN PHILLIPS, BART. AT OXON.

DEAR WAT,

ADVENTURES begin to thicken as we advance to the southward. Lismahago has now professed himself the admirer of our aunt, and carries on his addresses under the sanction of her brother's approbation; so that we shall certainly have a wedding by christmas. I should be glad you was present at the nuptials, to help me to throw the stocking, and perform other ceremonies peculiar to the occasion. I am sure it will be productive of some diversion; and truly, it would be worth your while to come across the country on purpose to see two such original figures in bed together, with their laced night caps; he the emblem of good cheer, and she the picture of good nature. All this agreeable prospect was clouded, and had well nigh vanished entirely, in consequence of a late misunderstanding between the future brothers-in-law, which, however, is now happily removed.

A few days ago, my uncle and I, going to visit a relation, met with Lord Oxmington at his house, who asked us to dine with him next day, and we accepted the invitation. Accordingly, leaving our women under the care of Captain Lismahago, at the inn where we had lodged the preceding night, in a little town, about a mile from his lordship's dwelling, we went at the hour appointed, and had a fashionable meal, served up with much ostentation, to a company of about a dozen persons, none of whom we had ever seen before. His lordship is much more remarkable for his pride, and caprice, than for his hospitality and understanding; and, indeed, it appeared that he considered his guests merely as objects to shine upon, so as to reflect the lustre of his own magnificence. There was much state, but no courtesy; and a great deal of compliment, without any conversation. Before the dessert was removed, our noble entertainer proposed three general toasts; then calling for a glass of wine, and bowing all round, wished us a good afternoon. This was the signal for the company to break up, and they obeyed it immediately, all except our squire, who was greatly shocked at the manner of this dismission. He changed countenance, bit his lip in silence, but still kept his seat, so that his lordship found himself obliged to give us another hint, by saying he should be glad to see us another time.— ' There is no time like the present time,' cried Mr Bramble; your lordship has not yet drank a bumper to *the best in Christendom*.' ' I'll drink no more bumpers to-day,' answered our landlord; ' and I am sorry to see you have drank too many.—Order the gentleman's carriage to the gate.' So saying, he rose and retired abruptly; our squire starting up at the same time, laying his hand upon his sword, and eyeing him with a most ferocious aspect. The master having vanished in this manner, our uncle bade one of the servants see what was to pay; and the fellow answering,—

'this is no inn;' 'I cry you mercy,' said the other, 'I perceive it is not; if it were the landlord would be more civil. There's a guinea, however; take it, and tell your lord, that I shall not leave the country till I have had an opportunity to thank him in person for his politeness and hospitality.'

We then walked down stairs through a double range of lacqueys, and, getting into the chaise, proceeded home-wards. Perceiving the 'squire much ruffled, I ventured to disapprove of his resentment, observing, that, as Lord Ox-mington was well known to have his brain very ill timbered, a sensible man should rather laugh than be angry at his ridi-culous want of breeding. Mr Bramble took umbrage at my presuming to be wiser than he upon this occasion; and told me, that, as he had always thought for himself in every oc-currence in life, he would still use the same privilege, with my good leave.

When we returned to our inn, he closeted Lismahago; and having explained his grievance, desired that gentleman to go and demand satisfaction of Lord Oxmington in his name. The lieutenant charged himself with this commission, and immediately set out a-horseback for his lordship's house, attended, at his own request, by my man Archy Macalpine, who had been used to military service; and truly, if Mac-alpine had been mounted upon an ass, this couple might have passed for the knight of La Mancha and his 'squire Panza. It was not till after some demur, that Lismahago obtained a private audience, at which he formally defied his lordship to single combat, in the name of Mr Bramble, and desired him to appoint the time and place. Lord Oxming-ton was so confounded at this unexpected message, that he could not, for some time, make any articulate reply; but stood staring at the lieutenant with manifest marks of pertur-bation. At length, ringing a bell with great vehemence, he exclaimed,—'what! a commoner send a challenge to a peer of the realm!—Privilege! privilege!—Here's a person brings me a challenge from the Welchman that dined at my table.' An impudent fellow!—My wine is not yet out of his head.'

The whole house was immediately in commotion. Macalpine made a soldierly retreat with the two horses; but the captain was suddenly surrounded and disarmed by the footmen, whom a French valet-de-chambre headed in this exploit; his sword was passed through a close-stool, and his person through the horse-pond. In this plight he returned to the inn, half mad with his disgrace. So violent was the rage of his indignation, that he mistook its object. He wanted to quarrel with Mr Bramble; he said, he had been dishonoured on his account, and he looked for reparation at his hands. My uncle's back was up in a moment; and he desired him to explain his pretensions. 'Either compel Lord Oxmington to give me satisfaction,' cried he, 'or give it me in your person.' 'The latter part of the alternative is the most easy and expeditious,' replied the 'squire, starting up; 'if you are disposed for a walk, I'll attend you this moment.'

Here they were interrupted by Mrs Tabby, who had overheard all that passed. She now burst into the room, and running betwixt them, in great agitation,—' is this your regard for me (said she to the lieutenant), to seek the life of my brother?' Lismahago, who seemed to grow as cool as my uncle grew hot, assured her he had a very great respect for Mr Bramble, but he had still more for his own honour, which had suffered pollution; but if that could be once purified, he should have no further cause of dissatisfaction. The 'squire said, he should have thought it incumbent upon him to vindicate the lieutenant's honour; but as he had now carved for himself, he might swallow and digest it as well as he could. In a word, what betwixt the mediation of Mrs Tabitha, the recollection of the captain, who perceived he had gone too far, and the remonstrances of your humble servant, who joined them at this juncture, those two originals were perfectly reconciled; and then we proceeded to deliberate upon the means of taking vengeance for the insults they had received from the petulant peer; for until that aim should be accomplished, Mr Bramble swore, with great emphasis, that he would not leave the inn where we now lodged, even if he should pass his christmas on the spot.

In consequence of our deliberations, we next day, in the forenoon, proceeded in a body to his lordship's house, all of us, with our servants, including the coachman, mounted a-horseback, with our pistols loaded and ready primed.—Thus prepared for action, we paraded solemnly and slowly before his lordship's gate, which we passed three times, in such a manner, that he could not but see us, and suspect the cause of our appearance.—After dinner we returned, and performed the same cavalcade, which was again repeated the morning following; but we had no occasion to persist in these manœuvres.—About noon we were visited by the gentleman at whose house we had first seen Lord Oxmington.—He now came to make apologies in the name of his lordship, who declared he had no intention to give offence to my uncle, in practising what had been always the custom of his house; and that as for the indignities which had been put upon the officer, they were offered without his lordship's knowledge, at the instigation of his valet-de-chambre. 'If that be the case,' said my uncle, in a peremptory tone, 'I shall be contented with Lord Oxmington's personal excuses; and I hope my friend will be satisfied with his lordship's turning that insolent rascal out of his service.' 'Sir,' cried Lismahago, 'I must insist upon taking personal vengeance for the personal injuries I have sustained.'

After some debate, the affair was adjusted in this manner. His lordship, meeting us at our friend's house, declared he was sorry for what had happened; and that he had no intention to give umbrage. The valet-de-chambre asked pardon of the lieutenant upon his knees, when Lismahago, to the astonishment of all present, gave him a violent kick on the face, which laid him on his back, exclaiming, in a furious tone,—' *oui je te pardonne, gens foutre.*'

Such was the fortunate issue of this perilous adventure, which threatened abundance of vexation to our family; for the squire is one of those who will sacrifice both life and fortune, rather than leave what he conceives to be the least speck or blemish upon his honour and reputation. His

lordship had no sooner pronounced his apology, with a
very bad grace, than he went away in some disorder, and,
I dare say, he will never invite another Welchman to his
table.

We forthwith quitted the field of this achievement, in
order to prosecute our journey; but we follow no determin-
ate course. We make small deviations, to see the remarkable
towns, villas, and curiosities, on each side of our route; so
that we advance by slow steps towards the borders of Monmouthshire: but, in the midst of these irregular motions,
there is no aberration nor eccentricity in that affection with
which I am, dear Wat, yours always,

September 28.   J. MELFORD.

TO DR LEWIS.

DEAR DICK,

AT what time of life may a man think himself exempted
from the necessity of sacrificing his repose to the punctilios
of a contemptible world? I have been engaged in a ridiculous adventure, which I shall recount at meeting; and this, I
hope, will not be much longer delayed, as we have now performed almost all our visits, and seen every thing that I think
has any right to retard us in our journey homewards.—A
few days ago, understanding, by accident, that my old
friend Baynard was in the country, I would not pass so
near his habitation without paying him a visit, though our
correspondence had been interrupted for a long course of
years.

I felt myself very sensibly affected by the ideas of our
past intimacy, as we approached the place where we had
spent so many happy days together; but when we arrived
at the house, I could not recognize any one of those objects
which had been so deeply impressed upon my remembrance.
The tall oaks that shaded the avenue had been cut down,
and the iron gates at the end of it removed, together with
the high wall that surrounded the court-yard. The house
itself, which was formerly a convent of Cistercian monks,
had a venerable appearance; and along the front that look-

ed into the garden, was a stone gallery, which afforded me
many an agreeable walk, when I was disposed to be con-
templative.—Now the old front is covered with a screen of
modern architecture; so that all without is Grecian, and
all within Gothic.—As for the garden, which was well stocked with the best fruit which England could produce, there
is not now the least vestige remaining of trees, walls, or
hedges.—Nothing appears but a naked circus of loose sand,
with a dry bason and a leaden Triton in the middle.

You must know, that Baynard, at his father's death,
had a clear estate of fifteen hundred pounds a-year, and
was in other respects extremely well qualified to make a respectable figure in the commonwealth; but, what with some
excesses of youth, and the expense of a contested election,
he, in a few years, found himself encumbered with a debt of
ten thousand pounds, which he resolved to discharge by
means of a prudent marriage. He accordingly married a
Miss Thomson, whose fortune amounted to double the sum
that he owed.—She was the daughter of a citizen who had
failed in trade; but her fortune came by an uncle, who died
in the East Indies.—Her own parents being dead, she lived
with a maiden aunt, who had superintended her education,
and, in all appearance, was well enough qualified for the
usual purposes of the married state.—Her virtues, however,
stood rather upon a negative than a positive foundation.—
She was neither proud, insolent, nor capricious, nor given
to scandal, nor addicted to gaming, nor inclined to gallantry.
She could read, and write, and dance, and sing, and play
at whist and ombre; but even these accomplishments she
possessed by halves.—She excelled in nothing. Her conversation was flat, her style mean, and her expression embarrassed—In a word, her character was totally insipid. Her
person was not disagreeable; but there was nothing graceful
in her address, nor engaging in her manners; and she was
so ill-qualified to do the honours of the house, that, when
she sat at the head of the table, one was always looking for
the mistress of the family in some other place.

Vol. VI.   X

Baynard had flattered himself that it would be no difficult matter to mould such a subject after his own fashion, and that she would cheerfully enter into his views, which were wholly turned to domestic happiness. He proposed to reside always in the country, of which he was fond to a degree of enthusiasm; to cultivate his estate, which was very improveable; to enjoy the exercise of rural diversions; to maintain an intimacy of correspondence with some friends that were settled in his neighbourhood; to keep a comfortable house, without suffering his expenses to exceed the limits of his income; and to find pleasure and employment for his wife in the management and avocations of her own family.—This, however, was a visionary scheme, which he never was able to realize.—His wife was as ignorant as a new-born babe of every thing that related to the conduct of a family; and she had no idea of a country life.—Her understanding did not reach so far as to comprehend the first principles of discretion; and indeed, if her capacity had been better than it was, her natural indolence would not have permitted her to abandon a certain routine to which she had been habituated. She had not taste enough to relish any rational enjoyment; but her ruling passion was vanity, not that species which arises from self-conceit of superior accomplishments, but that which is of a bastard and idiot nature, excited by show and ostentation, which implies not even the least consciousness of any personal merit.

The nuptial peal of noise and nonsense being rung out in all the usual changes, Mr Baynard thought it high time to make her acquainted with the particulars of the plan which he had projected.—He told her that his fortune, though sufficient to afford all the comforts of life, was not ample enough to command all the superfluities of pomp and pageantry, which, indeed, were equally absurd and intolerable.—He therefore hoped she would have no objection to their leaving London in the spring, when he would take the opportunity to dismiss some unnecessary domestics, whom he had hired for the occasion of their marriage.—She heard him in silence, and, after some pause,—' So,' said he, ' I am to be

buried in the country!' He was so confounded at this reply,
that he could not speak for some minutes: at length he told
her he was much mortified to find he had proposed any thing
that was disagreeable to her ideas.—' I am sure,' added he,
' I meant nothing more than to lay down a comfortable plan
of living within the bounds of our fortune, which is but
moderate.' ' Sir,' added she, ' you are the best judge of
your own affairs.—My fortune, I know, does not exceed
twenty thousand pounds.—Yet, even with that pittance, I
might have had a husband who would not have begrudged
me a house in London—' ' Good God! my dear,' cried poor
Baynard, in the utmost agitation, ' you don't think me so
sordid.—I only hinted what I thought—but I don't pretend
to impose—' ' Yes, sir,' resumed the lady; ' it is your
prerogative to command, and my duty to obey.'

So saying, she burst into tears, and retired to her chamber,
where she was joined by her aunt.—He endeavoured to recollect himself, and act with vigour of mind on this occasion; but was betrayed by the tenderness of his nature, which
was the greatest defect of his constitution. He found the
aunt in tears, and the niece in a fit, which held her the best
part of eight hours, at the expiration of which, she began
to talk incoherently about *death* and her *dear husband*, who
had sat by her all this time, and now pressed her hand to his
lips, in a transport of grief and penitence for the offence he
had given.—From thenceforward he carefully avoided mentioning the country; and they continued to be sucked deeper
and deeper into the vortex of extravagance and dissipation,
leading what is called a fashionable life in town.—About the
latter end of July, however, Mrs Baynard, in order to exhibit a proof of conjugal obedience, desired, of her own accord, that they might pay a visit to his country house, as
there was no company left in London. He would have excused himself from this excursion, which was no part of the
economical plan he had proposed; but she insisted upon
making this sacrifice to his taste and prejudices, and away
they went with such an equipage as astonished the whole
country.—All that remained of the season was engrossed by

receiving and returning visits in the neighbourhood; and, in this intercourse, it was discovered that Sir John Chickwell had a house steward, and one footman in livery more than the compliment of Mr Baynard's household.—This remark was made by the aunt at table, and assented to by the husband, who observed, that Sir John Chickwell might very well afford to keep more servants than were found in the family of a man who had not half his fortune. Mrs Baynard eat no supper that evening; but was seized with a violent fit, which completed her triumph over the spirit of her consort. The two supernumerary servants were added.—The family plate was sold for old silver, and a new service procured; fashionable furniture was provided, and the whole house turned topsy turvy.

At their return to London, in the beginning of winter, he, with a heavy heart, communicated these particulars to me in confidence. Before his marriage he had introduced me to the lady as his particular friend; and I now offered, in that character, to lay before her the necessity of reforming her economy, if she had any regard to the interest of her own family, or complaisance for the inclinations of her husband.—But Baynard declined my offer, on the supposition that his wife's nerves were too delicate to bear expostulation; and that it would only serve to overwhelm her with such distress as would make himself miserable.

Baynard is a man of spirit, and had she proved a termagant, he would have known how to deal with her; but, either by accident or instinct, she fastened upon the weak side of his soul, and held it so fast, that he has been in subjection ever since.—I afterwards advised him to carry her abroad to France and Italy, where he might gratify her vanity for half the expense it cost him in England; and this advice he followed accordingly.—She was agreeably flattered with the idea of seeing and knowing foreign parts, and foreign fashions, of being presented to sovereigns, and living familiarly with princes. She forthwith seized the hint, which I had thrown out on purpose, and even pressed Mr Baynard to hasten his departure; so that, in a few weeks, they

crossed the sea to France, with a moderate train, still including the aunt, who was her bosom counsellor, and abet-
ed her in all her opposition to her husband's will.—Since
that period I have had little or no opportunity to renew our
former correspondence.—All that I knew of his transactions
amounted to no more than that, after an absence of two years,
they returned so little improved in economy, that they
launched out into new oceans of extravagance, which at
length obliged him to mortgage his estate.—By this time she
had bore him three children, of which the last only survives,
a puny boy of twelve or thirteen, who will be ruined in his
education by the indulgence of his mother.

As for Baynard, neither his own good sense, nor the dread
of indigence, nor the consideration of his children, has been
of force sufficient to stimulate him into the resolution of
breaking at once the shameful spell by which he seems enchanted.—With a taste capable of the most refined enjoyment, a heart glowing with all the warmth of friendship and
humanity, and a disposition strongly turned to the more rational pleasures of a retired and country life, he is hurried
about in a perpetual tumult, amidst a mob of beings pleased
with rattles, baubles, and gewgaws, so void of sense and
distinction, that even the most acute philosophy would find
it a very hard task to discover for what wise purposes of
Providence they were created.—Friendship is not to be found,
nor can the amusements for which he sighs be enjoyed,
within the rotation of absurdity to which he is doomed for
life. He has long resigned all views of improving his fortune by management and attention to the exercise of husbandry, in which he delighted; and, as to domestic happiness, not the least glimpse of hope remains to amuse his
imagination. Thus blasted in all his prospects, he could
not fail to be overwhelmed with melancholy and chagrin,
which have preyed upon his health and spirits in such a
manner that he is now threatened with a consumption.

I have given you a sketch of the man whom the other day
I went to visit.—At the gate we found a great number of
powdered lacqueys, but no civility.—After we had sat a

considerable time in the coach, we were told, that Mr Baynard had rode out, and that his lady was dressing; but we
were introduced to a parlour, so very fine and delicate, that
in all appearance it was designed to be seen only, not inhabited.   The chairs and couches were carved, gilt, and covered with rich damask, so smooth and sleek, that they
looked as if they had never been sat upon.   There was no
carpet on the floor; but the boards were rubbed and waxed
in such a manner, that we could not walk, but were obliged
to slide along them; and, as for the stove, it was too bright
and polished to be polluted with sea-coal, or stained by the
smoke of any gross material fire.—When we had remained
above half an hour, sacrificing to the inhospitable powers in
this *temple of cold reception*, my friend Baynard arrived,
and, understanding we were in the house, made his appearance, so meagre, yellow, and dejected, that I really should
not have known him, had I met with him in any other place.
—Running up to me, with great eagerness, he strained me
in his embrace, and his heart was so full, that for some
minutes he could not speak.—Having saluted us all round,
he perceived our uncomfortable situation, and, conducting
us into another apartment, which had fire in the chimney,
called for chocolate; then withdrawing, he returned with a
compliment from his wife, and, in the meantime, presented
his son Harry, a shambling blear-eyed boy, in the habit of
a hussar, very rude, forward, and impertinent.—His father
would have sent him to a boarding-school, but his mamma
and aunt would not hear of his lying out of the house; so
that there was a clergyman engaged as his tutor in the family.

As it was but just turned of twelve, and the whole house
was in commotion to prepare a formal entertainment, I
foresaw it would be late before we dined, and proposed a
walk to Mr Baynard, that we might converse together
freely. In the course of this perambulation, when I expressed some surprise that he had returned so soon from Italy,
he gave me to understand, that his going abroad had not at
all answered the purpose for which he left England; that,

although the expense of living was not so great in Italy as at home, respect being had to the same rank of life in both countries, it had been found necessary for him to lift himself above his usual style, that he might be on some footing with the counts, marquisses, and cavaliers, with whom he kept company.—He was obliged to hire a great number of servants, to take off a great variety of rich clothes, and to keep a sumptuous table for the fashionable sorocconi of the country, who, without a consideration of this kind, would not have paid any attention to an untitled foreigner, let his family or fortune be ever so respectable.—Besides, Mrs Baynard was continually surrounded by a train of expensive loungers, under the denominations of language-masters, musicians, painters, and ciceroni; and had actually fallen into the disease of buying pictures and antiques upon her own judgment, which was far from being infallible.—At length she met with an affront, which gave her a disgust to Italy, and drove her back to England with some precipitation.—By means of frequenting the duchess of B———'s conversazione while her grace was at Rome, Mrs Baynard became acquainted with all the fashionable people of that city, and was admitted to their assemblies without scruple. Thus favoured, she conceived too great an idea of her own importance, and, when the duchess left Rome, resolved to have a conversazione that should leave the Romans no room to regret her grace's departure. She provided hands for a musical entertainment, and sent bighetti of invitation to every person of distinction; but not one Roman of the female sex appeared at her assembly.—She was that night seized with a violent fit, and kept her bed three days, at the expiration of which she declared that the air of Italy would be the ruin of her constitution. In order to prevent this catastrophe, she was speedily removed to Geneva, from whence they returned to England by the way of Lyons and Paris. By the time they arrived at Calais, she had purchased such a quantity of silks, stuffs, and laces, that it was necessary to hire a vessel to smuggle them over, and this vessel was taken by a custom-house cutter; so that they lost the whole cargo, which had cost them above eight hundred pounds.

It now appeared that her travels had produced no effect
upon her, but that of making her more expensive and fantastic than ever.   She affected to lead the fashion, not only
in point of female dress, but in every article of taste and con-
noisseurship.   She made a drawing of the new façade to the
house in the country ; she pulled up the trees, and pulled
down the walls of the garden, so as to let in the easterly
wind, which Mr Baynard's ancestors had been at great
pains to exclude.   To shew her taste in laying out ground,
she seized into her own hand a farm of two hundred acres,
about a mile from the house, which she parcelled out into
walks and shrubberies, having a great bason in the middle,
into which she poured a whole stream that turned two mills,
and afforded the best trout in the country.   The bottom of
the bason, however, was so ill secured, that it would not
hold the water, which strained through the earth, and made
a bog of the whole plantation.   In a word, the ground which
formerly paid him one hundred and fifty pounds a-year, now
cost him two hundred pounds a-year to keep it in tolerable
order, over and above the first expense of trees, shrubs,
flowers, turf, and gravel.   There was not an inch of garden
ground left about the house, nor a tree that produced fruit
of any kind ; nor did he raise a truss of hay or a bushel of
oats for his horses ; nor had he a single cow to afford milk
for his tea ; far less did he ever dream of feeding his own
mutton, pigs, and poultry : every article of house-keeping,
even the most inconsiderable, was brought from the next
market-town, at the distance of five miles ; and thither they
sent a courier every morning to fetch hot rolls for breakfast.
In short, Baynard fairly owned that he spent double his income, and that in a few years he should be obliged to sell
his estate for the payment of his creditors.   He said, his wife
had such delicate nerves, and such imbecility of spirit, that
she could neither bear remonstrance, be it ever so gentle, nor
practise any scheme of retrenchment, even if she perceived
the necessity of such a measure.   He had, therefore, ceased
struggling against the stream, and endeavoured to reconcile
himself to ruin, by reflecting, that his child at least would

inherit his mother's fortune, which was secured to him by
the contract of marriage.

The detail which he gave me of his affairs filled me at
once with grief and indignation. I inveighed bitterly against
the indiscretion of his wife, and reproached him with his
unmanly acquiescence under the absurd tyranny which she
exerted. I exhorted him to recollect his resolution, and
make one effectual effort to disengage himself from a thral-
dom equally shameful and pernicious. I offered him all the
assistance in my power. I undertook to regulate his affairs,
and even to bring about a reformation in his family, if he
would only authorize me to execute the plan I should form
for his advantage. I was so affected by the subject, that I
could not help mingling tears with my remonstrances; and
Baynard was so penetrated with these marks of my affection,
that he lost all power of utterance. He pressed me to his
breast with great emotion, and wept in silence. At length
he exclaimed,—' Friendship is undoubtedly the most precious balm of life! Your words, dear Bramble, have in a
great measure recalled me from an abyss of despondence, in
which I have been long overwhelmed. I will, upon honour,·
make you acquainted with a distinct state of my affairs, and,
as far as I am able to go, will follow the course you pre-
scribe. But there are certain lengths which my nature—
The truth is, there are tender connections, of which a ba-
chelor has no idea. Shall I own my weakness?—I cannot
bear the thoughts of making that woman uneasy.' ' And
yet,' cried I, she has seen you unhappy for a series of years
—unhappy from her misconduct, without ever shewing the
least inclination to alleviate your distress.' ' Nevertheless,'
said he, ' I am persuaded she loves me with the most warm
affection; but these are incongruities in the composition of·
the human mind which I hold to be inexplicable.'

I was shocked at his infatuation, and changed the subject,
after we had agreed to maintain a close correspondence for
the future. He then gave me to understand that he had two
neighbours, who, like himself, were driven by their wives at
full speed in the high road to bankruptcy and ruin. All the

three husbands were of dispositions very different from each
other, and, according to this variation, their consorts were
admirably suited to the purpose of keeping them all three in
subjection.   The views of the ladies were exactly the same.
They vied in grandeur, that is, in ostentation, with the wife
of Sir Charles Chickwell, who had four times their fortune;
and she again piqued herself upon making an equal figure
with a neighbouring peeress, whose revenue trebled her own.
Here then was the fable of the frog and the ox realised in
four different instances within the same county—one large
fortune and three moderate estates in a fair way of being
burst by the inflation of female vanity ; and, in three of these
instances, three different forms of female tyranny were exercised.   Mr Baynard was subjugated by practising upon the
tenderness of his nature.   Mr Milksan, being of a timorous
disposition, truckled to the insolence of a termagant.   Mr
Sowerby, who was of a temper neither to be moved by fits,
nor driven by menaces, had the fortune to be fitted with a
helpmate who assailed him with the weapons of irony and
satire ; sometimes sneering in the way of compliment ; sometimes throwing out sarcastic comparisons, implying reproaches upon his want of taste, spirit, and generosity ; by
which means she stimulated his passions from one act of extravagance to another, just as the circumstances of her vanity
required.

All these three ladies have at this time the same number
of horses, carriages, and servants in and out of livery ; the
same variety of dress ; the same quantity of plate and china ;
the like ornaments in furniture ; and in their entertainments
they endeavour to exceed one another in the variety, delicacy, and expense of their dishes.   I believe it will be found
upon inquiry, that nineteen out of twenty, who are ruined
by extravagance, fall a sacrifice to the ridiculous pride and
vanity of silly women, whose parts are held in contempt by
the very men whom they pillage and enslave.   Thank Heaven, Dick, that among all the follies and weaknesses of human nature, I have not yet fallen into that of matrimony.

After Baynard and I had discussed all these matters at

leisure, we returned towards the house,·and met Jery with
our two women, who had come forth to take the air, as the
lady of the mansion had not yet made her appearance. In
short, Mrs Baynard did not produce herself till about a
quarter of an hour before dinner was on the table. Then
her husband brought her into the parlour, accompanied by
her aunt and son, and she received us with a coldness of reserve sufficient to freeze the very soul of hospitality. Though
she knew I had been the intimate friend of her husband, and
had often seen me with him in London, she shewed no marks
of recognition or regard, when I addressed myself to her in
the most friendly terms of salutation. She did not express
the common compliment of, *I am glad to see you; or, I
hope you have enjoyed your health since we had the pleasure
of seeing you*; or some such words of course: nor did she
once open her mouth in the way of welcome to my sister
and my niece, but sat in silence like a statue, with an aspect
of insensibility. Her aunt, the model upon which she had
been formed, was indeed the very essence of insipid formality; but the boy was very pert and impudent, and prated
without ceasing.

At dinner the lady maintained the same ungracious indifference, never speaking but in whispers to her aunt; and
as to the repast, it was made up of a parcel of kickshaws,
contrived by a French cook, without one substantial article
adapted to the satisfaction of an English appetite. The
pottage was little better than bread soaked in dish-washings,
lukewarm. The ragouts looked·as if they had been once
eaten and half digested; the fricassees were involved in a
nasty yellow poultice; and the rotis were scorched and stinking, for the honour of the fumet: the dessert consisted of
faded fruit and iced froth, a good emblem of our landlady's
character; the table-beer was sour, the water foul, and the
wine vapid; but there was a parade of plate and china, and
a powdered lacquey stood behind every chair, except those
of the master and mistress of the house, who were served by
two valets dressed like gentlemen. We dined in a large old
Gothic parlour, which was formerly the hall. It was now

paved with marble, and, notwithstanding the fire, which had been kindled about an hour, struck me with such a chill sensation, that, when I entered it, the teeth chattered in my jaws. In short, every thing was cold, comfortless, and disgusting, except the looks of my friend Baynard, which declared the warmth of his affection and humanity.

After dinner, we withdrew into another apartment, where the boy began to be impertinently troublesome to my niece Liddy. He wanted a play-fellow, forsooth, and would have romped with her, had she encouraged his advances. He was even so impudent as to snatch a kiss, at which she changed countenance, and seemed uneasy; and though his father checked him for the rudeness of his behaviour, he became so outrageous as to thrust his hand in her bosom; an insult to which she did not tamely submit, though one of the mildest creatures upon earth. Her eyes sparkled with resentment; she started up, and lent him such a box in the ear, as sent him staggering to the other side of the room.

'Miss Melford,' cried his father, 'you have treated him with the utmost propriety: I am only sorry that the impertinence of any child of mine should have occasioned this exertion of your spirit, which I cannot but applaud and admire.' His wife was so far from assenting to the candour of his apology, that she rose from table, and, taking her son by the hand,—'Come, child,' said she, 'your father cannot abide you.' So saying, she retired with this hopeful youth, and was followed by her governante; but neither the one nor the other deigned to take the least notice of the company.

Baynard was exceedingly disconcerted; but I perceived his uneasiness was tinctured with resentment, and derived a good omen from this discovery. I ordered the horses to be put to the carriage; and, though he made some efforts to detain us all night, I insisted upon leaving the house immediately; but, before I went away, I took an opportunity of speaking again to him in private. I said every thing I could recollect to animate his endeavours in shaking off those shameful trammels. I made no scruple to declare that his wife was unworthy of that tender complaisance which he had shewn

for her foibles; that she was dead to all the genuine sentiments of conjugal affection, insensible of her own honour
and interest, and seemingly destitute of common sense and
reflection.   I conjured him to remember what he owed to his
father's house, to his own reputation, and to his family, including even this unreasonable woman herself, who was driving on blindly to her own destruction.   I advised him to form
a plan for retrenching superfluous expense, and try to convince the aunt of the necessity for such a reformation, that
she might gradually prepare her niece for its execution; and
I exhorted him to turn that disagreeable piece of formality
out of the house, if he should find her averse to his proposal.

Here he interrupted me with a sigh, observing, that such
a step would undoubtedly be fatal to Mrs Baynard—'I
shall lose all patience,' cried I, ' to hear you talk so weakly
—Mrs Baynard's fits will never hurt her constitution.   I
believe in my conscience they are all affected: I am sure she
has no feeling for your distresses ; and, when you are ruined,
she will appear to have no feeling for her own.'   Finally, I
took his word and honour that he would make an effort such
as I had advised ; that he would form a plan of economy,
and, if he found it impracticable without my assistance, he
would come to Bath in the winter, where I promised to give
him the meeting, and contribute all in my power to the.re-
trieval of his affairs.   With this mutual engagement we parted ; and I shall think myself supremely happy, if, by my
means, a worthy man, whom I love and esteem, can be saved
from misery, disgrace, and despair.

I have only one friend more to visit in this part of the
country, but he is of a complexion very different from that
of Baynard.   You have heard me mention Sir Thomas Bulford, whom I knew in Italy.   He is now become a country
gentleman ; but, being disabled by the gout from enjoying
any amusement abroad, he entertains himself within doors,
by keeping open house for all comers, and playing upon the
oddities and humours of his company ; but he himself is generally the greatest original at his table.   He is very good-
humoured, talks much, and laughs without ceasing.   I am

told, that all the use he makes of his understanding at present is to excite mirth, by exhibiting his guests in ludicrous attitudes. I know not how far we may furnish him with entertainment of this kind; but I am resolved to beat up his quarters, partly with a view to laugh with the knight himself, and partly to pay my respects to his lady, a good-natured sensible woman, with whom he lives upon very easy terms, although she has not had the good fortune to bring him an heir to his estate.

And now, dear Dick, I must tell you for your comfort, that you are the only man upon earth to whom I would presume to send such a long-winded epistle, which I could not find in my heart to curtail, because the subject interested the warmest passions of my heart; neither will I make any other apology to a correspondent who has been so long accustomed to the impertinence of

September 30.   MATT. BRAMBLE.

TO SIR WATKIN PHILLIPS, BART. AT OXON.

DEAR KNIGHT,

I BELIEVE there is something mischievous in my disposition, for nothing diverts me so much as to see certain characters tormented with false terrors.—We last night lodged at the house of Sir Thomas Bulford, an old friend of my uncle, a jolly fellow, of moderate intellects, who, in spite of the gout, which hath lamed him, is resolved to be merry to the last; and mirth he has a particular knack in extracting from his guests, let their humour be ever so caustic or refractory—besides our company, there was in the house a fat-headed justice of the peace, called Frogmore, and a country practitioner in surgery, who seemed to be our landlord's chief companion and confidant. We found the knight sitting on a couch, with his crutches by his side, and his feet supported on cushions; but he received us with a hearty welcome, and seemed greatly rejoiced at our arrival. After tea, we were entertained with a sonata on the harpsichord, by Lady Bulford, who sung and played to admiration; but Sir Thomas seemed to be a little asinine in the article of ears, though he affected to be in raptures; and begged his wife to favour us with an *arietta*, of her own composing. This *arietta*, however, she no sooner began to perform, than he and the justice fell asleep; but the moment she ceased playing, the knight waked snorting, and exclaimed,—' *O cara!* what d'ye think, gentlemen? Will you talk any more of your Pargolesi and your Corelli?'—At the same time, he thrust his tongue in one cheek, and leered with one eye at the doctor and me, who sat on his left hand—He concluded the pantomime with a loud laugh, which he could command at all times extempore—Notwithstanding his disorder, he did not do penance at supper, nor did he ever refuse his glass when the toast went round, but rather encouraged a quick circulation both by precept and example.

I soon perceived the doctor had made himself very necessary to the baronet—He was the whetstone of his wit, the butt of his satire, and his operator in certain experiments of humour which were occasionally tried upon strangers. Justice Frogmore was an excellent subject for this species of philosophy: sleek and corpulent, solemn and shallow, he had studied Burn with uncommon application; but he studied nothing so much as the art of living (that is, eating) well. This fat buck had often afforded good sport to our landlord; and he was frequently started with tolerable success, in the course of this evening; but the baronet's appetite for ridicule seemed to be chiefly excited by the appearance, address, and conversation of Lismahago, whom he attempted in all the different modes of exposition; but he put me in mind of a contest that I once saw betwixt a young hound and an old hedge-hog—The dog turned him over and over, and bounced, and barked, and mumbled; but as often as he attempted to bite, he felt a prickle in his jaws, and recoiled in manifest confusion—The captain, when left to himself, will not fail to turn his ludicrous side to the company; but if any man attempts to force him into that attitude, he becomes stubborn as a mule, and unmanageable as an elephant unbroke.

Divers tolerable jokes were cracked upon the justice, who

eat a most unconscionable supper, and among other things, a large plate of broiled mushrooms, which he had no sooner swallowed than the doctor observed, with great gravity, that they were of the kind called. *champignons,* which, in some constitutions, had a poisonous effect.—Mr Frogmore, startled at this remark, asked, in some confusion, why he had not been so kind as to give him that notice sooner? He answered, that he took it for granted, by his eating them so heartily, that he was used to the dish ; but as he seemed to be under some apprehension, he prescribed a bumper of plague-water, which the justice drank off immediately, and retired to rest, not without marks of terror and disquiet.

At midnight we were shewn to our different chambers, and in half an hour I was fast asleep in bed; but about three o'clock in the morning I was awaked with a dismal cry of *fire!* and starting up, ran to the window in my shirt.—The night was dark and stormy ; and a number of people, half-dressed, ran backwards and forwards through the court-yard, with links and lanterns, seemingly in the utmost hurry and trepidation.—Slipping on my clothes in a twinkling, I ran down stairs, and, upon inquiry, found the fire was confined to a back-stair, which led to a detached apart-ment where Lismahago lay.—By this time, the lieutenant was alarmed by a bawling at his window, which was in the second story, but he could not find his clothes in the dark, and his room-door was locked on the outside.—The servants called to him that the house had been robbed ; that without all doubt, the villains had taken away his clothes, fastened the door, and set the house on fire, for the stair-case was in flames. In this dilemma, the poor lieutenant ran about the room naked, like a squirrel in a cage, popping out his head at the window between whiles, and imploring assistance.— At length, the knight in person was brought out in his chair, attended by my uncle and all the family, including our aunt Tabitha, who screamed, and cried, and tore her hair, as if she had been distracted. —Sir Thomas had already ordered his people to bring a long ladder, which was applied to the captain's window, and now he exhorted him earnestly to descend. 'There was no need of much rhetoric to persuade Lismahago, who forthwith made his exit by the window, roaring all the time to the people below to hold fast the ladder.

Notwithstanding the gravity of the occasion, it was impossible to behold this scene without being seised with an inclination to laugh. The rueful aspect of the lieutenant in his shirt, with a quilted night-cap fastened under his chin, and his long lank limbs and posteriors exposed to the wind, made a very picturesque appearance, when illuminated by the links and torches which the servants held up to light him in his descent. All the company stood round the ladder, except the knight, who sat in his chair, exclaiming, from time to time,—' Lord have mercy upon us!—save the gentleman's life—mind your footing dear captain! softly !—stand fast !—clasp the ladder with both hands there !—well done, my dear boy !—O bravo !—an old soldier for ever !—bring a blanket—bring a warm blanket to comfort his poor carcase—warm the bed in the green room—give me your hand, dear captain,—I'm rejoiced to see thee safe and sound with all my heart.' Lismahago was received at the foot of the ladder by his inamorato, who snatching a blanket from one of the maids, wrapped it about his body; two men servants took him under the arms, and a female conducted him to the green room, still accompanied by Mrs Tabitha, who saw him fairly put to bed. During this whole transaction, he spoke not a syllable, but looked exceeding grim, sometimes at one, sometimes at another of the spectators, who now adjourned in a body to the parlour where we had supped, every one surveying another with marks of astonishment and curiosity.

The knight being seated in an easy chair, seized my uncle by the hand, and, bursting into a long and loud laugh,—' Mat,' cried he, ' crown me with oak, or ivy, or laurel, or parsley, or what you will, and acknowledge this to be a *coup de maitre* in the way of waggery—ha, ha, ha !—Such a *camisicata, scagliata beffata !—O che roba !—*O, what a subject !—O, what *caricatura !—*O, for a Rosa, a

Rembrandt, a Schalken !—Zooks, I'll give a hundred guineas
to have it painted—what a fine descent from the cross, or
ascent to the gallows !—what lights and shadows !—what a
group below !—what expression above !—what an aspect!
—did you mind the aspect ?—ha, ha, ha !—and the limbs,
and the muscles—every toe denoted terror !—ha, ha, ha !—
then the blanket !—O, what *costume!* S^t. Andrew ! S^t.
Lazarus ! S^t. Barnabas !—ha, ha, ha !'   ' After all then,'
cried Mr Bramble, very gravely, ' this was no more than a
false alarm.   We have been frightened out of our beds, and
almost out of our senses, for the joke's sake !'   ' Ay, and
such a joke !' cried our landlord, ' such a farce ! such a *de-
noument!* such a *catastrophe!*'

' Have a little patience,' replied our squire, ' we are not
yet come to the *catastrophe;* and pray God it may not turn
out a tragedy instead of a farce—The captain is one of those
saturnine subjects, who have no idea of humour.—He never
laughs in his own person ; nor can he bear that other people
should laugh at his expense.   Besides, if the subject had
been properly chosen, the joke was too severe in all conscience.'   ' 'Sdeath !' cried the knight, ' I could not have
bated him an ace, had he been my own father ; and as for
the subject such another does not present itself once in half
a century.'   Here Mrs Tabitha interposing, and bridling
up, declared, she did not see that Mr Lismahago was a
fitter subject for ridicule than the knight himself ; and that
she was very much afraid, he would very soon find he had
mistaken his man.   The baronet was a good deal disconcerted by this intimation, saying, that he must be a Goth and
a barbarian, if he did not enter into the spirit of such a happy
and humorous contrivance.   He begged, however, that Mr
Bramble and his sister would bring him to reason ; and this
request was reinforced by Lady Bulford, who did not fail
to read the baronet a lecture upon his indiscretion, which
lecture he received with submission on one side of the face,
and a leer upon the other.

We now went to bed for the second time ; and before I
got up, my uncle had visited Lismahago in the green room,

and used such arguments with him, that, when we met in the parlour, he seemed to be quite appeased.—He received the knight's apology with a good grace, and even professed himself pleased at finding he had contributed to the diversion of the company. Sir Thomas shook him by the hand, laughing heartily; and then desired a pinch of snuff, in token of perfect reconciliation. The lieutenant putting his hand in his waistcoat pocket, pulled out, instead of his own Scots mull, a very fine gold snuff-box, which he no sooner perceived than he said,—' here is a small mistake.' ' No mistake at all,' cried the baronet; ' a fair exchange is no robbery.—Oblige me so far, captain, as to let me keep your mull as a memorial.' ' Sir,' said the lieutenant, ' the mull is much at your service; but this machine I can by no means retain. It looks like compounding a ·sort of felony in the code of honour. Besides, I don't know but there may be another joke in this conveyance; and I don't find myself disposed to be brought upon the stage again—I won't presume to make free with your pockets, but I beg you will put it up again with your own hand.' So saying, with a certain austerity of aspect, he presented the snuff-box to the knight, who received it in some confusion, and restored the mull, which he would by no means keep, except on the terms of exchange.

. This transaction was like to give a grave cast to the conversation, when my uncle took notice that Mr Justice Frogmore had not made his appearance either at the night-alarm, or now at the general rendesvous. The baronet hearing Frogmore mentioned,—' odso!' cried he, ' I had forgot the justice. Pr'ythee, doctor, go and bring him out of his kennel.' Then laughing till his sides were well shaken, he said he would shew the captain, that he was not the only person of the drama exhibited for the entertainment of the company. As to the night scene, it could not affect the justice, who had been purposely lodged in the farther end of the house, remote from the noise, and lulled with a dose of opium into the bargain. In a few minutes, Mr Justice was led into the parlour in his night-cap, and loose morning-gown, rolling his head from side to side, and groaning piteously all the way.—'Jesu! neighbour Frogmore,' exclaimed the baronet, 'what is the matter;—you look as if you was not a man for this world.—Set him down softly on the couch— poor gentleman!—Lord have mercy upon us!—What makes him so pale, and yellow, and bloated?' 'Oh, Sir Thomas!' cried the justice, 'I doubt it is all over with me—those mushrooms I ate at your table have done my business—ah! oh! hey!'. 'Now the Lord forbid!' said the other.— 'what! man,—have a good heart. How does thy stomach feel?—hah!'

To this interrogation he made no reply, but throwing aside his night-gown, discovered that his waistcoat would not meet upon his belly by five good inches at least. 'Heaven protect us all!' cried Sir Thomas,—'what a melancholy spectacle!—never did I see a man so suddenly swelled, but when he was either just dead, or just dying.—Doctor, canst thou do nothing for this poor object?' 'I don't think the case is quite desperate,' said the surgeon, 'but I would advise Mr Frogmore to settle his affairs with all expedition; the parson may come and pray by him, while I prepare a clyster and an emetic draught.' The justice rolling his languid eyes, ejaculated with great fervency,—'Lord have mercy upon us! Christ have mercy upon us!'—Then he begged the surgeon, in the name of God, to dispatch.—'As for my worldly affairs,' said he, 'they are all settled but one mortgage, which must be left to my heirs—but, my poor soul! my poor soul! what will become of my poor soul?—miserable sinner that I am!' 'Nay, pr'ythee, my dear boy, compose thyself,' resumed the knight; 'consider the mercy of Heaven is infinite; thou canst not have any sins of a very deep dye on thy conscience, or the devil's in't.' 'Name not the devil,' exclaimed the terrified Frogmore, 'I have more sins to answer for than the world dreams of—Ah! friend, I have been sly—sly—damn'd sly!—Send for the parson without loss of time, and put me to bed, for I am posting to eternity.' He was accordingly raised from the couch, and supported by two servants, who led him

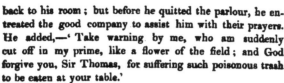

back to his room; but before he quitted the parlour, he entreated the good company to assist him with their prayers. He added,—' Take warning by me, who am suddenly cut off in my prime, like a flower of the field; and God forgive you, Sir Thomas, for suffering such poisonous trash to be eaten at your table.'

He was no sooner removed out of hearing than the baronet abandoned himself to a violent fit of laughing, in which he was joined by the greatest part of the company; but we could hardly prevent the good lady from going to undeceive the patient, by discovering, that, while he slept, his waistcoat had been straitened by the contrivance of the surgeon; and that the disorder in his stomach and bowels was occasioned by some antimonial wine, which he had taken over night, under the denomination of plague-water. She seemed to think that his apprehension might put an end to his life: the knight swore he was no such chicken, but a tough old rogue, that would live long enough to plague all his neighbours. Upon inquiry we found his character did not entitle him to much compassion or respect, and therefore we let our landlord's humour take its course. A clyster was actually administered by an old woman of the family, who had been Sir Thomas's nurse, and the patient took a draught made of oxymel of squills to forward the operation of the antimonial wine, which had been retarded by the opiate of the preceding night. He was visited by the vicar, who read prayers, and began to take an account of the state of his soul, when those medicines produced their effect: so that the parson was obliged to hold his nose while he poured forth spiritual consolation from his mouth. The same expedient was used by the knight and me, who, with the doctor, entered the chamber at this juncture, and found Frogmore enthroned on an easing-chair, under the pressure of a double evacuation. The short intervals betwixt every heave he employed in crying for mercy, confessing his sins, or asking the vicar's opinion of his case; and the vicar answered, in a solemn snuffling tone, that heightened the ridicule of the scene. The emetic having done its office, the

doctor interfered, and ordered the patient to be put in bed
again. When he examined the *egesta*, and felt his pulse,
he declared that much of the *virus* was discharged; and,
giving him a composing draught, assured him he had good
hopes of his recovery. This welcome hint he received with
the tears of joy in his eyes, protesting, that, if he should
recover, he would always think himself indebted for his life
to the great skill and tenderness of his doctor, whose hands
he squeezed with great fervour; and thus he was left to his
repose.

We were pressed to stay dinner, that we might be witnesses of his resuscitation; but my uncle insisted upon our
departing before noon, that we might reach this town before it should be dark. In the meantime, Lady Bulford
conducted us into the garden to see a fish-pond just finished,
which Mr Bramble censured as being too near the parlour,
where the knight now sat by himself, dosing in an elbow-
chair, after the fatigues of his morning achievement.—In
this situation he reclined, with his feet wrapped in flannel,
and supported in a line with his body, when the door flying open with a violent shock, Lieutenant Lismahago rushed into the room, with horror in his looks, exclaiming,—
' A mad dog! a mad dog!' and, throwing up the window-
sash, leaped into the garden. Sir Thomas, waked by this
tremendous exclamation, started up, and, forgetting his gout,
followed the lieutenant's example by a kind of instinctive
impulse. He not only bolted through the window like an
arrow from a bow, but ran up to his middle in the pond
before he gave the least sign of recollection. Then the captain began to bawl,—' Lord have mercy upon us! pray
take care of the gentleman!—for God's sake mind your footing my dear boy!—get warm blankets—comfort his poor
carcase—warm the bed in the green-room!'

Lady Bulford was thunderstruck at this phenomenon,
and the rest of the company gazed in silent astonishment,
while the servants hastened to assist their master, who suffered himself to be carried back into the parlour without
speaking a word. Being instantly accommodated with dry

clothes and flannels, comforted with a cordial, and replaced
in statu quo, one of the maids was ordered to chafe his lower extremities, an operation in consequence of which his
senses seemed to return, and his good humour to revive.——
As we had followed him into the room, he looked at every
individual in his turn, with a certain ludicrous expression
in his countenance, but fixed his eye in particular upon Lismahago, who presented him with a pinch of snuff; and
when he took it in silence,—'Sir Thomas Bulford,' said he,
'I am much obliged to you for all your favours, and some
of them I have endeavoured to repay in your own coin.'
'Give me thy hand,' cried the baronet; 'thou hast indeed
paid me *scot and lot*; and even left a balance in my hands,
for which, in presence of this company, I promise to be accountable.' So saying, he laughed very heartily, and even
seemed to enjoy the retaliation which had been exacted at
his own expense; but Lady Bulford looked very grave;
and, in all probability thought the lieutenant had carried
his resentment too far, considering that her husband was
valetudinary——but, according to the proverb, *he that will
play at bowls must expect to meet with rubbers.*

I have seen a tame bear, very diverting when properly
managed, become a very dangerous wild beast when teazed
for the entertainment of the spectators.——As for Lismahago,
he seemed to think the fright and the cold bath would have
a good effect upon his patient's constitution; but the doctor
hinted some apprehension that the gouty matter might, by
such a sudden shock, be repelled from the extremities, and
thrown upon some of the more vital parts of the machine.
I should be very sorry to see this prognostic verified upon
our facetious landlord, who told Mrs Tabitha at parting,
that he hoped she would remember him in the distribution
of the bride's favours, as he had taken so much pains to put
the captain's parts and mettle to the proof. After all, I am
afraid our squire will appear to be the greatest sufferer by
the baronet's wit; for his constitution is by no means calculated for night alarms.——He has yawned and shivered
all day, and gone to bed without supper; so that, as we

have got into good quarters, I imagine we shall make a halt to-morrow; in which case you will have at least one day's respite from the persecution of

J. MELFORD.

October 3.

TO MRS MARY JONES, AT BRAMBLETONHALL.

DEAR MARY,

MISS LIDDY is so good as to unclose me in a kiver as far as Gloster, and the carrier will bring it to hand.——God send us all safe to Monmouthshire, for I'm quite jaded with rambling.——'Tis true saying, *live and learn.*——O woman, what chuckling and changing have I seen!——Well there's nothin sartin in this world.——Who would have thought that mistriss, after all the pains taken for the good of her prusias sole, would go for to throw away her poor body? that she would cast the heys of infection upon such a carrying crow as Laahmyhago! as old as Mathewsullin, as dry as a red herring, and as pore as a starved veezel.——O, Molly! hadst thou seen him come down the ladder, in a shurt so scanty, that it could not kiver his nakedness! The young squire called him Dunquickset; but he looked for all the world like Cradock-ap-Morgan, the ould tinker that suffered at Abergany for stealing of kettle. Then he's a profane scuffle, and, as Mr Clinker says, no better than an impfiddle, continually playing upon the pyebill, and the new burth. I doubt he has as little manners as money; for he can't say a civil word, much more make me a present of a pair of gloves for good will; but he looks as if he wanted to be very forward and familiar. O! that ever a gentlewoman of years and discretion should tare her air, and cry and disporridge herself for such a nubjack! as the song goes—

I vow she would fain have a burd,
That bids such a price for an owl.

But, for sartain, he must have dealt with some Scotch musician to bring her to this pass.——As for me, I put my trust in the Lord; and I have got a slice of witchelm sowed in the gathers of my under petticoat; and Mr Clinker assures me, that, by the new light of grease, I may defy the devil and all his works.—But I nose what I nose.—If mistress should take up with Lashmyhago, this is no sarvice for me. Thank God, there's not want of places; and if I want for one thing, I would—but, no matter. Madam Baynar's woman has twenty good pounds a-year and parquisites; and dresses like a parson of distinkson. I dined with her and the valey de shambles, with bags and golden jackets: but there was nothing kimfittable to eat, being as how they live upon board; and having nothing but a piss of could cuddling tart and some blamangey, I was tuck with the cullick, and a murcy it was that mistress had her viol of assings in the cox.

But, as I was saying, I think for sartin this match will go forewood; for things are come to a creesus; and I have seen with my own heys such smuggling—But I scorn for to exclose the secrets of the family; and if it wance comes to marrying, who nose but the frolic may go round.—I believes as how Miss Liddy would have no reversion if her swan would appear; and you would be surprised, Molly, to receive a bride's fever from your humble sarvant.—But this is all suppository, dear girl; and I have sullenly promised to Mr Clinker, that neither man, woman, nor child, shall no that arrow said a civil thing to me in the way of infection.—I hopes to drink your health at Brambletonhall, in a horn of October, before the month be out. Pray let my bed be turned once a-day, and the windore opened, while the weather is dry; and burn a few billets with some brush in the footman's garret, and see their mattrash be dry as a bone; for both our gentlemen have got a sad could by lying in damp shits at Sir Tummus Ballfart's.—No more, at present, but my service to Saul and the rest of our fellow-sarvants, being, dear Mary Jones, always yours,

Oct. 4. WIN. JENKINS.

TO MISS LÆTITIA WILLIS, AT GLOUCESTER.

MY DEAR LETTY,

This method of writing to you from time to time, without any hopes of an answer, affords me, I own, some ease and satisfaction in the midst of my disquiet, as it in some degree lightens the burden of affliction; but it is at best a very imperfect enjoyment of friendship, because it admits of no return of confidence and good counsel.—I would give the whole world to have your company for a single day. I am heartily tired of this itinerant way of life. I am quite dizzy with a perpetual succession of objects. Besides, it is impossible to travel such a length of way, without being exposed to inconveniencies, dangers, and disagreeable accidents, which prove very grievous to a poor creature of weak nerves like me, and make me pay very dear for the gratification of my curiosity.

Nature never intended me for the busy world.—I long for repose and solitude, where I can enjoy that disinterested friendship which is not to be found among crowds, and indulge those pleasing reveries that shun the hurry and tumult of fashionable society. Unexperienced as I am in the commerce of life, I have seen enough to give me a disgust to the generality of those who carry it on.—There is such malice, treachery, and dissimulation, even among professed friends and intimate companions, as cannot fail to strike a virtuous mind with horror; and when vice quits the stage for a moment, her place is immediately occupied by folly, which is often too serious to excite any thing but compassion. Perhaps I ought to be silent on the foibles of my poor aunt; but with you, my dear Willis, I have no secrets; and truly, her weaknesses are such as cannot be concealed. Since the first moment we arrived at Bath, she has been employed constantly in spreading nets for the other sex; and, at length she has caught a superannuated lieutenant, who is in a fair way to make her change her name. My uncle and my brother seem to have no objection to this extraordinary match, which, I make no doubt, will afford abundance of matter of conversation and mirth: for my part, I am too sensible of my own weaknesses, to be diverted with those of other people. At present, I have something at heart that employs my whole attention, and keeps my mind in the utmost terror and suspense.

Yesterday, in the forenoon, as I stood with my brother at the parlour window of an inn, where we had lodged, a person passed a-horseback, whom (gracious heaven!) I instantly discovered to be Wilson! He wore a white riding coat, with the cap buttoned up to his chin; looked remarkably pale, and passed at a round trot, without seeming to observe us.—Indeed, he could not see us, for there was a blind that concealed us from the view. You may guess how I was affected at this apparition.—The light forsook my eyes; and I was seized with such a palpitation and trembling, that I could not stand. I sat down upon a couch, and strove to compose myself, that my brother might not perceive my agitation; but it was impossible to escape his prying eyes. —He had observed the object that alarmed me; and, doubtless knew him at the first glance. He now looked at me with a stern countenance; then he ran out into the street, to see what road the unfortunate horseman had taken. He afterwards dispatched his man for farther intelligence, and seemed to meditate some violent design. My uncle being out of order, we remained another night at the inn; and all day long Jery acted the part of an indefatigable spy upon my conduct—he watched my very looks with such eagerness of attention, as if he would have penetrated into the inmost recesses of my heart. This may be owing to his regard for my honour, if it is not the effect of his own pride; but he is so hot, and violent, and unrelenting, that the sight of him alone throws me into a flutter; and really it will not be in my power to afford him any share of my affection, if he persists in persecuting me at this rate. I am afraid he has formed some scheme of vengeance, which will make me completely wretched! I am afraid he suspects some collusion from this appearance of Wilson. Good God! did he really appear! or was it only a phantom, a pale spectre, to apprise me of his death?

O Letty, what shall I do?—Where shall I turn for advice and consolation?—Shall I implore the protection of my uncle, who has been always kind and compassionate?—This must be my last resource. I dread the thoughts of making

him uneasy; and would rather suffer a thousand deaths than
live the cause of dissension in the family.   I cannot perceive
the meaning of Wilson's coming hither: perhaps he was in
quest of us, in order to disclose his real name and situation.
—But wherefore pass without staying to make the least
inquiry?—My dear Willis, I am lost in conjecture—I have
not closed an eye since I saw him.   All night long have I
been tossed about from one imagination to another.—The reflection finds no resting-place.   I have prayed, and sighed,
and wept plentifully.   If this terrible suspense continues
much longer, I shall have another fit of illness, and then the
whole family will be in confusion.   If it was consistent with
the wise purposes of Providence, would I were in my grave.
But it is my duty to be resigned.   My dearest Letty, excuse
my weakness—excuse these blots—my tears fall so fast that
I cannot keep the paper dry—yet I ought to consider that I
have as yet no cause to despair—but I am such a faint-heart-
ed timorous creature!

Thank God, my uncle is much better than he was yesterday.—He is resolved to pursue our journey straight to
Wales.   I hope we shall take Gloucester in our way—that
hope cheers my poor heart.—I shall once more embrace my
best beloved Willis, and pour all my griefs into her friendly
bosom.   O heaven! is it possible that such happiness is reserved for the dejected and forlorn

October 4.   LYDIA MELFORD.

TO SIR WATKIN PHILLIPS, BART. OF JESUS COLLEGE, OXON.

DEAR WATKIN,

I YESTERDAY met with an accident which I believe you will
own to be very surprising.   As I stood with Liddy at the
window of the inn where we had lodged, who should pass
by but Wilson a-horseback?   I could not be mistaken in his
person, for I had a full view of him as he advanced; I plainly perceived by my sister's confusion that she recognized him
at the same time.   I was equally astonished and incensed at his appearance, which I could not but interpret into

an insult, or something worse. I ran out at the gate, and,
seeing him turn the corner of the street, I dispatched my
servant to observe his motions, but the fellow was too late to
bring me that satisfaction. He told me, however, that there
was an inn, called the Red lion, at that end of the town,
where he supposed the horseman had alighted, but that he
would not inquire without further orders. I sent him back
immediately to know what strangers were in the house, and
he returned with a report, that there was one Mr Wilson
lately arrived. In consequence of this information, I charged
him with a note directed to that gentleman, desiring him to
meet me in half an hour, in a certain field at the town's end,
with a case of pistols, in order to decide the difference which
could not be determined at our last rencounter: but I did
not think proper to subscribe the billet. My man assured
me he had delivered it into his own hand; and that, having
read it, he declared he would wait upon the gentleman at
the place and time appointed.

M‘Alpine being an old soldier, and luckily sober at the
time, I intrusted him with my secret. I ordered him to be
within call; and, having given him a letter to be delivered
to my uncle in case of accident, I repaired to the rendezvous,
which was an inclosed field at a little distance from the highway. I found my antagonist had already taken his ground,
wrapped in a dark horseman's coat, with a laced hat flapped over his eyes: but what was my astonishment, when,
throwing off this wrapper, he appeared to be a person whom
I had never seen before! He had one pistol stuck in a leather
belt, and another in his hand ready for action, and, advancing a few steps, called to know if I was ready. I answered,—‘ No;’ and desired a parley; upon which, he
turned the muzzle of his piece towards the earth, then replaced it in his belt, and met me half way. When I assured him he was not the man I expected to meet, he said, *it
might be so:* that he had received a slip of paper directed to
Mr Wilson, requesting him to come hither; and that, as
there was no other in the place of that name, he naturally
concluded the note was intended for him, and him only. I

then gave him to understand, that I had been injured by a
person who assumed that name; which person I had actually seen within the hour, passing through the street on
horseback; that hearing there was a Mr Wilson at the Red
lion, I took it for granted he was the man, and in that belief had writ the billet; and I expressed my surprise, that,
he, who was a stranger to me and my concerns, should give
me such a rendezvous, without taking the trouble to demand
a previous explanation.   He replied, that there was no other
of his name in the whole country; that no such horseman
had alighted at the Red lion since nine o'clock, when he
arrived; that having had the honour to serve his majesty,
he thought he could not decently decline any invitation of
this kind, from what quarter soever it might come; and that,
if any explanation was necessary, it did not belong to him
to demand it, but to the gentleman who summoned him into the field.——Vexed as I was at this adventure, I could not
help admiring the coolness of this officer, whose open countenance prepossessed me in his favour.   He seemed to be
turned of forty; wore his own short black hair, which curl-
ed naturally about his ears, and was very plain in his apparel.   When I begged pardon for the trouble I had given
him, he received my apology with great good humour.
He told me that he lived about ten miles off, at a small farm-
house, which would afford me tolerable lodging, if I would
come and take the diversion of hunting with him for a few
weeks; in which case, he might perhaps find out the man
who had given me offence.   I thanked him very sincerely
for his courteous offer, which, I told him, I was not at liberty to accept at present, on account of my being engaged in
a family party; and so we parted, with mutual professions
of good-will and esteem.

Now tell me, dear knight, what I am to make of this singular adventure?——Am I to suppose that the horseman I saw
was really a thing of flesh and blood, or a bubble that vanished into air?——or must I imagine Liddy knows more of the
matter than she chooses to disclose?——If I thought her capable of carrying on any clandestine correspondence with such

a fellow, I should at once discard all tenderness, and forget
that she was connected with me by the ties of blood. But
how is it possible that a girl of her simplicity and inexperience should maintain such an intercourse, surrounded, as
she is, with so many eyes, destitute of all opportunity, and
shifting quarters every day of her life?—Besides, she has
solemnly promised——No—I can't think the girl so base
—so insensible to the honour of her family. What dis-
turbs me chiefly is the impression which these occurrences
seem to make upon her spirits. These are the symptoms
from which I conclude that the rascal has still a hold on her
affection.—Surely I have a right to call him a rascal, and
to conclude that his designs are infamous.—But it shall be
my fault if he does not one day repent his presumption. I
confess I cannot think, much less write, on this subject,
with any degree of temper or patience: I shall therefore conclude with telling you, that we hope to be in Wales by the
latter end of the month; but before that period you will probably hear again from your affectionate

October 4.   J. MELFORD.

TO SIR WATKIN PHILLIPS, BART. AT OXON.

DEAR PHILLIPS,

WHEN I wrote you by last post, I did not imagine I
should be tempted to trouble you again so soon: but I now
sit down with a heart so full, that it cannot contain itself;
though I am under such agitation of spirits, that you are to
expect neither method nor connection in this address. We
have been this day within a hair's-breadth of losing honest
Matthew Bramble, in consequence of a cursed accident,
which I will endeavour to explain.—In crossing the country to get into the post-road, it was necessary to ford a river,
and we that were a-horseback passed without any danger or
difficulty; but a great quantity of rain having fallen last
night and this morning, there was such an accumulation of
water, that a mill head gave way, just as the coach was
passing under it, and the flood rushed down with such im-

petuosity, as first floated, and then fairly overturned the
carriage in the middle of the stream. Lismahago and I,
and the two servants, alighted instantaneously, ran into
the river to give all the assistance in our power. Our aunt,
Mrs Tabitha, who had the good fortune to be uppermost,
was already half way out of the coach window, when her
lover approaching, disengaged her entirely; but, whether
his foot slipt, or the burden was too great, they fell over
head and ears in each other's arms. He endeavoured more
than once to get up, and even to disentangle himself from
her embrace, but she hung about his neck like a millstone
(no bad emblem of matrimony); and if my man had not
proved a staunch auxiliary, those two lovers would in all
probability have gone hand in hand to the shades below.
For my part, I was too much engaged to take any cognisance of their distress.—I snatched out my sister by the hair
of the head, and dragging her to the bank, recollected that
my uncle had not yet appeared.—Rushing again into the
stream, I met Clinker hailing ashore Mrs Jenkins, who
looked like a mermaid with her hair dishevelled about her
ears; but, when I asked if his master was safe, he forthwith
shook her from him, and she must have gone to pot, if a
miller had not seasonably come to her relief. As for
Humphry, he flew like lightning to the coach, that was by this
time filled with water, and, diving into it, brought up the
poor squire, in all appearance, deprived of life.—It is not
in my power to describe what I felt at this melancholy spectacle. It was such an agony as baffles all description! The
faithful Clinker, taking him up in his arms, as if he had
been an infant of six months, carried him ashore, howling
most piteously all the way, and I followed him in a transport
of grief and consternation. When he was laid upon the
grass, and turned from side to side, a great quantity of water ran out at his mouth, then he opened his eyes, and
fetched a deep sigh. Clinker, perceiving these signs of life,
immediately tied up his arm with a garter, and, pulling
out a horse-fleam, let him blood in the farrier style.—At
first a few drops only issued from the orifice; but the arm

being chafed, in a little time the blood began to flow in a
continued stream; and he uttered some incoherent words,
which were the most welcome sounds that ever saluted my
ear. There was a country inn hard by, the landlord of
which had by this time come with his people to give their
assistance. Thither my uncle being carried, was undressed,
and put to bed wrapped in warm blankets; but having been
moved too soon, he fainted away, and once more lay without sense or motion, notwithstanding all the efforts of Clinker and the landlord, who bathed his temples with Hungary-
water, and held a smelling bottle to his nose. As I had heard
of the efficacy of salt in such cases, I ordered all that was in
the house to be laid under his head and body; and whether this
application had the desired effect, or Nature of herself prevailed, he, in less than a quarter of an hour, began to breathe
regularly, and soon retrieved his recollection, to the unspeakable joy of all the bystanders. As for Clinker, his brain
seemed to be affected.—He laughed and wept, and danced
about in such a distracted manner, that the landlord very
judiciously conveyed him out of the room. My uncle, seeing me dropping wet, comprehended the whole of what had
happened, and asked if all the company was safe?—Being
answered in the affirmative, he insisted upon my putting on
dry clothes; and having swallowed a little warm wine, desired he might be left to his repose. Before I went to shift
myself, I inquired about the rest of the family.—I found
Mrs Tabitha still delirious from her fright, discharging very
copiously the water she had swallowed. She was supported
by the captain, distilling drops from his uncurled periwig,
so lank and so dank that he looked like father Thame without his seges, embracing Isis, while she cascaded in his urn.
Mrs Jenkins was present also, in a loose bed-gown, without
either cap or handkerchief; but she seemed to be as little
compos mentis as her mistress, and acted so many cross purposes in the course of her attendance, that, between the two,
Lismahago had occasion for all his philosophy. As for Liddy, I thought the poor girl would have actually lost her
senses. The good woman of the house had shifted her linen,

and put her into bed; but she was seized with the idea that
her uncle had perished; and, in this persuasion, made a
dismal outcry; nor did she pay the least regard to what I
said, when I solemnly assured her he was safe.   Mr Bramble hearing the noise, and being informed of her apprehension, desired she might be brought into his chamber; and
she no sooner received this intimation, than she ran thither
half naked, with the wildest expression of eagerness in her
countenance.—Seeing the squire sitting up in the bed, she
sprung forwards, and throwing her arms about his neck, exclaimed, in a most pathetic tone,—' Are you—are you indeed my uncle!—My dear uncle!—My best friend! My
father!—Are you really living? or is it an illusion of my
poor brain?' Honest Matthew was so much affected, that he
could not help shedding tears, while he kissed her forehead,
saying,—' My dear Liddy, I hope I shall live long enough
to shew how sensible I am of your affection.—But your
spirits are fluttered, child—you want rest—go to bed and
compose yourself.'   ' Well, I will,' she replied, '—but still
methinks this cannot be real.—The coach was full of water
—my uncle was under us.—Gracious God!—You was under water—How did you get out?—Tell me that; or I shall
think this is all a deception.'   ' In what manner I was
brought out, I know as little as you do, my dear,' said the
squire: ' and truly that is a circumstance of which I want
to be informed.'   I would have given him a detail of the
whole adventure, but he would not hear me until I should
change my clothes; so that I had only time to tell him, that
he owed his life to the courage and fidelity of Clinker; and
having given him this hint, I conducted my sister to her
own chamber.

This accident happened about three o'clock in the afternoon, and in little more than half an hour the hurricane was
all over; but as the carriage was found to be so much damaged, that it could not proceed without considerable repairs,
a blacksmith and wheelwright were immediately sent for to
the next market-town, and we congratulated ourselves upon
being housed at an inn, which, though remote from the post-

road, afforded exceeding good lodging. The women being pretty well composed, and the men all afoot, my uncle sent for his servant, and, in the presence of Lismahago and me accosted him in these words.—' So, Clinker, I find you are resolved I shan't die by water. As you have fished me up from the bottom at your own risk, you are at least entitled to all the money that was in my pocket, and there it is,' So saying, he presented him with a purse containing thirty guineas, and a ring nearly of the same value. ' God forbid !' cried Clinker, ' your honour shall excuse me.—I am a poor fellow; but I have a heart—O ! if your honour did but know how I rejoiced to see—blessed be his holy name, that made me the humble instrument—but as for the lucre of gain, I renounce it—I have done no more than my duty —No more than I would have done for the most worthless of my fellow-creatures—No more than I would have done for Captain Lismahago, or Archy M'Alpine, or any sinner upon earth.—But for your worship, I would go through fire as well as water.' ' I do believe it Humphry,' said the squire ; ' but as you think it was your duty to save my life at the hazard of your own, I think it is mine to express the sense I have of your extraordinary fidelity and attachment— I insist upon your receiving this small token of my gratitude; but don't imagine that I look upon this as an adequate recompence for the service you have done me. I have determined to settle thirty pounds a-year upon you for life ; and I desire these gentlemen will bear witness to this my intention, of which I have a memorandum in my pocket-book.' ' Lord make me thankful for all these mercies !' cried Clinker, sobbing; ' I have been a poor bankrupt from the beginning. Your honour's goodness found me, when I was— naked—when I was—sick and forlorn—I understand your honour's looks—I would not give offence—but my heart is very full—and if your worship won't give me leave to speak —I must vent it in prayers to Heaven for my benefactor.' When he quitted the room, Lismahago said, he should have a much better opinion of his honesty, if he did not whine and cant so abominably ; but that he had always ob-

served those weeping and praying fellows were hypocrites at
bottom. Mr Bramble made no reply to this sarcastic remark, proceeding from the lieutenant's resentment of Clinker's having, in pure simplicity of heart, ranked him with
M'Alpine and the sinners of the earth. The landlord being
called to receive some orders about the beds, told the squire,
that his house was very much at his service, but he was sure
he should not have the honour to lodge him and his company. He gave us to understand, that his master, who
lived hard by, would not suffer us to be at a public-house,
when there was an accommodation for us at his own; and
that, if he had not dined abroad in the neighbourhood, he
would have undoubtedly come to offer his services at our
first arrival. He then launched out in praise of that gentleman, whom he had served as butler, representing him as a
perfect miracle of goodness and generosity. He said he was
a person of great learning, and allowed to be the best farmer
in the country—that he had a lady who was as much beloved as himself, and an only son, a very hopeful young
gentleman, just recovered from a dangerous fever, which
had like to have proved fatal to the whole family; for, if
the son had died, he was sure the parents would not have
survived their loss. He had not yet finished the encomium
of Mr Dennison, when this gentleman arrived in a post-
chaise, and his appearance seemed to justify all that had
been said in his favour. He is pretty well advanced in years,
but hale, robust, and florid, with an ingenuous countenance,
expressive of good sense and humanity. Having condoled
with us on the accident which had happened, he said he
was come to conduct us to his habitation, where we should
be less incommoded than at such a paltry inn, and expressed his hope that the ladies would not be the worse for
going thither in his carriage, as the distance was not above
a quarter of a mile. My uncle having made a proper return to this courteous exhibition, eyed him attentively, and
then asked if he had not been at Oxford, a commoner of
Queen's college? When Mr Dennison answered,—'yes,'
with some marks of surprise. 'Look at me then,' said our

'squire, and let us see if you can recollect the features of an old friend, whom you have not seen these forty years.' The gentleman, taking him by the hand, and gazing at him earnestly.—' I protest,' cried he, ' I do think I recal the idea of Matthew Lloyd of Glamorganshire, who was student of Jesus.' Well remembered, my dear friend Charles Dennison (exclaimed my uncle, pressing him to his breast), I am that very identical Matthew Llyod of Glamorgan.' Clinker, who had just entered the room with some coals for the fire, no sooner heard these words, than, throwing down the scuttle on the toes of Lismahago, he began to caper as if he was mad, crying,—' Matthew Lloyd, of Glamorgan!—O Providence!—Matthew Lloyd of Glamorgan!—Then, clasping my uncle's knees, he went on in this manner—' Your worship must forgive me—Matthew Lloyd of Glamorgan!—O Lord, sir!—I can't contain myself!—I shall lose my senses—' ' Nay, thou hast lost them already, I believe,' said the 'squire, peevishly ; ' pr'ythee, Clinker, be quiet—what is the matter?' Humphry, fumbling in his bosom, pulled out an old wooden snuff-box, which he presented in great trepidation to his master, who, opening it immediately, perceived a small cornelian seal, and two scraps of paper.—At sight of these articles he started, and changed colour, and casting his eye upon the inscriptions—' Ha!—how!—what!—where,' cried he, ' is the person here named!' Clinker, knocking his own breast, could hardly pronounce these words—' here—here—here is Matthew Lloyd, as the certificate sheweth.—Humphry Clinker was the name of the farrier that took me 'prentice.' ' And who gave you these tokens?' said my uncle, hastily. ' My poor mother on her death-bed,' replied the other. ' And who was your mother?' ' Dorothy Twyford, an' please your honour, heretofore bar-keeper at the Angel at Chippenham.' ' And why were not these tokens produced before?' ' My mother told me she had wrote to Glamorganshire, at the time of my birth, but had no answer; and that afterwards, when she made inquiry, there was no such person in that county.' ' And so, in consequence of my changing my name, and going abroad at that very time, thy poor mother and thou have been left to want and misery—I am really shocked at the consequence of my own folly.' Then, laying his hand on Clinker's head, he added,—' stand forth Matthew Lloyd—you see, gentlemen, how the sins of my youth rise up in judgment against me—here is my direction written with my own hand, and a seal which I left at the woman's request; and this is a certificate of the child's baptism, signed by the curate of the parish.' The company were not a little surprised at this discovery; upon which Mr Dennison facetiously congratulated both the father and the son: for my part, I shook my new found cousin heartily by the hand; and Lismahago complimented him with the tears in his eyes; for he had been hopping about the room, swearing in broad Scots, and bellowing with the pain occasioned by the fall of the coalscuttle upon his foot. He had even vowed to drive the soul out of the body of that mad rascal; but, perceiving the unexpected turn which things had taken, he wished him joy of his good fortune, observing that it went very near his heart, as he was like to be a great toe out of pocket by the discovery. Mr Dennison now desired to know for what reason my uncle had changed the name by which he knew him at Oxford; and our squire satisfied him, by answering to this effect.—' I took my mother's name, which was Lloyd, as heir to her lands in Glamorganshire; but, when I came of age, I sold that property, in order to clear my paternal estate, and resumed my real name; so that I am now Matthew Bramble of Brambletonhall, in Monmouthshire, at your service; and this is my nephew Jeremy Melford of Belfield, in the county of Glamorgan.' At that instant the ladies entering the room, he presented Mrs Tabitha as his sister, and Liddy as his niece. The old gentleman saluted them very cordially, and seemed struck with the appearance of my sister, whom he could not help surveying with a mixture of complacency and surprise. ' Sister,' said my uncle, there is a poor relation that recommends himself to your good graces. The quondam Humphry Clinker is metamorphosed into Matthew Lloyd, and claims the honour of being your carnal kinsman. In short, the rogue proves to be a crab of my own planting, in the days of hot blood and unrestrained libertinism.' Clinker had by this time dropped upon one knee, by the side of Mrs Tabitha, who, eyeing him askance, and flirting her fan with marks of agitation, thought proper, after some conflict, to hold out her hand for him to kiss, saying, with a demure aspect,—' brother, you have been very wicked ; but I hope you'll live to see the folly of your ways —I am very sorry to say, the young man, whom you have this day acknowledged, has more grace and religion, by the gift of God, than you wish all your profane learning, and repeated opportunity—I do think he has got the trick of the eye, and the tip of the nose of my uncle Llyod of Flhny-dwellin : and, as for the long chin, it is the very moral of the governor's. Brother, as you have changed his name, pray change his dress also; that livery doth not become any person that hath got our blood in his veins.' Liddy seemed much pleased with this acquisition to the family— she took him by the hand, declaring she should always be proud to own her connection with a virtuous young man, who had given so many proofs of his gratitude and affection to her uncle. Mrs Winifred Jenkins, extremely flattered between her surprise at this discovery, and the apprehension of losing her sweetheart, exclaimed, in a giggling tone,—' I wish you joy, Mr Clinker—Floyd, I would say—hi, hi, hi ! —you'll be so proud, you won't look at your poor fellow-servants, oh, oh !' Honest Clinker owned he was overjoyed at his good fortune, which was greater than he deserved—' but wherefore should I be proud,' said he; ' a poor object, con-ceived in sin, and brought forth in iniquity, nursed in a parish work-house, and bred in a smithy—whenever I seem proud, Mrs Jenkins, I beg of you to put me in mind of the condition I was in when I first saw you between Chippen-ham and Marlborough.'

When this momentous affair was discussed to the satis-faction of all parties concerned, the weather being dry, the ladies declined the carriage ; so that we walked altogether to Mr Dennison's house, where we found the tea ready pre-

pared by his lady, an amiable matron, who received us with
all the benevolence of hospitality.—The house is old fashion-
ed and irregular, but lodgeable and commodious.   To the
south it has the river in front, at the distance of a hundred
paces ; and on the north there is a rising ground, covered
with an agreeable plantation ; the greens and walks are kept
in the nicest order, and all is rural and romantic.   I have
not yet seen the young gentleman, who is on a visit to a
friend in the neighbourhood, from whose house he is not expected till to-morrow.

In the meantime, as there is a man going to the next market-town with letters for the post, I take this opportunity to
send you the history of this day, which has been remarkably
full of adventures ; and you will own I give you them like
a beef-stake at Dolly's, *hot and hot*, without ceremony and
parade, just as they come from the recollection of, yours,

J. MELFORD.

TO DR LEWIS.

DEAR DICK,

SINCE the last trouble I gave you, I have met with a variety
of incidents, some of them of a singular nature, which I reserve
as a fund for conversation ; but there are others so interesting, that they will not keep *in petto* till meeting.

Know then, it was a thousand pounds to a sixpence, that
you should now be executing my will, instead of perusing
my letter !—Two days ago, our coach was overturned in the
midst of a rapid river, where my life was saved with the utmost difficulty, by the courage, activity, and presence of
mind, of my servant Humphry Clinker.   But this is not the
most surprising circumstance of the adventure—The said
Humphry Clinker proves to be Matthew Lloyd, natural son
of one Matthew Lloyd of Glamorgan, if you know any such
person.—You see, doctor, that, notwithstanding all your
philosophy, it is not without some reason that we Welchmen
ascribe such energy to the force of blood.—But we shall dis-
cuss this point on some future occasion.

This is not the only discovery which I made in consequence of our disaster. We happened to be wrecked upon a friendly shore. The lord of the manor is no other than Charles Dennison, our fellow rake at Oxford. We are now happily housed with that gentleman, who has really attained to that pitch of rural felicity at which I have been aspiring these twenty years in vain. He is blessed with a consort, whose disposition is suited to his own in all respects; tender, generous, and benevolent. She, moreover, possesses an uncommon share of understanding, fortitude, and descretion, and is admirably qualified to be his companion, confidant, counsellor and coadjutrix. These excellent persons have an only son, about nineteen years of age, just such a youth as they could have wished that heaven would bestow; to fill up the measure of their enjoyment. In a word, they know no other allay to their happiness, but their apprehension and anxiety about the life and concerns of this beloved object.

Our old friend, who had the misfortune to be a second brother, was bred to the law, and even called to the bar; but he did not find himself qualified to shine in that province, and had very little inclination for his profession. He disobliged his father, by marrying for love, without any consideration of fortune; so that he had little or nothing to depend upon for some years but his practice, which afforded him a bare subsistence; and the prospect of an increasing family began to give him disturbance and disquiet. In the meantime, his father dying, was succeeded by his eldest brother, a fox-hunter and a sot, who neglected his affairs, insulted and oppressed his servants, and in a few years had well nigh ruined the estate, when he was happily carried off by a fever, the immediate consequence of a debauch. Charles, with the approbation of his wife, immediately determined to quit business, and retire into the country, although this resolution was strenuously and zealously opposed by every individual whom he consulted on the subject. Those who had tried the experiment assured him, that he could not pretend to breathe in the country for less than the double of what his estate produced; that, in order to be upon the footing of a gentleman, he would be obliged to keep horses, hounds, carriages, with a suitable number of servants, and maintain an elegant table for the entertainment of his neighbours; that farming was a mystery known only to those who had been bred up to it from the cradle, the success of it depending not only upon skill and industry, but also upon such attention and economy as no gentleman could be supposed to give or practise: accordingly, every attempt made by gentlemen miscarried, and not a few had been ruined by their prosecution of agriculture; nay, they affirmed, that he would find it cheaper to buy hay and oats for his cattle, and go to market for poultry, eggs, kitchen-herbs, and roots, and every the most inconsiderable article of house-keeping, than to have those articles produced on his own ground.

These objections did not deter Mr Dennison, because they were chiefly founded upon the supposition, that he would be obliged to lead a life of extravagance and dissipation, which he and his consort equally detested, despised, and determined to avoid.—The objects he had in view were, health of body, peace of mind, and the private satisfaction of domestic quiet, unallayed by actual want, and uninterrupted by the fears of indigence.   He was very moderate in his estimate of the necessaries, and even of the comforts of life : he required nothing but wholesome air, pure water, agreeable exercise, plain diet, convenient lodging, and decent apparel.   He reflected, that, if a peasant, without education, or any great share of natural sagacity, could maintain a large family, and even become opulent, upon a farm for which he paid an annual-rent of two or three hundred pounds to the landlord, surely he himself might hope for some success from his industry, having no rent to pay, but, on the contrary, three or four hundred pounds a-year to receive.   He considered that the earth was an indulgent mother, that yielded her fruits to all her children without distinction.   He had studied the theory of agriculture with a degree of eagerness and delight; and he could not conceive there was any mystery in the practise but what he should be able to disclose by dint of care and application.   With respect to household ex-pence, he entered into a minute detail and investigation, by which he perceived the assertions of his friends were altogether erroneous. He found he should save sixty pounds a-year in the single article of house-rent, and as much more in pocket-money and contingencies; that even butcher's meat was twenty per cent. cheaper in the country than in London; but that poultry, and almost every other circumstance of housekeeping might be had for less than one half of what they cost in town; besides a considerable saving on the side of dress, in being delivered from the oppressive imposition of ridiculous modes, invented by ignorance, and adopted by folly.

As to the danger of vying with the rich in pomp and equipage, it never gave him the least disturbance. He was now turned of forty, and having lived half that time in the busy scenes of life, was well skilled in the science of mankind. There cannot be in nature a more contemptible figure, than that of a man who, with five hundred pounds a-year, presumes to rival in expense a neighbour who possesses five times that income. His ostentation, far from concealing, serves only to discover his indigence, and render his vanity the more shocking; for it attracts the eyes of censure, and excites the spirit of inquiry. There is not a family in the county, nor a servant in his own house, nor a farmer in the parish, but what knows the utmost farthing that his lands produce; and all these behold him with scorn or compassion. I am surprised that these reflections do not occur to persons in this unhappy dilemma, and produce a salutary effect; but the truth is, of all the passions incident to human nature, vanity is that which most effectually perverts the faculties of the understanding; nay, it sometimes becomes so incredibly depraved, as to aspire at infamy, and find pleasure in bearing the stigmas of reproach.

I have now given you a sketch of the character and situation of Mr Dennison, when he came down to take possession of this estate; but as the messenger, who carries the letters to the next town, is just setting off, I shall reserve what farther

I have to say on this subject till the next post, when you shall certainly hear from, yours always, ·

October 3.   MATT. BRAMBLE.

TO DR LEWIS.

ONCE more, dear doctor, I resume the pen for your amusement. It was on the morning after our arrival, that, walking out with my friend Mr Dennison, I could not help breaking forth into the warmest expressions of applause, at the beauty of the scene, which is really enchanting; and I signified, in particular, how much I was pleased with the disposition of some detached groves, that afforded at once shelter and ornament to his habitation.

' When I took possession of these lands, about two-and-twenty years ago,' said he, ' there was not a tree standing within a mile of the house, except those of an old neglected orchard, which produced nothing but leaves and moss. It was in the gloomy month of November when I arrived, and found the house in such a condition, that it might have been justly styled *the tower of desolation*. The court-yard was covered with nettles and docks, and the garden exhibited such a rank plantation of weeds as I had never seen before; the window-shutters were falling in pieces; the sashes broke, and owls and jack-daws had taken possession of the chimneys. The prospect within was still more dreary. All was dark and damp, and dirty beyond description; the rain penetrated into several parts of the roof; in some apartments the very floors had given way; the hangings were parted from the walls, and shaking in mouldy remnants; the glasses were dropping out of their frames; the family pictures were covered with dust; and all the chairs and tables worm eaten and crazy. There was not a bed in the house that could be used, except one old-fashioned machine with a high gilt tester, and fringed curtains of yellow mohair, which had been, for aught I know, two centuries in the family. In short, there was no furniture but the utensils of the kitchen; and the cellar afforded nothing but a few empty butts and bar-

rels, that stunk so abominably, that I could not suffer any
body to enter it, until I had flashed a considerable quantity
of gunpowder, to qualify the foul air within.

'An old cottager and his wife, who were hired to lie in
the house, had left it with precipitation, alleging, among
other causes of retreat, that they could not sleep for frightful
noises, and that my poor brother certainly walked after his
death. In a word, the house appeared uninhabitable; the
barn, stable, and out-houses were in ruins, all the fences
broken down, and the fields lying waste.

'The farmer who kept the key, never dreamed I had any
intention to live upon the spot. He rented a farm of sixty
pounds, and his lease was just expiring. He had formed a
scheme of being appointed bailiff to the estate, and of converting the house and the adjacent grounds to his own use.
A hint of this intention I received from the curate, at my
first arrival; I therefore did not pay much regard to what he
said by way of discouraging me from coming to settle in the
country; but I was a little startled when he gave me warning that he should quit the farm at the expiration of his
lease, unless I would abate considerably in the rent.

'At this period I accidentally became acquainted with a
person, whose friendship laid the foundation of all my prosperity. In the next market town, I chanced to dine at an
inn with a Mr Wilson, who was lately come to settle in the
neighbourhood. He had been lieutenant of a man of war,
but quitted the sea in some disgust, and married the only
daughter of farmer Bland, who lives in this parish, and has
acquired a good fortune in the way of husbandry. Wilson
is one of the best-natured men I ever knew; brave, frank,
obliging, and ingenuous. He liked my conversation; I was
charmed with his liberal manner: an acquaintance immediately commenced, and this was soon improved into a friendship without reserve. There are characters, which, like similar particles of matter, strongly attract each other. He
forthwith introduced me to his father-in-law, farmer Bland,
who was well acquainted with every acre of my estate, of
consequence well qualified to advise me on this occasion.

Finding I was inclined to embrace a country life, and even to amuse myself with the occupations of farming, he approved of my design. He gave me to understand that all my farms were underlet, that the estate was capable of great improvement, that there was plenty of chalk in the neighbourhood, and that my own ground produced excellent marl for manure. With respect to the farm, which was like to fall into my hands, he said he would willingly take it at the present rent ; but at the same time owned, that if I would expend two hundred pounds in inclosures, it would be worth more than double the sum.

'Thus encouraged, I began the execution of my scheme without farther delay, and plunged into a sea of expense, though I had no fund in reserve, and the whole produce of the estate did not exceed three hundred pounds a-year. In one week my house was made weather-tight, and thoroughly cleansed from top to bottom ; then it was well ventilated, by throwing all the doors and windows open, and making blazing fires of wood in every chimney from the kitchen to the garrets. The floors were repaired, the sashes new glased, and, out of the old furniture of the whole house, I made shift to fit up a parlour and three chambers, in a plain, yet decent manner. The court-yard was cleared of weeds and rubbish, and my friend Wilson charged himself with the dressing of the garden. Bricklayers were set at work upon the barn and stable ; and labourers engaged to restore the fences, and begin the work of hedging and ditching, under the direction of farmer Bland, at whose recommendation I hired a careful hind to lie in the house, and keep constant fires in the apartments.

'Having taken these measures, I returned to London, where I forthwith sold off my household furniture, and, in three weeks from my first visit, brought my wife hither to keep her christmas. Considering the gloomy season of the year, the dreariness of the place, and the decayed aspect of our habitation, I was afraid that her resolution would sink under the sudden transition from a town life to such a melancholy state of rustication ; but I was agreeably disap-

pointed: she found the reality less uncomfortable than the
picture I had drawn. By this time, indeed, things were
mended in appearance. The out-houses had risen out of
their ruins; the pigeon-house was rebuilt, and replenished
by Wilson, who also put my garden in decent order, and
provided a good stock of poultry, which made an agreeable
figure in my yard; and the house, on the whole, looked like
the habitation of human creatures. Farmer Bland spared me
a milk-cow for my family, and an ordinary saddle-horse for
my servant to go to market at the next town. I hired a
country lad for a footman; the hind's daughter was my
house-maid, and my wife had brought a cook-maid from
London.

'Such was my family when I began house-keeping in this
place, with three hundred pounds in my pocket, raised from
the sale of my superfluous furniture. I knew we should find
occupation enough through the day to employ our time, but
I dreaded the long winter evenings; yet for these too we found
a remedy. The curate, who was a single man, soon became
so naturalized to the family, that he generally lay in the
house; and his company was equally agreeable and useful.
He was a modest man, a good scholar, and perfectly well
qualified to instruct me in such country matters as I wanted
to know. Mr Wilson brought his wife to see us, and she
became so fond of Mrs Dennison, that she said she was never so happy as when she enjoyed the benefit of her conversation. She was then a fine buxom country lass, exceedingly docile, and as good-natured as her husband Jack Wilson; so that a friendship ensued among the women, which
hath continued to this day.

'As for Jack, he hath been my constant companion,
counsellor, and commissary—I would not for a hundred
pounds you should leave my house without seeing him.
Jack is a universal genius—his talents are really astonishing. He is an excellent carpenter, joiner, and turner, and a
cunning artist in iron and brass. He not only superintended
my economy, but also presided over my pastimes. He taught
me to brew beer, to make cyder, perry, mead, usquebaugh,

and plague-water; to cook several outlandish delicacies,
such as *olias, pepper-pots, pillaws, corys, chabobs,* and
stuffatas. He understands all manner of games, from chess
down to chuck-farthing; sings a good song, plays upon the
violin, and dances a hornpipe with surprising agility. He
and I walked, and rode, and hunted, and fished together,
without minding the vicissitudes of the weather; and I am
persuaded, that in a raw moist climate, like this of England,
continual exercise is as necessary as food to the preservation
of the individual. In the course of two-and-twenty years
there has not been one hour's interruption or abatement in
the friendship subsisting between Wilson's family and mine;
and, what is a rare instance of good fortune, that friendship
is continued to our children. His son and mine are nearly
of the same age and the same disposition; they have been
bred up together at the same school and college, and love
each other with the warmest affection.

'By Wilson's means, I likewise formed an acquaintance
with a sensible physician, who lives in the next market
town; and his sister, an agreeable old maiden, passed the
christmas holidays at our house. Meanwhile, I began my
farming with great eagerness, and that very winter planted
these groves that please you so much. As for the neighbouring gentry, I had no trouble from that quarter during my
first campaign; they were all gone to town before I had
settled in the country; and by the summer I had taken measures to defend myself from their attacks. When a gay
equipage came to my gates, I was never at home; those who
visited me in a modest way, I received; and, according to
the remarks I made on their characters and conversation, either rejected their advances, or returned their civility. I
was in general despised among the fashionable company as
a low fellow, both in breeding and circumstances; nevertheless, I found a few individuals of moderate fortune, who gladly adopted my style of living; and many others would have
acceded to our society, had they not been prevented by the
pride, envy, and ambition, of their wives and daughters.
These, in times of luxury and dissipation, are the rocks upon
which all the small estates in the country are wrecked.

'I reserved in my own hands some acres of ground adjacent to the house, for making experiments in agriculture, according to the directions of Lyle, Tull, Hart, Duhamel, and others, who have written on this subject; and qualified their theory with the practical observations of farmer Bland, who was my great master in the art of husbandry. In short, I became enamoured of a country life; and my success greatly exceeded my expectation. I drained bogs, burned heath, grubbed up furze and fern; I planted copse and willows where nothing else would grow; I gradually inclosed all my farms, and made such improvements, that my estate now yields me clear twelve hundred pounds a-year. All this time my wife and I have enjoyed uninterrupted health, and a regular flow of spirits, except on a very few occasions, when our cheerfulness was invaded by such accidents as are inseparable from the condition of life. I lost two children in their infancy by the small-pox, so that I have one son only, in whom all our hopes are centered. He went yesterday to visit a friend, with whom he has staid all night, but he will be here to dinner. I shall this day have the pleasure of presenting him to you and your family; and I flatter myself you will find him not altogether unworthy of your affection.

'The truth is, either I am blinded by the partiality of a parent, or he is a boy of a very amiable character; and yet his conduct has given us unspeakable disquiet. You must know we had projected a match between him and a gentleman's daughter in the next county, who will in all probability be heiress of a considerable fortune; but it seems he had a personal disgust to the alliance. He was then at Cambridge, and tried to gain time on various pretences; but being pressed in letters by his mother and me to give a definitive answer, he fairly gave his tutor the slip, and disappeared about eight months ago. Before he took this rash step, he wrote me a letter, explaining his objections to the match, and declaring that he would keep himself concealed until he should understand that his parents would dispense with his contracting an engagement that must make him miserable for life; and he prescribed the form of advertising in a certain newspaper, by which he might be apprised of our sentiments on this subject.

'You may easily conceive how much we were alarmed and afflicted by this elopement, which he had made without dropping the least hint to his companion Charles Wilson, who belonged to the same college. We resolved to punish him with the appearance of neglect, in hopes that he would return of his own accord; but he maintained his purpose till the young lady chose a partner for herself; then he produced himself, and made his peace by the mediation of Wilson.—Suppose we should unite our families, by joining him with your niece, who is one of the most lovely creatures I ever beheld. My wife is already as fond of her as if she were her own child; and I have a presentiment that my son will be captivated by her at first sight.' 'Nothing could be more agreeable to all our family,' said I, 'than such an alliance; but, my dear friend, candour obliges me to tell you, that I am afraid Liddy's heart is not wholly disengaged—There is a cursed obstacle—' 'You mean the young stroller at Gloucester,' said he. 'You are surprised that I should know this circumstance; but you will be more surprised when I tell you that stroller is no other than my son George Dennison—that was the character he assumed in his eclipse.' 'I am indeed astonished and overjoyed,' cried I, 'and shall be happy beyond expression to see your proposal take effect.'

He then gave me to understand, that the young gentleman, at his emerging from concealment, had disclosed his passion for Miss Melford, the niece of Mr Bramble of Monmouthshire. Though Mr Dennison little dreamed that this was his old friend Matthew Lloyd, he nevertheless furnished his son with proper credentials; and he had been at Bath, London, and many other places, in quest of us, to make himself and his pretensions known. The bad success of his inquiry had such an effect upon his spirits, that, immediately at his return, he was seized with a dangerous fever, which overwhelmed his parents with terror and affliction; but he is now happily recovered, though still weak and disconsolate. My nephew joining us in our walk, I informed him of these circumstances, with which he was wonderfully pleased. He declared he would promote the match to the utmost of his power, and that he longed to embrace young Mr Dennison as his friend and brother. Meanwhile, the father went to desire his wife to communicate this discovery gradually to Liddy, that her delicate nerves might not suffer too sudden a shock; and I imparted the particulars to my sister Tabby, who expressed some surprise, not altogether unmixed, I believe, with an emotion of envy; for, though she could have no objection to an alliance at once so honourable and advantageous, she hesitated in giving her consent, on pretence of the youth and inexperience of the parties. At length, however, she acquiesced, in consequence of having consulted with Captain Lismahago.

Mr Dennison took care to be in the way when his son arrived at the gate, and without giving him time or opportunity to make any inquiry about the strangers, brought him up stairs to be presented to Mr Lloyd and his family.— The first person he saw, when he entered the room, was Liddy, who, notwithstanding all her preparation, stood trembling in the utmost confusion.—At sight of this object, he was fixed motionless to the floor, and, gazing at her with the utmost eagerness of astonishment, exclaimed,—'Sacred heaven! what is this!—ha! wherefore—' Here his speech failing, he stood straining his eyes, in the most emphatic silence. 'George,' said his father, 'this is my friend Mr Lloyd.' Roused at this intimation, he turned and received my salute, when I said,—'Young gentleman, if you had trusted me with your secret at our last meeting, we should have parted upon better terms.' Before he could make any answer, Jery came round and stood before him with open arms.—At first he started and changed colour; but, after a short pause, he rushed into his embrace, and they hugged one another as if they had been intimate friends from their infancy: then he paid his respects to Mrs Tabitha, and advancing to Liddy,—'Is it possible,' cried he, 'that my senses do not play me false!—that I see Miss Melford under my father's roof—that I am permitted to speak to her with-

out giving offence—and that her relations have honoured me
with their countenance and protection.' Liddy blushed,
and trembled, and faultered. ' To be sure, sir,' said she, 'it
is a very surprising circumstance—a great—a providential—
I really know not what I say—but I beg you will think I
have said what's agreeable.'

Mrs Dennison interposing, said,—' Compose yourselves,
my dear children.—Your mutual happiness shall be our peculiar care.' The son going up to his mother, kissed one
hand; my niece bathed the other with her tears; and the
good old lady pressed them both in their turns to her breast.
The lovers were too much affected to get rid of their embar-
rassment for one day; but the scene was much enlivened by
the arrival of Jack Wilson, who brought, as usual, some
game of his own killing. His honest countenance was a
good letter of recommendation. I received him like a dear
friend after a long separation; and I could not help wondering to see him shake Jery by the hand as an old acquaintance. They had, indeed, been acquainted some days, in
consequence of a diverting incident, which I shall explain
at meeting. That same night a consultation was held
upon the concerns of the lovers, when the match was formally agreed to, and all the marriage articles were settled
without the least dispute. My nephew and I promised to
make Liddy's fortune five thousand pounds. Mr Dennison
declared, he would make over one half of his estate immediately to his son, and that his daughter in-law should be secured in a jointure of four hundred. Tabby proposed, that
considering their youth, they should undergo one year at
least of probation, before the indissoluble knot should be
tied; but the young gentleman being very impatient and
importunate, and the scheme implying that the young couple should live in the house under the wings of his parents,
we resolved to make them happy without farther delay.

As the law requires that the parties should be some weeks
resident in the parish, we shall stay here till the ceremony is
performed. Mr Lismahago requests that he may take the
benefit of the same occasion; so that next Sunday the bands

will be published for all four together. I doubt I shall not
be able to pass my christmas with you at Brambletonhall.
Indeed, I am so agreeably situated in this place, that I have
no desire to shift my quarters; and I foresee, that, when the
day of separation comes, there will be abundance of sorrow
on all sides. In the meantime, we must make the most of
those blessings which Heaven bestows. Considering how
you are tethered by your profession, I cannot hope to see
you so far from home; yet the distance does not exceed a
summer day's journey, and Charles Dennison, who desires
to be remembered to you, would be rejoiced to see his old
compotator; but as I am now stationary, I expect regular
answers to the epistles of, yours invariably,

October 11.   ·   ·MATT. BRAMBLE.

TO SIR WATKIN PHILLIPS, BART. AT OXON.   ·

DEAR WAT,

Every day is now big with incident and discovery.—
Young Mr Dennison proves to be no other than that identical person whom I have execrated so long under the name
of Wilson. He had eloped from college at Cambridge, to
avoid a match that he detested, and acted in different parts
of the country as a stroller, until the lady in question made
choice of a husband for herself; then he returned to his father, and disclosed his passion for Liddy, which met with the
approbation of his parents, though the father little imagined
that Mr Bramble was his old companion Matthew Lloyd.
The young gentleman being empowered to make honourable
proposals to my uncle and me, had been in search of us all
over England without effect; and he it was whom I had seen
pass on horseback by the window of the inn, where I stood
with my sister; but he little dreamed that we were in the
house. As for the real Mr Wilson, whom I called forth to
combat, by mistake, he is the neighbour and intimate friend
of old Mr Dennison, and this connection had suggested to
the son the idea of taking that name while he remained in
obscurity.

You may easily conceive what pleasure I must have felt on discovering that the honour of our family was in no danger from the conduct of a sister whom I love with uncommon affection; that, instead of debasing her sentiments and views to a wretched stroller, she had really captivated the heart of a gentleman, her equal in rank, and superior in fortune; and that, as his parents approved of his attachment, I was on the eve of acquiring a brother-in-law so worthy of my friendship and esteem. George Dennison is, without all question, one of the most accomplished young fellows in England.—His person is at once elegant and manly, and his understanding highly cultivated. Though his spirit is lofty, his heart is kind; and his manner so engaging, as to command veneration and love, even from malice and indifference. When I weigh my own character with his, I am ashamed to find myself so light in the balance; but the comparison excites no envy—I propose him as a model for imitation.—I have endeavoured to recommend myself to his friendship, and hope I have already found a place in his affection. I am, however, mortified to reflect what flagrant injustice we every day commit, and what absurd judgment we form, in viewing objects through the falsifying medium of prejudice and passion. Had you asked me a few days ago the picture of Wilson the player, I should have drawn a portrait very unlike the real person and character of George Dennison. Without all doubt, the greatest advantage acquired in travelling and perusing mankind in the original, is that of dispelling those shameful clouds that darken the faculties of the mind, preventing it from judging with candour and precision.

The real Wilson is a great original, and the best tempered companionable man I ever knew.—I question if ever he was angry or low-spirited in his life. He makes no pretensions to letters; but he is an adept in every thing else that can be either useful or entertaining. Among other qualifications, he is a complete sportsman, and counted the best shot in the country. He and Dennison, and Lismahago and I, attended by Clinker, went a shooting yesterday, and made great havoc among the partridges. To-morrow we shall take the field against the woodcocks and snipes. In the evening we dance and sing, or play at commerce, loo, and quadrille.

Mr Dennison is an elegant poet, and has written some detached pieces on the subject of his passion for Liddy, which must be very flattering to the vanity of a young woman. Perhaps he is one of the greatest theatrical geniuses that ever appeared. He sometimes entertains us with reciting favourite speeches from our best plays. We are resolved to convert the great hall into a theatre, and get up the *Beaux Stratagem* without delay. I think I shall make no contemptible figure in the character of *Scrub;* and Lismahago will be very great in *Captain Gibbet.* Wilson undertakes to entertain the country people with *Harlequin Skeleton,* for which he has got a jacket ready painted with his own hand.

Our society is really enchanting. Even the severity of Lismahago relaxes, and the vinegar of Mrs Tabby is remarkably dulcified ever since it was agreed that she should take the precedency of her niece in being first noosed. For, you must know, the day is fixed for Liddy's marriage; and the bands for both couples have been already once published in the parish church. The captain earnestly begged that one trouble might serve for all, and Tabitha assented with a vile affectation of reluctance. Her inamorata, who came hither very slenderly equipt, has sent for his baggage to London, which, in all probability, will not arrive in time for the wedding; but it is of no great consequence, as every thing is to be transacted with the utmost privacy. Meanwhile, directions are given for making out the contracts of marriage, which are very favourable for both females. Liddy will be secured in a good jointure; and her aunt will remain mistress of her own fortune, except one half of the interest, which her husband shall have a right to enjoy for his natural life: I think this is as little in conscience as can be done with a man who yokes with such a partner for life.

These expectants seem to be so happy, that if Mr Den-

nison had an agreeable daughter, I believe I should be for
making the third couple in this country dance.   The humour seems to be infectious; for Clinker, alias Lloyd, has a
month's mind to play the fool in the same fashion with Mrs
Winifred Jenkins. He has even sounded me on the subject;
but I have given him no encouragement to prosecute this
scheme.—I told him I thought he might do better, as there
was no engagement nor promise subsisting; that I did not
know what designs my uncle might have formed for his advantage; but I was of opinion, that he should not at present run the risk of disobliging him by any premature application of this nature. Honest Humphry protested, he
would suffer death sooner than say or do any thing that
should give offence to the squire; but he owned he had a
kindness for the young woman, and had reason to think she
looked upon him with a favourable eye : that he considered
this mutual manifestation of good will as an engagement
understood, which ought to be binding to the conscience of
an honest man; and he hoped the 'squire and I would be of
the same opinion, when we should be at leisure to bestow
any thought about the matter. I believe he is in the right;
and we shall find time to take his case into consideration.
You see we are fixed for some weeks at least; and as you
have had a long respite, I hope you will begin immediately
to discharge the arrears due to your affectionate

October 14.   J. MELFORD.

TO MISS LÆTITIA WILLIS, AT GLOUCESTER.

MY DEAR DEAR LETTY,

NEVER did I sit down to write in such agitation as I now
feel.—In the course of a few days, we have met with a number of incidents so wonderful and interesting, that all my
ideas are thrown into confusion and perplexity. —You must
not expect either method or coherence in what I am going
to relate,—my dearest Willis. Since my last, the aspect
of affairs is totally changed!—and so changed! but I would
fain give you a regular detail. In passing a river, about

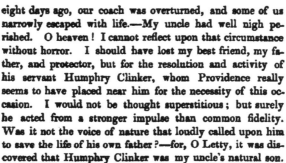

eight days ago, our coach was overturned, and some of us narrowly escaped with life.—My uncle had well nigh perished. O heaven! I cannot reflect upon that circumstance without horror. I should have lost my best friend, my father, and protector, but for the resolution and activity of his servant Humphry Clinker, whom Providence really seems to have placed near him for the necessity of this occasion. I would not be thought superstitious; but surely he acted from a stronger impulse than common fidelity. Was it not the voice of nature that loudly called upon him to save the life of his own father?—for, O Letty, it was discovered that Humphry Clinker was my uncle's natural son.

Almost at the same instant, a gentleman, who came to offer us his assistance, and invite us to his house, turned out to be a very old friend of Mr Bramble. His name is Mr Dennison, one of the worthiest men living; and his lady is a perfect saint upon earth. They have an only son. —Who do you think is this only son?—O Letty!—O gracious Heaven! how my heart palpitates, when I tell you, that this only son of Mr Dennison, is that very identical youth, who, under the name of Wilson, has made such ravage in my heart!—Yes, my dear friend! Wilson and I are now lodged in the same house, and converse together freely. His father approves of his sentiments in my favour; his mother loves me with all the tenderness of a parent; my uncle, my aunt, and my brother, no longer oppose my inclinations.—On the contrary, they have agreed to make us happy without delay; and, in three weeks or a month, if no unforeseen accident intervenes, your friend Lydia Melford will have changed her name and condition. I say, if *no accident intervenes*, because such a torrent of success makes me tremble!—I wish there may not be something treacherous in this sudden reconciliation of fortune.—I have no merit—I have no title to such felicity!—Far from enjoying the prospect that lies before me, my mind is harassed with a continued tumult, made up of hopes and wishes, doubts and apprehensions. I can neither eat nor sleep, and my spirits are in perpetual flutter. I more than ever feel that

vacancy in my heart, which your presence alone can fill.
The mind, in every disquiet, seeks to repose itself on the
bosom of a friend; and this is such a trial as I really know
not how to support without your company and counsel.—
I must therefore, dear Letty, put your friendship to the
test. I must beg you will come, and do the last offices of
maidenhood to your companion Lydia Melford.

This letter goes inclosed in one to our worthy governess,
from Mrs Dennison, entreating her to interpose with your
mamma, that you may be allowed to favour us with your
company on this occasion; and I flatter myself that no material objection can be made to our request. The distance
from hence to Gloucester does not exceed one hundred miles,
and the roads are good. Mr Clinket, *alias* Lloyd, shall
be sent over to attend your motions.—If you step into the
post-chaise, with your maid Betty Barker at seven in the
morning, you will arrive by four in the afternoon at the
half-way house, where there is good accommodation. There
you shall be met by my brother and myself, who will next
day conduct you to this place, where, I am sure, you will
find yourself perfectly at your ease in the midst of an agreeable society. Dear Letty, I will take no refusal—if you
have any friendship—any humanity—you will come. I desire that immediate application may be made to your mamma; and that the moment her permission is obtained, you
will apprise your ever faithful

October 14.   LYDIA MELFORD.

TO MRS JERMYN, AT HER HOUSE IN GLOUCESTER.

DEAR MADAM,

THOUGH I was not so fortunate as to be favoured with an
answer to the letter with which I troubled you in the spring,
I still flatter myself that you retain some regard for me and
my concerns. I am sure the care and tenderness with which
I was treated under your roof and tuition, demand the
warmest returns of gratitude and affection on my part; and
these sentiments, I hope, I shall cherish to my dying day.
At present I think it my duty to make you acquainted with

the happy issue of that indiscretion by which I incurred
your displeasure!—Ah! madam, the alighted Wilson is metamorphosed into George Dennison, only son and heir of a
gentleman, whose character is second to none in England,
as you may understand upon inquiry. My guardians, my
brother, and I, are now in his house; and an immediate
union of the two families is to take place in the persons of
the young gentleman and your poor Lydia Melford. You
will easily conceive how embarrassing this situation must be
to a young unexperienced creature like me, of weak nerves
and strong apprehensions; and how much the presence of a
friend and confidant would encourage and support me on
this occasion. You know that, of all the young ladies,
Miss Willis was she that possessed the greatest share of my
confidence and affection; and, therefore, I fervently wish
to have the happiness of her company at this interesting
crisis.

Mrs Dennison, who is the object of universal love and
esteem, has, at my request, written to you on this subject,
and I now beg leave to reinforce her solicitation. My dear
Mrs Jermyn! my ever-honoured governess! let me conjure
you by that fondness which once distinguished your favourite Liddy! by that benevolence of heart, which dis-
poses you to promote the happiness of your fellow creatures
in general! lend a favourable ear to my petition, and use
your influence with Letty's mamma, that my most earnest
desire may be gratified. Should I be indulged in this particular, I will engage to return her safe, and even to accompany her to Gloucester, where, if you will give me
leave, I will present to you, under another name, dear madam, your most affectionate humble servant, and penitent,

October 14.   LYDIA MELFORD.

TO MRS MARY JONES, AT BRAMBLETONHALL.

O MARY JONES! MARY JONES!

I HAVE met with so many axidents, surprisals, and terrifi-
cations, that I am in a perfect fantigo, and believe I shall
never be my own self again. Last week I was dragged out

of a river like a drowned rat, and lost a bran-new night-cap
with a sulfur stay-hook, that cost me a good half a crown,
and an odd shoe of green gallow-monkey; besides wetting
my clothes, and taring my smuck, and an ugly gash made
in the back part of my thy, by the stump of a tree.   To
be sure, Mr Clinker tuck me out of the cox; but he left me
on my back in the water, to go to the squire, and I mought
have had a watry grave, if a millar had not brought me to
the dry land.   But O! what choppings and changes, girl.
The player man that came after Miss Liddy, and frightened me with a beard at Bristol well, is now matthewmurphy'd
into a fine young gentleman, son and hare of Squire Dollison.   We are altogether in the same house, and all parties
have agreed to the match, and in a fortnite the surrymony
will be performed.

But this is not the only wedding we are to have.—Mistriss
is resolved to have the same frolick, in the naam of God!
Last Sunday in the parish crutch, if my own ars may be
trusted, the clerk called the banes of marridge betwixt Op-
aniah Lashmeyhago and Tapitha Brample, spinster; he
mought as well have called her inkle-weaver, for she never
spun an hank of yarn in her life.—Young Squire Dollison
and Miss Liddy made the second kipple; and there might
have been a turd, but times are changed with Mr Clinker.
—O, Molly! what do'st think? Mr Clinker is found to be
a pye-blow of our own squire, and his right naam is Mr
Mattew Loyd, (thof God he knose how that can be); and
he is now out of livery, and wares ruffles—but I knew him
when he was out at elbows, and had not a rag to kiver his
pistereroes; and he need not hold his head so high.—He is
for sartin very umble and compleasant, and purtests as how
he has the same regard as before; but that he is no longer
his own master, and cannot portend to marry without the
squire's consent.—He says we must wait with patience, and
trust to Providence, and such nonsense.   But if so be as
how his regard be the same, why stand shilly-shally? Why
not strike while the iron is hot, and speak to the squire without loss of time?—What subjection can the squire make to

our coming together ?—Thof my father wan't a gentleman, my mother was an honest woman. I did'nt come on the wrong side of the blanket girl. My parents were married according to the rights of holy mother crutch, in the face of men and angels—Mark that, Mary Jones.

Mr Clinker (Lloyd I would say) had best look to his tackle. There be other chaps in the market, as the saying is. What would he say if I should except the soot and sarvice of the young squire's valley? Mr Machappy is a gentleman born, and has been abroad in the wars. He has a world of buck learning, and speaks French, and Ditch, and Scotch, and all manner of outlandish lingos; to be sure he's a little the worse for the ware, and is much given to drink; but then he's good-tempered. in his liquor, and a prudent woman mought wind him about her finger. But I have no thoughts of him, I'l assure you—I scorn for to do, or to say, or to think any thing that might give umbreech to Mr Lloyd, without furder occasion. But then I have such vapours, Molly—I sit and cry by myself, and take ass of etida, and smill to burnt fathers, and kindal-snuffs; and I pray constantly for grease, that I may have a glimpse of the new light, to show me the way through this wretched veil of tares. And yet, I want for nothing in this family of love, where every sole is so kind and so courteous, that wan would think they are so many saints in haven. Dear Molly, I recommend myself to your prayers, being, with my sarvice to Saul, your ever loving, and discounselled friend,

October 14.   WIN. JENKINS.

TO DR LEWIS.

DEAR DICK,

You cannot imagine what pleasure I have in seeing your hand-writing, after such a long cessation on your side of our correspondence: yet, heaven knows, I have often seen your handwriting with disgust; I mean when it appeared in abbreviations of apothecary's Latin. I like your hint of making interest for the reversion of the collector's place for Lisma-

hago, who is much pleased with the scheme, and presents
you with his compliments and best thanks for thinking so
kindly of his concerns.   The man seems to mend upon further acquaintance.   That harsh reserve, which formed a
disagreeable husk about his character, begins to peel off in
the course of our communication.   I have great hopes that
he and Tabby will be as happily paired as any two draught
animals in the kingdom ; and I make no doubt but that he
will prove a valuable acquisition to our little society, in the
article of conversation by the fire-side in winter.

Your objection to my passing this season of the year at
such a distance from home, would have more weight if I did
not find myself perfectly at my ease where I am ; and my
health so much improved, that I am disposed to bid defiance
to the gout and rheumatism.—I begin to think I have put
myself on the superannuated list too soon, and absurdly
sought for health in the retreats of laziness.—I am persuaded, that all valetudinarians are too sedentary, too regular,
and too cautious.   We should sometimes increase the motion
of the machine, to *unclog the wheels of life;* and now and
then take a plunge amidst the waves of excess, in order to
case-harden the constitution.   I have even found a change
of company as necessary as a change of air, to promote a
vigorous circulation of the spirits, which is the very essence
and criterion of good health.

Since my last, I have been performing the duties of friendship, that required a great deal of exercise, from which I
hope to derive some benefit.   Understanding, by the greatest
accident in the world, that Mr Baynard's wife was dangerously ill of a pleuretic fever, I borrowed Dennison's post-
chaise, and went across the country to his habitation, attended only by Lloyd (quondam Clinker) on horseback.   As
the distance is not above thirty miles, I arrived about four in
the afternoon, and, meeting the physician at the door, was
informed that his patient had just expired.   I was instantly
seized with a violent emotion : but it was not grief.—The
family being in confusion, I ran up stairs into the chamber,
where, indeed, they were all assembled. The aunt stood wring-

ing her hands, in a state of stupefaction of sorrow, but my friend acted all the extravagancies of affliction. He held the body in his arms, and poured forth such a lamentation, that one would have thought he had lost the most amiable consort, and valuable companion upon earth.

Affection may certainly exist, independent of esteem ; nay, the same object may be lovely in one respect, and detestable in another. The mind has a surprising faculty of accommodating, and even attaching itself, in such a manner, by dint of use, to things that are in their own nature disagreeable, and even pernicious, that it cannot bear to be delivered from them without reluctance and regret. Baynard was so absorbed in his delirium, that he did not perceive me when I entered, and desired one of the women to conduct the aunt into her own chamber. At the same time, I begged the tutor to withdraw the boy, who stood gaping in a corner, very little affected with the distress of the scene. These steps being taken, I waited till the first violence of my friend's transport was abated, then disengaged him gently from the melancholy object, and led him by the hand into another apartment; though he struggled so hard, that I was obliged to have recourse to the assistance of his valet-de-chambre. In a few minutes, however, he recollected himself, and folding me in his arms—' This,' cried he, ' is a friendly office indeed !— I know not how you came hither, but, I think, heaven sent you to prevent my going distracted. O Matthew ! I have lost my dear Harriet !—my poor, gentle, tender creature, that loved me with such warmth and purity of affection— my constant companion of twenty years !—She's gone—she's gone for ever ! Heaven and earth, where is she ?—Death shall not part us !'

So saying, he started up, and could hardly be withheld from returning to the scene we had quitted. You will perceive it would have been very absurd for me to argue with a man that talked so madly. On all such occasions, the first torrent of passion must be allowed to subside gradually. I endeavoured to beguile his attention by starting little hints, and insinuating other objects of discourse imperceptibly; and being exceedingly pleased in my mind at this event, I exerted myself with such an extraordinary flow of spirits as was attended with success. In a few hours, he was calm enough to hear reason, and even to own that heaven could not have interposed more effectually to rescue him from disgrace and ruin. That he might not, however, relapse into weaknesses for want of company, I passed the night in his chamber, in a little tent-bed brought thither on purpose; and well it was that I took this precaution, for he started up in bed several times, and would have played the fool, if I had not been present.

Next day he was in a condition to talk of business, and vested me with full authority over his household, which I began to exercise without loss of time, though not before he knew and approved of the scheme I had projected for his advantage. He would have quitted the house immediately; but this retreat I opposed. Far from encouraging a temporary disgust, which might degenerate into an habitual aversion, I resolved, if possible to attach him more than ever to his household gods. I gave directions for the funeral to be as private as was consistent with decency; I wrote to London that an inventory and estimate might be made of the furniture and effects in his town-house, and gave notice to the landlord that Mr Baynard should quit the premises at lady-day; I set a person at work to take an account of every thing in the country-house, including horses, carriages, and harness; I settled the young gentleman at a boarding-school, kept by a clergyman in the neighbourhood, and thither he went without reluctance, as soon as he knew that he was to be troubled no more with his tutor, whom we dismissed. The aunt continued very sullen, and never appeared at table, though Mr Baynard paid his respects to her every day in her own chamber; there also she held conferences with the waiting women and other servants of the family: but the moment her niece was interred, she went away in a post-chaise prepared for that purpose: she did not leave the house, however, without giving Mr Baynard to understand, that the wardrobe of her niece was the perquisite of her woman;

accordingly, that worthless drab received all the clothes, laces, and linen, of her deceased mistress, to the value of five hundred pounds, at a moderate computation.

The next step I took was to disband that legion of super-numerary domestics, who had preyed so long upon the vitals of my friend ; a parcel of idle drones, so intolerably insolent, that they even treated their own master with the most con-temptuous neglect. They had been generally hired by his wife, according to the recommendation of her woman, and these were the only patrons to whom they paid the least de-ference. I had therefore uncommon satisfaction in clearing the house of those vermin. The woman of the deceased, and a chambermaid, a valet-de-chambre, a butler, a French cook, a master-gardener, two footmen, and a coachman, I paid off, and turned out of the house immediately, paying to each a month's wages in lieu of warning. Those whom I retained consisted of a female cook, who had been assistant to the Frenchman, a house-maid, an old lacquey, a postillion, and under-gardener. Thus I removed at once a huge moun-tain of expense and care from the shoulders of my friend, who could hardly believe the evidence of his own senses, when he found himself so suddenly and so effectually reliev-ed. His heart, however, was still subject to vibrations of tenderness, which returned at certain intervals, extorting sighs, and tears, and exclamations of grief and impatience ; but these fits grew every day less violent and less frequent, till at length his reason obtained a complete victory over the infirmities of his nature.

Upon an accurate inquiry into the state of his affairs, I find his debts amount to twenty thousand pounds, for eighteen thousand pounds of which sum his estate is mort-gaged ; and as he pays five per cent. interest, and some of his farms are unoccupied, he does not receive above two hundred pounds a-year clear from his lands, over and above the interest of his wife's fortune, which produced eight hun-dred pounds annually. For lightening this heavy burden, I devised the following expedient. His wife's jewels, toge-ther with his superfluous plate and furniture in both houses,

his horses and carriages, which are already advertised to be
sold by auction, will, according to the estimate, produce two
thousand five hundred pounds in ready money, with which
the debts will be immediately reduced to eighteen thousand
pounds. I have undertaken to find him ten thousand pounds
at four per cent, by which means he will save one hundred
a-year in the article of interest, and perhaps we shall be able
to borrow the other eight thousand on the same terms. According to his own scheme of a country life, he says he can
live comfortably for three hundred pounds a-year; but, as
he has a son to educate, we will allow him five hundred;
then there will be an accumulating fund of seven hundred
a-year, principal and interest, to pay off the encumbrance;
and, I think, we may modestly add three hundred on the
presumption of new-leasing and improving the vacant farms;
so that, in a couple of years, I suppose, there will be above
a thousand a-year appropriated to liquidate a debt of sixteen
thousand.

We forthwith began to class and set apart the articles designed for sale, under the direction of an upholder from London; and, that nobody in the house might be idle, commenced
our reformation without doors, as well as within. With
Baynard's good leave, I ordered the gardener to turn the ri-
vulet into its own channel, to refresh the fainting Naiads,
who had so long languished among mouldering roots, withered leaves, and dry pebbles. The shrubbery is condemned to
extirpation; and the pleasure-ground will be restored to its
original use of corn-field and pasture. Orders are given for
rebuilding the walls of the garden at the back of the house,
and for planting clumps of firs, intermingled with beech and
chesnut, at the east end, which is now quite exposed to the surly
blasts that come from that quarter. All these works being
actually begun, and the house and auction left to the care
and management of a reputable attorney, I brought Baynard
along with me in the chaise, and made him acquainted with
Dennison, whose goodness of heart would not fail to engage
his esteem and affection. He is indeed charmed with our
society in general, and declares that he never saw the theory

of true pleasure reduced to practice before.—I really believe it would not be an easy task to find such a number of individuals assembled under one roof more happy than we are at present.

I must tell you, however, in confidence, I suspect Tabby of tergiversation.—I have been so long accustomed to that original, that I know all the caprices of her heart, and can often perceive her designs, while they are yet in embryo.—. She attached herself to Lismahago for no other reason but that she despaired of making a more agreeable conquest.— At present if I am not much mistaken in my observation, she would gladly convert the widowhood of Baynard to her own advantage.—Since he arrived, she has behaved very coldly to the captain, and strove to fasten on the other's heart with the hooks of overstrained civility. These must be the instinctive efforts of her constitution, rather than the effects of any deliberate design; for matters are carried to such a length with the lieutenant, that she could not retract with any regard to conscience or reputation. Besides, she will meet with nothing but indifference or aversion on the side of Baynard, who has too much sense to think of such a partner at any time, and too much delicacy to admit a thought of any such connection at the present juncture. Meanwhile I have prevailed upon her to let him have four thousand pounds at four per cent. towards paying off his mortgage.—Young Dennison has agreed that Liddy's fortune shall be appropriated to the same purpose, on the same terms; his father will sell out three thousand pounds stock for his accommodation; Farmer Bland has, at the desire of Wilson, undertaken for two thousand; and I must make an effort to advance what farther will be required to take my friend out of the hands of the Philistines. He is so pleased with the improvements made on this estate, which is all cultivated like a garden, that he has entered himself as a pupil in farming to Mr Dennison, and resolved to attach himself wholly to the practice of husbandry.

Every thing is now prepared for our double wedding. The marriage articles for both couples are drawn and executed; and the ceremony only waits until the parties shall have been resident in the parish the term prescribed by law. Young Dennison betrays some symptoms of impatience; but Lismahago bears this necessary delay with the temper of a philosopher. You must know, the captain does not stand altogether on the foundation of personal merit. Besides his half-pay, amounting to two-and-forty pounds a-year, this indefatigable economist has amassed eight hundred pounds, which he has secured in the funds. This sum arises partly from his pay's running up while he remained among the Indians; partly from what he received as a consideration for the difference between his full appointment and the half-pay, to which he is now restricted; and partly from the profits of a little traffic he drove in peltry, during his sachemship among the Miamis.

Liddy's fears and perplexities have been much assuaged by the company of one Miss Willis, who had been her intimate companion at the boarding-school. Her parents had been earnestly solicited to allow her making this friendly visit on such an extraordinary occasion; and two days ago she arrived with her mother, who did not choose that she should come without a proper governante. The young lady is very handsome, sprightly, and agreeable, and the mother a mighty good sort of a woman; so that their coming adds considerably to our enjoyment. But we shall have a third couple yoked in the matrimonial chain. Mr Clinker Lloyd has made humble remonstrance, through the channel of my nephew, setting forth the sincere love and affection mutually subsisting between him and Mrs Winifred Jenkins, and praying my consent to their coming together for life. I would have wished that Mr Clinker had kept out of this scrape; but as the nymph's happiness is at stake, and she has had already some fits in the way of despondence, I, in order to prevent any tragical catastrophe, have given him leave to play the fool, in imitation of his betters; and I suppose we shall in time have a whole litter of his progeny at Brambletonhall. The fellow is stout and lusty, very sober and conscientious; and the wench seems to be as great an enthusiast in love as in religion.

I wish you would think of employing him some other way, that the parish may not be overstocked—you know he has been bred a farrier, consequently belongs to the faculty; and, as he is very docile, I make no doubt, but, with your good instruction, he may be, in a little time, qualified to act as a Welch apothecary. Tabby, who never did a favour with a good grace, has consented, with great reluctance, to this match. Perhaps it hurts her pride, as she now considers Clinker in the light of a relation; but I believe her objections are of a more selfish nature. She declares she cannot think of retaining the wife of Matthew Lloyd in the character of a servant; and she foresees, that, on such an occasion, the woman will expect some gratification for her past services. As for Clinker, exclusive of other considerations, he is so trusty, brave, affectionate, and alert, and I owe him such personal obligations, that he merits more than all the indulgence that possibly can be shewn him by yours,

MATT. BRAMBLE.

October 26.

TO SIR WATKIN PHILLIPS, BART. AT OXON.

DEAR KNIGHT,

THE fatal knots are now tied. The comedy is near a close, and the curtain is ready to drop; but the latter scenes of this act I shall recapitulate in order. About a fortnight ago, my uncle made an excursion across the country, and brought hither a particular friend, one Mr Baynard, who has just lost his wife, and was for some time disconsolate, though, by all accounts, he had much more cause for joy than for sorrow at this event. His countenance, however, clears up apace; and he appears to be a person of rare accomplishments; but we have received another still more agreeable reinforcement to our company, by the arrival of Miss Willis from Gloucester. She was Liddy's bosom-friend at boarding-school, and being earnestly solicited to assist at the nuptials, her mother was so obliging as to grant my sister's request, and even to come with her in person. Liddy, accompanied by George Dennison and me, gave them the meeting half way, and next day conducted them hither in safety. Miss Willis is a charming girl, and, in point of disposition, an agreeable contrast to my sister, who is rather too grave and sentimental for my turn of mind.—The other is gay, frank, a little giddy, and always good humoured. She has, moreover, a genteel fortune, is well born, and remarkably handsome. Ah Phillips! if these qualities were permanent—if her humour would never change, nor her beauties decay, what efforts would I not make—but these are idle reflections—my destiny must one day be fulfilled.

At present we pass the time as agreeably as we can.—We have got up several farces, which afforded unspeakable entertainment, by the effects they produced among the country people, who were admitted to all our exhibitions. Two nights ago, Jack Wilson acquired great applause in Harlequin Skeleton, and Lismahago surprised us all in the character of Pierot.—His long lank sides, and strong marked features, were all peculiarly adapted to his part. He appeared with a ludicrous stare, from which he had discharged all meaning: he adopted the impressions of fear and amazement so naturally, that many of the audience were infected by his looks; but when the skeleton had him in chase, his horror became most divertingly picturesque, and seemed to endow him with such preternatural agility, as confounded all the spectators. It was a lively representation of Death in pursuit of Consumption, and had such an effect upon the commonalty, that some of them shrieked aloud, and others ran out of the hall in the utmost consternation.

This is not the only instance in which the lieutenant had lately excited our wonder. His temper, which had been soured and shrivelled by disappointment and chagrin, is now swelled out and smoothed like a raisin in plum-porridge. From being reserved and punctilious, he is become easy and obliging. He cracks jokes, laughs, and banters, with the most facetious familiarity; and, in a word, enters into all our schemes of merriment and pastime. The other day his baggage arrived in the waggon from London, contained in two large trunks, and a long deal box, not unlike a coffin.

The trunks were filled with his wardrobe, which he displayed for the entertainment of the company; and he freely
owned, that it consisted chiefly of the *opima spolia* taken in
battle. What he selected for his wedding suit, was a tarnished white cloth, faced with blue velvet, embroidered with
silver; but he valued himself most upon a tye periwig, in
which he had made his first appearance as a lawyer, about
thirty years ago. This machine had been in buckle ever
since, and now all the servants in the family were employed
to friz it out for the ceremony, which was yesterday celebrated at the parish church. George Dennison and his
bride were distinguished by nothing extraordinary in their
apparel. His eyes lightened with eagerness and joy, and she
trembled with coyness and confusion. My uncle gave
her away, and her friend Willis supported her during the
ceremony.

But my aunt and her paramour took the *pas*, and formed
indeed such a pair of originals, as, I believe, all England
could not parallel. She was dressed in the style of 1739;
and, the day being cold, put on a mantle of green velvet
laced with gold: but this was taken off by the bridegroom,
who threw over her shoulders a fur cloak of American sables,
valued at fourscore guineas, a present equally agreeable and
unexpected. Thus accoutred, she was led up to the altar
by Mr Dennison, who did the office of her father. Lismahago advanced in the military step, with his French coat
reaching no farther than the middle of his thigh, his campaign wig that surpasses all description, and a languishing
leer upon his countenance, in which there seemed to be
something arch and ironical. The ring which he put upon her finger, he had concealed till the moment it was used.
He now produced it with an air of self-complacency. It
was a curious antique, set with rose diamonds; he told us
afterwards it had been in his family two hundred years, and
was a present from his grandmother. These circumstances
agreeably flattered the pride of our aunt Tabitha, which
had already found uncommon gratification in the captain's
generosity; for he had, in the morning, presented my uncle

with a fine bear's skin, and a Spanish fowling-piece, and
me with a case of pistols curiously mounted with silver. At
the same time, he gave Mrs Jenkins an Indian purse, made
of silk grass, containing twenty crown pieces. You must
know, this young lady, with the assistance of Mr Lloyd,
formed the third couple who yesterday sacrificed to Hymen.
I wrote you in my last that he had recourse to my mediation,
which I employed successfully with my uncle; but Mrs
Tabitha held out till the love-sick Jenkins had two fits of the
mother; then she relented, and those two cooing turtles
were caged for life.—Our aunt made an effort of generosity
in furnishing the bride with her superfluities of clothes and
linen, and her example was followed by my sister; nor did
Mr Bramble and I neglect her on this occasion. It was indeed a day of peace-offering—Mr Dennison insisted upon
Liddy's accepting two bank-notes of one hundred pounds
each, as pocket-money; and his lady gave her a diamond
necklace of double that value. There was, besides, a mutual exchange of tokens among the individuals of the two
families thus happily united.

As George Dennison and his partner were judged improper objects of mirth, Jack Wilson had resolved to execute some jokes on Lismahago, and, after supper, began
to ply him with bumpers, when the ladies had retired; but
the captain perceiving his drift, begged for quarter, alleging
that the adventure in which he had engaged was a very
serious matter; and that it would be more the part of a good
christian to pray that he might be strengthened, than to impede his endeavours to finish the adventure. He was spared
accordingly, and permitted to ascend the nuptial couch
with all his senses about him. There he and his consort sat
in state like Saturn and Cybele, while the benediction posset
was drank; and a cake being broken over the head of Mrs
Tabitha Lismahago, the fragments were distributed among
the by-standers, according to the custom of the ancient
Britons, on the supposition that every person who ate of
this hallowed cake should that night have a vision of the
man or woman whom Heaven designed should be his or her
wedded mate.

The weight of Wilson's waggery fell upon honest Humphry and his spouse, who were bedded in an upper room, with the usual ceremony of throwing the stocking. This being performed, and the company withdrawn, a sort of catter-wauling ensued, when Jack found means to introduce a real cat, shod with walnut-shells, which, galloping along the boards, made such a dreadful noise as effectually discom-posed our lovers.—Winifred screamed aloud, and shrunk under the bed-clothes.—Mr Lloyd, believing that Satan was come to buffet him *in propria persona*, laid aside all carnal thoughts, and began to pray aloud with great fervency.— At length, the poor animal being more afraid than either, leaped into the bed, and mewled with the most piteous ex-clamation. Lloyd, thus informed of the nature of the an-noyance, rose and set the door wide open, so that this troublesome visitant retreated with great expedition; then securing himself, by means of a double bolt, from a second intrusion, he was left to enjoy his good fortune without disturbance.

If one may judge from the looks of the parties, they are all very well satisfied with what has passed. George Den-nison and his wife are too delicate to exhibit any strong marked signs of their mutual satisfaction, but their eyes are sufficiently expressive. Mrs Tabitha Lismahago is rather fulsome in signifying her approbation of the captain's love; while his deportment is the very pink of gallantry. He sighs, and ogles, and languishes at this amiable object; he kisses her hand, mutters ejaculations of rapture, and sings tender airs; and, no doubt, laughs internally at her folly in be-lieving him sincere. In order to shew how little his vigour was impaired by the fatigues of the preceding day, he this morning danced a Highland saraband over a naked back-sword, and leaped so high, that I believe he would make no contemptible figure as a vaulter at Sadler's Wells.—Mr Matthew Lloyd, when asked how he relishes his bargain, throws up his eyes, crying,—'For what we have receiv-ed, Lord make us thankful: amen.' His help-mate gig-gles, and holds her hand before her eyes, affecting to be

ashamed of having been in bed with a man. Thus all these
widgeons enjoy the novelty of their situation; but perhaps
their note will be changed, when they are better acquainted
with the nature of the decoy.

As Mrs Willis cannot be persuaded to stay, and Liddy
is engaged by promise to accompany her daughter back to
Gloucester, I fancy there will be a general migration from
hence, and that most of us will spend the christmas holidays at Bath; in which case I shall certainly find an opportunity to beat up your quarters. By this time, I suppose,
you are sick of *alma mater*, and even ready to execute that
scheme of peregrination which was last year concerted between you and your affectionate

November 8. J. MELFORD.

TO DR LEWIS.

DEAR DOCTOR,

My niece Liddy is now happily settled for life; and Captain Lismahago has taken Tabby off my hands; so that I
have nothing farther to do, but to comfort my friend Baynard, and provide for my son Lloyd, who is also fairly joined to Mrs Winifred Jenkins. You are an excellent genius
at hints. Dr Arbuthnot was but a type of Dr Lewis in
that respect.——What you observe of the vestry-clerk deserves
consideration.——I make no doubt but Matthew Lloyd is well
enough qualified for the office; but, at present, you must
find room for him in the house. His incorruptible honesty
and indefatigable care will be serviceable in superintending
the economy of my farm, though I don't mean that he shall
interfere with Barnes, of whom I have no cause to complain.
——I am just returned with Baynard from a second trip to
his house, where every thing is regulated to his satisfaction.
He could not, however, review the apartments without tears
and lamentation, so that he is not yet in a condition to be
left alone; therefore, I will not part with him till the spring,
when he intends to plunge into the avocations of husbandry, which will at once employ and amuse his attention.——
Charles Dennison has promised to stay with him a fortnight,

to set him fairly afloat in his improvements; and Jack Wilson will see him from time to time; besides, he has a few friends in the country, whom his new plan of life will not exclude from his society. In less than a year, I make no doubt but he will find himself perfectly at ease, both in his mind and body, for the one had dangerously affected the other; and I shall enjoy the exquisite pleasure of seeing my friend rescued from misery and contempt.

Mrs Willis being determined to return with her daughter, in a few days, to Gloucester, our plan has undergone some alteration. Jerry has persuaded his brother-in-law to carry his wife to Bath; and I believe his parents will accompany him thither.—For my part I have no intention to take that route.—It must be something very extraordinary that will induce me either to revisit Bath or London. My sister and her husband, Baynard and I, will take leave of them at Gloucester, and make the best of our way to Brambletonhall, where I desire you will prepare a good chine and turkey for our christmas dinner.—You must also employ your medical skill in defending me from the attacks of the gout, that I may be in good case to receive the rest of our company, who promise to visit us in their return from the Bath. As I have laid in a considerable stock of health, it is to be hoped you will not have much trouble with me in the way of physic, but I intend to work you on the side of exercise.—I have got an excellent fowling-piece from Mr Lismahago, who is a keen sportsman, and we shall take the heath in all weathers.—That this scheme of life may be prosecuted the more effectually, I intend to renounce all sedentary amusements, particularly that of writing long letters; a resolution, which, had I taken it sooner, might have saved you the trouble which you have lately taken in reading the tedious epistles of

November 14.   MATT. BRAMBLE.

TO MRS GWYLLIM, AT BRAMBLETONHALL.

GOOD MRS GWYLLIM,

HEAVEN, for wise purposes, hath ordained that I should
change my name and citation in life, so that I am not to be
considered any more as manger of my brother's family: but
as I cannot surrender up my stewardship till I have settled
with you and Williams, I desire you will get your accounts
ready for inspection, as we are coming home without farther delay. My spouse, the captain, being subject to rum-
matticks, I beg you will take great care to have the bloo
chamber, up two pair of stairs, well warmed for his reception. Let the sashes be secured, the crevices stopt, the car-
pets laid, and the beds well tousled. Mrs Loyd, late Jenkins, being married to a relation of the family, cannot remain in the capacity of a sarvant; therefore, I wish you
would cast about for some creditable body to be with me in
her room. If she can spin, and is mistress of plain work,
so much the better—but she must not expect extravagant
wages—having a family of my own, I must be more œcu-
menical than ever. No more at present, but rests your loving friend,

November 20.   TAB. LISMAHAGO.

TO MRS MARY JONES, AT BRAMBLETONHALL.

MRS JONES,

PROVIDINCH hath bin pleased to make great halteration in
the pasture of our affairs. We were yesterday three kiple
chined by the grease of God, in the holy bands of matter-
money; and I now subscrive myself Loyd at your sarvice.
—All the parish allowed that young Squire Dallison and
his bride was a comely pear for to see.—As for Madam Lash-
imiheygo, you nose her picklearities—her head, to be sure,
was fintastical; and her spouse had rapt her with a long
marokin furse clock from the land of the selvedges, thof
they say it is of immense bally.—The captain himself had a
hudge hassock of air, with three tails, and a tumtawdry

coat, boddered with sulfur.—Wan said he was a monkey-
bank; and the ould botler swore he was the born imich of
Titidall.—For my part, I says nothing, being as how the
captain has done the handsome thing by me.—Mr Loyd
was dressed in a little frog and checket with gould binding;
and thof he don't enter in caparison with great folks of quality, yet he has got as good blood in his veins as arrow
private squire in the county; and then his pursing is far
from contentible.—Your humble sarvant had on a plain pea
green tabby sack, with my Runnela cap, rough toupee, and
side curls.—They said, I was the very moral of Lady Rick-
manstone, but not so pale—that may well be, for her ladyship is my elder by seven good years and more.—Now,
Mrs Mary, our satiety is to suppurate.—Mr Millfart goes
to Bath, along with the Dallisons, and the rest of us push
home to Wales, to pass our christmash at Brampletonhall.
—As our apartments is to be the yellow pepper, in the
thurd story, pray carry my things thither.—Present my
compliments to Mrs Gwillim, and I hope she and I will
live upon dissent terms of civility.—Being, by God's blessing, removed to a higher spear, you'll excuse my being
familiar with the lower sarvants of the family; but, as I
trust you'll behave respectful, and keep a proper distance,
you may always depend upon the good-will and purtection
of yours,

November 20.   W. LOYD.

THE END OF THE EXPEDITION OF HUMPHRY CLINKER.

THE

HISTORY & ADVENTURES

OF

AN ATOM.

ADVERTISEMENT

THE PUBLISHER TO THE READER.

In these ticklish times, it may be necessary to give such an account of the following sheets, as will exempt me from the plague of prosecution.

On the 7th of March, in the present year 1748, they were offered to me for sale by a tall thin woman, about the age of threescore, dressed in a gown of bombasin, with a cloak and bonnet of black silk, both a little the worse for the wear.—She called herself Dorothy Hatchet, spinster, of the parish of Old-street, administratrix of Mr Nathaniel Peacock, who died in the said parish on the 5th day of last April, and lies buried in the church-yard of Islington, in the north-west corner, where his grave is distinguished by a monumental board, inscribed with the following distich :

> *Hic, hæc, hoc,*
> Here lies the block
> Of old Nathaniel Peacock.

In this particular, any person whatever may satisfy himself, by taking an afternoon's walk to Islington, where, at the White house, he may recreate and refresh himself with excellent tea and hot rolls for so small a charge as eight pence.

As to the MS. before I would treat for it, I read it over attentively, and found it contained divers curious particulars of a foreign

history, without any allusion to, or resemblance with, the tran.
sactions of these times. I likewise turned over to Kempfer and the
Universal history, and found in their several accounts of Japan,
many of the names and much of the matter specified in the following sheets. Finally, that I might run no risk of misconstruction,
I had recourse to an eminent chamber-counsel of my acquaintance, who diligently perused the whole, and declared it was no
more actionable than the Vision of Ezekiel, or the Lamentations of
Jeremiah the prophet. Thus assured, I purchased the copy, which
I now present in print, with my best respects to the courteous
reader, being his very humble servant,

Bucklersburry.   S. ETHERINGTON.

Vivant Rex et Regina.

THE

ADVENTURES

OF

AN ATOM.

THE EDITOR'S DECLARATION.

I NATHANIEL PEACOCK, of the parish of St Giles's, haberdasher and author, solemnly declare, That, on the third of last August, sitting alone in my study, up three pair of stairs, between the hours of eleven and twelve at night, meditating upon the uncertainty of sublunary enjoyment, I heard a shrill, small voice, seemingly proceeding from a chink or crevice in my own pericranium, call distinctly three time,—' Nathaniel Peacock, Nathaniel Peacock, Nathaniel Peacock.'—Astonished, yea, even affrighted, at this citation, I replied, in a faultering tone,—' In the name of the Lord what art thou?' Thus adjured, the voice answered and said,—' I am an Atom.' I was now thrown into a violent perturbation of spirit, for I never could behold an atomy without fear and trembling, even when I knew it was no more than a composition of dry bones; but the conceit of being in presence of an atomy, informed with spirit, that is, animated by a ghost or goblin, increased my terrors exceedingly. I durst not lift up mine eyes, lest I should behold an apparition more dreadful than the hand-writing on the wall. My knees knocked together: my teeth chattered: mine hair bristled up so as to raise a cotton nightcap from the scalp: my tongue cleaved to the roof of my mouth : my temples were bedewed with a cold sweat. Verily I was for a season entranced.

At length, by the blessing of God, I recollected myself, and cried aloud,—'Avaunt, Satan, in the name of the Father, Son, and Holy Ghost.' 'White-livered caitiff!' said the voice, with a peculiar tartness of pronunciation, 'what art thou afraid of, that thou shouldst thus tremble, and diffuse around thee such an unsavory odour ?—What thou hearest is within thee—is part of thyself. I am one of those atoms, or constituent particles of matter, which can neither be annihilated, divided, nor impaired : the different arrangements of us, atoms, compose all the variety of objects and essences which nature exhibits, or art can obtain. Of the same shape, substance, and quality, are the component particles, that harden in rock, and flow in water; that blacken in the negro, and brighten in the diamond; that exhale from a rose, and steam from a dunghill. Even now, ten millions of atoms were dispersed in air by that odoriferous gale, which the commotion of thy fear produced; and I can foresee that one of them will be consolidated in a fibre of the olfactory nerve, belonging to a celebrated beauty, whose nostril is excoriated by the immoderate use of plain Spanish. Know, Nathaniel, that we, atoms, are singly endued with such efficacy of reason, as cannot be expected in an aggregate body, where we crowd and squeeze, and embarrass one another! Yet, those ideas which we singly possess, we cannot communicate, except once in a thousand years, and then only, when, we fill a certain place in the pineal gland of a human creature, the very station which I now maintain in thine.—For the benefit of you miserable mortals, I am determined to promulge the history of one period, during which I underwent some strange revolutions in the empire of Japan, and was conscious of some political anecdotes now to be divulged for the instruction of British ministers. Take up the pen, therefore, and write what I shall unfold.

By this time my first apprehensions vanished; but another fear, almost as terrible, usurped its place. I began to think myself insane, and concluded that the voice was no other than the fantastic undulation of a disturbed brain. I therefore preferred an earnest orison at the throne of grace, that I might be restored to the fruition of my right understanding and judgment. 'O incredulous wretch!' exclaimed the voice, 'I will now convince thee that this is no phantasma or hideous dream.—Answer me, dost thou know the meaning and derivation of the word atom?' I replied, —'No, verily.' 'Then I will tell thee,' said the voice; 'thou shalt write it down without delay, and consult the curate of the parish on the same subject. If his explanation and mine agree, thou wilt then be firmly persuaded that I am an actual, independent existence; and that this address is not the vague delirium of a disordered brain. *Atomos* is a Greek word, signifying an indivisible particle, derived from *alpha* privativa, and *temno* to cut.'

I marvelled much at this injunction, which, however, I literally obeyed; and next morning sallied forth to visit the habitation of the curate: but in going thither, it was my hap to encounter a learned physician of my acquaintance, who hath read all the books that ever were published in any nation or language; to him I referred for the derivation of the word atom. He paused a little, threw up his eyes to heaven, stroked his chin with great solemnity, and, heming three times,—'Greek, sir,' said he, 'is more familiar to me than my native tongue. I have conversed, sir, with Homer and Plato, Hesiod and Theophrastus, Herodotus, Thucydides, Hippocrates, Aretæus, Pindar, and Sophocles, and all the poets and historians of antiquity. Sir, my library cost me two thousand pounds. I have spent as much more in making experiments; and you must know that I have discovered certain chemical specifics, which I would not divulge for fifty times the sum.—As for the word *atomos*, or *atime*, it signifies a scoundrel, sir, or, as it were, sir, a thing of no estimation. It is derived, sir, from *alpha* privativa, and *time*, honour. Hence, we call a skeleton an atomy, because, sir, the bones are, as it were, dishonoured by being stript of their clothing, and exposed in their naked-ness.'

I was sorely vexed at this interpretation, and my appre-hension of lunacy recurred : nevertheless I proceeded in my way to the lodgings of the curate, and desired his explanation, which tallied exactly with what I had written. At my re-turn to my own house, I ascended to my study, asked par-don of my internal moniter ; and taking pen, ink, and pa-per, sat down to write what it dictated, in the following strain.——

It was in the era of * Foggien, one thousand years ago, that fate determined I should exist in the empire of Japan, where I underwent a great number of vicissitudes, till, at length, I was inclosed in a grain of rice, eaten by a Dutch mariner at Firando, and, becoming a particle of his body, brought to the Cape of Good Hope. There I was discharg-ed in a scorbutic dysentery, taken up in a heap of soil to manure a garden, raised to vegetation in a sallad, devoured by an English supercargo, assimulated to a certain organ of his body, which, at his return to London, being diseased in consequence of impure contact, I was again separated, with a considerable portion of putrified flesh, thrown upon a dunghill, gobbled up, and digested by a duck ; of which duck your father, Ephraim Peacock, having eaten plenti-fully at the feast of the cordwainers, I was mixed with his circulating juices, and finally fixed in the principal part of that animalcule, which, in process of time, expanded itself into thee, Nathaniel Peacock.'

Having thus particularised my transmigrations since my conveyance from Japan, I shall return thither, and unfold some curious particulars of state-intrigue, carried on during the short period, the history of which I mean to record. I need not tell thee that the empire of Japan consists of three large islands, or that the people who inhabit them are such inconsistent, capricious animals, that one would imagine

* The history of Japan is divided into three different eras, of which Foggien is the most considerable.

they were created for the purpose of ridicule. Their minds
are in continual agitation, like a shuttlecock tossed to and
fro, in order to divert the demons of philosophy and folly.
A Japanese, without the intervention of any visible motive,
is, by turns, merry and pensive, superficial and profound,
generous and illiberal, rash and circumspect, courageous
and fearful, benevolent and cruel. They seem to have no
fixed principle of action, no certain plan of conduct, no effectual rudder to steer them through the voyage of life, but
to be hurried down the rapid tide of each revolving whim,
or driven, the sport of every gust of passion that happens to
blow. A Japanese will sing at a funeral, and sigh at a wedding; he will this hour talk ribaldry with a prostitute, and
the next immerse himself in the study of metaphysics or
theology. In favour of one stranger, he will exert all
the virtues of hospitality; against another he will exercise all
the animosity of the most sordid prejudice: one minute sees
him hazarding his all on the success of the most extravagant
project; another beholds him hesitating in lending a few
copans* to his friend on undeniable security. To-day he is
afraid of paring his corns; to-morrow he scruples not to cut
his own throat. At one season he will give half his fortune
to the poor; at another he will not bestow the smallest pittance to save his brother from indigence and distress. He is
elated to insolence by the least gleam of success; he is dejected to despondence by the slightest turn of adverse fortune. One hour he doubts the best established truths; the
next he swallows the most improbable fiction. His praise
and his censure are what a wise man would choose to avoid,
as evils equally pernicious: the first is generally raised without foundation, and carried to such extravagance, as to expose the object to the ridicule of mankind; the last is often
unprovoked, yet usually inflamed to all the rage of the most
malignant persecution. He will extol above Alexander the
Great, a petty officer who robs a hen-roost; and damn to
infamy a general for not performing impossibilities. The
same man whom he yesterday flattered with the most ful-

* Copan is a gold coin used in Japan, value about 43 shillings.

some adulation, he will to-morrow revile with the most bitter abuse; and, at the turning of a straw, take into his bosom the very person whom he has formerly defamed as the most perfidious rascal.

The Japanese value themselves much upon their constitution, and are very clamorous about the words liberty and property; yet, in fact, the only liberty they enjoy is to get drunk whenever they please, to revile the government, and quarrel with one another. With respect to their property, they are the tamest animals in the world; and, if properly managed, undergo, without wincing, such impositions as no other nation in the world would bear. In this particular, they may be compared to an ass, that will crouch under the most unconscionable burden, provided you scratch his long ears, and allow him to bray his bellyful. They are so practicable, that they have suffered their pockets to be drained, their veins to be emptied, and their credit to be cracked, by the most bungling administration, to gratify the avarice, pride, and ambition, of the most sordid and contemptible sovereigns that ever sat upon the throne.

The methods used for accomplishing these purposes are extremely simple. You have seen a dancing bear incensed to a dangerous degree of rage, and all at once appeased by firing a pistol over his nose. The Japanese, even in their most ferocious moods, when they denounce vengeance against the cuboy, or minister, and even threaten the throne itself, are easily softened into meekness and condescension. A set of tall fellows, hired for the purpose, tickle them under the noses with long straws into a gentle convulsion, during which they shut their eyes, and smile, and quietly suffer their pockets to be turned inside out. Nay, what is still more remarkable, the ministry is in possession of a pipe, or rather bullock's horn, which, being sounded to a particular pitch, has such an effect on the ears and understanding of the people, that they allow their pockets to be picked with their eyes open, and are bribed to betray their own interests with their own money, as easily as if the treasure had come from the remotest corner of the globe. Notwithstanding these capricious peculiarities, the Japanese are become a wealthy and powerful people, partly from their insular situation, and partly from a spirit of commercial adventure, sustained by all the obstinacy of perseverance, and conducted by repeated flashes of good sense, which almost incessantly gleam through the chaos of their absurdities.

Japan was originally governed by monarchs who possessed an absolute power, and succeeded by hereditary right, under the title of Dairo. But in the beginning of the period Foggien, this emperor became a cypher, and the whole administration devolved into the hands of the prime minister, or cuboy, who now exercises all the power and authority, leaving the trappings of royalty to the inactive dairo. The prince, who held the reins of government in the short period which I intend to record, was not a lineal descendant of the ancient dairos, the immediate succession having failed, but sprung from a collateral branch which was invited from a foreign country in the person of *Bupo*, in honour of whom the Japanese erected Fakku-basi *, or the temple of the white horse. So much were all his successors devoted to the culture of this idol, which, by-the-by, was made of the vilest materials, that, in order to enrich his shrine, they impoverished the whole empire, yet still with the connivance and by the influence of the cuboy, who gratified this sordid passion or superstition of the dairo, with a view to prevent him from employing his attention on matters of greater consequence.

Nathaniel, you have heard of the transmigration of souls, a doctrine avowed by one Pythagoras, a philosopher of Crotona. This doctrine, though discarded and reprobated by christians, is nevertheless sound and orthodox, I affirm on the integrity of an atom. Further I shall not explain myself on this subject, though I might with safety set the convocation and the whole hierarchy at defiance, knowing, as I do, that it is not in their power to make me bate one particle of what I advance; or, if they should endeavour to reach me through your organs, and even condemn you to the stake

* *Vid.* Kempfer, lib. 1.

at Smithfield, verily, I say unto thee, I should be a gainer
by the next remove.   I should shift my quarters from a very
cold and empty tenement which I now occupy in the brain
of a poor haberdasher, to the nervous plexus situated at the
mouth of the stomach of a fat alderman fed with venison and
turtle.

But to return to Pythagoras, whom one of your wise countrymen denominated *Peter Gore, the wise-acre* of Croton,
you must know that philosopher was a type, which hath
not yet been fully unveiled.   That he taught the metempsychosis, explained the nature and property of harmonies,
demonstrated the motion of the earth, discovered the elements of geometry and arithmetic, enjoined his disciples silence, and abstained from eating any thing that was ever informed by the breath of life, are circumstances known to all
the learned world; but his veneration for beans, which cost
him his life, his golden thigh, his adventures in the character of a courtesan, his golden verses, his epithet of ἀντὶ ἴρα,
the fable of his being born of a virgin, and his descent into
hell, are mysteries in which some of the most important
truths are concealed.   Between friends, honest Nathaniel,
I myself constituted part of that sage's body ; and I could
say a great deal—but there is a time for all things.   I shall
only observe, that Philip Tessier had some reason for supposing Pythagoras to have been a monk ; and there are
shrewd hints in Meyer's dissertation, *Utrum Pythagoras
Judæus fuit. an monachus Carmelita.*

Waving these intricate discussions for the present (though
I cannot help disclosing that Pythagoras was actually cir-
cumcised), know, Peacock, that the metempsychosis, or
transmigration of souls, is the method which nature and fate
constantly pursue in animating the creatures produced on the
face of the earth ; and this process, with some variation, is
such as the Eleusinian mysteries imported, and such as you
have read in Dryden's translation of the sixth book of Vir-
gil's Æneid.   The gods have provided a great magazine or
diversorium, to which the departed souls of all animals repair
at their dismission from the body.   Here they are bathed in

the waters of oblivion until they retain no memory of the scenes through which they have passed; but they still preserve their original crasis and capacity. From this repository all new created beings are supplied with souls; and these souls transmigrate into different animals, according to the pleasure of the great disposer. For example, my good friend Nathaniel Peacock, your own soul has, within these hundred years, threaded a goat, a spider, and a bishop; and its next stage will be the carcase of a brewer's horse.

In what manner we atoms come by these articles of intelligence, whether by intuition, or communication of ideas, it is not necessary that you should conceive. Suffice it to say, the gods were merry on the follies of mankind, and Mercury undertook to exhibit a mighty nation, ruled and governed by the meanest intellects that could be found in the repository of pre-existing spirits. He laid the scene in Japan, about the middle of the period Foggien, when that nation was at peace with all her neighbours. Into the mass, destined to sway the sceptre, he infused, at the very article of conception, the spirit, which in course of strangulation had been expelled *a posteriori* from a goose, killed on purpose to regale the appetite of the mother. The animalcule, thus inspired, was born, and succeeded to the throne, under the name of Got-hama-baba. His whole life and conversation was no other than a repetition of the humours he had displayed in his last character. He was rapacious, shallow, hot-headed and perverse; in point of understanding, just sufficient to appear in public without a slavering bib; imbued with no knowledge, illumed by no sentiment, and warmed with no affection, except a blind attachment to the worship of Fakku-basi, which seemed indeed to be a disease in his constitution. His heart was meanly selfish, and his disposition altogether unprincely.

Of all his recreations, that which he delighted in most, was kicking the breech of his cuboy, or prime minister, an exercise which he every day performed in private. It was therefore necessary that a cuboy should be found to undergo this diurnal operation without repining. This was a circumstance foreseen and provided for by Mercury, who, a little after the conception of Got-hama-baba, impregnated the ovum of a future cuboy, and implanted in it a chang-ling soul, which had successively passed through the bodies of an ass, a dotteril, an apple-woman, and a cow-boy. It was diverting enough to see the rejoicings with which the birth of this quanbuku * was celebrated; and still more so to observe the marks of fond admiration in the parents, as the soul of the cow-boy proceeded to expand itself in the young cuboy. This is a species of diversion we atoms often enjoy. We at different times behold the same spirit, hunted down in a hare, and cried up in an Hector; fawning in a prostitute, and bribing in a minister; breaking forth in a whistle at the plough, and in a sermon from the pulpit; impelling a hog to the stye, and a counsellor to the cabinet; prompting a shoe-boy to filch, and a patriot to harangue; squinting in a goat, and smiling in a matron.

Tutors of all sorts were provided betimes for the young quanbuku, but his genius rejected all cultivation; at least the crops it produced were barren and ungrateful. He was distinguished by the name of Fika-kaka, and caressed as the heir of an immense fortune. Nay, he was really considered as one of the most hopeful young quanbukus in the empire of Japan; for his want of ideas was attended with a total absence of pride, insolence, or any other disagreeable vice: indeed his character was founded upon negatives. He had no understanding, no economy, no courage, no industry, no steadiness, no discernment, no vigour, no retention. He was reputed generous and good-humoured; but was really profuse, chicken-hearted, negligent, fickle, blundering, weak, and leaky. All these qualifications were agitated by an eagerness, haste, and impatience, that completed the most ludicrous composition, which human nature ever produced. He appeared always in hurry and confusion, as if he had lost his wits in the morning, and was in quest of them all day.—Let me whisper a secret to you, my good friend Pea-cock. All this bustle and trepidation proceeded from a

* Quanbuku is a dignity of the first order in Japan.

hollowness in the brain, forming a kind of eddy, in which
his animal spirits were hurried about in a perpetual swirl.
Had it not been for this *lusus naturæ* the circulation would
not have been sufficient for the purposes of animal life.
Had the whole world been searched by the princes thereof,
it would not have produced another to have matched this
half-witted original, to whom the administration of a mighty
empire was wholly consigned.   Notwithstanding all the care
that was taken of his education, Fika-kaka never could
comprehend any art or science, except that of dancing bare-
headed among the bonzas, at the great festival of Cambadoxi.
The extent of his knowledge in arithmetic went no farther
than the numeration of his ten fingers.   In history, he had
no idea of what preceded a certain treaty with the Chinese,
in the reign of queen Syko, who died within his own remembrance; and was so ignorant of geography, that he did not
know that his native country was surrounded by the sea.
No system of morality could he ever understand; and of the
fourteen sects of religion that are permitted in Japan, the
only discipline he could imbibe was a superstitious devotion
for Fauk-basi, the temple of the white horse.   This, indeed,
was neither the fruit of doctrine, nor the result of reason;
but a real instinct, implanted in his nature for fulfilling the
ends of Providence.   His person was extremely awkward;
his eye vacant, though alarmed; his speech thick, and embarrassed; his utterance ungraceful; and his meaning perplexed.
With much difficulty he learned to write his own name, and
that of the dairo; and picked up a smattering of the Chinese
language, which was sometimes used at court.   In his youth,
he freely conversed with women; but, as he advanced in
age he placed his chief felicity in the delights of the table.
He hired cooks from China at an enormous expense, and
drank huge quantities of the strong liquor distilled from rice,
which, by producing repeated intoxication, had an unlucky
effect upon his brain, that was naturally of a loose flimsy
texture.   The immoderate use of this potation was likewise
said to have greatly impaired his retentive faculty; inasmuch as he was subject upon every extraordinary emotion

of spirit, to an involuntary discharge from the last of the intestines.

Such was the character of Fika-kaka, entitled by his birth to a prodigious estate, as well as to the honours of quanbuku, the first hereditary dignity in the empire. In consequence of his high station, he was connected with all the great men in Japan, and used to the court from his infancy. Here it was he became acquainted with young Gothama-baba, his future sovereign; and their souls being congenial, they soon contracted an intimacy, which endured for life. They were like twin particles of matter, which having been divorced from one another by a most violent shock, had floated many thousand years in the ocean of the universe, till at length meeting by accident, and approaching within the spheres of each other's attraction, they rush together with an eager embrace, and continue united ever after.

The favour of the sovereign, added to the natural influence arising from a vast fortune and great alliances, did not fail to elevate Fika-kaka to the most eminent offices of the state, until, at length, he attained to the dignity of cuboy, or chief minister, which virtually comprehends all the rest. Here then was the strangest phenomenon that ever appeared in the political world. A statesman without capacity, or the smallest tincture of human learning : a secretary who could not write ; a financier who did not understand the multiplication table ; and the treasurer of a vast empire who never could balance accounts with his own butler.

He was no sooner, for the diversion of the gods, promoted to the cuboyship, than his vanity was pampered with all sorts of adulation. He was in magnificence extoled above the first Meckaddo, or line of emperors, to whom divine honours had been paid ; equal in wisdom to Tensio-dai-sin, the first founder of the Japanese monarchy ; braver than Whey-vang, of the dynasty of Chew ; more learned than Jacko, the chief pontiff of Japan ; more liberal than Shi-wang-ti, who was possessed of the universal medicine ; and more religious than *Bupo*, alias *Kobot*, who, from a foreign

country, brought with him on a white horse, a book called
Kio, containing the mysteries of his religion.

But by none was he more cultivated than by the bonzas,
or clergy, especially those of the university Frenoxena*, so
renowned for their learning, sermons, and oratory, who actually chose him their supreme director, and every morning
adored him with a very singular rite of worship. This attachment was the more remarkable, as Fika-kaka was known
to favour the sect of Nem-buds-ju, who distinguished themselves by the ceremony of circumcision. Some malicious
people did not scruple to whisper about, that he himself had
privately undergone the operation: but these, to my certain
knowledge, were the suggestions of falsehood and slander.
A slight scarification, indeed, it was once necessary to make,
on account of his health; but this was no ceremony of any
religious worship. The truth was this.—The Nem-buds-ju,
being few in number, and generally hated by the whole nation, had recourse to the protection of Fika-kaka, which
they obtained for a valuable consideration. Then a law was
promulgated in their favour; a step which was so far from
exciting the jealousy of the bonzas, that there was not above
three, out of one hundred and fifty-nine thousand, that
opened their lips in disapprobation of the measure. Such
were the virtue and moderation of the bonzas, and so loth
were they to disoblige their great director Fika-kaka.

What rendered the knot of connection between Dairo
Got-hama-baba, and this cuboy, altogether indissoluble,
was a singular circumstance, which I shall now explain.—
Fika-kaka not only devoted himself entirely to the gratification of his master's prejudices and rapacity, even when they
interfered the most with the interest and reputation of Japan;
but he also submitted personally to his capricious humours
with the most placid resignation. He presented his posteriors to be kicked as regularly as the day revolved; and
presented them not barely with submission, but with all the
appearance of fond desire: and truly this diurnal exposure
was attended with such delectation as he never enjoyed in
any other attitude.

* Vid. Hist. Eccles. Japan, Vol. i.

To explain this matter, I must tell thee, Peacock, that Fika-kaka was from his infancy afflicted with an itching of the podex, which the learned Dr Woodward would have termed *immanis αιδοῖον pruritus*. That great naturalist would have imputed it to a redundancy of cholicy salts, got out of the stomach and guts into the blood, and thrown upon these parts, and he would have attempted to break their collactations with oil, &c. but I, who know the real causes of this disorder, smile at these whims of philosophy.

Be that as it may, certain it is, all the most eminent physicians in Japan were consulted about this strange tickling and tingling, and among these the celebrated Fansey, whose spirit afterwards informed the body of Rabelais. This experienced leech, having prescribed a course of cathartics, balsamics, and sweetners, on the supposition that the blood was tainted with a scorbutical itch, at length found reason to believe that the disease was local. He therefore tried the method of gentle friction: for which purpose he used almost the very same substances which were many centuries after applied by Gargantua to his own posteriors; such as a nightcap, a pillow-bier, a slipper, a poke, a pannier, a beaver, a hen, a cock, a chicken, a calf-skin, a hare-skin, a pigeon, a cormorant, a lawyer's bag, a lamprey, a coif, a lure; nay, even a goose's neck, without finding that *volupté merifique au trou de cul*, which was the portion of the son of Grangousier. In short, there was nothing that gave Fika-kaka such respite from this tormenting titillation as did smearing the parts with thick cream, which was afterwards licked up by the rough tongue of a boar-cat. But the administration of this remedy was once productive of a disagreeable incident. In the meantime, the distemper gaining ground, became so troublesome, that the unfortunate quanbuku was incessantly in the fidgets, and ran about distracted, cackling like a hen in labour.

The source of all this misfortune was the juxta position of two atoms quarrelling for precedency, in this the cuboy's seat of honour. Their pressing and squeesing, and elbowing and jostling, though of no effect in discomposing one another, occasioned all this irritation and titillation in the posteriors of Fika-kaka.—What! dost thou mutter, Peacock? dost thou presume to question my veracity? now, by the indivisible rotundity of an atom, I have a good mind, caitiff, to raise such a buzzing commotion in thy glandula pinealis, that thou shalt run distracted over the face of the earth, like Io when she was stung by Juno's gad-fly! What! thou who has been wrapt from the cradle in visions of mystery and revelation, swallowed impossibilities like lamb's wool, and digested doctrines harder than iron three times quenched in the Ebro! thou to demur at what I assert upon the evidence and faith of my own consciousness and consistency!—Oh! you capitulate! well, then beware of a relapse—you know a relapsed heretic finds no mercy.

I say, while Fika-kaka's podex was the scene of contention between two turbulent atoms, I had the honour to be posted immediately under the nail of the dairo's great toe, which happened one day to itch more than usual for occupation. The cuboy presenting himself at that instant, and turning his face from his master, Got-hama-baba performed the exercise with such uncommon vehemence, that first his slipper, and then his toe-nail flew off, after having made a small breach in the perineum of Fika-kaka. By the same effort, I was divorced from the great toe of the sovereign, and lodged near the great gut of his minister, exactly in the interstice between the two hostile particles, which were thus in some measure restrained from wrangling; though it was not in my power to keep the peace entirely. Nevertheless, Fika-kaka's torture was immediately suspended; and he was even seized with an orgasm of pleasure, analogous to that which characterises the ecstasy of love.

Think not, however, Peacock, that I would adduce this circumstance as a proof that pleasure and pain are mere relations, which can exist only as they are contrasted. No: pleasure and pain are simple independent ideas, incapable of definition; and this which Fika-kaka felt was an ecstasy compounded of positive pleasure ingrafted upon the removal of pain; but whether this positive pleasure depended upon a particular centre of percussion hit upon by accident, or was the inseparable effect of a kicking and scratching conferred by a royal foot and toe, I shall not at present unfold: neither will I demonstrate the *modus operandi* on the nervous papillœ of Fika-kaka's breech, whether by irritation, relaxation, undulation, or vibration.—Were these essential discoveries communicated, human philosophy would become too arrogant. It was but the other day that Newton made shift to dive into some subaltern laws of matter; to explain the revolution of the planets, and analyze the composition of light; and ever since, that reptile man has believed itself a demi-god.—I hope to see the day when the petulant philosopher shall be driven back to his Categories, and the Organum universale of Aristotle, his οὐσία, his ὕλη, and his ἐντελέμανον.

But waving these digressions, the pleasure which the cuboy felt from the application of the dairo's toe-nail was succeeded by a kind of tension or stiffness, which began to grow troublesome just as he reached his own palace, where the bonzas were assembled to offer up their diurnal incense. Instinct, on this occasion, performed what could hardly have been expected from the most extraordinary talents. At sight of a grizzled beard belonging to one of those venerable doctors, he was struck with the idea of a powerful assuage; and taking him into his cabinet, proposed that he should make oral application to the part affected. The proposal was embraced without hesitation, and the effect even transcended the hope of the cuboy. The osculation itself was soft, warm, emollient, and comfortable; but when the nervous papillæ were gently stroked, and, as it were, fondled by the long elastic, peristaltic, abstersive fibres that composed this reverend verriculum, such a deleetable titillation ensued, that Fika-kaka was quite in raptures.

That which he intended at first for a medicine he now converted into an article of luxury. All the bonzas who enrolled themselves in the number of his dependants, whether old or young, black or fair, rough or smooth, were enjoined every day to perform this additional and posterior rite of worship, so productive of delight to the cuboy, that he was every morning impatient to receive the dairo's calcitration, or rather his pedestrian digitation; after which he flew with all the eagerness of desire to the subsequent part of his entertainment.

The transports thus produced seemed to disarrange his whole nervous system, and produce an odd kind of revolution in his fancy; for though he was naturally grave, and indeed overwhelmed with constitutional hebetude, he became, in consequence of this periodical tickling, the most giddy pert buffoon in nature. All was grinning, giggling, laughing, and pratting, except when his fears intervened; then he started and stared, and cursed and prayed, by turns. There was but one barber in the whole empire, that would undertake to shave him, so ticklish and unsteady he was under the hands of the operator.—He could not sit above one minute in the same attitude, or on the same seat; but shifted about from couch to chair, from chair to stool, from stool to close-stool, with incessant rotation; and all the time gave audience to those who solicited his favour and protection. To all and several he promised his best offices, and confirmed these promises with oaths and protestations. One he shook by the hand; another he hugged; a third he kissed on both sides the face; with a fourth he whispered; a fifth he honoured with a familiar horse-laugh. He never had courage to refuse even that which he could not possibly grant; and at last his tongue actually forgot how to pronounce the negative particle: but as in the English language two negatives amount to an affirmative, five hundred affirmatives in the mouth of Fika-kaka did not altogether destroy the efficacy of simple negation. A promise five hundred times repeated, and at every repetition confirmed by an oath, barely amounted to a computable chance of performance.

It must be allowed, however, he promoted a great number of bonzas, and in this promotion he manifested an uncommon taste. They were preferred according to the colour of their beards. He found, by experience, that beards of different colours yielded him different degrees of pleasure in the fric-

tion we have described above; and the provision he made
for each was in proportion to the satisfaction the candidate
could afford.   The sensation ensuing from the contact of a
grey beard was soft and delicate, and agreeably demulcent,
when the parts were unusually inflamed; a red, yellow, or
brindled beard was in request when the business was to thrill
or tingle; but a black beard was of all others the most honoured by Fika-kaka, not only on account of its fleecy feel,
equally spirited and balsamic, but also for another philosophical reason, which I shall now explain.   You know, Peacock, that black colour absorbs the rays of light, and detains
them, as it were, in a repository.   Thus a black beard, like
the back of a black cat, becomes a phosphorus in the dark,
and emits sparkles upon friction.   You must know, that one
of the gravest doctors of the bonzas, who had a private request to make, desired an audience of Fika-kaka in his closet
at night, and the taper falling down by accident, that very
instant, when his beard was in contact with the cuboy's seat
of honour, the electrical snap was heard, and the part illuminated, to the astonishment of the spectators, who looked upon it as a prelude to the apotheosis of Fika-kaka.   Being
made acquainted with this phenomenon, the minister was
exceedingly elevated in his own mind.   He rejoiced in it, as a
communication of some divine efficacy, and raised the happy
bonza to the rank of pontifex maximus, or chief priest, in
the temple of Faku-basi.   In the course of experiments, he
found that all black beards were electrical in the same degree, and being ignorant of philosophy, ascribed it to some
supernatural virtue, in consequence of which, they were promoted as the holiest of the bonzas.   But you and I know,
that such a phosphorus is obtained from the most worthless
and corrupted materials, such as rotten wood, putrified veal,
and stinking whiting.

Fika-kaka, such as I described him, could not possibly
act in the character of cuboy, without the assistance of
counsellors and subalterns, who understood the detail of
government and the forms of business.   He was accordingly
surrounded by a number of satelites, who reflected his lustre

in their several spheres of rotation; and though their immersions and emersions were apparently abrupt and irregular, formed a kind of luminous belt as pale and comfortless as the ring of Saturn, the most distant, cold, and baleful of all the planets.

The most remarkable of these subordinates, was Sti-phi-rum-poo, a man, who, from a low plebeian origin, had raised himself to one of the first offices of the empire, to the dignity of *quo*, or nobleman, and a considerable share of the dairo's personal regard. He owed his whole success to his industry, assiduity, and circumspection. During the former part of his life, he studied the laws of Japan with such severity of application, that, though unassisted by the least gleam of genius, and destitute of the smallest pretension to talent, he made himself master of all the written ordinances, all the established customs, and forms of proceeding in the different tribunals of the empire. In the progress of his vocation, he became an advocate of some eminence, and even acquired reputation for polemical eloquence, though his manner was ever dry, laboured, and unpleasant.—Being elevated to the station of a judge, he so far justified the interest by which he had been promoted, that his honesty was never called in question; and his sentences were generally allowed to be just and upright. He heard causes with the most painful attention, seemed to be indefatigable in his researches after truth; and though he was forbidding in his aspect, slow in deliberation, tedious in discussion, and cold in his address; yet I must own, he was also unbiassed in his decisions. I mean, unbiassed, by any consciousness of sinister motive: for a man may be biassed by the nature of his disposition, as well as by prejudices acquired, and yet not guilty of intentional partiality. Sti-phi-rum-poo was scrupulously just, according to his own ideas of justice, and consequently well qualified to decide in common controversies. But in delicate cases, which required an uncommon share of penetration; when the province of a supreme judge is to mitigate the severity, and sometimes even deviate from the dead letter of the common law, in favour of particular

institutions, or of humanity in general; he had neither
genius to enlighten his understanding, sentiment to elevate
his mind, nor courage to surmount the petty inclosures of
ordinary practice. He was accused of avarice and cruelty;
but, in fact, these were not active passions in his heart. The
conduct which seemed to justify these imputations, was
wholly owing to a total want of taste and generosity. The
nature of his post furnished him with opportunities to accumulate riches; and as the narrowness of his mind admitted
no ideas of elegance or refined pleasure, he knew not how
to use his wealth so as to avoid the charge of a sordid disposition. His temper was not rapacious but attentive: he
knew not the use of wealth, and therefore did not use it at
all; but was in this particular neither better nor worse than
a strong-box for the convenience and advantage of his heir.
The appearance of cruelty remarkable in his counsels, re-
lating to some wretched insurgents who had been taken in
open rebellion, and the rancorous pleasure he seemed to feel
in pronouncing sentence of death by self-exenteration,* was
in fact the gratification of a dastardly heart, which had never
acknowledged the least impulse of any liberal sentiment.
This being the case, mankind ought not to impute that to
his guilt which was, in effect, the consequence of his infirmity. A man might, with equal justice, be punished for
being purblind. Sti-phi-ram-poo was much more culpable
for seeking to shine in a sphere for which nature never intended him; I mean for commencing statesman, and inter-
meddling in the machine of government; yet even into this
character he was forced, as it were, by the opinion and injunctions of Fika-kaka, who employed him at first in making speeches for the dairo, which that prince used to pronounce in public at certain seasons of the year. These
speeches being tolerably well received by the populace, the
cuboy conceived an extraordinary opinion of his talents,
and thought him extremely well qualified to ease him of
great part of the burden of government. He found him very

* A gentleman capitally convicted in Japan is allowed the privilege of anti-
cipating the common executioner, by ripping out his own bowels

well disposed to engage heartily in his interests. Then he
was admitted to the obsculation *a posteriori*: and though
his beard was not black, but rather of a subfuscan hue, he
managed it with such dexterity, that Fika-kaka declared
the salute gave him unspeakable pleasure; while the by-
standers protested that the contact produced, not simply
electrical sparks or scintillations, but even a perfect irradia-
tion, which seemed altogether supernatural. From this moment Sti-phi-rum-poo was initiated in the mysteries of the
cabinet, and even introduced to the person of the dairo Got-
hama-baba, whose pedestrian favours he shared with his
new patron. It was observed, however, that even after his
promotion and nobilitation, he still retained his original
awkwardness, and never could acquire that graceful ease
of attitude with which the cuboy presented his parts averse
to the contemplation of his sovereign. Indeed the minister's
body was so well moulded for the celebration of the rite, that
one would have imagined nature had formed him expressly
for that purpose, with his head and body projecting forwards,
so as to form an angle of forty-five with the horizon, while
the gluteal muscles swelled backwards as if ambitious to meet
half-way the imperial encounter.

The third connection that strengthened this political band
was Nin-kom-poo-po, commander of the *fund*, or navy of
Japan, who, if ever man was, might surely be termed the
child of fortune. He was bred to the sea from his infancy,
and, in the course of pacific service, rose to the command of
a jonkh, when he was so lucky as to detect a crew of pirates
employed on a desolate shore, in concealing a hoard of money which they had taken from the merchants of Corea.
Nin-kom-poo-po falling in with them at night, attacked
them unawares, and having obtained an easy victory, carried off the treasure. I cannot help being amused at the
folly of you silly mortals, when I recollect the transports of
the people at the return of this fortunate officer, with a paltry
mass of silver, parading in covered waggons, escorted by
his crew in arms. The whole city of Meaco resounded with
acclamation; and Nin-kom-poo-po was extolled as the

greatest hero that ever the empire of Japan produced. The cuboy honoured him with five kisses in public; accepted of the osculation in private, recommended him in the strongest terms to the dairo, who promoted him to the rank of Sey-seo-gun, or general at sea. He professed himself as adherent to the cuboy, entered into a strict alliance with Sti-phi-rum poo, and the whole management of the *fune* was consigned into his hands. With respect to his understanding, it was just sufficient to comprehend the duties of a common mariner, and to follow the ordinary route of the most sordid avarice. As to his heart, he might be said to be in a state of total apathy, without principle or passion; for I cannot afford the name of passion to such a vile appetite as an insatiable thrist for lucre. He was, indeed, so cold and forbidding, that, in Japan, the people distinguished him by a nick-name equivalent to the English word Salamander; not that he was inclined to live in fire, but that the coldness of his heart would have extinguished any fire it had approached. Some individuals imagined he had been begot upon a mermaid by a sailor of Kamschatka; but this was a mere fable. I can assure you, however, that when his lips were in contact with the cuboy's posteriors, Fika-kaka's teeth were seen to chatter. The pride of this animal was equal to his frigidity. He affected to establish new regulations at the council where he presided: he treated his equals with insolence, and his superiors with contempt. Other people generally rejoice in obliging their fellow-creatures, when they can do it without prejudice to their own interest. Nin-com-poo-po had a repulsive power in his disposition; and seemed to take pleasure in denying a request. When this vain creature, selfish, inelegant, arrogant, and uncouth, appeared in all his trappings at the dairo's court, upon a festival, he might have been justly compared to a Lapland idol of ice, adorned with a profusion of brass leaf and trinkets of pewter. In the direction of the *fune*, he was provided with a certain number of assessors, counsellors, or co-adjutors; but these he never consulted, more than if they had been wooden images. He distributed his commands among his own dependants; and left all the forms of the office to the care of the scribe, who thus became so necessary, that his influence sometimes had well nigh interfered with that of the president; nay, they have been seen, like the electrical spheres of two bodies, repelling each other. Hence, it was observed, that the office of the sey-seo-gun-siality resembled the serpent called amphisbæna, which, contrary to the formation of other animals in head and tail, has a head where the tail should be. Well, indeed, might they compare them to a serpent, in creeping, cunning, coldness, and venom; but the comparison would have held with more propriety had nature produced a serpent without ever a head at all.

The fourth who contributed his credit and capacity to this coalition, was Foksi-roku, a man who greatly surpassed them all in the science of politics, bold, subtle, interested, insinuating, ambitious, and indefatigable. An adventurer from his cradle; a latitudinarian in principle, a libertine in morals, without the advantages of birth, fortune, character, or interest; by his own natural sagacity, a close attention to the follies and foibles of mankind, a projecting spirit, an invincible assurance, and an obstinacy of perseverance, proof against all the shocks of disappointment and repulse; he forced himself, as it were, into the scale of preferment; and being found equally capable and compliant, rose to high offices of trust and profit, detested by the people, as one of the most desperate tools of a wicked administration; and odious to his colleagues in the m——y, for his superior talents, his restless ambition, and the uncertainty of his attachment.

As interest prompted him, he hovered between the triumvirate we have described, and another knot of competitors for the ad——n, headed by Quamba-cun-dono, a great quo, related to the dairo, who had bore the supreme command in the army, and was styled fatsman*, κατ' ἐξοχὴν, or by way of eminence. This accomplished prince was not only the greatest in his mind, but also the greatest in his person of all the subjects of Japan; and whereas your Shak-

* Vide Kempfer, Amœnitat. Japan.

speare makes Falstaff urge it as a plea in his own favour,
that as he had more flesh, so likewise he had more frailty
than other men: I may justly convert the proposition in favour of Quamba-cun-dono, and affirm, that as he had
more flesh, so he had more virtue than any other Japanese;
more bowels, more humanity, more beneficence, more affability. He was undoubtedly, for a fatsman, the most courteous, the most gallant, the most elegant, generous, and
munificent quo that ever adorned the court of Japan. So
consummate in the art of war, that the whole world could
not produce a general to match him in foresight, vigilance,
conduct, and ability. Indeed his intellects were so extraordinary and extensive, that he seemed to sentimentise at
every pore, and to have the faculty of thinking diffused all over his frame, even to his fingers ends; or, as the
Latins call it *ad unguem:* nay, so wonderful was his or-
ganical conformation, that, in the opinion of many Japanese
philosophers, his whole body was enveloped in a kind of
poultice of brain, and that if he had lost his head in battle
the damage with regard to his power of reflection would
have been scarce perceptible. After he had achieved many
glorious exploits in a war against the Chinese on the continent, he was sent with a strong army to quell a dangerous insurrection in the northern parts of Ximo, which is
one of the Japanese islands. He accordingly by his valour
crushed the rebellion; and afterwards, by dint of clemency
and discretion, extinguished the last embers of disaffection.
When the insurgents were defeated, dispersed, and disarmed, and a sufficient number selected for example, his humanity emerged, and took full possession of his breast. He
considered them as wretched men misled by false principles
of honour, and sympathized with their distress: he pitied
them as men and fellow-citizens: he regarded them as useful fellow-subjects, who might be reclaimed and remitted to
the community. Instead of sending out the ministers of
blood, rapine, and revenge, to ravage, burn, and destroy,
without distinction of age, sex, or principle; he extended
the arms of mercy to all who would embrace that indulg-

once : he protected the lives and habitations of the helpless, and diminished the number of the malcontents much more effectually by his benevolence than by his sword.

The southern Japanese had been terribly alarmed at this insurrection, and, in the first transports of their deliverance, voluntarily taxed themselves with a considerable yearly tribute to the hero Quamba-cun-dono. In all probability, they would not have appeared so grateful, had they staid to see the effects of his merciful disposition towards the vanquished rebels ; for mercy is surely no attribute of the Japanese, considered as a people. Indeed, nothing could form a more striking contrast than appeared in the transactions in the northern and southern parts of the empire at this juncture. While the amiable Quamba-cun-dono, was employed in the godlike office of gathering together, and cherishing under his wings the poor, dispersed, forlorn widows and orphans, whom the savage hand of war had deprived of parent, husband, home, and sustenance ; while he, in the north, gathered these miserable creatures, even as a hen gathereth her chickens ; Sti-phi-rum-poo, and other judges in the south, were condemning such of their parents and husbands, as survived the sword, to crucifixion, cauldrons of boiling oil, or exenteration ; and the people were indulging their appetites by feasting upon the viscera thus extracted. The liver of a Ximian was in such request at this period, that if the market had been properly managed and supplied, this delicacy would have sold for two obans a pound, or about four pounds sterling. The troops in the north might have provided at the rate of a thousand head per month for the demand of Meaco ; and though the other parts of the carcase would not have sold at so high price as the liver, heart, harrigals, sweet-bread, and pope's eye ; yet the whole, upon an average, would have fetched at the rate of three hundred pounds a-head ; especially if those animals, which are but poorly fed in their own country, had been fattened up and kept upon hard meat for the slaughter. This new branch of traffic would have produced about three hundred and sixty thousand pounds annually ; for the rebellion might easily have been fomented from year to year; and consequently it would have yielded a considerable addition to the emperor's revenue, by a proper taxation.

The philosophers of Japan were divided in their opinions concerning this new taste for Ximian flesh, which suddenly sprung up among the Japanese. Some ascribed it to a principle of hatred and revenge, agreeable to the common expression of animosity among the multitude,—'You dog, I'll have your liver.' Others imputed it to a notion analogous to the vulgar conceit, that the liver of a mad dog being eaten, is a preventive against madness; ergo, the liver of a traitor is an antidote against treason. A third sort derived this strange appetite from the belief of the Americans, who imagine they shall inherit all the virtues of the enemies they devour; and a fourth affirmed, that the demand for this dainty arose from a very high and peculiar flavour in Ximian flesh, which flavour was discovered by accident: moreover, there were not wanting some who supposed this banquet was a kind of sacrifice to the powers of sorcery; as we find that one of the ingredients of the charm prepared in Shakspeare's cauldron was 'the liver of a blaspheming Jew:' and indeed it is not at all improbable that the liver of a rebellious Ximian might be altogether as effectual. I know that Fika-kaka was stimulated by curiosity to try the experiment, and held divers consultations with his cooks on this subject. They all declared in favour of the trial; and it was accordingly presented at the table, where the cuboy eat of it to such excess as to produce a surfeit. He underwent a severe evacuation both ways, attended with cold sweats and swoonings. In a word, his agony was so violent, that he ever after loathed the sight of Ximian flesh, whether dead or alive.

With the fatsman Quamba-cun-dono was connected another quo called Gotto-mio, viceroy of Xicoco, one of the islands of Japan. If his understanding had been as large as his fortune, and his temper a little more tractable, he would have been a dangerous rival to the cuboy. But if their brains had been weighed against each other, the nineteenth part of a grain would have turned either scale; and as Fika-kaka had negative qualities, which supported and extended his personal influence, so Gotto-mio had positive powers, that defended him from all approaches of popularity. His pride was of the insolent order; his temper extremely irrascible; and his avarice quite rapacious; nay, he is said to have once declined the honour of a kicking from the dairo. Conceited of his own talents, he affected to harangue in the council of twenty-eight; but his ideas were embarrassed; his language was mean; and his elocution more discordant than the braying of fifty asses. When Fika-kaka addressed himself to speech, an agreeable simper played upon the countenances of all the audience; but soon as Gotto-mio stood up, every spectator raised his thumbs to his ears, as it were instinctively. The dairo Got-hama-baba, by the advice of the cuboy, sent him over to govern the people of Xicoco, and a more effectual method could not have been taken to mortify his arrogance. His deportment was so insolent, his economy so sordid, and his government so arbitrary, that those islanders, who are remarkably ferocious and impatient, expressed their hatred and contempt of him on every occasion. His quanbukuship was hardly safe from outrage in the midst of his guards; and a cross was actually erected for the execution of his favourite kow-kin, who escaped with some difficulty to the island of Niphon, whither also his patron soon followed him, attended by the curses of the people whom he had been sent to rule.

He who presided at the council of twenty-eight was called Soo-san-sin-o, an old experienced shrewd politician, who conveyed more sense in one single sentence, than could have been distilled from all the other brains in council, had they been macerated in one alembic. He was a man of extensive learning and elegant taste. He saw through the characters of his fellow-labourers in the ad——n. He laughed at the folly of one faction, and detested the arrogance and presumption of the other. In an assembly of sensible men, his talents would have shone with superior lustre: but at the council of twenty-eight, they were obscured by the thick clouds of ignorance that enveloped his brethren. The dairo had a personal respect for him, and is said to have conferred frequent favours on his posteriors in private. He kicked the cuboy often *ex officio*, as a husband thinks it incumbent upon him to caress his wife: but he kicked the president for pleasure, as a voluptuary embraces his mistress. Soo-san-sin-o, conscious that he had no family interest to support him in cabals among the people, and, careless of his country's fate, resolved to enjoy the comforts of life in quiet. He laughed and quaffed with his select companions in private; received his appointments thankfully; and swam with the tide of politics as it happened to flow. It was pretty extraordinary that the wisest man should be the greatest cypher: but such was the will of the gods.

Besides these great luminaries that enlightened the cabinet of Japan, I shall have occasion, in the course of my narrative, to describe many other stars of an inferior order. At this board there was as great a variety of characters as we find in the celebrated table of Cebes. Nay, indeed, what was objected to the philosopher, might have been more justly said of the Japanese councils. There was neither invention, unity, nor design, among them. They consisted of mobs of sauntering, strolling, vagrant, and ridiculous, politicians. Their schemes were absurd, and their deliberations like the sketches of anarchy. All was bellowing, bleating, braying, grinning, grumbling, confusion, and uproar. It was more like a dream of chaos than a picture of human life. If the ΔAIMON, or genius, was wanting, it must be owned that Fika-kaka exactly answered Cebe's description of ΤΥΧΗ, or fortune, blind and frantic, running about every where; giving to some, and taking from others, without rule or distinction; while her emblem of the round stone fairly shew his *giddy* nature; καλῶς μηνύει φύσιν αὐτῆς. Here, however, one might have seen many other figures of the painter's allegory; such as Deception tendering the cup of ignorance and error, opinions, and appetites; Disappointment and Anguish; Debauchery, Profligacy, Gluttony, and Adulation; Luxury, Fraud, Rapine, Perjury, and Sacrilege; but not the least traces of the virtues which are described in the group of true education, and in the grove of happiness.

The two factions that divided the council of Japan, though inveterate enemies to each other, heartily and cordially concurred in one particular, which was the worship established in the temple of Fakku-basi, or the white horse. This was the orthodox faith in Japan, and was certainly founded, as S^t. Paul saith of the christian religion, upon the evidence of things not seen. All the votaries of this superstition of Fakku-basi subscribed and swore to the following creed implicitly, without hesitation or mental reservation.—
' I believe in the white horse, that he descended from heaven, and sojourned in Jeddo, which is the land of promise. I believe in *Bupo* his apostle, who first declared to the children of Niphon the glad tidings of the gospel of Fakku-basi. I believe that the white horse was begot by a black mule, and brought forth by a green dragon; that his head is of silver, and his hoofs are of brass; that he eats gold as provender, and discharges diamonds as dung; that the Japanese are ordained and predestined to furnish him with food, and the people of Jeddo to clear away his litter. I believe that the island of Niphon is joined to the continent of Jeddo, and that whoever thinks otherwise shall be damned to all eternity. I believe that the smallest portion of matter may be practically divided *ad infinitum*; that equal quantities taken from equal quantities, an unequal quantity will remain; that two and two make seven; that the sun rules the night, the stars the day; and the moon is made of green cheese. Finally, I believe that a man cannot be saved without devoting his goods and his chattels, his children, relations, and friends; his senses and ideas, his soul and his body, to the religion of the white horse, as it is prescribed in the ritual of Fakku-basi.' These are the tenets which the Japanese ministers swallowed as glib as the English clergy swallowed the thirty-nine articles.

Having thus characterised the chiefs that disputed the administration, or, in other words, the empire of Japan, I shall now proceed to a plain narration of historical incidents, with-

out pretending to philosophise like H——e, or dogmatise
like S——tt. I shall only tell thee, Nathaniel, that Britain
never gave birth but to two historians worthy of credit, and
they were Taliessin and Geoffrey of Monmouth. I'll tell you
another secret: the whole world has never been able to produce six good historians. Herodotus is fabulous even to a
proverb; Thucydides is perplexed, obscure, and unimportant; Polybius is dry and inelegant, Livy superficial, and
Tacitus a coxcomb; Guicciardini wants interest, Davila digestion, and Sarpi truth. In the whole catalogue of French
historians, there is not one of tolerable authenticity.

In the year of the period Foggien one hundred and fifty-
four, the tranquillity of Japan was interrupted by the encroachments of the Chinese adventurers, who made descents
upon certain islands belonging to the Japanese, a great way
to the southward of Xicoco. They even settled colonies, and
built forts on some of them, while the two empires were at
peace with each other. When the Japanese governors ex-
postulated with the Chinese officers on this intrusion, they
were treated with ridicule and contempt: then they had recourse to force of arms, and some skirmishes were fought
with various success. When the tidings of these hostilities
arrived at Meaco, the whole council of twenty-eight was
overwhelmed with fear and confusion. The dairo kicked
them all round, not from passion, but by way of giving an
animating fillip to their deliberative faculties. The disputes
had happened in the island of Fatsissio; but there were only
three members of the council who knew that Fatsissio was an
island, although the commerce there carried on was of the
utmost importance to the empire of Japan. They were so
much in the dark with respect to its situation. Fika-kaka,
on the supposition that it adjoined to the coast of Corea, expressed his apprehension that the Chinese would invade it
with a numerous army; and was so transported when Foksi-
roku assured him it was an island at a vast distance from any
continent, that he kissed him five times in the face of the
whole council; and his royal master, Got-hama-baba, swore
he should be indulged with a double portion of kicking at

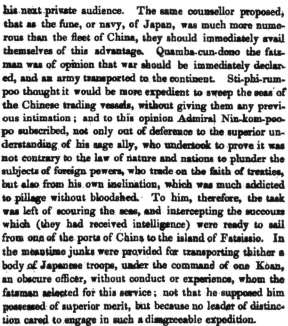

his next private audience. The same counsellor proposed, that as the fune, or navy, of Japan, was much more numerous than the fleet of China, they should immediately avail themselves of this advantage. Quamba-cun-dono the fatsman was of opinion that war should be immediately declared, and an army transported to the continent. Sti-phi-rumpoo thought it would be more expedient to sweep the seas' of the Chinese trading vessels, without giving them any previous intimation; and to this opinion Admiral Nin-kom-poo-po subscribed, not only out of deference to the superior understanding of his sage ally, who undertook to prove it was not contrary to the law of nature and nations to plunder the subjects of foreign powers, who trade on the faith of treaties, but also from his own inclination, which was much addicted to pillage without bloodshed. To him, therefore, the task was left of scouring the seas, and intercepting the succours which (they had received intelligence) were ready to sail from one of the ports of China to the island of Fatsissio. In the meantime junks were provided for transporting thither a body of Japanese troops, under the command of one Koan, an obscure officer, without conduct or experience, whom the fatsman selected for this service; not that he supposed him possessed of superior merit, but because no leader of distinction cared to engage in such a disagreeable expedition.

Nin-kom-poo-po acted according to the justest ideas which had been formed of his understanding. He let loose his cruisers among the merchant ships of China, and the harbours of Japan were quickly filled with prizes and prisoners. The Chinese exclaimed against these proceedings as the most perfidious acts of piracy; and all the other powers of Asia beheld them with astonishment. But the consummate wisdom of the sea sey-seo-gun appeared most conspicuous in another stroke of generalship which he now struck. Instead of blocking up in the Chinese harbour the succours destined to reinforce the enemy in Fatsissio, until they should be driven from their encroachments on that island, he very wisely sent a strong squadron of fune to cruise in the open sea, midway between China and Fatsissio, in the most tempestuous season of the year, when the fogs are so thick and so constant in that latitude as to rival the darkness of a winter night; and supported the feasibility of this scheme in council, by observing, that the enemy would be thus decoyed from their harbour, and undoubtedly intercepted in their passage by the Japanese squadron. This plan was applauded as one of the most ingenious stratagems that ever was devised; and Fika-kaka insisted upon kissing his posteriors, as the most honourable mark of his approbation.

Philosophers have observed, that the motives of actions are not to be estimated by events. Fortune did not altogether fulfil the expectations of the council. General Koan suffered himself and his army to be decoyed into the middle of a wood, where they stood like sheep in the shambles, to be slaughtered by an unseen enemy. The Chinese succours perceiving their harbour open, set sail for Fatsissio, which they reached in safety, by changing their course about one degree from the common route; while the Japanese fune continued cruising among the fogs, until the ships were shattered by storms, and the crews more than half destroyed by cold and distemper.

When the news of these disasters arrived, great commotion arose in the council. The dairo Got-hama-baba fluttered, and clucked, and cackled, and hissed, like a goose disturbed in the act of incubation. Quamba-cun-dono shed bitter tears, the cuboy snivelled and sobbed, Sti-phi-rum-poo groaned, Gotto-mio swore, but the sea sey-seo-gun Nin-kom-poo-po underwent no alteration. He sat as the emblem of insensibility, fixed as the north star, and as cold as that luminary, sending forth emanations of frigidity. Fika-kaka mistaking this congelation for fortitude, went round and embraced him where he sat, exclaiming,—'My dear day, sey-seo-gun, what would you advise in this dilemma?' But the contact had almost cost him his life; for the touch of Nin-kom-poo-po, thus congealed, had the same effect as that of the fish called torpor. The cuboy's whole body was instantly benumbed; and if his friends had not instantly poured down his throat a considerable quantity of strong spirit, the circulation would have ceased. This is what philosophers call a generation of cold, which became so intense, that the mercury in a Japanese thermometer, constructed on the same principles that were afterwards adopted by Fahrenheit, and fixed in the apartment, immediately sank thirty degrees below the freezing point.

The first astonishment of the council was succeeded by critical remarks and argumentation. The dairo consoled himself by observing, that his troops made a very soldierly appearance as they lay on the field in their new clothing, smart caps and clean buskins; and that the enemy allowed they had never seen beards and whiskers in better order. He then declared, that, should a war ensue with China, he would go abroad and expose himself for the glory of Japan. Foksi-roku expressed his surprise that a general should march his army through a wood in an unknown country, without having it first reconnoitered; but the fatzman assured him that was a practice never admitted into the discipline of Japan. Gotto-mio swore the man was mad to stand with his men, like oxen in a stall, to be knocked on the head, without using any means of defence. 'Why the devil,' said he, 'did not he either retreat, or advance to close engagement with the handful of Chinese who formed the ambuscade?' 'I hope, my dear Quanbuku,' replied the fatzman, 'that the troops of Japan will always stand without flinching. I should have been mortified beyond measure had they retreated without seeing the face of the enemy: that would have been a disgrace which never befel any troops formed under my direction; and as for advancing, the ground would not permit any manœuvre of that nature. They were engaged in a *cul de sac,* where they could not form either in hollow square, front line, potence, column, or platoon. It was the fortune of war, and they bore it like men:—we shall be more fortunate on another occasion.' The president Soo-san-sin-o took notice, that if there had been one spaniel in the whole Japanese army, this disaster could not have happened, as the animal would have beat the bushes, and discovered the ambuscade. He therefore proposed, that if the war was to be prosecuted in Fatsissio, which is a country overgrown with wood, a number of blood-hounds might be provided and sent over, to run upon the foot in the front and on the flanks of the army, when it should be on its march through such impediments. Quamba-cun-dono declared, that soldiers had much better die in the bed of honour, than be saved and victorious by such an unmilitary expedient; that such a proposal was so contrary to the rules of war, and the scheme of inlisting dogs so derogatory from the dignity of the service, that, if ever it should be embraced, he would resign his command, and spend the remainder of his life in retirement. This canine project was equally disliked by the dairo, who approved of the fatzman's objection, and sealed his approbation with a pedestrian salute of such momentum, that the fatzman could hardly stand under the weight of the compliment. It was agreed that new levies should be made, and a new squadron of fune equipped with all expedition; and thus the assembly broke up.

Fortune had not yet sufficiently humbled the pride of Japan. That body of Chinese which defeated Koan, made several conquests in Fatsissio, and seemed to be in a fair way of reducing the whole island. Yet the court of China, not satisfied with this success, resolved to strike a blow that should be equally humiliating to the Japanese, in another part of the world. Having by specious remonstrances already prepossessed all the neighbouring nations against the government of Japan, as the patrons of perfidy and piracy, they fitted out an armament, which was intended to subdue the island of Motao on the coast of Corea, which the Japanese had taken in a former war, and now occupied at a very great expense, as a place of the utmost importance to the commerce of the empire. Repeated advices of the enemy's design were sent from different parts to the m——y of Japan; but they seemed all overwhelmed by such a lethargy of infatuation, that no measures of prevention were concerted.

Such was the opinion of the people; but the truth is, they were fast asleep. The Japanese hold with the ancient Greeks and modern Americans, that dreams are from heaven; and in any perplexing emergency, they, like the Indians, Jews, and natives of Madagascar, have recourse to dreaming as to an oracle. These dreams or divinations are preceded by certain religious rites, analogous to the ceremony of the ephod, the urim and the thummim. The rites were religiously performed in the council of twenty-eight; and a deep sleep overpowered the dairo and all his counsellors.

Got-hama-baba, the emperor, who reposed his head upon the pillowy sides of Quamba-cun-dono, dreamed that he was sacrificing in the temple of Fakka-basi, and saw the deity of the white horse devouring pearls by the bushel at one end, and voiding corruption by the ton at the other. The fatsman dreamed that a great number of Chinese cooks were busy buttering his brains. Gotto-mio dreamed of lending money, and borrowing sense. Sti-phi-rum-poo thought he had procured a new law for clapping padlocks upon the chastity of all the females of Japan, under twenty, of which padlocks he himself kept the keys. Nin-kom-poo-po dreamed he was metamorphosed into a sea-lion, in pursuit of a shole of golden gudgeons. *One did laugh in't sleep, and one cried murder.* The first was Soo-san-sin-o, who had precisely the same vision that disturbed the imagination of the cuboy. He thought he saw the face of a right reverend prelate of the bonzas united with, and growing to, the posteriors of the minister. Fika-kaka underwent the same disagreeable illusion, with this aggravating circumstance, that he already felt the teeth of the said bonza. The president laughed aloud at the ridiculous phenomenon: the cuboy exclaimed, in the terror of being encumbered with such a monstrous appendage. It was not without some reason he cried ' murder !' Fok-si-roku, who happened to sleep on the next chair, dreamed of money-bags, places, and reversions; and, in the transport of his eagerness, laid fast hold on the trunk-breeches of the cuboy, including certain fundamentals, which he grasped so violently, as to excite pain, and extort the exclamation from Fika-kaka, even in his sleep.

The council being at last waked by the clamours of the people, who surrounded the palace, and proclaimed that

Motao was in danger of an invasion; the sea sey-seo-gun
Nin-kom-poo-po, was ordered to fit out a fleet of fune, for
the relief of that island; and directions were given that the
commander of these fune should, in his voyage, touch at the
garrison of Foutao, and take on board from thence a certain
number of troops, to reinforce the Japanese governor of the
place that was in danger. Nin-kom-poo-po for this service
chose the commander Bihn-goh, a man who had never signalised himself by any act of valour. He sent him out with
a squadron of fune ill-manned, wretchedly provided, and
inferior in number to the fleet of China, which was by this
time known to be assembled, in order to support the invasion
of the island of Motao. He sailed, nevertheless, on this expedition, and touched at the garrison of Foutao, to take in
the reinforcement; but the orders sent for this purpose from
Nob-od-i, minister for the department of war, appeared so
contradictory and absurd, that they could not possibly be
obeyed; so that Bihn-goh proceeded without the reinforcement towards Motao, the principal fortress of which was by
this time invested. He had been accidentally joined by a
few cruisers, which rendered him equal in strength to the Chinese squadron, which he now descried. Both commanders
seemed afraid of each other. The fleets, however, engaged;
but little damage was done to either. They parted, as if by
consent. Bihn-goh made the best of his way back to Foutao,
without making the least attempt to succour, or open a communication with Fi-de-ta-da, the governor of Motao, who,
looking upon himself as abandoned by his country, surren-
dered his fortress with the whole island, to the Chinese general. These disgraces happening on the back of the Fatsissian disasters, raised a prodigious ferment in Japan, and
the ministry had almost sunk under the first fury of the people's resentment. They not only exclaimed against the folly
of the administration, but they also accused them of treachery; and seemed to think that the glory and advantage of
the empire had been betrayed. What increased the commotion, was the terror of an invasion, with which the Chinese threatened the islands of Japan. The terrors of Fiks-

kaka had already cost him two pair of trunk hose, which
were defiled by sudden sallies or irruptions from the postern
of his microcosm; and these were attended with such noisome effluvia, that the bonzas could not perform the barbal
abstersion without marks of abhorrence.   The emperor himself was seen to stop his nose, and turn away his head, when
he approached him to perform the pedestrian exercise.

Here I intended to insert a dissertation on trowsers, or trunk-
breeches, called by the Greeks, βραχω, et περιζωματα ; by the
Latins, *braccæ laxæ ;* by the Spaniards, *bragas anchas ;* by
the Italians, *calzone largo ;* by the French, *haut de chaussees ;*
by the Saxons, *brœcce ;* by the Swedes, *brackor ;* by the Irish,
briechan ; by the Celtæ, *brag ;* and by the Japenese, *bra-ak.*
I could make some curious discoveries touching the analogy
between the Περιζωματα and Ζωναι γυναϊαν, and point out the
precise time at which the Grecian women began to wear the
breeches.   I would have demonstrated that the *cingulum
muliebre* was originally no other than the wife's literally
wearing the husband's trowsers at certain *orgia,* as a mark of
dominion transferred, *pro tempore,* to the female.   I would
have drawn a curious parallel between the Ζωναι of the Greek,
and the *shim* or middle cloth worn by the black ladies in
Guinea.   I would have proved that breeches were not first used
to defend the central parts from the injuries of the weather,
inasmuch as they were first worn by the orientals in a warm
climate; as you may see in Persius, *braccatis illita medis—
porticus.* I would have shewn that breeches were first brought
from Asia to the northern parts of Europe, by the Celtæ,
sprung from the ancient Gomanaus: that trowsers were
worn in Scotland long before the time of Pythagoras ; and
indeed we are told by Jamblycus, that Abaris, the famous
Highland philosopher, contemporary, and personally acquainted with the sage of Crotona, wore long trowsers.   I myself can attest the truth of that description, as I well remember the person and habit of that learned mountaineer.   I
would have explained the reasons that compelled the posterity of those mountaineers to abandon the breeches of their
forefathers, and expose their posteriors to the wind.   I would

have convinced the English antiquaries that the inhabitants
of Yorkshire came originally from the Highlands of Scotland,
before the Scots had laid aside their breeches, and wore this
part of dress, long after their ancestors, as well as the southern Britons, were unbreeched by the Romans.   From this
distinction they acquired the name of *Brigantes, quasi Brag-
antes*; and hence came the verb *to brag*, or boast contemptuously; for the neighbours of the Brigantes being at variance
with that people, used, by way of contumelious defiance,
when they saw any of them passing or repassing, to clap
their hands on their posteriors, and cry *Brag-Brag.*—I
would have drawn a learned comparison between the shield
of Ajax and the sevenfold breeches of a Dutch skipper. Finally, I would have promulgated the original use of trunk-
breeches, which would have led me into a discussion of the
rites of Cloacina, so differently worshipped by the southern
and northern inhabitants of this kingdom.   These disquisitions would have unveiled the mysteries that now conceal
the origin, migration, superstition, language, laws, and connections, of different nations—*sed nunc non erit his locus.* I
shall only observe, that Linschot and others are mistaken in
deriving the Japanese from their neighbours the Chinese;
and that Dr Kempfer is right in his conjecture, supposing
them to have come from Media immediately after the confusion of Babel.   It is no wonder, therefore, that being
Braccatorum filii, they should retain the wide breeches of
their progenitors.

Having dropped these hints concerning the origin of
breeches, I shall now return to the great personage that turned me into this train of thinking.   The council of twenty-
eight being assembled in a great hurry, Fika-kaka sat about
five seconds in silence, having in his countenance nearly the
same expression which you have seen in the face and attitude of Felix on his tribunal, as represented by the facetious
Hogarth, in his print done after the Dutch taste. After
some pause, he rose, and surveying every individual of the
council through a long tube, began a speech to this effect—
' Imperial Got-hama-baba, my ever-glorious master; and

you, ye illustrious nobles of Japan, quanbukus, quos, days, and daygos, my fellows and colleagues, in the work of administration; it is well known to you all, and they are rascals that deny it, I have watched and fasted for the public weal—By G—d, I have deprived myself of two hours of my natural rest, every night for a week together.—Then I have been so hurried with state affairs, that I could not eat a comfortable meal in a whole fortnight: and what rendered this misfortune the greater, my chief cook had dressed an olio *a la Chine*. —I say an olio, my lords, such an olio as never appeared before upon a table in Japan—by the Lord, it cost me fifty obans; and I had not time to taste a morsel.—Well, then, I have watched, that my fellow-subjects should sleep; I have fasted, that they should feed.—I have not only watched and fasted, but I have prayed—no, not much of that—yes, by the Lord, I have prayed, as it were—I have ejaculated.—I have danced and sung at the matsuris, which, you know, are religious rites—I have headed the multitude, and treated all the raggamuffins in Japan.—To be certain, I could not do too much for our most excellent and sublime emperor, an emperor unequalled in wisdom, and unrivalled in generosity. Were I to expatiate from the rising of the sun to the setting thereof, I should not speak half his praise.—O happy nation! O fortunate Japan! happy in such a dairo to wield the sceptre; and, let me add (vanity apart), fortunate in such a cuboy to conduct the administration.—Such a prince! and such a minister!—a ha! my noble friend Soo-san-sin-o, I see your dayship smile.—I know what you think, ha! ha!— Very well, my lord—you may think what you please, but two such head pieces—pardon, my royal master, my presumption in laying our heads together, you wo'n't find again in the whole universe, ha! ha!—I'll be damn'd if you do, ha! ha! ha!'—The tumult without doors was, by this time, increased to such a degree, that the cuboy could utter nothing more *ab anteriori*; and the majority of the members sat aghast in silence. The dairo declared he would throw his cap out of the window into the midst of the populace, and challenge any single man of them to bring it up; but he was dissuaded from hazarding his sacred person in such a manner. Quamba-cun-dono proposed to let loose the guards among the multitude; but Fika-kaka protested he could never agree to an expedient so big with danger to the persons of all present. Sti-phi-rum-poo was of opinion that they should proceed according to law, and indict the leaders of the mob for a riot. Nin kom-poo-po exhorted the dairo and the whole council to take refuse on board the fleet. Gotto-mio sweated in silence: he trembled for his money-bags, and dreaded another encounter with the mob, by whom he had suffered severely in the flesh, upon a former occasion. The president shrugged up his shoulders, and kept his eye fixed upon a postern or back-door. In this general consternation, Foksi-roku stood up, and offered a scheme, which was immediately put in execution. 'The multitude, my lords,' said he, 'is a many-headed monster—it is a Cerberus that must have a sop:—it is a wild-beast, so ravenous that nothing but blood will appease its appetite: it is a whale that must have a barrel for its amusement:—it is a demon to which we must offer up human sacrifice. Now, the question is, who is to be this sop, this barrel, this scape-goat?—Tremble not, illustrious Fika-kaka—be not afraid—your life is of too much consequence. But I perceive that the cuboy is moved—an unsavoury odour assails my nostrils—brief let me be—Bihn-goh must be the victim—happy, if the sacrifice of his single life can appease the commotions of his country. To him let us impute the loss of Matso—Let us, in the meantime, soothe the rabble with solemn promises that national justice shall be done;—let us employ emissaries to mingle in all places of plebeian resort; to puzzle, perplex, and prevaricate: to exaggerate the misconduct of Bihn-goh; to traduce his character with retrospective reproach; strain circumstances to his prejudice; inflame the resentment of the vulgar against that devoted officer; and keep up the flame, by feeding it with continual fuel.'

The speech was heard with universal applause: Foksi-roku was kicked by the dairo, and kissed by the cuboy in token of approbation. The populace were dispersed by means of fair promises. Bihn-goh was put under arrest, and kept as a malefactor in close prison. Agents were employed through the whole metropolis, to vilify his character, and accuse him of cowardice and treachery. Authors were inlisted to defame him in public writings; and mobs hired to hang and burn him in effigy. By these means, the revenge of the people was artfully transferred, and their attention effectually diverted from the ministry, which was the first object of their indignation. At length matters being duly prepared for the exhibition of such an extraordinary spectacle, Bihn-goh underwent a public trial, was unanimously found guilty, and unanimously declared innocent; by the same mouths condemned to death, and recommended to mercy; but mercy was incompatible with the designs of the ad——n. The unfortunate Bihn-goh was crucified for cowardice, and bore his fate with the most heroic courage. His behaviour at his death was so inconsistent with the crime for which he was doomed to die, that the emissaries of the cuboy were fain to propagate a report, that Bihn-goh had bribed a person to represent him at his execution, and be crucified in his stead.

This was a stratagem very well calculated for the meridian of the Japanese populace; and it would have satisfied them entirely, had not their fears been concerned. But the Chinese had for some time been threatening an invasion, the terror of which kept the people of Japan in perpetual agitation and disquiet. They neglected their business, and ran about in distraction, inquiring news, listening to reports, staring, whispering, whimpering, clamouring, neglecting their food, and renouncing their repose. The dairo, who believed the Tartars of Yesso (from whom he himself was descended) had more valour, and skill and honesty, than was possessed by any other nation on earth, took a large body of them into his pay, and brought them over to the island of Niphon, for the defence of his Japanese dominions. The truth is, he had a strong predilection for that people: he had been nursed among them, and sucked it from the nipple. His father had succeeded as heir to a paltry farm in that country,

and there he fitted up a cabin which he preferred to all the
palaces of Meaco and Jeddo.   The son received the first
rudiments of his education among these Tartars, whose
country had given birth to his progenitor Bupo.   He therefore loved their country; he admired their manners, because they were conformable to his own; and he was in
particular captivated by the taste they shewed in trimming
and curling their mustachios.

In full belief that the Yessites stood as high in the estimation of his Japanese subjects as in his own, he imported a
body of them into Niphon, where at first they were received
as saviours and protectors ; but the apprehension of danger
no sooner vanished, than they were exposed to a thousand
insults and mortifications, arising from the natural prejudice
to foreigners, which prevails among the people of Japan.
They were reviled, calumniated, and maltreated in every
different form, by every class of people; and when the
severe season set in, the Japanese refused shelter from the
extremities of the weather, to those very auxiliaries they
had hired to defend every thing that was dear to them, from
the swords of an enemy whom they themselves durst not look
in the face.   In vain Fika-kaka employed a double band of
artists to tickle their noses.   They shut their eyes indeed, as
usual : but their eyes no sooner closed, than their mouths
opened, and out flew the tropes and figures of obloquy and
execretion.   They exclaimed, that they had not bought but
caught the Tartar ; that they had hired the wolves to guard
the sheep ; that they were simple beasts who could not defend themselves from the dog with their own horns; but
what could be expected from a flock which was led by such
a pusillanimous bell-weather ?—In a word, the Yessites were
sent home in disgrace : but the ferment did not subside ; and
the conduct of the administration was summoned before the
venerable tribunal of the populace.

There was one Taycho who had raised himself to great
consideration in this self-constituted college of the mob.   He
was distinguished by a loud voice, an unabashed countenance, a fluency of abuse, and an intrepidity of opposition

to the measures of the cuboy, who was far from being a favourite with the plebeians. Orator Taycho's eloquence was admirably suited to his audience; he roared and he brayed, and he bellowed against the m——r: he threw out personal sarcasms against the dairo himself. He inveighed against his partial attachment to the land of Yesso, which he had more than once manifested to the detriment of Japan: ho inflamed the national prejudice against foreigners; and as he professed an inviolable zeal for the commons of Japan, he became the first demagogue of the empire. The truth is, he generally happened to be on the right side. The partiality of the dairo, the errors, absurdities, and corruption of the ministry, presented such a palpable mark as could not be missed by the arrows of his declamation. This Cerberus had been silenced more than once with a sop; but whether his appetite was not satisfied to the full, or he was still stimulated by the turbulence of his disposition, which would not allow him to rest, he began to shake his chains anew, and open in the old cry; which was a species of music to the mob, as agreeable as the sound of a bag-pipe to a mountaineer of North Briton, or the strum-strum to the swarthy natives of Angola. It was a strain which had the wonderful effect of effacing from the memory of his hearers every idea of his former fickleness and apostacy.

In order to weaken the effect of orator Taycho's harangues, the cuboy had found means to intrude upon the councils of the mob, a native of Ximo called Murat-clami, who had acquired some reputation for eloquence, as an advocate in the tribunals of Japan. He certainly possessed an uncommon share of penetration, with a silver tone of voice, and a great magazine of words and phrases, which flowed from him in a pleasing tide of elocution. He had withal the art of soothing, wheedling, insinuating, and misrepresenting, with such a degree of plausibility, that his talents were admired even by the few who had sense enough to detect his sophistry. He had no idea of principle, and no feeling of humanity. He had renounced the maxims of his family, after having turned them to the best account by execrating the rites of Fakku-basi, or the white horse, in private among malcontents, while he worshipped him in public with the appearance of enthusiastic devotion. When detected in this double dealing, he fairly owned to the cuboy, that he cursed the white horse in private for his private interest, but that he served him in public from inclination.

The cuboy had just sense enough to perceive that he would always be true to his own interest; and therefore he made it his interest to serve the m——y to the full extent of his faculties. Accordingly Mura-clami fought a good battle with orator Taycho, in the occasional assemblies of the populace. But as it is much more easy to inflame than to allay, to accuse than to acquit, to asperse than to purify, to unveil truth than to varnish falsehood; in a word, to patronise a good cause than to support a bad one; the majesty of the mob snuffed up the excrementitious salts of Taycho's invective, until their juglars ached, while they rejected with signs of loathing the flowers of Mura-clami's elocution; just as a citizen of Edinburgh stops his nose when he passes by the shop of a perfumer.

While the constitution of human nature remains unchanged, satire will always be better received than panegyric, in those popular harangues. The Athenians and Romans were better pleased with the philippics of Demosthenes and Tully, than they would have been with all the praise those two orators could have culled from the stores of their eloquence. A man feels a secret satisfaction in seeing his neighbour treated as a rascal. If he be a knave himself (which ten to one is the case), he rejoices to see a character brought down to the level of his own, and a new member added to his society; if he be one degree removed from actual roguery (which is the case with nine-tenths of those who enjoy the reputation of virtue), he indulges himself with the pharisaical consolation, of thanking God he is not like that publican.

But to return from this digression, Mura-clami, though he could not with all his talents maintain any sort of competition with Taycho, in the opinion of the mob; he never-

theless took a more effectual method to weaken the force of
his opposition. He pointed out to Fika-kaka the proper
means for amending the errors of his administration; he
proposed measures for prosecuting the war with vigour; he
projected plans of conquest in Fatsissio; recommended
active officers; forwarded expeditions, and infused such a
spirit into the councils of Japan, as had not before appeared
for some centuries.

But his patron was precluded from the benefit of these
measure, by the obstinate prejudice and precipitation of
the dairo, who valued his Yessian farm above all the empire
of Japan. This precious morsel of inheritance bordered
upon the territories of a Tartar chief called Brut-an-tiffi, a
famous freebooter, who had inured his kurd to bloodshed,
and enriched himself with rapine. Of all mankind he hated
most the dairo, though his kinsman; and sought a pretence
for seizing the farm, which in three days he could have
made his own. The dairo Got-hama-baba was not ignorant
of his sentiments. He trembled for his cabin, when he considered its situation between hawk and buzzard; exposed on
one side to the talons of Brut-an-tiffi, and open on the
other to the incursions of the Chinese, under whose auspices
the said Brut-an-tiffi had acted formerly as a zealous partisan. He had, indeed, in a former quarrel exerted himself
with such activity and rancour, to thwart the politics of the
dairo, and accumulate expenses on the subjects of Niphon,
that he was universally detested through the whole empire of
Japan as a lawless robber, deaf to every suggestion of humanity, respecting no law, restricted by no treaty, scoffing
at all religion, goaded by ambition, instigated by cruelty,
and attended by rapine.

In order to protect the farm from such a dangerous neighbour, Got-hama-baba, by an effort of sagacity peculiar to
himself, granted a large subsidy from the treasury of Japan,
to a remote nation of Mantchoux Tartars, on condition that
they should march to the assistance of his farm, whenever it
should be attacked. With the same sanity of foresight, the
Dutch might engage in a defensive league with the Ottoman

porte, to screen them from the attempts of the most christian king, who is already on their frontiers. Brut-an-tiffi knew his advantage, and was resolved to enjoy it. He had formed a plan of usurpation, which could not be executed without considerable sums of money. He gave the dairo to understand, he was perfectly sensible how much the farm lay at his mercy: then proposed that Got-hama-baba should renounce his subsidiary treaty with the Mantchoux; pay a yearly tribute to him Brut-an-tiffi, in consideration of his forbearing to seize the farm; and maintain an army to protect it on the other side from the irruptions of the Chinese.

Got-hama-baba, alarmed at this declaration, began by his emissaries to sound the inclinations of his Japanese subjects touching a continental war, for the preservation of the farm; but he found them totally averse to this wise system of politics. Taycho, in particular, began to bawl and bellow among the mob, upon the absurdity of attempting to defend a remote cabin, which was not defensible; upon the iniquity of ruining a mighty empire, for the sake of preserving a few barren acres, a naked common, a poor, pitiful, pelting farm, the interest of which, like Aaron's rod, had already, on many occasions, swallowed up all regard and consideration for the advantage of Japan. He inveighed against the shameful and senseless partiality of Got-hama-baba: he mingled menaces with his representations. He expatiated on the folly and pernicious tendency of a continental war: he enlarged upon the independence of Japan, secure in her insular situation. He declared, that not a man should be sent to the continent, nor a subsidy granted to any greedy, mercenary, freebooting Tartar; and threatened, that if any corrupt minister should dare to form such a connection, he would hang it about his neck like a millstone, to sink him to perdition. The bellows of Taycho's oratory blew up such a flame in the nation, that the cuboy and all his partisans were afraid to whisper one syllable about the farm.

Meanwhile, Brut-an-tiffi, in order to quicken their determinations, withdrew the garrison he had in a town on the

frontiers of China, and it was immediately occupied by the
Chinese; an army of whom poured in, like a deluge, through
this opening, upon the lands adjoining to the farm. Got-
hama-baba was now seised with a fit of temporary distraction.
He foamed and raved, and cursed and swore in the Tartarian language: he declared he would challenge Brut-an-tiffi
to single combat. He not only kicked, but also cuffed the
whole council of twenty-eight, and played at foot-ball with
his imperial tiara. Fika-kaka was dumb-founded: Sti-phi-
rum-poo muttered something about a commission of lunacy:
Nin-com-poo-po pronounced the words, flat-bottomed junks;
but his teeth chattered so much that his meaning could not
be understood. The fatsman offered to cross the sea and
put himself at the head of a body of light horse, to observe the motions of the enemy; and Gotto-mio prayed fervently within himself, that God Almighty would be pleased
to annihilate that accursed farm, which had been productive
of such mischief to Japan. Nay, he even ventured to exclaim,—' Would to God the farm was sunk in the middle
of the Tartarian ocean!' ' Heaven forbid!' cried the president Soo-san-sin-o; ' for, in that case, Japan must be at the
expense of weighing it up again.'

In the midst of this perplexity, they were suddenly surprised at the apparition of Taycho's head nodding from a
window that overlooked their deliberations. At sight of this
horrid spectacle the council broke up. The dairo fled to
the inmost recesses of the palace, and all his counsellors
vanished, except the unfortunate Fika-kaka, whose fear had
rendered him incapable of any sort of motion but one, and
that he instantly had to a very efficacious degree. Taycho
bolting in at the window advanced to the cuboy without
ceremony, and accosted him in these words,—' It depends
upon the cuboy, whether Taycho continues to oppose his
measures, or becomes his most obsequious servant. Arise,
illustrious quanbuku, and cast your eyes upon the steps by
which I ascended.' Accordingly Fika-kaka looked, and
saw a multitude of people who had accompanied their orator
into the court of the palace, and raised for him an occasional

stair of various implements. The first step was made by an old fig-box, the second by a nightman's bucket, the third by a cask of hemp-seed, the fourth by a tar barrel, the fifth by an empty kilderkin, the sixth by a keg, the seventh by a bag of soot, the eighth by a fishwoman's basket, the ninth by a rotten pack-saddle, and the tenth by a block of hard wood from the island of Fatsissio. It was supported on one side by a varnished lettered post, and on the other by a crazy hogshead. The artificers who erected this climax, and now exulted over it with hideous clamour, consisted of grocers, scavengers, halter-makers, carpenters, draymen, distillers, chimney-sweepers, oyster-women, ass-drivers, aldermen, and dealers in waste paper.—To make myself understood, I am obliged, Peacock, to make use of those terms and denominations which are known in this metropolis.

Fika-kaka, having considered this work with astonishment, and heard the populace declare upon oath, that they would exalt their orator above all competition, was again addressed by the invincible Taycho. ' Your quanbukuship perceives how bootless it will be to strive against the torrent. What need is there of many words? admit me to a share of the administration.—I will commence your humble slave.—I will protect the farm at the expense of Japan, while there is an oban left in the island of Niphon; and I will muzzle these bears so effectually that they shall not shew their teeth, except in applauding our proceedings.' An author who sees the apparition of a bailiff standing before him in his garret, and instead of being shewn a *capias*, is presented with a bank-note; an impatient lover stopped upon Bagshot heath by a person in a mask, who proves to be his sweetheart come to meet him in disguise, for the sake of the frolic; a condemned criminal, who, on the morning of execution-day, instead of being called upon by the finisher of the law, is visited by the sheriff with a free pardon; could not be more agreeably surprised than was Fika-kaka at the demagogue's declaration. He flew into his embrace, and wept aloud with joy, calling him his dear Taycho. He squeezed his hand, kissed him on both cheeks, and swore he should share the

better half of all his power : then he laughed and snivelled
by turns, lolled out his tongue, waddled about the chamber,
wriggled, and niggled, and noddled.   Finally, he undertook
to prepare the dairo for his reception ; and it was agreed,
that the orator should wait on his new colleague next morning.——This matter being settled to their mutual satisfaction, Taycho retreated through the window in the court-
yard, and was convoyed home in triumph by that many-
headed hydra, the mob, which shook its multitudinous tail,
and brayed through every throat with hideous exultation.

The cuboy, meanwhile, had another trial to undergo ; a
trial which he had not foreseen.   Taycho was no sooner departed, than he hied him to the dairo's cabinet, in order to
communicate the happy success of his negociation.   But at
certain periods, Got-hama-baba's resentment was more than
a match for any other passion that belonged to his disposition, and now it was its turn to reign.   The dairo was made
of very combustible materials, and these had been kindled
up by the appearance of orator Taycho, who (he knew)
had treated his person with indecent freedoms, and publicly
vilified the worship of the white horse.   When Fika-kaka,
therefore, told him he had made peace with the demagogue,
the dairo, instead of giving him the kick of approbation,
turned his own back upon the cuboy, and silenced him
with a *boh!*   Had Fika-kaka assailed him with the same
syllogistical sophism, which was used by the Stagyrite
to Alexander in a passion, perhaps he might have listened
to reason :—ἡ ὀργὴ πρὸς ἴσας, ἀλλὰ πρὸς τὰς κρεττονας γινεται,
σοι δε ουδεις ἴσος.——' Anger should be raised not by our
equals, but by our superiors ; but you have no equal.'——
Certain it is, that Got-hama-baba had no equal ; but Fika-
kaka was no more like Aristotle, than his master resembled Alexander.   The dairo remained deaf to all his remonstrances, tears, and entreaties, until he declared that there
was no other way of saving the farm, but that of giving
charte blanche to Taycho.   This agreement seemed at once
to dispel the clouds which had been compelled by his in-

dignation: he consented to receive the orator in quality of minister, and next day was appointed for his introduction.

In the morning, Taycho the great, repaired to the palace of the cuboy, where he privately performed the ceremony of osculation *a posteriori*, sung a solemn palinodia on the subject of political system, repeated and signed the Buposian creed, embraced the religion of Fakku-busi, and adored the white horse with marks of unfeigned piety and contrition. Then he was conducted to the anti-chamber of the emperor, who could not, without great difficulty, so far master his personal dislike, as to appear before him with any degree of composure. He was brought forth by Fika-kaka like a tame bear to the stake, if that epithet of *tame* can be given with any propriety to an animal which nobody but his keeper dares approach. The orator, perceiving him advance, made him a low obeisance, according to the custom of Japan; that is, by bending the body averse from the dairo, and laying the right hand upon the left buttock; and pronounced, with an audible voice,—' Behold, invincible Got-. hama-baba, a sincere penitent come to make atonement for his virulent opposition to your government, for his atrocious insolence to your sacred person. I have calumniated your favourite farm, I have questioned your integrity, I have vilified your character, ridiculed your understanding, and despised your authority.'—This recapitulation was so disagreeable to the dairo, that he suddenly flew off at a tangent, and retreated growling to his den; from whence he could by no means be lugged again by the cuboy, until Taycho, exalting his voice, uttered these words.— ' But I will exalt your authority more than ever it was debased.—I will extol your wisdom, and expatiate on your generosity; I will glorify the white horse, and sacrifice all the treasures of Japan, if needful, for the protection of the farm of Yesso.' By these cabalistical sounds the wrath of Got-hama-baba was entirely appeased. He now returned with an air of gaiety, strutting, sideling, circling, fluttering, and gobbling like a turkey-cock in his pride, when he displays his feathers to the sun. Taycho hailed the omen; and, turning his face from the emperor, received such a salutation on the *os sacrum* that the parts continued vibrating and tingling for several days.

An indenture tripartite was now drawn up and executed. Fika-kaka was continued treasurer, with his levees, his bonzas, and his places; and orator Taycho undertook, in the character of chief scribe, to protect the farm of Yesso, as well as to bridle and manage the blatant beast whose name was Legion. That a person of this kidney should have the presumption to undertake such an affair, is not at all surprising; the wonder is, that his performance should even exceed his promise. The truth is, he promised more than he could have performed, had not certain unforeseen incidents in which he had no concern, contributed towards the infatuation of the people.

The first trial to which he brought his ascendency over the mob, was his procuring from them a free gift, to enable the dairo to arm his own private tenants in Yesso, together with some raggamuffin Tartars in the neighbourhood, for the defence of the farm. They winked so hard upon this first overt-act of his apostacy, that he was fully persuaded they had resigned up all their senses to his direction; and resolved to shew them to all Europe, as a surprising instance of his art in monster-taming. This furious beast not only suffered itself to be bridled and saddled, but frisked and fawned, and purred and yelped, and crouched before the orator, licking his feet, and presenting its back to the burdens which he was pleased to impose. Immediately after this first essay, Quamba-cun-dono, the fatsman, was sent over to assemble and command a body of light horse in Yesso, in order to keep an eye on the motions of the enemy; and indeed this vigilant and sagacious commander conducted himself with such activity and discretion, that he soon brought the war in those parts to a point of termination.

Meanwhile, Brut-an-tiffi continuing to hover on the skirts of the farm, at the head of his myrmidons, and demanding of the dairo a categorical answer to the hints he had given,

Got-hama-baba underwent several successive fits of impatience and distraction.   The cuboy, instigated by his own partizans, and in particular by Mura-clami, who hoped to see Taycho take some desperate step that would ruin his popularity : I say, the cuboy thus stimulated, began to ply the orator with such pressing entreaties as he could no longer resist ; and now he exhibited such a specimen of his own power and the people's insanity, as transcends the flight of ordinary faith.   Without taking the trouble to scratch their long ears, tickle their noses, drench them with mandragora or geneva, or make the least apology for his own turning tail to the principles which he had all his life so strenuously inculcated, he crammed down their throats an obligation to pay a yearly tribute to Brut-an-tiffi, in consideration of his forbearing to seize the dairo's farm ; a tribute which amounted to seven times the value of the lands, for the defence of which it was paid.   When I said *crammed*, I ought to have used another phrase.   The beast, far from shewing any signs of loathing, closed its eyes, opened its hideous jaws, and as it swallowed the inglorious bond, wagged its tail in token of entire satisfaction.

No fritter on Shrove Tuesday was ever more dexterously turned, than were the hydra's brains by this mountebank in patriotism, this juggler in politics, this cat in pan, or cake in pan, or *xara sas* in principle.   Some people gave out that he dealt with a conjurer, and others scrupled not to insinuate that he had sold himself to the evil spirit.   But there was no occasion for a conjurer to deceive those whom the demon of folly had previously confounded ; and as to selling, he sold nothing but the interest of his country ; and of that he made a very bad bargain.   Be that as it may, the Japanese now viewed Brut-an-tiffi either through a new perspective, or else surveyed him with organs entirely metamorphosed.   Yesterday they detested him as a profligate ruffian, lost to all sense of honesty and shame, addicted to all manner of vice, a scoffer at religion, particularly that of Fakku-basi, the scourge of human nature, and the inveterate enemy of Japan.   To-day, they glorified him as an

unblemished hero, the protector of good faith, the mirror
of honesty, the pattern of every virtue, a saint in piety, a
devout votary to the white horse, a friend to mankind, the
fast ally and the firmest prop of the Japanese empire. The
farm of Yesso, which they had so long execrated as a putrid and painful excrescence upon the breech of their country, which would never be quiet until this cursed wart was
either exterminated or taken away, they now fondled as a
favourite mole, nay, and cherished as the apple of their eye.
One would have imagined that all the inconsistencies and
absurdities which characterise the Japanese nation, had
taken their turns to reign, just as the interest of Taycho's
ambition required. When it was necessary for him to establish new principles, at that very instant their levity prompted them to renounce their former maxims. Just as he had
occasion to facinate their senses, the demon of caprice instigated them to shut their eyes, and hold out their necks,
that they might be led by the nose. At the very nick of
time when he adopted the cause of Brut-an-tiffi, in a dia-
metrical opposition to all his former professions, the spirit
of whim and singularity disposed them to kick against the
shins of common sense, deny the light of day at noon, and
receive in their bosoms as a dove, the man whom before they
had shunned as a serpent. Thus every thing concurred
to establish for orator, Taycho, a despotism of popularity;
and that not planned by reason, or raised by art, but founded on fatality, and finished by accident. *Quos Jupiter vult
perdere prius dementat.*

Brut-an-tiffi being so amply gratified by the Japanese for
his promise of forbearance with respect to the farm of Yesso,
and determined at all events to make some new acquisition,
turned his eyes upon the domains of Pol-hassan-akoutsi, another of his neighbours, who had formed a most beautiful
colony in this part of Tartary; and rushed upon it at a
minute's warning. His resolution in this respect was so
suddenly taken, and quickly executed, that he had not yet
formed any excuse for this outrage, in order to save appearances. Without giving himself the trouble to invent a pre-

tence, he drove old Pol-hassan-akousti out of his residence, compelled the domestics of that prince to enter among his own banditti, plundered his house, seized the archives of his family, threatened to shoot the ancient gentlewoman his wife, exacted heavy contribution from the tenants, then dispersed a manifesto, in which he declared himself the best friend of the said Akousti and his spouse, assuring him he would take care of his estate as a precious deposit, to be restored to him in due season. In the meantime, he thought proper to sequester the rents, that they might not enable Pol-hassan to take any measures that should conduce to his own prejudice. As for the articles of meat, drink, clothing, and lodging, for him and his wife, and a large family of small children, he had nothing to do but depend upon Providence, until the present troubles should be appeased. His behaviour on this occasion, Peacock, puts me in mind of the Spaniard whom Philip II. employed to assassinate his own son Don Carlos. This compassionate Castilian, when the prince began to deplore his fate, twirled his mustachio, pronouncing, with great gravity, these words of comfort, —' *Calla, calla, senor, todo que se haze es por su bien.*' 'I beg your highness won't make any noise, this is all for your own good;' or the politeness of Gibbet, in the play called the Beaux Stratagem, who says to Mrs Sullen, —' Your jewels, madam, if you please—don't be under any uneasiness, madam—if you make any noise I shall blow your brains out—I have a particular regard for the ladies, madam.'

But the possession of Pol-hassan's demesnes was not the ultimate aim of Brut-an-tiffi. He had an eye to a fair and fertile province belonging to a Tartar princess of the house of Ostrog. He saw himself at the head of a numerous banditti trained to war, fleshed in carnage, and eager for rapine; his coffers were filled with the spoils he had gathered in his former freebooting expeditions; and the incredible sums paid him as an annual tribute from Japan, added to his other advantages, rendered him one of the most formidable chiefs in all Tartary. Thus elated with the consciousness of his own

strength, he resolved to make a sudden irruption into the
dominions of Ostrog, at a season of the year when that house
could not avail itself of the alliances they had formed with
the other powers; and he did not doubt but that, in a few
weeks, he should be able to subdue the whole country belonging to the amazonian princess. But I can tell thee,
Peacock, his views extended even farther than the conquest
of the Ostrog dominions. He even aspired at the empire of
Tartary, and had formed the design of deposing the great
cham, who was intimately connected with the princess of
Ostrog. Inspired by these projects, he, at the beginning of
winter, suddenly poured like a deluge into one of the provinces that owned this amazon's sway; but he had hardly
gained the passes of the mountains, when he found himself
opposed by a numerous body of forces, assembled under the
command of a celebrated general, who gave him battle without hesitation, and handled him so roughly, that he was fain
to retreat into the demesnes of Pol-hassan, where he spent
the greatest part of the winter in exacting contributions and
extending the reign of desolation.

All the petty princes and states who hold of the great
cham began to tremble for their dominions; and the cham
himself was so much alarmed at the lawless proceedings of
Brut-an-tiffi, that he convoked a general assembly of all the
potentates who possessed fiefs in the empire, in order to deliberate upon measures for restraining the ambition of this
ferocious freebooter. Among others, the dairo of Japan, as
lord of the farm of Yesso, sent a deputy to this convention,
who, in his master's name, solemnly disclaimed and professed his detestation of Brut-an-tiffi's proceedings, which indeed were universally condemned. The truth is, he at this
period dreaded the resentment of all the other co-estates rather more than he feared the menaces of Brut-an-tiffi; and,
in particular, apprehended a sentence of outlawry from the
cham, by which at once he would have forfeited all legal
title to his beloved farm. Brut-an-tiffi, on the other hand,
began to raise a piteous clamour, as if he meant to excite
compassion. He declared himself a poor injured prince,
who had been a dupe to the honesty and humanity of his

own heart. He affirmed that the amazon of Ostrog had entered into a conspiracy against him, with the Mantchoux Tartars, and Prince Akoosti. He published particulars of this dreadful conjuration, which appeared to be no other than a defensive alliance formed in the apprehension that he would fall upon some of them, without any regard to treaty, as he had done on a former occasion, when he seised one of the amazon's best provinces. He publicly taxed the dairo of Japan with having prompted him to commence hostilities, and hinted that the said dairo was to have shared his conquests. He openly entreated his co-estates to interpose their influence towards the re-establishment of peace in the empire; and gave them privately to understand, that he would ravage their territories without mercy, should they concur with the cham in any sentence to his prejudice.

As he had miscarried in his first attempt, and perceived a terrible cloud gathering around him, in all probability he would have been glad to compound matters at this juncture, on condition of being left in *statu quo*; but this was a condition not to be obtained. The princess of Ostrog had by this time formed such a confederacy as threatened him with utter destruction. She had contracted an offensive and defensive alliance with the Chinese, the Mantchoux, and the Serednee Tartars; and each of these powers engaged to furnish a separate army to humble the insolence of Brut-an-tiffi. The majority of the Tartar fiefs agreed to raise a body of forces to act against him as a disturber of the public peace, the great cham threatened him with a decree of outlawry and rebellion, and the amazon herself opposed him at the head of a very numerous and warlike tribe, which had always been considered as the most formidable in that part of Tartary. Thus powerfully sustained, she resolved to enjoy her revenge, and at any rate retrieve the province which had been ravished from her by Brut-an-tiffi, at a time when she was embarrassed with other difficulties. Brut-an-tiffi did not think himself so reduced as to purchase peace with such a sacrifice. The Mantchoux were at a great distance, naturally slow in their motions, and had a very long march

through a desert country, which they would not attempt
without having first provided prodigious magazines. The
Serednee were a divided people, among whom he had made
shift to foment intestine divisions, that would impede the
national operations of the war. The Japanese fatsman formed a strong barrier between him and the Chinese; the army
furnished by the fiefs, he despised as raw, undisciplined militia; besides, their declaring against him afforded a specious
pretence for laying their respective dominions under contribution. But he chiefly depended upon the coffers of Japan,
which he firmly believed would hold out until all his enemies should be utterly exhausted.

As this freebooter was a principal character in the drama
which I intend to rehearse, I shall sketch his portrait according to the information I received from a fellow-atom who
once resided at his court, constituting part in one of the organs belonging to his first chamberlain. His stature was
under the middle size; his aspect mean and forbidding, with
a certain expression which did not at all prepossess the spectator in favour of his morals. Had an accurate observer beheld him without any exterior distinctions in the streets of
this metropolis, he would have naturally clapped his hands
to his pockets. Thou hast seen the character of Gibbet represented on the stage by a late comedian of expressive
feature. Nature sometimes makes a strange contrast between
the interior workmanship and the exterior form; but here
the one reflected a true image of the other. His heart never
felt an impression of tenderness; his notions of right and
wrong did not refer to any idea of benevolence, but were
founded entirely on the convenience of human commerce;
and there was nothing social in the turn of his disposition.
By nature he was stern, insolent, and rapacious; uninflu-
enced by any motive of humanity, unawed by any precept
of religion. With respect to religion, he took all opportunities of exposing it to ridicule and contempt. Liberty of
conscience he allowed to such extent, as exceeded the bounds
of decorum, and disgraced all legislation. He pardoned a
criminal convicted of bestiality; and publicly declared, that

all modes of religion, and every species of amour, might be
freely practised and prosecuted through all his dominions.
His capacity was of the middling mould, and he had taken
some pains to cultivate his understanding.   He had studied
the Chinese language, which he spoke with fluency ; and
piqued himself upon his learning, which was but superficial.
His temper was so capricious and inconstant, that it was impossible even for those who knew him best to foresee any one
particular of his personal demeanour.   The same individual
he would caress and insult by. turns, without the least apparent change of circumstance.   He has been known to dismiss one of his favourites with particular marks of regard,
and the most flattering professions of affection ; and, before
he had time to pull off his buskins at his own house, he has
been hurried on horseback by a detachment of cavalry, and
conveyed to the frontiers.   Thus harassed, without refresh-
ment or repose, he was brought back by another party, and
re-conveyed to the presence of Brut-an-tiffi, who embraced
him at meeting, and gently chid him for having been so
long absent.—The fixed principles of this Tartar were these:
insatiable rapacity, restless ambition, and an insuperable
contempt for the Japanese nation.—His maxims of government were entirely despotic.   He considered his subjects as
slaves, to be occasionally sacrificed to the accomplishment
of his capital designs ; but, in the meantime, he indulged
them with the protection of equitable laws, and encouraged
them to industry for his own emolument.

His virtues consisted of temperance, vigilance, activity,
and perseverance.   His folly chiefly appeared in childish
vanity and self-conceit.   He amused himself with riding,
reviewing his troops, reading Chinese authors, playing on
a musical instrument in use among the Tartars, trifling with
buffoons, conversing with supposed wits, and reasoning with
pretended philosophers ; but he had no communication with
the female sex ; nor indeed, was there any ease, comfort, or
enjoyment, to be derived from a participation of his pastime.   His wits, philosophers, and buffoons, were composed
of Chinese refugees, who soon discovered his weak side, and

flattered his vanity to an incredible pitch of infatuation. They persuaded him that he was an universal genius, an invincible hero, a sage legislator, a sublime philosopher, a consummate politician, a divine poet, and an elegant historian. They wrote systems, compiled memoirs, and composed poems, which were published in his name; nay, they contrived witticisms, which he uttered as his own. They had, by means of commercial communication with the banks of the Ganges, procured the history of a western hero, called Raskalander, which, indeed, was no other than the memoirs of Alexander, wrote by Quintus Curtius, translated from the Indian language, with an intermixture of oriental fables. This they recommended, with many hyperbolical encomiums, to the perusal of Brut-an-tiffi, who became enamoured of the performance, and was fired with the ambition of rivalling, if not excelling, Raskalander, not only as a warrior, but likewise as a patron of taste, and a protector of the liberal arts. As Alexander deposited Homer's Iliad in a precious casket, so Brut-an-tiffi procured a golden box for preserving this sophistication of Quintus Curtius. It was his constant companion; he affected to read it in public, and to lay it under his pillow at night.

Thus pampered with adulation, and intoxicated with dreams of conquest, he made no doubt of being able to establish a new empire in Tartary, which should entirely eclipse the kingdom of Tum-ming-qua, and raise a reputation that should infinitely transcend the fame of Yan, or any emperor that ever sat upon the throne of Thibet. He now took the field against the amazon of the house of Ostrog, penetrated into her dominions, defeated one of her generals in a pitched battle, and undertook the siege of one of her principal cities, in full confidence of seeing her kneeling at his gate before the end of the campaign. In the meantime, her scattered troops were rallied, and reinforced by another old experienced commander, who, being well acquainted with the genius of his adversary, pitched upon an advantageous situation, where he waited for another attack. Brut-an-tiffi, flushed with his former victory, and firmly persuaded that no mortal power could withstand his prowess, gave him battle at a very great disadvantage. The consequence was natural; he lost great part of his army, was obliged to abandon the siege, and retreat with disgrace. A separate body, commanded by one of his ablest captains, met with the same fate in a neighbouring country; and a third detachment at the farthest extremity of his dominions, having attacked an army of the Mantchoux, was repulsed with great loss.

· These were not all the mortifications to which he was exposed about this period. The fatsman of Japan, who had formed an army for the defence of the farm of Yesso against the Chinese, met with a terrible disaster. Notwithstanding his being outnumbered by the enemy he exhibited many proofs of uncommon activity and valour. At length they came to blows with him, and handled him so roughly, that he was fain to retreat from post to pillar, and leave the farm at their mercy. Had he pursued his route to the right, he might have found shelter in the dominions of Brut-an-tiffi; and this was his intention; but instead of marching in a straight line, he revolved to the right, like a planet round the sun, impelled as it were by a compound impulse, until he had described a regular semicircle; and then he found himself with all his followers engaged in a sheep-pen, from whence there was no egress; for the enemy, who followed his steps, immediately blocked up the entrance. The unfortunate fatsman being thus pounded, must have fallen a sacrifice to his centripetal force, had he not been delivered by the interposition of a neighbouring chief, who prevailed upon the Chinese general to let Qumba-cun dona escape, provided his followers would lay down their arms, and return peaceably to their own habitations. This was a bitter pill, which the fatsman was obliged to swallow, and is said to have cost him five stone of suet. He returned to Japan in obscurity; the Chinese general took possession of the farm in the name of his emperor; and all the damage which the tenants sustained was nothing more than a change of masters, which they had no great cause to regret.

To the thinking part of the Japanese, nothing could be more agreeable than this event, by which they were at once delivered from a pernicious excrescence, which, like an ulcerated tumour, exhausted the juices of the body by which it was fed. Brut-an-tiffi considered the transaction in a different point of view. He foresaw that the Chinese forces would now be at liberty to join his enemies, the tribe of Ostrog, with whom the Chinese emperor was intimately connected; and that it would be next to impossible to withstand the joint efforts of the confederacy, which he had brought upon his own head. He therefore raised a hideous clamour. He accused the fatzman of misconduct, and insisted, not without a mixture of menaces, upon the dairo's re-assembling his forces in the county of Yesso.

The dairo himself was inconsolable. He neglected his food, and refused to confer with his ministers. He dismissed the fatzman from his service. He locked himself in his cabinet, and spent the hours in lamentation.—'O my dear farm of Yesso!' cried he, 'shall I never more enjoy thy charms!—Shall I never more regale my eye with thy beauteous prospects, thy hills of heath; thy meads of broom: and thy wastes of sand! shall I never more eat thy black bread, drink thy brown beer, and feast upon thy delicate porkers! Shall I never more receive the homage of the sallow Yessites with their meagre faces, ragged skirts, and wooden shoes! Shall I never more improve their huts and regulate their pigstyes! O cruel Fate! in vain did I face thy mud-walled mansion with a new freestone front! In vain did I cultivate thy turnip-garden! In vain did I inclose a piece of ground at a great expense, and raise a crop of barley, the first that ever was seen in Yesso! In vain did I send over a breed of mules and black cattle for the purposes of husbandry! In vain did I supply you with all the implements of agriculture! In vain did I sow grass and grain for food, and plant trees, and furze and fern for shelter to the game, which could not otherwise subsist upon your naked downs! In vain did I furnish your houseless sides, and fill your hungry bellies with the good things of Japan! In vain did I expend the treasures of my empire for thy melioration and defence! In vain did I incur the execrations of my people, if I must now lose thee for ever; if thou must now fall into the hands of an insolent alien, who has no affection for thy soil, and no regard for thy interest! O Quamba-cun-dono! Quamba-cun-dono! how hast thou disappointed my hope! I thought thou wast too ponderous to flinch; that thou wouldst have stood thy ground, fixed as the temple of Fakku-basi, and larded the lean earth with thy carcase, rather than leave my farm uncovered; but, alas! thou hast fled before the enemy like a partridge on the mountains; and suffered thyself at last to be taken in a snare like a foolish dotterel!'

The cuboy, who overheard this exclamation, attempted to comfort him through the key-hole. He soothed, and whined, and wheedled, and laughed, and wept all in a breath. He exhorted the illustrious Got-hama-baba to bear this misfortune with his wonted greatness of mind. He offered to present his imperial majesty with lands in Japan that should be equal in value to the farm he had lost; or, if that should not be agreeable, to make good at the peace, all the damage that should be done to it by the enemy. Finally, he cursed the farm, as the cause of his master's chagrin, and fairly wished it at the devil. Here he was suddenly interrupted with a—' Bub-ub-ub-boh! my lord cuboy, your grace talks like an apothecary.—Go home to your own palace, and direct your cooks; and may your bonzes kiss your a— to your heart's content.—I swear by the horns of the moon and the hoofs of the white horse, that my foot shall not touch your posteriors these three days.' Fika-kaka, having received this severe check, craved pardon in a whimpering tone, for the liberty he had taken, and retired to consult with Mura-clami, who advised him to summon orator Taycho to his assistance.

This mob-driver being made acquainted with the passion of the dairo, and the cause of his distress, readily undertook to make such a speech through the key-hole, as should effectually dispel the emperor's despondence; and to this en-

terprise he was encouraged by the hyperbolical praises of
Mura-clami, who exhausted all the tropes of his own rhetoric in extolling the eloquence of Taycho.—This triumvirate immediately adjourned to the door of the apartment in
which Got-hama-baba was sequestered, where the orator,
kneeling upon a cushion, with his mouth applied to the
key-hole, opened the sluices of his elocution to this effect.—
'Most gracious!' 'Bo, bo, boh!' 'Most illustrious!'
'Bo, boh!' 'Most invincible Got-hama-baba!' 'Boh!'
'When the sun, that glorious luminary, is obscured by
envious clouds, all nature saddens, and seems to sympathise
with his apparent distress. Your imperial majesty is the
sun of our hemisphere, whose splendour illuminates our
throne; and whose genial warmth enlivens our hearts; and
shall we your subjects, your slaves, the creatures of your
nod—shall we, unmoved, behold your ever-glorious effulgence
overcast? No! while the vital stream bedews our veins,
while our souls retain the faculty of reason, and our tongues
the power of speech, we shall not cease to embalm your sorrow with our tears; we shall not cease to pour the overflowings of our affection—our filial tenderness, which will always be reciprocal with your parental care: these are the
inexhaustible sources of the nation's happiness. They may
be compared to the rivers Jodo and Jodo-gava, which derive their common origin from the vast lake of Ami. The
one winds its silent course, calm, clear, and majestic, reflecting the groves and palaces that adorn its banks, and
fertilising the delightful country through which it runs: the
other gushes impetuous through a rugged channel and less
fertile soil; yet serves to beautify a number of wild romantic
scenes; to fill an hundred aqueducts, and to turn a thousand mills: at length they join their streams below the imperial city of Meaco, and form a mighty flood devolving to
the bay of Osaca, bearing on its spacious bosom the riches of
Japan.' Here the orator paused for breath:—the cuboy
clapped him on the back, whispering,—' super-excellent!
O charming simile! Another such will sink the dairo's grief
to the bottom of the sea: and his heart will float like a blown

Vol. VI. G g

bladder upon the waves of Kugava.' Mura-clami was not
silent in his praise, while he squeezed an orange between the
lips of Taycho; and Got-hama-baba seemed all attention:
at length the orator resumed his subject.—'Think not,
august emperor, that the cause of your disquiet is unknown,
or unlamented by your weeping servants. We have not
only perceived your eclipse, but discovered the invidious
body by whose interposition that eclipse is effected. The
rapacious arms of the hostile Chinese have seized the farm
of Yesso!' 'Oh, oh, oh!' 'That farm so cherished by
your imperial favour; that farm which, in the north of Tartary, shone like a jewel in an Æthiop's ear;—yes, that
jewel hath been snatched by the savage hand of a Chinese
freebooter:—but, dry your tears, my prince: that jewel
shall detect his theft, and light us to revenge. It shall become a rock to crush him in his retreat;—a net of iron to
entangle his steps; a fallen trunk over which his feet shall
stumble. It shall hang like a weight about his neck, and
sink him to the lowest gulf of perdition.——Be comforted,
then, my liege! your farm is rooted to the centre; it can
neither be concealed nor removed. Nay, should he hide it
at the bottom of the ocean, or place it among the constellations in the heavens, your faithful Taycho would fish it up
entire, or tear it headlong from the starry firmament.—We
will retrive the farm of Yesso.' 'But, how, how, how,
dear orator Taycho?' 'The empire of Japan shall be mort-
gaged for the sake of that precious—that sacred spot, which
produced the patriarch apostle *Bupo*, and resounded under
the hoofs of the holy steed.—Your people of Japan shall
chaunt the litany of Fakku-basi.—They shall institute Cru-
sades for the recovery of the farm; they shall pour their
treasury at your imperial feet;—they shall clamour for imposition; they shall load themselves with tenfold burdens,
desolate their country, and beggar their posterity in behalf
of Yesso. With these funds I could undertake even to
overturn the councils of Pekin.—While the Tartar princes
deal in the trade of blood, there will be no want of hands to
cut away those noxious weeds which have taken root in the

farm of Yesso: those vermin that have preyed upon her delightful blossoms! Amidst such a variety of remedies, there can be no difficulty in choosing. Like a weary traveller, I will break a bough from the first pine that presents, and brush away those troublesome insects that gnaw the fruits of Yesso.—Should not the mercenary bands of Tartary suffice to repel those insolent invaders, I will engage to chain this island to the continent; to build a bridge from shore to shore, that shall afford a passage more free and ample than the road to hell. Through this avenue I will ride the mighty beast whose name is Legion. I have studied the art of war, my liege:—I had once the honour to serve my country as lance-presado in the militia of Niphon.—I will unpeople these realms, and overspread the land of Yesso with the forces of Japan.'

Got-hama-baba could no longer resist the energy of such expressions. He flew to the door of his cabinet, and embraced the orator in a transport of joy; while Fika-kaka fell upon his neck and wept aloud; and Mura-clami kissed the hem of his garment.'

You must know, Peacock, I had by this time changed my situation. I was discharged in the perspiratory vapour from the perinæum of the cuboy, and sucked into the lungs of Mura-clami, through which I pervaded into the course of the circulation, and visited every part of his composition, I found the brain so full and compact, that there was not room for another particle of matter. But instead of a heart, he had a membranous sac, or hollow viscus, cold and callous, the habitation of sneaking caution, servile flattery, griping avarice, creeping malice, and treacherous deceit. Among these tenants it was my fate to dwell; and there I discovered the motives by which the lawyer's conduct was influenced. He now secretly rejoiced at the presumption of Taycho, which he hoped had already prompted him to undertake more than he could perform; in which case he would infallibly incur disgrace either with the dairo or the people. It is not impossible but this hope might have been realized, had not fortune unexpectedly interposed, and operated as an

auxiliary to the orator's presumption. Success began to
dawn upon the arms of Japan in the island of Fatsissio; and
towards the end of the campaign, Brut-an-tiffi obtained two
petty advantages in Tartary against one body of Chinese,
another of the Ostrog. All these were magnified into
astonishing victories, and ascribed to the wisdom and courage
of Taycho, because during his ministry they were obtained;
though he neither knew why, nor wherefore; and was in
this respect, as innocent as his master Got-hama-baba, and
his colleague Fika-kaka. He had penetration enough to perceive, however, that these events had intoxicated the rabble,
and began to pervert their ideas. Success of any kind is
apt to perturb the weak brain of a Japanese; but the acquisition of any military trophy produces an actual delirium.
The streets of Meaco were filled with multitudes who shouted,
whooped, and hallooed. They made processions with flags
and banners; they illuminated their houses; they extolled
Ian-on-i, a provincial captain of Fatsissio, who, had by accident, repulsed a body of the enemy, and reduced an old
barn which they had fortified. They magnified Brut-an-
tiffi; they deified orator Taycho; they drank, they damned,
they squabbled, and acted a thousand extravagancies, which
I shall not pretend to enumerate or particularise. Taycho,
who knew their trim, seized this opportunity to strike while
the iron was hot.—He forthwith mounted an old tub, which
was his public rostrum, and, waving his hand in an oratorial
attitude, was immediately surrounded with the thronging
populace.—I have already given you a specimen of his
manner, and therefore shall not repeat the tropes and figures
of his harangue; but only sketch out the plan of his address,
and specify the chain of his argument alone. He assailed
them in the way of paradox, which never fails to produce a
wonderful effect upon a heated imagination and a shallow
understanding. Having, in his exordium, artfully fascinated
their faculties like a juggler in Bartholomew fair, by means
of an assemblage of words without meaning or import, he
proceeded to demonstrate, that a wise and good man ought
to discard his maxims, the moment he finds they are cer-

tainly established on the foundation of eternal truth: that
the people of Japan ought to preserve the farm of Yesso,
as the apple of their eye, because nature had disjoined it
from their empire; and the maintenance of it would involve
them in all the quarrels of Tartary: that it was to be preserved at all hazards, because it was not worth preserving:
that all the power and opulence of Japan ought to be exerted
and employed in its defence, because, by the nature of its
situation, it could not possibly be defended: that Brut-an-
tiffi was the great protector of the religion of the bonzas,
because he had never shewn the least regard to any religion
at all: that he was the fast friend of Japan, because he had
more than once acted as a rancorous enemy to this empire,
and never let slip the least opportunity of expressing his
contempt for the subjects of Niphon: that he was an invincible hero, because he had been thrice beaten, and once
compelled to raise a siege, in the course of two campaigns:
that he was a prince of consummate honour, because he had,
in the time of profound peace, usurped the dominions, and
ravaged the countries of his neighbours, in defiance of common honesty; in violation of the most solemn treaties: that
he was the most honourable and important ally that the
empire of Japan could choose, because his alliance was to
be purchased with an enormous annual tribute, for which he
was bound to perform no earthly office of friendship or assistance; because connection with him effectually deprived
Japan of the friendship of all the other princes and states of
Tartary: and the utmost exertion of his power could never
conduce, in the smallest degree, to the interest or advantage
of the Japanese empire.

Such were the propositions orator Taycho undertook to
demonstrate, and the success justified his undertaking. After
a weak mind has been duly prepared, and turned, as it were,
by opening a sluice or torrent of high-sounding words, the
greater the contradiction proposed, the stronger impression
it makes, because it increases the puzzle, and lays fast hold
on the admiration; depositing the small proportion of reason
with which it was before impregnated, like the vitriol acid

in the copper mines of Wicklow, into which, if you immerse iron, it immediately quits the copper which it had before dissolved, and unites with the other metal, to which it has a stronger attraction.   Orator Taycho was not so well skilled in logic as to amuse his audience with definitions of concrete and abstract terms; or expatiate upon the genus and the difference; or state propositions by the subject, the predicate and the copula; or form syllogisms by mood and figure; but he was perfectly well acquainted with all the equivocal or synonymous words in his own language, and could ring the changes on them with great dexterity.   He knew perfectly well how to express the same ideas by words that literally implied opposition: for example, a valuable conquest or an invaluable conquest; a shameful rascal or a shameful villain; a hard head or a soft head: a large conscience or no conscience; immensely great or immensely little; damned high or damned low; damned bitter, damned sweet; damned severe, damned insipid; and damned fulsome.   He knew how to invert the sense of words by changing the manner of pronunciation; *e. g.* 'You are a very pretty fellow!' to signify, ' you are a very dirty scoundrel.' ' You have *always* spoke respectfully of the higher power!' to express, ' you have often insulted your betters, and even your sovereign.' ' You have *never* turned tail to the principles you professed!' to declare, ' you have acted the part of an infamous apostate.'   He was well aware that words alter their signification according to the circumstances of times, customs, and the difference of opinion.   Thus the name of Jack, who used to turn the spit, and pull off his master's boots, was transferred to an iron machine and a wooden instrument now substituted for these purposes: thus a stand for the tea-kettle acquired the name of footman; and the words canon and ordinance, signifying originally a rule or law, were extended to a piece of artillery, which is counted the *ultima lex*, or *ultima ratio regum*.   In the same manner, the words infidel, heresy, good man, and political orthodoxy, imply very different significations, among different classes of people.   A mussulman is an infidel at Rome, and a christian is distinguished as an unbeliever at Constantinople. A papist by protestantism understands heresy; to a Turk the same idea is conveyed by the sect of Ali. The term *good man* at Edinburgh implies fanaticism, upon the Exchange of London it signifies cash, and in the general acceptation benevolence. Political orthodoxy has different, nay opposite, definitions, at different places in the same kingdom; at O— and C—, at the Cocoa-tree in Pall-mall, and at Garraway's in Exchange alley. Our orator was well acquainted with all the legerdemain of his own language, as well as with the nature of the beast he had to rule. He knew when to distract its weak brain with a tumult of incongruous and contradictory ideas: he knew when to overwhelm its feeble faculty of thinking, by pouring in a torrent of words without any ideas annexed. These throng in like city-milliners to a Mile-end assembly, while it happens to be under the direction of a conductor without strength and authority. Those that have ideas annexed may be compared to the females provided with partners, which, though they may crowd the place, do not absolutely destroy all regulation and decorum; but those that are uncoupled press in promiscuously with such impetuosity, and in such numbers, that the puny master of the ceremonies is unable to withstand the irruption, far less to distinguish their quality, or accommodate them with partners: thus they fall into the dance without order, and immediately anarchy ensues. Taycho having kept the monster's brain on a simmer, until, like the cow-heel in Don Quixote, it seemed to cry *comenme, comenme*,—come eat me, come eat me; then told them in plain terms, that it was expedient they should part with their wives and their children, their souls and their bodies, their substance and their senses, their blood and their suet, in order to defend the indefensible farm of Yesso, and to support Brut-an-tiffi, their insupportable ally. The hydra, rolling itself in the dust, turned up its huge unwieldy paunch, and wagged its forky tail; then licked the feet of Taycho, and through all its hoarse discordant throats began to bray applause. The dairo rejoiced in his success, the first fruits of which consisted in their agreeing to maintain an army of twenty thousand Tartar mercenaries, who were reinforced by the flower of the national troops of Japan, sent over to defend the farm of Yesso; and in their consenting to prolong the annual tribute granted to Brut-an-tiffi, who, in return for this condescension, accommodated the dairo with one of his freebooting captains to command the Yessite army. This new general had seen some service, and was counted a good officer: but it was not so much on account of his military character that he obtained this command, as for his dexterity in prolonging the war, his skill in exercising all the different arts of peculation, and his attachment to Brut-an-tiffi, with whom he had agreed to co-operate in milking the Japanese cow. This plan they executed with such effect, as could not possibly result from address alone, unassisted by the infatuation of those whom they pillaged. Every article of contingent expense for draught-horses, waggons, postage, forage, provision, and secret service, was swelled to such a degree, as did violence to common sense as well as to common honesty. The general had a fellow-feeling with all the contractors in the army, who were connected with him in such a manner as seemed to preclude all possibility of detection. In vain some of the Japanese officers endeavoured to pry into this mysterious commerce; in vain inspectors were appointed by the government of Japan. The first were removed on different pretences; the last were encountered by such disgraces and discouragements, as in a little time compelled them to resign the office they had undertaken. In a word, there was not a private mercenary Tartar soldier in this army who did not cost the empire of Japan as much as any subaltern officer of its own: and the annual charge of this continental war, undertaken for the protection of the farm of Yesso, exceeded the whole expense of any former war which Japan had ever maintained on its own account since the beginning of the empire: nay, it was attended with one circumstance which rendered it still more insupportable. The money expended in armaments and operations, equipped and prosecuted on the side of Japan, was all circulated within the empire; so that it still remained useful to the community in general; but no instance could be produced of a single copan that ever returned from the continent of Tartary; therefore all the sums sent thither were clear loss to the subjects of Japan. Orator Taycho acted as a faithful ally to Brut-antiffi, by stretching the bass-strings of the mobile in such a manner, as to be always in concert with the extravagance of the Tartar's demands, and the absurdity of the dairo's predilection. Fika-kaka was astonished at these phenomena; while Mura-clami hoped in secret that the orator's brain was disordered, and that his insanity would soon stand confessed, even to the conviction of the people. 'If,' said he to himself, 'they are not altogether destitute of human reason, they must, of their own accord, perceive and comprehend this plain proposition: a cask of water that discharges *three* by one pipe, and receives no more than *two* by another must infallibly be emptied at the long-run. Japan discharges *three* millions of obans every year for the defence of that blessed farm, which, were it put up to sale, would not fetch one sixth part of the sum; and the annual balance of her trade with all the world brings in *two* millions: *ergo* it runs out faster than it runs in, and the vessel at the long-run must be empty.' Mura-clami was mistaken. He had studied philosophy only in profile. He had endeavoured to investigate the sense, but he had never fathomed the absurdities of human nature. All that Taycho had done for Yesso amounted not to one third of what was required for the annual expense of Japan while it maintained the war against China in different quarters of Asia. A former cuboy (rest his soul!) finding it impossible to raise within the year the exorbitant supplies that were required to gratify the avarice and ambition of the dairo, had contrived the method of funding, which hath been lately adopted with such remarkable success in this kingdom. You know, Peacock, this is no more than borrowing a certain sum on the credit of the nation, and laying a fresh tax upon the public, to defray the interest of every sum thus borrowed; an excellent expedient,

when kept within due bounds, for securing the established
government, multiplying the dependents of the m——ry, and
throwing all the money of the empire into the hands of the
administration.   But those loans were so often repeated, that
the national debt had already swelled to an enormous burden : such a variety of taxes was laid upon the subject, as
grievously enhanced all the necessaries of life ; consequently
the poor were distressed, and the price of labour was raised
to such a degree, that the Japanese manufactures were everywhere undersold by the Chinese traders, who employed their
workmen at a more moderate expense.

Taycho, in this dilemma, was seized with a strange conceit.   Alchemy was at that period become a favourite study
in Japan.   Some bonzas having more learning and avarice
than their brethren, applied themselves to the study of certain Chaldean manuscripts, which their ancestors had
brought from Assyria ; and in these they found the substance of all that is contained in the works of Hermes Tris-
megistus, Geber, Zosymus, the Panopolite, Olympiodorus,
Heliodorus, Agathodæmon, Morienus, Albertus Magnus,
and, above all, your countryman Roger Bacon, who adopted Geber's opinion, that mercury is the common basis, and
sulphur the cement of all metals.   By-the-by, this same
Friar Bacon was well acquainted with the composition of
gunpowder, though the reputation arising from the discovery has been given to Swartz, who lived many years after that monk of Westminster.   Whether the philosopher's
stone, otherwise called the gift azoth, the fifth essence,
or the alkahest ; which last Van Helmont pilfered from the
tenth book of the Archidoxa, that treasure so long deposited in the occiput of the renowned Aureolus, Philippus,
Paracelsus, Theophrastus, Bombast, de Hohenheim ; was
ever really attained by human adept, I am not at liberty
to disclose ; but certain it is, the philosophers and alchemists
of Japan, employed by orator Taycho to transmute baser
metals into gold, miscarried in all their experiments.   The
whole evaporated in smoke, without leaving so much as the
scrapings of a crucible for a specific against the itch.

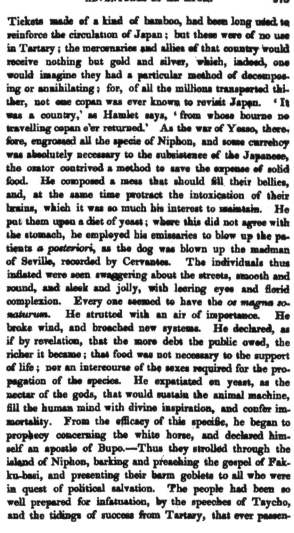

Tickets made of a kind of bamboo, had been long used to
reinforce the circulation of Japan; but these were of no use
in Tartary; the mercenaries and allies of that country would
receive nothing but gold and silver, which, indeed, one
would imagine they had a particular method of decompos-
ing or annihilating; for, of all the millions transported thither, not one copan was ever known to revisit Japan. ‘It
was a country,’ as Hamlet says, ‘from whose bourne no
travelling copan e'er returned.’ As the war of Yesso, therefore, engrossed all the specie of Niphon, and some currehcy
was absolutely necessary to the subsistence of the Japanese,
the orator contrived a method to save the expense of solid
food. He composed a mess that should fill their bellies,
and, at the same time protract the intoxication of their
brains, which it was so much his interest to maintain.   He
put them upon a diet of yeast; where this did not agree with
the stomach, he employed his emissaries to blow up the patients *a posteriori*, as the dog was blown up the madman
of Seville, recorded by Cervantes.   The individuals thus
inflated were seen swaggering about the streets, smooth and
round, and sleek and jolly, with leering eyes and florid
complexion.   Every one seemed to have the *os magna so-
naturum*.   He strutted with an air of importance.   He
broke wind, and broached new systems.   He declared, as
if by revelation, that the more debt the public owed, the
richer it became; that food was not necessary to the support
of life; nor an intercourse of the sexes required for the propagation of the species.   He expatiated on yeast, as the
nectar of the gods, that would sustain the animal machine,
fill the human mind with divine inspiration, and confer immortality.   From the efficacy of this specific, he began to
prophecy concerning the white horse, and declared himself an apostle of Bupo.—Thus they strolled through the
island of Niphon, barking and preaching the gospel of Fakku-basi, and presenting their barm goblets to all who were
in quest of political salvation.   The people had been so
well prepared for infatuation, by the speeches of Taycho,
and the tidings of success from Tartary, that ever passen-

get greedily swallowed the drench, and in a little time the whole nation was converted: that is, they were totally freed from those troublesome and impertinent faculties of reason and reflection, which could have served no other purpose but to make them miserable under the burdens to which their backs were now subjected. They offered up all their gold and silver, their jewels, their furniture and apparel, at the shrine of Fakku-basi, singing psalms and hymns in praise of the white horse. They put arms into the hands of their children, and drove them into Tartary, in order to fatten the land of Yesso with their blood. They grew fanatics in that cause, and worshipped Brut-an-tiffi, as the favourite prophet of the beatified Bupo. All was staggering, staring, incoherence, and contortion, exclamation and eructation. Still this was no more than a temporary delirium, which might vanish as the intoxicating effects of the yeast subsided. Taycho, therefore, called in two reinforcements to the drench. He resolved to satiate their appetite for blood, and to amuse their infantine vanity with the gew-gaws of triumph. He equipped out one armament at a considerable expense to make a descent on the coast of China, and sent another at a much greater, to fight the enemy in Fatsissio. The commander of the first disembarked upon a desolate island, demolished an unfinished cottage, and brought away a few bunches of wild grapes. He afterwards hovered on the Chinese coast; but was deterred from landing by a very singular phenomenon. In surveying the shore, through spying glasses, he perceived the whole beach instantaneously fortified, as it were, with parapets of sand, which had escaped the naked eye; and at one particular part, there appeared a body of giants with very hideous features, peeping, as it were, from behind those parapets: from which circumstance the Japanese general concluded there was a very formidable ambuscade, which he thought it would be madness to encounter, and even folly to ascertain. One would imagine he had seen Homer's account of the Cyclops, and did not think himself safe, even at the distance of some miles from the shore; for he pressed the com-

mander of the fune to weigh anchor immediately, and retire to a place of more safety.—I shall now, Peacock, let
you into the whole secret. This great officer was deceived
by the carelessness of the commissary, who, instead of perspectives, had furnished him with glasses peculiar to Japan,
that magnified and multiplied objects at the same time.
They are called pho-beron-tia.—The large parapets of sand
were a couple of mole-hills; and the gigantic faces of grim
aspect, were the posteriors of an old woman sacrificing *sub
dio*, to the powers of digestion. There was another circumstance which tended to the miscarriage of this favourite expedition. The principal design was against a trading town,
situated on a navigable river; and at the place where this
river disembogued itself into the sea, there was a Chinese
fort called Sa-rouf. The admiral of the fune sent the second in command, whose name was Sel-uon, to lay this fort
in ashes, that the embarkation might pass without let or
molestation. A Chinese pilot offered to bring his junk within a cable length of the walls; but he trusted to the light of
his own penetration. He ran his junk a-ground, and solemnly declared there was not water sufficient to float any
vessel of force, within three miles of Sa rouf. This discovery he had made by sounding, and it proved two very
surprising paradoxes: first, that the Chinese junks drew
little or no water, otherwise they could not have arrived at
the town where they were laid up: secondly, that the fort
So-rouf was raised in a spot where it neither could offend,
nor be offended. But the sey-seo-gun Sel-uon was a mighty
man for paradoxes. His superior in command was a plain
man, who did not understand these niceties: he therefore
grumbled, and began to be troublesome; upon which, a
council of war was held; and he being over-ruled by a majority of voices, the whole embarkation returned to Niphon
re infecta. You have been told how the beast called Legion
brayed, and bellowed, and kicked, when the fate of Byn-
goh's expedition was known; it was disposed to be very
unruly at the return of this armament; but Taycho lulled
it with a double dose of his mandragora. It growled at the

giants, the sand-hills, and the paradoxes of Sel-uon: then brayed aloud, *Taycho for ever!* rolled itself up like a blubberly hydra, yawned, and fell fast asleep. The other armament equipped for the operations in Fatsissio, did not arrive at the place of destination till the opportunity for action was lost. The object was the reduction of a town and island belonging to the Chinese: but before the fune with the troops arrived from Niphon, the enemy, having received intimation of their design, had reinforced the garrison and harbour with a greater number of forces and fune than the Japenese commander could bring against them. He therefore wisely declined an enterprise which must have ended in his own disgrace and destruction. The Chinese were successful in other parts of Fatsissio. They demolished some forts, they defeated some parties, and massacred some people, belonging to the colonies of Japan. Perhaps the tidings of these disasters would have roused the people of Niphon from the lethargy of intoxication in which they were overwhelmed, had not their delirium been kept up by some fascinating amulets from Tartary : these were no other than the bubbles which Brut-an-tiffi swelled into mighty victories over the Chinese and Ostrog; though, in fact, he had been severely cudgelled, and more than once in very great danger of crucifixion. Taycho presented the monster with a bowl of blood, which he told it this invincible ally had drawn from its enemies the Chinese, and, at the same time, blowed the gay bubbles athwart its numerous eyes. The hydra lapped the gore with signs of infinite relish; groaned and grunted to see the blubbles dance; exclaimed, —' O rare Taycho!' and relapsed into the arms of slumber. Thus passed the first campaign of Taycho's administration.

By this time Fika-kaka was fully convinced that the orator actually dealt with the devil, and had even sold him his soul for this power of working miracles on the understanding of the populace. He began to be invaded with fears, that the same consideration would be demanded of him for the ease and pleasure he now enjoyed in partnership with that

magician. He no longer heard himself scoffed, ridiculed,
and reviled in the assemblies of the people. He no longer
saw his measures thwarted, nor his person treated with disdain. He no longer racked his brains for pretences to extort
money; nor trembled with terror, when he used these pretences to the public. The mouth of the opposition was now
glewed to his own posteriors. Many a time, and often, when
he heard orator Taycho declaiming against him from his
rostrum, he cursed him in his heart, and was known to eja-
culate,—' Kiss my a——, Taycho ;' but little did he think
the orator would one day stoop to this compliance. He now
saw that insolent foul-mouthed demagogue ministering with
the utmost servility to his pleasure and ambition. He filled
his bags with the treasures of Japan, as if by enchantment ;
so that he could now gratify his own profuse temper without
stint or controul. He took upon himself the whole charge
of the administration ; and left Fika-kaka to the full enjoyment of his own sensuality, thus divested of all its thorns.
It was the contemplation of these circumstances, which inspired the cuboy with a belief that the devil was concerned
in producing this astonishing calm of felicity ; and that his
infernal highness would require of him some extraordinary sacrifice for the extraordinary favours he bestowed. He could
not help suspecting the sincerity of Taycho's attachment, because it seemed altogether unnatural ; and if his soul was to
be the sacrifice, he wished to treat with Satan as a principal.
Full of this idea, he had recourse to his bonzas, as the most
likely persons to procure him such an interview with the prince
of darkness, as should not be attended with immediate danger
to his corporeal parts : but, upon inquiry, he found there
was not one conjurer among them all.—Some of them made
a merit of their ignorance ; pretending they could not in
conscience give application to an art which must have led
them into communication with demons : others insisted there
was no such thing as the devil ; and this opinion seemed to
be much relished by the cuboy : the rest frankly owned they
knew nothing at all of the matter. For my part, Peacock,
I not only know there is a devil, but I likewise know that

he has marked out nineteen-twentieths of the people of this
metropolis for his prey.—How now! you shake, sirrah!—
You have some reason, considering the experiments you
have been trying in the way of sorcery; turning the sieve
and shears; mumbling gibberish over a goose's liver
stuck with pins; pricking your thumbs, and writing mystical characters with your blood; forming spells with sticks
laid across; reading prayers backwards; and invoking the
devil by the name, style, and title of *Sathan, Abrasax,
Adonai.* I know what communication you had with goody
Thrusk at Camberwell, who undertook, for three shillings
and fourpence, to convey you on a broomstick to Norway,
where the devil was to hold a conventicle; but you boggled
at crossing the sea, without such security for your person as
the beldame could not give. I remember you poring over
the treatise *De volucri arborea,* until you had well nigh lost
your wits; and your intention to enrol yourself in the Rosi-
crusian society, until your intrigue with the tripe-woman
in Thieving lane destroyed your pretension to chastity.
Then you cloaked your own wickedness with an affectation of
scepticism, and declared there never was any such existence
as devil, demon, spirit, or goblin; nor any such art as
magic, necromancy, sorcery, or witchcraft.—O infidel!
hast thou never heard of the three divisions of magic into
natural, artificial, and diabolical? The first of these is no
more than medicine; hence the same word Pharmacopola
signified both a wiseacre and apothecary. To the second
belong the glass sphere of Archimedes, the flying wooden
pigeon of Archytus, the emperor Leo's singing birds of gold,
Boetius the consolator's flying birds of brass, hissing serpents
of the same metal, and the famous speaking head of Albertus
Magnus. The last, which we call diabolical, depends upon the evocation of spirits; such was the art exercised by
the magicians of Pharaoh; as well as by that conjurer recorded by Gasper Peucerus, who animated the dead carcase
of a famous female harper in Bologna, in such a manner,
that she played upon her instrument as well as ever she had
done in her life, until another magician removing the charm,

which had been placed in her arm-pits, the body fell down deprived of all motion. It is by such means that conjurers cure distempers with charms and amulets; that, according to S*t*. Isidore, they confound the elements, disturb the understanding, slay without poison or any perceptible wound, call up devils, and learn from them how to torment their enemies. Magic was known even to the ancient Romans. Cato teaches us how to charm a dislocated bone, by repeating these mystical words,—*Incipe, cantare in alto, S. F. motas danata dardaries, Astotaries, die una parite dum coeunt, &c.* Besides, the virtues of ABRACADABRA are well known; though the meaning of the word has puzzled some of the best critics of the last age; such as Wendelinus, Scaliger, Saumaise, and father Kircher; not to mention the ancient physician Serenus Sammonicus, who describes the disposition of these characters in hexameter verse. I might here launch out into a very learned dissertation, to prove that this very Serenus formed the word ABRACADABRA from the Greek word Αβρασαξ, a name by which Basilides the Egyptian heretic defined the Deity, as the letters of it imply 365, the number of days in the year. This is the word still fair and legible on one of the two talismans found in the seventeenth century, of which Baronius gives us the figure in the second volume of his Annals. By-the-by, Peacock, you must take notice, that the figure of S*t*. George, encountering the dragon, which is the symbol of the order of the garter, and at this day distinguishes so many inns, taverns, and ale-houses, in this kingdom, was no other originally than the device of an abraxas or amulet wore by the Basilidians, as a charm against infection; for, by the man on horseback killing the dragon, was typified the sun purifying the air, and dispersing the noxious vapours from the earth. An abraxas marked with this device, is exhibited by Montfaucon out of the collection of Sig. Capello. This symbol, improved by the cross on the top of the spear, was afterwards adopted by the christian crusards, as a badge of their religious warfare, as well as an amulet to ensure victory; the cross alluding to Constantine's labarum

Vol. VI.　　　　　　H h

with the motto,—*ιν τουτ νικα*, ' In this you shall conquer.'
The figure on horseback they metamorphosed into S^t. George,
the same with George the Arian, who at one time was reckoned a martyr, and maintained a place in the Roman mar-
tyrology, from which he and others were erased by Pope
Gelasius, in the fifth century, because the accounts of their
martyrdom were written by heretics.   This very George,
while he officiated as bishop of Alexandria, having ordered
a temple of the god *Mythras* to be purified, and converted
into a christian church, found in the said temple this emblem
of the sun, which the Persians adored under the name of
Mythras; and with the addition of the cross, metamorphosed it into a symbol of christian warfare against idolatry.   It
was on this occasion that the pagans rose against George,
and murdered him with the utmost barbarity; and from this
circumstance he became a saint and martyr, and the amulet
or abraxas became his badge of distinction.   The cross was
considered as such a sure protection in battle, that every
sword-hilt was made in this form, and every warrior, before
he engaged, kissed it, in token of devotion: hence, the
phrase,—' I kiss your hilt,' which is sometimes used even at
this day.—With respect to the mystical words, ABRACAλ,
IAΩ, AOΩNAI, which are found upon those amulets, and
supposed to be of Hebrew extract, though in the Greek character of termination; if thou wouldst know their real signification, thou mayest consult the learned De Croy, in his
treatise concerning the genealogies of the *Gnostics*.   Thou
wilt find it at the end of S^t. Irenæus's works, published by
Grabius at Oxford.

But, to return to magic, thou must have heard of the
famous Albertus Magnus de Boldstadt, who indifferently
exercised the professions of conjurer, bawd, and man-mid-
wife; who forged the celebrated *Androids*, or brazen head,
which pronounced oracles, and solved questions of the utmost difficulty: nor can the fame of Henry Cornelius Agrippa
have escaped thee; he, who wrote the Treatises *De occulta
Philosophia; et de cæcis Ceremoniis;* who kept his demon
secured with an enchanted iron collar, in the shape of a

black dog; which black dog being dismissed in his last moments with these words,—*Abi perdita bestia quæ me totum perdidisti*, plunged itself in the river Soame, and immediately disappeared. But what need of those profane instances, to prove the existence of magicians who held communication with the devil? Don't we read in the Scripture of the magicians of Pharaoh and Manasses; of the witch of Endor; of Simon and Barjesus, magicians; and of that sorceress, of whose body the apostle Paul dispossessed the devil? Have not the fathers mentioned magicians and sorcerers? Have not different councils denounced anathemas against them? Hath not the civil law decreed punishments to be inflicted upon those convicted of the black art? Have not all the tribunals in France, England, and particularly in Scotland, condemned many persons to the stake for sorceries, on the fullest evidence, nay, even on their own confession? Thou thyself mayest almost remember the havoc that was made among the sorcerers in one of the English colonies in North America, by Dr Encrease Mather, and Dr Cotton Mather, those luminaries of the New-England church, under the authority and auspices of Sir William Phipps, that flower of knighthood, and mirror of governors, who, not contented with living witnesses, called in the assistance of spectral evidence, to the conviction of those diabolical delinquents. This was a hint, indeed, which he borrowed from the famous trial of Urban Grandier, canon of Loudun in France, who was duly convicted of magic, upon the depositions of the devils *Astaroth, Eusas, Celsus, Acaos, Cedon, Asmodeus, Alix, Zabulon, Nephthalim, Cham, Uriel,* and *Achas.* I might likewise refer thee to King James's history of witchcraft, wherein it appears, upon uncontrovertible evidence, that the devil not only presided in person at the assemblies of those wise women, but even condescended to be facetious, and often diverted them by dancing and playing gambols with a lighted candle in his breech. I might bid thee recollect the authenticated account of the earl of Gowry's conspiracy against the said king, in which appears the deposition of a certain person, certifying that the earl of Gowry had studied the black art; that he wore an amulet about his person, of such efficacy, that although he was run several times through the body, not one drop of blood flowed from the wounds until those mystical characters were removed.— Finally, I could fill whole volumes with undeniable facts, to prove the existence of magic; but what I have said shall suffice. I must only repeat it again, that there was not one magician, conjurer, wizard, or witch, among all the bonzas of Japan, whom the cuboy consulted: a circumstance that astonished him the more, as divers of them, notwithstanding their beards, were shrewdly suspected to be old women; and till that time, an old woman with a beard upon her chin had been always considered as an agent of the devil. It was the nature of Fika-kaka to be impatient and impetuous. Perceiving that none of his bonzas had any communication with the devil, and that many of them doubted whether there was any such personage as the devil, he began to have some doubts about his own soul :—'for if there is no devil,' said he, ' there is no soul to be damned; and it would be a reproach to the justice of heaven, to suppose that all souls are to be saved, considering what rascally stuff mankind are made of.' This was an inference which gave him great disturbance; for he was one of those who would rather encounter eternal damnation, than run any risk of being annihilated. He therefore assembled all those among the bonzas who had the reputation of being great philosophers and metaphysicians, in order to hear their opinions concerning the nature of the soul. The first reverend sage who delivered himself on this mysterious subject, having stroked his grey beard, and hemmed thrice with great solemnity, declared that the soul was an animal; a second pronounced it to be the number *three*, or proportion; a third contended for the number *seven*, or harmony; a fourth defined the soul the *universe*; a fifth affirmed it was a mixture of elements; a sixth asserted it was composed of *fire*; a seventh opined it was formed of *water*; an eighth called it an *essence*; a ninth, an *idea*; a tenth stickled for *substance without extension*; an eleventh, for *extension without substance*; a

twelfth cried it was an *accident;* a thirteenth called it a
reflecting mirror; a fourteenth, the *image reflected;* a
fifteenth insisted upon its being a *tune;* a sixteenth believed
it was the instrument that played the tune; a seventeenth
undertook to prove it was *material;* an eighteenth exclaimed
it was *immaterial;* a nineteenth allowed it was *something;*
and a twentieth swore it was *nothing.*—By this time all the
individuals that composed this learned assembly, spoke together, with equal eagerness and vociferation. The volubility with which a great number of abstruse and unintelligible terms and definitions were pronounced and repeated,
not only resembled the confusion of Babel, but they had just
the same effect upon the brain of Fika-kaka, as is generally
produced in weak heads, by looking stedfastly at a mill-
wheel or a vortex, or any other object in continual rotation.
He grew giddy, ran three times round, and dropped down
in the midst of the bonzas, deprived of sense and motion.
When he recovered so far as to be able to reflect upon what
had happened, he was greatly disturbed with the terror of
annihilation, as he had heard nothing said in the consultation which could give him any reason to believe there was
such a thing as an immortal soul.—In this emergency, he
sent for his counsellor Mura-clami, and when that lawyer
entered his chamber, exclaimed,—' my dear Mura, as I
have a soul to be saved!—A soul to be saved!—ay, there's
the rub!—the devil a soul have I!—Those bonzas are good
for nothing but to kiss my a——;—a parcel of ignorant asses!
—Pox on their philosophy!—Instead of demonstrating
the immortality of the soul, they have plainly proved the
soul is a chimera, a Will-o'-the-wisp, a bubble, a term, a
word, a nothing!—My dear Mura! prove but that I have a
soul, and I shall be contented to be damned to all eternity!'
' If that be the case,' said the other, ' your quambukuship
may set your heart at rest: for, if you proceed to govern
this empire, in conjunction with Taycho, as you have begun, it will become a point of eternal justice to give you an
immortal soul (if you have not one already), that you may
undergo eternal punishment, according to your demerits.

The cuboy was much comforted by this assurance, and returned to his former occupations with redoubled ardour. He continued to confer benefices on his back-friends the bonzas; to regulate the whole army of tax-gatherers; to bribe the tribunes, the centurions, the decuriones, and all the inferior mob-drivers of the empire; to hire those pipers who were best skilled in making the multitude dance, and find out the ablest artists to scratch their long ears, and tickle their noses. These toils were sweetened by a variety of enjoyments. He possessed all the pomp of ostentation; the vanity of levees, the pride of power, the pleasure of adulation, the happiness of being kicked by his sovereign and kissed by his bonzas; and above all, the delights of the stomach and the close-stool, which recurred in perpetual succession, and which he seemed to enjoy with a particular relish: for it must be observed, to the honour of Fika-kaka, that what he eagerly received at one end, he as liberally refunded at the other. But as the faculties of his mind were insufficient to digest the greatness of power which had fallen to his share, so were the organs of his body unable to concoct the enormous mass of aliments which he so greedily swallowed. He laboured under an indigestion of both; and the vague promises which went upwards, as well as the murmurs that passed the other way, were no other than eruptive crudities arising from the defects of his soul and body.

As for Taycho, he confined himself to the management of the war. He recalled the general in chief from Fatsissio, because he had not done that which he could not possibly do; but, instead of sending another on whose abilities he could depend, he allowed the direction of the armaments to devolve upon the second in command, whose character he could not possibly know; because, indeed, he was too obscure to have any character at all. The fruits of his sagacity soon appeared. The new general Abra-moria, having reconnoitred a post of the enemy, which was found too strong to be forced, attacked it without hesitation, and his troops were repulsed and routed with considerable slaughter. It was lucky for Taycho that the tidings of this disaster were qualified by the news of two other advantages which the arms of Japan had gained. A separate corps of troops, under Yaf-frai and Ya-loff, reduced a strong Chinese fortress in the neighbourhood of Fatsissio; and a body of Japanese, headed by a factor called Ka-liff, obtained a considerable victory at Fla-sao, in the farther extremity of Tartary, where a trading company of Meaco possessed a commercial settlement. The Hydra of Meaco began to shake its numerous heads, and growl, when it heard of Abra-moria's defeat. At that instant, one of its leaders exclaimed,—' Bless thy long ears! It was not Taycho that recommended Abra-moria to this command. He was appointed by the fatsman.' This was true. It was likewise true that Taycho had allowed him quietly to succeed to the command, without knowing any thing of his abilities; it was equally true that Taycho was an utter stranger to Yaf-frai and Ya-loff, who took the fortress, as well as to the factor Ka-liff, who obtained the victory at the farther end of Tartary. Nevertheless, the beast cried aloud,—' Hang Abra-moria! and a fig for the fatsman. But let the praise of Taycho be magnified! It was Taycho that subdued the fortress in the isle Ka-frit-o. It was Taycho that defeated the enemy at Fla-sao. Yaf-frai has slain his thousands; Ya-loff has slain his five thousands; but Taycho has slain his ten thousands.'

Taycho had credit not only for the success of the Japanese arms, but likewise for the victories of Brut-an-tiffi, who had lately been much beholden to fortune. I have already observed what a noise that Tartar made when the fatsman of Japan found himself obliged to capitulate with the Chinese general. In consequence of that event, the war was already at an end with respect to the Japanese, on the continent of Tartary. The emperor of China took possession of the farm of Yesso; the peasants quietly submitted to their new masters; and those very free-booting Tartar chiefs, who had sold their subjects as soldiers, to serve under the fatsman, had already agreed to send the very same mercenaries into the army of China. It was at this juncture that Brut-an-tiffi exalted his throat. In the preceding campaign he had fought with various success. One of his generals had given battle to the Mantchoux Tartars, and each side claimed the victory. Another of his leaders had been defeated and taken by the Ostrog. The Chinese had already advanced to the frontiers of Brut-an-tiffi's dominions. In this dilemma he exerted himself with equal activity and address: he repulsed the Chinese army with considerable loss; and, in the space of one month after this action, gained a victory over the general of the Ostrog. These advantages rendered him insufferably arrogant. He exclaimed against the fatzman; he threatened the dairo; and, as I have taken notice above, a new army was raised at the expense of Japan, to defend him from all future invasions of the Chinese. Already the Tartar general Bron-xi-tic, who was vested at his desire with the command of the mercenary army of Japan, had given a severe check to a strong body of the Chinese, and even threatened to carry the war into the empire of China; but his progress was soon stopt, and he was forced to retreat in his turn towards the farm of Yesso. But from nothing did orator Taycho reap a fuller harvest of praise, than from the conquest of Tsin-khall, a settlement of the Chinese on the coast of Terra Australis; which conquest was planned by a Banyan merchant of Meaco, who had traded on that coast, and was particularly known to the king of the country. This royal savage was uneasy at the neighbourhood of the Chinese, and conjured the merchant, whose name was Thum-Khumm-qua, to use his influence at the court of Meaco, that an armament should be equipped against the settlement of Tsin-khall, he himself solemnly promising to co-operate in the reduction of it with all his forces. Thum-Khumm-qua, whose zeal for the good of his country got the better of all his prudential maxims, did not fail to represent this object in the most interesting points of view. He demonstrated to Taycho the importance of the settlement; that it abounded with slaves, ivory, gold, and a precious gum which was not to be found in any other part of the world; a gum in great request all over Asia, and par-

ticularly among the Japanese, who were obliged to purchase
it in time of war at second-hand from their enemies the
Chinese, at an exorbitant price. He demonstrated that
the loss of this settlement would be a terrible wound to the
emperor of China; and proved that the conquest of it could
be achieved at a very trifling expense. He did more.
Though by the maxims of his sect he was restrained from
engaging in any military enterprise, he offered to conduct
the armament in person, in order the more effectually to
keep the king of the country steady to his engagements.
Though the scheme was in itself plausible and practicable,
Mr Orator Taycho shuffled and equivocated until the season
for action was past. But Thum-Khumm-qua was indefatigable: he exhorted, he pressed, he remonstrated, he complained, and besieged the orator's house in such a manner,
that Taycho at length, in order to be rid of his importunity,
granted his request. A small armament was fitted out; the
banyan embarked in it, leaving his own private affairs in
confusion; and the settlement was reduced according to his
prediction. When the news of this conquest arrived at
Meaco, the multifarious beast breathed hoarse applause, and
the minister Taycho was magnified exceedingly. As for
Thum-Khumm-qua, whose private fortune was consumed in
the expedition, all the recompence he received, was the consciousness of having served his country. In vain he reminded Taycho of his promises; in vain he recited the minister's
own letters, in which he had given his word that the banyan should be liberally rewarded, according to the importance of his services: Taycho was both deaf and blind to all
his remonstrances and representations; and, at last, fairly
flung the door in his face.

Such was the candour and the gratitude of the incomparable Taycho. The poor projector Thum-Khumm-qua
found himself in a piteous case, while the whole nation resounded with joy for the conquest which his sagacity had
planned, and his zeal carried into execution. He was not
only abandoned by the minister Taycho, but also renounced
by the whole sect of the banyans, who looked upon him as

a wicked apostate, because he had been concerned with those
who fought with the arm of flesh.   It was lucky for him that
he afterwards found favour with a subsequent minister, who
had not adopted all the maxims of his predecessor Taycho.
The only measures which this eggregious demagogue could
hitherto properly call his own, were these : his subsidiary
treaty with Brut an-tiffi ; his raising an immense army of
mercenaries to act in Tartary for the benefit of that prince ;
his exacting an incredible sum of money from the people of
Japan ; and, finally, two successive armaments which he
had sent to annoy the sea-coasts of China.   I have already
given an account of the first, the intent of which was frustrated by a mistake in the perspectives.   The other was more
fortunate in the beginning.   Taycho had, by the force of
his genius, discovered that nothing so effectually destroyed
the oiled paper which the Chinese use in their windows instead of glass, as the gold coin called oban, when discharged
from a military engine at a proper distance.   He found that
gold was more compact, more heavy, more malleable, and
more manageable, than any other metal or substance that
he knew : he therefore provided a great quantity of obans,
and a good body of slingers ; and these being conveyed to
the coast of China in a squadron of fune, as none of the Chinese appeared to oppose these hostilities, a select number of
the troops were employed to make ducks and drakes with
the obans, on the supposition that this diversion would al-
lure the enemy to the sea-side, where they might be knocked on the head without further trouble ; but the care of their
own safety got the better of their curiosity on this occasion ;
and fifty thousand obans were expended in this manner,
without bringing one Chinese from his lurking-hole.   Considerable damage was done to the windows of the enemy.
Then the forces were landed in a village, which they found
deserted.   Here they burned some fishing-boats ; and from
hence they carried off some military machines, which were
brought to Meaco, and conveyed through the streets in procession, amidst the acclamations of the hydra, who sung the
praise of Taycho.   Elevated by this triumph, the minister

sent forth the same armament a second time, under a new
general of his own choosing, whose name was Hylib-bib,
who had long entertained an opinion that the inhabitants of
China were not beings of flesh and blood, but mere fantastic
shadows, who could neither offend nor be offended. Full
of this opinion, he made a descent on the coast of that empire; and, to convince his followers that his notion was right,
he advanced some leagues into the country, without having
taken any precautions to secure a retreat, leaving the fune
at anchor upon an open beach. Some people alleged that
he depended upon the sagacity of an engineer recommended
to him by Taycho; which engineer had such an excellent
nose, that he could smell a Chinese at the distance of ten
leagues; but it seems the scent failed him at this juncture.
Perhaps the Chinese general had trailed rusty bacon and
other odoriferous substances to confound his sense of smelling. Perhaps no dew had fallen over-night, and a strong
breeze blew towards the enemy. Certain it is, Hylib-bib, in
the evening, received repeated intelligence that he was within half a league of the Chinese general, at the head of a body
of troops greatly superior in number to the Japanese forces
which he himself commanded. He still believed it was all
illusion; and, when he heard their drums beat, declared it
was no more than a ridiculous enchantment. He thought
proper, however, to retreat towards the sea-side; but this he
did with great deliberation, after having given the enemy
fair notice by beat of drum. His motions were so slow, that
he took seven hours to march three miles. When he reached the shore where the fune were at anchor, he saw the whole
body of the Chinese drawn up on a rising ground, ready to
begin the attack. He ordered his rear-guard to face about,
on the supposition that the phantoms would disappear as
soon as they shewed their faces; but finding himself mistaken, and perceiving some of his own people to drop in
consequence of missiles that came from the enemy, he very
calmly embarked with his van, leaving his rear to amuse the
Chinese, by whom they were, in less than five minutes, either massacred or taken. From this small disgrace the ge-

neral deduced two important corollaries; first, that the Chinese were actually material beings, capable of impulsion; and, secondly, that his engineer's nose was not altogether infallible. The people of Meaco did not seem to relish the experiments by which these ideas were ascertained. The monster was heard to grunt in different streets of the metropolis; and these notes of discontent produced the usual effect in the bowels of Fika-kaka; but orator Taycho had his flowers of rhetoric and his bowl of mandragora in readiness. He assured them that Hylib-bib should be employed for the future in keeping sheep on the island of Xicoco, and the engineer be sent to hunt truffles on the mountains of Ximo. Then he tendered his dose, which the hydra swallowed with signs of pleasure; and, lastly, he mounted upon its back, and rode in triumph under the windows of the astonished cuboy, who, while he shifted his trowsers, exclaimed, in a rapture of joy,—' All hail, Taycho, thou prince of monster-taming men! the dairo shall kick thy posteriors, and I will kiss them in token of approbation and applause.'

The time was now come when fortune, which had hitherto smiled upon the Chinese arms, resolved to turn tail to that vain-glorious nation; and precisely at the same instant Taycho undertook to display his whole capacity in the management of the war. But before he assumed this province, it was necessary that he should establish a despotism in the council of twenty-eight, some members of which had still the presumption to offer their advice towards the administration of affairs. This council being assembled by the dairo's order, to deliberate upon the objects of the next campaign, the president began by asking the opinion of Taycho, who was the youngest member; upon which the orator made no articulate reply, but cried,—' Ba-ba-ba-ba!' The dairo exclaimed,—' Boh!' The fatsman ejaculated the interjection ' pish!' The cuboy sat in silent astonishment. Gotto-mio swore the man was dumb, and hinted something of lunacy. Foksi-roku shook his head, and Soo-san-sin-o shrugged up his shoulders. At length Fika-kaka going round, and kissing Taycho on the forehead,—' My dear

boy!' cried he, ' Gad's curse! what's the matter? Do but
open the sluices of your eloquence once more, my dear orator; let us have one simile—one dear simile, and then I
shall die contented. With respect to the operations of the
campaign, don't you think—' Here he was interrupted with
—'Ka, ka, ka, ka!' 'Heighday!' cried the cuboy, ' Ba-
ba-ba, ka-ka-ka! that's the language of children!' ' And
children you shall be,' exclaimed the orator. ' Here is a
two-penny trumpet for the amusement of the illustrious Got-
hama-baba, a sword of gingerbread covered with gold leaf
for the fatsman, and a rattle for my lord cuboy. I have
likewise sugar-plumbs for the rest of the council.' So saying, he, without ceremony, advanced to the dairo, and tied
a scarf round the eyes of his imperial majesty; then he produced a number of padlocks, and sealed up the lips of every
quo in council, before they could recollect themselves from
their first astonishment. The assembly broke up abruptly;
and the dairo was conducted to his cabinet by the fatsman
and the cuboy, which last endeavoured to divert the chagrin
of his royal master, by blowing the trumpet and shaking the
rattle in his ears; but Got-hama-baba could not be so easily
appeased. He growled like an enraged bear at the indignity
which had been offered to him, and kicked the cuboy before
as well as behind. Mr Orator Taycho was fain to come to
an explanation. He assured the dairo it was necessary that
his imperial majesty should remain in the dark, and that the
whole council should be muzzled for a season, otherwise he
could not accomplish the great things he had projected in
favour of the farm of Yesso. He declared, that, while his
majesty remained blindfold, he would enjoy all his other
senses in greater perfection; that his ears would be every day
regaled with the shouts of triumph, conveyed in notes of uncommon melody; and that the less quantity of animal spirits
was expended in vision, the greater proportion would flow
to his extremities; consequently, his pleasure would be more
acute in his pedestrian exercitations upon the cuboy and
others, whom he delighted to honour. He therefore exhorted
him to undergo a total privation of eye-sight, which was at

best a troublesome faculty, that exposed mankind to a great
variety of disagreeable spectacles.   This was a proposal
which the dairo did not relish ; on the contrary, he waxed
exceedingly wroth, and told the orator he would rather enjoy one transient glance of the farm of Yesso, than the most
exquisite delights that could be procured for all the other
senses.   ' To gratify your majesty with that ineffable pleasure,' cried Taycho, ' I have devoted myself, soul and body,
and even reconciled contradictions.   I have renounced all
my former principles, without forfeiting the influence which,
by professing those principles, I had gained.   I have obtained the most astonishing victories over common sense, and
even refuted mathematical demonstration.   The many-headed mob, which no former demagogue could ever tame, I
have taught to fetch and to carry, to dance to my pipe, to
bray to my tune, to swallow what I present without murmuring, to lick my feet when I am angry, and kiss the rod when
I think proper to chastise it.   I have done more, my liege :
I have prepared a drench for it, which, like Lethe, washes
away the remembrance of what is past, and takes away all
sense of its own condition.   I have swept away all the money
of the empire ; and persuaded the people not only to beggar
themselves, but likewise to entail indigence upon their latest
posterity ; and all for the sake of Yesso.   It is by dint of these
efforts I have been able to subsidize Brut-an-tiffi, and raise
an army of one hundred thousand men to defend your imperial majesty's farm, which, were the entire property of it
brought to market, would not fetch one third part of the
sums which are now yearly expended in its defence.   I shall
strike but one great stroke in the country of Fatsissio, and
then turn the whole stream of the war into the channel of
Tartary, until the barren plains of Yesso are fertilized with
human blood.   In the meantime, I must insist upon your
majesty's continuing in the dark, and amusing yourself in
your cabinet with the trumpet and other gewgaws which I
have provided for your diversion, otherwise I quit the reins
of administration, and turn the monster out of my trammels ; in which case, like the dog that returns to its vomit,

it will not fail to take up its former prejudices against Yes-so, which I have with such pains obliged it to resign.' ' O my dear Taycho!' cried the affrighted dairo; ' talk not of leaving me in such a dreadful dilemma. Rather than the dear farm should fall into the hands of the Chinese, I would be contented to be led about blindfold all the days of my life.—Proceed in your own way.—I invest you with full power and authority, not only to gag my whole council, but even to nail their ears to the pillory, should it be found necessary for the benefit of Yesso. In token of which dele-gation, present your posteriors, and I will bestow upon you a double portion of my favour.' Taycho humbly thanked his imperial majesty for the great honour he intended him; but begged leave to decline the ceremony, on account of the hemorrhoids, which at that time gave him great disturb-ance.

The orator having thus annihilated all opposition in the council of twenty-eight, repaired to his own house, in order to plan the operations of the ensuing campaign. Though he had reinforced the army in Tartary with the flower of the Japanese soldiery, and destined a strong squadron of fune, as usual, to parade on the coast of China, he foresaw it would be necessary to amuse the people with some new stroke on the side of Fatsissio, which indeed was the original and the most natural scene of the war. He locked himself up in his closet; and consulting the map of Fatsissio, he found that the principal Chinese settlement of that island was a fortified town called Quib-quab, to which there was access by two different avenues; one by a broad, rapid, navigable river, on the banks of which the town was situated; and the other by an inland route over moun-tains, lakes, and dangerous torrents. He measured the map with his compass, and perceived that both routes were near-ly of the same length; and therefore, he resolved, that the forces in Fatsissio, being divided into two equal bodies, should approach the place by the two different avenues, on the supposition that they would both arrive before the walls of Quib-quab at the same instant of time. The conduct of the inland expedition was given to Yaff-rai, who now commanded in chief in Fatsissio; and the rest of the troops were sent up the great river under the auspices of Ya-loff, who had so eminently distinguished himself in the course of the preceding year.

Orator Taycho had received some articles of intelligence which embarrassed him a little at first; but these difficulties soon vanished before the vigour of his resolutions. He knew that not only the town of Quib-quab was fortified by art, but also that the whole adjacent country was almost impregnable by nature: that one Chinese general blocked up the passes with a strong body of forces, in the route which was to be followed by Yaff-rai; and that another commanded a separate corps in the neighbourhood of Quib-quab, equal, at least, in number to the detachment of Ya-loff, whom he might therefore either prevent from landing, or attack after he should be landed: or, finally, should neither of these attempts succeed, he might reinforce the garrison of Quib-quab, so as to make it more numerous than the besieging army, which, according to the rules of war, ought to be ten times the number of the besieged. On the other hand, in order to invalidate these objections, he reflected that fortune, which had such a share in all military events, is inconstant and variable; that as the Chinese had been so long successful in Fatsissio, it was now their turn to be unfortunate. He reflected that the demon of folly was capricious; and that as it had so long possessed the rulers and generals of Japan, it was high time it should shift its quarters, and occupy the brains of the enemy; in which case they would quit their advantageous posts, and commit some blunder that would lay them at the mercy of the Japanese.—With respect to the reduction of Quib-quab, he had heard, indeed, that the besiegers ought to be ten times the number of the garrison besieged; but as every Japanese was equivalent to ten subjects of China, he thought the match was pretty equal. He reflected, that even if this expedition should not succeed, it would be of little consequence to his reputation, as he could plead at home, that he neither conceived the original plan, nor appointed any of the officers concerned in the execution. It is true, he might have reinforced the army in Fatsissio, so as to leave very little to fortune: but then he must have subtracted something from the strength of the operations in Tartary, which was now become the favourite scene of the war; or he must have altogether suspended the execution of another darling scheme, which was literally his own conception. There was an island in the great Indian ocean at a considerable distance from Fatsissio; and here the Chinese had a strong settlement. Taycho was inflamed with the ambition of reducing this island, which was called Thin-quo; and for this purpose he resolved to embark a body of forces which should co-operate with the squadron of fune, destined to cruise in those latitudes. The only difficulty that remained, was to choose a general to direct this enterprise. He perused a list of all the military officers in Japan; and as they were all equal in point of reputation, he began to examine their names, in order to pitch upon that which should appear to be the most significant: and in this particular, Taycho was a little superstitious. Not but that surnames, when properly bestowed, might be rendered very useful terms of distinction: but I must tell thee, Peacock, nothing can be more preposterously absurd than the practice of inheriting *cognomina*, which ought ever to be purely personal. I would ask thee, for example, what propriety there was in giving the name *Xenophon*, which signifies *one that speaks a foreign language*, to the celebrated Greek who distinguished himself, not only as a consummate captain, but also as an elegant writer in his mother tongue? What could be more ridiculous than to denominate the great philosopher of Cretona, *Pythagoras*, which implies a *stinking speech?* Or what could be more misapplied than the name of the weeping philosopher *Heraclitus*, signifying *military glory?* The inheritance of surnames among the Romans, produced still more ludicrous consequences. The best and noblest families in Rome derived their names from the coarsest employments, or else from the corporeal blemishes of their aneesters. The *Pisones* were millers: the *Cicerones* and the *Lentuli* were so called from the *vetches* and the *lentils* which their forefathers dealt in. The *Fabii* were so denominated from a dung-pit, in which the first of the family was begot by stealth in the way of fornication. A ploughman gave rise to the great family of the *Serrani*, the ladies of which always went without smocks. The *Suilli*, the *Bubulci*, and the *Porci*, were descended from a swine-herd, a cow-herd, and hog-butcher.—What could be more disgraceful than to call the senator *Strabo*, *Squintum;* or a fine young lady of the house of *Pæti*, *Pigsnies?* or to distinguish a matron of the *Limi*, by the appellation of *Sheep's-eye?*—What could be more dishonourable than to give the surname of *Snub-nose* to P. *Silius*, the proprætor, because his great-great-great-grandfather had a nose of that make? *Ovid*, indeed, had a long nose, and therefore was justly denominated *Naso:* but why should Horace be called *Flaccus*, as if his ears had been stretched in the pillory. I need not mention the *Burrhi*, *Nigri*, *Rufi*, *Aquilli*, and *Rutilii*, because we have the same foolish surnames in England; and even the *Lappa;* for I myself know a very pretty miss called *Rough-head*, though in fact there is not a young lady in the bills of mortality, who takes more pains to dress her hair to the best advantage. The famous dictator, when the deputies of Rome found at the plough, was known by the name of *Cincinnatus*, or *Ragged-head*. Now I leave you to judge how it would sound in these days, if a footman at the play-house should call out,—' *My Lady Ragged-head's coach. Room for my Lady Ragged-head.* I am doubtful whether the English name of *Hale* does not come from the Roman cognomen *Hala*, which signified *stinking breath*. What need I mention the *Plauti*, *Panci*, *Valgi*, *Vari*, *Vatiæ*, and *Scauri;* the *Tuditani*, the *Malici*, *Cenestellæ*, and *Leccæ;* in other words, the *Splay-foots*, *Bandy-legs*, *Shamble-shins*, *Baker-knees*, *Club-foots*, *Hammer-heads*, *Chubby-cheeks*, *Bald-heads*, and *Letchers.* I shall not say a word of the *Buteo* or *Buzzard*, that I may not be obliged to explain the meaning of the word *Triorchis*,

from whence it takes its denomination; yet all those were
great families in Rome. But I cannot help taking notice of
some of the same improprieties which have crept into the
language and customs of this country. Let us suppose, for
example, a foreigner reading an English newspaper in these
terms.—Last Tuesday the Right Honourable *Timothy Silly-
man*, secretary of state for the southern department, gave a
grand entertainment to the nobility and gentry at his house in
Knave's acre. The evening was concluded with a ball, which
was opened by Sir *Samuel Hog*, and Lady *Diana Rough-head.*
—We hear there is purpose of marriage between Mr Alderman *Small-cock* and Miss *Harriot Hair-stones*, a young lady
of great fortune and superlative merit.—By the last mail from
Germany, we have certain advice of a complete victory
which General *Coward* has obtained over the enemy. On
this occasion the general displayed all the intrepidity of the
most renowned hero: by the same canal we are informed,
that Lieutenant *Little-fear* has been broke by a court-martial
for cowardice. We hear that *Edward West*, esquire, will
be elected president of the directors of the *East-India* company for the ensuing year. It is reported that Commodore
North will be sent with a squadron into the *South sea.*
Captains *East* and *South* are appointed by the lords of the
admiralty, commanders of two frigates, to sail on the discovery of the *North-west* passage. Yesterday morning Sir
John Summer, baronet, lay dangerously ill at his house in
Spring-garden: he is attended by Dr *Winter ;* but there
are no hopes of his recovery. Saturday last *Philip Frost*,
a dealer in *gunpowder*, died at his house in *Snow-hill*, of
a high fever caught by overheating himself, in walking for
a wager from *No Man's land* to the *World's End.* Last
week Mr *John Fog*, teacher of astronomy in Rotherhithe,
was married to the widow *Fairweather* of *Puddledock.* We
hear from Bath, that on Thursday last a duel was fought
on Lansdown, by Captain *Sparrow* and *Richard Hawke*,
esquire, in which the latter was mortally wounded. Friday
last ended the sessions at the Old-bailey, when the following

persons received sentence of death.—*Leonard Lamb*, for
the murder of *Julius Wolf*; and *Henry Grave*, for robbing
and assaulting Dr *Death*, whereby the said *Death* was put
in fear of his life. *Giles Gosling*, for defrauding *Simon
Fox* of four guineas and his watch, by subtle craft, was
transported for seven years; and *David Drinkwater* was ordered to be set in the stocks, as an habitual drunkard. The
trial of *Thomas Green*, whitster at Fulham, for a rape on
the body of *Flora White*, a mulatto, was put off til next
sessions, on account of the absence of two material evidences,
viz. *Sarah Brown*, clear-starcher of *Pimlico*, and *Anthony
Black*, scarlet-dyer of *Wandsworth*.' I ask thee, *Peacock*,
whether a sensible foreigner, who understood the literal meaning of these names, which are all truly British, would not
think ye were a nation of humourists, who delighted in
cross-purposes and ludicrous singularity? But, indeed, ye
are not more absurd in this particular, than some of your
neighbours. I knew a Frenchman of the name of *Bouvier*,
which signifies *cow-keeper*, pique himself upon his noblesse;
and a general called *Valavoir*, is said to have lost his life by
the whimsical impropriety of his surname, which signifies
go and see. You may remember an Italian minister called *Grossa-testa*, or *Great-head*, though in fact he had
scarce any head at all. That nation has, likewise, its
Sforzas, Malatestas, Boccanigras, Porcinas, Giudices; its
Colonnas, Muratorios, Medicis, and *Goxxi*; *endeavours,
chuckle-heads, black muzzles, hogs, judges, pillars, masons,
leeches*, and *chubby chops*. Spain has its *Almohadas, Gi-
rones, Utreras, Ursinas*, and *Zapatus*; signifying, cushions, gores, bullocks, bears, and slippers. The Turks,
in other respects a sensible people, fall into the same extravagance, with respect to the inheritance of surnames. An
Armenian merchant, to whom I once belonged at Aleppo,

---

* The general, taking a solitary walk in the evening, was questioned by a
sentinel, and answered,—' Va la voir.' The soldier, taking the words in
the literal sense, repeated the challenge: he was answered in the same
manner; and being affronted, fired upon the general, who fell dead on the
spot.

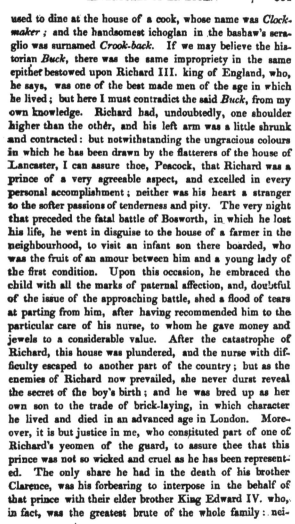

used to dine at the house of a cook, whose name was *Clock-maker* ; and the handsomest ichoglan in the bashaw's seraglio was surnamed *Crook-back*.   If we may believe the historian *Buck*, there was the same impropriety in the same epithet bestowed upon Richard III. king of England, who, he says, was one of the best made men of the age in which he lived; but here I must contradict the said *Buck*, from my own knowledge.   Richard had, undoubtedly, one shoulder higher than the other, and his left arm was a little shrunk and contracted : but notwithstanding the ungracious colours in which he has been drawn by the flatterers of the house of Lancaster, I can assure thee, Peacock, that Richard was a prince of a very agreeable aspect, and excelled in every personal accomplishment ; neither was his heart a stranger to the softer passions of tenderness and pity.   The very night that preceded the fatal battle of Bosworth, in which he lost his life, he went in disguise to the house of a farmer in the neighbourhood, to visit an infant son there boarded, who was the fruit of an amour between him and a young lady of the first condition.   Upon this occasion, he embraced the child with all the marks of paternal affection, and, doubtful of the issue of the approaching battle, shed a flood of tears at parting from him, after having recommended him to the particular care of his nurse, to whom he gave money and jewels to a considerable value.   After the catastrophe of Richard, this house was plundered, and the nurse with difficulty escaped to another part of the country ; but as the enemies of Richard now prevailed, she never durst reveal the secret of the boy's birth ; and he was bred up as her own son to the trade of brick-laying, in which character he lived and died in an advanced age in London.   Moreover, it is but justice in me, who constituted part of one of Richard's yeomen of the guard, to assure thee that this prince was not so wicked and cruel as he has been represented.   The only share he had in the death of his brother Clarence, was his forbearing to interpose in the behalf of that prince with their elder brother King Edward IV. who, in fact, was the greatest brute of the whole family : neither did he poison his own wife; nor employ assasins to murder his two nephews in the Tower. Both the boys were given by Tyrrel in charge to a German Jew, with directions to breed them up as his own children, in a remote country; and the eldest died of a fever at Embden, and the other afterwards appeared as claimant of the English crown; all the world knows how he finished his career under the name of Perkin Warbeck. So much for the abuse of surnames, in the investigation of which I might have used thy own by way of illustration; for, if thou and all thy generation were put to the rack, they would not be able to give any tolerable reason why thou shouldst be called *Peacock* rather than *Crab-louse*. But it is now high time to return to the thread of our narration. Taycho, having considered the list of officers, without finding one name which implied any active virtue, resolved that the choice should depend upon accident. He hustled them altogether in his cap, and putting in his hand at random, drew forth that of Hob-nob; a person who had grown old in obscurity, without ever having found an opportunity of being concerned in actual service. His very name was utterly unknown to Fika-ka-ka; and this circumstance the orator considered as a lucky omen; for the cuboy had such a remarkable knack at finding out the least qualified subjects, and overlooking merit, his new colleague concluded, not without some shadow of reason, that Hob-nob's being unknown to the prime minister, was a sort of negative presumption in favour of his character. This officer was accordingly placed at the head of an armament, and sent against the island of Thin-quo, in the conquest of which he was to be supported by a squadron of fune already in those latitudes, under the command of the chief He-rhumn.

The voyage was performed without loss; the troops were landed without opposition. They had already advanced towards a rising ground which commanded the principal town of the island, and He-rhumn had offered to land and draw the artillery by the mariners of his squadron, when Hob-nob had a dream which disconcerted all his measures,

He dreamed that he entertained all the islanders in the temple of the white horse; and that his own grandmother did the honours of the table. Indeed he could not have performed a greater act of charity; for they were literally in danger of perishing by famine. Having consulted his interpreter on this extraordinary dream, he was given to understand that the omen was unlucky; that if he persisted in his hostilities, he himself would be taken prisoner, and offered up as a sacrifice to the idol of the place. While he ruminated on this unfavourable response, the principal inhabitants of the island assembled, in order to deliberate upon their own deplorable situation. They had neither troops, arms, fortifications, nor provision, and despaired of supplies, as the fleet of Japan surrounded the island. In this emergency, they determined to submit without opposition; and appointed a deputation to go and make a tender of the island to general Hob-nob. This deputation, preceded by white flags of truce, the Japanese commander no sooner descried, than he thought upon the interpretation of his dream. He mistook the deputies with their white flags for the bonzas of the idol to which he was to be sacrificed; and, being sorely troubled in mind, ordered the troops to be immediately re-embarked, notwithstanding the exhortations of He-rhumn, and the remonstrances of Rha-rin-tumm, the second in command, who used a number of arguments to dissuade him from his purpose. The deputies seeing the enemy in motion, made a halt, and after they were fairly on board, returned to the town, singing hymns in praise of the idol Fo, who, they imagined, had confounded the understanding of the Japanese general.

The attempt upon Thin-quo having thus miscarried, Hob-nob declared he would return to Japan; but was with great difficulty persuaded by the commander of the fune and his own second, to make a descent upon another island belonging to the Chinese, called *Qua-chu,* where they assured him he would meet with no opposition. As he had no dream to deter him from this attempt, he suffered himself to be persuaded, and actually made good his landing; but the hor-

ror occasioned by the apparition of his grandmother had
made such an impression upon his mind, as affected the
constitution of his body. Before he was visited by another
such vision, he sickened and died; and in consequence of
his death, Rha-rin-tumm and He-rhumn made a conquest
of the island of Qua-chu, which was much more valuable
than Thin-quo, the first and sole object of the expedition.
When the first news of this second descent arrived in Japan,
the ministry were in the utmost confusion.   Mr Orator
Taycho did not scruple to declare that general Hob-nob had
misbehaved; first, in relinquishing Thin-quo, upon such a frivolous pretence as the supposed apparition of an old woman;
secondly, in attempting the conquest of another place, which
was not so much as mentioned in his instructions. The truth
is, the importance of Qua-chu was not known to the cabinet
of Japan. Fika-kaka believed it was some place on the continent of Tartary, and exclaimed, in a violent passion,—
' Rot the blockhead, Hob-nob; he'll have an army of Chinese on his back in a twinkling !'   When the president Soo-
san-sin-o assured him that Qua-chu was a rich island at an
immense distance from the continent of Tartary, the cuboy
insisted upon kissing his excellency's posteriors for the agreeable information he had received. In a few weeks arrived
the tidings of the island's being totally reduced by Rha-rin-
tumm and He-rhumn.—Then the conquest was published
throughout the empire of Japan, with every circumstance of
exaggeration.   The blatant beast brayed applause. The
rites of Fakku-basi were celebrated with unusual solemnity;
and hymns of triumph were sung to the glory of the great
Taycho.   Even the cuboy arrogated to himself some share
of the honour gained by this expedition; inasmuch as the
general Rha-rin-tumm was the brother of his friend Mr Secretary *No-bo-dy*. Fika-kaka gave a grand entertainment
at his palace, where he appeared crowned with a garland of
the *tsikk-burasiba*, or laurel of Japan ; and eat so much of
the soup of *Joniku*, or famous *swallow's-nest*, that he was
for three days troubled with flatulencies and indigestion.

In the midst of all this festivity, the emperor still growled and grumbled about Yesso. His new ally Brut-an-tiffi had met with a variety of fortune, and even suffered some shocks, which Orator Taycho, with all his art, could not keep from the knowledge of the dairo.—He had been severely drubbed by the Mantchoux, who had advanced for that purpose even to his court-yard; but this was nothing in comparison to another disaster, from which he had a hair-breadth escape. The great khan had employed one of his most wily and entesprising chiefs to seize Brut-an-tiffi by surprise, that he might be brought to justice, and executed as a felon and perturbator of the public peace. Kunt-than, who was the partisan pitched upon for this service, practised a thousand stratagems to decoy Brut-an-tiffi into a careless security; but he was still baffled by the vigilance of Yam-a-kheit, a famous soldier of fortune, who had engaged in the service of the outlawed Tartar. At length the opportunity offered, when this captain was sent out to lay the country under contribution. Then Kunt-than marching solely in the dead of night, caught Brut-an-tiffi napping. He might have slain him upon the spot; but his orders were to take him alive, that he might be made a public example. Accordingly, his sentinels being dispatched, he was pulled out of bed, and his hands were already tied with cords, like those of a common malefactor, when, by his roaring and bellowing, he gave the alarm to Yam-a-kheit, who chanced to be in the neighbourhood, returning from his excursion.—He made all the haste he could, and came up in the very nick of time to save his master. He fell upon the party of Kunt-than with such fury, that they were fain to quit their prey: then he cut the fetters of Brut-an-tiffi, who took to his heels and fled with incredible expedition, leaving his preserver in the midst of his enemies, by whom he was overpowered, struck from his horse, and trampled to death. The grateful Tartar not only deserted his brave captain in such extremity, but he also took care to asperse his memory, by insinuating that Yam-a-hkeit had undertaken to watch him while he took his repose, and had himself fallen asleep upon his post, by which neglect of duty the Ostrog had been enabled to penetrate into his quarters. 'Tis an ill wind that blows nobody good:—the same disaster that deprived him of a good officer, afforded him an opportunity to shift the blame of neglect from his own shoulders to those of a person who could not answer for himself. In the same manner, your general A———y acquitted himself of the charge of misconduct for the attack of T———a, by accusing his engineer, who, having fallen in the battle, could not contradict his assertion. In regard to the affair with the Mantchoux, Brut-an-tiffi was resolved to swear truth out of Tartary by mere dint of impudence. In the very article of running away, he began to propagate the report of the great victory he had obtained. He sent the dairo a circumstantial detail of his own prowess, and expatiated upon the cowardice of the Mantchoux, who, he said, had vanished from him like quick-silver, at the very time when they were quietly possessed of the field of battle, and he himself was calling upon the mountains to cover him. It must have been in imitation of this great original, that the inspector of tympanitical memory, assured the public, in one of his lucubrations, that a certain tall Hibernian was afraid of looking him in the face, because the said poltroon had kicked his breech the night before, in presence of five hundred people.

Fortune had now abandoned the Chinese in good earnest. Two squadrons of their fune had been successively taken, destroyed, or dispersed, by the Japanese commanders, Or-nbos and Fas-khan; and they had lost such a number of single junks, that they were scarce able to keep the sea. On the coast of Africa, they were driven from the settlement of Kho-rhe, by the commander Kha-fell. In the extremity of Asia, they had an army totally defeated by the Japanese captain Khutt-whang, and many of their settlements were taken. In Fatsissio, they lost another battle to Yan-oni, and divers strong holds. In the neighbourhood of Yesso, Bronxi-tic, who commanded the mercenary army of Japan on that continent, had been obliged to retreat before the Chinese from post to pillar, till at length he found it absolutely necessary to maintain his position, even at the risk of being

attacked by the enemy, that outnumbered him greatly. He
chose an advantageous post, where he thought himself secure, and went to sleep at his usual time of rest. The
Chinese general resolving to beat up his quarters in the night,
selected a body of horse for that purpose, and put them in
motion accordingly. It was happy for Bron-xi-tic that this
detachment fell upon a quarter, where there happened to be
a kennel of Japanese dogs, which are as famous as the bull-
dogs of England. These animals, ever on the watch, not
only gave the alarm, but at the same time fell upon the
Chinese horses with such impetuosity, that the enemy were
disordered, and had actually fled before Bron-xi-tic could
bring up his troops to action. All that he saw of the battle,
when he came up, was a small number of killed and wounded, and the cavalry of the enemy scampering off in confusion, though at a great distance from the field. No matter;
he found means to paint this famous battle of Myn-than in
such colours as dazzled the weak eye-sight of the Japanese
monster, which bellowed hoarse applause through all its
throats; and in its hymns of triumph equalled Bron-xi-tic
even to the unconquerable Brut-an-tiffi; which last, about
the time, received at his own door another beating from the
Mantchoux, so severe, that he lay for some time without exhibiting any signs of life; and, indeed, owed his safety to
a very extraordinary circumstance. An Ostrog chief, called
Llha-dahn, who had reinforced the Mantchoux with a very
considerable body of horse before the battle, insisted upon
carrying off the carcase of Brut-an-tiffi, that it might be
hung up on a gibbet *in terrorem*, before the pavilion of the
great khan. The general of the Mantchoux, on the other
hand, declared he would have it flayed upon the spot, and
the skin sent as a trophy to his sovereign. This dispute
produced a great deal of abuse betwixt those barbarians; and
it was with great difficulty some of their inferior chiefs
who were wiser than themselves, prevented them from
going by the ears together. In a word, the confusion and
anarchy that ensued, afforded an opportunity to one of
Brut-an-tiffi's partisans to steal away the body of his master,

whom the noise of the contest had just roused from his swoon.
Llha-dahn perceiving he was gone, rode off in disgust with
all his cavalry; and the Mantchoux, instead of following
the blow, made a retrograde motion towards their own country, which allowed Brut-an-tiffi time to breathe.   Three successive disasters of this kind would have been sufficient to
lower the military character of any warrior, in the opinion
of any public that judged from their own senses and reflection; but by this time the Japanese had quietly resigned all
their natural perceptions, and paid the most implicit faith
to every article broached by their apostle Taycho.   The
more it seemed to contradict common reason and common
evidence, the more greedily was it swallowed as a mysterious
dogma of the political creed.   Taycho then assured them
that the whole army of the Mantchoux was put to the sword;
and that Bron-xi-tic would carry the war within three weeks
into the heart of China; he gave them goblets of horse-blood
from Myn-than; and tickled their ears and their noses;
they snorted approbation, licked his toes, and sunk into a
profound lethargy.

From this, however, they were soon aroused by unwel-
come tidings from Fatsissio.   Yaff-rai had proceeded in his
route until he was stopped by a vast lake, which he could
not possibly traverse without boats, cork-jackets, or some
such expedient, which could not be supplied for that campaign.   Ya-loff had sailed up the river to Quib-quab, which
he found so strongly fortified by nature, that it seemed rash-
ness even to attempt a landing, especially in the face of an
enemy more numerous than his own detachment.   Land,
however, he did, and even attacked a fortified camp of the
Chinese; but, in spite of all his efforts, he was repulsed
with considerable slaughter.   He sent an account of this
miscarriage to Taycho, giving him to understand, at the
same time, that he had received no intelligence of Yaff-rai's
motions; that his troops were greatly diminished; that the
season was too far advanced to keep the field much longer;
and that nothing was left them but a choice of difficulties,
every one of which seemed more insurmountable than an-

other. Taycho having deliberated on this subject, thought
it was necessary to prepare the monster for the worst that
could happen, as he now expected to hear by the first
opportunity that the grand expedition of Fatsissio had totally miscarried.   He resolved, therefore, to throw the blame
upon the shoulders of Ya-loff and Yaff-rai, and stigmatise
them as the creatures of Fika-kaka, who had neither ability to
comprehend the instructions he had given, nor resolution to
execute the plan he had projected.   For this purpose he
ascended the rostrum, and, with a rueful length of face,
opened his harangue upon the defeat of Ya-loff.   The hydra
no sooner understood that the troops of Japan had been discomfited, than it was seized with a kind of hysteric fit, and
uttered a yell so loud and horrible, that the blindfold dairo
trembled in the most internal recesses of his palace : the cuboy Fika-kaka had such a profuse evacuation, that the discharge is said to have weighed five boll-ab, equal to eight-
and-forty-pounds three ounces and two penny-weight avoir-
dupois of Great Britain.   Even Taycho himself was discomposed.   In vain he presented the draught of yeast, and the
goblet of blood :—in vain his pipers soothed the ears, and
his tall fellows tickled the nose of the blatant beast.   It continued to howl and grin, and gnash its teeth, and writhe itself into a thousand contortions, as if it had been troubled
with that twisting of the guts called the iliac passion. Taycho
began to think its case desperate, and sent for the dairo's
chief physician, who prescribed a glyster of the distilled
spirit analogous to your geneva; but no apothecary nor
old woman in Meaco would undertake to administer it on
any consideration, the patient was such a filthy, awkward,
lubberly, unmanageable beast.   ‘ If what comes from
its mouth,’ said they, ‘ be foul, virulent, and pestilential,
how nauseous, poisonous, and intolerable, must that be
which takes the other course ?’   When Taycho's art and
foresight were at a stand, accident came to his assistance.
A courier arrived, preceded by twelve postillions blowing
horns ; and he brought the news that Quib-quab was taken.
The orator commanded them to place their horns within as

many of the monster's long-ears, and blow with all their
might, until it should exhibit some signs of hearing. The
experiment succeeded.   The hydra waking from its trance,
opened its eyes; and Taycho seizing this opportunity, hallooed in his loudest tone,—' Quib-quab is taken.' This
note being repeated, the beast started up; then raising itself on its hind legs, began to wag its tail, to frisk and
fawn, to lick Taycho's sweaty socks; in fine, crouching
on its belly, it took the orator on its back, and, proceeding
through the streets of Meaco, brayed aloud,—' Make way
for the divine Taycho! Make way for the conqueror of
Quib-quab!' But the gallant Ya-loff, the real conqueror of
Quib-quab, was no more. He fell in the battle by which the
conquest was achieved, yet not before he saw victory declare
in his favour. He had made incredible efforts to surmount the
difficulties that surrounded him. At length he found means
to scale a perpendicular rock, which the enemy had left
unguarded, on the supposition that nature had made it inaccessible. This exploit was performed in the night, and in
the morning the Chinese saw his troops drawn up in order
of battle on the plains of Quib-quab. As their numbers
greatly exceeded the Japanese, they did not decline the
trial; and in a little time both armies were engaged. The
contest, however, was not of long duration, though it
proved fatal to the general on each side. Ya-loff being slain,
the command devolved upon Tohn-syn, who pursued the
enemy to the walls of Quib-quab, which was next day sur-
rendered to him by capitulation. Nothing was now seen
and heard in the capital but jubilee, triumph, and intoxication; and indeed the nation had not for some centuries seen
such an occasion for joy and satisfaction. The only person
that did not heartily rejoice was the dairo Got-hama-baba.
By this time he was so tartarised, that he grudged his subjects every advantage obtained in Fatsissio; and when Fika-
kaka hobbled up to him with the news of the victory, instead of saluting him with the kick of approbation, he turned his back upon him, saying,—' Boh! boh! What do you
tell me of Quib-quab? The damned Chinese are still on the

frontiers of Yesso.' As to the beast, it was doomed to undergo a variety of agitation. Its present gambols were interrupted by a fresh alarm from China. It was reported
that two great armaments were equipped for a double descent upon the dominions of Japan; that one of these had already sailed north about for the island of Xicoco, to make a
diversion in favour of the other, which, being the most considerable, was designed for the southern coast of Japan.
These tidings, which were not without foundation, had such
an effect upon the multitudinous monster, that it was first of
all seized with an universal shivering. Its teeth chattered
so loud, that the sound was heard at the distance of half a
league; and for some time it was struck dumb. During this
paroxysm, it crawled silently on its belly to a sand-hill just
without the walls of Meaco, and began to scratch the earth
with great eagerness and perseverance. Some people imagined it was digging for gold; but the truth is, the beast was
making a hole to hide itself from the enemy, whom it durst
not look in the face; for, it must be observed of this beast,
it was equally timorous and cruel, equally cowardly and insolent. So hard it laboured at this cavern, that it had actually burrowed itself all but the tail, when its good angel
Taycho whistled it out, with the news of another complete
victory gained over the Chinese at sea by the sey-seo-gun
Phal-khan, who had, sure enough, discomfited or destroyed
the great armament of the enemy. As for the other small
squadron which had steered the northerly course to Xicoco,
it was encountered, defeated, taken, and brought into the
harbours of Japan, by three light fune, under the command
of a young chief called Hel-y-otte, who happened to be
cruising on that part of the coast. The beast hearing Taycho's auspicious whistle, crept out with its buttocks foremost,
and, having done him homage in the usual style, began to
re-act its former extravagancies. It now considered this demagogue as the supreme giver of all good, and adored him
accordingly. The apostle Bupo was no longer invoked. The
temple of Fakku-basi was almost forgotten, and the bonzas
were universally despised. The praise of the prophet Tay-

cho had swallowed up all other worship.   Let us inquire
how far he merited this adoration, how justly the unparal-
leled success of this year was ascribed to his conduct and
sagacity.   Kho-rhé was taken by Kha-fell, and Quib-quab
by Ya-loff and Thou-syn.   By land the Chinese were defeated in Fatsissio by Yan-o-ni, in the extremity of Asia by
Khutt-whang, and in Tartary by the Japanese bull-dogs,
without command or direction.   At sea one of their squadrons had been destroyed by Or-nbos, a second by Fas-khan,
a third was taken by Hel-y-otte, a fourth was worsted and
put to flight in three successive engagements near the land
of Kamtschatka by the chief Bak-kakh, and their grand armament defeated by the sey-seo-gun Phal-khan.   But Kha-
fell was a stranger to Orator Taycho ; Ya-loff he had never
seen ; the bull-dogs had been collected at random from the
shambles of Meaco ; he had never heard of Yan-o-ni's name,
till he distinguished himself by his first victory ; nor did he
know there was any such person as Khutt-whang existing.
As for Or-nbos, Fas-khan, Phal-khan, and Bak-kakh, they
had been sey-seo-guns in constant employment under the
former administration ; and the youth Hel-y-otte owed his
promotion to the interest of his own family.   But it may be
alleged that Taycho projected in his closet those plans that
were crowned with success.   We have seen how he mutilated and frittered the original scheme of the campaign in
Fatsissio, so as to leave it at the caprice of fortune.   The
reduction of Kho-rhé was part of the design formed by the
banyan Thum-khumm-qua, which Taycho did all that lay
in his power to render abortive.   The plan of operations in
the extremity of Tartary he did not pretend to meddle with ;
it was the concern of the officers appointed by the trading
company their settled : and as to the advantages obtained
at sea, they naturally resulted from the disposition of cruises,
made and regulated by the board of sey-seo-gun-sealty, with
which no minister ever interfered.   He might indeed have
recalled the chiefs and officers whom he found already appointed when he took the reins of administration, and filled
their places with others of his own choosing.   How far he

was qualified to make such a choice, and plan new expeditions, appears from the adventures of the generals he did appoint; Moria-tanti, who was deterred from landing by a perspective view of whiskers; Hylib-bib, who left his rear in the lurch; and Hob-nob, who made such a masterly retreat from the supposed bonzas of Thin-quo. These three were literally commanders of his own creation, employed in executing schemes of his own projecting; and these three were the only generals he made, and the only military plans he projected, if we except the grand scheme of subsidizing Brut-an-tiffi, and forming an army of one hundred thousand men in Tartary, for the defence of the farm of Yesso. Things being so circumstanced, it may be easily conceived that the orator could ask nothing which the mobile would venture to refuse; and indeed he tried his influence to the utmost stretch; he milked the dugs of the monster till the blood came. For the service of the ensuing year, he squeezed from them near twelve millions of obans, amounting to near twenty-four millions sterling, about four times as much as had ever been raised by the empire of Japan in any former war. But by this time Taycho was become not only a convert to the system of Tartary, which he had formerly persecuted, but also an enthusiast in love and admiration of Brut-an-tiffi, who had lately sent him his poetical works in a present. This, however, would have been of no use, as he could not read them, had not he discovered that they were printed on a very fine, soft, smooth, Chinese paper, made of silk, which he happily converted to another fundamental purpose. In return for this compliment, the orator sent him a bullock's horn, bound with brass, value fifteen pence, which had long served him as a pitch-pipe when he made harangues to the mobile: it was the same kind of instrument which Horace describes, *tibia vincta orichalco:* and pray take notice, Peacock, this was the only present Taycho ever bestowed on any man, woman, or child, through the whole course of his life, I mean out of his own pocket; for he was extremely liberal of the public money, in his subsidies to the Tartar chiefs, and in the prosecution of the war upon that continent. The orator was a genius self-taught, without the help of human institution. He affected to undervalue all men of literary talents; and the only book he ever read with any degree of pleasure, was a collection of rhapsodies preached by one Ab-ren-thi, an obscure fanatic bonza, a native of the island Xicoco. Certain it is, Nature seemed to have produced him for the sole purpose of fascinating the mob, and endued him with faculties accordingly.

Notwithstanding all his efforts in behalf of the Tartarian scheme, the Chinese still lingered on the frontiers of Yesso. The views of the court of Pekin exactly coincided with the interest of Bron-xi-tic, the mercenary general of Japan. The Chinese, confounded at the unheard-of success of the Japanese in Fatsissio and other parts of the globe, and extremely mortified at the destruction of their fleets and the ruin of their commerce, saw no other way of distressing the enemy, but that of prolonging the war on the continent of Tartary, which they could support for little more than their ordinary expense; whereas Japan could not maintain it without contracting yearly immense loads of debt, which must have crushed it at the long-run. It was the business of the Chinese, therefore, not to finish the war in Tartary by taking the farm of Yesso, because, in that case, the annual expense of it would have been saved to Japan; but to keep it alive by forced marches, predatory excursions, and undecisive actions; and this was precisely the interest of General Bron-xi-tic, who, in the continuance of the war, enjoyed the continuance of all his emoluments. All that he had to do, then, was to furnish Taycho from time to time with a cask of human blood, for the entertainment of the blatant beast; and to send over a few horse tails, as trophies of pretended victories, to be waved before the monster in its holiday processions. He and the Chinese general seemed to act in concert. They advanced and retreated in their turns betwixt two given lines, and the campaign always ended on the same spot where it began. The only difference between them was in the motives of their conduct; the Chinese commander acted for the benefit of his sovereign, and Bon-xi-tic acted for his own.

The continual danger to which the farm of Yesso was exposed, produced such apprehensions and chagrin in the mind of the dairo Got-hama-baba, that his health began to decline. He neglected his food and his rattle, and no longer took any pleasure in kicking the cuboy. He frequently muttered ejaculations about the farm of Yesso; nay, once or twice, in the transports of his impatience, he pulled the bandage from his eyes, and cursed Taycho in the Tartarian language. At length he fell into a lethargy, and, even when roused a little by blisters and caustics, seemed insensible of every thing that was done about him. These blisters were raised by burning the moxa upon his scalp. The powder of *menoki* was also injected in a glyster; and the operation of acupuncture, called *senkei*, performed without effect. His disorder was so stubborn, that the cuboy began to think he was bewitched, and suspected Taycho of having practised sorcery on his sovereign. He communicated this suspicion to Mura-clami, who shook his head, and advised that, with the orator's good leave, the council should be consulted. Taycho, who had gained an absolute empire over the mind of the dairo, and could not foresee how his interest might stand with his successor, was heartily disposed to concur in any feasible experiment for the recovery of Got-hama-baba; he therefore consented that the mouths of the council should be unpadlocked *pro hac vice*, and the members were assembled without delay; with this express proviso, however, that they were to confine their deliberations to the subject of the dairo and his distemper. By this time the physicians had discovered the cause of the disorder, which was no other than his being stung by a poisonous insect produced in the land of Yesso, analogous to the tarantula, which is said to do so much mischief in some parts of Apuglia, as we are told by Ælian, Epiphanius Ferdinandus, and Boglivi. In both cases the only effectual remedy was music; and now the council was called to determine what sort of music should be administered. You must know, Peacock, the Japanese are but indifferently skilled in this art, though in general they affect to be connoisseurs. They are utterly ignorant of the theory, and in the practice are excelled by all their neighbours, the Tartars not excepted. For my own part, I studied music under Pythagoras at Crotona. He found the scale of seven tones imperfect, and added the octave as a fixed, sensible, and intelligent, termination of an interval, which included every possible division, and determined all the relative differences of sounds; besides, he taught us how to express the octave by $\frac{1}{2}$, &c. &c. But why should I talk to thee of the ancient digramma, the genera, &c. of music, which, with their colours, were constructed by a division of the diatessaron. Thou art too dull and ignorant to comprehend the chromatic species, the construction of the tetrachord, the Phrygian, the Lydian, and other modes of the ancient music; and for distinction of ear, thou mightest be justly ranked amongst the braying tribe that graze along the ditches of Tottenham-court, or Hockley-i'the-hole. I know that nothing exhilarates thy spirits so much as a sonata on the salt-box, or a concert of marrow-bones and cleavers. The ears of the Japanese were much of the same texture; and their music was suited to their ears. They neither excelled in the melopœia, and rhyme or cadence; nor did they know any thing of the true science of harmony, compositions in parts, and those combinations of sounds, the invention of which, with the improvement of the scale, is erroneously ascribed to a Benedictine monk. The truth is, the ancients understood composition perfectly well. Their scale was founded upon perfect consonances; they were remarkably nice in tempering sounds, and had reduced their intervals and concords to mathematical demonstration.

But, to return to the council of twenty-eight, they convened in the same apartment where the dairo lay; and as the business was to determine what kind of music was most likely to make an impression upon his organs, every member came provided with his expedient. First and foremost, Mr Orator Tayeho pronounced an oration upon the excellencies of the land of Yesso, of energy (as the cuboy said) sufficient to draw the moon from her sphere; it drew nothing, however, from the patient but a single groan: then

the fatzman caused a drum to beat, without producing any
effect at all upon the dairo; though it deprived the whole
council of their hearing for some time. The third essay was
made by Fika-kaka; first with a rattle, and then with tongs
and gridiron, which last was his favourite music; but here
it failed, to his great surprise and consternation. Sti-phi-
rum-poo brought the crier of his court to promulgate a decree against Yesso, in a voice that is wont to make the culprit tremble; but the dairo was found *ignoramus*. Nin-
com-poo-po blew a blast with a kind of boatswain's whistle,
which discomposed the whole audience without affecting
the emperor. Fokh-si-rokhu said he would try his imperial
majesty with a sound which he had always been known to
prefer to every species of music; and pulling out a huge
purse of golden obans, began to chink them in his ear.
This experiment so far succeeded, that the dairo was perceived to smile, and even to contract one hand : but further
effect it had none. At last Goto-mio starting up, threw a
small quantity of *aurum fulminans* into the fire, which went
off with such an explosion, that in the same instant Fika-
kaka fell flat upon his face, and Got-hama-baba started upright in his bed. This, however, was no more than a convulsion that put an end to his life; for he fell back again, and
expired in the twinkling of an eye. As for the cuboy,
though he did not die, he underwent a surprising transformation or metamorphosis, which I shall record in due season. .

Taycho was no sooner certified that Got-hama-baba had
actually breathed his last, than he vanished from the council in the twinkling of an eye, and mounting the beast whose
name is Legion, rod full speed to the habitation of *Gio-gio*,
the successor and descendant of the deceased dairo. Gio-
gio was a young prince who-had been industriously sequestered from the public view, and excluded from all share in
the affairs of state by the jealousy of the last emperor. He
lived retired under the wings of his grandmother, and had
divers preceptors to teach him the rudiments of every art

but the art of reigning. Of all those who superintended his education, he who insinuated himself the farthest in his favour, was one *Yak-strot*, from the mountains of Ximo, who valued himself much upon the ancient blood that ran in his veins, and still more upon his elevated ideas of patriotism. Yak-strot was honest at bottom, but proud, reserved, vain, and affected. He had a turn for nick-nacks and gim-cracks, and once made and mounted an iron jack and a wooden clock with his own hands. But it was his misfortune to set up for a connoisseur in painting and other liberal arts, and to announce himself an universal patron of genius. He did not fail to infuse his own notions and conceits into the tender mind of Gio-gio, who gradually imbibed his turn of thinking, and followed the studies which he recommended. With respect to his lessons on the art of government, he reduced them to a very few simple principles. His maxims were these:—That the emperor of Japan ought to cherish the established religion, both by precept and example: that he ought to abolish corruption, discourage faction, and balance the two parties, by admitting an equal number from each to places and offices of trust in the administration: that he should make peace as soon as possible, even in despite of the public, which seemed insensible of the burden it sustained, and was indeed growing delirious by the illusions of Taycho, and the cruel evacuations he had prescribed: that he should retrench all superfluous expense in his household and government, and detach himself entirely from the accursed farm of Yesso, which some evil genius had fixed upon the breech of Japan, as a cancerous ulcer through which all her blood and substance would be discharged. These maxims were generally just enough in speculation, but some of them were altogether impracticable:—for example, that of forming an administration equally composed of the two factions, was as absurd as it would be to yoke two stone-horses and two jack-asses in the same carriage, which, instead of drawing one way, would do nothing but bite and kick one another, while the machine of government would stand stock-still, or perhaps be torn

in pieces by their dragging in opposite directions. The
people of Japan had been long divided between two inveterate parties known by the names of *Shit-tilk-ums-heit*, and
She-it-kums-he-til, the first signifying *more fool than knave*;
and the other, *more knave than fool*. Each had predominated in its turn, by securing a majority in the assemblies
of the people; for the majority had always interest to force
themselves into the administration; because the constitution
being partly democratic, the dairo was still obliged to
truckle to the prevailing faction. To obtain this majority,
each side had employed every art of corruption, calumny,
infatuation, and priest-craft; for nothing is such an effectual ferment in all popular commotions as religious fanaticism. No sooner one party accomplished its aim, than it
reprobated the other, branding it with the epithets of traitors to their country, or traitors to their prince; while the
minority retorted upon them the charge of corruption, ra-
paciousness, and abject servility. In short, both parties
were equally abusive, rancorous, uncandid, and illiberal.
Taycho had been of both factions more than once. He made
his first appearance as a *Shit-tilk-ums-heit* in the minority,
and displayed his talent for scurrility against the dairo to
such advantage, that an old rich hag, who loved nothing
so well as money, except the gratification of her revenge,
made him a present of five thousand obans, on condition he
should continue to revile the dairo till his dying-day. After her death, the ministry, intimidated by the boldness of
his tropes, and the fame he began to acquire as a malcontent orator, made him such offers as he thought proper to
accept; and then he turned *She-it-kums-hi-til*. Being disgusted in the sequel, at his own want of importance in the
council, he opened once more at the head of his old friends
the *Shi-tilk-ums-hi-tites*; and once more he deserted them
to rule the roast, as chief of the *She-it-kums-hi-ti-lites*, in
which predicament he now stood. And, indeed, this was
the most natural posture in which he could stand; for this
party embraced all the scum of the people, constituting the
blatant beast, which his talents were so peculiarly adapted

to manage and govern.   Another impracticable maxim of
Yak-strot, was the abolition of corruption, the ordure of
which is as necessary to anoint the wheels of government in
Japan, as grease is to smear the axle-tree of a loaded waggon.   His third impolitic (though not impracticable) maxim, was that of making peace while the populace were intoxicated with the steams of blood, and elated with the
shews of triumph.   Be that as it will, Gio-gio, attended by
Yak-strot, was drawing plans of wind-mills, when orator
Taycho, opening the door, advanced towards him, and
falling on his knees, addressed him in these words.—' The
empire of Japan, magnanimous prince! resembles, at this
instant, a benighted traveller, who by the light of the star
Hesperus continued his journey without repining, until that
glorious luminary setting, left him bewildered in darkness
and consternation : but scarce had he time to bewail his fate,
when the more glorious sun, the ruler of a fresh day, appearing on the tops of the eastern hills, dispelled his terrors
with the shades of night, and filled his soul with transports
of pleasure and delight.   The illustrious Got-hama-baba, of
honoured memory, is the glorious star which hath set on our
hemisphere.   His soul, which took wing about two hours ago,
is now happily nestled in the bosom of the blessed Bupo;
and you, my prince, are the more glorious rising sun, whose
genial influence will cheer the empire, and gladden the
hearts of your faithful Japanese.   I therefore hail your succession to the throne, and cry aloud, Long live the ever-
glorious Gio-gio, emperor of the three islands of Japan.'
To this salutation the beast below brayed hoarse applause;
and all present kissed the hand of the new emperor, who,
kneeling before his venerable grandame, craved her blessing,
desiring the benefit of her prayers, that God would make
him a good king, and establish his throne in righteousness.
Then he ascended his chariot, accompanied by the orator
and his beloved Yak-strot, and, proceeding to the palace of
Meaco, was proclaimed with the usual ceremonies, his relation the fatsman and other princes of the blood assisting
on this occasion.

The first step he took after his elevation, was to publish a decree, or rather exhortation, to honour religion and the bonzas; and this was no impolitic expedient: for it firmly attached that numerous and powerful tribe to his interest. His next measures did not seem to be directed by the same spirit of discretion. He admitted a parcel of raw boys, and even some individuals of the faction of *Shi-tilk-ums-heit* into his council; and though Taycho still continued to manage the reins of administration, Yak-strot was associated with him in office, to the great scandal and dissatisfaction of the Niphonites, who hate all the Ximians with a mixture of jealousy and contempt.

. Fika-kaka was not the last who paid his respects to his new sovereign, by whom he was graciously received, although he did not seem quite satisfied; because when he presented himself in his usual attitude, he had not received the kick of approbation. New reigns, new customs: this dairo never dreamed of kicking those whom he delighted to honour. It was a secret of state which had not yet come to his knowledge: and Yak-strot had always assured him, that kicking the breech always and every where implied disgrace, as kicking the parts before, betokens ungovernable passion. Yak-strot, however, in this particular, seems to have been too confined in his notions of the *etiquette:* for it had been the custom time immemorial for the dairos of Japan to kick their favourites and prime ministers. Besides, there are at this day different sorts of kicks used even in England, without occasioning any dishonour to the *kickee.* It is sometimes a misfortune to be *kicked* out of place, but no dishonour. A man is often *kicked* up in the way of preferment, in order that his place may be given to a person of more interest. Then there is the amorous kick, called *kick'um jenny*, which every gallant undergoes with pleasure; hence the old English appellation of *kicksy-wicksy*, bestowed on a wanton leman who knew all her paces. As for the familiar kick, it is no other than a mark of friendship; nor is it more dishonourable to be cuffed and cudgelled. Every body knows that the *alapa* or box o' the ear, among the Romans, was a

particular mark of favour by which their slaves were made
free: and the favourite gladiator, when he obtained his dismission from the service, was honoured with a sound cudgel-
ling; this being the true meaning of the phrase *rude donatus*.
In the times of chivalry, the knight when dubbed, was well
thwacked across the shoulders by his god-father in arms.
Indeed, *dubbing* is no other than a corruption of *drubbing*.
It was the custom formerly here and elsewhere, for a man to
drub his son or apprentice as a mark of his freedom, and of
his being admitted to the exercise of arms.   The Paraschis-
tes, who practised *embalming* in Egypt, which was counted
a very honourable profession, was always severely drubbed
after the operation, by the friends and relations of the defunct;
and to this day, the patriarch of the Greeks once a-year, on
Easter-eve, when he carries out the sacred fire from the holy
sepulchre of Jerusalem, is heartily cudgelled by the infidels,
a certain number of whom he hires for that purpose; and
he thinks himself very unhappy and much disgraced, if he
is not beaten into all the colours of the rain-bow.   You know
the quakers of this country think it no dishonour to receive
a slap o' the face, but when you smite them on one cheek,
they present the other, that it may have the same salutation.
The venerable father Lactantius falls out with Cicero for
saying,—' A good man hurts nobody unless he is justly provoked;' *nisi lacessitur injuria*.. ' O,' cries the good father,
' *quam simplicem veramque sententiam duorum verborum
adjectione corrupit!—non minus enim mali est, referre injuri-
am, quam inferre.*' The great philosopher Socrates thought
it no disgrace to be kicked by his wife Xantippe; nay, he
is said to have undergone the same discipline from other people, without making the least resistance, it being his opinion
that it was more courageous, consequently more honourable,
to bear a drubbing patiently, than to attempt any thing either
in the way of self-defence or retaliation.   The judicious and
learned Puffendorf, in his book *De Jure Gentium et Natu-
rali*, declares that a man's honour is not so fragile as to be
hurt either by a box on the ear, or a kick on the breech,
otherwise it would be in the power of every saucy fellow to

diminish or infringe it. It must be owned, indeed, Grotius, *De Jure Belli et Pacis*, says, that charity does not of itself require our patiently suffering such an affront. The English have, with a most servile imitation, borrowed their *punto*, as well as other modes, from the French nation. Now kicking and cuffing were counted infamous among those people for these reasons: a box on the ear destroys the whole economy of their *frisure*, upon which they bestow the greatest part of their time and attention; and a kick on the breech is attended with great pain and danger, as they are generally subject to the piles. This is so truly the case, that they have no less than two saints to patrónise and protect the individuals afflicted with this disease. One is St. *Fiacre*, who was a native of the kingdom of Ireland. He presides over the blind piles. The other is a female saint, *Hæmorrhoissa*, and she comforts those who are distressed with the bleeding piles. No wonder, therefore, that a Frenchman put to the torture by a kick on those tender parts should be provoked to vengeance; and that this vengeance should gradually become an article in their system of punctilio.

But to return to the thread of my narration.—Whatever inclination the dairo and Yak-strot had to restore the blessings of peace, they did not think proper as yet to combat the disposition and schemes of orator Taycho; in consequence of whose remonstrances, the tributary treaty was immediately renewed with Brut-an-tiffi, and Gio-gio declared in the assembly of the people, that he was determined to support that illustrious ally, and carry on the war with vigour. By this time the Chinese were in a manner expelled from their chief settlements in Fatsissio, where they now retained nothing but an inconsiderable colony, which would have submitted on the first summons: but this Taycho left as a nest-egg to produce a new brood of disturbance to the Japanese settlements, that they might not rust with too much peace and security. To be plain with you, Peacock, his thoughts were entirely alienated from this Fatsissian war, in which the interest of his country was chiefly concerned, and converted wholly to the continent of Tartary, where all his

cares centered in schemes for the success of his friend Brut-
an-tiffi. This freebooter had lately undergone strange vicissitudes of fortune. He had seen his chief village possessed
and plundered by the enemy; but he found means, by surprise, to beat up their quarters in the beginning of winter,
which always proved his best ally, because then the Mantchoux Tartars were obliged to retire to their own country,
at a vast distance from the seat of war. As for Bron-xi-tic,
who commanded the Japanese army on that continent, he
continued to play booty with the Chinese general, over
whom he was allowed to obtain some petty advantages,
which, with the trophies won by Brut-an-tiffi, were swelled
up into mighty victories, to increase the infatuation of the
blatant beast. On the other hand, Bron-xi-tic obliged the
generals of China with the like indulgencies, by now and
then sacrificing a detachment of his Japanese troops, to keep
up the spirits of that nation.

Taycho had levied upon the people of Japan an immense
sum of money for the equipment of a naval armament, the
destination of which was kept a profound secret. Some politicians imagined it was designed for the conquest of Thin-
quo, and all the other settlements which the Chinese possessed in the Indian ocean: others conjectured the intention
was to attack the king of Corea, who had since the beginning of this war, acted with a shameful partiality in favour
of the emperor of China, his kinsman and ally. But the
truth of the matter was this, Taycho kept the armament in
the harbours of Japan ready for a descent upon the coast of
China, in order to make a diversion in favour of his friend
Brut-an-tiffi, in case he had run any risk of being oppressed
by his enemies. However, the beast of many heads having
growled and grumbled, during the best part of the summer,
at the inactivity of this expensive armament, it was now
thought proper to send it to sea in the beginning of winter:
but it was soon driven back in great distress, by contrary
winds and storms;—and this was all the monster had for its
ten millions of obans.

While Taycho amused the mobile with this winter expedition, Yak-strot resolved to plan the scheme of economy which he had projected. He dismissed from the dairo's service about a dozen of cooks and scullions ; shut up one of the kitchens, after having sold the grates, hand-irons, spits, and saucepans ; deprived the servants and officers of the household of their breakfast ; took away their usual allowance of oil and candles ; retrenched their tables ; reduced their proportion of drink ; and persuaded his pupil the dairo to put himself upon a diet of soup-meagre thickened with oatmeal. In a few days there was no smoke seen to ascend from the kitchens of the palace ; nor did any fuel, torch, or taper, blaze in the chimneys, courts, and apartments thereof, which now became the habitation of cold, darkness, and hunger. Gio-gio himself, who now turned peripatetic philosopher merely to keep himself in heat, fell into a wash-tub as he groped his way in the dark through one of the lower galleries. Two of his body guard had their whiskers gnawed off by the rats, as they slept in his anti-chamber ; and their captain presented a petition, declaring, that neither he nor his men could undertake the defence of his imperial majesty's person, unless their former allowance of provision should be restored. They and all the individuals of the household were not only punished in their bellies, but likewise curtailed in their clothing, and abridged in their stipends.—The palace of Meaco, which used to be the temple of mirth, jollity, and good cheer was now so dreary and deserted, that a certain wag fixed up a ticket on the outward gate with this inscription.—' This tenement to let, the proprietor having left off house-keeping.'

Yak-strot, however, was resolved to shew, that if the new dairo retrenched the superfluities of his domestic expense, he did not act from avarice or poorness of spirit, inasmuch as he should now display his liberality in patronizing genius and the arts. A general jubilee was now promised to all those who had distinguished themselves by their talents or erudition. The emissaries of Yak-strot declared that Mæcenas was but a type of this Ximian mountaineer ; and that he was determined to search for merit, even in the thickest shades of obscurity. All these researches, however, proved so unsuccessful, that not above four or five men of genius could be found in the whole empire of Japan, and these were gratified with pensions of about one hundred obans each. One was a secularised bonsa from Ximo; another a malcontent poet of Niphon; a third, a reformed comedian of Xicoco; a fourth, an empyric, who had outlived his practice; and a fifth, a decayed apothecary, who was bard, quack, author, chymist, philosopher, and simpler, by profession. The whole of the expense arising from the favour and protection granted by the dairo to these men of genius, did not exceed seven or eight hundred obans per annum, amounting to about fifteen hundred pounds sterling; whereas many a private quo in Japan expended more money on a kennel of hounds. I do not mention those men of singular merit, whom Yak-strot fixed in established places under the government; such as architects, astronomers, painters, physicians, barbers, &c. because their salaries were included in the ordinary expense of the crown: I shall only observe, that a certain person who could not read, was appointed librarian to his imperial majesty.

These were all the men of superlative genius, that Yak-strot could find at this period in the empire of Japan.

Whilst this great patriot was thus employed in executing his schemes of economy with more zeal than discretion, and in providing his poor relations with lucrative offices under the government, a negociation for peace was brought upon the carpet by the mediation of certain neutral powers; and orator Taycho arrogated to himself the province of discussing the several articles of the treaty.—Upon this occasion he shewed himself surprisingly remiss and indifferent in whatever related to the interest of Japan, particularly in regulating and fixing the boundaries of the Chinese and Japanese settlements in Fatsissio, the uncertainty of which had given rise to the war: but when the business was to determine the claims and pretensions of his ally Brut-an-tiffi, on the continent of Tartary, he appeared stiff and immovable as mount Athos. He actually broke off the negociation, because the emperor of China would not engage to drive by force of arms the troops of his ally the princess of Ostrog, from a village or two belonging to the Tartarian freebooter, who, by-the-by, had left them defenceless at the beginning of the war, on purpose that his enemies might, by taking possession of them, quicken the resolutions of the dairo to send over an army for the protection of Yesso.

The court of Pekin perceiving that the Japanese were rendered intolerably insolent and overbearing by success, and that an equitable peace could not be obtained while orator Taycho managed the reins of government at Meaco, and his friend Brut-an-tiffi found any thing to plunder in Tartary, resolved to fortify themselves with a new alliance. They actually entered into closser connections with the king of Corea, who was nearly related to the Chinese emperor, had some old scores to settle with Japan, and because he desired those disputes might be amicably compromised in the general pacification, had been grossly insulted by Taycho, in the person of his ambassador. He had for some time dreaded the ambition of the Japanese ministry, which seemed to aim at universal empire; and he was, moreover, stimulated by this outrage to conclude a defensive alliance with the emperor of China; a measure which all the caution of the two courts could not wholly conceal from the knowledge of the Japanese politicians.

Meanwhile a dreadful cloud big with ruin and disgrace seemed to gather round the head of Brut-an-tiffi. The Mantchoux Tartars, sensible of the inconvenience of their distant situation from the scene of action, which rendered it impossible for them to carry on their operations vigorously in conjunction with the Ostrog, resolved to secure winter quarters in some part of the enemy's territories, from whence they should be able to take the field, and act against him early in the spring. With this view they besieged and took a frontier fortress belonging to Brut-an-tiffi, situated upon a great inland lake, which extended as far as the capital of the Mantchoux, who were thus enabled to send thither by water-carriage all sorts of provisions and military stores for the use of their army, which took up their winter-quarters accordingly in and about this new acquisition. It was now that the ruin of Brut-an-tiffi seemed inevitable. Orator Taycho saw with horror the precipice, to the brink of which his dear ally was driven. Not that his fears were actuated by sympathy or friendship. Such emotions had never possessed the heart of Taycho. No; he trembled because he saw his own popularity connected with the fate of the Tartar. It was the success and petty triumphs of this adventurer which had dazzled the eyes of the blatant beast, so as to disorder its judgment, and prepare it for the illusions of the orator: but, now that Fortune seemed ready to turn tail to Brut-an-tiffi, and leave him a prey to his adversaries, Taycho knew the dispositions of the monster so well as to prognosticate that its applause and affection would be immediately turned into grumbling and disgust; and that he himself, who had led it blindfold into this unfortunate connection, might possibly fall a sacrifice to its resentment, provided he could not immediately project some scheme to divert its attention, and transfer the blame from his own shoulders.

For this purpose he employed his invention, and succeeded to his wish. Having called a council of the twenty-eight, at which the dairo assisted in person, he proposed, and insisted upon it, that a strong squadron of fune should be immediately ordered to scour the seas, and kidnap all the vessels and ships belonging to the king of Corea, who had acted during the whole war with the most scandalous partiality in favour of the Chinese emperor, and was now so intimately connected with that potentate, by means of a secret alliance, that he ought to be prosecuted with the same hostilities which the other had severely felt. The whole council were confounded at this proposal: the dairo stood aghast: the cuboy trembled: Yak-strot stared like a skewered pig. After some pause, the president Soo-san-sin-o ventured to observe, that the measure seemed to be a little abrupt and premature: that the nation was already engaged in a very expensive war, which had absolutely drained it of its wealth, and even loaded it with enormous debts; therefore little able

to sustain such additional burdens as would, in all probability, be occasioned by a rupture with a prince so rich and
powerful. Gotto-mio swore the landholders were already so
impoverished by the exactions of Taycho, that he himself,
ere long, should be obliged to come upon the parish. Fika-
kaka got up to speak; but could only cackle. Sti-phi-rum-
poo was for proceeding in form by citation. Nin-kom-poo-
po declared he had good intelligence of a fleet of merchant
ships belonging to Corea, laden with treasure, who were
then on their return from the Indian isles; and he gave it as
his opinion, that they should be way-laid and brought into
the harbours of Japan; not by way of declaring war, but
only with a view to prevent the money's going into the coffers of the Chinese emperor. Fokh-si-rokhu started two objections to this expedient; first, the uncertainty of falling in
with the Corean fleet at sea, alleging, as an instance, the
disappointment and miscarriage of the squadron which the
sey-seo-gun had sent some years ago to intercept the Chinese
fune on the coast of Fatsissio: secondly, the loss and hardship it would be to many subjects of Japan who dealt in
commerce, and had great sums embarked in those very Corean bottoms. Indeed Fokh-si-rokhu himself was interested
in this very commerce. The fatsman sat silent. Yak-strot,
who had some romantic notions of honour and honesty, represented that the nation had already incurred the censure
of all its neighbours, by seizing the merchant ships of China,
without any previous declaration of war: that the law of
nature and nations, confirmed by repeated treaties, prescribed a more honourable method of proceeding, than that of
plundering like robbers, the ships of pacific merchants, who
trade on the faith of such laws and such treaties: he was
therefore of opinion, that if the king of Corea had in any
shape deviated from the neutrality which he professed, satisfaction should be demanded in the usual form; and when
that should be refused, it might be found necessary to proceed to compulsive measures. The dairo acquiesced in this
advice, and assured Taycho that an ambassador should
be forthwith dispatched to Corea, with instructions to de-

mand an immediate and satisfactory explanation of that prince's conduct and designs with regard to the empire of Japan.

This regular method of practice would by no means suit the purposes of Taycho, who rejected it with great insolence and disdain. He bit his thumb at the president; forked out his fingers on his forehead at Gotto-mio; wagged his under jaw at the cuboy; snapt his fingers at Sti-phi-rum-poo; grinned at the sey-seo-gun; made the sign of the cross or gallows to Fokh-si-rokhu; then turning to Yak-strot, he clapped his thumbs in his ears, and began to bray like an ass: finally, pulling out the badge of his office, he threw it at the dairo, who in vain entreated him to be pacified; and wheeling to the right about, stalked away, slapping the flat of his hand upon a certain part that shall be nameless. He was followed by his kinsman the quo Lob-kob, who worshipped him with the most humble adoration. He now imitated this great original in the signal from behind at parting, and in him it was attended by a rumbling sound; but whether this was the effect of contempt or compunction, I could never learn.

Taycho having thus carried his point, which was to have a pretence for quitting the reins of government, made his next appeal to the blatant beast. He reminded the many-headed monster of the uninterrupted success which had attended his administration; of his having supported the glorious Brut-an-tiffi, the great bulwark of the religion of Bupo, who had kept the common enemy at bay, and filled all Asia with the fame of his victories. He told them, that for his own part, he pretended to have subdued Fatsissio in the heart of Tartary: that he despised honours, and had still a greater contempt for riches; and that all his endeavours had been solely exerted for the good of his country, which was now brought to the very verge of destruction. He then gave the beast to understand that he had formed a scheme against the king of Corea, which would not only have disabled that monarch from executing his hostile intentions with respect to Japan, but also have indemnified this nation for the whole

expense of the war: but that his proposal having been rejected by the council of twenty-eight, who were influenced
by Yak-strot, a Ximian mountaineer without spirit or understanding, he had resigned his office with intention to retire to some solitude, where he should in silence deplore the
misfortunes of his country, and the ruin of the Buponian
religion, which must fall of course with its great protector
Brut-an-tiffi, whom he foresaw the new ministry would immediately abandon.

This address threw Legion into such a quandary, that it
rolled itself in the dirt, and yelled hideously.   Meanwhile
the orator retreating to a cell in the neighbourhood of Meaco,
hired the common crier to go round the streets, and proclaim
that Taycho, being no longer in a condition to afford any
thing but the bare necessaries of life, would by public sale
dispose of his ambling mule and furniture, together with an
ermined robe of his wife, and the greater part of his kitchen
utensils.   At this time he was well known to be worth upwards of twenty thousand gold obans; nevertheless, the
mobile discharging this circumstance entirely from their reflection, attended to nothing but the object which the orator
was pleased to present.—They thought it was a pitious case,
and a great scandal upon the government, that such a patriot,
who had saved the nation from ruin and disgrace, should be
reduced to the cruel necessity of selling his mule and his
household furniture.   Accordingly they raised a clamour
that soon rung in the ears of Gio-gio and his favourite.

It was supposed that Mura-clami suggested on this occasion to his countryman Yak-strot the hint of offering a pension to Taycho, by way of remuneration for his past services.—' If he refuses it,' said he, ' the offer will at least reflect some credit upon the dairo and the administration; but,
should he accept of it (which is much more likely), it will
either stop his mouth entirely, or expose him to the censure
of the people, who now adore him as a mirror of disinterested integrity.'   The advice was instantly complied with: the
dairo signed a patent for a very ample pension to Taycho·
and his heirs; which patent Yak-strot delivered to him next

day at his cell in the country. This miracle of patriotism received the bounty as a turnpike-man receives the toll, and then slapped his door full in the face of the favourite; yet nothing of what Mura-clami had prognosticated came to pass. The many-tailed monster, far from calling in question the orator's disinterestedness, considered his acceptance of the pension as a proof of his moderation, in receiving such a trifling reward for the great services he had done his country; and the generosity of the dairo, instead of exciting the least emotion of gratitude in Taycho's own breast, acted only as a golden key to unlock all the sluices of his virulence and abuse.

These, however, he kept within bounds until he should see what would be the fate of Brut-an-tiffi, who now seemed to be in the condition of a criminal at the foot of the ladder. In this dilemma, he obtained a very unexpected reprieve. Before the army of the Mantchoux could take the least advantage of the settlement they had made on his frontiers, their empress died, and was succeeded by a weak prince, who no sooner ascended the throne than he struck up a peace with the Tartar freebooter, and even ordered his troops to join him against the Ostrog, to whom they had hitherto acted as auxiliaries. Such an accession of strength would have cast the balance greatly in his favour, had not Providence once more interposed, and brought matters again to an equilibrium.

Taycho no sooner perceived his ally thus unexpectedly delivered from the dangers that surrounded him, than he began to repent of his own resignation ; and resolved once more to force his way to the helm, by the same means he had so successfully used before. He was, indeed, of such a turbulent disposition as could not relish the repose of private life, and his spirit so corrosive, that it would have preyed upon himself, if he could not have found external food for it to devour. He therefore began to prepare his engines, and provide proper emissaries, to bespatter, and raise a hue-and-cry against Yak-strot at a convenient season ; not doubting but an occasion would soon present itself, considering

the temper, inexperience, and prejudices of this Ximian
politician, together with the pacific system he had adopted
so contrary to the present spirit of the blatant beast.

In these preparations he was much comforted and assisted
by his kinsman and pupil Lob-kob, who entered into his
measures with surprising zeal; and had the good luck to light
on such instruments as were admirably suited to the work in
hand. Yak-strot was extremely pleased at the secession of
Taycho, who had been a very troublesome colleague to him in
the administration, and run counter to all the schemes he had
projected for the good of the empire. He now found himself at liberty to follow his own inventions, and being naturally an enthusiast, believed himself born to be the saviour of
Japan. Some efforts, however, he made to acquire popularity, proved fruitless. Perceiving the people were, by the
orator's instigations, exasperated against the king of Corea,
he sent a peremptory message to that prince, demanding a
categorical answer; and this being denied, declared war
against him, according to the practice of all civilized nations; but even this measure failed of obtaining that approbation for which it was taken. The monster, tutored by
Taycho and his ministers, exclaimed, that the golden opportunity was lost, inasmuch as, during the observance of those
useless forms, the treasures of Corea were safely brought home
to that kingdom; treasures which, had they been interrupted
by the fune of Japan, would have paid off the debts of the
nation, and enabled the inhabitants of Meaco to pave their
streets with silver. By-the-by, this treasure existed no where
but in the fiction of Taycho, and the imagination of the blatant beast, which never attempted to use the evidence of sense
or reason to examine any assertion, how absurd and improbable soever it might be, which proceeded from the mouth of
the orator.

Yak-strot having now taken upon himself the task of steering the political bark, resolved to shew the Japanese, that,
although he recommended peace, he was as well qualified as
his predecessor for conducting the war. He therefore, with
the assistance of the fatzman, projected three naval enter-

prises ; the first against Thin-quo, the conquest of which had been unsuccessfully attempted by Taycho ; the second was destined for the reduction of Fan-yah, one of the most considerable settlements belonging to the king of Corea, in the Indian ocean ; and the third armament was sent to plunder and destroy a flourishing colony called Lli-nam, which the same prince had established almost as far to the southward as the Terra Australis Incognita. Now the only merit which either Yak-strot, or any other minister could justly claim from the success of such expeditions, is that of adopting the most feasible of those schemes which are presented by different projectors, and of appointing such commanders as are capable of conducting them with vigour, and sagacity.

The next step which the favourite took was to provide a help-mate for the young dairo ; and a certain Tartar princess, of the religion of Bupo, being pitched upon for this purpose, was formally demanded, brought over to Niphon, espoused by Gio-gio, and installed empress, with the usual solemnities. But, lest the choice of a Tartarian princess should subject the dairo to the imputation of inheriting his predecessor's predilection for the land of Yesso, which had given such sensible umbrage to all the sensible Japanese who made use of their own reason, he determined to detach his master gradually from those continental connections, which had been the source of such enormous expense, and such continual vexation to the empire of Japan. In these sentiments, he withheld the annual tribute which had been lately paid to Brut-an-tiffi ; by which means he saved a very considerable sum to the nation, and, at the same time, rescued it from the infamy of such a disgraceful imposition. He expected the thanks of the public for this exertion of his influence in favour of his country ; but he reckoned without his host. What he flattered himself would yield him an abundant harvest of honour and applause, produced nothing but odium and reproach, as we shall see in the sequel.

These measures pursued with an eye to the advantage of the public, which seemed to argue a considerable share of spirit and capacity, were strangely chequered with others of a more domestic nature, which savoured strongly of childish vanity, rash ambition, littleness of mind, and lack of understanding. He purchased a vast wardrobe of tawdry clothes, and fluttered in all the finery of Japan : he prevailed upon his master to vest him with the badges and trappings of all the honorary institutions of the empire, although this multiplication of orders in the person of one man was altogether without precedent or prescription. This was only setting himself up as the more conspicuous mark for envy and detraction.

Not contented with engrossing the personal favour and confidence of his sovereign, and, in effect, directing the whole machine of government, he thought his fortune still imperfect while the treasure of the empire passed through the hands of the cuboy, enabling that minister to maintain a very extensive influence, which might one day interfere with his own. He therefore employed all his invention, together with that of his friends, to find out some specious pretext for removing the old cuboy from his office ; and in a little time accident afforded what all their intrigues had not been able to procure.

Ever since the demise of Got-hama-baba, poor Fika-kaka had been subject to a new set of vagaries. The death of his old master gave him a rude shock : then the new dairo encroached upon his province, by prefering a bonza without his consent or knowledge : finally, he was prevented by the express order of Gio-gio from touching a certain sum out of the treasury, which he had been accustomed to throw out of his windows at stated periods, in order to keep up an interest among the dregs of the people. All these mortifications had an effect upon the weak brain of the cuboy. He began to loath his usual food, and sometimes even declined, shewing himself to the bonzas at his levee ; symptoms that alarmed all his friends and dependants. Instead of frequenting the assemblies of the great, he now attended assiduously at all groanings and christenings, grew extremely fond of caudle, and held conferences with practitioners, both male and female, in the art of midwifery. When business or

ceremony obliged him to visit any of the quos or quanbukus of Meaco, he, by surprising instinct, ran directly
to the nursery, where, if there happened to be a child in
the cradle, he took it up, and, if it was foul, wiped it with
great care and seeming satisfaction. He, moreover, learned of the good women to sing lullabies, and practised them ·
with uncommon success : but the most extravagant of all his
whims, was what he exhibited one day in his own court-
yard. Observing a nest with some eggs, which the goose
had quitted, he forthwith dropped his trowsers, and squat-
ting down in the attitude of incubation, began to stretch
out his neck, to hiss and to cackle, as if he had been
really metamorphosed into the animal whose place he now
supplied.

It was on the back of this adventure that one of the bonzas,
as prying, and as great a gossip, as the barber of Midas, in
paying his morning worship to the cuboy's posteriors, spied
something, or rather nothing, and was exceedingly affrighted. He communicated his discovery and apprehension to
divers others of the cloth ; and they were all of opinion that
some effectual inquisition should be held on this phenomenon,
lest the clergy of Japan should hereafter be scandalised, as
having knowingly kissed the breech of an old woman, perhaps a monster or magician. Information was accordingly
made to the dairo, who gave orders for immediate inspection ; and Fika-kaka was formally examined by a jury of
matrons. Whether these were actuated by undue influence,
I shall not at present explain ; certain it is, they found their
verdict, the cuboy *non mas ;* and among other evidences
produced to attest this metamorphosis, a certain Ximian,
who pretended to have the second sight, made oath that he
had one evening seen the said Fika-kaka in a female dress,
riding through the air on a broom-stick. The unhappy
cuboy being thus convicted, was divested of his office, and
confined to his palace in the country ; while Gio-gio, by the
advice of his favourite, published a proclamation, declaring
it was not for the honour of Japan that her treasury should
be managed either by a witch or an old woman.

Fika-kaka being thus removed, Yak-strot was appointed treasurer and cuboy in his place, and now ruled the roast with uncontrouled authority. On the very threshold of his greatness, however, he made a false step, which was one cause of his tottering during the whole sequel of his administration. In order to refute the calumnies and defeat the intrigues of Taycho in the assemblies of the people, he chose as an associate in the ministry Fokhsi-rokhu, who was at that instant the most unpopular man in the whole empire of Japan; and at the instigation of this colleague, deprived of bread a great number of poor families, who subsisted on petty places which had been bestowed upon them by the former cuboy. Those were so many mouths opened to augment the clamour against his own person and administration.

It might be imagined, that while he thus set one part of the nation at defiance, he would endeavour to cultivate the other; and, in particular, strive to conciliate the good will of the nobility, who did not see his exultation without umbrage. But, instead of ingratiating himself with them by a liberal turn of demeanour; by treating them with frankness and affability; granting them favours with a good grace; making entertainments for them at his palace; and mixing in their social parties of pleasure; Yak-strot always appeared on the reserve, and, under all his finery, continually wore a doublet of buckram, which gave an air of stiffness and constraint to his whole behaviour. He studied postures, and, in giving audience, generally stood in the attitude of the idol Fo; so that he sometimes was mistaken for an image of stone. He formed a scale of gesticulation in a great variety of divisions, comprehending the slightest inclination of the head, the front-nod, the side-nod, the bow, the half, the semi-demi-bow, with the shuffle, the slide, the circular, semi-circular, and quadrant sweep of the right foot. With equal care and precision did he model the economy of his looks into the divisions and sub-divisions of the full stare, the side glance, the pensive look, the pouting look, the gay look, the vacant look, and the solid look. To these different expressions of the eye he suited the corresponding features of the nose and mouth; such as the wrinkled nose, the retorted nose, the sneer, the grin, the simper, and the smile. All these postures and gesticulations he practised, and distributed occasionally, according to the difference of rank and importance of the various individuals with whom he had communication.

But these affected airs being assumed in despite of nature, he appeared as awkward as a native of Angola, when he is first hampered with clothes, or a Highlander, obliged by act of parliament to wear breeches. Indeed, the distance observed by Yak-strot in his behaviour to the nobles of Niphon, was imputed to his being conscious of a sulphureous smell which came from his own body; so that greater familiarity on his side might have bred contempt. He took delight in no other conversation but that of two or three obscure Ximians, his companions and counsellors, with whom he spent all his leisure time, in conferences upon politics, patriotism, philosophy, and the belles lettres. Those were the oracles he consulted in all the emergencies of state; and with these he spent many an attic evening.

The gods, not yet tired of sporting with the farce of human government, were still resolved to shew by what inconsiderable springs a mighty empire may be moved. The new cuboy was vastly well disposed to make his Ximian favourites great men. It was in his power to bestow places and pensions upon them; but it was not in his power to give them consequence in the eyes of the public. The administration of Yak-strot could not fail of being propitious to his own family and poor relations, who were very numerous. Their naked backs and hungry bellies were now clothed with the richest stuffs, and fed with the fat things of Japan. Every department, civil and military, was filled with Ximians. Those islanders came over in shoals to Niphon, and swarmed in the streets of Meaco, where they were easily distinguished by their lank sides, gaunt looks, lanthorn jaws, and long sharp teeth. There was a fatality that attended the whole conduct of this unfortunate cuboy. His very partiality to his own countrymen brought upon him at last the curses of his whole clan.

Mr Orator Taycho and his kinsman Lob-kob were not idle in the meantime. They provided their emissaries, and primed all their engines. Their understrappers filled every corner of Meaco with rumours, jealousies, and suspicions. Yak-strot was represented as a statesman without discernment, a minister without knowledge, and a man without humanity. He was taxed with insupportable pride, indiscretion, pusillanimity, rapacity, partiality, and breach of faith. It was affirmed that he had dishonoured the nation, and endangered the very existence of the Buponian religion, in withdrawing the annual subsidy from the great Brut-an-tiffi: that he wanted to starve the war, and betray the glory and advantage of the empire by a shameful peace: that he had avowedly shared his administration with the greatest knave in Japan: that he treated the nobles of Niphon with insolence and contempt: that he had suborned evidence against the ancient cuboy Fika-kaka, who had spent a long life and immense fortune in supporting the temple of Fakku-basi; that he had cruelly turned adrift a great number of helpless families, in order to gratify his own worthless dependants with their spoils: that he had enriched his relations and countrymen with the plunder of Niphon: that his intention was to bring over the whole nation of Ximians, a savage race, who had been ever perfidious, greedy, and hostile, towards the natives of the other Japanese islands. Nay, they were described as monsters in nature, with cloven feet, long tails, saucer eyes, iron fangs and claws, who would first devour the substance of the Niphonites, and then feed upon their blood.

Taycho had Legion's understanding so much in his power, that he actually made it believe Yak-strot had formed a treasonable scheme in favour of a foreign adventurer who pretended to the throne of Japan, and that the reigning dairo was an accomplice in this project for his own deposition. Indeed, they did not scruple to say that Gio-gio was no more than a puppet moved by his own grandmother and this vile Ximian, between whom they hinted there was a secret correspondence which reflected very little honour on the family of the dairo.

Mr Orator Taycho and his associate Lob-kob left no stone unturned to disgrace the favourite, and drive him from the helm. They struck up an alliance with the old cuboy Fika-kaka; and, fetching him from his retirement, produced him to the beast as a martyr to loyalty and virtue. They had often before this period exposed him to the derision of the populace; but now they set him up as the object of veneration and esteem; and every thing succeeded to their wish. Legion hoisted Fika-kaka on his back, and paraded through the streets of Meaco, braying hoarse encomiums on the great talents and great virtues of the ancient cuboy. His cause was now espoused by his old friend Sti-phi-rum-poo and Nin-kim-poo-po, who had been turned adrift along with him, and by several other quos who had nestled themselves in warm places, under the shadow of his protection: but it was remarkable, that not one of all the bonzas who owed their preferment to his favour, had gratitude enough to follow his fortune, or pay the least respect to him in the day of his disgrace. Advantage was also taken of the disgust occasioned by Yak-strot's reserve among the nobles of Japan. Even the fatsman was estranged from the councils of his kinsman Gio-gio, and lent his name and countenance to the malcontents, who now formed themselves into a very formidable cabal, comprehending a great number of the first quos in the empire.

In order to counterbalance this confederacy, which was a strange coalition of jarring interests, the new cuboy endeavoured to strengthen his administration, by admitting into a share of it Gotto-mio, who dreaded nothing so much as the continuation of the war, and divers other noblemen, whose alliance contributed very little to his interest or advantage. Gotto-mio was universally envied for his wealth, and detested for his avarice: the rest were either of the She-it-kun-sheit-el faction, which had been long in disgrace with the mobile, or men of desperate fortunes and loose morals, who attached themselves to the Ximian favourite solely on account of the posts and pensions he had to bestow.

During these domestic commotions, the arms of Japan,

continued to prosper in the Indian ocean. Thin-quo
was reduced almost without opposition; and news arrived
that the conquest of Fan-yah was already more than half
achieved. At the same time, some considerable advantages
were gained over the enemy on the continent of Tartary, by
the Japanese forces under the command of Bron-xi-tic. It
might be naturally supposed that these events would have
in some measure reconciled the Niphonites to the new ministry; but they produced rather a contrary effect. The blatant beast was resolved to rejoice at no victories but those
that were obtained under the auspices of its beloved Taycho;
and now took it highly amiss that Yak-strot should presume
to take any step which might redound to the glory of the
empire. Nothing could have pleased the monster at this
juncture so much as the miscarriage of both expeditions,
and a certain information that all the troops and ships employed in them had miserably perished. The king of Corea,
however, was so alarmed at the progress of the Japanese
before Fan-yah, that he began to tremble for all his distant
colonies, and earnestly craved the advice of the cabinet of
Pekin touching some scheme to make a diversion in their
favour.

The councils of Pekin have been ever fruitful of intrigues
to embroil the rest of Asia. They suggested a plan to the
king of Corea, which he forthwith put in execution. The
land of Fumma, which borders on the Correan territories,
was governed by a prince nearly allied to the king of Corea,
although his subjects had very intimate connections in the
way of commerce with the empire of Japan, which indeed
had entered into an offensive and defensive alliance with this
country. The emperor of China and the king of Corea
having sounded the sovereign of Fumma, and found him
well disposed to enter into their measures, communicated
their scheme, in which he immediately concurred. They
called upon him in public, as their friend and ally, to join
them against the Japanese, as the inveterate enemy of the
religion of Fo, and as an insolent people, who affected a
despotism at sea, to the detriment and destruction of all their

neighbours; plainly declaring, that he must either immediately break with the dairo, or expect an invasion on the side of Corea. The prince of Fumma affected to complain loudly of this iniquitous proposal; he made a merit of rejecting the alternative; and immediately demanded of the court of Meaco the succours stipulated in the treaty of alliance, in order to defend his dominions. In all appearance, indeed, there was no time to be lost; for the monarchs of China and Corea declared war against him without further hesitation; and, uniting their forces on that side, ordered them to enter the land of Fumma, after having given satisfactory assurances in private that the prince had nothing to fear from their hostilities.

Yak-strot was not much embarrassed on this occasion. Without suspecting the least collusion among the parties, he resolved to take the prince of Fumma under his protection, thereunto moved by divers considerations. First and foremost, he piqued himself upon his good faith; secondly, he knew that the trade with Fumma was of great consequence to Japan, and therefore concluded that his supporting the sovereign of it would be a popular measure; thirdly, he hoped that the multiplication of expense incurred by this new war would make the blatant beast wince under its burden, and, of consequence, reconcile it to the thoughts of a general pacification, which he had very much at heart. Meanwhile he hastened the necessary succours to the land of Fumma, and sent hither an old general, called Le-yaw-ter, in order to concert with the prince and his ministers the operations of the campaign.

This officer was counted one of the shrewdest politicians in Japan; and, having resided many years as ambassador in Fumma, was well acquainted with the genius of that people. He immediately discovered the scene which had been acted behind the curtain. He found that the prince of Fumma, far from having made any preparations for his own defence, had actually withdrawn his garrisons from the frontier places, which were by this time peaceably occupied by the invading army of Chinese and Coreans; that the few troops he had were without clothes, arms, and discipline; and that he had amused the court of Meaco with false musters, and a specious account of levies and preparations which had been made. In a word, though he could not learn the particulars, he comprehended the whole mystery of the secret negociations. He upbraided the minister of Fumma with perfidy; refused to assume the command of the Japanese auxiliaries when they arrived; and, returning to Meaco communicated his discoveries and suspicions to the new euboy. But he did not meet with that reception which he thought he deserved for intelligence of such importance. Yak-strot affected to doubt; perhaps he was not really convinced; or, if he was, thought proper to temporize; and he was in the right for so doing. A rupture with Fumma at this juncture would have forced the prince to declare openly for the enemies of Japan; in which case, the inhabitants of Niphon would have lost the benefit of a very advantageous trade. They had already been great sufferers in commerce by the breach with the king of Corea, whose subjects had been used to take off great quantities of the Japanese manufactures, for which they paid in gold and silver; and they could ill bear such an additional loss as an interruption of the trade with Fumma would have occasioned. The cuboy, therefore, continued to treat the prince of that country as a staunch ally, who had sacrificed every other consideration to his good faith; and, far from restricting himself to the number of troops and fune stipulated in the treaty, sent over a much more numerous body of forces, and ships of war; declaring, at the same time, he would support the people of Fumma with the whole power of Japan.

Such a considerable diversion of the Japanese strength could not fail to answer in some measure the expectation of the two sovereigns of China and Corea; but it did not prevent the success of the expeditions which were actually employed against their colonies in the Indian ocean. It was not in his power, however, to protect Fumma, had the invaders been in earnest; but the combined army of the Chinese and Coreans had orders to protract the war; and, in-

stead of penetrating to the capital, at a time when the Fum-
mians, though joined with the auxiliaries of Japan, were
not numerous enough to look them in the face, they made a
full stop in the middle of their march, and quietly retired
into summer quarters.

The additional encumbrance of a new continental war
redoubled the cuboy's desire of peace; and his inclination
being known to the enemy, who were also sick of the war,
they had recourse to the good offices of a certain neutral
power, called Sab-oi, sovereign of the mountains of Cam-
bodia. This prince accordingly offered his mediation at the
court of Meaco, and it was immediately accepted. The negociation for peace which had been broke off in the ministry
of Taycho was now resumed; an ambassador plenipotentiary
arrived from Pekin; and Gotto-mio was sent thither in the
same capacity, in order to adjust the articles, and sign the
preliminaries of peace.

While this new treaty was on the carpet the armament
equipped against Fan-yah, under the command of the quo
Kep-marl, and the brave admiral who had signalized himself in the sea of Kamtschatka, reduced that important place,
where they became masters of a strong squadron of fune belonging to the king of Corea, together with a very considerable treasure, sufficient to indemnify Japan for the expense
of the expedition. This, though the most grievous, was not
the only disaster which the war brought upon the Coreans.
Their distant settlement of Lli-nam was likewise taken by
General Tra-rep, and the inhabitants paid an immense sum
in order to redeem their capital from plunder.

These successes did not at all retard the conclusion of the
treaty, which was indeed become equally necessary to all the
parties concerned. Japan in particular was in danger of
being ruined by her conquests. The war had destroyed so
many men, that the whole empire could not afford a sufficiency of recruits for the maintenance of the land forces.
All those who had conquered Fatsissio and Fan-yah were
already destroyed by hard duty and the diseases of those
unhealthy climates; above two thirds of the fune were rot-

ten in the course of service, and the complements of mariners reduced to less than one half of their original numbers. Troops were actually wanting to garrison the new conquests. The finances of Japan were by this time drained to the bottom. One of her chief resources was stopped by the rupture with Corea, while her expences were considerably augmented, and her national credit was stretched even to cracking. All these considerations stimulated more and more the dairo and his cuboy to conclude the work of peace.

Meanwhile the enemies of Yak-strot gave him no quarter nor respite. They vilified his parts, traduced his morals, endeavoured to intimidate him with threats which did not even respect the dairo, and never failed to insult him whenever he appeared in public. It had been the custom, time immemorial, for the chief magistrate of Meaco to make an entertainment for the dairo and his empress immediately after their nuptials, and to this banquet all the great quos in Japan were invited. The person who filled the chair at present was Rhum-kikh, an half-witted politician, self-conceited, headstrong, turbulent, and ambitious ; a professed worshipper of Taycho, whose oratorial talents he admired, and attempted to imitate in the assemblies of the people, where he generally excited the laughter of his audience. By dint of great wealth and extensive traffic, he became a man of consequence among the mob, notwithstanding an illiberal turn of mind, and an ungracious address ; and now he resolved to use this influence for the glory of Taycho, and the disgrace of the Ximian favourite. Legion was tutored for the purpose, and, moreover, well primed with a fiery caustic spirit, in which Rhum-kikh was a considerable dealer. The dairo and his young empress were received by him and his council with a sullen formality in profound silence. The cuboy was pelted as he passed along, and his litter almost overturned by the monster, which yelled, and brayed, and hooted, without ceasing, until he was housed in the city-hall, where he met with every sort of mortification from the entertainer, as well as the spectators. At length Mr Orator Taycho, with his cousin Lob-kob, appearing in a triumph-

al car at the city-gate, the blatant beast received them with
loud huzzas, unharnessed their horses, and, putting itself in
the traces, drew them through the streets of Meaco, which
resounded with acclamation. They were received with the
same exultation within the hall of entertainment, where their
sovereign and his consort sat altogether unhonoured and unnoticed.

A small squadron of Chinese fune having taken possession of a defenceless fishery belonging to Japan, in the
neighbourhood of Fatsissio, the emissaries of Taycho magnified this event into a terrible misfortune, arising from the
mal-administration of the new cuboy; nay, they did not
scruple to affirm that he had left the fishing-town defenceless, on purpose that it might be taken by the enemy. This
clamour, however, was of short duration. The quo Phyll-
Kholl, who commanded a few fune in one of the harbours
of Fatsissio, no sooner received intelligence of what had happened, than he embarked what troops were at hand, and,
sailing directly to the place, obliged the enemy to abandon
their conquest with precipitation and disgrace.

In the midst of these transactions, the peace was signed,
ratified, and even approved, in the great national council of
the quos, as well as in the assembly of the people. The truth
is, the minister of Japan has it always in his power to secure
a majority in both these conventions, by means that may be
easily guessed; and those were not spared on this occasion.
Yak-strot in a speech harangued the great council, who
were not a little surprised to hear him speak with such propriety and extent of knowledge; for he had been represented as tongue-tied, and, in point of elocution, little better than
the palfrey he rode.   He now vindicated all the steps he had
taken since his accession to the helm: he demonstrated the
necessity of a pacification; explained and descanted upon
every article of the treaty; and, finally, declared his conscience was so clear in this matter, that, when he died, he
should desire no other encomium to be engraved on his
tomb, but that he was the author of this peace.

Nevertheless, the approbation of the council was not ob-

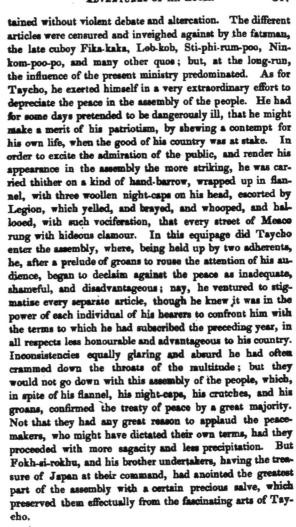

tained without violent debate and altercation. The different articles were censured and inveighed against by the fatsman, the late cuboy Fika-kaka, Lob-kob, Sti-phi-rum-poo, Nin-kom-poo-po, and many other quos; but, at the long-run, the influence of the present ministry predominated. As for Taycho, he exerted himself in a very extraordinary effort to depreciate the peace in the assembly of the people. He had for some days pretended to be dangerously ill, that he might make a merit of his patriotism, by shewing a contempt for his own life, when the good of his country was at stake. In order to excite the admiration of the public, and render his appearance in the assembly the more striking, he was carried thither on a kind of hand-barrow, wrapped up in flannel, with three woollen night-caps on his head, escorted by Legion, which yelled, and brayed, and whooped, and hallooed, with such vociferation, that every street of Meaco rung with hideous clamour. In this equipage did Taycho enter the assembly, where, being held up by two adherents, he, after a prelude of groans to rouse the attention of his audience, began to declaim against the peace as inadequate, shameful, and disadvantageous; nay, he ventured to stigmatise every separate article, though he knew it was in the power of each individual of his hearers to confront him with the terms to which he had subscribed the preceding year, in all respects less honourable and advantageous to his country. Inconsistencies equally glaring and absurd he had often crammed down the throats of the multitude; but they would not go down with this assembly of the people, which, in spite of his flannel, his night-caps, his crutches, and his groans, confirmed the treaty of peace by a great majority. Not that they had any great reason to applaud the peace-makers, who might have dictated their own terms, had they proceeded with more sagacity and less precipitation. But Fokh-si-rokhu, and his brother undertakers, having the treasure of Japan at their command, had anointed the greatest part of the assembly with a certain precious salve, which preserved them effectually from the fascinating arts of Taycho.

This orator, incensed at his bad success within doors, renewed and redoubled his operations without.   He exasperated Legion against Yak-strot to such a pitch of rage, that
the monster could not hear the cuboy's name three times
pronounced without falling into fits.   His confederate Lob-
kob, in the course of his researches, found out two originals
admirably calculated for executing his vengence against
the Ximian favourite.   One of them, called Llur-chir, a
profligate bonza, degraded for his lewd life, possessed a wonderful talent of exciting different passions in the blatant
beast, by dint of quaint rhymes, which were said to be inspirations of the demon of obloquy, to whom he had sold his
soul.   These oracles not only commanded the passions, but
even influenced the organs of the beast in such a manner, as
to occasion an evacuation either upwards or downwards, at
the pleasure of the operator.   The other, known by the name
of Jan-ki-dtzin, was counted the best marksman in Japan in
the art and mystery of dirt-throwing.   He possessed the art
of making balls of filth, which were famous for sticking and
stinking; and these he threw with such dexterity, that they
very seldom missed their aim.   Being reduced to a low ebb
of fortune by his debaucheries, he had made advances to the
new cuboy, who had rejected his proffered services on account of his immoral character; a prudish punctilio, which
but ill became Yak-strot, who had paid very little regard to
reputation in choosing some of the colleagues he had associated in his administration.   Be that as it may, he no sooner
understood that Mr Orator Taycho was busy in preparing
for an active campaign, than he likewise began to put himself in a posture of defence.   He hired a body of mercenaries,
and provided some dirt-men and rhymers.   Then, taking
the field, a sharp contest and pelting match ensued; but the
dispute was soon terminate.   Yak-strot's versifiers turned
out no great conjurers on the trial.   They were not such favourites of the demon as Llur chir.   The rhymes they used
produced no other effect upon Legion but that of setting it
a-braying.   The cuboy's dirt-men, however, played their
parts tolerably well.   Though their balls were inferior in

point of composition to those of Jan-ki-dtsin, they did not
fail to discompose Orator Taycho and his friend Lob-kob,
whose eyes were seen to water with the smart occasioned by
those missiles; but these last had a great advantage over
their adversaries, in the zeal and attachment of Legion,
whose numerous tongues were always ready to lick off the
ordure that stuck to any part of their leaders; and this they
did with such signs of satisfaction, as seemed to indicate an
appetite for all manner of filth.

Yak-strot having suffered woefully in his own person,
and seeing his partizans in confusion, thought proper to retreat. Yet, although discomfited, he was not discouraged.
On the contrary, having at bottom a fund of fanaticism,
which, like chamomile, grows the faster for being trod upon,
he became more obstinately bent than ever upon prosecuting
his own schemes for the good of the people in their own despite. His vanity was likewise buoyed up by the flattery of
his creatures, who extolled the passive courage he had shewn
in the late engagement. Though every part of him still
tingled and stunk, from the balls of the enemy, he persuaded himself that not one of their missiles had taken place;
and, of consequence, that there was something of divinity in
his person. Full of this notion, he discarded his rhymsters
and his dirt-casters as unnecessary, and resolved to bear the
brunt of the battle in his own individual person.

Fokh-si-rokhu advised him, nevertheless, to fill his trowsers with gold obans, which he might throw at Legion, in
case of necessity, assuring him that this was the only am-
munition which the monster could not withstand. The advice was good; and the cuboy might have followed it, without being obliged to the treasury of Japan; for he was by
this time become immensely rich, in consequence of having found a hoard in digging his garden: but this was an
expedient which Yak-strot could never be prevailed-upon
to use, either on this or any other occasion. Indeed, he
was now so convinced of his own personal energy, that he
persuaded his master Gio-gio to come forth, and see it
operate on the blatant beast. Accordingly the dairo ascend-

ed his car of state, while the cuboy, arrayed in all his trappings, stood before him with the reins in his own hand, and drove directly to the enemy, who waited for him without flinching.   Being arrived within dung-shot of Jan-ki-dtzin, he made a halt, and putting himself in the attitude of the idol Fo, with a simper in his countenance, seemed to invite the warrior to make a full discharge of his artillery. He did not long wait in suspense.   The balls soon began to whiz about his ears; and a great number took effect upon his person.   At length he received a shot upon his right temple, which brought him to the ground.   All his gewgaws fluttered, and his buckram doublet rattled as he fell. —Llur-chir no sooner beheld him prostrate, than, advancing with the monster, he began to repeat his rhymes, at which every mouth and every tail of Legion was opened and lifted up; and such a torrent of filth squirted from these channels, that the unfortunate cuboy was quite overwhelmed. Nay, he must have been actually suffocated where he lay, had not some of the dairo's attendants interposed, and rescued him from the vengeance of the monster.   He was carried home in such an unsavoury pickle, that his family smelled his disaster long before he came in sight; and when he appeared in this woful condition, covered with ordure, blinded with dirt, and even deprived of sense and motion, his wife was seized with *hysterica passio*.   He was immediately stripped and washed, and other means being used for his recovery, he in a little time retrieved his recollection.

He was now pretty well undeceived, with respect to the divinity of his person; but his enthusiasm took a new turn. He aspired to the glory of martyrdom, and resolved to devote himself as a victim to patriotic virtue.   While his attendants were employed in washing off the filth that stuck to his beard, he recited, in a theatrical tone, the stanza of a famous Japanese bard, whose soul afterwards transmigrated into the body of a Roman poet, Horatius Flaccus, and inspired him with the same sentiment, in the Latin tongue,—

Virtus repulsæ nescia sordidæ
Intaminatis fulget honoribus ;
Nec sumit, aut ponit secures
Arbitrio popularis auræ.

His friends hearing him declare his resolution of dying
for his country, began to fear that his understanding was
disturbed. They advised him to yield to the torrent, which
was become too impetuous to stem ; to resign the cuboyship
quietly, and reserve his virtues for a more favourable occasion. In vain his friends remonstrated : in vain his wife
and children employed their tears and entreaties to the same
purpose. He lent a deaf ear to all their solicitations, until they
began to drop some hints that seemed to imply a suspicion
of his insanity, which alarmed him exceedingly ; and the
dairo himself signifying to him in private, that it was become absolutely necessary to temporise, he resigned the reins
of government with a heavy heart, though not before he was
assured that he should still continue to exert his influence
behind the curtain.

Gio-gio's own person had not escaped untouched in the
last skirmish. Jan-ki-dtsin was transported to such a pitch
of insolence, that he aimed some balls at the dairo, and one
of them taking place exactly betwixt the eyes, defiled his
whole visage. Had the laws of Japan been executed in
all their severity against this audacious plebeian, he would
have suffered crucifixion on the spot : but Gio-gio, being
good-natured even to a fault, contented himself with ordering some of his attendants to apprehend and put him in the
public stocks, after having seized the whole cargo of filth
which he had collected at his habitation, for the manufacture of his balls. Legion was no sooner informed of his
disgrace, than it released him by force, being therein comforted and abetted by the declaration of a puny magistrate,
called Praff-patt-phogg, who seized this, as the only opportunity he should ever find of giving himself any consequence
in the commonwealth. Accordingly, the monster hoisting
him and Jan-kid-dtin on their shoulders, went in procession
through the streets of Meaco, hallooing, huzzaing, and

extolling this venerable pair of patriots, as the *palladia of* the liberty of Japan.

The monster's officious zeal on this occasion, was far from being agreeable to Mr. Orator Taycho, who took umbrage at this exaltation of his two understrappers, and from that moment devoted Jan-ki-dtzin to destruction.—The dairo finding it absolutely necessary for the support of his government, that this dirt-monger should be punished, gave directions for trying him according to the laws of the land. He was ignominiously expelled from the assembly of the people, where his old patron Taycho not only disclaimed him, but even represented him as a worthless atheist and sower of sedition : but he escaped the weight of a more severe sentence in another tribunal, by retreating, without beat of drum, into the territories of China, where he found an asylum, from whence he made divers ineffectual appeals to the multitudinous beast at Niphon.

As for Yak-strot, he was every thing but a downright martyr to the odium of the public which produced a ferment all over the nation. His name was become a term of reproach. He was burnt or crucified in effigy in every city, town, village, and district, of Niphon. Even his own countrymen, the Ximians, held him in abhorrence and execration. Notwithstanding his partiality to the *natale solum*, he had not been able to provide for all those adventurers who came from thence, in consequence of his promotion. The whole number of the disappointed became his enemies of course ; and the rest finding themselves exposed to the animosity and ill offices of their fellow-subjects of Niphon, who hated the whole community for his sake, inveighed against Yak-strot as the curse of their nation.

In the midst of all this detestation and disgrace, it must be owned, for the sake of truth, that Yak-strot was one of the honestest men in Japan, and certainly the greatest benefactor to the empire. Just, upright, sincere, and charitable ; his heart was susceptible of friendship and tenderness. He was a virtuous husband, a fond father, a kind master, and a zealous friend. In his public capacity, he had nothing in view but the advantage of Japan, in the prosecution of which, he flattered himself he should be able to display all the abilities of a profound statesman, and all the virtues of the most sublime patriotism. It was here he over-rated his own importance. His virtue became the dupe of his vanity. Nature had denied him shining talents, as well as that easiness of deportment, that affability, liberal turn, and versatile genius, without which no man can ever figure at the head of an adminstration. Nothing could be more absurd than his being charged with want of parts and understanding to guide the helm of government, considering how happily it had been conducted for many years by Fika-kaka, whose natural genius would have been found unequal even to the art and mystery of wool-combing. Besides, the war had prospered in his hands as much as it ever did under the auspices of his predecessor; though, as I have before observed, neither the one nor the other could justly claim any merit from its success.

But Yak-strot's services to the public were much more important in another respect. He had the resolution to dissolve the shameful and pernicious engagements which the empire had contracted on the continent of Tartary.—He lightened the intolerable burdens of the empire: he saved its credit, when it was stretched even to bursting. He made a peace, which, if not the most glorious that might have been obtained, was at least, the most solid and advantageous that ever Japan had concluded with any power whatsoever; and, in particular, much more honourable, useful, and ascertained, than that which Taycho had agreed to subscribe the preceding year; and, by this peace he put an end to all the horrors of a cruel war, which had ravaged the best parts of Asia, and destroyed the lives of six hundred thousand men every year. On the whole, Yak-strot's good qualities were respectable.—There was very little vicious in his composition; and as to his follies, they were rather the subjects of ridicule, than of resentment.

Yak-strot's subalterns in the ministry rejoiced in secret at his running so far into the north of Legion's displeasure. Nay, it was shrewdly suspected that some of their emis-

saries had been very active against him in the day of his dis-
comfiture.   They flattered themselves, that if he could be
effectually driven from the presence of the dairo, they would
succeed to his influence; and, in the meantime, would acquire popularity, by turning tail to, and kicking at the
Ximian favourite, who had associated them in the administration, in consequence of their vowing eternal attachment
to his interest, and constant submission to his will.   Having
held a secret conclave, to concert their operations, they began to execute their plan, by seducing Yak-strot into certain odious measures of raising new impositions on the people, which did not fail, indeed, to increase the clamour of
the blatant beast, and promote its filthy discharge upwards
and downwards; but then the torrents were divided, and
many a tail was lifted up against the real projectors of the
scheme which the favourite had adopted.   They now resolved to make a merit with the mobile, by picking a German quarrel with Strot, and insulting him in public.   Getto-
mio caused a scrubbing-post to be set up in the night at the
cuboy's door.   The scribe Zan-ti-fic presented him with a
scheme for the importation of brimstone into the island of
Ximo: the other scribe pretended he could not spell the
barbarous names of the cuboy's relations and countrymen,
who were daily thrust into the most lucrative employments.
As for Twitz-er, the financier, he never approached Yak-
strot without clawing his knuckles in derision.   At the
council of twenty-eight, they thwarted every plan he proposed, and turned into ridicule every word he spoke.   At
length they bluntly told the dairo, that as Yak-strot resigned
the reins of administration in public, he must likewise give
up his management behind the curtain; for they were not
at all disposed to answer to the people for measures dictated
by an invisible agent.   This was but a reasonable demand,
in which the emperor seemed to acquiesce.   But the new
ministers thought it was requisite that they should commit
some overt act of contempt for the abdicated cuboy.   One
of his nearest relations had obtained a profitable office in the
island of Ximo; and of this, the new cabal insisted he

should be immediately deprived. The dairo remonstrated against the injustice of turning a man out of his place, for no other reason but to satisfy their caprice; and plainly told them he could not do it without infringing his honour, as he had given his word that the possessor should enjoy the post for life. Far from being satisfied with this declaration, they urged their demand with redoubled importunity, mixed with menaces, which equally embarrassed and incensed the good-natured dairo. At last, Yak-strot, taking compassion upon his indulgent master, prevailed upon his kinsman to release him from the obligation of his word, by making a voluntary resignation of his office. The dairo fell sick of vexation: his life was despaired of; and all Japan was filled with alarm and apprehension at the prospect of an infant's ascending the throne: for the heir-apparent was still in the cradle.

Their fears, however, were happily disappointed by the recovery of the emperor, who, to prevent as much as possible, the inconveniencies that might attend his demise, during the minority of his son, resolved that a regency should be established and ratified by the states of the empire. The plan of this regency he concerted in private with the venerable princess his grandmother, and his friend Yak-strot; and then communicated the design to his ministers, who, knowing the quarter from whence it had come, treated it with coldness and contempt. They were so elevated by their last triumph over the Ximian favourite, that they overlooked every obstacle to their ambition; and determined to render the dairo dependant on them, and them only. With this view, they threw cold water on the present measure; and to mark their hatred of the favourite more strongly in the eyes of Legion, they endeavoured to exclude the name of his patroness the dairo's grandmother from the deed of regency, though their malice was frustrated by the vigilance of Yak-strot, and the indignation of the states, who resented this affront offered to the family of their sovereign.

The tyranny of this junto became so intolerable to Giogio, that he resolved to shake off their yoke, whatever

might be the consequence : but before any effectual step
was taken for that purpose, Yak-strot, who understood mechanics, and had studied the art of puppet playing, tried
an experiment on the organs of the cabal, which he tampered with individually without success.   Instead of uttering
what he prompted, the sounds came out quite altered in their
passage.   Gotto-mio grunted ; the financier Twitz-er bleat-
ed, or rather brayed ; one scribe mewed like a cat ; the other
yelped like a jackall.   In short, they were found so perverse
and refractory, that the master of the motion kicked them
off the stage, and supplied the scene with a new set of puppets made of very extraordinary materials.   They were the
very figures through whose pipes the charge of mal-administration had been so loudly sounded against the Ximian favourite.   They were now mustered by the fatsman, and hung
upon the pegs of the very same puppet-show-man against
whom they had so vehemently inveighed.   Even the superannuated Fika-kaka appeared again upon the stage as an
actor of some consequence ; and insisted upon it, that his
metamorphosis was a mere calumny.   But Taycho and Lob-
kob kept aloof, because Yak-strot had not yet touched them
on the proper keys.

   The first exhibition of the new puppets was called *topsy-
turvy*, a farce in which they overthrew all the paper houses
which their predecessors had built : but they performed their
parts in such confusion, that Yak-strot interposing to keep
them in order, received divers contusions and severe kicks
on the shins, which made his eyes water ; and, indeed, he
had in a little time reason enough to repent of the revolution
he had brought about.   The new sticks of administration
proved more stiff and unmanageable than the former ; and
those he had discarded, associating with the blatant beast, be-
daubed him with such a variety of filth, drained from all the
sewers of scurrility, that he really became a public nuisance.
Gotto-mio pretended remorse of conscience, and declared he
would impeach Yak-strot for the peace which he himself
had negociated.   Twits er snivelled and cried, and cast
figures, to prove that Yak-strot was born for the destruc-

tion of Japan; and Zan-ti-fic lured an incendiary bonze, called Toks, to throw fire-balls by night into the palace of the
favourite.

In this distress, Strot cast his eyes on Taycho the monster-
tamer, who alone seemed able to overbalance the weight of
all their opposition; and to him he made large advances
accordingly; but his offers were still inadequate to the expectations of that demagogue, who, nevertheless, put on a
face of capitulation.   He was even heard to say, that Yak-
strot was an honest man, and a good minister: nay, he declared he would ascend the highest pinacle of the highest
pagod in Japan, and proclaim that Yak-strot had never,
directly or indirectly, meddled with administration since he
resigned the public office of minister.   Finding him, however, tardy and phlegmatic in his proposals, he thought
proper to change his phrase, and, in the next assembly of
the people, swore, with great vociferation, that the said
Yak-strot was the greatest rogue that ever escaped the gallows.   This was a necessary fillip to Yak-strot, and operated upon him so effectually, that he forthwith sent a charte
blanche to the great Taycho, and a treaty was immediately
ratified on the following conditions: that the said Taycho
should be raised to the rank of quambuku, and be appointed
conservator of the dairo's signet: that no state measure should
be taken without his express approbation: that his creature
the lawyer, Praff-fog should be enobled and preferred to the
most eminent place in the tribunals of Japan; and that all
his friends and dependants should be provided for at the
public expense, in such a manner as he himself should propose.   His kinsman Lob-kob, however, was not comprehended in this treaty, the articles of which he inveighed
against with such acrimony, that a rupture ensued betwixt
these two originals.   The truth is, Lob-kob was now so full
of his own importance, that nothing less than an equal share
of administration would satisfy his ambition; and this was
neither in Taycho's power nor inclination to grant.

The first consequence of this treaty was a new shift of
hands, and a new dance of ministers.   The chair of prece-

dency was pulled from under the antiquated Fika-kaka;
who fell upon his back; and his heels flying up, discovered
but too plainly the melancholy truth of his metamorphosis.
All his colleagues were discarded, except those who thought
proper to temporise and join in dancing the hay, according
as they were actuated by the new partners of the puppet-show.
This coalition was the greatest masterpiece in politics that
Yak-strot ever performed. Taycho, the formidable Taycho!
whom in his single person he dreaded more than all his
other enemies of Japan united, was now become his coadju-
tor, abettor, and advocate; and which was still of more
consequence to Strot, that demagogue was forsaken of his
good genius Legion.

The many-headed monster would have swallowed down
every other species of tergiversation in Taycho, except a
coalition with the detested favourite, and the title of quo, by
which he formerly renounced its society; but these were articles which the mongrel could not digest. The tidings of
this union threw the beast into a kind of stupor, from which
it was roused by blisters and cauteries applied by Gotto-mio,
Twitz-er, Zan-ti-fic, with his understrapper Toks, now
reinforced by Fika-kaka, and his discarded associates; for
their common hatred to Yak-strot, like the rod of Moses,
swallowed up every distinction of party, and every suggestion of former animosity; and they concurred with incredible zeal, in rousing Legion to a due sense of Taycho's apos-
tasy. The beast, so stimulated, howled three days and
three nights successively at Taycho's gate; then was seized
with a convulsion, that went off with an evacuation upwards and downwards, so offensive that the very air was
infected.

The horrid sounds of the beast's lamentations, the noxious
effluvia of its filthy discharge, joined to the poignant remorse which Taycho felt at finding his power over Legion
dissolved, occasioned a commotion in his brain; and this
led him into certain extravagancies, which give his enemies
a handle to say he was actually insane. His former friends
and partizans thought the best apology they could make for

the inconsistency of his conduct, was to say he was *non compos*; and this report was far from being disagreeable to Yak-strot, because it would at any time furnish him with a plausible pretence to dissolve the partnership, at which he inwardly repined; for it was necessity alone that drove him to a partition of his power with a man so incapable of acting in concert with any colleague whatsoever.

In the meantime Gotto-mio and his associates left no stone unturned to acquire the same influence over Legion, which Taycho had so eminently possessed; but the beast's faculties, slender as they were, seemed now greatly impaired, in consequence of that arch empiric's practises upon its constitution. In vain did Gotto-mio hoop and halloo; in vain did Twits-er tickle its long ears; in vain did Zan-ti-fic apply sternutatories, and his bonze administer inflammatory glysters; the monster could never be brought to a right understanding, or at all concur with their designs, except in one instance, which was its antipathy to the Ximian favourite. This had become so habitual, that it acted mechanically upon its organs even after it had lost all other signs of recognition. As often as the name of Yak-strot was pronounced, the beast began to yell; and all the usual consequences ensued; but when ever his new friends presumed to mount him, he threw himself on his back, and rolled them in the kennel at the hazard of their lives.

One would imagine there was some leaven in the nature of Yak-strot, that soured all his subalterns who were natives of Niphon; for, howsoever they promised all submission to his will before they were admitted into his motion, they no sooner found themselves acting characters in his drama, than they began to thwart him in his measures; so that he was plagued by those he had taken in, and persecuted by those he had driven out. The two great props, which he had been at so much pains to provide, now failed him. Taycho was grown crazy, and could no longer manage the monster; and Quam-ba-cundono the fatsman, whose authority had kept several puppets in awe, died about this period. These two circumstances were the more alarming, as Gotto-

mio and his crew began to gain ground, not only in their
endeavours to rouse the monster, but also in tampering with
some of the acting puppets, to join their cabal, and make
head against their master.   These exoterics grew so refractory, that when he tried to wheel them to the right, they
turned to the left about ; and, instead of joining hands in
the dance of politics, rapped their heads against each other
with such violence, that the noise of the collision was heard
in the street ; and, if they had not been made of the hardest
wood in Japan, some of them would certainly have been
split in the encounter.

By this time Legion began to have some sense of its own
miserable condition.   The effects of the yeast potions which
it had drank so liberally from the hands of Taycho, now
wore off.   The fumes dispersed ; the illusion vanished ; the
flatulent tumour of its belly disappeared with innumerable
explosions, leaving a hideous lankness and such a canine
appetite as all the eatables of Japan could not satisfy.   After
having devoured the whole harvest, it yawned for more, and
grew quite outrageous in its hunger, threatening to feed on
human flesh, if not plentifully supplied with other viands.
In this dilemma, Yak-strot convened the council of twenty-
eight, where, in consideration of the urgency of the case, it
was resolved to suspend the law against the importation of
foreign provisions, and open the ports of Japan for the relief
of the blatant beast.

As this was vesting the dairo with a dispensing power unknown to the constitution of Japan, it was thought necessary, at the next assembly of the quos and quanbukus,
that constitute the legislature, to obtain a legal sanction for
that extraordinary exercise of prerogative, which nothing
but the *salus populi* could excuse.   Upon this occasion, it
was diverting to see with what effrontery individuals changed their principles with their places.   Taycho the quo,
happening to be in one of his lucid intervals, went to the
assembly, supported by his two creatures Praff-fog, and
another limb of the law, called Lley-nah, surnamed Gurg-
grog, or Curse-mother ; and this triumvirate, who had

raised themselves from nothing to the first rank in the state, by vilifying and insulting the kingly power, and affirming that the dairo was the slave of the people, now had the impudence to declare in the face of day, that in some cases the emperor's power was absolute, and that he had an inherent right to suspend and supersede the laws and ordinances of the legislature.

Mura-clami, who had been for some time eclipsed in his judicial capacity by the popularity of Praff-fog, did not fail to seize this opportunity of exposing the character of his upstart rival. Though he had been all his life an humble retainer to the prerogative, he now made a parade of patriotism, and, in a tide of eloquence, bore down all the flimsy arguments which the triumvirate advanced. He demonstrated the futility of their reasoning, from the express laws and customs of the empire; he expatiated on the pernicious tendency of their doctrine, and exhibited the inconsistency of their conduct in such colours, that they must have hid their heads in confusion, had they not happily conquered all sense of shame, and been well convinced that the majority of the assembly were not a whit more honest than themselves. Mura-clami enjoyed a momentary triumph; but his words made a very slight impression; for it was his misfortune to be a Ximian; and if his virtues had been more numerous than the hairs in his beard, this very circumstance would have shaved them clean away from the consideration of the audience.

Taycho, opening the flood-gates of his abuse, bespattered all that opposed him. Lley-nah, alias Curse-mother, swore that he had got into the wrong box; then turning to Praff-fog,—' Brother Praff,' cried he, ' thou hast now let down thy trowsers, and every rascal in Japan will whip thy a——e !' Praff was afraid of the beast's resentment : but Taycho bestrid him like a colossus, and he crept through between his legs into a place of safety. This was the last time that the orator appeared in public. Immediately after this occurrence, it was found necessary to confine him to a dark chamber, and Yak-strot was left to his own inventions.

In this dilemma he had recourse to the old expedient of changing hands; and, as a prelude to this reform, made advances to Gotto-mio, whom he actually detached from the opposition, by providing his friends and dependents with lucrative offices, and promising to take no steps of consequence without his privity and approbation. A sop was at the same time thrown to Twits-er; Zan-ti-fic, lulled with specious promises, discarded Toks the incendiary bonza; Lob-kob signed a neutrality; and old F.ka kaka was deprived of the use of speech:—in a word, the ill-cemented confederacy of Strot's exoteric foes fell asunder; and Legion had now no rage but the rage of hunger to be appeased. But the Ximian favourite was still thwarted in his operations behind the curtain; for he had so often chopped and changed the figures that composed his motion, that they were all of different materials; so wretchedly sorted and so ill-toned, that, when they came upon the scene, they produced nothing but discord and disorder.

The Japanese colony of Fatsissio had been settled above a century; and, in the face of a thousand dangers and difficulties, raised themselves to such consideration, that they consumed infinite quantities of the manufactures of Japan, for which they paid their mother country in gold and silver, and precious drugs, the produce of their plantations. The advantages which Japan reaped from this traffic with her own colonists, almost equalled the amount of what she gained by her commerce with all the other parts of Asia. Twits-er, when he managed the finances of Japan, had, in his great wisdom, planned, procured, and promulgated a law, saddling the Fatsissians, with a grievous tax, to answer the occasions of the Japanese government; an imposition which struck at the very vitals of their constitution, by which they were exempt from all burdens but such as they fitted for their own shoulders. They raised a mighty clamour at this innovation, in which they were joined by Legion, at that time under the influence of Taycho, who, in the assembly of the people, bitterly inveighed against the authors and abettors of such an arbitrary and tyrannical measure. Their reproach and execration did not stop at Twitz-er, but proceeded, as usual, to Yak-strot, who was the general butt at which all the arrows of slander, scurrility, and abuse, were levelled. The puppets with which he supplied the places of Twitz-er and his associates, in order to recommend themselves to Legion, and perhaps with a view to mortify the favourite who had patronised the Fatsissian tax, insisted upon withdrawing this imposition, which was accordingly abrogated, to the no small disgrace and contempt of the lawgivers; but when these new ministers were turned out, to make way for Taycho and his friends, the interest of the Fatsissians was again abandoned. Even the orator himself declaimed against them with an unembarrassed countenance, after they had raised statues to him as their friend and patron; and measures were taken to make them feel all the severity of an abject dependence upon the legislature of Japan. Finally, Gotto-mio acceded to this system, which he had formerly approved in conjunction with Twitz-er; and preparations were made for using compulsory measures, should the colonists refuse to submit with a good grace.

The Fatsissians, far from acquiescing in these proceedings, resolved to defend to the last extremity those liberties which they had hitherto preserved; and, as a proof of their independence, agreed among themselves to renounce all the superfluities with which they had so long been furnished, at a vast expense, from the manufactures of Japan, since that nation had begun to act towards them with all the cruelty of a stepmother. It was amazing to see and to hear how Legion raved, and slabbered, and snapped his multitudinous jaws in the streets of Meaco, when it understood that the Fatsissians were determined to live on what their own country afforded. They were represented and reviled as ruffians, barbarians, and unnatural monsters, who clapped the dagger to the breast of their indulgent mother, in presuming to save themselves the expense of those superfluities, which, by the bye, her cruel impositions had left them no money to purchase. Nothing was heard in Japan but threats of punishing those ungrateful colonists with whips and scorpions.

For this purpose troops were assembled and fleets equipped; and the blatant beast yawned with impatient expectation of being drenched with the blood of its fellow-subjects.

Yak-strot was seized with horror at the prospect of such extremities; for, to give the devil his due, his disposition was neither arbitrary nor cruel; but he had been hurried by evil counsellors into a train of false politics, the consequences of which he did not foresee. He now summoned council after council to deliberate upon conciliatory expedients, but found the motely crew so divided by self-interest, faction, and mutual rancour, that no consistent plan could be formed; all was nonsense, clamour, and contradiction. The Ximian favourite now wished all his puppets at the devil, and secretly cursed the hour in which he first undertook the motion. He even fell sick of chagrin, and resolved in good earnest to withdraw himself entirely from the political helm, which he was now convinced he had no talents to guide. In the mean time, he tried to find some temporary alleviation to the evils occasioned by the monstrous incongruity of the members and materials that composed his administration. But before any effectual measures could be taken, his evil genius, ever active, brewed up a new storm in another quarter, which had well nigh swept him and all his projects into the gulf of perdition.

THE END.

LEITH:
Printed by Ogle, Allardice & Thomson.